DOCUMENTS SUPPLEMENT TO

INTERNATIONAL COMMERCIAL ARBITRATION

A TRANSNATIONAL PERSPECTIVE

Sixth Edition

■ ■ ■

by

Tibor Várady

Professor of Law, Central European University, Budapest, and Emeritus Professor, Emory University School of Law

John J. Barceló III

William Nelson Cromwell Professor of International and Comparative Law, Cornell Law School

Stefan Kröll

Honorary Professor, Bucerius Law Schoool, Hamburg, and Director VIS-Arbitration Moot

AMERICAN CASEBOOK SERIES®

WEST
ACADEMIC
PUBLISHING

American Casebook Series is a trademark registered in the U.S. Patent and Trademark Office.

© 2015 LEG, Inc. d/b/a West Academic
    444 Cedar Street, Suite 700
    St. Paul, MN 55101
    1-877-888-1330

West, West Academic Publishing, and West Academic are trademarks of West Publishing Corporation, used under license.

Printed in the United States of America

ISBN: 978-0-314-28541-6

TABLE OF CONTENTS

DOCUMENTS SUPPLEMENT TO
INTERNATIONAL COMMERCIAL ARBITRATION
A TRANSNATIONAL PERSPECTIVE

Sixth Edition

CHAPTER I

INTERNATIONAL CONVENTIONS ON ARBITRATION

■ ■ ■

A. UNITED NATIONS CONVENTION ON THE RECOGNITION AND ENFORCEMENT OF FOREIGN ARBITRAL AWARDS (NEW YORK CONVENTION OF 1958)*

(Done at New York, June 10, 1958.)

Article I

1.   This Convention shall apply to the recognition and enforcement of arbitral awards made in the territory of a State other than the State where the recognition and enforcement of such awards are sought, and arising out of differences between persons, whether physical or legal. It shall also apply to arbitral awards not considered as domestic awards in the State where their recognition and enforcement are sought.

2.   The term "arbitral awards" shall include not only awards made by arbitrators appointed for each case but also those made by permanent arbitral bodies to which the parties have submitted.

3.   When signing, ratifying or acceding to this Convention, or notifying extension under article X hereof, any State may on the basis of reciprocity declare that it will apply the Convention to the recognition and enforcement of awards made only in the territory of another Contracting State. It may also declare that it will apply the Convention only to differences arising out of legal relationships, whether contractual or not, which are considered as commercial under the national law of the State making such declaration.

Article II

1.   Each Contracting State shall recognize an agreement in writing under which the parties undertake to submit to arbitration all or any differences which have arisen or which may arise between them in respect of a defined legal relationship, whether contractual or not, concerning a subject matter capable of settlement by arbitration.

---

*   The Convention can be found at the UNCITRAL Website at http://www.uncitral.org/pdf/ english/texts/arbitration/NY-conv/XXII_1_e.pdf. Reprinted with permission of UNCITRAL.

2.   The term "agreement in writing" shall include an arbitral clause in a contract or an arbitration agreement, signed by the parties or contained in an exchange of letters or telegrams.

3.   The court of a Contracting State, when seized of an action in a matter in respect of which the parties have made an agreement within the meaning of this article, shall, at the request of one of the parties, refer the parties to arbitration, unless it finds that the said agreement is null and void, inoperative or incapable of being performed.

Article III

Each Contracting State shall recognize arbitral awards as binding and enforce them in accordance with the rules of procedure of the territory where the award is relied upon, under the conditions laid down in the following articles. There shall not be imposed substantially more onerous conditions or higher fees or charges on the recognition or enforcement of arbitral awards to which this Convention applies than are imposed on the recognition or enforcement of domestic arbitral awards.

Article IV

1.   To obtain the recognition and enforcement mentioned in the preceding article, the party applying for recognition and enforcement shall, at the time of the application, supply:

(a)   The duly authenticated original award or a duly certified copy thereof;

(b)   The original agreement referred to in article II or a duly certified copy thereof.

2.   If the said award or agreement is not made in an official language of the country in which the award is relied upon, the party applying for recognition and enforcement of the award shall produce a translation of these documents into such language. The translation shall be certified by an official or sworn translator or by a diplomatic or consular agent.

Article V

1.   Recognition and enforcement of the award may be refused, at the request of the party against whom it is invoked, only if that party furnishes to the competent authority where the recognition and enforcement is sought, proof that:

(a)   The parties to the agreement referred to in article II were, under the law applicable to them, under some incapacity, or the said agreement is not valid under the law to which the parties have subjected it or, failing any indication thereon, under the law of the country where the award was made; or

(b)   The party against whom the award is invoked was not given proper notice of the appointment of the arbitrator or of the arbitration proceedings or was otherwise unable to present his case; or

(c)   The award deals with a difference not contemplated by or not falling within the terms of the submission to arbitration, or it contains decisions on matters beyond the scope of the submission to arbitration, provided that, if the decisions on matters submitted to arbitration can be separated from those not so submitted, that part of the award which contains decisions on matters submitted to arbitration may be recognized and enforced; or

(d)   The composition of the arbitral authority or the arbitral procedure was not in accordance with the agreement of the parties, or, failing such agreement, was not in accordance with the law of the country where the arbitration took place; or

(e)   The award has not yet become binding on the parties, or has been set aside or suspended by a competent authority of the country in which, or under the law of which, that award was made.

2.   Recognition and enforcement of an arbitral award may also be refused if the competent authority in the country where recognition and enforcement is sought finds that:

(a)   The subject matter of the difference is not capable of settlement by arbitration under the law of that country; or

(b)   The recognition or enforcement of the award would be contrary to the public policy of that country.

Article VI

If an application for the setting aside or suspension of the award has been made to a competent authority referred to in article V(1)(e), the authority before which the award is sought to be relied upon may, if it considers it proper, adjourn the decision on the enforcement of the award and may also, on the application of the party claiming enforcement of the award, order the other party to give suitable security.

Article VII

1.   The provisions of the present Convention shall not affect the validity of multilateral or bilateral agreements concerning the recognition and enforcement of arbitral awards entered into by the Contracting States nor deprive any interested party of any right he may have to avail himself of an arbitral award in the manner and to the extent allowed by the law or the treaties of the country where such award is sought to be relied upon.

2.   The Geneva Protocol on Arbitration Clauses of 1923 and the Geneva Convention on the Execution of Foreign Arbitral Awards of 1927

shall cease to have effect between Contracting States on their becoming bound and to the extent that they become bound, by this Convention.

Article VIII

1.   This Convention shall be open until 31 December 1958 for signature on behalf of any Member of the United Nations and also on behalf of any other State which is or hereafter becomes a member of any specialized agency of the United Nations, or which is or hereafter becomes a party to the Statute of the International Court of Justice, or any other State to which an invitation has been addressed by the General Assembly of the United Nations.

2.   This Convention shall be ratified and the instrument of ratification shall be deposited with the Secretary-General of the United Nations.

Article IX

1.   This Convention shall be open for accession to all States referred to in article VIII.

2.   Accession shall be effected by the deposit of an instrument of accession with the Secretary-General of the United Nations.

Article X

1.   Any State may, at the time of signature, ratification or accession, declare that this Convention shall extend to all or any of the territories for the international relations of which it is responsible. Such a declaration shall take effect when the Convention enters into force for the State concerned.

2.   At any time thereafter any such extension shall be made by notification addressed to the Secretary-General of the United Nations and shall take effect as from the ninetieth day after the day of receipt by the Secretary-General of the United Nations of this notification, or as from the date of entry into force of the Convention for the State concerned, whichever is the later.

3.   With respect to those territories to which this Convention is not extended at the time of signature, ratification or accession, each State concerned shall consider the possibility of taking the necessary steps in order to extend the application of this Convention to such territories, subject, where necessary for constitutional reasons, to the consent of the Governments of such territories.

Article XI

In the case of a federal or non-unitary State the following provisions shall apply:

(a) With respect to those articles of this Convention that come within the legislative jurisdiction of the federal authority, the obligations of the federal Government shall to this extent be the same as those of Contracting States which are not federal States;

(b)   With respect to those articles of this Convention that come within the legislative jurisdiction of constituent states or provinces which are not, under the constitutional system of the federation, bound to take legislative action, the federal Government shall bring such articles with a favorable recommendation to the notice of the appropriate authorities of constituent states or provinces at the earliest possible moment;

(c)   A federal State Party to this Convention shall, at the request of any other Contracting State transmitted through the Secretary-General of the United Nations, supply a statement of the law and practice of the federation and its constituent units in regard to any particular provision of this Convention, showing the extent to which effect has been given to that provision by legislative or other action.

Article XII

1.   This Convention shall come into force on the ninetieth day following the date of deposit of the third instrument of ratification or accession.

2.   For each State ratifying or acceding to this Convention after the deposit of the third instrument of ratification or accession, this Convention shall enter into force on the ninetieth day after deposit by such State of its instrument of ratification or accession.

Article XIII

1.   Any Contracting State may denounce this Convention by a written notification to the Secretary-General of the United Nations. Denunciation shall take effect one year after the date of receipt of the notification by the Secretary-General.

2.   Any State which has made a declaration or notification under article X may, at any time thereafter, by notification to the Secretary-General of the United Nations, declare that this Convention shall cease to extend to the territory concerned one year after the date of the receipt of the notification by the Secretary-General.

3.   This Convention shall continue to be applicable to arbitral awards in respect of which recognition or enforcement proceedings have been instituted before the denunciation takes effect.

Article XIV

A Contracting State shall not be entitled to avail itself of the present Convention against other Contracting States except to the extent that it is itself bound to apply the Convention.

Article XV

The Secretary-General of the United Nations shall notify the States contemplated in article VIII of the following:

(a)   Signatures and ratifications in accordance with article VIII;

(b)   Accessions in accordance with article IX;

(c)   Declarations and notifications under articles I, X and XI;

(d)   The date upon which this Convention enters into force in accordance with article XII;

(e)   Denunciations and notifications in accordance with article XIII.

Article XVI

1.   This Convention, of which the Chinese, English, French, Russian and Spanish texts shall be equally authentic, shall be deposited in the archives of the United Nations.

2.   The Secretary-General of the United Nations shall transmit a certified copy of this Convention to the States contemplated in article VIII.

LIST OF PARTIES TO THE NEW YORK CONVENTION AS OF FEBRUARY 2015*[1]

STATUS: Parties: 154.

All dates: DD/MM/YYYY

State	Notes	Signature	Ratification, Accession(*), Approval(†), Acceptance(‡) or Succession(§)	Entry into force
Afghanistan	(a), (c)		30/11/2004(*)	28/02/2005

    *   List can be found at the UN Website at http://www.uncitral.org/uncitral/en/uncitral_texts/arbitration/NYConvention_status.html. Reprinted with permission of UNCITRAL.

    [1]   a) The following States, having adopted the "reciprocity declaration," will restrict application of the Convention to recognition and enforcement of awards made in the territory of another Contracting State: Afghanistan, Algeria, Antigua and Barbuda, Argentina, Armenia, Bahrain, Barbados, Belgium, Bhutan, Bosnia and Herzegovina, Botswana, Brunei Darussalam, Bulgaria, Central African Republic, China, Croatia, Cuba, Cyprus, Czech Republic, Denmark, Djibouti, Ecuador, France, Greece, Guatemala, Holy See, Honduras, Hungary, India, Indonesia, Iran (Islamic Republic of), Ireland, Jamaica, Japan, Kenya, Kuwait, Lebanon, Liechtenstein, Luxembourg, Madagascar, Malaysia, Malta, Monaco, Mongolia, Montenegro, Morocco, Mozambique, Nepal, Netherlands, New Zealand, Nigeria, Norway, Pakistan, Philippines, Poland, Portugal, Republic of Korea, Republic of Moldova, Romania, Saint Vincent and the Grenadines, Saudi Arabia, Serbia, Singapore, Slovakia, Tajikistan, Trinidad and Tobago, Tunisia, Turkey, Uganda, United Kingdom of Great Britain and Northern Ireland, United Republic of Tanzania, United States of America, Venezuela (Bolivarian Republic of), Viet Nam.

Nine other States (Belarus, Bulgaria, Czech Republic, Romania, Lithuania, the Russian Federation, Slovakia, Ukraine and Viet Nam) have stated that they will apply the Convention with respect to non-contracting States as well, but on the condition of reciprocal treatment.

Five States (Bulgaria, Czech Republic, Romania, Slovakia and Viet Nam) have declared that they will only apply the Convention with regard to awards made in a Contracting State, but have added that they will nevertheless apply the Convention with regard to awards rendered in non-contracting States on the condition of reciprocal treatment.

b) The following States have adopted the "commercial declaration": Afghanistan, Algeria, Antigua and Barbuda, Argentina, Armenia, Bahrain, Barbados, Bhutan, Bosnia and Herzegovina, Botswana, Burundi, Central African Republic, China, Croatia, Cuba, Cyprus, Denmark, Djibouti, Ecuador, Greece, Guatemala, Holy See, Honduras, Hungary, India, Indonesia, Iran (Islamic

State	Notes	Signature	Ratification, Accession(*), Approval(†), Acceptance(‡) or Succession(§)	Entry into force
Albania			27/06/2001(*)	25/09/2001
Algeria	(a), (c)		07/02/1989(*)	08/05/1989
Antigua and Barbuda	(a), (c)		02/02/1989(*)	03/05/1989
Argentina	(a), (c)	26/08/1958	14/03/1989	12/06/1989
Armenia	(a), (c)		29/12/1997(*)	29/03/1998
Australia			26/03/1975(*)	24/06/1975
Austria			02/05/1961(*)	31/07/1961
Azerbaijan			29/02/2000(*)	29/05/2000
Bahamas			20/12/2006(*)	20/03/2007
Bahrain	(a), (c)		06/04/1988(*)	05/07/1988
Bangladesh			06/05/1992(*)	04/08/1992
Barbados	(a), (c)		16/03/1993(*)	14/06/1993
Belarus	(b)	29/12/1958	15/11/1960	13/02/1961
Belgium	(a)	10/06/1958	18/08/1975	16/11/1975
Benin			16/05/1974(*)	14/08/1974
Bhutan	(a), (c)		25/09/2014(*)	24/12/2014
Bolivia (Plurinational State of)			28/04/1995(*)	27/07/1995
Bosnia and Herzegovina	(a), (c), (i)		01/09/1993(§)	06/03/1992
Botswana	(a), (c)		20/12/1971(*)	19/03/1972
Brazil			07/06/2002(*)	05/09/2002
Brunei Darussalam	(a)		25/07/1996(*)	23/10/1996
Bulgaria	(a), (b)	17/12/1958	10/10/1961	08/01/1962
Burkina Faso			23/03/1987(*)	21/06/1987
Burundi	(c)		23/06/2014(*)	21/09/2014

Republic of), Jamaica, Madagascar, Malaysia, Monaco, Mongolia, Montenegro, Nepal, Nigeria, Philippines, Poland, Republic of Korea, Romania, Saint Vincent and the Grenadines, Serbia, The former Yugoslav Republic of Macedonia, Trinidad and Tobago, Tunisia, Turkey, United States of America, Venezuela (Bolivarian Republic of), Vietnam. These States will apply the Convention only with regard to differences arising out of a legal relationship which is considered commercial under the municipal law of the State making the declaration.

State	Notes	Signature	Ratification, Accession(*), Approval(†), Acceptance(‡) or Succession(§)	Entry into force
Cambodia			05/01/1960(*)	04/04/1960
Cameroon			19/02/1988(*)	19/05/1988
Canada	(d)		12/05/1986(*)	10/08/1986
Central African Republic	(a), (c)		15/10/1962(*)	13/01/1963
Chile			04/09/1975(*)	03/12/1975
China	(a), (c), (h)		22/01/1987(*)	22/04/1987
Colombia			25/09/1979(*)	24/12/1979
Cook Islands			12/01/2009(*)	12/04/2009
Costa Rica		10/06/1958	26/10/1987	24/01/1988
Côte d'Ivoire			01/02/1991(*)	02/05/1991
Croatia	(a), (c), (i)		26/07/1993(§)	08/10/1991
Cuba	(a), (c)		30/12/1974(*)	30/03/1975
Cyprus	(a), (c)		29/12/1980(*)	29/03/1981
Czech Republic	(a), (b)		30/09/1993(§)	01/01/1993
Democratic Republic of the Congo			05/11/2014(*)	03/02/2015
Denmark	(a), (c), (f)		22/12/1972(*)	22/03/1973
Djibouti	(a), (c)		14/06/1983(§)	27/06/1977
Dominica			28/10/1988(*)	26/01/1989
Dominican Republic			11/04/2002(*)	10/07/2002
Ecuador	(a), (c)	17/12/1958	03/01/1962	03/04/1962
Egypt			09/03/1959(*)	07/06/1959
El Salvador		10/06/1958	26/02/1998	27/05/1998
Estonia			30/08/1993(*)	28/11/1993
Fiji			27/09/2010(*)	26/12/2010
Finland		29/12/1958	19/01/1962	19/04/1962
France	(a)	25/11/1958	26/06/1959	24/09/1959
Gabon			15/12/2006(*)	15/03/2007

State	Notes	Signature	Ratification, Accession(*), Approval(†), Acceptance(‡) or Succession(§)	Entry into force
Georgia			02/06/1994(*)	31/08/1994
Germany		10/06/1958	30/06/1961	28/09/1961
Ghana			09/04/1968(*)	08/07/1968
Greece	(a), (c)		16/07/1962(*)	14/10/1962
Guatemala	(a), (c)		21/03/1984(*)	19/06/1984
Guinea			23/01/1991(*)	23/04/1991
Guyana			25/09/2014(*)	24/12/2014
Haiti			05/12/1983(*)	04/03/1984
Holy See	(a), (c)		14/05/1975(*)	12/08/1975
Honduras	(a), (c)		03/10/2000(*)	01/01/2001
Hungary	(a), (c)		05/03/1962(*)	03/06/1962
Iceland			24/01/2002(*)	24/04/2002
India	(a), (c)	10/06/1958	13/07/1960	11/10/1960
Indonesia	(a), (c)		07/10/1981(*)	05/01/1982
Iran (Islamic Republic of)	(a), (c)		15/10/2001(*)	13/01/2002
Ireland	(a)		12/05/1981(*)	10/08/1981
Israel		10/06/1958	05/01/1959	07/06/1959
Italy			31/01/1969(*)	01/05/1969
Jamaica	(a), (c)		10/07/2002(*)	08/10/2002
Japan	(a)		20/06/1961(*)	18/09/1961
Jordan		10/06/1958	15/11/1979	13/02/1980
Kazakhstan			20/11/1995(*)	18/02/1996
Kenya	(a)		10/02/1989(*)	11/05/1989
Kuwait	(a)		28/04/1978(*)	27/07/1978
Kyrgyzstan			18/12/1996(*)	18/03/1997
Lao People's Democratic Republic			17/06/1998(*)	15/09/1998
Latvia			14/04/1992(*)	13/07/1992
Lebanon	(a)		11/08/1998(*)	09/11/1998
Lesotho			13/06/1989(*)	11/09/1989
Liberia			16/09/2005(*)	15/12/2005

State	Notes	Signature	Ratification, Accession(*), Approval(†), Acceptance(‡) or Succession(§)	Entry into force
Liechtenstein	(a)		07/07/2011(*)	05/10/2011
Lithuania	(b)		14/03/1995(*)	12/06/1995
Luxembourg	(a)	11/11/1958	09/09/1983	08/12/1983
Madagascar	(a), (c)		16/07/1962(*)	14/10/1962
Malaysia	(a), (c)		05/11/1985(*)	03/02/1986
Mali			08/09/1994(*)	07/12/1994
Malta	(a), (i)		22/06/2000(*)	20/09/2000
Marshall Islands			21/12/2006(*)	21/03/2007
Mauritania			30/01/1997(*)	30/04/1997
Mauritius			19/06/1996(*)	17/09/1996
Mexico			14/04/1971(*)	13/07/1971
Monaco	(a), (c)	31/12/1958	02/06/1982	31/08/1982
Mongolia	(a), (c)		24/10/1994(*)	22/01/1995
Montenegro	(a), (c), (i)		23/10/2006(§)	03/06/2006
Morocco	(a)		12/02/1959(*)	07/06/1959
Mozambique	(a)		11/06/1998(*)	09/09/1998
Myanmar			16/04/2013(*)	15/07/2013
Nepal	(a), (c)		04/03/1998(*)	02/06/1998
Netherlands	(a), (e)	10/06/1958	24/04/1964	23/07/1964
New Zealand	(a)		06/01/1983(*)	06/04/1983
Nicaragua			24/09/2003(*)	23/12/2003
Niger			14/10/1964(*)	12/01/1965
Nigeria	(a), (c)		17/03/1970(*)	15/06/1970
Norway	(a), (j)		14/03/1961(*)	12/06/1961
Oman			25/02/1999(*)	26/05/1999
Pakistan	(a)	30/12/1958	14/07/2005	12/10/2005
Panama			10/10/1984(*)	08/01/1985
Paraguay			08/10/1997(*)	06/01/1998
Peru			07/07/1988(*)	05/10/1988
Philippines	(a), (c)	10/06/1958	06/07/1967	04/10/1967
Poland	(a), (c)	10/06/1958	03/10/1961	01/01/1962

State	Notes	Signature	Ratification, Accession(*), Approval(†), Acceptance(‡) or Succession(§)	Entry into force
Portugal	(a)		18/10/1994(*)	16/01/1995
Qatar			30/12/2002(*)	30/03/2003
Republic of Korea	(a), (c)		08/02/1973(*)	09/05/1973
Republic of Moldova	(a), (i)		18/09/1998(*)	17/12/1998
Romania	(a), (b), (c)		13/09/1961(*)	12/12/1961
Russian Federation	(b)	29/12/1958	24/08/1960	22/11/1960
Rwanda			31/10/2008(*)	29/01/2009
Saint Vincent and the Grenadines	(a), (c)		12/09/2000(*)	11/12/2000
San Marino			17/05/1979(*)	15/08/1979
Sao Tome and Principe			20/11/2012(*)	18/02/2013
Saudi Arabia	(a)		19/04/1994(*)	18/07/1994
Senegal			17/10/1994(*)	15/01/1995
Serbia	(a), (c), (i)		12/03/2001(§)	27/04/1992
Singapore	(a)		21/08/1986(*)	19/11/1986
Slovakia	(a), (b)		28/05/1993(§)	01/01/1993
Slovenia	(i)		06/07/1992(§)	25/06/1991
South Africa			03/05/1976(*)	01/08/1976
Spain			12/05/1977(*)	10/08/1977
Sri Lanka		30/12/1958	09/04/1962	08/07/1962
State of Palestine			02/01/2015(*)	02/04/2015
Sweden		23/12/1958	28/01/1972	27/04/1972
Switzerland		29/12/1958	01/06/1965	30/08/1965
Syrian Arab Republic			09/03/1959(*)	07/06/1959
Tajikistan	(a), (i), (j)		14/08/2012(*)	12/11/2012
Thailand			21/12/1959(*)	20/03/1960

State	Notes	Signature	Ratification, Accession(*), Approval(†), Acceptance(‡) or Succession(§)	Entry into force
The former Yugoslav Republic of Macedonia	(c), (i)		10/03/1994(§)	17/11/1991
Trinidad and Tobago	(a), (c)		14/02/1966(*)	15/05/1966
Tunisia	(a), (c)		17/07/1967(*)	15/10/1967
Turkey	(a), (c)		02/07/1992(*)	30/09/1992
Uganda	(a)		12/02/1992(*)	12/05/1992
Ukraine	(b)	29/12/1958	10/10/1960	08/01/1961
United Arab Emirates			21/08/2006(*)	19/11/2006
United Kingdom of Great Britain and Northern Ireland	(a), (g)		24/09/1975(*)	23/12/1975
United Republic of Tanzania	(a)		13/10/1964(*)	11/01/1965
United States of America	(a), (c)		30/09/1970(*)	29/12/1970
Uruguay			30/03/1983(*)	28/06/1983
Uzbekistan			07/02/1996(*)	07/05/1996
Venezuela (Bolivarian Republic of)	(a), (c)		08/02/1995(*)	09/05/1995
Viet Nam	(a), (b), (c)		12/09/1995(*)	11/12/1995
Zambia			14/03/2002(*)	12/06/2002
Zimbabwe			29/09/1994(*)	28/12/1994

Parties: 154

Notes

Declarations or other notifications pursuant to article I(3) and article X(1)

(a)   This State will apply the Convention only to recognition and enforcement of awards made in the territory of another contracting State.

(b)   With regard to awards made in the territory of non-contracting States, this State will apply the Convention only to the extent to which those States grant reciprocal treatment.

(c)   This State will apply the Convention only to differences arising out of legal relationships, whether contractual or not, that are considered commercial under the national law.

(d)   Canada declared that it would apply the Convention only to differences arising out of legal relationships, whether contractual or not, that were considered commercial under the laws of Canada, except in the case of the Province of Quebec, where the law did not provide for such limitation.

(e)   On 24 April 1964, the Netherlands declared that the Convention shall apply to the Netherlands Antilles.

(f)   On 10 February 1976, Denmark declared that the Convention shall apply to the Faeroe Islands and Greenland.

(g)   On 24 February 2014, the United Kingdom submitted a notification to extend territorial application of the Convention to the British Virgin Islands. For the following territories, the United Kingdom has submitted notifications extending territorial application and declaring that the Convention shall apply only to the recognition and enforcement of awards made in the territory of another Contracting State: Gibraltar (24 September 1975), Isle of Man (22 February 1979), Bermuda (14 November 1979), Cayman Islands (26 November 1980), Guernsey (19 April 1985), Bailiwick of Jersey (28 May 2002).

(h)   Upon resumption of sovereignty over Hong Kong on 1 July 1997, the Government of China extended the territorial application of the Convention to Hong Kong, Special Administrative Region of China, subject to the statement originally made by China upon accession to the Convention. On 19 July 2005, China declared that the Convention shall apply to the Macao Special Administrative Region of China, subject to the statement originally made by China upon accession to the Convention.

Reservations or other notifications

(i)   This State formulated a reservation with regards to retroactive application of the Convention.

(j)   This State formulated a reservation with regards to the application of the Convention in cases concerning immovable property.

B. EUROPEAN (GENEVA) CONVENTION ON INTERNATIONAL COMMERCIAL ARBITRATION OF 1961*

[Done at Geneva, 21 April 1961. Entered into force, 7 January 1964. United Nations Treaty Series, vol. 484, p. 364 No. 7041 (1963–1964)]

Article I.   Scope of the Convention

1.   This Convention shall apply:

(a)   to arbitration agreements concluded for the purpose of settling disputes arising from international trade between physical or legal persons having, when concluding the agreement, their habitual place of residence or their seat in different Contracting States;

(b)   to arbitral procedures and awards based on agreements referred to in paragraph 1(a) above.

2.   For the purpose of this Convention,

(a)   the term "arbitration agreement" shall mean either an arbitral clause in a contract or an arbitration agreement being signed by the parties, or contained in an exchange of letters, telegrams, or in a communication by teleprinter and, in relations between States whose laws do not require that an arbitration agreement be made in writing, any arbitration agreement concluded in the form authorized by these laws;

(b)   the term "arbitration" shall mean not only settlement by arbitrators appointed for each case (ad hoc arbitration) but also by permanent arbitral institutions;

(c)   the term "seat" shall mean the place of the situation of the establishment that has made the arbitration agreement.

Article II.   Right of legal persons of public law to resort to arbitration

1.   In the cases referred to in Article I, paragraph 1, of this Convention, legal persons considered by the law which is applicable to them as "legal persons of public law" have the right to conclude valid arbitration agreements.

2.   On signing, ratifying or acceding to this Convention any State shall be entitled to declare that it limits the above faculty to such conditions as may be stated in its declaration.

---

* The Convention can be found at https://treaties.un.org/doc/Treaties/1964/01/19640107%20 02-01%20AM/Ch_XXII_02p.pdf.

Article III. Right of foreign nationals to be designated as arbitrators

In arbitration covered by this Convention, foreign nationals may be designated as arbitrators.

Article IV. Organization of the arbitration

1.   The parties to an arbitration agreement shall be free to submit their disputes:

   (a)   to a permanent arbitral institution; in this case, the arbitration proceedings shall be held in conformity with the rules of the said institution;

   (b)   to an ad hoc arbitral procedure; in this case, they shall be free inter alia

   (i)   to appoint arbitrators or to establish means for their appointment in the event of an actual dispute;

   (ii)   to determine the place of arbitration; and

   (iii) to lay down the procedure to be followed by the arbitrators.

2.   Where the parties have agreed to submit any disputes to an ad hoc arbitration, and where within thirty days of the notification of the request for arbitration to the respondent one of the parties fails to appoint his arbitrator, the latter shall, unless otherwise provided, be appointed at the request of the other party by the President of the competent Chamber of Commerce of the country of the defaulting party's habitual place of residence or seat at the time of the introduction of the request for arbitration. This paragraph shall also apply to the replacement of the arbitrator(s) appointed by one of the parties or by the President of the Chamber of Commerce above referred to.

3.   Where the parties have agreed to submit any disputes to an ad hoc arbitration by one or more arbitrators and the arbitration agreement contains no indication regarding the organization of the arbitration, as mentioned in paragraph 1 of this article, the necessary steps shall be taken by the arbitrator(s) already appointed, unless the parties are able to agree thereon and without prejudice to the case referred to in paragraph 2 above. Where the parties cannot agree on the appointment of the sole arbitrator or where the arbitrators appointed cannot agree on the measures to be taken, the claimant shall apply for the necessary action, where the place of arbitration has been agreed upon by the parties, at his option to the President of the Chamber of Commerce of the place of arbitration agreed upon or to the President of the competent Chamber of Commerce of the respondent's habitual place of residence or seat at the time of the introduction of the request for arbitration. Where such a place has not been agreed upon, the claimant shall be entitled at his option to apply for the

necessary action either to the President of the competent Chamber of Commerce of the country of the respondent's habitual place of residence or seat at the time of the introduction of the request for arbitration, or to the Special Committee whose composition and procedure are specified in the Annex to this Convention. Where the claimant fails to exercise the rights given to him under this paragraph the respondent or the arbitrator(s) shall be entitled to do so.

4.   When seized of a request the President or the Special Committee shall be entitled as need be:

(a) to appoint the sole arbitrator, presiding arbitrator, umpire, or referee;

(b) to replace the arbitrator(s) appointed under any procedure other than that referred to in paragraph 2 above;

(c) to determine the place of arbitration, provided that the arbitrator(s) may fix another place of arbitration;

(d) to establish directly or by reference to the rules and statutes of a permanent arbitral institution the rules of procedure to be followed by the arbitrator(s), provided that the arbitrators have not established these rules themselves in the absence of any agreement thereon between the parties.

5.   Where the parties have agreed to submit their disputes to a permanent arbitral institution without determining the institution in question and cannot agree thereon, the claimant may request the determination of such institution in conformity with the procedure referred to in paragraph 3 above.

6.   Where the arbitration agreement does not specify the mode of arbitration (arbitration by a permanent arbitral institution or an ad hoc arbitration) to which the parties have agreed to submit their dispute, and where the parties cannot agree thereon, the claimant shall be entitled to have recourse in this case to the procedure referred to in paragraph 3 above to determine the question. The President of the competent Chamber of Commerce or the Special Committee, shall be entitled either to refer the parties to a permanent arbitral institution or to request the parties to appoint their arbitrators within such time-limits as the President of the competent Chamber of Commerce or the Special Committee may have fixed and to agree within such time-limits on the necessary measures for the functioning of the arbitration. In the latter case, the provisions of paragraphs 2, 3 and 4 of this Article shall apply.

7.   Where within a period of sixty days from the moment when he was requested to fulfil one of the functions set out in paragraphs 2, 3, 4, 5 and 6 of this Article, the President of the Chamber of Commerce designated by virtue of these paragraphs has not fulfilled one of these

functions, the party requesting shall be entitled to ask the Special Committee to do so.

Article V.   Plea as to arbitral jurisdiction

1.   The party which intends to raise a plea as to the arbitrator's jurisdiction based on the fact that the arbitration agreement was either non-existent or null and void or had lapsed shall do so during the arbitration proceedings, not later than the delivery of its statement of claim or defense relating to the substance of the dispute; those based on the fact that an arbitrator has exceeded his terms of reference shall be raised during the arbitration proceedings as soon as the question on which the arbitrator is alleged to have no jurisdiction is raised during the arbitral procedure. Where the delay in raising the plea is due to a cause which the arbitrator deems justified, the arbitrator shall declare the plea admissible.

2.   Pleas to the jurisdiction referred to in paragraph 1 above that have not been raised during the time-limits there referred to, may not be entered either during a subsequent stage of the arbitral proceedings where they are pleas left to the sole discretion of the parties under the law applicable by the arbitrator, or during subsequent court proceedings concerning the substance or the enforcement of the award where such pleas are left to the discretion of the parties under the rule of conflict of the court seized of the substance of the dispute or the enforcement of the award. The arbitrator's decision on the delay in raising the plea, will, however, be subject to judicial control.

3.   Subject to any subsequent judicial control provided for under the lex fori, the arbitrator whose jurisdiction is called in question shall be entitled to proceed with the arbitration, to rule on his own jurisdiction and to decide upon the existence or the validity of the arbitration agreement or of the contract of which the agreement forms part.

Article VI.   Jurisdiction of courts of law

1.   A plea as to the jurisdiction of the court made before the court seized by either party to the arbitration agreement, on the basis of the fact that an arbitration agreement exists shall, under penalty of estoppel, be presented by the respondent before or at the same time as the presentation of his substantial defense, depending upon whether the law of the court seized regards this plea as one of procedure or of substance.

2.   In taking a decision concerning the existence or the validity of an arbitration agreement, courts of Contracting States shall examine the validity of such agreement with reference to the capacity of the parties, under the law applicable to them, and with reference to other questions

(a) under the law to which the parties have subjected their arbitration agreement;

(b) failing any indication thereon, under the law of the country in which the award is to be made;

(c) failing any indication as to the law to which the parties have subjected the agreement, and where at the time when the question is raised in court the country in which the award is to be made cannot be determined, under the competent law by virtue of the rules of conflict of the court seized of the dispute. The courts may also refuse recognition of the arbitration agreement if under the law of their country the dispute is not capable of settlement by arbitration.

3.   Where either party to an arbitration agreement has initiated arbitration proceedings before any resort is had to a court, courts of Contracting States subsequently asked to deal with the same subject-matter between the same parties or with the question whether the arbitration agreement was non-existent or null and void or had lapsed, shall stay their ruling on the arbitrator's jurisdiction until the arbitral award is made, unless they have good and substantial reasons to the contrary.

4.   A request for interim measures or measures of conservation addressed to a judicial authority shall not be deemed incompatible with the arbitration agreement, or regarded as a submission of the substance of the case to the court.

Article VII.   Applicable law

1.   The parties shall be free to determine, by agreement, the law to be applied by the arbitrators to the substance of the dispute. Failing any indication by the parties as to the applicable law, the arbitrators shall apply the proper law under the rule of conflict that the arbitrators deem applicable. In both cases the arbitrators shall take account of the terms of the contract and trade usages.

2.   The arbitrators shall act as amiables compositeurs if the parties so decide and if they may do so under the law applicable to the arbitration.

Article VIII.   Reasons for the award

The parties shall be presumed to have agreed that reasons shall be given for the award unless they

(a) either expressly declare that reasons shall not be given; or

(b) have assented to an arbitral procedure under which it is not customary to give reasons for awards, provided that in this case neither party requests before the end of the hearing, or if there has not been a hearing then before the making of the award, that reasons be given.

Article IX.   Setting aside of the arbitral award

1.   The setting aside in a Contracting State of an arbitral award covered by this Convention shall only constitute a ground for the refusal of recognition or enforcement in another Contracting State where such setting aside took place in a State in which, or under the law of which, the award has been made and for one of the following reasons:

(a)   the parties to the arbitration agreement were under the law applicable to them, under some incapacity or the said agreement is not valid under the law to which the parties have subjected it or, failing any indication thereon, under the law of the country where the award was made; or

(b)   the party requesting the setting aside of the award was not given proper notice of the appointment of the arbitrator or of the arbitration proceedings or was otherwise unable to present his case; or

(c)   the award deals with a difference not contemplated by or not falling within the terms of the submission to arbitration, or it contains decisions on matters beyond the scope of the submission to arbitration, provided that, if the decisions on matters submitted to arbitration can be separated from those not so submitted, that part of the award which contains decisions on matters submitted to arbitration need not be set aside;

(d)   the composition of the arbitral authority or the arbitral procedure was not in accordance with the agreement of the parties, or failing such agreement, with the provisions of Article IV of this Convention.

2.   In relations between Contracting States that are also parties to the New York Convention on the Recognition and Enforcement of Foreign Arbitral Awards of 10th June 1958, paragraph 1 of this Article limits the application of Article V(1)(e) of the New York Convention solely to the cases of setting aside set out under paragraph 1 above.

Article X.   Final clauses

1.   This Convention is open for signature or accession by countries members of the Economic Commission for Europe and countries admitted to the Commission in a consultative capacity under paragraph 8 of the Commission's terms of reference.

2.   Such countries as may participate in certain activities of the Economic Commission for Europe in accordance with paragraph 11 of the

Commission's terms of reference may become Contracting Parties to this Convention by acceding thereto after its entry into force.

3.   The Convention shall be open for signature until 31 December 1961 inclusive. Thereafter, it shall be open for accession.

4.   This Convention shall be ratified.

5.   Ratification or accession shall be effected by the deposit of an instrument with the Secretary-General of the United Nations.

6.   When signing, ratifying or acceding to this Convention, the Contracting Parties shall communicate to the Secretary-General of the United Nations a list of the Chambers of Commerce or other institutions in their country who will exercise the functions conferred by virtue of Article IV of this Convention on Presidents of the competent Chambers of Commerce.

7.   The provisions of the present Convention shall not affect the validity of multilateral or bilateral agreements concerning arbitration entered into by Contracting States.

8.   This Convention shall come into force on the ninetieth day after five of the countries referred to in paragraph 1 above have deposited their instruments of ratification or accession. For any country ratifying or acceding to it later this Convention shall enter into force on the ninetieth day after the said country has deposited its instrument of ratification or accession.

9.   Any Contracting Party may denounce this Convention by so notifying the Secretary-General of the United Nations. Denunciation shall take effect twelve months after the date of receipt by the Secretary-General of the notification of denunciation.

10. If, after the entry into force of this Convention, the number of Contracting Parties is reduced, as a result of denunciations, to less than five, the Convention shall cease to be in force from the date on which the last of such denunciations takes effect.

11. The Secretary-General of the United Nations shall notify the countries referred to in paragraph 1, and the countries which have become Contracting Parties under paragraph 2 above, of

(a)   declarations made under Article II, paragraph 2;

(b)   ratifications and accessions under paragraphs 1 and 2 above;

(c)   communications received in pursuance of paragraph 6 above;

(d)   the dates of entry into force of this Convention in accordance with paragraph 8 above;

(e) denunciations under paragraph 9 above;

(f) the termination of this Convention in accordance with paragraph 10 above.

12. After 31 December 1961, the original of this Convention shall be deposited with the Secretary-General of the United Nations, who shall transmit certified true copies to each of the countries mentioned in paragraphs 1 and 2 above.

IN WITNESS WHEREOF the undersigned, being duly authorized thereto, have signed this Convention.

DONE at Geneva, this twenty-first day of April, one thousand nine hundred and sixty-one, in a single copy in the English, French and Russian languages, each text being equally authentic.

LIST OF PARTIES TO THE 1961 GENEVA CONVENTION ON INTERNATIONAL COMMERCIAL ARBITRATION AS OF OCTOBER 2014*

STATUS: Signatories: 16. Parties: 31.

Participant	Signature	Ratification, Accession(a), Succession(d)
Albania		27 June 2001 a
Austria	21 April 1961	6 March 1964
Azerbaijan		17 January 2005 a
Belarus	21 April 1961	14 October 1963
Belgium	21 April 1961	9 October 1975
Bosnia and Herzegovina		1 September 1993 d
Bulgaria	21 April 1961	13 May 1964
Burkina Faso		26 January 1965 a
Croatia		26 July 1993 d
Cuba		1 September 1965 a
Czech Republic		30 September 1993 d
Denmark	21 April 1961	22 December 1972
Finland	21 December 1961	
France	21 April 1961	16 December 1966
Germany	21 April 1961	27 October 1964
Hungary	21 April 1961	9 October 1963
Italy	21 April 1961	3 August 1970
Kazakhstan		20 November 1995 a
Latvia		20 March 2003 a

---

*   The list of participants can be found at the website of the UN https://treaties.un.org/pages/ViewDetails.aspx?src=TREATY&mtdsg_no=XXII-2&chapter=22&lang=en.

Participant	Signature	Ratification, Accession(a), Succession(d)
Luxembourg		26 March 1982 a
Montenegro		23 October 2006 d
Poland	21 April 1961	15 September 1964
Republic of Moldova		5 March 1998 a
Romania	21 April 1961	16 August 1963
Russian Federation	21 April 1961	27 June 1962
Serbia		12 March 2001 d
Slovakia		28 May 1993 d
Slovenia		6 July 1992 d
Spain	14 December 1961	12 May 1975
The former Yugoslav Republic of Macedonia		10 March 1994 d
Turkey	21 April 1961	24 January 1992
Ukraine	21 April 1961	18 March 1963

C.   INTER-AMERICAN CONVENTION ON INTERNATIONAL COMMERCIAL ARBITRATION*

[Done at Panama City, 30 January, 1975; entered into force January 16, 1976; *reprinted in* 14 I.L.M. 336 (1975)]

The Governments of the Member States of the Organization of American States, desirous of concluding a convention on international commercial arbitration, have agreed as follows:

Article 1

An agreement in which the parties undertake to submit to arbitral decision any differences that may arise or have arisen between them with respect to a commercial transaction is valid. The agreement shall be set forth in an instrument signed by the parties, or in the form of an exchange of letters, telegrams, or telex communications.

Article 2

Arbitrators shall be appointed in the manner agreed upon by the parties. Their appointment may be delegated to a third party, whether a natural or juridical person.

Arbitrators may be nationals or foreigners.

---

*   The Convention can be found at the Website of the Organization of American States at http://www.oas.org/juridico/english/treaties/b-35.html.

Article 3

In the absence of an express agreement between the parties, the arbitration shall be conducted in accordance with the rules of procedure of the Inter-American Commercial Arbitration Commission.

Article 4

An arbitral decision or award that is not appealable under the applicable law or procedural rules shall have the force of a final judicial judgement. Its execution or recognition may be ordered in the same manner as that of decisions handed down by national or foreign ordinary courts, in accordance with the procedural laws of the country where it is to be executed and the provisions of international treaties.

Article 5

1. The recognition and execution of the decision may be refused, at the request of the party against which it is made, only if such party is able to prove to the competent authority of the State in which recognition and execution are requested:

   a. That the parties to the agreement were subject to some incapacity under the applicable law or that the agreement is not valid under the law to which the parties have submitted it, or, if such law is not specified, under the law of the State in which the decision was made; or

   b. That the party against which the arbitral decision has been made was not duly notified of the appointment of the arbitrator or of the arbitration procedure to be followed, or was unable, for any other reason, to present his defense; or

   c. That the decision concerns a dispute not envisaged in the agreement between the parties to submit to arbitration; nevertheless, if the provisions of the decision that refer to issues submitted to arbitration can be separated from those not submitted to arbitration, the former may be recognized and executed; or

   d. That the constitution of the arbitral tribunal or the arbitration procedure has not been carried out in accordance with the terms of the agreement signed by the parties or, in the absence of such agreement, that the constitution of the arbitral tribunal or the arbitration procedure has not been carried out in accordance with the law of the State where the arbitration took place; or

   e. That the decision is not yet binding on the parties or has been annulled or suspended by a competent authority of the State in which, or according to the law of which, the decision has been made.

2.   The recognition and execution of an arbitral decision may also be refused if the competent authority of the State in which the recognition and execution is requested finds:

    a.   That the subject of the dispute cannot be settled by arbitration under the law of that State; or

    b.   That the recognition or execution of the decision would be contrary to the public policy ("ordre public") of that State.

Article 6

If the competent authority mentioned in Article 5. 1. e has been requested to annual or suspend the arbitral decision, the authority before which such decision is invoked may, if it deems it appropriate, postpone a decision on the execution of the arbitral decision and, at the request of the party requesting execution, may also instruct the other party to provide appropriate guaranties.

Article 7

This Convention shall be open for signature by the Member States of the Organization of American States.

Article 8

This Convention is subject to ratification. The instruments of ratification shall be deposited with the General Secretariat of the Organization of American States.

Article 9

This Convention shall remain open for accession by any other State. The instruments of accession shall be deposited with the General Secretariat of the Organization of American States.

Article 10

This Convention shall enter into force on the thirtieth day following the date of deposit of the second instrument of ratification.

For each State ratifying or acceding to the Convention after the deposit of the second instrument of ratification, the Convention shall enter into force on the thirtieth day after deposit by such State of its instrument of ratification or accession.

Article 11

If a State Party has two or more territorial units in which different systems of law apply in relation to the matters dealt with in this Convention, it may, at the time of signature, ratification or accession, declare that this Convention shall extend to all its territorial units or only to one or more of them.

Such declaration may be modified by subsequent declarations, which shall expressly indicate the territorial unit or units to which the Convention applies. Such subsequent declarations shall be transmitted to the General Secretariat of the Organization of American States, and shall become effective thirty days after the date of their receipt.

Article 12

This Convention shall remain in force indefinitely, but any of the States Parties may denounce it. The instrument of denunciation shall be deposited with the General Secretariat of the Organization of American States. After one year from the date of deposit of the instrument of denunciation, the Convention shall no longer be in effect for the denouncing State, but shall remain in effect for the other States Parties.

Article 13

The original instrument of this Convention, the English, French, Portuguese and Spanish texts of which are equally authentic, shall be deposited with the General Secretariat of the Organization of American States. The Secretariat shall notify the Member States of the Organization of American States and the States that have acceded to the Convention of the signatures, deposits of instruments of ratification, accession, and denunciation as well as of reservations, if any. It shall also transmit the declarations referred to in Article 11 of this Convention.

LIST OF PARTIES TO THE INTER-AMERICAN CONVENTION ON INTERNATIONAL COMMERCIAL ARBITRATION AS OF OCTOBER 2014*

Signatory Countries	Signature	Ratification	Deposit of Instrument
Argentina	03/15/91	11/03/94	01/05/95
Bolivia	08/02/83	10/08/98	04/29/99
Brazil	01/30/75	08/31/95	11/27/95
Chile	01/30/75	04/08/76	05/17/76
Colombia	01/30/75	11/18/86	12/29/86
Costa Rica	01/30/75	01/02/78	01/20/78
Dominican Republic	04/18/77	02/11/08	07/07/08
Ecuador	01/30/75	08/06/91	10/23/91
El Salvador	01/30/75	06/27/80	08/11/80
Guatemala	01/30/75	07/07/86	08/20/86
Honduras	01/30/75	01/08/79	03/22/79
Mexico	10/27/77	02/15/78	03/27/78
Nicaragua	01/30/75	07/15/03	10/02/03
Panama	01/30/75	11/11/75	12/17/75

* List can be found at the website of the Organization of American States http://www.oas.org/juridico/english/treaties/b-35.html.

Signatory Countries	Signature	Ratification	Deposit of Instrument
Paraguay	08/26/75	12/02/76	12/15/76
Peru	04/21/88	05/02/89	05/22/89
United States	06/09/78	11/10/86	09/27/90
Uruguay	01/30/75	03/29/77	04/25/77
Venezuela	01/30/75	03/22/85	05/16/85

CHAPTER II

UNCITRAL (UN COMMISSION ON INTERNATIONAL TRADE LAW) ENACTMENTS AND OTHER MODEL NORMS

■ ■ ■

A. UNCITRAL MODEL LAW ON INTERNATIONAL COMMERCIAL ARBITRATION [A PROPOSAL FOR NATIONAL LEGISLATION]

A.1. THE 1985 TEXT OF THE UNCITRAL MODEL LAW ON INTERNATIONAL COMMERCIAL ARBITRATION*

Chapter I

General Provisions

Article 1

Scope of application[1]

(1)   This Law applies to international commercial[2] arbitration, subject to any agreement in force between this State and any other State or States.

(2)   The provisions of this Law, except articles 8, 9, 35 and 36, apply only if the place of arbitration is in the territory of this State.

(3)   An arbitration is international if:

(a)   the parties to an arbitration agreement have, at the time of the conclusion of that agreement, their places of business in different States; or

---

*   Reprinted with permission from UNCITRAL.

[1]   *Article headings are for reference purposes only and are not to be used for purposes of interpretation.*

[2]   The term "commercial" should be given a wide interpretation so as to cover matters arising from all relationships of a commercial nature, whether contractual or not. Relationships of a commercial nature include, but are not limited to, the following transactions: any trade transaction for the supply or exchange of goods or services; distribution agreement; commercial representation or agency; factoring; leasing; construction of works; consulting; engineering; licensing; investment; financing; banking; insurance; exploitation agreement or concession; joint venture and other forms of industrial or business co-operation; carriage of goods or passengers by air, sea, rail or road.

(b) one of the following places is situated outside the State in which the parties have their places of business:

    (i) the place of arbitration if determined in, or pursuant to, the arbitration agreement;

    (ii) any place where a substantial part of the obligations of the commercial relationship is to be performed or the place with which the subject-matter of the dispute is most closely connected; or

(c) the parties have expressly agreed that the subject-matter of the arbitration agreement relates to more than one country.

(4) For the purposes of paragraph (3) of this article:

(a) if a party has more than one place of business, the place of business is that which has the closest relationship to the arbitration agreement;

(b) if a party does not have a place of business, reference is to be made to his habitual residence.

(5) This Law shall not affect any other law of this State by virtue of which certain disputes may not be submitted to arbitration or may be submitted to arbitration only according to provisions other than those of this Law.

Article 2

Definitions and rules of interpretation

For the purposes of this Law:

(a) "arbitration" means any arbitration whether or not administered by a permanent arbitral institution;

(b) "arbitral tribunal" means a sole arbitrator or a panel of arbitrators;

(c) "court" means a body or organ of the judicial system of a State;

(d) where a provision of this Law, except article 28, leaves the parties free to determine a certain issue, such freedom includes the right of the parties to authorize a third party, including an institution, to make that determination;

(e) where a provision of this Law refers to the fact that the parties have agreed or that they may agree or in any other way refers to an agreement of the parties, such agreement includes any arbitration rules referred to in that agreement;

(f) where a provision of this Law, other than in articles 25 (a) and 32 (2) (a), refers to a claim, it also applies to a counter-claim, and where it refers to a defense, it also applies to a defense to such counter-claim.

Article 3

Receipt of written communications

(1) Unless otherwise agreed by the parties:

(a) any written communication is deemed to have been received if it is delivered to the addressee personally or if it is delivered at his place of business, habitual residence or mailing address; if none of these can be found after making a reasonable inquiry, a written communication is deemed to have been received if it is sent to the addressee's last-known place of business, habitual residence or mailing address by registered letter or any other means which provides a record of the attempt to deliver it;

(b) the communication is deemed to have been received on the day it is so delivered.

(2) The provisions of this article do not apply to communications in court proceedings.

Article 4

Waiver of right to object

A party who knows that any provision of this Law from which the parties may derogate or any requirement under the arbitration agreement has not been complied with and yet proceeds with the arbitration without stating his objection to such non-compliance without undue delay or, if a time-limit is provided therefore, within such period of time, shall be deemed to have waived his right to object.

Article 5

Extent of court intervention

In matters governed by this Law, no court shall intervene except where so provided in this Law.

Article 6

Court or other authority for certain functions of arbitration assistance and supervision

The functions referred to in articles 11(3), 11(4), 13(3), 14, 16(3) and 34(2) shall be performed by . . . [Each State enacting this model law specifies the court, courts or, where referred to therein, other authority competent to perform these functions.]

Chapter II

Arbitration Agreement

Article 7

Definition and form of arbitration agreement

(1) "Arbitration agreement" is an agreement by the parties to submit to arbitration all or certain disputes which have arisen or which may arise between them in respect of a defined legal relationship, whether contractual or not. An arbitration agreement may be in the form of an arbitration clause in a contract or in the form of a separate agreement.

(2) The arbitration agreement shall be in writing. An agreement is in writing if it is contained in a document signed by the parties or in an exchange of letters, telex, telegrams or other means of telecommunication which provide a record of the agreement, or in an exchange of statements of claim and defense in which the existence of an agreement is alleged by one party and not denied by another. The reference in a contract to a document containing an arbitration clause constitutes an arbitration agreement provided that the contract is in writing and the reference is such as to make that clause part of the contract.

Article 8

Arbitration agreement and substantive claim before court

(1) A court before which an action is brought in a matter which is the subject of an arbitration agreement shall, if a party so requests not later than when submitting his first statement on the substance of the dispute, refer the parties to arbitration unless it finds that the agreement is null and void, inoperative or incapable of being performed.

(2) Where an action referred to in paragraph (1) of this article has been brought, arbitral proceedings may nevertheless be commenced or continued, and an award may be made, while the issue is pending before the court.

Article 9

Arbitration agreement and interim court measures

It is not incompatible with an arbitration agreement for a party to request, before or during arbitral proceedings, from a court an interim measure of protection and for a court to grant such measure.

Chapter III

Composition of Arbitral Tribunal

Article 10

Number of arbitrators

(1) The parties are free to determine the number of arbitrators.

(2) Failing such determination, the number of arbitrators shall be three.

Article 11

Appointment of arbitrators

(1) No person shall be precluded by reason of his nationality from acting as an arbitrator, unless otherwise agreed by the parties.

(2) The parties are free to agree on a procedure of appointing the arbitrator or arbitrators, subject to the provisions of paragraphs (4) and (5) of this article.

(3) Failing such agreement,

(a) in an arbitration with three arbitrators, each party shall appoint one arbitrator, and the two arbitrators thus appointed shall appoint the third arbitrator; if a party fails to appoint the arbitrator within thirty days of receipt of a request to do so from the other party, or if the two arbitrators fail to agree on the third arbitrator within thirty days of their appointment, the appointment shall be made, upon request of a party, by the court or other authority specified in article 6;

(b) in an arbitration with a sole arbitrator, if the parties are unable to agree on the arbitrator, he shall be appointed, upon request of a party, by the court or other authority specified in article 6.

(4) Where, under an appointment procedure agreed upon by the parties,

(a) a party fails to act as required under such procedure, or

(b) the parties, or two arbitrators, are unable to reach an agreement expected of them under such procedure, or

(c) a third party, including an institution, fails to perform any function entrusted to it under such procedure, any party may request the court or other authority specified in article 6 to take the necessary measure, unless the agreement on the appointment procedure provides other means for securing the appointment.

(5) A decision on a matter entrusted by paragraph (3) or (4) of this article to the court or other authority specified in article 6 shall be subject

to no appeal. The court or other authority, in appointing an arbitrator, shall have due regard to any qualifications required of the arbitrator by the agreement of the parties and to such considerations as are likely to secure the appointment of an independent and impartial arbitrator and, in the case of a sole or third arbitrator, shall take into account as well the advisability of appointing an arbitrator of a nationality other than those of the parties.

Article 12

Grounds for challenge

(1) When a person is approached in connection with his possible appointment as an arbitrator, he shall disclose any circumstances likely to give rise to justifiable doubts as to his impartiality or independence. An arbitrator, from the time of his appointment and throughout the arbitral proceedings, shall without delay disclose any such circumstances to the parties unless they have already been informed of them by him.

(2) An arbitrator may be challenged only if circumstances exist that give rise to justifiable doubts as to his impartiality or independence, or if he does not possess qualifications agreed to by the parties. A party may challenge an arbitrator appointed by him, or in whose appointment he has participated, only for reasons of which he becomes aware after the appointment has been made.

Article 13

Challenge procedure

(1) The parties are free to agree on a procedure for challenging an arbitrator, subject to the provisions of paragraph (3) of this article.

(2) Failing such agreement, a party who intends to challenge an arbitrator shall, within fifteen days after becoming aware of the constitution of the arbitral tribunal or after becoming aware of any circumstance referred to in article 12(2), send a written statement of the reasons for the challenge to the arbitral tribunal. Unless the challenged arbitrator withdraws from his office or the other party agrees to the challenge, the arbitral tribunal shall decide on the challenge.

(3) If a challenge under any procedure agreed upon by the parties or under the procedure of paragraph (2) of this article is not successful, the challenging party may request, within thirty days after having received notice of the decision rejecting the challenge, the court or other authority specified in article 6 to decide on the challenge, which decision shall be subject to no appeal; while such a request is pending, the arbitral tribunal, including the challenged arbitrator, may continue the arbitral proceedings and make an award.

Article 14

Failure or impossibility to act

(1) If an arbitrator becomes de jure or de facto unable to perform his functions or for other reasons fails to act without undue delay, his mandate terminates if he withdraws from his office or if the parties agree on the termination. Otherwise, if a controversy remains concerning any of these grounds, any party may request the court or other authority specified in article 6 to decide on the termination of the mandate, which decision shall be subject to no appeal.

(2) If, under this article or article 13 (2), an arbitrator withdraws from his office or a party agrees to the termination of the mandate of an arbitrator, this does not imply acceptance of the validity of any ground referred to in this article or article 12 (2).

Article 15

Appointment of substitute arbitrator

Where the mandate of an arbitrator terminates under article 13 or 14 or because of his withdrawal from office for any other reason or because of the revocation of his mandate by agreement of the parties or in any other case of termination of his mandate, a substitute arbitrator shall be appointed according to the rules that were applicable to the appointment of the arbitrator being replaced.

Chapter IV

Jurisdiction of Arbitral Tribunal

Article 16

Competence of arbitral tribunal to rule on its jurisdiction

(1) The arbitral tribunal may rule on its own jurisdiction, including any objections with respect to the existence or validity of the arbitration agreement. For that purpose, an arbitration clause which forms part of a contract shall be treated as an agreement independent of the other terms of the contract. A decision by the arbitral tribunal that the contract is null and void shall not entail ipso jure the invalidity of the arbitration clause.

(2) A plea that the arbitral tribunal does not have jurisdiction shall be raised not later than the submission of the statement of defense. A party is not precluded from raising such a plea by the fact that he has appointed, or participated in the appointment of, an arbitrator. A plea that the arbitral tribunal is exceeding the scope of its authority shall be raised as soon as the matter alleged to be beyond the scope of its authority is raised during the arbitral proceedings. The arbitral tribunal may, in either case, admit a later plea if it considers the delay justified.

(3)   The arbitral tribunal may rule on a plea referred to in paragraph (2) of this article either as a preliminary question or in an award on the merits. If the arbitral tribunal rules as a preliminary question that it has jurisdiction, any party may request, within thirty days after having received notice of that ruling, the court specified in article 6 to decide the matter, which decision shall be subject to no appeal; while such a request is pending, the arbitral tribunal may continue the arbitral proceedings and make an award.

Article 17

Power of arbitral tribunal to order interim measures

Unless otherwise agreed by the parties, the arbitral tribunal may, at the request of a party, order any party to take such interim measure of protection as the arbitral tribunal may consider necessary in respect of the subject-matter of the dispute. The arbitral tribunal may require any party to provide appropriate security in connection with such measure.

Chapter V

Conduct of Arbitral Proceedings

Article 18

Equal treatment of parties

The parties shall be treated with equality and each party shall be given a full opportunity of presenting his case.

Article 19

Determination of rules of procedure

(1)   Subject to the provisions of this Law, the parties are free to agree on the procedure to be followed by the arbitral tribunal in conducting the proceedings.

(2)   Failing such agreement, the arbitral tribunal may, subject to the provisions of this Law, conduct the arbitration in such manner as it considers appropriate. The power conferred upon the arbitral tribunal includes the power to determine the admissibility, relevance, materiality and weight of any evidence.

Article 20

Place of arbitration

(1)   The parties are free to agree on the place of arbitration. Failing such agreement, the place of arbitration shall be determined by the arbitral tribunal having regard to the circumstances of the case, including the convenience of the parties.

(2)   Notwithstanding the provisions of paragraph (1) of this article, the arbitral tribunal may, unless otherwise agreed by the parties, meet at

any place it considers appropriate for consultation among its members, for hearing witnesses, experts or the parties, or for inspection of goods, other property or documents.

Article 21

Commencement of arbitral proceedings

Unless otherwise agreed by the parties, the arbitral proceedings in respect of a particular dispute commence on the date on which a request for that dispute to be referred to arbitration is received by the respondent.

Article 22

Language

(1)   The parties are free to agree on the language or languages to be used in the arbitral proceedings. Failing such agreement, the arbitral tribunal shall determine the language or languages to be used in the proceedings. This agreement or determination, unless otherwise specified therein, shall apply to any written statement by a party, any hearing and any award, decision or other communication by the arbitral tribunal.

(2)   The arbitral tribunal may order that any documentary evidence shall be accompanied by a translation into the language or languages agreed upon by the parties or determined by the arbitral tribunal.

Article 23

Statements of claim and defense

(1)   Within the period of time agreed by the parties or determined by the arbitral tribunal, the claimant shall state the facts supporting his claim, the points at issue and the relief or remedy sought, and the respondent shall state his defense in respect of these particulars, unless the parties have otherwise agreed as to the required elements of such statements. The parties may submit with their statements all documents they consider to be relevant or may add a reference to the documents or other evidence they will submit.

(2)   Unless otherwise agreed by the parties, either party may amend or supplement his claim or defense during the course of the arbitral proceedings, unless the arbitral tribunal considers it inappropriate to allow such amendment having regard to the delay in making it.

Article 24

Hearings and written proceedings

(1)   Subject to any contrary agreement by the parties, the arbitral tribunal shall decide whether to hold oral hearings for the presentation of evidence or for oral argument, or whether the proceedings shall be conducted on the basis of documents and other materials. However, unless

the parties have agreed that no hearings shall be held, the arbitral tribunal shall hold such hearings at an appropriate stage of the proceedings, if so requested by a party.

(2) The parties shall be given sufficient advance notice of any hearing and of any meeting of the arbitral tribunal for the purposes of inspection of goods, other property or documents.

(3) All statements, documents or other information supplied to the arbitral tribunal by one party shall be communicated to the other party. Also any expert report or evidentiary document on which the arbitral tribunal may rely in making its decision shall be communicated to the parties.

Article 25

Default of a party

Unless otherwise agreed by the parties, if, without showing sufficient cause,

(a) the claimant fails to communicate his statement of claim in accordance with article 23(1), the arbitral tribunal shall terminate the proceedings;

(b) the respondent fails to communicate his statement of defense in accordance with article 23(1), the arbitral tribunal shall continue the proceedings without treating such failure in itself as an admission of the claimant's allegations;

(c) any party fails to appear at a hearing or to produce documentary evidence, the arbitral tribunal may continue the proceedings and make the award on the evidence before it.

Article 26

Expert appointed by arbitral tribunal

(1) Unless otherwise agreed by the parties, the arbitral tribunal

(a) may appoint one or more experts to report to it on specific issues to be determined by the arbitral tribunal;

(b) may require a party to give the expert any relevant information or to produce, or to provide access to, any relevant documents, goods or other property for his inspection.

(2) Unless otherwise agreed by the parties, if a party so requests or if the arbitral tribunal considers it necessary, the expert shall, after delivery of his written or oral report, participate in a hearing where the parties have the opportunity to put questions to him and to present expert witnesses in order to testify on the points at issue.

Article 27

Court assistance in taking evidence

The arbitral tribunal or a party with the approval of the arbitral tribunal may request from a competent court of this State assistance in taking evidence. The court may execute the request within its competence and according to its rules on taking evidence.

Chapter VI

Making of Award and Termination of Proceedings

Article 28

Rules applicable to substance of dispute

(1) The arbitral tribunal shall decide the dispute in accordance with such rules of law as are chosen by the parties as applicable to the substance of the dispute. Any designation of the law or legal system of a given State shall be construed, unless otherwise expressed, as directly referring to the substantive law of that State and not to its conflict of laws rules.

(2) Failing any designation by the parties, the arbitral tribunal shall apply the law determined by the conflict of laws rules which it considers applicable.

(3) The arbitral tribunal shall decide ex aequo et bono or as amiable compositeur only if the parties have expressly authorized it to do so.

(4) In all cases, the arbitral tribunal shall decide in accordance with the terms of the contract and shall take into account the usages of the trade applicable to the transaction.

Article 29

Decision-making by panel of arbitrators

In arbitral proceedings with more than one arbitrator, any decision of the arbitral tribunal shall be made, unless otherwise agreed by the parties, by a majority of all its members. However, questions of procedure may be decided by a presiding arbitrator, if so authorized by the parties or all members of the arbitral tribunal.

Article 30

Settlement

(1) If, during arbitral proceedings, the parties settle the dispute, the arbitral tribunal shall terminate the proceedings and, if requested by the parties and not objected to by the arbitral tribunal, record the settlement in the form of an arbitral award on agreed terms.

(2)   An award on agreed terms shall be made in accordance with the provisions of article 31 and shall state that it is an award. Such an award has the same status and effect as any other award on the merits of the case.

Article 31

Form and contents of award

(1)   The award shall be made in writing and shall be signed by the arbitrator or arbitrators. In arbitral proceedings with more than one arbitrator, the signatures of the majority of all members of the arbitral tribunal shall suffice, provided that the reason for any omitted signature is stated.

(2)   The award shall state the reasons upon which it is based, unless the parties have agreed that no reasons are to be given or the award is an award on agreed terms under article 30.

(3)   The award shall state its date and the place of arbitration as determined in accordance with article 20(1). The award shall be deemed to have been made at that place.

(4)   After the award is made, a copy signed by the arbitrators in accordance with paragraph (1) of this article shall be delivered to each party.

Article 32

Termination of proceedings

(1)   The arbitral proceedings are terminated by the final award or by an order of the arbitral tribunal in accordance with paragraph (2) of this article.

(2)   The arbitral tribunal shall issue an order for the termination of the arbitral proceedings when:

(a)   the claimant withdraws his claim, unless the respondent objects thereto and the arbitral tribunal recognizes a legitimate interest on his part in obtaining a final settlement of the dispute;

(b)   the parties agree on the termination of the proceedings;

(c)   the arbitral tribunal finds that the continuation of the proceedings has for any other reason become unnecessary or impossible.

(3)   The mandate of the arbitral tribunal terminates with the termination of the arbitral proceedings, subject to the provisions of articles 33 and 34(4).

Article 33

Correction and interpretation of award; additional award

(1)   Within thirty days of receipt of the award, unless another period of time has been agreed upon by the parties:

(a)   a party, with notice to the other party, may request the arbitral tribunal to correct in the award any errors in computation, any clerical or typographical errors or any errors of similar nature;

(b)   if so agreed by the parties, a party, with notice to the other party, may request the arbitral tribunal to give an interpretation of a specific point or part of the award.

If the arbitral tribunal considers the request to be justified, it shall make the correction or give the interpretation within thirty days of receipt of the request. The interpretation shall form part of the award.

(2)   The arbitral tribunal may correct any error of the type referred to in paragraph (1)(a) of this article on its own initiative within thirty days of the date of the award.

(3)   Unless otherwise agreed by the parties, a party, with notice to the other party, may request, within thirty days of receipt of the award, the arbitral tribunal to make an additional award as to claims presented in the arbitral proceedings but omitted from the award. If the arbitral tribunal considers the request to be justified, it shall make the additional award within sixty days.

(4)   The arbitral tribunal may extend, if necessary, the period of time within which it shall make a correction, interpretation or an additional award under paragraph (1) or (3) of this article.

(5)   The provisions of article 31 shall apply to a correction or interpretation of the award or to an additional award.

Chapter VII

Recourse Against Award

Article 34

Application for setting aside as exclusive recourse against arbitral award

(1)   Recourse to a court against an arbitral award may be made only by an application for setting aside in accordance with paragraphs (2) and (3) of this article.

(2)   An arbitral award may be set aside by the court specified in article 6 only if:

(a)   the party making the application furnishes proof that:

    (i)   a party to the arbitration agreement referred to in article 7 was under some incapacity; or the said agreement is not valid under the law to which the parties have subjected it or, failing any indication thereon, under the law of this State; or

    (ii)   the party making the application was not given proper notice of the appointment of an arbitrator or of the arbitral proceedings or was otherwise unable to present his case; or

    (iii) the award deals with a dispute not contemplated by or not falling within the terms of the submission to arbitration, or contains decisions on matters beyond the scope of the submission to arbitration, provided that, if the decisions on matters submitted to arbitration can be separated from those not so submitted, only that part of the award which contains decisions on matters not submitted to arbitration may be set aside; or

    (iv) the composition of the arbitral tribunal or the arbitral procedure was not in accordance with the agreement of the parties, unless such agreement was in conflict with a provision of this Law from which the parties cannot derogate, or, failing such agreement, was not in accordance with this Law; or

(b)   the court finds that:

    (i)   the subject-matter of the dispute is not capable of settlement by arbitration under the law of this State; or

    (ii)   the award is in conflict with the public policy of this State.

(3)   An application for setting aside may not be made after three months have elapsed from the date on which the party making that application had received the award or, if a request had been made under article 33, from the date on which that request had been disposed of by the arbitral tribunal.

(4)   The court, when asked to set aside an award, may, where appropriate and so requested by a party, suspend the setting aside proceedings for a period of time determined by it in order to give the arbitral tribunal an opportunity to resume the arbitral proceedings or to take such other action as in the arbitral tribunal's opinion will eliminate the grounds for setting aside.

Chapter VIII

Recognition and Enforcement of Awards

Article 35

Recognition and enforcement

(1) An arbitral award, irrespective of the country in which it was made, shall be recognized as binding and, upon application in writing to the competent court, shall be enforced subject to the provisions of this article and of article 36.

(2) The party relying on an award or applying for its enforcement shall supply the duly authenticated original award or a duly certified copy thereof, and the original arbitration agreement referred to in article 7 or a duly certified copy thereof. If the award or agreement is not made in an official language of this State, the party shall supply a duly certified translation thereof into such language.[3]

Article 36

Grounds for refusing recognition or enforcement

(1) Recognition or enforcement of an arbitral award, irrespective of the country in which it was made, may be refused only:

(a) at the request of the party against whom it is invoked, if that party furnishes to the competent court where recognition or enforcement is sought proof that:

(i) a party to the arbitration agreement referred to in article 7 was under some incapacity; or the said agreement is not valid under the law to which the parties have subjected it or, failing any indication thereon, under the law of the country where the award was made; or

(ii) the party against whom the award is invoked was not given proper notice of the appointment of an arbitrator or of the arbitral proceedings or was otherwise unable to present his case; or

(iii) the award deals with a dispute not contemplated by or not falling within the terms of the submission to arbitration, or it contains decisions on matters beyond the scope of the submission to arbitration, provided that, if the decisions on matters submitted to arbitration can be separated from those not so submitted, that part of the award which contains

---

[3] The conditions set forth in this paragraph are intended to set maximum standards. It would, thus, not be contrary to the harmonization to be achieved by the model law if a State retained even less onerous conditions.

decisions on matters submitted to arbitration may be recognized and enforced; or

(iv) the composition of the arbitral tribunal or the arbitral procedure was not in accordance with the agreement of the parties or, failing such agreement, was not in accordance with the law of the country where the arbitration took place; or

(v) the award has not yet become binding on the parties or has been set aside or suspended by a court of the country in which, or under the law of which, that award was made; or

(b) if the court finds that:

(i) the subject-matter of the dispute is not capable of settlement by arbitration under the law of this State; or

(ii) the recognition or enforcement of the award would be contrary to the public policy of this State.

(2) If an application for setting aside or suspension of an award has been made to a court referred to in paragraph (1)(a)(v) of this article, the court where recognition or enforcement is sought may, if it considers it proper, adjourn its decision and may also, on the application of the party claiming recognition or enforcement of the award, order the other party to provide appropriate security.

A.2. THE 2006 AMENDMENTS TO THE UNCITRAL MODEL LAW ON INTERNATIONAL COMMERCIAL ARBITRATION*

Article 1

Scope of application

* * *

(2) The provisions of this Law, except articles 8, 9, 17 H, 17 I, 17 J, 35 and 36, apply only if the place of arbitration is in the territory of this State.

* * *

Article 2 A.

International origin and general principles

(1) In the interpretation of this Law, regard is to be had to its international origin and to the need to promote uniformity in its application and the observance of good faith.

---

*   The consolidated text of the amended Model Law can be found at the UNCITRAL Website at http://www.uncitral.org/pdf/english/texts/arbitration/ml-arb/07-86998_Ebook.pdf.   Reprinted with permission of UNCITRAL.

(2) Questions concerning matters governed by this Law which are not expressly settled in it are to be settled in conformity with the general principles on which this Law is based.

* * *

CHAPTER II

Arbitration Agreement

Option I

Article 7.

Definition and form of arbitration agreement

(1) "Arbitration agreement" is an agreement by the parties to submit to arbitration all or certain disputes which have arisen or which may arise between them in respect of a defined legal relationship, whether contractual or not. An arbitration agreement may be in the form of an arbitration clause in a contract or in the form of a separate agreement.

(2) The arbitration agreement shall be in writing.

(3) An arbitration agreement is in writing if its content is recorded in any form, whether or not the arbitration agreement or contract has been concluded orally, by conduct, or by other means.

(4) The requirement that an arbitration agreement be in writing is met by an electronic communication if the information contained therein is accessible so as to be useable for subsequent reference; "electronic communication" means any communication that the parties make by means of data messages; "data message" means information generated, sent, received or stored by electronic, magnetic, optical or similar means, including, but not limited to, electronic data interchange (EDI), electronic mail, telegram, telex or telecopy.

(5) Furthermore, an arbitration agreement is in writing if it is contained in an exchange of statements of claim and defence in which the existence of an agreement is alleged by one party and not denied by the other.

(6) The reference in a contract to any document containing an arbitration clause constitutes an arbitration agreement in writing, provided that the reference is such as to make that clause part of the contract.

Option II

Article 7.

Definition of arbitration agreement

"Arbitration agreement" is an agreement by the parties to submit to arbitration all or certain disputes which have arisen or which may arise between them in respect of a defined legal relationship, whether contractual or not.

* * *

CHAPTER IV A

Interim measures and preliminary orders

Section 1.   Interim measures

Article 17.

Power of arbitral tribunal to order interim measures

1)   Unless otherwise agreed by the parties, the arbitral tribunal may, at the request of a party, grant interim measures.

2)   An interim measure is any temporary measure, whether in the form of an award or in another form, by which, at any time prior to the issuance of the award by which the dispute is finally decided, the arbitral tribunal orders a party to:

(a) Maintain or restore the status quo pending determination of the dispute;

(b) Take action that would prevent, or refrain from taking action that is likely to cause, current or imminent harm or prejudice to the arbitral process itself;

(c) Provide a means of preserving assets out of which a subsequent award may be satisfied; or

(d) Preserve evidence that may be relevant and material to the resolution of the dispute.

Article 17 A.

Conditions for granting interim measures

(1) The party requesting an interim measure under article 17(2)(a), (b) and (c) shall satisfy the arbitral tribunal that:

(a) Harm not adequately reparable by an award of damages is likely to result if the measure is not ordered, and such harm substantially outweighs the harm that is likely to result to the party against whom the measure is directed if the measure is granted; and *(b)* There is a reasonable possibility that the requesting party will succeed on the merits of the claim. The determination on this possibility shall not affect the discretion of the arbitral tribunal in making any subsequent determination.

(2) With regard to a request for an interim measure under article 17(2)*(d)*, the requirements in paragraphs (1)*(a)* and *(b)* of this article shall apply only to the extent the arbitral tribunal considers appropriate.

Section 2.   Preliminary orders

Article 17 B.

Applications for preliminary orders and conditions for granting preliminary orders

(1) Unless otherwise agreed by the parties, a party may, without notice to any other party, make a request for an interim measure together with an application for a preliminary order directing a party not to frustrate the purpose of the interim measure requested.

(2) The arbitral tribunal may grant a preliminary order provided it considers that prior disclosure of the request for the interim measure to the party against whom it is directed risks frustrating the purpose of the measure.

(3) The conditions defined under article 17A apply to any preliminary order, provided that the harm to be assessed under article 17A(1)*(a)*, is the harm likely to result from the order being granted or not.

Article 17 C.

Specific regime for preliminary orders

(1) Immediately after the arbitral tribunal has made a determination in respect of an application for a preliminary order, the arbitral tribunal shall give notice to all parties of the request for the interim measure, the application for the preliminary order, the preliminary order, if any, and all other communications, including by indicating the content of any oral communication, between any party and the arbitral tribunal in relation thereto.

(2) At the same time, the arbitral tribunal shall give an opportunity to any party against whom a preliminary order is directed to present its case at the earliest practicable time.

(3) The arbitral tribunal shall decide promptly on any objection to the preliminary order.

(4) A preliminary order shall expire after twenty days from the date on which it was issued by the arbitral tribunal. However, the arbitral tribunal may issue an interim measure adopting or modifying the

preliminary order, after the party against whom the preliminary order is directed has been given notice and an opportunity to present its case.

(5) A preliminary order shall be binding on the parties but shall not be subject to enforcement by a court. Such a preliminary order does not constitute an award.

Section 3. Provisions applicable to interim measures and preliminary orders

Article 17 D.

Modification, suspension, termination

The arbitral tribunal may modify, suspend or terminate an interim measure or a preliminary order it has granted, upon application of any party or, in exceptional circumstances and upon prior notice to the parties, on the arbitral tribunal own initiative.

Article 17 E.

Provision of security

(1) The arbitral tribunal may require the party requesting an interim measure to provide appropriate security in connection with the measure.

(2) The arbitral tribunal shall require the party applying for a preliminary order to provide security in connection with the order unless the arbitral tribunal considers it inappropriate or unnecessary to do so.

Article 17 F.

Disclosure

(1) The arbitral tribunal may require any party promptly to disclose any material change in the circumstances on the basis of which the measure was requested or granted.

(2) The party applying for a preliminary order shall disclose to the arbitral tribunal all circumstances that are likely to be relevant to the arbitral tribunal determination whether to grant or maintain the order, and such obligation shall continue until the party against whom the order has been requested has had an opportunity to present its case. Thereafter, paragraph (1) of this article shall apply.

Article 17 G.

Costs and damages

The party requesting an interim measure or applying for a preliminary order shall be liable for any costs and damages caused by the measure or the order to any party if the arbitral tribunal later determines that, in the circumstances, the measure or the order should not have been granted. The arbitral tribunal may award such costs and damages at any point during the proceedings.

Section 4.   Recognition and enforcement of interim measures

Article 17 H.

Recognition and enforcement

(1) An interim measure issued by an arbitral tribunal shall be recognized as binding and, unless otherwise provided by the arbitral tribunal, enforced upon application to the competent court, irrespective of the country in which it was issued, subject to the provisions of article 17 I.

(2) The party who is seeking or has obtained recognition or enforcement of an interim measure shall promptly inform the court of any termination, suspension or modification of that interim measure.

(3) The court of the State where recognition or enforcement is sought may, if it considers it proper, order the requesting party to provide appropriate security if the arbitral tribunal has not already made a determination with respect to security or where such a decision is necessary to protect the rights of third parties.

Article 17 I.

Grounds for refusing recognition or enforcement†

(1) Recognition or enforcement of an interim measure may be refused only:

(a) At the request of the party against whom it is invoked if the court is satisfied that:

(i) Such refusal is warranted on the grounds set forth in article 36(1)*(a)*(i), (ii), (iii) or (iv); or

(ii) The arbitral tribunal decision with respect to the provision of security in connection with the interim measure issued by the arbitral tribunal has not been complied with; or

(iii)The interim measure has been terminated or suspended by the arbitral tribunal or, where so empowered, by the court of the State in which the arbitration takes place or under the law of which that interim measure was granted; or

(b) If the court finds that:

(i) The interim measure is incompatible with the powers conferred upon the court unless the court decides to reformulate the interim measure to the extent necessary to adapt it to its own powers and procedures for the

---

† *The conditions set forth in article 17 I are intended to limit the number of circumstances in which the court may refuse to enforce an interim measure. It would not be contrary to the level of harmonization sought to be achieved by these model provisions if a State were to adopt fewer circumstances in which enforcement may be refused.*

purposes of enforcing that interim measure and without modifying its substance; or

(ii) Any of the grounds set forth in article 36(1)*(b)*(i) or (ii), apply to the recognition and enforcement of the interim measure.

(2) Any determination made by the court on any ground in paragraph (1) of this article shall be effective only for the purposes of the application to recognize and enforce the interim measure. The court where recognition or enforcement is sought shall not, in making that determination, undertake a review of the substance of the interim measure.

Section 5. Court-ordered interim measures

Article 17 J.

Court-ordered interim measures

A court shall have the same power of issuing an interim measure in relation to arbitration proceedings, irrespective of whether their place is in the territory of this State, as it has in relation to proceedings in courts. The court shall exercise such power in accordance with its own procedures in consideration of the specific features of international arbitration.

* * *

Article 35

Recognition and enforcement

* * *

(2) The party relying on an award or applying for its enforcement shall supply the original award or a copy thereof. If the award is not made in an official language of this State, the court may request the party to supply translation thereof into such language.‡

B. UNCITRAL ARBITRATION RULES (AS REVISED IN 2010)*

Section I.   Introductory rules

Scope of application

Article 1

1.   Where parties have agreed that disputes between them in respect of a defined legal relationship, whether contractual or not, shall be referred to

---

‡ The conditions set forth in this paragraph are intended to set maximum standards. It would, thus, not be contrary to the harmonization to be achieved by the model law if a State retained even less onerous conditions.

* Document can be found at the UNCITRAL website at http://www.uncitral.org/pdf/english/texts/arbitration/arb-rules-revised/arb-rules-revised-2010-e.pdf. Reprinted with permission of UNCITRAL.

arbitration under the UNCITRAL Arbitration Rules, then such disputes shall be settled in accordance with these Rules subject to such modification as the parties may agree.

2.   The parties to an arbitration agreement concluded after 15 August 2010 shall be presumed to have referred to the Rules in effect on the date of commencement of the arbitration, unless the parties have agreed to apply a particular version of the Rules. That presumption does not apply where the arbitration agreement has been concluded by accepting after 15 August 2010 an offer made before that date.

3.   These Rules shall govern the arbitration except that where any of these Rules is in conflict with a provision of the law applicable to the arbitration from which the parties cannot derogate, that provision shall prevail.

Notice and calculation of periods of time

Article 2

1.   A notice, including a notification, communication or proposal, may be transmitted by any means of communication that provides or allows for a record of its transmission.

2.   If an address has been designated by a party specifically for this purpose or authorized by the arbitral tribunal, any notice shall be delivered to that party at that address, and if so delivered shall be deemed to have been received. Delivery by electronic means such as facsimile or e-mail may only be made to an address so designated or authorized.

3.   In the absence of such designation or authorization, a notice is:

(a)   Received if it is physically delivered to the addressee; or

(b)   Deemed to have been received if it is delivered at the place of business, habitual residence or mailing address of the addressee.

4.   If, after reasonable efforts, delivery cannot be effected in accordance with paragraphs 2 or 3, a notice is deemed to have been received if it is sent to the addressee's last-known place of business, habitual residence or mailing address by registered letter or any other means that provides a record of delivery or of attempted delivery.

5.   A notice shall be deemed to have been received on the day it is delivered in accordance with paragraphs 2, 3 or 4, or attempted to be delivered in accordance with paragraph 4. A notice transmitted by electronic means is deemed to have been received on the day it is sent, except that a notice of arbitration so transmitted is only deemed to have been received on the day when it reaches the addressee's electronic address.

6.   For the purpose of calculating a period of time under these Rules, such period shall begin to run on the day following the day when a notice is received. If the last day of such period is an official holiday or a non-business day at the residence or place of business of the addressee, the period is extended until the first business day which follows. Official holidays or non-business days occurring during the running of the period of time are included in calculating the period.

Notice of arbitration

Article 3

1.   The party or parties initiating recourse to arbitration (hereinafter called the "claimant") shall communicate to the other party or parties (hereinafter called the "respondent") a notice of arbitration.

2.   Arbitral proceedings shall be deemed to commence on the date on which the notice of arbitration is received by the respondent.

3.   The notice of arbitration shall include the following:

  (a)   A demand that the dispute be referred to arbitration;
  (b)   The names and contact details of the parties;
  (c)   Identification of the arbitration agreement that is invoked;
  (d)   Identification of any contract or other legal instrument out of or in relation to which the dispute arises or, in the absence of such contract or instrument, a brief description of the relevant relationship;
  (e)   A brief description of the claim and an indication of the amount involved, if any;
  (f)   The relief or remedy sought;
  (g)   A proposal as to the number of arbitrators, language and place of arbitration, if the parties have not previously agreed thereon.

4.   The notice of arbitration may also include:

  (a)   A proposal for the designation of an appointing authority referred to in article 6, paragraph 1;
  (b)   A proposal for the appointment of a sole arbitrator referred to in article 8, paragraph 1;
  (c)   Notification of the appointment of an arbitrator referred to in article 9 or 10.

5.   The constitution of the arbitral tribunal shall not be hindered by any controversy with respect to the sufficiency of the notice of arbitration, which shall be finally resolved by the arbitral tribunal.

Response to the notice of arbitration

Article 4

1.   Within 30 days of the receipt of the notice of arbitration, the respondent shall communicate to the claimant a response to the notice of arbitration, which shall include:

   (a)   The name and contact details of each respondent;

   (b)   A response to the information set forth in the notice of arbitration, pursuant to article 3, paragraphs 3 (c) to (g).

2.   The response to the notice of arbitration may also include:

   (a)   Any plea that an arbitral tribunal to be constituted under these Rules lacks jurisdiction;

   (b)   A proposal for the designation of an appointing authority referred to in article 6, paragraph 1;

   (c)   A proposal for the appointment of a sole arbitrator referred to in article 8, paragraph 1;

   (d)   Notification of the appointment of an arbitrator referred to in article 9 or 10;

   (e)   A brief description of counterclaims or claims for the purpose of a set-off, if any, including where relevant, an indication of the amounts involved, and the relief or remedy sought;

   (f)   A notice of arbitration in accordance with article 3 in case the respondent formulates a claim against a party to the arbitration agreement other than the claimant.

3.   The constitution of the arbitral tribunal shall not be hindered by any controversy with respect to the respondent's failure to communicate a response to the notice of arbitration, or an incomplete or late response to the notice of arbitration, which shall be finally resolved by the arbitral tribunal.

Representation and assistance

Article 5

Each party may be represented or assisted by persons chosen by it. The names and addresses of such persons must be communicated to all parties and to the arbitral tribunal. Such communication must specify whether the appointment is being made for purposes of representation or assistance. Where a person is to act as a representative of a party, the arbitral tribunal, on its own initiative or at the request of any party, may at any time require proof of authority granted to the representative in such a form as the arbitral tribunal may determine.

Designating and appointing authorities

Article 6

1.   Unless the parties have already agreed on the choice of an appointing authority, a party may at any time propose the name or names of one or more institutions or persons, including the Secretary-General of the Permanent Court of Arbitration at The Hague (hereinafter called the "PCA"), one of whom would serve as appointing authority.

2.   If all parties have not agreed on the choice of an appointing authority within 30 days after a proposal made in accordance with paragraph 1 has been received by all other parties, any party may request the Secretary-General of the PCA to designate the appointing authority.

3.   Where these Rules provide for a period of time within which a party must refer a matter to an appointing authority and no appointing authority has been agreed on or designated, the period is suspended from the date on which a party initiates the procedure for agreeing on or designating an appointing authority until the date of such agreement or designation.

4.   Except as referred to in article 41, paragraph 4, if the appointing authority refuses to act, or if it fails to appoint an arbitrator within 30 days after it receives a party's request to do so, fails to act within any other period provided by these Rules, or fails to decide on a challenge to an arbitrator within a reasonable time after receiving a party's request to do so, any party may request the Secretary-General of the PCA to designate a substitute appointing authority.

5.   In exercising their functions under these Rules, the appointing authority and the Secretary-General of the PCA may require from any party and the arbitrators the information they deem necessary and they shall give the parties and, where appropriate, the arbitrators, an opportunity to present their views in any manner they consider appropriate. All such communications to and from the appointing authority and the Secretary-General of the PCA shall also be provided by the sender to all other parties.

6.   When the appointing authority is requested to appoint an arbitrator pursuant to articles 8, 9, 10 or 14, the party making the request shall send to the appointing authority copies of the notice of arbitration and, if it exists, any response to the notice of arbitration.

7.   The appointing authority shall have regard to such considerations as are likely to secure the appointment of an independent and impartial arbitrator and shall take into account the advisability of appointing an arbitrator of a nationality other than the nationalities of the parties.

Section II.   Composition of the arbitral tribunal

Number of arbitrators

Article 7

1.   If the parties have not previously agreed on the number of arbitrators, and if within 30 days after the receipt by the respondent of the notice of arbitration the parties have not agreed that there shall be only one arbitrator, three arbitrators shall be appointed.

2.   Notwithstanding paragraph 1, if no other parties have responded to a party's proposal to appoint a sole arbitrator within the time limit provided for in paragraph 1 and the party or parties concerned have failed to appoint a second arbitrator in accordance with article 9 or 10, the appointing authority may, at the request of a party, appoint a sole arbitrator pursuant to the procedure provided for in article 8, paragraph 2, if it determines that, in view of the circumstances of the case, this is more appropriate.

Appointment of arbitrators (articles 8 to 10)

Article 8

1.   If the parties have agreed that a sole arbitrator is to be appointed and if within 30 days after receipt by all other parties of a proposal for the appointment of a sole arbitrator the parties have not reached agreement thereon, a sole arbitrator shall, at the request of a party, be appointed by the appointing authority.

2.   The appointing authority shall appoint the sole arbitrator as promptly as possible. In making the appointment, the appointing authority shall use the following list-procedure, unless the parties agree that the list-procedure should not be used or unless the appointing authority determines in its discretion that the use of the list-procedure is not appropriate for the case:

   (a)   The appointing authority shall communicate to each of the parties an identical list containing at least three names;

   (b)   Within 15 days after the receipt of this list, each party may return the list to the appointing authority after having deleted the name or names to which it objects and numbered the remaining names on the list in the order of its preference;

   (c)   After the expiration of the above period of time the appointing authority shall appoint the sole arbitrator from among the names approved on the lists returned to it and in accordance with the order of preference indicated by the parties;

   (d)   If for any reason the appointment cannot be made according to this procedure, the appointing authority may exercise its discretion in appointing the sole arbitrator.

Article 9

1.   If three arbitrators are to be appointed, each party shall appoint one arbitrator. The two arbitrators thus appointed shall choose the third arbitrator who will act as the presiding arbitrator of the arbitral tribunal.

2.   If within 30 days after the receipt of a party's notification of the appointment of an arbitrator the other party has not notified the first party of the arbitrator it has appointed, the first party may request the appointing authority to appoint the second arbitrator.

3.   If within 30 days after the appointment of the second arbitrator the two arbitrators have not agreed on the choice of the presiding arbitrator, the presiding arbitrator shall be appointed by the appointing authority in the same way as a sole arbitrator would be appointed under article 8.

Article 10

1.   For the purposes of article 9, paragraph 1, where three arbitrators are to be appointed and there are multiple parties as claimant or as respondent, unless the parties have agreed to another method of appointment of arbitrators, the multiple parties jointly, whether as claimant or as respondent, shall appoint an arbitrator.

2.   If the parties have agreed that the arbitral tribunal is to be composed of a number of arbitrators other than one or three, the arbitrators shall be appointed according to the method agreed upon by the parties.

3.   In the event of any failure to constitute the arbitral tribunal under these Rules, the appointing authority shall, at the request of any party, constitute the arbitral tribunal and, in doing so, may revoke any appointment already made and appoint or reappoint each of the arbitrators and designate one of them as the presiding arbitrator.

Disclosures by and challenge of arbitrators (articles 11 to 13)

Article 11

When a person is approached in connection with his or her possible appointment as an arbitrator, he or she shall disclose any circumstances likely to give rise to justifiable doubts as to his or her impartiality or independence. An arbitrator, from the time of his or her appointment and throughout the arbitral proceedings, shall without delay disclose any such circumstances to the parties and the other arbitrators unless they have already been informed by him or her of these circumstances.

Article 12

1.   Any arbitrator may be challenged if circumstances exist that give rise to justifiable doubts as to the arbitrator's impartiality or independence.

2.   A party may challenge the arbitrator appointed by it only for reasons of which it becomes aware after the appointment has been made.

3.   In the event that an arbitrator fails to act or in the event of the de jure or de facto impossibility of his or her performing his or her functions, the procedure in respect of the challenge of an arbitrator as provided in article 13 shall apply.

Article 13

1.   A party that intends to challenge an arbitrator shall send notice of its challenge within 15 days after it has been notified of the appointment of the challenged arbitrator, or within 15 days after the circumstances mentioned in articles 11 and 12 became known to that party

2.   The notice of challenge shall be communicated to all other parties, to the arbitrator who is challenged and to the other arbitrators. The notice of challenge shall state the reasons for the challenge.

3.   When an arbitrator has been challenged by a party, all parties may agree to the challenge. The arbitrator may also, after the challenge, withdraw from his or her office. In neither case does this imply acceptance of the validity of the grounds for the challenge.

4.   If, within 15 days from the date of the notice of challenge, all parties do not agree to the challenge or the challenged arbitrator does not withdraw, the party making the challenge may elect to pursue it. In that case, within 30 days from the date of the notice of challenge, it shall seek a decision on the challenge by the appointing authority.

Replacement of an arbitrator

Article 14

1.   Subject to paragraph 2, in any event where an arbitrator has to be replaced during the course of the arbitral proceedings, a substitute arbitrator shall be appointed or chosen pursuant to the procedure provided for in articles 8 to 11 that was applicable to the appointment or choice of the arbitrator being replaced. This procedure shall apply even if during the process of appointing the arbitrator to be replaced, a party had failed to exercise its right to appoint or to participate in the appointment.

2.   If, at the request of a party, the appointing authority determines that, in view of the exceptional circumstances of the case, it would be justified for a party to be deprived of its right to appoint a substitute arbitrator, the appointing authority may, after giving an opportunity to the parties and the remaining arbitrators to express their views: (a) appoint the substitute arbitrator; or (b) after the closure of the hearings, authorize the other arbitrators to proceed with the arbitration and make any decision or award.

Repetition of hearings in the event of the replacement of an arbitrator

Article 15

If an arbitrator is replaced, the proceedings shall resume at the stage where the arbitrator who was replaced ceased to perform his or her functions, unless the arbitral tribunal decides otherwise.

Exclusion of liability

Article 16

Save for intentional wrongdoing, the parties waive, to the fullest extent permitted under the applicable law, any claim against the arbitrators, the appointing authority and any person appointed by the arbitral tribunal based on any act or omission in connection with the arbitration.

Section III. Arbitral proceedings

General provisions

Article 17

1.   Subject to these Rules, the arbitral tribunal may conduct the arbitration in such manner as it considers appropriate, provided that the parties are treated with equality and that at an appropriate stage of the proceedings each party is given a reasonable opportunity of presenting its case. The arbitral tribunal, in exercising its discretion, shall conduct the proceedings so as to avoid unnecessary delay and expense and to provide a fair and efficient process for resolving the parties' dispute.

2.   As soon as practicable after its constitution and after inviting the parties to express their views, the arbitral tribunal shall establish the provisional timetable of the arbitration. The arbitral tribunal may, at any time, after inviting the parties to express their views, extend or abridge any period of time prescribed under these Rules or agreed by the parties.

3.   If at an appropriate stage of the proceedings any party so requests, the arbitral tribunal shall hold hearings for the presentation of evidence by witnesses, including expert witnesses, or for oral argument. In the absence of such a request, the arbitral tribunal shall decide whether to hold such hearings or whether the proceedings shall be conducted on the basis of documents and other materials.

4.   All communications to the arbitral tribunal by one party shall be communicated by that party to all other parties. Such communications shall be made at the same time, except as otherwise permitted by the arbitral tribunal if it may do so under applicable law.

5.   The arbitral tribunal may, at the request of any party, allow one or more third persons to be joined in the arbitration as a party provided such person is a party to the arbitration agreement, unless the arbitral tribunal

finds, after giving all parties, including the person or persons to be joined, the opportunity to be heard, that joinder should not be permitted because of prejudice to any of those parties. The arbitral tribunal may make a single award or several awards in respect of all parties so involved in the arbitration.

Place of arbitration

Article 18

1.   If the parties have not previously agreed on the place of arbitration, the place of arbitration shall be determined by the arbitral tribunal having regard to the circumstances of the case. The award shall be deemed to have been made at the place of arbitration.

2.   The arbitral tribunal may meet at any location it considers appropriate for deliberations. Unless otherwise agreed by the parties, the arbitral tribunal may also meet at any location it considers appropriate for any other purpose, including hearings.

Language

Article 19

1.   Subject to an agreement by the parties, the arbitral tribunal shall, promptly after its appointment, determine the language or languages to be used in the proceedings. This determination shall apply to the statement of claim, the statement of defence, and any further written statements and, if oral hearings take place, to the language or languages to be used in such hearings.

2.   The arbitral tribunal may order that any documents annexed to the statement of claim or statement of defence, and any supplementary documents or exhibits submitted in the course of the proceedings, delivered in their original language, shall be accompanied by a translation into the language or languages agreed upon by the parties or determined by the arbitral tribunal.

Statement of claim

Article 20

1.   The claimant shall communicate its statement of claim in writing to the respondent and to each of the arbitrators within a period of time to be determined by the arbitral tribunal. The claimant may elect to treat its notice of arbitration referred to in article 3 as a statement of claim, provided that the notice of arbitration also complies with the requirements of paragraphs 2 to 4 of this article.

2.   The statement of claim shall include the following particulars:

    (a)   The names and contact details of the parties;

(b)   A statement of the facts supporting the claim;

(c)   The points at issue;

(d)   The relief or remedy sought;

(e)   The legal grounds or arguments supporting the claim.

3.   A copy of any contract or other legal instrument out of or in relation to which the dispute arises and of the arbitration agreement shall be annexed to the statement of claim.

4.   The statement of claim should, as far as possible, be accompanied by all documents and other evidence relied upon by the claimant, or contain references to them.

Statement of defence

Article 21

1.   The respondent shall communicate its statement of defence in writing to the claimant and to each of the arbitrators within a period of time to be determined by the arbitral tribunal. The respondent may elect to treat its response to the notice of arbitration referred to in article 4 as a statement of defence, provided that the response to the notice of arbitration also complies with the requirements of paragraph 2 of this article.

2.   The statement of defence shall reply to the particulars (b) to (e) of the statement of claim (art. 20, para. 2). The statement of defence should, as far as possible, be accompanied by all documents and other evidence relied upon by the respondent, or contain references to them.

3.   In its statement of defence, or at a later stage in the arbitral proceedings if the arbitral tribunal decides that the delay was justified under the circumstances, the respondent may make a counterclaim or rely on a claim for the purpose of a set-off provided that the arbitral tribunal has jurisdiction over it.

4.   The provisions of article 20, paragraphs 2 to 4, shall apply to a counterclaim, a claim under article 4, paragraph 2 (f), and a claim relied on for the purpose of a set-off.

Amendments to the claim or defence

Article 22

During the course of the arbitral proceedings, a party may amend or supplement its claim or defence, including a counterclaim or a claim for the purpose of a set-off, unless the arbitral tribunal considers it inappropriate to allow such amendment or supplement having regard to the delay in making it or prejudice to other parties or any other circumstances. However, a claim or defence, including a counterclaim or a claim for the purpose of a set-off, may not be amended or supplemented in such a manner that the amended or supplemented claim or defence falls outside the jurisdiction of the arbitral tribunal. Pleas as to the jurisdiction of the arbitral tribunal

Article 23

1.   The arbitral tribunal shall have the power to rule on its own jurisdiction, including any objections with respect to the existence or validity of the arbitration agreement. For that purpose, an arbitration clause that forms part of a contract shall be treated as an agreement independent of the other terms of the contract. A decision by the arbitral tribunal that the contract is null shall not entail automatically the invalidity of the arbitration clause.

2.   A plea that the arbitral tribunal does not have jurisdiction shall be raised no later than in the statement of defence or, with respect to a counterclaim or a claim for the purpose of a set-off, in the reply to the counterclaim or to the claim for the purpose of a set-off. A party is not precluded from raising such a plea by the fact that it has appointed, or participated in the appointment of, an arbitrator. A plea that the arbitral tribunal is exceeding the scope of its authority shall be raised as soon as the matter alleged to be beyond the scope of its authority is raised during the arbitral proceedings. The arbitral tribunal may, in either case, admit a later plea if it considers the delay justified.

3.   The arbitral tribunal may rule on a plea referred to in paragraph 2 either as a preliminary question or in an award on the merits. The arbitral tribunal may continue the arbitral proceedings and make an award, notwithstanding any pending challenge to its jurisdiction before a court.

Further written statements

Article 24

The arbitral tribunal shall decide which further written statements, in addition to the statement of claim and the statement of defence, shall be required from the parties or may be presented by them and shall fix the periods of time for communicating such statements.

Periods of time

Article 25

The periods of time fixed by the arbitral tribunal for the communication of written statements (including the statement of claim and statement of defence) should not exceed 45 days. However, the arbitral tribunal may extend the time limits if it concludes that an extension is justified.

Interim measures

Article 26

1.   The arbitral tribunal may, at the request of a party, grant interim measures.

2.   An interim measure is any temporary measure by which, at any time prior to the issuance of the award by which the dispute is finally decided, the arbitral tribunal orders a party, for example and without limitation, to:

   (a)   Maintain or restore the status quo pending determination of the dispute;

   (b)   Take action that would prevent, or refrain from taking action that is likely to cause, (i) current or imminent harm or (ii) prejudice to the arbitral process itself;

   (c)   Provide a means of preserving assets out of which a subsequent award may be satisfied; or

   (d)   Preserve evidence that may be relevant and material to the resolution of the dispute.

3.   The party requesting an interim measure under paragraphs 2 (a) to (c) shall satisfy the arbitral tribunal that:

   (a)   Harm not adequately reparable by an award of damages is likely to result if the measure is not ordered, and such 18 harm substantially outweighs the harm that is likely to result to the party against whom the measure is directed if the measure is granted;

   and

   (b)   There is a reasonable possibility that the requesting party will succeed on the merits of the claim. The determination on this possibility shall not affect the discretion of the arbitral tribunal in making any subsequent determination.

4.   With regard to a request for an interim measure under paragraph 2 (d), the requirements in paragraphs 3 (a) and (b) shall apply only to the extent the arbitral tribunal considers appropriate.

5.   The arbitral tribunal may modify, suspend or terminate an interim measure it has granted, upon application of any party or, in exceptional circumstances and upon prior notice to the parties, on the arbitral tribunal's own initiative.

6.   The arbitral tribunal may require the party requesting an interim measure to provide appropriate security in connection with the measure.

7.   The arbitral tribunal may require any party promptly to disclose any material change in the circumstances on the basis of which the interim measure was requested or granted.

8.   The party requesting an interim measure may be liable for any costs and damages caused by the measure to any party if the arbitral tribunal later determines that, in the circumstances then prevailing, the measure should not have been granted. The arbitral tribunal may award such costs and damages at any point during the proceedings.

9.   A request for interim measures addressed by any party to a judicial authority shall not be deemed incompatible with the agreement to arbitrate, or as a waiver of that agreement.

Evidence

Article 27

1.   Each party shall have the burden of proving the facts relied on to support its claim or defence.

2.   Witnesses, including expert witnesses, who are presented by the parties to testify to the arbitral tribunal on any issue of fact or expertise may be any individual, notwithstanding that the individual is a party to the arbitration or in any way related to a party. Unless otherwise directed by the arbitral tribunal, statements by witnesses, including expert witnesses, may be presented in writing and signed by them.

3.   At any time during the arbitral proceedings the arbitral tribunal may require the parties to produce documents, exhibits or other evidence within such a period of time as the arbitral tribunal shall determine.

4.   The arbitral tribunal shall determine the admissibility, relevance, materiality and weight of the evidence offered.

Hearings

Article 28

1.   In the event of an oral hearing, the arbitral tribunal shall give the parties adequate advance notice of the date, time and place thereof.

2.   Witnesses, including expert witnesses, may be heard under the conditions and examined in the manner set by the arbitral tribunal.

3.   Hearings shall be held in camera unless the parties agree otherwise. The arbitral tribunal may require the retirement of any witness or witnesses, including expert witnesses, during the testimony of such other witnesses, except that a witness, including an expert witness, who is a party to the arbitration shall not, in principle, be asked to retire.

4.   The arbitral tribunal may direct that witnesses, including expert witnesses, be examined through means of telecommunication that do not require their physical presence at the hearing (such as videoconference).

Experts appointed by the arbitral tribunal

Article 29

1.   After consultation with the parties, the arbitral tribunal may appoint one or more independent experts to report to it, in writing, on specific issues to be determined by the arbitral tribunal. A copy of the expert's terms of reference, established by the arbitral tribunal, shall be communicated to the parties.

2.   The expert shall, in principle before accepting appointment, submit to the arbitral tribunal and to the parties a description of his or her qualifications and a statement of his or her impartiality and independence. Within the time ordered by the arbitral tribunal, the parties shall inform the arbitral tribunal whether they have any objections as to the expert's qualifications, impartiality or independence. The arbitral tribunal shall decide promptly whether to accept any such objections. After an expert's appointment, a party may object to the expert's qualifications, impartiality or independence only if the objection is for reasons of which the party becomes aware after the appointment has been made. The arbitral tribunal shall decide promptly what, if any, action to take.

3.   The parties shall give the expert any relevant information or produce for his or her inspection any relevant documents or goods that he or she may require of them. Any dispute between a party and such expert as to the relevance of the required information or production shall be referred to the arbitral tribunal for decision.

4.   Upon receipt of the expert's report, the arbitral tribunal shall communicate a copy of the report to the parties, which shall be given the opportunity to express, in writing, their opinion on the report. A party shall be entitled to examine any document on which the expert has relied in his or her report.

5.   At the request of any party, the expert, after delivery of the report, may be heard at a hearing where the parties shall have the opportunity to be present and to interrogate the expert. At this hearing, any party may present expert witnesses in order to testify on the points at issue. The provisions of article 28 shall be applicable to such proceedings.

Default

Article 30

1.   If, within the period of time fixed by these Rules or the arbitral tribunal, without showing sufficient cause:

(a) The claimant has failed to communicate its statement of claim, the arbitral tribunal shall issue an order for the termination of the arbitral proceedings, unless there are remaining matters that may need to be decided and the arbitral tribunal considers it appropriate to do so;

(b) The respondent has failed to communicate its response to the notice of arbitration or its statement of defence, the arbitral tribunal shall order that the proceedings continue, without treating such failure in itself as an admission of the claimant's allegations; the provisions of this subparagraph also apply to a claimant's failure to submit a defence to a counterclaim or to a claim for the purpose of a set-off.

2. If a party, duly notified under these Rules, fails to appear at a hearing, without showing sufficient cause for such failure, the arbitral tribunal may proceed with the arbitration.

3. If a party, duly invited by the arbitral tribunal to produce documents, exhibits or other evidence, fails to do so within the established period of time, without showing sufficient cause for such failure, the arbitral tribunal may make the award on the evidence before it.

Closure of hearings

Article 31

1. The arbitral tribunal may inquire of the parties if they have any further proof to offer or witnesses to be heard or submissions to make and, if there are none, it may declare the hearings closed.

2. The arbitral tribunal may, if it considers it necessary owing to exceptional circumstances, decide, on its own initiative or upon application of a party, to reopen the hearings at any time before the award is made.

Waiver of right to object

Article 32

A failure by any party to object promptly to any non-compliance with these Rules or with any requirement of the arbitration agreement shall be deemed to be a waiver of the right of such party to make such an objection, unless such party can show that, under the circumstances, its failure to object was justified.

Section IV. The award

Decisions

Article 33

1. When there is more than one arbitrator, any award or other decision of the arbitral tribunal shall be made by a majority of the arbitrators.

2.   In the case of questions of procedure, when there is no majority or when the arbitral tribunal so authorizes, the presiding arbitrator may decide alone, subject to revision, if any, by the arbitral tribunal.

Form and effect of the award

Article 34

1.   The arbitral tribunal may make separate awards on different issues at different times.

2.   All awards shall be made in writing and shall be final and binding on the parties. The parties shall carry out all awards without delay.

3.   The arbitral tribunal shall state the reasons upon which the award is based, unless the parties have agreed that no reasons are to be given.

4.   An award shall be signed by the arbitrators and it shall contain the date on which the award was made and indicate the place of arbitration. Where there is more than one arbitrator and any of them fails to sign, the award shall state the reason for the absence of the signature.

5.   An award may be made public with the consent of all parties or where and to the extent disclosure is required of a party by legal duty, to protect or pursue a legal right or in relation to legal proceedings before a court or other competent authority.

6.   Copies of the award signed by the arbitrators shall be communicated to the parties by the arbitral tribunal.

Applicable law, amiable compositeur

Article 35

1.   The arbitral tribunal shall apply the rules of law designated by the parties as applicable to the substance of the dispute. Failing such designation by the parties, the arbitral tribunal shall apply the law which it determines to be appropriate.

2.   The arbitral tribunal shall decide as amiable compositeur or ex aequo et bono only if the parties have expressly authorized the arbitral tribunal to do so.

3.   In all cases, the arbitral tribunal shall decide in accordance with the terms of the contract, if any, and shall take into account any usage of trade applicable to the transaction.

Settlement or other grounds for termination

Article 36

1.   If, before the award is made, the parties agree on a settlement of the dispute, the arbitral tribunal shall either issue an order for the termination of the arbitral proceedings or, if requested by the parties and accepted by the arbitral tribunal, record the settlement in the form of an arbitral award

on agreed terms. The arbitral tribunal is not obliged to give reasons for such an award.

2. If, before the award is made, the continuation of the arbitral proceedings becomes unnecessary or impossible for any reason not mentioned in paragraph 1, the arbitral tribunal shall inform the parties of its intention to issue an order for the termination of the proceedings. The arbitral tribunal shall have the power to issue such an order unless there are remaining matters that may need to be decided and the arbitral tribunal considers it appropriate to do so.

3. Copies of the order for termination of the arbitral proceedings or of the arbitral award on agreed terms, signed by the arbitrators, shall be communicated by the arbitral tribunal to the parties. Where an arbitral award on agreed terms is made, the provisions of article 34, paragraphs 2, 4 and 5, shall apply.

Interpretation of the award

Article 37

1. Within 30 days after the receipt of the award, a party, with notice to the other parties, may request that the arbitral tribunal give an interpretation of the award.

2. The interpretation shall be given in writing within 45 days after the receipt of the request. The interpretation shall form part of the award and the provisions of article 34, paragraphs 2 to 6, shall apply.

Correction of the award

Article 38

1. Within 30 days after the receipt of the award, a party, with notice to the other parties, may request the arbitral tribunal to correct in the award any error in computation, any clerical or typographical error, or any error or omission of a similar nature. If the arbitral tribunal considers that the request is justified, it shall make the correction within 45 days of receipt of the request.

2. The arbitral tribunal may within 30 days after the communication of the award make such corrections on its own initiative.

3. Such corrections shall be in writing and shall form part of the award. The provisions of article 34, paragraphs 2 to 6, shall apply.

Additional award

Article 39

1. Within 30 days after the receipt of the termination order or the award, a party, with notice to the other parties, may request the arbitral tribunal

to make an award or an additional award as to claims presented in the arbitral proceedings but not decided by the arbitral tribunal.

2.   If the arbitral tribunal considers the request for an award or additional award to be justified, it shall render or complete its award within 60 days after the receipt of the request. The arbitral tribunal may extend, if necessary, the period of time within which it shall make the award.

3.   When such an award or additional award is made, the provisions of article 34, paragraphs 2 to 6, shall apply.

Definition of costs

Article 40

1.   The arbitral tribunal shall fix the costs of arbitration in the final award and, if it deems appropriate, in another decision.

2.   The term "costs" includes only:

(a)   The fees of the arbitral tribunal to be stated separately as to each arbitrator and to be fixed by the tribunal itself in accordance with article 41;

(b)   The reasonable travel and other expenses incurred by the arbitrators;

(c)   The reasonable costs of expert advice and of other assistance required by the arbitral tribunal;

(d)   The reasonable travel and other expenses of witnesses to the extent such expenses are approved by the arbitral tribunal;

(e)   The legal and other costs incurred by the parties in relation to the arbitration to the extent that the arbitral tribunal determines that the amount of such costs is reasonable;

(f)   Any fees and expenses of the appointing authority as well as the fees and expenses of the Secretary-General of the PCA.

3.   In relation to interpretation, correction or completion of any award under articles 37 to 39, the arbitral tribunal may charge the costs referred to in paragraphs 2 (b) to (f), but no additional fees.

Fees and expenses of arbitrators

Article 41

1.   The fees and expenses of the arbitrators shall be reasonable in amount, taking into account the amount in dispute, the complexity of the subject matter, the time spent by the arbitrators and any other relevant circumstances of the case.

2.   If there is an appointing authority and it applies or has stated that it will apply a schedule or particular method for determining the fees for

arbitrators in international cases, the arbitral tribunal in fixing its fees shall take that schedule or method into account to the extent that it considers appropriate in the circumstances of the case.

3.   Promptly after its constitution, the arbitral tribunal shall inform the parties as to how it proposes to determine its fees and expenses, including any rates it intends to apply. Within 15 days of receiving that proposal, any party may refer the proposal to the appointing authority for review. If, within 45 days of receipt of such a referral, the appointing authority finds that the proposal of the arbitral tribunal is inconsistent with paragraph 1, it shall make any necessary adjustments thereto, which shall be binding upon the arbitral tribunal.

4.   (a) When informing the parties of the arbitrators' fees and expenses that have been fixed pursuant to article 40, paragraphs 2 (a) and (b), the arbitral tribunal shall also explain the manner in which the corresponding amounts have been calculated;

(b)   Within 15 days of receiving the arbitral tribunal's determination of fees and expenses, any party may refer for review such determination to the appointing authority.

If no appointing authority has been agreed upon or designated, or if the appointing authority fails to act within the time specified in these Rules, then the review shall be made by the Secretary-General of the PCA;

(c)   If the appointing authority or the Secretary-General of the PCA finds that the arbitral tribunal's determination is inconsistent with the arbitral tribunal's proposal (and any adjustment thereto) under paragraph 3 or is otherwise manifestly excessive, it shall, within 45 days of receiving such a referral, make any adjustments to the arbitral tribunal's determination that are necessary to satisfy the criteria in paragraph 1. Any such adjustments shall be binding upon the arbitral tribunal;

(d)   Any such adjustments shall either be included by the arbitral tribunal in its award or, if the award has already been issued, be implemented in a correction to the award, to which the procedure of article 38, paragraph 3, shall apply.

5.   Throughout the procedure under paragraphs 3 and 4, the arbitral tribunal shall proceed with the arbitration, in accordance with article 17, paragraph 1.

6.   A referral under paragraph 4 shall not affect any determination in the award other than the arbitral tribunal's fees and expenses; nor shall it delay the recognition and enforcement of all parts of the award other than those relating to the determination of the arbitral tribunal's fees and expenses.

Allocation of costs

Article 42

1.   The costs of the arbitration shall in principle be borne by the unsuccessful party or parties. However, the arbitral tribunal may apportion each of such costs between the parties if it determines that apportionment is reasonable, taking into account the circumstances of the case.

2.   The arbitral tribunal shall in the final award or, if it deems appropriate, in any other award, determine any amount that a party may have to pay to another party as a result of the decision on allocation of costs.

Deposit of costs

Article 43

1.   The arbitral tribunal, on its establishment, may request the parties to deposit an equal amount as an advance for the costs referred to in article 40, paragraphs 2 (a) to (c).

2.   During the course of the arbitral proceedings the arbitral tribunal may request supplementary deposits from the parties.

3.   If an appointing authority has been agreed upon or designated, and when a party so requests and the appointing authority consents to perform the function, the arbitral tribunal shall fix the amounts of any deposits or supplementary deposits only after consultation with the appointing authority, which may make any comments to the arbitral tribunal that it deems appropriate concerning the amount of such deposits and supplementary deposits.

4.   If the required deposits are not paid in full within 30 days after the receipt of the request, the arbitral tribunal shall so inform the parties in order that one or more of them may make the required payment. If such payment is not made, the arbitral tribunal may order the suspension or termination of the arbitral proceedings.

5.   After a termination order or final award has been made, the arbitral tribunal shall render an accounting to the parties of the deposits received and return any unexpended balance to the parties.

ANNEX

Model arbitration clause for contracts

Any dispute, controversy or claim arising out of or relating to this contract, or the breach, termination or invalidity thereof, shall be settled by arbitration in accordance with the UNCITRAL Arbitration Rules.

Note: Parties should consider adding:

(a)   The appointing authority shall be . . . [name of institution or person];

(b)   The number of arbitrators shall be . . . [one or three];

(c)   The place of arbitration shall be . . . [town and country];

(d)   The language to be used in the arbitral proceedings shall be. . . .

Possible waiver statement

Note. If the parties wish to exclude recourse against the arbitral award that may be available under the applicable law, they may consider adding a provision to that effect as suggested below, considering, however, that the effectiveness and conditions of such an exclusion depend on the applicable law.

Waiver

The parties hereby waive their right to any form of recourse against an award to any court or other competent authority, insofar as such waiver can validly be made under the applicable law.

Model statements of independence pursuant to article 11 of the Rules

No circumstances to disclose

I am impartial and independent of each of the parties and intend to remain so. To the best of my knowledge, there are no circumstances, past or present, likely to give rise to justifiable doubts as to my impartiality or independence. I shall promptly notify the parties and the other arbitrators of any such circumstances that may subsequently come to my attention during this arbitration.

Circumstances to disclose

I am impartial and independent of each of the parties and intend to remain so. Attached is a statement made pursuant to article 11 of the UNCITRAL Arbitration Rules of (a) my past and present professional, business and other relationships with the parties and (b) any other relevant circumstances. [Include statement.]

I confirm that those circumstances do not affect my independence and impartiality. I shall promptly notify the parties and the other arbitrators of any such further relationships or circumstances that may subsequently come to my attention during this arbitration.

Note. Any party may consider requesting from the arbitrator the following addition to the statement of independence:

I confirm, on the basis of the information presently available to me, that I can devote the time necessary to conduct this arbitration diligently, efficiently and in accordance with the time limits in the Rules.

C. UNCITRAL NOTES ON ORGANIZING ARBITRAL PROCEEDINGS, 1996*

INTRODUCTION

Purpose of the Notes

1.   The purpose of the Notes is to assist arbitration practitioners by listing and briefly describing questions on which appropriately timed decisions on organizing arbitral proceedings may be useful. The text, prepared with a particular view to international arbitrations, may be used whether or not the arbitration is administered by an arbitral institution.

Non-binding character of the Notes

2.   No legal requirement binding on the arbitrators or the parties is imposed by the Notes. The arbitral tribunal remains free to use the Notes as it sees fit and is not required to give reasons for disregarding them.

3.   The Notes are not suitable to be used as arbitration rules, since they do not establish any obligation of the arbitral tribunal or the parties to act in a particular way. Accordingly, the use of the Notes cannot imply any modification of the arbitration rules that the parties may have agreed upon.

Discretion in conduct of proceedings and usefulness of timely decisions organizing proceedings

4.   Laws governing the arbitral procedure and arbitration rules that parties may agree upon typically allow the arbitral tribunal broad discretion and flexibility in the conduct of arbitral proceedings. This is useful in that it enables the arbitral tribunal to take decisions on the organization of proceedings that take into account the circumstances of the case, the expectations of the parties and of the members of the arbitral tribunal, and the need for a just and cost-efficient resolution of the dispute.

5.   Such discretion may make it desirable for the arbitral tribunal to give the parties a timely indication as to the organization of the proceedings and the manner in which the tribunal intends to proceed. This is particularly desirable in international arbitrations, where the participants may be accustomed to differing styles of conducting arbitrations. Without such guidance, a party may find aspects of the proceedings unpredictable and difficult to prepare for. That may lead to misunderstandings, delays and increased costs.

Multi-party arbitration

6.   These Notes are intended for use not only in arbitrations with two parties but also in arbitrations with three or more parties. Use of the Notes

---

*   The Notes can be found at the UNCITRAL Website at http://www.uncitral.org/pdf/english/ texts/arbitration/arb-notes/arb-notes-e.pdf. Reprinted with permission of UNCITRAL.

in multi-party arbitration is referred to below in paragraphs 86–88 (item 18).

Process of making decisions on organizing arbitral proceedings

7.   Decisions by the arbitral tribunal on organizing arbitral proceedings may be taken with or without previous consultations with the parties. The method chosen depends on whether, in view of the type of the question to be decided, the arbitral tribunal considers that consultations are not necessary or that hearing the views of the parties would be beneficial for increasing the predictability of the proceedings or improving the procedural atmosphere.

8.   The consultations, whether they involve only the arbitrators or also the parties, can be held in one or more meetings, or can be carried out by correspondence or telecommunications such as telefax or conference telephone calls or other electronic means. Meetings may be held at the venue of arbitration or at some other appropriate location.

9.   In some arbitrations a special meeting may be devoted exclusively to such procedural consultations; alternatively, the consultations may be held in conjunction with a hearing on the substance of the dispute. Practices differ as to whether such special meetings should be held and how they should be organized. Special procedural meetings of the arbitrators and the parties separate from hearings are in practice referred to by expressions such as "preliminary meeting", "pre-hearing conference", "preparatory conference", "pre-hearing review", or terms of similar meaning. The terms used partly depend on the stage of the proceedings at which the meeting is taking place.

List of matters for possible consideration in organizing arbitral proceedings

10.   The Notes provide a list, followed by annotations, of matters on which the arbitral tribunal may wish to formulate decisions on organizing arbitral proceedings.

11.   Given that procedural styles and practices in arbitration vary widely, that the purpose of the Notes is not to promote any practice as best practice, and that the Notes are designed for universal use, it is not attempted in the Notes to describe in detail different arbitral practices or express a preference for any of them.

12.   The list, while not exhaustive, covers a broad range of situations that may arise in an arbitration. In many arbitrations, however, only a limited number of the matters mentioned in the list need to be considered. It also depends on the circumstances of the case at which stage or stages of the proceedings it would be useful to consider matters concerning the organization of the proceedings. Generally, in order not to create

opportunities for unnecessary discussions and delay, it is advisable not to raise a matter prematurely, i.e. before it is clear that a decision is needed.

13. When the Notes are used, it should be borne in mind that the discretion of the arbitral tribunal in organizing the proceedings may be limited by arbitration rules, by other provisions agreed to by the parties and by the law applicable to the arbitral procedure. When an arbitration is administered by an arbitral institution, various matters discussed in the Notes may be covered by the rules and practices of that institution.

ANNOTATIONS

1. Set of arbitration rules

If the parties have not agreed on a set of arbitration rules, would they wish to do so

14. Sometimes parties who have not included in their arbitration agreement a stipulation that a set of arbitration rules will govern their arbitral proceedings might wish to do so after the arbitration has begun. If that occurs, the UNCITRAL Arbitration Rules may be used either without modification or with such modifications as the parties might wish to agree upon. In the alternative, the parties might wish to adopt the rules of an arbitral institution; in that case, it may be necessary to secure the agreement of that institution and to stipulate the terms under which the arbitration could be carried out in accordance with the rules of that institution.

15. However, caution is advised as consideration of a set of arbitration rules might delay the proceedings or give rise to unnecessary controversy.

16. It should be noted that agreement on arbitration rules is not a necessity and that, if the parties do not agree on a set of arbitration rules, the arbitral tribunal has the power to continue the proceedings and determine how the case will be conducted.

2. Language of proceedings

17. Many rules and laws on arbitral procedure empower the arbitral tribunal to determine the language or languages to be used in the proceedings, if the parties have not reached an agreement thereon.

(a) Possible need for translation of documents, in full or in part

18. Some documents annexed to the statements of claim and defense or submitted later may not be in the language of the proceedings. Bearing in mind the needs of the proceedings and economy, it may be considered whether the arbitral tribunal should order that any of those documents or parts thereof should be accompanied by a translation into the language of the proceedings.

(b) Possible need for interpretation of oral presentations

19. If interpretation will be necessary during oral hearings, it is advisable to consider whether the interpretation will be simultaneous or consecutive and whether the arrangements should be the responsibility of a party or the arbitral tribunal. In an arbitration administered by an institution, interpretation as well as translation services are often arranged by the arbitral institution.

(c) Cost of translation and interpretation

20. In taking decisions about translation or interpretation, it is advisable to decide whether any or all of the costs are to be paid directly by a party or whether they will be paid out of the deposits and apportioned between the parties along with the other arbitration costs.

3. Place of arbitration

(a) Determination of the place of arbitration, if not already agreed upon by the parties

21. Arbitration rules usually allow the parties to agree on the place of arbitration, subject to the requirement of some arbitral institutions that arbitrations under their rules be conducted at a particular place, usually the location of the institution. If the place has not been so agreed upon, the rules governing the arbitration typically provide that it is in the power of the arbitral tribunal or the institution administering the arbitration to determine the place. If the arbitral tribunal is to make that determination, it may wish to hear the views of the parties before doing so.

22. Various factual and legal factors influence the choice of the place of arbitration, and their relative importance varies from case to case. Among the more prominent factors are: (a) suitability of the law on arbitral procedure of the place of arbitration; (b) whether there is a multilateral or bilateral treaty on enforcement of arbitral awards between the State where the arbitration takes place and the State or States where the award may have to be enforced; (c) convenience of the parties and the arbitrators, including the travel distances; (d) availability and cost of support services needed; and (e) location of the subject-matter in dispute and proximity of evidence.

(b) Possibility of meetings outside the place of arbitration

23. Many sets of arbitration rules and laws on arbitral procedure expressly allow the arbitral tribunal to hold meetings elsewhere than at the place of arbitration. For example, under the UNCITRAL Model Law on International Commercial Arbitration "the arbitral tribunal may, unless otherwise agreed by the parties, meet at any place it considers appropriate for consultation among its members, for hearing witnesses, experts or the parties, or for inspection of goods, other property or documents" (article

20(2)). The purpose of this discretion is to permit arbitral proceedings to be carried out in a manner that is most efficient and economical.

4.   Administrative services that may be needed for the arbitral tribunal to carry out its functions

24.   Various administrative services (e.g. hearing rooms or secretarial services) may need to be procured for the arbitral tribunal to be able to carry out its functions. When the arbitration is administered by an arbitral institution, the institution will usually provide all or a good part of the required administrative support to the arbitral tribunal. When an arbitration administered by an arbitral institution takes place away from the seat of the institution, the institution may be able to arrange for administrative services to be obtained from another source, often an arbitral institution; some arbitral institutions have entered into cooperation agreements with a view to providing mutual assistance in servicing arbitral proceedings.

25.   When the case is not administered by an institution, or the involvement of the institution does not include providing administrative support, usually the administrative arrangements for the proceedings will be made by the arbitral tribunal or the presiding arbitrator; it may also be acceptable to leave some of the arrangements to the parties, or to one of the parties subject to agreement of the other party or parties. Even in such cases, a convenient source of administrative support might be found in arbitral institutions, which often offer their facilities to arbitrations not governed by the rules of the institution. Otherwise, some services could be procured from entities such as chambers of commerce, hotels or specialized firms providing secretarial or other support services.

26.   Administrative services might be secured by engaging a secretary of the arbitral tribunal (also referred to as registrar, clerk, administrator or rapporteur), who carries out the tasks under the direction of the arbitral tribunal. Some arbitral institutions routinely assign such persons to the cases administered by them. In arbitrations not administered by an institution or where the arbitral institution does not appoint a secretary, some arbitrators frequently engage such persons, at least in certain types of cases, whereas many others normally conduct the proceedings without them.

27.   To the extent the tasks of the secretary are purely organizational (e.g. obtaining meeting rooms and providing or coordinating secretarial services), this is usually not controversial. Differences in views, however, may arise if the tasks include legal research and other professional assistance to the arbitral tribunal (e.g. collecting case law or published commentaries on legal issues defined by the arbitral tribunal, preparing summaries from case law and publications, and sometimes also preparing drafts of procedural decisions or drafts of certain parts of the award, in

particular those concerning the facts of the case). Views or expectations may differ especially where a task of the secretary is similar to professional functions of the arbitrators. Such a role of the secretary is in the view of some commentators inappropriate or is appropriate only under certain conditions, such as that the parties agree thereto. However, it is typically recognized that it is important to ensure that the secretary does not perform any decision-making function of the arbitral tribunal.

5. Deposits in respect of costs

(a) Amount to be deposited

28. In an arbitration administered by an institution, the institution often sets, on the basis of an estimate of the costs of the proceedings, the amount to be deposited as an advance for the costs of the arbitration. In other cases it is customary for the arbitral tribunal to make such an estimate and request a deposit. The estimate typically includes travel and other expenses by the arbitrators, expenditures for administrative assistance required by the arbitral tribunal, costs of any expert advice required by the arbitral tribunal, and the fees for the arbitrators. Many arbitration rules have provisions on this matter, including on whether the deposit should be made by the two parties (or all parties in a multi-party case) or only by the claimant.

(b) Management of deposits

29. When the arbitration is administered by an institution, the institution's services may include managing and accounting for the deposited money. Where that is not the case, it might be useful to clarify matters such as the type and location of the account in which the money will be kept and how the deposits will be managed.

(c) Supplementary deposits

30. If during the course of proceedings it emerges that the costs will be higher than anticipated, supplementary deposits may be required (e.g. because the arbitral tribunal decides pursuant to the arbitration rules to appoint an expert).

6. Confidentiality of information relating to the arbitration; possible agreement thereon

31. It is widely viewed that confidentiality is one of the advantageous and helpful features of arbitration. Nevertheless, there is no uniform answer in national laws as to the extent to which the participants in an arbitration are under the duty to observe the confidentiality of information relating to the case. Moreover, parties that have agreed on arbitration rules or other provisions that do not expressly address the issue of confidentiality cannot assume that all jurisdictions would recognize an implied commitment to confidentiality. Furthermore, the participants in an

arbitration might not have the same understanding as regards the extent of confidentiality that is expected. Therefore, the arbitral tribunal might wish to discuss that with the parties and, if considered appropriate, record any agreed principles on the duty of confidentiality.

32. An agreement on confidentiality might cover, for example, one or more of the following matters: the material or information that is to be kept confidential (e.g. pieces of evidence, written and oral arguments, the fact that the arbitration is taking place, identity of the arbitrators, content of the award); measures for maintaining confidentiality of such information and hearings; whether any special procedures should be employed for maintaining the confidentiality of information transmitted by electronic means (e.g. because communication equipment is shared by several users, or because electronic mail over public networks is considered not sufficiently protected against unauthorized access); circumstances in which confidential information may be disclosed in part or in whole (e.g. in the context of disclosures of information in the public domain, or if required by law or a regulatory body).

7. Routing of written communications among the parties and the arbitrators

33. To the extent the question how documents and other written communications should be routed among the parties and the arbitrators is not settled by the agreed rules, or, if an institution administers the case, by the practices of the institution, it is useful for the arbitral tribunal to clarify the question suitably early so as to avoid misunderstandings and delays.

34. Among various possible patterns of routing, one example is that a party transmits the appropriate number of copies to the arbitral tribunal, or to the arbitral institution, if one is involved, which then forwards them as appropriate. Another example is that a party is to send copies simultaneously to the arbitrators and the other party or parties. Documents and other written communications directed by the arbitral tribunal or the presiding arbitrator to one or more parties may also follow a determined pattern, such as through the arbitral institution or by direct transmission. For some communications, in particular those on organizational matters (e.g. dates for hearings), more direct routes of communication may be agreed, even if, for example, the arbitral institution acts as an intermediary for documents such as the statements of claim and defense, evidence or written arguments.

8. Telefax and other electronic means of sending documents

(a) Telefax

35. Telefax, which offers many advantages over traditional means of communication, is widely used in arbitral proceedings. Nevertheless,

should it be thought that, because of the characteristics of the equipment used, it would be preferable not to rely only on a telefacsimile of a document, special arrangements may be considered, such as that a particular piece of written evidence should be mailed or otherwise physically delivered, or that certain telefax messages should be confirmed by mailing or otherwise delivering documents whose facsimile were transmitted by electronic means. When a document should not be sent by telefax, it may, however, be appropriate, in order to avoid an unnecessarily rigid procedure, for the arbitral tribunal to retain discretion to accept an advance copy of a document by telefax for the purposes of meeting a deadline, provided that the document itself is received within a reasonable time thereafter.

(b) Other electronic means (e.g. electronic mail and magnetic or optical disk)

36. It might be agreed that documents, or some of them, will be exchanged not only in paper-based form, but in addition also in an electronic form other than telefax (e.g. as electronic mail, or on a magnetic or optical disk), or only in electronic form. Since the use of electronic means depends on the aptitude of the persons involved and the availability of equipment and computer programs, agreement is necessary for such means to be used. If both paper-based and electronic means are to be used, it is advisable to decide which one is controlling and, if there is a time-limit for submitting a document, which act constitutes submission.

37. When the exchange of documents in electronic form is planned, it is useful, in order to avoid technical difficulties, to agree on matters such as: data carriers (e.g. electronic mail or computer disks) and their technical characteristics; computer programs to be used in preparing the electronic records; instructions for transforming the electronic records into human-readable form; keeping of logs and back-up records of communications sent and received; information in human-readable form that should accompany the disks (e.g. the names of the originator and recipient, computer program, titles of the electronic files and the back-up methods used); procedures when a message is lost or the communication system otherwise fails; and identification of persons who can be contacted if a problem occurs.

9. Arrangements for the exchange of written submissions

38. After the parties have initially stated their claims and defenses, they may wish, or the arbitral tribunal might request them, to present further written submissions so as to prepare for the hearings or to provide the basis for a decision without hearings. In such submissions, the parties, for example, present or comment on allegations and evidence, cite or explain law, or make or react to proposals. In practice such submissions are referred to variously as, for example, statement, memorial, counter-memorial, brief, counter-brief, reply, réplique, duplique, rebuttal or

rejoinder; the terminology is a matter of linguistic usage and the scope or sequence of the submission.

(a) Scheduling of written submissions

39. It is advisable that the arbitral tribunal set time-limits for written submissions. In enforcing the time-limits, the arbitral tribunal may wish, on the one hand, to make sure that the case is not unduly protracted and, on the other hand, to reserve a degree of discretion and allow late submissions if appropriate under the circumstances. In some cases the arbitral tribunal might prefer not to plan the written submissions in advance, thus leaving such matters, including time-limits, to be decided in light of the developments in the proceedings. In other cases, the arbitral tribunal may wish to determine, when scheduling the first written submissions, the number of subsequent submissions.

40. Practices differ as to whether, after the hearings have been held, written submissions are still acceptable. While some arbitral tribunals consider post-hearing submissions unacceptable, others might request or allow them on a particular issue. Some arbitral tribunals follow the procedure according to which the parties are not requested to present written evidence and legal arguments to the arbitral tribunal before the hearings; in such a case, the arbitral tribunal may regard it as appropriate that written submissions be made after the hearings.

(b) Consecutive or simultaneous submissions

41. Written submissions on an issue may be made consecutively, i.e. the party who receives a submission is given a period of time to react with its counter-submission. Another possibility is to request each party to make the submission within the same time period to the arbitral tribunal or the institution administering the case; the received submissions are then forwarded simultaneously to the respective other party or parties. The approach used may depend on the type of issues to be commented upon and the time in which the views should be clarified. With consecutive submissions, it may take longer than with simultaneous ones to obtain views of the parties on a given issue. Consecutive submissions, however, allow the reacting party to comment on all points raised by the other party or parties, which simultaneous submissions do not; thus, simultaneous submissions might possibly necessitate further submissions.

10. Practical details concerning written submissions and evidence (e.g. method of submission, copies, numbering, references)

42. Depending on the volume and kind of documents to be handled, it might be considered whether practical arrangements on details such as the following would be helpful:

- Whether the submissions will be made as paper documents or by electronic means, or both (see paragraphs 35–37);

- The number of copies in which each document is to be submitted;

- A system for numbering documents and items of evidence, and a method for marking them, including by tabs;

- The form of references to documents (e.g. by the heading and the number assigned to the document or its date);

- Paragraph numbering in written submissions, in order to facilitate precise references to parts of a text;

- When translations are to be submitted as paper documents, whether the translations are to be contained in the same volume as the original texts or included in separate volumes.

11. Defining points at issue; order of deciding issues; defining relief or remedy sought

(a) Should a list of points at issue be prepared

43. In considering the parties' allegations and arguments, the arbitral tribunal may come to the conclusion that it would be useful for it or for the parties to prepare, for analytical purposes and for ease of discussion, a list of the points at issue, as opposed to those that are undisputed. If the arbitral tribunal determines that the advantages of working on the basis of such a list outweigh the disadvantages, it chooses the appropriate stage of the proceedings for preparing a list, bearing in mind also that subsequent developments in the proceedings may require a revision of the points at issue. Such an identification of points at issue might help to concentrate on the essential matters, to reduce the number of points at issue by agreement of the parties, and to select the best and most economical process for resolving the dispute. However, possible disadvantages of preparing such a list include delay, adverse effect on the flexibility of the proceedings, or unnecessary disagreements about whether the arbitral tribunal has decided all issues submitted to it or whether the award contains decisions on matters beyond the scope of the submission to arbitration. The terms of reference required under some arbitration rules, or in agreements of parties, may serve the same purpose as the above-described list of points at issue.

(b) In which order should the points at issue be decided

44. While it is often appropriate to deal with all the points at issue collectively, the arbitral tribunal might decide to take them up during the proceedings in a particular order. The order may be due to a point being preliminary relative to another (e.g. a decision on the jurisdiction of the arbitral tribunal is preliminary to consideration of substantive issues, or the issue of responsibility for a breach of contract is preliminary to the issue of the resulting damages). A particular order may be decided also when the

breach of various contracts is in dispute or when damages arising from various events are claimed.

45. If the arbitral tribunal has adopted a particular order of deciding points at issue, it might consider it appropriate to issue a decision on one of the points earlier than on the other ones. This might be done, for example, when a discrete part of a claim is ready for decision while the other parts still require extensive consideration, or when it is expected that after deciding certain issues the parties might be more inclined to settle the remaining ones. Such earlier decisions are referred to by expressions such as "partial", "interlocutory" or "interim" awards or decisions, depending on the type of issue dealt with and on whether the decision is final with respect to the issue it resolves. Questions that might be the subject of such decisions are, for example, jurisdiction of the arbitral tribunal, interim measures of protection, or the liability of a party.

(c) Is there a need to define more precisely the relief or remedy sought

46. If the arbitral tribunal considers that the relief or remedy sought is insufficiently definite, it may wish to explain to the parties the degree of definiteness with which their claims should be formulated. Such an explanation may be useful since criteria are not uniform as to how specific the claimant must be in formulating a relief or remedy.

12. Possible settlement negotiations and their effect on scheduling proceedings

47. Attitudes differ as to whether it is appropriate for the arbitral tribunal to bring up the possibility of settlement. Given the divergence of practices in this regard, the arbitral tribunal should only suggest settlement negotiations with caution. However, it may be opportune for the arbitral tribunal to schedule the proceedings in a way that might facilitate the continuation or initiation of settlement negotiations.

13. Documentary evidence

(a) Time-limits for submission of documentary evidence intended to be submitted by the parties; consequences of late submission

48. Often the written submissions of the parties contain sufficient information for the arbitral tribunal to fix the time-limit for submitting evidence. Otherwise, in order to set realistic time periods, the arbitral tribunal may wish to consult with the parties about the time that they would reasonably need.

49. The arbitral tribunal may wish to clarify that evidence submitted late will as a rule not be accepted. It may wish not to preclude itself from accepting a late submission of evidence if the party shows sufficient cause for the delay.

(b) Whether the arbitral tribunal intends to require a party to produce documentary evidence

50. Procedures and practices differ widely as to the conditions under which the arbitral tribunal may require a party to produce documents. Therefore, the arbitral tribunal might consider it useful, when the agreed arbitration rules do not provide specific conditions, to clarify to the parties the manner in which it intends to proceed.

51. The arbitral tribunal may wish to establish time-limits for the production of documents. The parties might be reminded that, if the requested party duly invited to produce documentary evidence fails to do so within the established period of time, without showing sufficient cause for such failure, the arbitral tribunal is free to draw its conclusions from the failure and may make the award on the evidence before it.

(c) Should assertions about the origin and receipt of documents and about the correctness of photocopies be assumed as accurate

52. It may be helpful for the arbitral tribunal to inform the parties that it intends to conduct the proceedings on the basis that, unless a party raises an objection to any of the following conclusions within a specified period of time: (a) a document is accepted as having originated from the source indicated in the document; (b) a copy of a dispatched communication (e.g. letter, telex, telefax or other electronic message) is accepted without further proof as having been received by the addressee; and (c) a copy is accepted as correct. A statement by the arbitral tribunal to that effect can simplify the introduction of documentary evidence and discourage unfounded and dilatory objections, at a late stage of the proceedings, to the probative value of documents. It is advisable to provide that the time-limit for objections will not be enforced if the arbitral tribunal considers the delay justified.

(d) Are the parties willing to submit jointly a single set of documentary evidence

53. The parties may consider submitting jointly a single set of documentary evidence whose authenticity is not disputed. The purpose would be to avoid duplicate submissions and unnecessary discussions concerning the authenticity of documents, without prejudicing the position of the parties concerning the content of the documents. Additional documents may be inserted later if the parties agree. When a single set of documents would be too voluminous to be easily manageable, it might be practical to select a number of frequently used documents and establish a set of "working" documents. A convenient arrangement of documents in the set may be according to chronological order or subject-matter. It is useful to keep a table of contents of the documents, for example, by their short headings and dates, and to provide that the parties will refer to documents by those headings and dates.

(e)   Should voluminous and complicated documentary evidence be presented through summaries, tabulations, charts, extracts or samples

54. When documentary evidence is voluminous and complicated, it may save time and costs if such evidence is presented by a report of a person competent in the relevant field (e.g. public accountant or consulting engineer). The report may present the information in the form of summaries, tabulations, charts, extracts or samples. Such presentation of evidence should be combined with arrangements that give the interested party the opportunity to review the underlying data and the methodology of preparing the report.

14. Physical evidence other than documents

55. In some arbitrations the arbitral tribunal is called upon to assess physical evidence other than documents, for example, by inspecting samples of goods, viewing a video recording or observing the functioning of a machine.

(a)   What arrangements should be made if physical evidence will be submitted

56. If physical evidence will be submitted, the arbitral tribunal may wish to fix the time schedule for presenting the evidence, make arrangements for the other party or parties to have a suitable opportunity to prepare itself for the presentation of the evidence, and possibly take measures for safekeeping the items of evidence.

(b)   What arrangements should be made if an on-site inspection is necessary

57. If an on-site inspection of property or goods will take place, the arbitral tribunal may consider matters such as timing, meeting places, other arrangements to provide the opportunity for all parties to be present, and the need to avoid communications between arbitrators and a party about points at issue without the presence of the other party or parties.

58. The site to be inspected is often under the control of one of the parties, which typically means that employees or representatives of that party will be present to give guidance and explanations. It should be borne in mind that statements of those representatives or employees made during an on-site inspection, as contrasted with statements those persons might make as witnesses in a hearing, should not be treated as evidence in the proceedings.

15. Witnesses

59. While laws and rules on arbitral procedure typically leave broad freedom concerning the manner of taking evidence of witnesses, practices on procedural points are varied. In order to facilitate the preparations of the parties for the hearings, the arbitral tribunal may consider it

appropriate to clarify, in advance of the hearings, some or all of the following issues.

(a) Advance notice about a witness whom a party intends to present; written witnesses' statements

60. To the extent the applicable arbitration rules do not deal with the matter, the arbitral tribunal may wish to require that each party give advance notice to the arbitral tribunal and the other party or parties of any witness it intends to present. As to the content of the notice, the following is an example of what might be required, in addition to the names and addresses of the witnesses: (a) the subject upon which the witnesses will testify; (b) the language in which the witnesses will testify; and (c) the nature of the relationship with any of the parties, qualifications and experience of the witnesses if and to the extent these are relevant to the dispute or the testimony, and how the witnesses learned about the facts on which they will testify. However, it may not be necessary to require such a notice, in particular if the thrust of the testimony can be clearly ascertained from the party's allegations.

61. Some practitioners favour the procedure according to which the party presenting witness evidence submits a signed witness's statement containing testimony itself. It should be noted, however, that such practice, which implies interviewing the witness by the party presenting the testimony, is not known in all parts of the world and, moreover, that some practitioners disapprove of it on the ground that such contacts between the party and the witness may compromise the credibility of the testimony and are therefore improper (see paragraph 67). Notwithstanding these reservations, signed witness's testimony has advantages in that it may expedite the proceedings by making it easier for the other party or parties to prepare for the hearings or for the parties to identify uncontested matters. However, those advantages might be outweighed by the time and expense involved in obtaining the written testimony.

62. If a signed witness's statement should be made under oath or similar affirmation of truthfulness, it may be necessary to clarify by whom the oath or affirmation should be administered and whether any formal authentication will be required by the arbitral tribunal.

(b) Manner of taking oral evidence of witnesses

(i)   Order in which questions will be asked and the manner in which the hearing of witnesses will be conducted

63. To the extent that the applicable rules do not provide an answer, it may be useful for the arbitral tribunal to clarify how witnesses will be heard. One of the various possibilities is that a witness is first questioned by the arbitral tribunal, whereupon questions are asked by the parties, first by the party who called the witness. Another possibility is for the

witness to be questioned by the party presenting the witness and then by the other party or parties, while the arbitral tribunal might pose questions during the questioning or after the parties on points that in the tribunal's view have not been sufficiently clarified. Differences exist also as to the degree of control the arbitral tribunal exercises over the hearing of witnesses. For example, some arbitrators prefer to permit the parties to pose questions freely and directly to the witness, but may disallow a question if a party objects; other arbitrators tend to exercise more control and may disallow a question on their initiative or even require that questions from the parties be asked through the arbitral tribunal.

(ii) Whether oral testimony will be given under oath or affirmation and, if so, in what form an oath or affirmation should be made

64. Practices and laws differ as to whether or not oral testimony is to be given under oath or affirmation. In some legal systems, the arbitrators are empowered to put witnesses on oath, but it is usually in their discretion whether they want to do so. In other systems, oral testimony under oath is either unknown or may even be considered improper as only an official such as a judge or notary may have the authority to administer oaths.

(iii) May witnesses be in the hearing room when they are not testifying

65. Some arbitrators favour the procedure that, except if the circumstances suggest otherwise, the presence of a witness in the hearing room is limited to the time the witness is testifying; the purpose is to prevent the witness from being influenced by what is said in the hearing room, or to prevent that the presence of the witness would influence another witness. Other arbitrators consider that the presence of a witness during the testimony of other witnesses may be beneficial in that possible contradictions may be readily clarified or that their presence may act as a deterrent against untrue statements. Other possible approaches may be that witnesses are not present in the hearing room before their testimony, but stay in the room after they have testified, or that the arbitral tribunal decides the question for each witness individually depending on what the arbitral tribunal considers most appropriate. The arbitral tribunal may leave the procedure to be decided during the hearings, or may give guidance on the question in advance of the hearings.

(c)   The order in which the witnesses will be called

66. When several witnesses are to be heard and longer testimony is expected, it is likely to reduce costs if the order in which they will be called is known in advance and their presence can be scheduled accordingly. Each party might be invited to suggest the order in which it intends to present the witnesses, while it would be up to the arbitral tribunal to approve the scheduling and to make departures from it.

(d) Interviewing witnesses prior to their appearance at a hearing

67. In some legal systems, parties or their representatives are permitted to interview witnesses, prior to their appearance at the hearing, as to such matters as their recollection of the relevant events, their experience, qualifications or relation with a participant in the proceedings. In those legal systems such contacts are usually not permitted once the witness's oral testimony has begun. In other systems such contacts with witnesses are considered improper. In order to avoid misunderstandings, the arbitral tribunal may consider it useful to clarify what kind of contacts a party is permitted to have with a witness in the preparations for the hearings.

(e) Hearing representatives of a party

68. According to some legal systems, certain persons affiliated with a party may only be heard as representatives of the party but not as witnesses. In such a case, it may be necessary to consider ground rules for determining which persons may not testify as witnesses (e.g. certain executives, employees or agents) and for hearing statements of those persons and for questioning them.

16. Experts and expert witnesses

69. Many arbitration rules and laws on arbitral procedure address the participation of experts in arbitral proceedings. A frequent solution is that the arbitral tribunal has the power to appoint an expert to report on issues determined by the tribunal; in addition, the parties may be permitted to present expert witnesses on points at issue. In other cases, it is for the parties to present expert testimony, and it is not expected that the arbitral tribunal will appoint an expert.

(a) Expert appointed by the arbitral tribunal

70. If the arbitral tribunal is empowered to appoint an expert, one possible approach is for the tribunal to proceed directly to selecting the expert. Another possibility is to consult the parties as to who should be the expert; this may be done, for example, without mentioning a candidate, by presenting to the parties a list of candidates, soliciting proposals from the parties, or by discussing with the parties the "profile" of the expert the arbitral tribunal intends to appoint, i.e. the qualifications, experience and abilities of the expert.

(i) The expert's terms of reference

71. The purpose of the expert's terms of reference is to indicate the questions on which the expert is to provide clarification, to avoid opinions on points that are not for the expert to assess and to commit the expert to a time schedule. While the discretion to appoint an expert normally includes the determination of the expert's terms of reference, the arbitral

tribunal may decide to consult the parties before finalizing the terms. It might also be useful to determine details about how the expert will receive from the parties any relevant information or have access to any relevant documents, goods or other property, so as to enable the expert to prepare the report. In order to facilitate the evaluation of the expert's report, it is advisable to require the expert to include in the report information on the method used in arriving at the conclusions and the evidence and information used in preparing the report.

(ii) The opportunity of the parties to comment on the expert's report, including by presenting expert testimony

72. Arbitration rules that contain provisions on experts usually also have provisions on the right of a party to comment on the report of the expert appointed by the arbitral tribunal. If no such provisions apply or more specific procedures than those prescribed are deemed necessary, the arbitral tribunal may, in light of those provisions, consider it opportune to determine, for example, the time period for presenting written comments of the parties, or, if hearings are to be held for the purpose of hearing the expert, the procedures for interrogating the expert by the parties or for the participation of any expert witnesses presented by the parties.

(b) Expert opinion presented by a party (expert witness)

73. If a party presents an expert opinion, the arbitral tribunal might consider requiring, for example, that the opinion be in writing, that the expert should be available to answer questions at hearings, and that, if a party will present an expert witness at a hearing, advance notice must be given or that the written opinion must be presented in advance, as in the case of other witnesses (see paragraphs 60–62).

17. Hearings

(a) Decision whether to hold hearings

74. Laws on arbitral procedure and arbitration rules often have provisions as to the cases in which oral hearings must be held and as to when the arbitral tribunal has discretion to decide whether to hold hearings.

75. If it is up to the arbitral tribunal to decide whether to hold hearings, the decision is likely to be influenced by factors such as, on the one hand, that it is usually quicker and easier to clarify points at issue pursuant to a direct confrontation of arguments than on the basis of correspondence and, on the other hand, the travel and other cost of holding hearings, and that the need of finding acceptable dates for the hearings might delay the proceedings. The arbitral tribunal may wish to consult the parties on this matter.

(b) Whether one period of hearings should be held or separate periods of hearings

76. Attitudes vary as to whether hearings should be held in a single period of hearings or in separate periods, especially when more than a few days are needed to complete the hearings. According to some arbitrators, the entire hearings should normally be held in a single period, even if the hearings are to last for more than a week. Other arbitrators in such cases tend to schedule separate periods of hearings. In some cases issues to be decided are separated, and separate hearings set for those issues, with the aim that oral presentation on those issues will be completed within the allotted time. Among the advantages of one period of hearings are that it involves less travel costs, memory will not fade, and it is unlikely that people representing a party will change. On the other hand, the longer the hearings, the more difficult it may be to find early dates acceptable to all participants. Furthermore, separate periods of hearings may be easier to schedule, the subsequent hearings may be tailored to the development of the case, and the period between the hearings leaves time for analyzing the records and negotiations between the parties aimed at narrowing the points at issue by agreement.

(c) Setting dates for hearings

77. Typically, firm dates will be fixed for hearings. Exceptionally, the arbitral tribunal may initially wish to set only "target dates" as opposed to definitive dates. This may be done at a stage of the proceedings when not all information necessary to schedule hearings is yet available, with the understanding that the target dates will either be confirmed or rescheduled within a reasonably short period. Such provisional planning can be useful to participants who are generally not available on short notice.

(d) Whether there should be a limit on the aggregate amount of time each party will have for oral arguments and questioning witnesses

78. Some arbitrators consider it useful to limit the aggregate amount of time each party has for any of the following: (a) making oral statements; (b) questioning its witnesses; and (c) questioning the witnesses of the other party or parties. In general, the same aggregate amount of time is considered appropriate for each party, unless the arbitral tribunal considers that a different allocation is justified. Before deciding, the arbitral tribunal may wish to consult the parties as to how much time they think they will need.

79. Such planning of time, provided it is realistic, fair and subject to judiciously firm control by the arbitral tribunal, will make it easier for the parties to plan the presentation of the various items of evidence and arguments, reduce the likelihood of running out of time towards the end of the hearings and avoid that one party would unfairly use up a disproportionate amount of time.

(e) The order in which the parties will present their arguments and evidence

80. Arbitration rules typically give broad latitude to the arbitral tribunal to determine the order of presentations at the hearings. Within that latitude, practices differ, for example, as to whether opening or closing statements are heard and their level of detail; the sequence in which the claimant and the respondent present their opening statements, arguments, witnesses and other evidence; and whether the respondent or the claimant has the last word. In view of such differences, or when no arbitration rules apply, it may foster efficiency of the proceedings if the arbitral tribunal clarifies to the parties, in advance of the hearings, the manner in which it will conduct the hearings, at least in broad lines.

(f) Length of hearings

81. The length of a hearing primarily depends on the complexity of the issues to be argued and the amount of witness evidence to be presented. The length also depends on the procedural style used in the arbitration. Some practitioners prefer to have written evidence and written arguments presented before the hearings, which thus can focus on the issues that have not been sufficiently clarified. Those practitioners generally tend to plan shorter hearings than those practitioners who prefer that most if not all evidence and arguments are presented to the arbitral tribunal orally and in full detail. In order to facilitate the parties' preparations and avoid misunderstandings, the arbitral tribunal may wish to clarify to the parties, in advance of the hearings, the intended use of time and style of work at the hearings.

(g) Arrangements for a record of the hearings

82. The arbitral tribunal should decide, possibly after consulting with the parties, on the method of preparing a record of oral statements and testimony during hearings. Among different possibilities, one method is that the members of the arbitral tribunal take personal notes. Another is that the presiding arbitrator during the hearing dictates to a typist a summary of oral statements and testimony. A further method, possible when a secretary of the arbitral tribunal has been appointed, may be to leave to that person the preparation of a summary record. A useful, though costly, method is for professional stenographers to prepare verbatim transcripts, often within the next day or a similarly short time period. A written record may be combined with tape-recording, so as to enable reference to the tape in case of a disagreement over the written record.

83. If transcripts are to be produced, it may be considered how the persons who made the statements will be given an opportunity to check the transcripts. For example, it may be determined that the changes to the record would be approved by the parties or, failing their agreement, would be referred for decision to the arbitral tribunal.

(h) Whether and when the parties are permitted to submit notes summarizing their oral arguments

84. Some legal counsel are accustomed to giving notes summarizing their oral arguments to the arbitral tribunal and to the other party or parties. If such notes are presented, this is usually done during the hearings or shortly thereafter; in some cases, the notes are sent before the hearing. In order to avoid surprise, foster equal treatment of the parties and facilitate preparations for the hearings, advance clarification is advisable as to whether submitting such notes is acceptable and the time for doing so.

85. In closing the hearings, the arbitral tribunal will normally assume that no further proof is to be offered or submission to be made. Therefore, if notes are to be presented to be read after the closure of the hearings, the arbitral tribunal may find it worthwhile to stress that the notes should be limited to summarizing what was said orally and in particular should not refer to new evidence or new argument.

18. Multi-party arbitration

86. When a single arbitration involves more than two parties (multi-party arbitration), considerations regarding the need to organize arbitral proceedings, and matters that may be considered in that connection, are generally not different from two-party arbitrations. A possible difference may be that, because of the need to deal with more than two parties, multi-party proceedings can be more complicated to manage than bilateral proceedings. The Notes, notwithstanding a possible greater complexity of multi-party arbitration, can be used in multi-party as well as in two-party proceedings.

87. The areas of possibly increased complexity in multi-party arbitration are, for example, the flow of communications among the parties and the arbitral tribunal (see paragraphs 33, 34 and 38–41); if points at issue are to be decided at different points in time, the order of deciding them (paragraphs 44–45); the manner in which the parties will participate in hearing witnesses (paragraph 63); the appointment of experts and the participation of the parties in considering their reports (paragraphs 70–72); the scheduling of hearings (paragraph 76); the order in which the parties will present their arguments and evidence at hearings (paragraph 80).

88. The Notes, which are limited to pointing out matters that may be considered in organizing arbitral proceedings in general, do not cover the drafting of the arbitration agreement or the constitution of the arbitral tribunal, both issues that give rise to special questions in multi-party arbitration as compared to two-party arbitration.

19. Possible requirements concerning filing or delivering the award

89. Some national laws require that arbitral awards be filed or registered with a court or similar authority, or that they be delivered in a particular manner or through a particular authority. Those laws differ with respect to, for example, the type of award to which the requirement applies (e.g. to all awards or only to awards not rendered under the auspices of an arbitral institution); time periods for filing, registering or delivering the award (in some cases those time periods may be rather short); or consequences for failing to comply with the requirement (which might be, for example, invalidity of the award or inability to enforce it in a particular manner).

Who should take steps to fulfil any requirement

90. If such a requirement exists, it is useful, some time before the award is to be issued, to plan who should take the necessary steps to meet the requirement and how the costs are to be borne.

D. IBA RULES ON THE TAKING OF EVIDENCE IN INTERNATIONAL COMMERCIAL ARBITRATION*

(Adopted by a resolution of the IBA Council 29 May 2010, International Bar Association)

Preamble

1. These IBA Rules on the Taking of Evidence in International Arbitration are intended to provide an efficient, economical and fair process for the taking of evidence in international arbitrations, particularly those between Parties from different legal traditions. They are designed to supplement the legal provisions and the institutional, ad hoc or other rules that apply to the conduct of the arbitration.

2. Parties and Arbitral Tribunals may adopt the IBA Rules of Evidence, in whole or in part, to govern arbitration proceedings, or they may vary them or use them as guidelines in developing their own procedures. The Rules are not intended to limit the flexibility that is inherent in, and an advantage of, international arbitration, and Parties and Arbitral Tribunals are free to adapt them to the particular circumstances of each arbitration.

3. The taking of evidence shall be conducted on the principles that each Party shall act in good faith and be entitled to know, reasonably in advance

of any Evidentiary Hearing or any fact or merits determination, the evidence on which the other Parties rely.

Definitions In the IBA Rules of Evidence:

'Arbitral Tribunal' means a sole arbitrator or a panel of arbitrators;

'Claimant' means the Party or Parties who commenced the arbitration and any Party who, through joinder or otherwise, becomes aligned with such Party or Parties;

'Document' means a writing, communication, picture, drawing, program or data of any kind, whether recorded or maintained on paper or by electronic, audio, visual or any other means;

'Evidentiary Hearing' means any hearing, whether or not held on consecutive days, at which the Arbitral Tribunal, whether in person, by teleconference, videoconference or other method, receives oral or other evidence;

'Expert Report' means a written statement by a Tribunal-Appointed Expert or a Party-Appointed Expert;

'General Rules' mean the institutional, ad hoc or other rules that apply to the conduct of the arbitration;

'IBA Rules of Evidence' or 'Rules' means these IBA Rules on the Taking of Evidence in International Arbitration, as they may be revised or amended from time to time;

'Party' means a party to the arbitration;

'Respondent' means the Party or Parties against whom the Claimant made its claim, and any Party who, through joinder or otherwise, becomes aligned with such Party or Parties, and includes a Respondent making a counter-claim;

'Tribunal-Appointed Expert' means a person or organization appointed by the Arbitral Tribunal in order to report to it on specific issues determined by the Arbitral Tribunal;

and

'Witness Statement' means a written statement of testimony by a witness of fact.

Article 1

Scope of Application

1.   Whenever the Parties have agreed or the Arbitral Tribunal has determined to apply the IBA Rules of Evidence, the Rules shall govern the taking of evidence, except to the extent that any specific provision of them may be found to be in conflict with any mandatory provision of law

determined to be applicable to the case by the Parties or by the Arbitral Tribunal.

2.   Where the Parties have agreed to apply the IBA Rules of Evidence, they shall be deemed to have agreed, in the absence of a contrary indication, to the version as current on the date of such agreement.

3.   In case of conflict between any provisions of the IBA Rules of Evidence and the General Rules, the Arbitral Tribunal shall apply the IBA Rules of Evidence in the manner that it determines best in order to accomplish the purposes of both the General Rules and the IBA Rules of Evidence, unless the Parties agree to the contrary.

4.   In the event of any dispute regarding the meaning of the IBA Rules of Evidence, the Arbitral Tribunal shall interpret them according to their purpose and in the manner most appropriate for the particular arbitration.

5.   Insofar as the IBA Rules of Evidence and the General Rules are silent on any matter concerning the taking of evidence and the Parties have not agreed otherwise, the Arbitral Tribunal shall conduct the taking of evidence as it deems appropriate, in accordance with the general principles of the IBA Rules of Evidence.

Article 2

Consultation on Evidentiary Issues

1.   The Arbitral Tribunal shall consult the Parties at the earliest appropriate time in the proceedings and invite them to consult each other with a view to agreeing on an efficient, economical and fair process for the taking of evidence.

2.   The consultation on evidentiary issues may address the scope, timing and manner of the taking of evidence, including:

(a)   the preparation and submission of Witness Statements and Expert Reports;

(b)   the taking of oral testimony at any Evidentiary Hearing;

(c)   the requirements, procedure and format applicable to the production of Documents;

(d)   the level of confidentiality protection to be afforded to evidence in the arbitration; and

(e)   the promotion of efficiency, economy and conservation of resources in connection with the taking of evidence.

3.   The Arbitral Tribunal is encouraged to identify to the Parties, as soon as it considers it to be appropriate, any issues:

(a)   that the Arbitral Tribunal may regard as relevant to the case and material to its outcome; and/or

(b) for which a preliminary determination may be appropriate.

Article 3

Documents

1.   Within the time ordered by the Arbitral Tribunal, each Party shall submit to the Arbitral Tribunal and to the other Parties all Documents available to it on which it relies, including public Documents and those in the public domain, except for any Documents that have already been submitted by another Party.

2.   Within the time ordered by the Arbitral Tribunal, any Party may submit to the Arbitral Tribunal and to the other Parties a Request to Produce.

3.   A Request to Produce shall contain:

(a) *(i)* a description of each requested Document sufficient to identify it, or

   (ii) a description in sufficient detail (including subject matter) of a narrow and specific requested category of Documents that are reasonably believed to exist; in the case of Documents maintained in electronic form, the requesting Party may, or the Arbitral Tribunal may order that it shall be required to, identify specific files, search terms, individuals or other means of searching for such Documents in an efficient and economical manner;

(b) a statement as to how the Documents requested are relevant to the case and material to its

outcome; and

(c) *(i)* a statement that the Documents requested are not in the possession, custody or control of the requesting Party or a statement of the reasons why it would be unreasonably burdensome for the requesting Party to produce such Documents, and

   (ii) a statement of the reasons why the requesting Party assumes the Documents requested are in the possession, custody or control of another Party.

4.   Within the time ordered by the Arbitral Tribunal, the Party to whom the Request to Produce is addressed shall produce to the other Parties and, if the Arbitral Tribunal so orders, to it, all the Documents requested in its possession, custody or control as to which it makes no objection.

5.   If the Party to whom the Request to Produce is addressed has an objection to some or all of the Documents requested, it shall state the objection in writing to the Arbitral Tribunal and the other Parties within

the time ordered by the Arbitral Tribunal. The reasons for such objection shall be any of those set forth in Article 9.2 or a failure to satisfy any of the requirements of Article 3.3.

6.   Upon receipt of any such objection, the Arbitral Tribunal may invite the relevant Parties to consult with each other with a view to resolving the objection.

7.   Either Party may, within the time ordered by the Arbitral Tribunal, request the Arbitral Tribunal to rule on the objection. The Arbitral Tribunal shall then, in consultation with the Parties and in timely fashion, consider the Request to Produce and the objection. The Arbitral Tribunal may order the Party to whom such Request is addressed to produce any requested Document in its possession, custody or control as to which the Arbitral Tribunal determines that *(i)* the issues that the requesting Party wishes to prove are relevant to the case and material to its outcome; *(ii)* none of the reasons for objection set forth in Article 9.2 applies; and *(iii)* the requirements of Article 3.3 have been satisfied. Any such Document shall be produced to the other Parties and, if the Arbitral Tribunal so orders, to it.

8.   In exceptional circumstances, if the propriety of an objection can be determined only by review of the Document, the Arbitral Tribunal may determine that it should not review the Document. In that event, the Arbitral Tribunal may, after consultation with the Parties, appoint an independent and impartial expert, bound to confidentiality, to review any such Document and to report on the objection. To the extent that the objection is upheld by the Arbitral Tribunal, the expert shall not disclose to the Arbitral Tribunal and to the other Parties the contents of the Document reviewed.

9.   If a Party wishes to obtain the production of Documents from a person or organisation who is not a Party to the arbitration and from whom the Party cannot obtain the Documents on its own, the Party may, within the time ordered by the Arbitral Tribunal, ask it to take whatever steps are legally available to obtain the requested Documents, or seek leave from the Arbitral Tribunal to take such steps itself. The Party shall submit such request to and to the other Parties in writing, and the request shall contain the particulars set forth in Article 3.3, as applicable. The Arbitral Tribunal shall decide on this request and shall take, authorize the requesting Party to take, or order any other Party to take, such steps as the Arbitral Tribunal considers appropriate if, in its discretion, it determines that *(i)* the Documents would be relevant to the case and material to its outcome, *(ii)* the requirements of Article 3.3, as applicable, have been satisfied and *(iii)* none of the reasons for objection set forth in Article 9.2 applies.

10.   At any time before the arbitration is concluded, the Arbitral Tribunal may *(i)* request any Party to produce Documents, *(ii)* request any Party to

use its best efforts to take or *(iii)* itself take, any step that it considers appropriate to obtain Documents from any person or organisation. A Party to whom such a request for Documents is addressed may object to the request for any of the reasons set forth in Article 9.2. In such cases, Article 3.4 to Article 3.8 shall apply correspondingly.

11. Within the time ordered by the Arbitral Tribunal, the Parties may submit to the Arbitral Tribunal and to the other Parties any additional Documents on which they intend to rely or which they believe have become relevant to the case and material to its outcome as a consequence of the issues raised in Documents, Witness Statements or Expert Reports submitted or produced, or in other submissions of the Parties.

12. With respect to the form of submission or production of Documents:

(a) copies of Documents shall conform to the originals and, at the request of the Arbitral Tribunal, any original shall be presented for inspection;

(b) Documents that a Party maintains in electronic form shall be submitted or produced in the form most convenient or economical to it that is reasonably usable by the recipients, unless the Parties agree otherwise or, in the absence of such agreement, the Arbitral Tribunal decides otherwise;

(c) a Party is not obligated to produce multiple copies of Documents which are essentially identical unless the Arbitral Tribunal decides otherwise; and

(d) translations of Documents shall be submitted together with the originals and marked as translations with the original language identified.

13. Any Document submitted or produced by a Party or non-Party in the arbitration and not otherwise in the public domain shall be kept confidential by the Arbitral Tribunal and the other Parties, and shall be used only in connection with the arbitration. This requirement shall apply except and to the extent that disclosure may be required of a Party to fulfil a legal duty, protect or pursue a legal right, or enforce or challenge an award in bona fide legal proceedings before a state court or other judicial authority. The Arbitral Tribunal may issue orders to set forth the terms of this confidentiality. This requirement shall be without prejudice to all other obligations of confidentiality in the arbitration.

14. If the arbitration is organised into separate issues or phases (such as jurisdiction, preliminary determinations, liability or damages), the Arbitral Tribunal may, after consultation with the Parties, schedule the submission of Documents and Requests to Produce separately for each issue or phase.

Article 4

Witnesses of Fact

1.   Within the time ordered by the Arbitral Tribunal, each Party shall identify the witnesses on whose testimony it intends to rely and the subject matter of that testimony.

2.   Any person may present evidence as a witness, including a Party or a Party's officer, employee or other representative.

3.   It shall not be improper for a Party, its officers, employees, legal advisors or other representatives to interview its witnesses or potential witnesses and to discuss their prospective testimony with them.

4.   The Arbitral Tribunal may order each Party to submit within a specified time to the Arbitral Tribunal and to the other Parties Witness Statements by each witness on whose testimony it intends to rely, except for those witnesses whose testimony is sought pursuant to Articles 4.9 or 4.10. If Evidentiary Hearings are organised into separate issues or phases (such as jurisdiction, preliminary determinations, liability or damages), the Arbitral Tribunal or the Parties by agreement may schedule the submission of Witness Statements separately for each issue or phase.

5.   Each Witness Statement shall contain:

    (a)   the full name and address of the witness, a statement regarding his or her present and past relationship (if any) with any of the Parties, and a description of his or her background, qualifications, training and experience, if such a description may be relevant to the dispute or to the contents of the statement;

    (b)   a full and detailed description of the facts, and the source of the witness's information as to those facts, sufficient to serve as that witness's evidence in the matter in dispute. Documents on which the witness relies that have not already been submitted shall be provided;

    (c)   a statement as to the language in which the Witness Statement was originally prepared and the language in which the witness anticipates giving testimony at the Evidentiary Hearing;

    (d)   an affirmation of the truth of the Witness Statement; and

    (e)   the signature of the witness and its date and place.

6.   If Witness Statements are submitted, any Party may, within the time ordered by the Arbitral Tribunal, submit to the Arbitral Tribunal and to the other Parties revised or additional Witness Statements, including statements from persons not previously named as witnesses, so long as any such revisions or additions respond only to matters contained in another Party's Witness Statements, Expert Reports or other submissions that have not been previously presented in the arbitration.

7.   If a witness whose appearance has been requested pursuant to Article 8.1 fails without a valid reason to appear for testimony at an Evidentiary Hearing, the Arbitral Tribunal shall disregard any Witness Statement related to that Evidentiary Hearing by that witness unless, in exceptional circumstances, the Arbitral Tribunal decides otherwise.

8.   If the appearance of a witness has not been requested pursuant to Article 8.1, none of the other Parties shall be deemed to have agreed to the correctness of the content of the Witness Statement.

9.   If a Party wishes to present evidence from a person who will not appear voluntarily at its request, the Party may, within the time ordered by the Arbitral Tribunal, ask it to take whatever steps are legally available to obtain the testimony of that person, or seek leave from the Arbitral Tribunal to take such steps itself. In the case of a request to the Arbitral Tribunal, the Party shall identify the intended witness, shall describe the subjects on which the witness's testimony is sought and shall state why such subjects are relevant to the case and material to its outcome. The Arbitral Tribunal shall decide on this request and shall take, authorize the requesting Party to take or order any other Party to take, such steps as the Arbitral Tribunal considers appropriate if, in its discretion, it determines that the testimony of that witness would be relevant to the case and material to its outcome.

10.   At any time before the arbitration is concluded, the Arbitral Tribunal may order any Party to provide for, or to use its best efforts to provide for, the appearance for testimony at an Evidentiary Hearing of any person, including one whose testimony has not yet been offered. A Party to whom such a request is addressed may object for any of the reasons set forth in Article 9.2.

Article 5

Party-Appointed Experts

1.   A Party may rely on a Party-Appointed Expert as a means of evidence on specific issues. Within the time ordered by the Arbitral Tribunal, (i) each Party shall identify any Party-Appointed Expert on whose testimony it intends to rely and the subject-matter of such testimony; and (ii) the Party-Appointed Expert shall submit an Expert Report.

2.   The Expert Report shall contain:

   (a)   the full name and address of the Party-Appointed Expert, a statement regarding his or her present and past relationship (if any) with any of the Parties, their legal advisors and the Arbitral Tribunal, and a description of his or her background, qualifications, training and experience;

   (b)   a description of the instructions pursuant to which he or she is providing his or her opinions and conclusions;

(c) a statement of his or her independence from the Parties, their legal advisors and the Arbitral Tribunal;

(d) a statement of the facts on which he or she is basing his or her expert opinions and conclusions;

(e) his or her expert opinions and conclusions, including a description of the methods, evidence and information used in arriving at the conclusions. Documents on which the Party-Appointed Expert relies that have not already been submitted shall be provided;

(f) if the Expert Report has been translated, a statement as to the language in which it was originally prepared, and the language in which the Party-Appointed Expert anticipates giving testimony at the Evidentiary Hearing;

(g) an affirmation of his or her genuine belief in the opinions expressed in the Expert Report;

(h) the signature of the Party-Appointed Expert and its date and place; and

(i) if the Expert Report has been signed by more than one person, an attribution of the entirety or specific parts of the Expert Report to each author.

3. If Expert Reports are submitted, any Party may, within the time ordered by the Arbitral Tribunal, submit to the Arbitral Tribunal and to the other Parties revised or additional Expert Reports, including reports or statements from persons not previously identified as Party-Appointed Experts, so long as any such revisions or additions respond only to matters contained in another Party's Witness Statements, Expert Reports or other submissions that have not been previously presented in the arbitration.

4. The Arbitral Tribunal in its discretion may order that any Party-Appointed Experts who will submit or who have submitted Expert Reports on the same or related issues meet and confer on such issues. At such meeting, the Party-Appointed Experts shall attempt to reach agreement on the issues within the scope of their Expert Reports, and they shall record in writing any such issues on which they reach agreement, any remaining areas of disagreement and the reasons therefore.

5. If a Party-Appointed Expert whose appearance has been requested pursuant to Article 8.1 fails without a valid reason to appear for testimony at an Evidentiary Hearing, the Arbitral Tribunal shall disregard any Expert Report by that Party-Appointed Expert related to that Evidentiary Hearing unless, in exceptional circumstances, the Arbitral Tribunal decides otherwise.

6. If the appearance of a Party-Appointed Expert has not been requested pursuant to Article 8.1, none of the other Parties shall be deemed to have agreed to the correctness of the content of the Expert Report.

Article 6

Tribunal-Appointed Experts

1.   The Arbitral Tribunal, after consulting with the Parties, may appoint one or more independent Tribunal-Appointed Experts to report to it on specific issues designated by the Arbitral Tribunal. The Arbitral Tribunal shall establish the terms of reference for any Tribunal-Appointed Expert Report after consulting with the Parties. A copy of the final terms of reference shall be sent by the Arbitral Tribunal to the Parties.

2.   The Tribunal-Appointed Expert shall, before accepting appointment, submit to the Arbitral Tribunal and to the Parties a description of his or her qualifications and a statement of his or her independence from the Parties, their legal advisors and the Arbitral Tribunal. Within the time ordered by the Arbitral Tribunal, the Parties shall inform the Arbitral Tribunal whether they have any objections as to the Tribunal-Appointed Expert's qualifications and independence. The Arbitral Tribunal shall decide promptly whether to accept any such objection. After the appointment of a Tribunal-Appointed Expert, a Party may object to the expert's qualifications or independence only if the objection is for reasons of which the Party becomes aware after the appointment has been made. The Arbitral Tribunal shall decide promptly what, if any, action to take.

3.   Subject to the provisions of Article 9.2, the Tribunal-Appointed Expert may request a Party to provide any information or to provide access to any Documents, goods, samples, property, machinery, systems, processes or site for inspection, to the extent relevant to the case and material to its outcome. The authority of a Tribunal-Appointed Expert to request such information or access shall be the same as the authority of the Arbitral Tribunal. The Parties and their representatives shall have the right to receive any such information and to attend any such inspection. Any disagreement between a Tribunal-Appointed Expert and a Party as to the relevance, materiality or appropriateness of such a request shall be decided by the Arbitral Tribunal, in the manner provided in Articles 3.5 through 3.8. The Tribunal-Appointed Expert shall record in the Expert Report any non-compliance by a Party with an appropriate request or decision by the Arbitral Tribunal and shall describe its effects on the determination of the specific issue.

4.   The Tribunal-Appointed Expert shall report in writing to the Arbitral Tribunal in an Expert Report. The Expert Report shall contain:

   (a)   the full name and address of the Tribunal-Appointed Expert, and a description of his or her background, qualifications, training and experience;

   (b)   a statement of the facts on which he or she is basing his or her expert opinions and conclusions;

    (c)   his or her expert opinions and conclusions, including a description of the methods, evidence and information used in arriving at the conclusions. Documents on which the Tribunal-Appointed Expert relies that have not already been submitted shall be provided;

    (d)   if the Expert Report has been translated, a statement as to the language in which it was originally prepared, and the language in which the Tribunal-Appointed Expert anticipates giving testimony at the Evidentiary Hearing;

    (e)   an affirmation of his or her genuine belief in the opinions expressed in the Expert Report;

    (f)   the signature of the Tribunal-Appointed Expert and its date and place; and

    (g)   if the Expert Report has been signed by more than one person, an attribution of the entirety or specific parts of the Expert Report to each author.

5.   The Arbitral Tribunal shall send a copy of such Expert Report to the Parties. The Parties may examine any information, Documents, goods, samples, property, machinery, systems, processes or site for inspection that the Tribunal-Appointed Expert has examined and any correspondence between the Arbitral Tribunal and the Tribunal-Appointed Expert. Within the time ordered by the Arbitral Tribunal, any Party shall have the opportunity to respond to the Expert Report in a submission by the Party or through a Witness Statement or an Expert Report by a Party-Appointed Expert. The Arbitral Tribunal shall send the submission, Witness Statement or Expert Report to the Tribunal-Appointed Expert and to the other Parties.

6.   At the request of a Party or of the Arbitral Tribunal, the Tribunal-Appointed Expert shall be present at an Evidentiary Hearing. The Arbitral Tribunal may question the Tribunal-Appointed Expert, and he or she may be questioned by the Parties or by any Party-Appointed Expert on issues raised in his or her Expert Report, the Parties' submissions or Witness Statement or the Expert Reports made by the Party-Appointed Experts pursuant to Article 6.5.

7.   Any Expert Report made by a Tribunal-Appointed Expert and its conclusions shall be assessed by the Arbitral Tribunal with due regard to all circumstances of the case.

8.   The fees and expenses of a Tribunal-Appointed Expert, to be funded in a manner determined by the Arbitral Tribunal, shall form part of the costs of the arbitration.

Article 7

Inspection

Subject to the provisions of Article 9.2, the Arbitral Tribunal may, at the request of a Party or on its own motion, inspect or require the inspection by a Tribunal-Appointed Expert or a Party-Appointed Expert of any site, property, machinery or any other goods, samples, systems, processes or Documents, as it deems appropriate. The Arbitral Tribunal shall, in consultation with the Parties, determine the timing and arrangement for the inspection. The Parties and their representatives shall have the right to attend any such inspection.

Article 8

Evidentiary Hearing

1.   Within the time ordered by the Arbitral Tribunal, each Party shall inform the Arbitral Tribunal and the other Parties of the witnesses whose appearance it requests. Each witness (which term includes, for the purposes of this Article, witnesses of fact and any experts) shall, subject to Article 8.2, appear for testimony at the Evidentiary Hearing if such person's appearance has been requested by any Party or by the Arbitral Tribunal. Each witness shall appear in person unless the Arbitral Tribunal allows the use of videoconference or similar technology with respect to a particular witness.

2.   The Arbitral Tribunal shall at all times have complete control over the Evidentiary Hearing. The Arbitral Tribunal may limit or exclude any question to, answer by or appearance of a witness, if it considers such question, answer or appearance to be irrelevant, immaterial, unreasonably burdensome, duplicative or otherwise covered by a reason for objection set forth in Article 9.2. Questions to a witness during direct and re-direct testimony may not be unreasonably leading.

3.   With respect to oral testimony at an Evidentiary Hearing:

   (a)   the Claimant shall ordinarily first present the testimony of its witnesses, followed by the Respondent presenting the testimony of its witnesses;

   (b)   following direct testimony, any other Party may question such witness, in an order to be determined by the Arbitral Tribunal. The Party who initially presented the witness shall subsequently have the opportunity to ask additional questions on the matters raised in the other Parties' questioning;

   (c)   thereafter, the Claimant shall ordinarily first present the testimony of its Party-Appointed Experts, followed by the Respondent presenting the testimony of its Party-Appointed Experts. The Party who initially presented the Party-Appointed

Expert shall subsequently have the opportunity to ask additional questions on the matters raised in the other Parties' questioning;

(d)   the Arbitral Tribunal may question a Tribunal-Appointed Expert, and he or she may be questioned by the Parties or by any Party-Appointed Expert, on issues raised in the Tribunal-Appointed Expert Report, in the Parties' submissions or in the Expert Reports made by the Party-Appointed Experts;

(e)   if the arbitration is organised into separate issues or phases (such as jurisdiction, preliminary determinations, liability and damages), the Parties may agree or the Arbitral Tribunal may order the scheduling of testimony separately for each issue or phase;

(f)   the Arbitral Tribunal, upon request of a Party or on its own motion, may vary this order of proceeding, including the arrangement of testimony by particular issues or in such a manner that witnesses be questioned at the same time and in confrontation with each other (witness conferencing);

(g)   the Arbitral Tribunal may ask questions to a witness at any time.

4.   A witness of fact providing testimony shall first affirm, in a manner determined appropriate by the Arbitral Tribunal, that he or she commits to tell the truth or, in the case of an expert witness, his or her genuine belief in the opinions to be expressed at the Evidentiary Hearing. If the witness has submitted a Witness Statement or an Expert Report, the witness shall confirm it. The Parties may agree or the Arbitral Tribunal may order that the Witness Statement or Expert Report shall serve as that witness's direct testimony.

5.   Subject to the provisions of Article 9.2, the Arbitral Tribunal may request any person to give oral or written evidence on any issue that the Arbitral Tribunal considers to be relevant to the case and material to its outcome. Any witness called and questioned by the Arbitral Tribunal may also be questioned by the Parties.

Article 9

Admissibility and Assessment of Evidence

1.   The Arbitral Tribunal shall determine the admissibility, relevance, materiality and weight of evidence.

2.   The Arbitral Tribunal shall, at the request of a Party or on its own motion, exclude from evidence or production any Document, statement, oral testimony or inspection for any of the following reasons:

(a)   lack of sufficient relevance to the case or materiality to its outcome;

(b) legal impediment or privilege under the legal or ethical rules determined by the Arbitral Tribunal to be applicable;

(c) unreasonable burden to produce the requested evidence;

(d) loss or destruction of the Document that has been shown with reasonable likelihood to have occurred;

(e) grounds of commercial or technical confidentiality that the Arbitral Tribunal determines to be compelling;

(f) grounds of special political or institutional sensitivity (including evidence that has been classified as secret by a government or a public international institution) that the Arbitral Tribunal determines to be compelling; or

(g) considerations of procedural economy, proportionality, fairness or equality of the Parties that the Arbitral Tribunal determines to be compelling.

3.   In considering issues of legal impediment or privilege under Article 9.2(b), and insofar as permitted by any mandatory legal or ethical rules that are determined by it to be applicable, the Arbitral Tribunal may take into account:

(a) any need to protect the confidentiality of a Document created or statement or oral communication made in connection with and for the purpose of providing or obtaining legal advice;

(b) any need to protect the confidentiality of a Document created or statement or oral communication made in connection with and for the purpose of settlement negotiations;

(c) the expectations of the Parties and their advisors at the time the legal impediment or privilege is said to have arisen;

(d) any possible waiver of any applicable legal impediment or privilege by virtue of consent, earlier disclosure, affirmative use of the Document, statement, oral communication or advice contained therein, or otherwise; and

(e) the need to maintain fairness and equality as between the Parties, particularly if they are subject to different legal or ethical rules.

4.   The Arbitral Tribunal may, where appropriate, make necessary arrangements to permit evidence to be presented or considered subject to suitable confidentiality protection.

5.   If a Party fails without satisfactory explanation to produce any Document requested in a Request to Produce to which it has not objected in due time or fails to produce any Document ordered to be produced by the Arbitral Tribunal, the Arbitral Tribunal may infer that such document would be adverse to the interests of that Party.

6.   If a Party fails without satisfactory explanation to make available any other relevant evidence, including testimony, sought by one Party to which

the Party to whom the request was addressed has not objected in due time or fails to make available any evidence, including testimony, ordered by the Arbitral Tribunal to be produced, the Arbitral Tribunal may infer that such evidence would be adverse to the interests of that Party.

7.   If the Arbitral Tribunal determines that a Party has failed to conduct itself in good faith in the taking of evidence, the Arbitral Tribunal may, in addition to any other measures available under these Rules, take such failure into account in its assignment of the costs of the arbitration, including costs arising out of or in connection with the taking of evidence.

E. UNCITRAL MODEL LAW ON INTERNATIONAL COMMERCIAL CONCILIATION (2002)*

Resolution adopted by the General Assembly

[on the report of the Sixth Committee (A/57/562 and Corr.1)]

57/18 *Model Law on International Commercial Conciliation of the United Nations Commission on International Trade Law*

The General Assembly,

Recognizing the value for international trade of methods for settling commercial disputes in which the parties in dispute request a third person or persons to assist them in their attempt to settle the dispute amicably,

Noting that such dispute settlement methods, referred to by expressions such as conciliation and mediation and expressions of similar import, are increasingly used in international and domestic commercial practice as an alternative to litigation,

Considering that the use of such dispute settlement methods results in significant benefits, such as reducing the instances where a dispute leads to the termination of a commercial relationship, facilitating the administration of international transactions by commercial parties and producing savings in the administration of justice by States,

Convinced that the establishment of model legislation on these methods that is acceptable to States with different legal, social and economic systems would contribute to the development of harmonious international economic relations,

Noting with satisfaction the completion and adoption by the United Nations Commission on International Trade Law of the Model Law on International Commercial Conciliation,**

---

*   Text can be found at UNCITRAL website http://www.uncitral.org/.

**   Official Records of the General Assembly, Fifty-seventh Session, Supplement No. 17 (A/57/17), annex I.

Believing that the Model Law will significantly assist States in enhancing their legislation governing the use of modern conciliation or mediation techniques and in formulating such legislation where none currently exists,

Noting that the preparation of the Model Law was the subject of due deliberation and extensive consultations with Governments and interested circles,

Convinced that the Model Law, together with the Conciliation Rules recommended by the General Assembly in its resolution 35/52 of 4 December 1980,contributes significantly to the establishment of a harmonized legal framework for the fair and efficient settlement of disputes arising in international commercial relations,

1.   *Expresses its appreciation* to the United Nations Commission on International Trade Law for completing and adopting the Model Law on International Commercial Conciliation, the text of which is contained in the annex to the present resolution, and for preparing the Guide to Enactment and Use of the Model Law;

2.   *Requests* the Secretary-General to make all efforts to ensure that the Model Law, together with its Guide to Enactment, becomes generally known and available;

3.   *Recommends* that all States give due consideration to the enactment of the Model Law, in view of the desirability of uniformity of the law of dispute settlement procedures and the specific needs of international commercial conciliation practice.

UNCITRAL Model Law on International Commercial Conciliation (2002)

Article 1.   Scope of application and definitions

1.   This Law applies to international[1] commercial[2] conciliation.

2.   For the purposes of this Law, "conciliator" means a sole conciliator or two or more conciliators, as the case may be.

3.   For the purposes of this Law, "conciliation" means a process, whether referred to by the expression conciliation, mediation or an

---

[1]   States wishing to enact this Model Law to apply to domestic as well as international conciliation may wish to consider the following changes to the text:

—Delete the word "international" in paragraph 1 of article 1; and

—Delete paragraphs 4, 5 and 6 of article 1.

[2]   The term "commercial" should be given a wide interpretation so as to cover matters arising from all relationships of a commercial nature, whether contractual or not. Relationships of a commercial nature include, but are not limited to, the following transactions: any trade transaction for the supply or exchange of goods or services; distribution agreement; commercial representation or agency; factoring; leasing; construction of works; consulting; engineering; licensing; investment; financing; banking; insurance; exploitation agreement or concession; joint venture and other forms of industrial or business cooperation; carriage of goods or passengers by air, sea, rail or road.

expression of similar import, whereby parties request a third person or persons ("the conciliator") to assist them in their attempt to reach an amicable settlement of their dispute arising out of or relating to a contractual or other legal relationship. The conciliator does not have the authority to impose upon the parties a solution to the dispute.

4.   A conciliation is international if:

(a) The parties to an agreement to conciliate have, at the time of the conclusion of that agreement, their places of business in different States; or

(b) The State in which the parties have their places of business is different from either:

(i)   The State in which a substantial part of the obligations of the commercial relationship is to be performed; or

(ii)   The State with which the subject matter of the dispute is most closely connected.

5.   For the purposes of this article:

(a) If a party has more than one place of business, the place of business is that which has the closest relationship to the agreement to conciliate;

(b) If a party does not have a place of business, reference is to be made to the party's habitual residence.

6.   This Law also applies to a commercial conciliation when the parties agree that the conciliation is international or agree to the applicability of this Law.

7.   The parties are free to agree to exclude the applicability of this Law.

8.   Subject to the provisions of paragraph 9 of this article, this Law applies irrespective of the basis upon which the conciliation is carried out, including agreement between the parties whether reached before or after a dispute has arisen, an obligation established by law, or a direction or suggestion of a court, arbitral tribunal or competent governmental entity.

9.   This Law does not apply to:

(a) Cases where a judge or an arbitrator, in the course of judicial or arbitral proceedings, attempts to facilitate a settlement; and

(b)   [. . .]

Article 2.   Interpretation

1.   In the interpretation of this Law, regard is to be had to its international origin and to the need to promote uniformity in its application and the observance of good faith.

2.   Questions concerning matters governed by this Law which are not expressly settled in it are to be settled in conformity with the general principles on which this Law is based.

Article 3.   Variation by agreement

Except for the provisions of article 2 and article 6, paragraph 3, the parties may agree to exclude or vary any of the provisions of this Law.

Article 4.   Commencement of conciliation proceedings[3]

1.   Conciliation proceedings in respect of a dispute that has arisen commence on the day on which the parties to that dispute agree to engage in conciliation proceedings.

2.   If a party that invited another party to conciliate does not receive an acceptance of the invitation within thirty days from the day on which the invitation was sent, or within such other period of time as specified in the invitation, the party may elect to treat this as a rejection of the invitation to conciliate.

Article 5.   Number and appointment of conciliators

1.   There shall be one conciliator, unless the parties agree that there shall be two or more conciliators.

2.   The parties shall endeavor to reach agreement on a conciliator or conciliators, unless a different procedure for their appointment has been agreed upon.

3.   Parties may seek the assistance of an institution or person in connection with the appointment of conciliators. In particular:

(a) A party may request such an institution or person to recommend suitable persons to act as conciliator; or

(b) The parties may agree that the appointment of one or more conciliators be made directly by such an institution or person.

4.   In recommending or appointing individuals to act as conciliator, the institution or person shall have regard to such considerations as are likely to secure the appointment of an independent and impartial conciliator and, where appropriate, shall take into account the advisability of appointing a conciliator of a nationality other than the nationalities of the parties.

---

[3]   The following text is suggested for States that might wish to adopt a provision on the suspension of the limitation period:

Article X. Suspension of limitation period:

1. When the conciliation proceedings commence, the running of the limitation period regarding the claim that is the subject matter of the conciliation is suspended.

2. Where the conciliation proceedings have terminated without a settlement agreement, the limitation period resumes running from the time the conciliation ended without a settlement agreement.

5.   When a person is approached in connection with his or her possible appointment as conciliator, he or she shall disclose any circumstances likely to give rise to justifiable doubts as to his or her impartiality or independence. A conciliator, from the time of his or her appointment and throughout the conciliation proceedings, shall without delay disclose any such circumstances to the parties unless they have already been informed of them by him or her.

Article 6.   Conduct of conciliation

1.   The parties are free to agree, by reference to a set of rules or otherwise, on the manner in which the conciliation is to be conducted.

2.   Failing agreement on the manner in which the conciliation is to be conducted, the conciliator may conduct the conciliation proceedings in such a manner as the conciliator considers appropriate, taking into account the circumstances of the case, any wishes that the parties may express and the need for a speedy settlement of the dispute.

3.   In any case, in conducting the proceedings, the conciliator shall seek to maintain fair treatment of the parties and, in so doing, shall take into account the circumstances of the case.

4.   The conciliator may, at any stage of the conciliation proceedings, make proposals for a settlement of the dispute.

Article 7.   Communication between conciliator and parties

The conciliator may meet or communicate with the parties together or with each of them separately.

Article 8.   Disclosure of information

When the conciliator receives information concerning the dispute from a party, the conciliator may disclose the substance of that information to any other party to the conciliation. However, when a party gives any information to the conciliator, subject to a specific condition that it be kept confidential, that information shall not be disclosed to any other party to the conciliation.

Article 9.   Confidentiality

Unless otherwise agreed by the parties, all information relating to the conciliation proceedings shall be kept confidential, except where disclosure is required under the law or for the purposes of implementation or enforcement of a settlement agreement.

Article 10.   Admissibility of evidence in other proceedings

1.   A party to the conciliation proceedings, the conciliator and any third person, including those involved in the administration of the conciliation proceedings, shall not in arbitral, judicial or similar

proceedings rely on, introduce as evidence or give testimony or evidence regarding any of the following:

(a) An invitation by a party to engage in conciliation proceedings or the fact that a party was willing to participate in conciliation proceedings;

(b) Views expressed or suggestions made by a party in the conciliation in respect of a possible settlement of the dispute;

(c) Statements or admissions made by a party in the course of the conciliation proceedings;

(d) Proposals made by the conciliator;

(e) The fact that a party had indicated its willingness to accept a proposal for settlement made by the conciliator;

(f) A document prepared solely for purposes of the conciliation proceedings.

2.   Paragraph 1 of this article applies irrespective of the form of the information or evidence referred to therein.

3.   The disclosure of the information referred to in paragraph 1 of this article shall not be ordered by an arbitral tribunal, court or other competent governmental authority and, if such information is offered as evidence in contravention of paragraph 1 of this article, that evidence shall be treated as inadmissible. Nevertheless, such information may be disclosed or admitted in evidence to the extent required under the law or for the purposes of implementation or enforcement of a settlement agreement.

4.   The provisions of paragraphs 1, 2 and 3 of this article apply whether or not the arbitral, judicial or similar proceedings relate to the dispute that is or was the subject matter of the conciliation proceedings.

5.   Subject to the limitations of paragraph 1 of this article, evidence that is otherwise admissible in arbitral or judicial or similar proceedings does not become inadmissible as a consequence of having been used in a conciliation.

Article 11. Termination of conciliation proceedings

The conciliation proceedings are terminated:

(a) By the conclusion of a settlement agreement by the parties, on the date of the agreement;

(b) By a declaration of the conciliator, after consultation with the parties, to the effect that further efforts at conciliation are no longer justified, on the date of the declaration;

(c) By a declaration of the parties addressed to the conciliator to the effect that the conciliation proceedings are terminated, on the date of the declaration; or

(d) By a declaration of a party to the other party or parties and the conciliator, if appointed, to the effect that the conciliation proceedings are terminated, on the date of the declaration.

Article 12.   Conciliator acting as arbitrator

Unless otherwise agreed by the parties, the conciliator shall not act as an arbitrator in respect of a dispute that was or is the subject of the conciliation proceedings or in respect of another dispute that has arisen from the same contract or legal relationship or any related contract or legal relationship.

Article 13.   Resort to arbitral or judicial proceedings

Where the parties have agreed to conciliate and have expressly undertaken not to initiate during a specified period of time or until a specified event has occurred arbitral or judicial proceedings with respect to an existing or future dispute, such an undertaking shall be given effect by the arbitral tribunal or the court until the terms of the undertaking have been complied with, except to the extent necessary for a party, in its opinion, to preserve its rights. Initiation of such proceedings is not of itself to be regarded as a waiver of the agreement to conciliate or as a termination of the conciliation proceedings.

Article 14.   Enforceability of settlement agreement[4]

If the parties conclude an agreement settling a dispute, that settlement agreement is binding and enforceable . . . [*the enacting State may insert a description of the method of enforcing settlement agreements or refer to provisions governing such enforcement*].

---

[4]   When implementing the procedure for enforcement of settlement agreements, an enacting State may consider the possibility of such a procedure being mandatory.

CHAPTER III

NATIONAL LEGISLATION ON ARBITRATION

■ ■ ■

A. UNITED STATES FEDERAL ARBITRATION ACT OF 1925*

(as last amended in 2002)

FEDERAL ARBITRATION ACT

United States Code

TITLE 9. ARBITRATION

CHAPTER 1.

GENERAL PROVISIONS

§ 1. "Maritime transactions" and "commerce" defined; exceptions to operation of title

"Maritime transactions", as herein defined, means charter parties, bills of lading of water carriers, agreements relating to wharfage, supplies furnished vessels or repairs to vessels, collisions, or any other matters in foreign commerce which, if the subject of controversy, would be embraced within admiralty jurisdiction; "commerce", as herein defined, means commerce among the several States or with foreign nations, or in any Territory of the United States or in the District of Columbia, or between any such Territory and another, or between any such Territory and any State or foreign nation, or between the District of Columbia and any State or Territory or foreign nation, but nothing herein contained shall apply to contracts of employment of seamen, railroad employees, or any other class of workers engaged in foreign or interstate commerce.

§ 2. Validity, irrevocability and enforcement of agreements to arbitrate

A written provision in any maritime transaction or a contract evidencing a transaction involving commerce to settle by arbitration a controversy thereafter arising out of such contract or transaction, or the refusal to perform the whole or any part thereof, or an agreement in writing

---

* Unofficial compilation available at: https://www.law.cornell.edu/. The Federal Arbitration Act is codified in Title 9 of the U.S. Code, chapters 1,2, and 3. The provisions can be found at https://www.law.cornell.edu/uscode/text/9/ chapter 1 [(chapter 2); (chapter 3)].

to submit to arbitration an existing controversy arising out of such a contract, transaction, or refusal, shall be valid, irrevocable, and enforceable, save upon such grounds as exist at law or in equity for the revocation of any contract.

§ 3. Stay of proceedings where issue therein referable to arbitration

If any suit or proceeding be brought in any of the courts of the United States upon any issue referable to arbitration under an agreement in writing for such arbitration, the court in which such suit is pending, upon being satisfied that the issue involved in such suit or proceeding is referable to arbitration under such an agreement, shall on application of one of the parties stay the trial of the action until such arbitration has been had in accordance with the terms of the agreement, providing the applicant for the stay is not in default in proceeding with such arbitration.

§ 4. Failure to arbitrate under agreement; petition to United States court having jurisdiction for order to compel arbitration; notice and service thereof; hearing and determination

A party aggrieved by the alleged failure, neglect, or refusal of another to arbitrate under a written agreement for arbitration may petition any United States district court which, save for such agreement, would have jurisdiction under Title 28 [28 U.S.C. §§ 1 et seq.], in a civil action or in admiralty of the subject matter of a suit arising out of the controversy between the parties, for an order directing that such arbitration proceed in the manner provided for in such agreement. Five days' notice in writing of such application shall be served upon the party in default. Service thereof shall be made in the manner provided by the Federal Rules of Civil Procedure. The court shall hear the parties, and upon being satisfied that the making of the agreement for arbitration or the failure to comply therewith is not in issue, the court shall make an order directing the parties to proceed to arbitration in accordance with the terms of the agreement. The hearing and proceedings, under such agreement, shall be within the district in which the petition for an order directing such arbitration is filed. If the making of the arbitration agreement or the failure, neglect, or refusal to perform the same be in issue, the court shall proceed summarily to the trial thereof. If no jury trial be demanded by the party alleged to be in default, or if the matter in dispute is within admiralty jurisdiction, the court shall hear and determine such issue. Where such an issue is raised, the party alleged to be in default may, except in cases of admiralty, on or before the return day of the notice of application, demand a jury trial of such issue, and upon such demand the court shall make an order referring the issue or issues to a jury in the manner provided by the Federal Rules of Civil Procedure, or may specially call a jury for that purpose. If the jury find that no agreement in writing for arbitration was made or that there is no default in proceeding thereunder, the proceeding shall be dismissed. If the jury find that an agreement for arbitration was made in writing and that there is a default in proceeding thereunder, the court shall make an order summarily directing the parties to proceed with the arbitration in accordance with the terms thereof.

§ 5. Appointment of arbitrators or umpire

If in the agreement provision be made for a method of naming or appointing an arbitrator or arbitrators or an umpire, such method shall be followed; but if no method be provided therein, or if a method be provided and any party thereto shall fail to avail himself of such method, or if for any other reason there shall be a lapse in the naming of an arbitrator or arbitrators or umpire, or in filling a vacancy, then upon the application of either party to the controversy the court shall designate and appoint an arbitrator or arbitrators or umpire, as the case may require, who shall act under the said agreement with the same force and effect as if he or they had been specifically named therein; and unless otherwise provided in the agreement the arbitration shall be by a single arbitrator.

§ 6. Application heard as motion

Any application to the court hereunder shall be made and heard in the manner provided by law for the making and hearing of motions, except as otherwise herein expressly provided.

§ 7. Witnesses before arbitrators; fees; compelling attendance

The arbitrators selected either as prescribed in this title [9 U.S.C. §§ 1 et seq.] or otherwise, or a majority of them, may summon in writing any person to attend before them or any of them as a witness and in a proper case to bring with him or them any book, record, document, or paper which may be deemed material as evidence in the case. The fees for such attendance shall be the same as the fees of witnesses before masters of the United States courts. Said summons shall issue in the name of the arbitrator or arbitrators, or a majority of them, and shall be signed by the arbitrators, or a majority of them, and shall be directed to the said person and shall be served in the same manner as subpoenas to appear and testify before the court; if any person or persons so summoned to testify shall refuse or neglect to obey said summons, upon petition the United States district court for the district in which such arbitrators, or a majority of them, are sitting may compel the attendance of such person or persons before said arbitrator or arbitrators, or punish said person or persons for contempt in the same manner provided by law for securing the attendance of witnesses or their punishment for neglect or refusal to attend in the courts of the United States.

§ 8. Proceedings begun by libel in admiralty and seizure of vessel or property

If the basis of jurisdiction be a cause of action otherwise justiciable in admiralty, then, notwithstanding anything herein to the contrary, the party claiming to be aggrieved may begin his proceeding hereunder by libel and seizure of the vessel or other property of the other party according to the usual course of admiralty proceedings, and the court shall then have jurisdiction to direct the parties to proceed with the arbitration and shall retain jurisdiction to enter its decree upon the award.

§ 9. Award of arbitrators; confirmation; jurisdiction; procedure

If the parties in their agreement have agreed that a judgment of the court shall be entered upon the award made pursuant to the arbitration, and shall specify the court, then at any time within one year after the award is made any party to the arbitration may apply to the court so specified for an order confirming the award, and thereupon the court must grant such an order unless the award is vacated, modified, or corrected as prescribed in sections 10 and 11 of this title [9 U.S.C. §§ 10, 11]. If no court is specified in the agreement of the parties, then such application may be made to the United States court in and for the district within which such award was made. Notice of the application shall be served upon the adverse party, and thereupon the court shall have jurisdiction of such party as though he had appeared generally in the proceeding. If the adverse party is a resident of the district within which the award was made, such service shall be made upon the adverse party or his attorney as prescribed by law for service of notice of motion in an action in the same court. If the adverse party shall be a nonresident, then the notice of the application shall be served by the marshal of any district within which the adverse party may be found in like manner as other process of the court.

§ 10. Same; vacation; grounds; rehearing

   (a) In any of the following cases the United States court in and for the district wherein the award was made may make an order vacating the award upon the application of any party to the arbitration—

      (1) Where the award was procured by corruption, fraud, or undue means.

      (2) Where there was evident partiality or corruption in the arbitrators, or either of them.

      (3) Where the arbitrators were guilty of misconduct in refusing to postpone the hearing, upon sufficient cause shown, or in refusing to hear evidence pertinent and material to the controversy; or of any other misbehavior by which the rights of any party have been prejudiced, or

(4) Where the arbitrators exceeded their powers, or so imperfectly executed them that a mutual, final, and definite award upon the subject matter submitted was not made.

(b) if an award is vacated and the time within which the agreement required the award to be made has not expired, the court may, in its discretion, direct a rehearing by the arbitrators.

(c) The United States district court for the district wherein an award was made that was issued pursuant to section 580 of title 5 may make an order vacating the award upon the application of a person, other than a party to the arbitration, who is adversely affected or aggrieved by the award, if the use of arbitration or the award is clearly inconsistent with the factors set forth in section 572 of title 5.

§ 11. Same; modification or correction; grounds; order

In either of the following cases the United States court in and for the district wherein the award was made may make an order modifying or correcting the award upon the application of any party to the arbitration—

(a) Where there was an evident material miscalculation of figures or an evident material mistake in the description of any person, thing, or property referred to in the award.

(b) Where the arbitrators have awarded upon a matter not submitted to them, unless it is a matter not affecting the merits of the decision upon the matter submitted.

(c) Where the award is imperfect in matter of form not affecting the merits of the controversy.

The order may modify and correct the award, so as to effect the intent thereof and promote justice between the parties.

§ 12. Notice of motions to vacate or modify; service; stay of proceedings

Notice of a motion to vacate, modify, or correct an award must be served upon the adverse party or his attorney within three months after the award is filed or delivered. If the adverse party is a resident of the district within which the award was made, such service shall be made upon the adverse party or his attorney as prescribed by law for service of notice of motion in an action in the same court. If the adverse party shall be a nonresident then the notice of the application shall be served by the marshal of any district within which the adverse party may be found in like manner as other process of the court. For the purposes of the motion any judge who might make an order to stay the proceedings in an action brought in the same court may make an order, to be served with the notice of motion, staying the proceedings of the adverse party to enforce the award.

§ 13. Papers filed with order on motions; judgment; docketing; force and effect; enforcement

The party moving for an order confirming, modifying, or correcting an award shall, at the time such order is filed with the clerk for the entry of judgment thereon, also file the following papers with the clerk:

(a) The agreement; the selection or appointment, if any, of an additional arbitrator or umpire; and each written extension of the time, if any, within which to make the award.

(b) The award.

(c) Each notice, affidavit, or other paper used upon an application to confirm, modify, or correct the award, and a copy of each order of the court upon such an application.

The judgment shall be docketed as if it was rendered in an action.

The judgment so entered shall have the same force and effect, in all respects, as, and be subject to all the provisions of law relating to, a judgment in an action; and it may be enforced as if it had been rendered in an action in the court in which it is entered.

§ 14. Contracts not affected

This title [9 U.S.C. §§ 1 et seq.] shall not apply to contracts made prior to January 1, 1926.

§ 15. Inapplicability of the Act of State doctrine

Enforcement of arbitral agreements, confirmation of arbitral awards, and execution upon judgments based on orders confirming such awards shall not be refused on the basis of the Act of State doctrine.

§ 16. Appeals

(a) An appeal may be taken from—

(1) an order—

refusing a stay of any action under section 3 of this title,

denying a petition under section 4 of this title to order arbitration to proceed,

denying an application under section 206 of this title to compel arbitration,

confirming or denying confirmation of an award or partial award, or

modifying, correcting, or vacating an award;

(2) an interlocutory order granting, continuing, or modifying an injunction against an arbitration that is subject to this title; or

(3) a final decision with respect to an arbitration that is subject to this title.

(b) Except as otherwise provided in section 1292(b) of title 28, an appeal may not be taken from an interlocutory order—

(1) granting a stay of any action under section 3 of this title;

(2) directing arbitration to proceed under section 4 of this title;

(3) compelling arbitration under section 206 of this title; or

(4) refusing to enjoin an arbitration that is subject to this title.

CHAPTER 2.

CONVENTION ON THE RECOGNITION AND ENFORCEMENT OF FOREIGN ARBITRAL AWARDS

§ 201.   Enforcement of Convention

The Convention on the Recognition and Enforcement of Foreign Arbitral Awards of June 10, 1958, shall be enforced in United States courts in accordance with this chapter [9 U.S.C. §§ 201 et seq.].

§ 202.   Agreement or award falling under the Convention

An arbitration agreement or arbitral award arising out of a legal relationship, whether contractual or not, which is considered as commercial, including a transaction, contract, or agreement described in section 2 of this title [9 U.S.C. § 2], falls under the Convention. An agreement or award arising out of such a relationship which is entirely between citizens of the United States shall be deemed not to fall under the Convention unless that relationship involves property located abroad, envisages performance or enforcement abroad, or has some other reasonable relation with one or more foreign states. For the purpose of this section a corporation is a citizen of the United States if it is incorporated or has its principal place of business in the United States.

§ 203.   Jurisdiction; amount in controversy

An action or proceeding falling under the Convention shall be deemed to arise under the laws and treaties of the United States. The district courts of the United States (including the courts enumerated in section 460 of title 28 [28 U.S.C. § 460]) shall have original jurisdiction over such an action or proceeding, regardless of the amount in controversy.

§ 204.   Venue

An action or proceeding over which the district courts have jurisdiction pursuant to section 203 of this title [9 U.S.C. § 203] may be brought in any such court in which save for the arbitration agreement an action or proceeding with respect to the controversy between the parties could be brought, or in such court for the district and division which embraces the place designated in the agreement as the place of arbitration if such place is within the United States.

§ 205.   Removal of cases from State courts

Where the subject matter of an action or proceeding pending in a State court relates to an arbitration agreement or award falling under the Convention, the defendant or the defendants may, at any time before the trial thereof, remove such action or proceeding to the district court of the United States for the district and division embracing the place where the action or proceeding is pending. The procedure for removal of causes otherwise provided by law shall apply, except that the ground for removal provided in this section need not appear on the face of the complaint but may be shown in the petition for removal. For the purposes of Chapter 1 of this title [9 U.S.C. §§ 1 et seq.] any action or proceeding removed under this section shall be deemed to have been brought in the district court to which it is removed.

§ 206.   Order to compel arbitration; appointment of arbitrators

A court having jurisdiction under this chapter [9 U.S.C. §§ 201 et seq.] may direct that arbitration be held in accordance with the agreement at any place therein provided for, whether that place is within or without the United States. Such court may also appoint arbitrators in accordance with the provisions of the agreement.

§ 207.   Award of arbitrators; confirmation; jurisdiction; proceeding

Within three years after an arbitral award falling under the Convention is made, any party to the arbitration may apply to any court having jurisdiction under this chapter [9 U.S.C. §§ 201 et seq.] for an order confirming the award as against any other party to the arbitration. The court shall confirm the award unless it finds one of the grounds for refusal or deferral of recognition or enforcement of the award specified in the said Convention.

§ 208.   Chapter 1 [9 U.S.C. §§ 1 et seq.]; residual application

Chapter 1 [9 U.S.C. §§ 1 et seq.] applies to actions and proceedings brought under this chapter [9 U.S.C. §§ 201 et seq.] to the extent that chapter is not in conflict with this chapter [9 U.S.C. §§ 201 et seq.] or the Convention as ratified by the United States.

CHAPTER 3.

INTER-AMERICAN CONVENTION ON INTERNATIONAL COMMERCIAL ARBITRATION

§ 301.   Enforcement of Convention

The Inter-American Convention on International Commercial Arbitration of January 30, 1975, shall be enforced in United States courts in accordance with this chapter [9 U.S.C. §§ 301 et seq.].

§ 302.   Incorporation by reference

Sections 202, 203, 204, 205, and 207 of this title shall apply to this chapter [9 U.S.C. §§ 301 et seq.] as if specifically set forth herein, except that for the purposes of this chapter [9 U.S.C. §§ 301 et seq.] "the Convention" shall mean the Inter-American Convention.

§ 303.   Order to compel arbitration; appointment of arbitrators; locale

(a)   A court having jurisdiction under this chapter [9 U.S.C. §§ 301 et seq.] may direct that arbitration be held in accordance with the agreement at any place therein provided for, whether that place is within or without the United States. The court may also appoint arbitrators in accordance with the provisions of the agreement.

(b)   In the event the agreement does not make provision for the place of arbitration or the appointment of arbitrators, the court shall direct that the arbitration shall be held and the arbitrators be appointed in accordance with Article 3 of the Inter-American Convention.

§ 304.   Recognition and enforcement of foreign arbitral decisions and awards; reciprocity

Arbitral decisions or awards made in the territory of a foreign State shall, on the basis of reciprocity, be recognized and enforced under this chapter [9 U.S.C. §§ 301 et seq.] only if that State has ratified or acceded to the Inter-American Convention.

§ 305.   Relationship between the Inter-American Convention and the Convention on the Recognition and Enforcement of Foreign Arbitral Awards of June 10, 1958

When the requirements for application of both the Inter-American Convention and the Convention on the Recognition and Enforcement of Foreign Arbitral Awards of June 10, 1958, are met, determination as to which Convention applies shall, unless otherwise expressly agreed, be made as follows:

(1)   If a majority of the parties to the arbitration agreement are citizens of a State or States that have ratified or acceded to the Inter-American Convention and are member States of the Organization of American States, the Inter-American Convention shall apply.

(2) In all other cases the Convention on the Recognition and Enforcement of Foreign Arbitral Awards of June 10, 1958, shall apply.

§ 306. Applicable rules of Inter-American Commercial Arbitration Commission

(a) For the purposes of this chapter [9 U.S.C. §§ 301 et seq.] the rules of procedure of the Inter-American Commercial Arbitration Commission referred to in Article 3 of the Inter-American Convention shall, subject to subsection (b) of this section, be those rules as promulgated by the Commission on July 1, 1988.

(b) In the event the rules of procedure of the Inter-American Commercial Arbitration Commission are modified or amended in accordance with the procedures for amendment of the rules of that Commission, the Secretary of State, by regulation in accordance with section 553 of title 5, consistent with the aims and purposes of this Convention, may prescribe that such modifications or amendments shall be effective for purposes of this chapter [9 U.S.C. §§ 301 et seq.].

§ 307. Chapter 1; residual application

Chapter 1 [9 U.S.C. §§ 1 et seq.] applies to actions and proceedings brought under this chapter [9 U.S.C. §§ 301 et seq.] to the extent chapter 1 [9 U.S.C. §§ 1 et seq.] is not in conflict with this chapter [9 U.S.C. §§ 301 et seq.] or the Inter-American Convention as ratified by the United States.

B. FRENCH CODE OF CIVIL PROCEDURE, BOOK FOUR (ARBITRATION LEGISLATION OF 1981)*

(as amended in 2011)
BOOK IV—ARBITRATION
Title I—Domestic Arbitration**
CHAPTER I—THE ARBITRATION AGREEMENT
Article 1442

An arbitration agreement may be in the form of an arbitration clause or a submission agreement.

---

*   English translation is prepared by Emmanuel Gaillard, Nanou Leleu-Knobil and Daniela Pellarini of Shearman & Sterling LLP. and text is available on http://www.iaiparis.com/.

**   Articles or paragraphs preceded by three asterisks (* * *) also apply to international arbitration and all text shown in bold indicates mandatory provisions.

An arbitration clause is an agreement by which the parties to one or more contracts undertake to submit to arbitration disputes which may arise in relation to such contract(s).

A submission agreement is an agreement by which the parties to a dispute submit such dispute to arbitration.

Article 1443

In order to be valid, an arbitration agreement shall be in writing. It can result from an exchange of written communications or be contained in a document to which reference is made in the main agreement.

Article 1444

An arbitration agreement shall designate, including by reference to arbitration rules, the arbitrator or arbitrators, or provide for a procedure for their appointment. Alternatively, Articles 1451 through 1454 shall apply.

Article 1445

In order to be valid, a submission agreement shall define the subject matter of the dispute.

* * * Article 1446

Parties may submit their dispute to arbitration even where proceedings are already pending before a court.

* * * Article 1447

An arbitration agreement is independent of the contract to which it relates. It shall not be affected if such contract is void.

If an arbitration clause is void, it shall be deemed not written.

Article 1448

* * * When a dispute subject to an arbitration agreement is brought before a court, such court shall decline jurisdiction, except if an arbitral tribunal has not yet been seized of the dispute and if the arbitration agreement is manifestly void or manifestly not applicable.

* * * A court may not decline jurisdiction on its own motion.

Any stipulation contrary to the present article shall be deemed not written.

* * * Article 1449

The existence of an arbitration agreement, insofar as the arbitral tribunal has not yet been constituted, shall not preclude a party from applying to a court for measures relating to the taking of evidence or provisional or conservatory measures.

Subject to the provisions governing conservatory attachments and judicial security, application shall be made to the President of the Tribunal de grande instance or of the Tribunal de commerce who shall rule on the measures relating to the taking of evidence in accordance with the provisions of Article 1452 and, where the matter is urgent, on the provisional or conservatory measures requested by the parties to the arbitration agreement. * * *

CHAPTER II—THE ARBITRAL TRIBUNAL

Article 1450

Only a natural person having full capacity to exercise his or her rights may act as an arbitrator.

Where an arbitration agreement designates a legal person, such person shall only have the power to administer the arbitration.

Article 1451

An arbitral tribunal shall be composed of a sole arbitrator or an uneven number of arbitrators.

If an arbitration agreement provides for an even number of arbitrators, an additional arbitrator shall be appointed.

If the parties cannot agree on the appointment of the additional arbitrator, he or she shall be appointed by the other arbitrators within one month of having accepted their mandate or, if they fail to do so, by the judge acting in support of the arbitration (*juge d'appui*) referred to in Article 1459.

* * * Article 1452

If the parties have not agreed on the procedure for appointing the arbitrator(s):

(1)   Where there is to be a sole arbitrator and if the parties fail to agree on the arbitrator, he or she shall be appointed by the person responsible for administering the arbitration or, where there is no such person, by the judge acting in support of the arbitration;

(2)   Where there are to be three arbitrators, each party shall appoint an arbitrator and the two arbitrators so appointed shall appoint a third arbitrator. If a party fails to appoint an arbitrator within one month following receipt of a request to that effect by the other party, or if the two arbitrators fail to agree on the third arbitrator within one month of having accepted their mandate, the person responsible for administering the arbitration or, where there is no such person, the judge acting in support of the arbitration, shall appoint the third arbitrator.

* * * Article 1453

If there are more than two parties to the dispute and they fail to agree on the procedure for constituting the arbitral tribunal, the person responsible for administering the arbitration or, where there is no such person, the judge acting in support of the arbitration, shall appoint the arbitrator(s).

* * * Article 1454

Any other dispute relating to the constitution of an arbitral tribunal shall be resolved, if the parties cannot agree, by the person responsible for administering the arbitration or, where there is no such person, by the judge acting in support of the arbitration.

* * * Article 1455

If an arbitration agreement is manifestly void or manifestly not applicable, the judge acting in support of the arbitration shall declare that no appointment need be made.

* * * Article 1456

The constitution of an arbitral tribunal shall be complete upon the arbitrators' acceptance of their mandate. As of that date, the tribunal is seized of the dispute.

Before accepting a mandate, an arbitrator shall disclose any circumstance that may affect his or her independence or impartiality. He or she also shall disclose promptly any such circumstance that may arise after accepting the mandate.

If the parties cannot agree on the removal of an arbitrator, the issue shall be resolved by the person responsible for administering the arbitration or, where there is no such person, by the judge acting in support of the arbitration to whom application must be made within one month following the disclosure or the discovery of the fact at issue.

* * * Article 1457

Arbitrators shall carry out their mandate until it is completed, unless they are legally incapacitated or there is a legitimate reason for them to refuse to act or to resign.

If there is disagreement as to the materiality of the reason invoked, the matter shall be resolved by the person responsible for administering the arbitration or, where there is no such person, by the judge acting in support of the arbitration to whom application must be made within one month following such incapacity, refusal to act or resignation.

* * *Article 1458

An arbitrator may only be removed with the unanimous consent of the parties. Where there is no unanimous consent, the provisions of the final paragraph of Article 1456 shall apply.

Article 1459

The judge acting in support of the arbitration shall be the President of a Tribunal de grande instance.

However, the President of a Tribunal de commerce shall have jurisdiction to rule on applications made on the basis of Articles 1451 through 1454 if there is an express provision to that effect in the arbitration agreement. In that case, he or she may apply Article 1455.

The arbitration agreement shall determine which court has territorial jurisdiction, failing which, jurisdiction shall lie with the court of the place where the seat of the arbitral tribunal has been set. Where the arbitration agreement is silent, territorial jurisdiction shall lie with the court of the place where the party or one of the parties resisting the application resides or, if that party does not reside in France, with the court of the place where the applicant resides.

* * *Article 1460

Application to the judge acting in support of the arbitration shall be made either by a party or by the arbitral tribunal or one of its members.

Such application shall be made, heard and decided as for expedited proceedings (_référé_).

The judge acting in support of the arbitration shall rule by way of an order against which no recourse can be had. However, such order may be appealed where the judge holds that no appointment need be made for one of the reasons stated in Article 1455.

Article 1461

Subject to the provisions of Article 1456, paragraph 1, any stipulation contrary to the rules set forth in the present chapter shall be deemed not written.

CHAPTER III—THE ARBITRAL PROCEEDINGS

* * * Article 1462

A dispute shall be submitted to the arbitral tribunal either jointly by the parties or by the most diligent party.

Article 1463

If an arbitration agreement does not specify a time limit, the duration of the arbitral tribunal's mandate shall be limited to six months as of the date on which the tribunal is seized of the dispute.

* * * The statutory or contractual time limit may be extended by agreement between the parties or, where there is no such agreement, by the judge acting in support of the arbitration.

Article 1464

Unless otherwise agreed by the parties, the arbitral tribunal shall define the procedure to be followed in the arbitration. It is under no obligation to abide by the rules governing court proceedings.

However, the fundamental principles governing court proceedings set forth in Articles 4, 10, Article 11, paragraph 1, Article 12, paragraphs 2 and 3, Articles 13 through 21, 23 and 23–1 shall apply.

* * * Both parties and arbitrators shall act diligently and in good faith in the conduct of the proceedings.

Subject to legal requirements, and unless otherwise agreed by the parties, arbitral proceedings shall be confidential.

* * * Article 1465

The arbitral tribunal has exclusive jurisdiction to rule on objections to its jurisdiction.

* * * Article 1466

A party which, knowingly and without a legitimate reason, fails to object to an irregularity before the arbitral tribunal in a timely manner shall be deemed to have waived its right to avail itself of such irregularity.

* * * Article 1467

The arbitral tribunal shall take all necessary steps concerning evidentiary and procedural matters, unless the parties authorise it to delegate such tasks to one of its members.

The arbitral tribunal may call upon any person to provide testimony. Witnesses shall not be sworn in.

If a party is in possession of an item of evidence, the arbitral tribunal may enjoin that party to produce it, determine the manner in which it is to be produced and, if necessary, attach penalties to such injunction.

* * * Article 1468

The arbitral tribunal may order upon the parties any conservatory or provisional measures that it deems appropriate, set conditions for such measures and, if necessary, attach penalties to such order. However, only courts may order conservatory attachments and judicial security.

The arbitral tribunal has the power to amend or add to any provisional or conservatory measure that it has granted.

* * * Article 1469

If one of the parties to arbitral proceedings intends to rely on an official (*acte authentique*) or private (*acte sous seing privé*) deed to which it was not a party, or on evidence held by a third party, it may, upon leave of the arbitral tribunal, have that third party summoned before the President of the Tribunal de grande instance for the purpose of obtaining a copy thereof (*expédition*) or the production of the deed or item of evidence.

Articles 42 through 48 shall determine which Tribunal de grande instance has territorial jurisdiction in this regard.

Application shall be made, heard and decided as for expedited proceedings (*référé*).

If the president considers the application well-founded, he or she shall order that the relevant original, copy or extract of the deed or item of evidence be issued or produced, under such conditions and guarantees as he or she determines, and, if necessary, attach penalties to such order.

Such order is not readily enforceable.

It may be appealed within fourteen days following service (*signification*) of the order.

* * * Article 1470

Unless otherwise stipulated, the arbitral tribunal shall have the power to rule on a request for verification of handwriting or claim of forgery in accordance with Articles 287 through 294 and Article 299.

Where an incidental claim of forgery of official documents is raised, Article 313 shall apply.

Article 1471

Abatement of proceedings shall be governed by Articles 369 through 372.

* * * Article 1472

Where necessary, the arbitral tribunal may stay the proceedings. The proceedings shall be stayed for the period of time set forth in the stay order or until such time as the event prescribed in the order has occurred.

The arbitral tribunal may, as the circumstances require, lift or shorten the stay.

Article 1473

Unless otherwise stipulated, arbitral proceedings shall also be stayed in the event of the death, legal incapacity, refusal to act, resignation, challenge or removal of an arbitrator, and until such time as a substitute arbitrator has accepted his or her mandate.

The substitute arbitrator shall be appointed in accordance with the procedure agreed upon by the parties or, failing that, in accordance with the procedure followed for the appointment of the original arbitrator.

Article 1474

An abatement or stay of the proceedings shall not put an end to the arbitral tribunal's mandate.

The arbitral tribunal may ask the parties to report any steps taken towards resuming the proceedings or putting an end to the situation having caused the abatement or stay. If the parties fail to take action, the tribunal may terminate the proceedings.

Article 1475

The arbitral proceedings shall resume at the stage reached before the abatement or stay, once the underlying causes for such abatement or stay cease to exist.

When the proceedings resume, and by way of an exception to Article 1463, the arbitral tribunal may extend the duration of the proceedings for a period not exceeding six months.

Article 1476

The arbitral tribunal shall set the date on which the award is to be rendered.

During the course of the deliberations, no claim may be made, no argument raised, nor evidence produced, except at the request of the arbitral tribunal.

Article 1477

Arbitral proceedings shall come to an end upon expiration of the time limit set for the arbitration.

CHAPTER IV—THE ARBITRAL AWARD

Article 1478

The arbitral tribunal shall decide the dispute in accordance with the law, unless the parties have empowered it to rule as amiable compositeur.

* * * Article 1479

The arbitral tribunal's deliberations shall be confidential.

Article 1480

The arbitral award shall be made by majority decision.

It shall be signed by all the arbitrators.

If a minority among them refuses to sign, the award shall so state and shall have the same effect as if it had been signed by all the arbitrators.

* * * Article 1481

The arbitral award shall state:

(1) the full names of the parties, as well as their domicile or corporate headquarters;

(2) if applicable, the names of the counsel or other persons who represented or assisted the parties;

(3) the names of the arbitrators who made it;

(4) the date on which it was made;

(5) the place where the award was made.

* * * Article 1482

The arbitral award shall succinctly set forth the respective claims and arguments of the parties.

The award shall state the reasons upon which it is based.

Article 1483

An arbitral award which fails to comply with the provisions of Article 1480, the provisions of Article 1481 regarding the names of the arbitrators and the date of the award, and those contained in Article 1482 regarding the reasons for the award, shall be void.

However, no omission or inaccuracy in the particulars required for the award to be valid shall render the award void if it can be established, through the case record or any other means, that it does, in fact, comply with the relevant legal requirements.

Article 1484

* * * As soon as it is made, an arbitral award shall be res judicata with regard to the claims adjudicated in that award.

* * * The award may be declared provisionally enforceable.

The award shall be notified by service (signification) unless the parties agree otherwise.

Article 1485

* * * Once an award is made, the arbitral tribunal shall no longer be vested with the power to rule on the claims adjudicated in that award.

* * * However, on application of a party, the arbitral tribunal may interpret the award, rectify clerical errors and omissions, or make an additional award where it failed to rule on a claim. The arbitral tribunal shall rule after having heard the parties or having given them the opportunity to be heard.

If the arbitral tribunal cannot be reconvened and if the parties cannot agree on the constitution of a new tribunal, this power shall vest in the court which would have had jurisdiction had there been no arbitration.

* * * Article 1486

Applications under Article 1485, paragraph 2, shall be filed within three months of notification of the award.

Unless otherwise agreed, the decision amending the award or the additional award shall be made within three months of application to the arbitral tribunal. This time limit may be extended in accordance with Article 1463, paragraph 2.

The decision amending the award or the additional award shall be notified in the same manner as the initial award.

CHAPTER V—EXEQUATUR

Article 1487

An arbitral award may only be enforced by virtue of an enforcement order (exequatur) issued by the Tribunal de grande instance of the place where the award was made.

Exequatur proceedings shall not be adversarial.

Application for exequatur shall be filed by the most diligent party with the Court Registrar, together with the original award and arbitration agreement, or duly authenticated copies of such documents.

The enforcement order shall be affixed to the original or, if the original is not produced, to a duly authenticated copy of the arbitral award, as per the previous paragraph.

Article 1488

No enforcement order may be granted where an award is manifestly contrary to public policy.

An order denying enforcement shall state the reasons upon which it is based.

CHAPTER VI—RECOURSE
SECTION 1—APPEAL
Article 1489

An arbitral award shall not be subject to appeal, unless otherwise agreed by the parties.

Article 1490

An appeal may seek to obtain either the reversal or the setting aside of an award.

The court shall rule in accordance with the law or as amiable compositeur, within the limits of the arbitral tribunal's mandate.

SECTION 2—ACTIONS TO SET ASIDE
Article 1491

An action to set aside an award may be brought except where the parties have agreed that the award may be appealed.

Any provision to the contrary shall be deemed not written.

Article 1492

An award may only be set aside where:

(1)   the arbitral tribunal wrongly upheld or declined jurisdiction; or

(2)   the arbitral tribunal was not properly constituted; or

(3)   the arbitral tribunal ruled without complying with the mandate conferred upon it; or

(4)   due process was violated; or

(5)   the award is contrary to public policy; or

(6)   the award failed to state the reasons upon which it is based, the date on which it was made, the names or signatures of the arbitrator(s) having made the award; or where the award was not made by majority decision.

Article 1493

When a court sets aside an arbitral award, it shall rule on the merits within the limits of the arbitrator's mandate, unless otherwise agreed by the parties.

SECTION 3—APPEALS AND ACTIONS
TO SET ASIDE-COMMON PROVISIONS
Article 1494

Appeals and actions to set aside shall be brought before the Court of Appeal of the place where the award was made.

Such recourse can be had as soon as the award is rendered. If no application is made within one month following notification of the award, recourse shall no longer be admissible.

Article 1495

Appeals and actions to set aside shall be brought, heard and decided in accordance with the rules applicable to adversarial proceedings set forth in Articles 900 through 930–1.

Article 1496

Unless an arbitral award is provisionally enforceable, enforcement shall be stayed until expiration of the time limit set for appeals or actions to set aside, or upon the filing of an appeal or action to set aside during this period.

Article 1497

The first president ruling in expedited proceedings (*référé*) or, once the matter is referred to him or her, the judge assigned to the case (*conseiller de la mise en état*) may:

(1)   if the award is provisionally enforceable and where enforcement may lead to manifestly excessive consequences, stay or set conditions for enforcement of the award; or

(2)   if the award is not provisionally enforceable, order that the award or any part thereof be provisionally enforceable.

Article 1498

If an award is provisionally enforceable or if it has been made provisionally enforceable as per Article 1497(2), the first president or, once the matter is referred to him or her, the judge assigned to the case may grant enforcement (exequatur) of the arbitral award.

A decision denying an appeal or an application to set aside an award shall be deemed an enforcement order of the arbitral award or the parts thereof that were not overturned by the court.

SECTION 4—RECOURSE AGAINST ORDERS GRANTING OR DENYING ENFORCEMENT

Article 1499

No recourse may be had against an order granting enforcement of an award.

However, an appeal or an action to set aside an award shall be deemed to constitute recourse against the order of the judge having ruled on enforcement or shall bring an end to said judge's jurisdiction, as regards the parts of the award which are challenged.

Article 1500

An order denying enforcement may be appealed within one month following service (signification) thereof.

If it is appealed, and if one of the parties so requests, the Court of Appeal shall rule on an appeal or application to set aside the award, provided that the time limit for such appeal or application has not expired.

SECTION 5—OTHER MEANS OF RECOURSE

Article 1501

Third parties may challenge an arbitral award by petitioning the court which would have had jurisdiction had there been no arbitration, subject to the provisions of Article 588, paragraph 1.

Article 1502

* * * Application for revision of an arbitral award may be made in the circumstances provided in Article 595 for court judgments,3 and under the conditions set forth in Articles 594, 596, 597 and 601 through 603.

* * * Application shall be made to the arbitral tribunal.

However, if the arbitral tribunal cannot be reconvened, application shall be made to the Court of Appeal which would have had jurisdiction to hear other forms of recourse against the award.

* * * Article 1503

No opposition may be filed against an arbitral award, nor may the Cour de Cassation be petitioned to quash the award.

Title II—International Arbitration

Article 1504

An arbitration is international when international trade interests are at stake.

Article 1505

In international arbitration, and unless otherwise stipulated, the judge acting in support of the arbitration shall be the President of the Tribunal de grande instance of Paris when:

  (1) the arbitration takes place in France; or

  (2) the parties have agreed that French procedural law shall apply to the arbitration; or

  (3) the parties have expressly granted jurisdiction to French courts over disputes relating to the arbitral procedure; or

  (4) one of the parties is exposed to a risk of a denial of justice

Article 1506

Unless the parties have agreed otherwise, and subject to the provisions of the present Title, the following Articles shall apply to international arbitration:

(1) 1446, 1447, 1448 (paragraphs 1 and 2) and 1449, regarding the arbitration agreement;

(2) 1452 through 1458 and 1460 regarding the constitution of the arbitral tribunal and the procedure governing application to the judge acting in support of the arbitration;

(3) 1462, 1463 (paragraph 2), 1464 (paragraph 3), 1465 through 1470 and 1472 regarding arbitral proceedings;

(4) 1479, 1481, 1482, 1484 (paragraphs 1 and 2), 1485 (paragraphs 1 and 2) and 1486 regarding arbitral awards;

(5) 1502 (paragraphs 1 and 2) and 1503 regarding means of recourse other than appeals or actions to set aside.

CHAPTER I—INTERNATIONAL ARBITRATION AGREEMENTS

Article 1507

An arbitration agreement shall not be subject to any requirements as to its form.

Article 1508

An arbitration agreement may designate the arbitrator(s) or provide for the procedure for their appointment, directly or by reference to arbitration rules or to procedural rules.

CHAPTER II—ARBITRAL PROCEEDINGS AND AWARDS

Article 1509

An arbitration agreement may define the procedure to be followed in the arbitral proceedings, directly or by reference to arbitration rules or to procedural rules.

Unless the arbitration agreement provides otherwise, the arbitral tribunal shall define the procedure as required, either directly or by reference to arbitration rules or to procedural rules.

Article 1510

Irrespective of the procedure adopted, the arbitral tribunal shall ensure that the parties are treated equally and shall uphold the principle of due process.

Article 1511

The arbitral tribunal shall decide the dispute in accordance with the rules of law chosen by the parties or, where no such choice has been made, in accordance with the rules of law it considers appropriate.

In either case, the arbitral tribunal shall take trade usages into account.

Article 1512

The arbitral tribunal shall rule as amiable compositeur if the parties have empowered it to do so.

Article 1513

Unless the arbitration agreement provides otherwise, the award shall be made by majority decision. It shall be signed by all the arbitrators.

However, if a minority among them refuses to sign, the others shall so state in the award.

If there is no majority, the chairman of the arbitral tribunal shall rule alone. Should the other arbitrators refuse to sign, the chairman shall so state in the award, which only he or she shall sign.

An award made under the circumstances described in either of the two preceding paragraphs shall have the same effect as if it had been signed by all the arbitrators or made by majority decision.

CHAPTER III—RECOGNITION AND ENFORCEMENT OF ARBITRAL AWARDS MADE ABROAD OR IN INTERNATIONAL ARBITRATION

Article 1514

An arbitral award shall be recognised or enforced in France if the party relying on it can prove its existence and if such recognition or enforcement is not manifestly contrary to international public policy.

Article 1515

The existence of an arbitral award shall be proven by producing the original award, together with the arbitration agreement, or duly authenticated copies of such documents.

If such documents are in a language other than French, the party applying for recognition or enforcement shall produce a translation. The applicant may be requested to provide a translation by a translator whose name appears on a list of court experts or a translator accredited by the administrative or judicial authorities of another Member State of the European Union, a Contracting Party to the European Economic Area Agreement or the Swiss Confederation.

Article 1516

An arbitral award may only be enforced by virtue of an enforcement order (*exequatur*) issued by the Tribunal de grande instance of the place where the award was made or by the Tribunal de grande instance of Paris if the award was made abroad.

Exequatur proceedings shall not be adversarial.

Application for exequatur shall be filed by the most diligent party with the Court Registrar, together with the original award and arbitration agreement, or duly authenticated copies of such documents.

Article 1517

The enforcement order shall be affixed to the original or, if the original is not produced, to a duly authenticated copy of the arbitral award, as per the final paragraph of Article 1516.

Where an arbitral award is in a language other than French, the enforcement order shall also be affixed to the translation produced as per Article 1515.

An order denying enforcement of an arbitral award shall state the reasons upon which it is based.

CHAPTER IV—RECOURSE

SECTION 1—AWARDS MADE IN FRANCE

Article 1518

The only means of recourse against an award made in France in an international arbitration is an action to set aside.

Article 1519

An action to set aside shall be brought before the Court of Appeal of the place where the award was made.

Such recourse can be had as soon as the award is rendered. If no application is made within one month following notification of the award, recourse shall no longer be admissible.

The award shall be notified by service (*signification*), unless otherwise agreed by the parties.

Article 1520

An award may **only** be set aside **where**:

(1) the arbitral tribunal wrongly upheld or declined jurisdiction; or

(2) the arbitral tribunal was not properly constituted; or

(3) the arbitral tribunal ruled without complying with the mandate conferred upon it; or

(4) due process was violated; or

(5) recognition or enforcement of the award is contrary to international public policy.

Article 1521

The first president or, once the matter is referred to him or her, the judge assigned to the case (conseiller de la mise en état) may grant enforcement (exequatur) of the award.

Article 1522

By way of a specific agreement the parties may, at any time, expressly waive their right to bring an action to set aside.

Where such right has been waived, the parties nonetheless retain their right to appeal an enforcement order on one of the grounds set forth in Article 1520.

Such appeal shall be brought within one month following notification of the award bearing the enforcement order. The award bearing the enforcement order shall be notified by service (signification), unless otherwise agreed by the parties.

Article 1523

An order denying recognition or enforcement of an international arbitral award made in France may be appealed.

The appeal shall be brought within one month following service (signification) of the order.

If the order is appealed, and if one of the parties so requests, the Court of Appeal shall rule on an action to set aside unless the parties have waived the right to bring such action **or the time limit to bring such action has expired.**

Article 1524

No recourse may be had against an order granting enforcement of an award, except as provided in Article 1522, paragraph 2.

However, an action to set aside an award shall be deemed to constitute recourse against the order of the judge having ruled on enforcement or shall bring an end to said judge's jurisdiction, as regards the parts of the award which are challenged.

SECTION 2—AWARDS MADE ABROAD
Article 1525

An order granting or denying recognition or enforcement of an arbitral award made abroad may be appealed.

The appeal shall be brought within one month following service (signification) of the order.

However, the parties may agree on other means of notification when an appeal is brought against an award bearing an enforcement order.

The Court of Appeal may only deny recognition or enforcement of an arbitral award on the grounds listed in Article 1520.

SECTION 3—AWARDS MADE IN FRANCE AND ABROAD-COMMON PROVISIONS
Article 1526

Neither an action to set aside an award nor an appeal against an enforcement order shall suspend enforcement of an award.

However, the first president ruling in expedited proceedings (*référé*) or, once the matter is referred to him or her, the judge assigned to the matter (*conseiller de la mise en état*), may stay or set conditions for enforcement of an award where enforcement could severely prejudice the rights of one of the parties.

Article 1527

Appeals against orders granting or denying enforcement and actions to set aside awards shall be brought, heard and decided in accordance with the rules applicable to adversarial proceedings set forth in Articles 900 through 930–1.

A decision denying an appeal or application to set aside an award shall be deemed an enforcement order of the arbitral award or of the parts of the award that were not overturned by the court.

C. SWISS FEDERAL STATUTE ON PRIVATE INTERNATIONAL LAW, CHAPTER 12, INTERNATIONAL ARBITRATION*

Chapter 12: International Arbitration

Article 176

I.   Field of application; seat of the arbitral tribunal

1   The provisions of this chapter shall apply to all arbitrations if the seat of the arbitral tribunal is in Switzerland and if, at the time of the conclusion of the arbitration agreement, at least one of the parties had neither its domicile nor its habitual residence in Switzerland.

2   The parties may exclude the application of this chapter by an explicit declaration in the arbitration agreement or by an agreement at a later date and agree on the application of the third part of the CPC.

3   The seat of the arbitral tribunal shall be determined by the parties, or the arbitral institution designated by them, or, failing both, by the arbitrators.

Article 177

II.   Arbitrability

1   Any dispute of financial interest may be the subject of an arbitration.

2   A state, or an enterprise held by, or an organization controlled by a state, which is party to an arbitration agreement, cannot invoke its own law in order to contest its capacity to arbitrate or the arbitrability of a dispute covered by the arbitration agreement.

Article 178

III. Arbitration agreement

1   The arbitration agreement must be made in writing, by telegram, telex, telecopier or any other means of communication which permits it to be evidenced by a text.

2   Furthermore, an arbitration agreement is valid if it conforms either to the law chosen by the parties, or to the law governing the subject-matter of the dispute, in particular the main contract, or to Swiss law.

3   The arbitration agreement cannot be contested on the grounds that the main contract is not valid or that the arbitration agreement concerns a dispute which had not as yet arisen.

---

*   The Chapter 12 on International Arbitration of the Swiss Federal Statute on Private International Law can be found on https://www.swissarbitration.org/sa/download/IPRG_english.pdf.

Article 179

IV. Arbitrators

1. Constitution of the arbitral tribunal

1 The arbitrators shall be appointed, removed or replaced in accordance with the agreement of the parties.

2 In the absence of such agreement, the judge where the arbitral tribunal has its seat may be seized with the question; he shall apply, by analogy, the provisions of the CPC on appointment, removal or replacement of arbitrators.

3 If a judge has been designated as the authority for appointing an arbitrator, he shall make the appointment unless a summary examination shows that no arbitration agreement exists between the parties.

Article 180

2. Challenge of an arbitrator

1 An arbitrator may be challenged:

a) if he does not meet the qualifications agreed upon by the parties;

b) if a ground for challenge exists under the rules of arbitration agreed upon by the parties; c) if circumstances exist that give rise to justifiable doubts as to his independence.

2 No party may challenge an arbitrator nominated by it, or whom it was instrumental in appointing, except on a ground which came to that party's attention after such appointment. The ground for challenge must be notified to the arbitral tribunal and the other party without delay.

3 To the extent that the parties have not made provisions for this challenge procedure, the judge at the seat of the arbitral tribunal shall make the final decision.

Article 181

V. Lis Pendens

1 The arbitral proceedings shall be pending from the time when one of the parties seizes with a claim either the arbitrator or arbitrators designated in the arbitration agreement or, in the absence of such designation in the arbitration agreement, from the time when one of the parties initiates the procedure for the appointment of the arbitral tribunal.

Article 182

VI. Procedure

1. Principle

1   The parties may, directly or by reference to rules of arbitration, determine the arbitral procedure; they may also submit the arbitral procedure to a procedural law of their choice.

2   If the parties have not determined the procedure, the arbitral tribunal shall determine it to the extent necessary, either directly or by reference to a statute or to rules of arbitration.

3   Regardless of the procedure chosen, the arbitral tribunal shall ensure equal treatment of the parties and the right of both parties to be heard in adversarial proceedings.

Article 183

2. Provisional and conservatory measures

1   Unless the parties have otherwise agreed, the arbitral tribunal may, on motion of one party, order provisional or conservatory measures.

2   If the party concerned does not voluntarily comply with these measures, the arbitral tribunal may request the assistance of the state judge; the judge shall apply his own law.

3   The arbitral tribunal or the state judge may make the granting of provisional or conservatory measures subject to appropriate sureties.

Article 184

3. Taking of evidence

1   The arbitral tribunal shall itself conduct the taking of evidence.

2   If the assistance of state judiciary authorities is necessary for the taking of evidence, the arbitral tribunal or a party with the consent of the arbitral tribunal may request the assistance of the state judge at the seat of the arbitral tribunal; the judge shall apply his own law.

Article 185

4. Other judicial assistance

For any further judicial assistance the state judge at the seat of the arbitral tribunal shall have jurisdiction.

Article 186

VII. Jurisdiction

1   The arbitral tribunal shall itself decide on its jurisdiction.

1bis It shall decide on its jurisdiction notwithstanding an action on the same matter between the same parties already pending before a state court or another arbitral tribunal, unless there are serious reasons to stay the proceedings.

2   A plea of lack of jurisdiction must be raised prior to any defence on the merits.

3   The arbitral tribunal shall, as a rule, decide on its jurisdiction by preliminary award.

Article 187

VIII. Decision on the merits

1.   Applicable law

1   The arbitral tribunal shall decide the case according to the rules of law chosen by the parties or, in the absence thereof, according to the rules of law with which the case has the closest connection.

2   The parties may authorize the arbitral tribunal to decide ex aequo et bono.

Article 188

2.   Partial award

Unless the parties otherwise agree, the arbitral tribunal may render partial awards.

Article 189

3.   Arbitral award

1   The arbitral award shall be rendered in conformity with the rules of procedure and in the form agreed upon by the parties.

2   In the absence of such an agreement, the arbitral award shall be made by a majority, or, in the absence of a majority, by the chairman alone. The award shall be in writing, supported by reasons, dated and signed. The signature of the chairman is sufficient.

Article 190

IX. Finality; Action for annulment

1.   Principle

1   The award is final from its notification.

2   The award may only be annulled:

a)   if the sole arbitrator was not properly appointed or if the arbitral tribunal was not properly constituted;

b)   if the arbitral tribunal wrongly accepted or declined jurisdiction;

c)   if the arbitral tribunal's decision went beyond the claims submitted to it, or failed to decide one of the items of the claim;

d)   if the principle of equal treatment of the parties or the right of the parties to be heard was violated;

e)   if the award is incompatible with public policy.

3   Preliminary awards can be annulled on the grounds of the above paras. 2(a) and 2(b) only; the time limit runs from the notification of the preliminary award.

Article 191

2.   Judicial authority to set aside

The sole judicial authority to set aside is the Swiss Federal Supreme Court. The procedure follows Art. 77 of the Swiss Federal Statute on the Swiss Federal Supreme Court of June 17, 2005.

Article 192

X.   Waiver of annulment

1   If none of the parties have their domicile, their habitual residence, or a business establishment in Switzerland, they may, by an express statement in the arbitration agreement or by a subsequent written agreement, waive fully the action for annulment or they may limit it to one or several of the grounds listed in Art. 190(2).

2   If the parties have waived fully the action for annulment against the awards and if the awards are to be enforced in Switzerland, the New York Convention of June 10, 1958 on the Recognition and Enforcement of Foreign Arbitral Awards applies by analogy.

Article 193

XI.   Deposit and certificate of enforceability

1   Each party may at its own expense deposit a copy of the award with the Swiss court at the seat of the arbitral tribunal.

2   On request of a party, the court shall certify the enforceability of the award.

3   On request of a party, the arbitral tribunal shall certify that the award has been rendered pursuant to the provisions of this statute; such certificate has the same effect as the deposit of the award.

Article 194

XII.   Foreign arbitral awards

The recognition and enforcement of a foreign arbitral award is governed by the New York Convention of June 10, 1958 on the Recognition and Enforcement of Foreign Arbitral Awards.

D. ENGLAND: ARBITRATION ACT 1996*

PART I

ARBITRATION PURSUANT TO
AN ARBITRATION AGREEMENT

Introductory

1.—General principles.

The provisions of this Part are founded on the following principles, and shall be construed accordingly—

    (a)   the object of arbitration is to obtain the fair resolution of disputes by an impartial tribunal without unnecessary delay or expense;

    (b)   the parties should be free to agree how their disputes are resolved, subject only to such safeguards as are necessary in the public interest;

    (c)   in matters governed by this Part the court should not intervene except as provided by this Part.

2.—Scope of application of provisions.

(1)   The provisions of this Part apply where the seat of the arbitration is in England and Wales or Northern Ireland.

(2)   The following sections apply even if the seat of the arbitration is outside England and Wales or Northern Ireland or no seat has been designated or determined—

    (a)   sections 9 to 11 (stay of legal proceedings, & c.), and

    (b)   section 66 (enforcement of arbitral awards).

(3)   The powers conferred by the following sections apply even if the seat of the arbitration is outside England and Wales or Northern Ireland or no seat has been designated or determined—

    (a)   section 43 (securing the attendance of witnesses), and

    (b)   section 44 (court powers exercisable in support of arbitral proceedings);

but the court may refuse to exercise any such power if, in the opinion of the court, the fact that the seat of the arbitration is outside England and Wales or Northern Ireland, or that when designated or determined the seat is likely to be outside England and Wales or Northern Ireland, makes it inappropriate to do so.

---

   * UK Statutes Crown Copyright. Reproduced by permission of the Controller of Her Majesty's Stationery Office.

(4)   The court may exercise a power conferred by any provision of this Part not mentioned in subsection (2) or (3) for the purpose of supporting the arbitral process where—

(a)   no seat of the arbitration has been designated or determined, and

(b)   by reason of a connection with England and Wales or Northern Ireland the court is satisfied that it is appropriate to do so.

(5)   Section 7 (separability of arbitration agreement) and section 8 (death of a party) apply where the law applicable to the arbitration agreement is the law of England and Wales or Northern Ireland even if the seat of the arbitration is outside England and Wales or Northern Ireland or has not been designated or determined.

3.—The seat of the arbitration.

In this Part "the seat of the arbitration" means the juridical seat of the arbitration designated—

(a)   by the parties to the arbitration agreement, or

(b)   by any arbitral or other institution or person vested by the parties with powers in that regard, or

(c)   by the arbitral tribunal if so authorised by the parties, or determined, in the absence of any such designation, having regard to the parties' agreement and all the relevant circumstances.

4.—Mandatory and non-mandatory provisions.

(1)   The mandatory provisions of this Part are listed in Schedule 1 and have effect notwithstanding any agreement to the contrary.

(2)   The other provisions of this Part (the "non-mandatory provisions") allow the parties to make their own arrangements by agreement but provide rules which apply in the absence of such agreement.

(3)   The parties may make such arrangements by agreeing to the application of institutional rules or providing any other means by which a matter may be decided.

(4)   It is immaterial whether or not the law applicable to the parties' agreement is the law of England and Wales or, as the case may be, Northern Ireland.

(5)   The choice of a law other than the law of England and Wales or Northern Ireland as the applicable law in respect of a matter provided for by a non-mandatory provision of this Part is equivalent to an agreement making provision about that matter.

For this purpose an applicable law determined in accordance with the parties' agreement, or which is objectively determined in the absence of any express or implied choice, shall be treated as chosen by the parties.

5.—Agreements to be in writing.

(1)   The provisions of this Part apply only where the arbitration agreement is in writing, and any other agreement between the parties as to any matter is effective for the purposes of this Part only if in writing.

The expressions "agreement", "agree" and "agreed" shall be construed accordingly.

(2)   There is an agreement in writing—

    (a)   if the agreement is made in writing (whether or not it is signed by the parties),

    (b)   if the agreement is made by exchange of communications in writing, or

    (c)   if the agreement is evidenced in writing.

(3)   Where parties agree otherwise than in writing by reference to terms which are in writing, they make an agreement in writing.

(4)   An agreement is evidenced in writing if an agreement made otherwise than in writing is recorded by one of the parties, or by a third party, with the authority of the parties to the agreement.

(5)   An exchange of written submissions in arbitral or legal proceedings in which the existence of an agreement otherwise than in writing is alleged by one party against another party and not denied by the other party in his response constitutes as between those parties an agreement in writing to the effect alleged.

(6)   References in this Part to anything being written or in writing include its being recorded by any means.

6.—Definition of arbitration agreement.

(1)   In this Part an "arbitration agreement" means an agreement to submit to arbitration present or future disputes (whether they are contractual or not).

(2)   The reference in an agreement to a written form of arbitration clause or to a document containing an arbitration clause constitutes an arbitration agreement if the reference is such as to make that clause part of the agreement.

7.—Separability of arbitration agreement.

Unless otherwise agreed by the parties, an arbitration agreement which forms or was intended to form part of another agreement (whether or not in writing) shall not be regarded as invalid, non-existent or ineffective because that other agreement is invalid, or did not come into existence or has become ineffective, and it shall for that purpose be treated as a distinct agreement.

8.—Whether agreement discharged by death of a party.

(1) Unless otherwise agreed by the parties, an arbitration agreement is not discharged by the death of a party and may be enforced by or against the personal representatives of that party.

(2) Subsection (1) does not affect the operation of any enactment or rule of law by virtue of which a substantive right or obligation is extinguished by death.

9.—Stay of legal proceedings.

(1) A party to an arbitration agreement against whom legal proceedings are brought (whether by way of claim or counterclaim) in respect of a matter which under the agreement is to be referred to arbitration may (upon notice to the other parties to the proceedings) apply to the court in which the proceedings have been brought to stay the proceedings so far as they concern that matter.

(2) An application may be made notwithstanding that the matter is to be referred to arbitration only after the exhaustion of other dispute resolution procedures.

(3) An application may not be made by a person before taking the appropriate procedural step (if any) to acknowledge the legal proceedings against him or after he has taken any step in those proceedings to answer the substantive claim.

(4) On an application under this section the court shall grant a stay unless satisfied that the arbitration agreement is null and void, inoperative, or incapable of being performed.

(5) If the court refuses to stay the legal proceedings, any provision that an award is a condition precedent to the bringing of legal proceedings in respect of any matter is of no effect in relation to those proceedings.

10.—Reference of interpleader issue to arbitration.

(1) Where in legal proceedings relief by way of interpleader is granted and any issue between the claimants is one in respect of which there is an arbitration agreement between them, the court granting the relief shall direct that the issue be determined in accordance with the agreement unless the circumstances are such that proceedings brought by a claimant in respect of the matter would not be stayed.

(2) Where subsection (1) applies but the court does not direct that the issue be determined in accordance with the arbitration agreement, any provision that an award is a condition precedent to the bringing of legal proceedings in respect of any matter shall not affect the determination of that issue by the court.

11.—Retention of security where Admiralty proceedings stayed.

(1) Where Admiralty proceedings are stayed on the ground that the dispute in question should be submitted to arbitration, the court granting the stay may, if in those proceedings property has been arrested or bail or other security has been given to prevent or obtain release from arrest—

   (a) order that the property arrested be retained as security for the satisfaction of any award given in the arbitration in respect of that dispute, or

   (b) order that the stay of those proceedings be conditional on the provision of equivalent security for the satisfaction of any such award.

(2) Subject to any provision made by rules of court and to any necessary modifications, the same law and practice shall apply in relation to property retained in pursuance of an order as would apply if it were held for the purposes of proceedings in the court making the order.

12.—Power of court to extend time for beginning arbitral proceedings, & c.

(1) Where an arbitration agreement to refer future disputes to arbitration provides that a claim shall be barred, or the claimant's right extinguished, unless the claimant takes within a time fixed by the agreement some step—

   (a) to begin arbitral proceedings, or

   (b) to begin other dispute resolution procedures which must be exhausted before arbitral proceedings can be begun, the court may by order extend the time for taking that step.

(2) Any party to the arbitration agreement may apply for such an order (upon notice to the other parties), but only after a claim has arisen and after exhausting any available arbitral process for obtaining an extension of time.

(3) The court shall make an order only if satisfied—

   (a) that the circumstances are such as were outside the reasonable contemplation of the parties when they agreed the provision in question, and that it would be just to extend the time, or

   (b) that the conduct of one party makes it unjust to hold the other party to the strict terms of the provision in question.

(4) The court may extend the time for such period and on such terms as it thinks fit, and may do so whether or not the time previously fixed (by agreement or by a previous order) has expired.

(5) An order under this section does not affect the operation of the Limitation Acts (see section 13).

(6)   The leave of the court is required for any appeal from a decision of the court under this section.

13.—Application of Limitation Acts.

(1)   The Limitation Acts apply to arbitral proceedings as they apply to legal proceedings.

(2)   The court may order that in computing the time prescribed by the Limitation Acts for the commencement of proceedings (including arbitral proceedings) in respect of a dispute which was the subject matter—

(a)   of an award which the court orders to be set aside or declares to be of no effect, or

(b)   of the affected part of an award which the court orders to be set aside in part, or declares to be in part of no effect, the period between the commencement of the arbitration and the date of the order referred to in paragraph (a) or (b) shall be excluded.

(3)   In determining for the purposes of the Limitation Acts when a cause of action accrued, any provision that an award is a condition precedent to the bringing of legal proceedings in respect of a matter to which an arbitration agreement applies shall be disregarded.

(4)   In this Part "the Limitation Acts" means—

(a)   in England and Wales, the Limitation Act 1980, the Foreign Limitation Periods Act 1984 and any other enactment (whenever passed) relating to the limitation of actions;

(b)   in Northern Ireland, the Limitation (Northern Ireland) Order 1989, the Foreign Limitation Periods (Northern Ireland) Order 1985 and any other enactment (whenever passed) relating to the limitation of actions.

14.—Commencement of arbitral proceedings.

(1)   The parties are free to agree when arbitral proceedings are to be regarded as commenced for the purposes of this Part and for the purposes of the Limitation Acts.

(2)   If there is no such agreement the following provisions apply.

(3)   Where the arbitrator is named or designated in the arbitration agreement, arbitral proceedings are commenced in respect of a matter when one party serves on the other party or parties a notice in writing requiring him or them to submit that matter to the person so named or designated.

(4)   Where the arbitrator or arbitrators are to be appointed by the parties, arbitral proceedings are commenced in respect of a matter when one party serves on the other party or parties notice in writing requiring him or them

to appoint an arbitrator or to agree to the appointment of an arbitrator in respect of that matter.

(5)   Where the arbitrator or arbitrators are to be appointed by a person other than a party to the proceedings, arbitral proceedings are commenced in respect of a matter when one party gives notice in writing to that person requesting him to make the appointment in respect of that matter.

15.—The arbitral tribunal.

(1)   The parties are free to agree on the number of arbitrators to form the tribunal and whether there is to be a chairman or umpire.

(2)   Unless otherwise agreed by the parties, an agreement that the number of arbitrators shall be two or any other even number shall be understood as requiring the appointment of an additional arbitrator as chairman of the tribunal.

(3)   If there is no agreement as to the number of arbitrators, the tribunal shall consist of a sole arbitrator.

16.—Procedure for appointment of arbitrators.

(1)   The parties are free to agree on the procedure for appointing the arbitrator or arbitrators, including the procedure for appointing any chairman or umpire.

(2)   If or to the extent that there is no such agreement, the following provisions apply.

(3)   If the tribunal is to consist of a sole arbitrator, the parties shall jointly appoint the arbitrator not later than 28 days after service of a request in writing by either party to do so.

(4)   If the tribunal is to consist of two arbitrators, each party shall appoint one arbitrator not later than 14 days after service of a request in writing by either party to do so.

(5)   If the tribunal is to consist of three arbitrators—

(a)   each party shall appoint one arbitrator not later than 14 days after service of a request in writing by either party to do so, and

(b)   the two so appointed shall forthwith appoint a third arbitrator as the chairman of the tribunal.

(6)   If the tribunal is to consist of two arbitrators and an umpire—

(a)   each party shall appoint one arbitrator not later than 14 days after service of a request in writing by either party to do so, and

(b)   the two so appointed may appoint an umpire at any time after they themselves are appointed and shall do so before any substantive hearing or forthwith if they cannot agree on a matter relating to the arbitration.

(7)   In any other case (in particular, if there are more than two parties) section 18 applies as in the case of a failure of the agreed appointment procedure.

17.—Power in case of default to appoint sole arbitrator.

(1)   Unless the parties otherwise agree, where each of two parties to an arbitration agreement is to appoint an arbitrator and one party ("the party in default") refuses to do so, or fails to do so within the time specified, the other party, having duly appointed his arbitrator, may give notice in writing to the party in default that he proposes to appoint his arbitrator to act as sole arbitrator.

(2)   If the party in default does not within 7 clear days of that notice being given—

    (a)   make the required appointment, and

    (b)   notify the other party that he has done so, the other party may appoint his arbitrator as sole arbitrator whose award shall be binding on both parties as if he had been so appointed by agreement.

(3)   Where a sole arbitrator has been appointed under subsection (2), the party in default may (upon notice to the appointing party) apply to the court which may set aside the appointment.

(4)   The leave of the court is required for any appeal from a decision of the court under this section.

18.—Failure of appointment procedure.

(1)   The parties are free to agree what is to happen in the event of a failure of the procedure for the appointment of the arbitral tribunal.

There is no failure if an appointment is duly made under section 17 (power in case of default to appoint sole arbitrator), unless that appointment is set aside.

(2)   If or to the extent that there is no such agreement any party to the arbitration agreement may (upon notice to the other parties) apply to the court to exercise its powers under this section.

(3)   Those powers are—

    (a)   to give directions as to the making of any necessary appointments;

    (b)   to direct that the tribunal shall be constituted by such appointments (or any one or more of them) as have been made;

    (c)   to revoke any appointments already made;

    (d)   to make any necessary appointments itself.

(4)   An appointment made by the court under this section has effect as if made with the agreement of the parties.

(5)   The leave of the court is required for any appeal from a decision of the court under this section.

19. Court to have regard to agreed qualifications.

In deciding whether to exercise, and in considering how to exercise, any of its powers under section 16 (procedure for appointment of arbitrators) or section 18 (failure of appointment procedure), the court shall have due regard to any agreement of the parties as to the qualifications required of the arbitrators.

20.—Chairman.

(1)   Where the parties have agreed that there is to be a chairman, they are free to agree what the functions of the chairman are to be in relation to the making of decisions, orders and awards.

(2)   If or to the extent that there is no such agreement, the following provisions apply.

(3)   Decisions, orders and awards shall be made by all or a majority of the arbitrators (including the chairman).

(4)   The view of the chairman shall prevail in relation to a decision, order or award in respect of which there is neither unanimity nor a majority under subsection (3).

21.—Umpire.

(1)   Where the parties have agreed that there is to be an umpire, they are free to agree what the functions of the umpire are to be, and in particular—

    (a)   whether he is to attend the proceedings, and

    (b)   when he is to replace the other arbitrators as the tribunal with power to make decisions, orders and awards.

(2)   If or to the extent that there is no such agreement, the following provisions apply.

(3)   The umpire shall attend the proceedings and be supplied with the same documents and other materials as are supplied to the other arbitrators.

(4)   Decisions, orders and awards shall be made by the other arbitrators unless and until they cannot agree on a matter relating to the arbitration. In that event they shall forthwith give notice in writing to the parties and the umpire, whereupon the umpire shall replace them as the tribunal with power to make decisions, orders and awards as if he were sole arbitrator.

(5)   If the arbitrators cannot agree but fail to give notice of that fact, or if any of them fails to join in the giving of notice, any party to the arbitral

proceedings may (upon notice to the other parties and to the tribunal) apply to the court which may order that the umpire shall replace the other arbitrators as the tribunal with power to make decisions, orders and awards as if he were sole arbitrator.

(6)   The leave of the court is required for any appeal from a decision of the court under this section.

22.—Decision-making where no chairman or umpire.

(1)   Where the parties agree that there shall be two or more arbitrators with no chairman or umpire, the parties are free to agree how the tribunal is to make decisions, orders and awards.

(2)   If there is no such agreement, decisions, orders and awards shall be made by all or a majority of the arbitrators.

23.—Revocation of arbitrator's authority.

(1)   The parties are free to agree in what circumstances the authority of an arbitrator may be revoked.

(2)   If or to the extent that there is no such agreement the following provisions apply.

(3)   The authority of an arbitrator may not be revoked except—

   (a)   by the parties acting jointly, or

   (b)   by an arbitral or other institution or person vested by the parties with powers in that regard.

(4)   Revocation of the authority of an arbitrator by the parties acting jointly must be agreed in writing unless the parties also agree (whether or not in writing) to terminate the arbitration agreement.

(5)   Nothing in this section affects the power of the court—

   (a)   to revoke an appointment under section 18 (powers exercisable in case of failure of appointment procedure), or

   (b)   to remove an arbitrator on the grounds specified in section 24.

24.—Power of court to remove arbitrator.

(1)   A party to arbitral proceedings may (upon notice to the other parties, to the arbitrator concerned and to any other arbitrator) apply to the court to remove an arbitrator on any of the following grounds—

   (a)   that circumstances exist that give rise to justifiable doubts as to his impartiality;

   (b)   that he does not possess the qualifications required by the arbitration agreement;

(c)   that he is physically or mentally incapable of conducting the proceedings or there are justifiable doubts as to his capacity to do so;

(d)   that he has refused or failed—

(i)   properly to conduct the proceedings, or

(ii)   to use all reasonable despatch in conducting the proceedings or making an award, and that substantial injustice has been or will be caused to the applicant.

(2)   If there is an arbitral or other institution or person vested by the parties with power to remove an arbitrator, the court shall not exercise its power of removal unless satisfied that the applicant has first exhausted any available recourse to that institution or person.

(3)   The arbitral tribunal may continue the arbitral proceedings and make an award while an application to the court under this section is pending.

(4)   Where the court removes an arbitrator, it may make such order as it thinks fit with respect to his entitlement (if any) to fees or expenses, or the repayment of any fees or expenses already paid.

(5)   The arbitrator concerned is entitled to appear and be heard by the court before it makes any order under this section.

(6)   The leave of the court is required for any appeal from a decision of the court under this section.

25.—Resignation of arbitrator.

(1)   The parties are free to agree with an arbitrator as to the consequences of his resignation as regards—

(a)   his entitlement (if any) to fees or expenses, and

(b)   any liability thereby incurred by him.

(2)   If or to the extent that there is no such agreement the following provisions apply.

(3)   An arbitrator who resigns his appointment may (upon notice to the parties) apply to the court—

(a)   to grant him relief from any liability thereby incurred by him, and

(b)   to make such order as it thinks fit with respect to his entitlement (if any) to fees or expenses or the repayment of any fees or expenses already paid.

(4)   If the court is satisfied that in all the circumstances it was reasonable for the arbitrator to resign, it may grant such relief as is mentioned in subsection (3)(a) on such terms as it thinks fit.

(5)   The leave of the court is required for any appeal from a decision of the court under this section.

26.—Death of arbitrator or person appointing him.

(1)   The authority of an arbitrator is personal and ceases on his death.

(2)   Unless otherwise agreed by the parties, the death of the person by whom an arbitrator was appointed does not revoke the arbitrator's authority.

27.—Filling of vacancy, etc.

(1)   Where an arbitrator ceases to hold office, the parties are free to agree—

(a)   whether and if so how the vacancy is to be filled,

(b)   whether and if so to what extent the previous proceedings should stand, and

(c)   what effect (if any) his ceasing to hold office has on any appointment made by him (alone or jointly).

(2)   If or to the extent that there is no such agreement, the following provisions apply.

(3)   The provisions of sections 16 (procedure for appointment of arbitrators) and 18 (failure of appointment procedure) apply in relation to the filling of the vacancy as in relation to an original appointment.

(4)   The tribunal (when reconstituted) shall determine whether and if so to what extent the previous proceedings should stand. This does not affect any right of a party to challenge those proceedings on any ground which had arisen before the arbitrator ceased to hold office.

(5)   His ceasing to hold office does not affect any appointment by him (alone or jointly) of another arbitrator, in particular any appointment of a chairman or umpire.

28.—Joint and several liability of parties to arbitrators for fees and expenses.

(1)   The parties are jointly and severally liable to pay to the arbitrators such reasonable fees and expenses (if any) as are appropriate in the circumstances.

(2)   Any party may apply to the court (upon notice to the other parties and to the arbitrators) which may order that the amount of the arbitrators' fees and expenses shall be considered and adjusted by such means and upon such terms as it may direct.

(3)   If the application is made after any amount has been paid to the arbitrators by way of fees or expenses, the court may order the repayment of such amount (if any) as is shown to be excessive, but shall not do so

unless it is shown that it is reasonable in the circumstances to order repayment.

(4) The above provisions have effect subject to any order of the court under section 24(4) or 25(3)(b) (order as to entitlement to fees or expenses in case of removal or resignation of arbitrator).

(5) Nothing in this section affects any liability of a party to any other party to pay all or any of the costs of the arbitration (see sections 59 to 65) or any contractual right of an arbitrator to payment of his fees and expenses.

(6) In this section references to arbitrators include an arbitrator who has ceased to act and an umpire who has not replaced the other arbitrators.

29.—Immunity of arbitrator.

(1) An arbitrator is not liable for anything done or omitted in the discharge or purported discharge of his functions as arbitrator unless the act or omission is shown to have been in bad faith.

(2) Subsection (1) applies to an employee or agent of an arbitrator as it applies to the arbitrator himself.

(3) This section does not affect any liability incurred by an arbitrator by reason of his resigning (but see section 25).

30.—Competence of tribunal to rule on its own jurisdiction.

(1) Unless otherwise agreed by the parties, the arbitral tribunal may rule on its own substantive jurisdiction, that is, as to—

    (a) whether there is a valid arbitration agreement,

    (b) whether the tribunal is properly constituted, and

    (c) what matters have been submitted to arbitration in accordance with the arbitration agreement.

(2) Any such ruling may be challenged by any available arbitral process of appeal or review or in accordance with the provisions of this Part.

31.—Objection to substantive jurisdiction of tribunal.

(1) An objection that the arbitral tribunal lacks substantive jurisdiction at the outset of the proceedings must be raised by a party not later than the time he takes the first step in the proceedings to contest the merits of any matter in relation to which he challenges the tribunal's jurisdiction. A party is not precluded from raising such an objection by the fact that he has appointed or participated in the appointment of an arbitrator.

(2) Any objection during the course of the arbitral proceedings that the arbitral tribunal is exceeding its substantive jurisdiction must be made as soon as possible after the matter alleged to be beyond its jurisdiction is raised.

(3) The arbitral tribunal may admit an objection later than the time specified in subsection (1) or (2) if it considers the delay justified.

(4) Where an objection is duly taken to the tribunal's substantive jurisdiction and the tribunal has power to rule on its own jurisdiction, it may—

(a) rule on the matter in an award as to jurisdiction, or

(b) deal with the objection in its award on the merits.

If the parties agree which of these courses the tribunal should take, the tribunal shall proceed accordingly.

(5) The tribunal may in any case, and shall if the parties so agree, stay proceedings whilst an application is made to the court under section 32 (determination of preliminary point of jurisdiction).

32.—Determination of preliminary point of jurisdiction.

(1) The court may, on the application of a party to arbitral proceedings (upon notice to the other parties), determine any question as to the substantive jurisdiction of the tribunal.

A party may lose the right to object (see section 73).

(2) An application under this section shall not be considered unless—

(a) it is made with the agreement in writing of all the other parties to the proceedings, or

(b) it is made with the permission of the tribunal and the court is satisfied—

(i) that the determination of the question is likely to produce substantial savings in costs,

(ii) that the application was made without delay, and

(iii) that there is good reason why the matter should be decided by the court.

(3) An application under this section, unless made with the agreement of all the other parties to the proceedings, shall state the grounds on which it is said that the matter should be decided by the court.

(4) Unless otherwise agreed by the parties, the arbitral tribunal may continue the arbitral proceedings and make an award while an application to the court under this section is pending.

(5) Unless the court gives leave, no appeal lies from a decision of the court whether the conditions specified in subsection (2) are met.

(6) The decision of the court on the question of jurisdiction shall be treated as a judgment of the court for the purposes of an appeal.

But no appeal lies without the leave of the court which shall not be given unless the court considers that the question involves a point of law which is one of general importance or is one which for some other special reason should be considered by the Court of Appeal.

33.—General duty of the tribunal.

(1) The tribunal shall—

    (a) act fairly and impartially as between the parties, giving each party a reasonable opportunity of putting his case and dealing with that of his opponent, and

    (b) adopt procedures suitable to the circumstances of the particular case, avoiding unnecessary delay or expense, so as to provide a fair means for the resolution of the matters falling to be determined.

(2) The tribunal shall comply with that general duty in conducting the arbitral proceedings, in its decisions on matters of procedure and evidence and in the exercise of all other powers conferred on it.

34.—Procedural and evidential matters.

(1) It shall be for the tribunal to decide all procedural and evidential matters, subject to the right of the parties to agree any matter.

(2) Procedural and evidential matters include—

    (a) when and where any part of the proceedings is to be held;

    (b) the language or languages to be used in the proceedings and whether translations of any relevant documents are to be supplied;

    (c) whether any and if so what form of written statements of claim and defence are to be used, when these should be supplied and the extent to which such statements can be later amended;

    (d) whether any and if so which documents or classes of documents should be disclosed between and produced by the parties and at what stage;

    (e) whether any and if so what questions should be put to and answered by the respective parties and when and in what form this should be done;

    (f) whether to apply strict rules of evidence (or any other rules) as to the admissibility, relevance or weight of any material (oral, written or other) sought to be tendered on any matters of fact or opinion, and the time, manner and form in which such material should be exchanged and presented;

(g) whether and to what extent the tribunal should itself take the initiative in ascertaining the facts and the law;

(h) whether and to what extent there should be oral or written evidence or submissions.

(3) The tribunal may fix the time within which any directions given by it are to be complied with, and may if it thinks fit extend the time so fixed (whether or not it has expired).

35.—Consolidation of proceedings and concurrent hearings.

(1) The parties are free to agree—

(a) that the arbitral proceedings shall be consolidated with other arbitral proceedings, or

(b) that concurrent hearings shall be held, on such terms as may be agreed.

(2) Unless the parties agree to confer such power on the tribunal, the tribunal has no power to order consolidation of proceedings or concurrent hearings.

36.—Legal or other representation.

Unless otherwise agreed by the parties, a party to arbitral proceedings may be represented in the proceedings by a lawyer or other person chosen by him.

37.—Power to appoint experts, legal advisers or assessors.

(1) Unless otherwise agreed by the parties—

(a) the tribunal may—

(i) appoint experts or legal advisers to report to it and the parties, or

(ii) appoint assessors to assist it on technical matters, and may allow any such expert, legal adviser or assessor to attend the proceedings; and

(b) the parties shall be given a reasonable opportunity to comment on any information, opinion or advice offered by any such person.

(2) The fees and expenses of an expert, legal adviser or assessor appointed by the tribunal for which the arbitrators are liable are expenses of the arbitrators for the purposes of this Part.

38.—General powers exercisable by the tribunal.

(1) The parties are free to agree on the powers exercisable by the arbitral tribunal for the purposes of and in relation to the proceedings.

(2)   Unless otherwise agreed by the parties the tribunal has the following powers.

(3)   The tribunal may order a claimant to provide security for the costs of the arbitration.

This power shall not be exercised on the ground that the claimant is—

(a)   an individual ordinarily resident outside the United Kingdom, or

(b)   a corporation or association incorporated or formed under the law of a country outside the United Kingdom, or whose central management and control is exercised outside the United Kingdom.

(4)   The tribunal may give directions in relation to any property which is the subject of the proceedings or as to which any question arises in the proceedings, and which is owned by or is in the possession of a party to the proceedings—

(a)   for the inspection, photographing, preservation, custody or detention of the property by the tribunal, an expert or a party, or

(b)   ordering that samples be taken from, or any observation be made of or experiment conducted upon, the property.

(5)   The tribunal may direct that a party or witness shall be examined on oath or affirmation, and may for that purpose administer any necessary oath or take any necessary affirmation.

(6)   The tribunal may give directions to a party for the preservation for the purposes of the proceedings of any evidence in his custody or control.

39.—Power to make provisional awards.

(1)   The parties are free to agree that the tribunal shall have power to order on a provisional basis any relief which it would have power to grant in a final award.

(2)   This includes, for instance, making—

(a)   a provisional order for the payment of money or the disposition of property as between the parties, or

(b)   an order to make an interim payment on account of the costs of the arbitration.

(3)   Any such order shall be subject to the tribunal's final adjudication; and the tribunal's final award, on the merits or as to costs, shall take account of any such order.

(4)   Unless the parties agree to confer such power on the tribunal, the tribunal has no such power. This does not affect its powers under section 47 (awards on different issues, & c.).

40.—General duty of parties.

(1)   The parties shall do all things necessary for the proper and expeditious conduct of the arbitral proceedings.

(2)   This includes—

(a)   complying without delay with any determination of the tribunal as to procedural or evidential matters, or with any order or directions of the tribunal, and

(b)   where appropriate, taking without delay any necessary steps to obtain a decision of the court on a preliminary question of jurisdiction or law (see sections 32 and 45).

41.—Powers of tribunal in case of party's default.

(1)   The parties are free to agree on the powers of the tribunal in case of a party's failure to do something necessary for the proper and expeditious conduct of the arbitration.

(2)   Unless otherwise agreed by the parties, the following provisions apply.

(3)   If the tribunal is satisfied that there has been inordinate and inexcusable delay on the part of the claimant in pursuing his claim and that the delay—

(a)   gives rise, or is likely to give rise, to a substantial risk that it is not possible to have a fair resolution of the issues in that claim, or

(b)   has caused, or is likely to cause, serious prejudice to the respondent, the tribunal may make an award dismissing the claim.

(4)   If without showing sufficient cause a party—

(a)   fails to attend or be represented at an oral hearing of which due notice was given, or

(b)   where matters are to be dealt with in writing, fails after due notice to submit written evidence or make written submissions, the tribunal may continue the proceedings in the absence of that party or, as the case may be, without any written evidence or submissions on his behalf, and may make an award on the basis of the evidence before it.

(5)   If without showing sufficient cause a party fails to comply with any order or directions of the tribunal, the tribunal may make a peremptory order to the same effect, prescribing such time for compliance with it as the tribunal considers appropriate.

(6)   If a claimant fails to comply with a peremptory order of the tribunal to provide security or costs, the tribunal may make an award dismissing his claim.

(7) If a party fails to comply with any other kind of peremptory order, then, without prejudice to section 42 (enforcement by court of tribunal's peremptory orders), the tribunal may do any of the following—

(a) direct that the party in default shall not be entitled to rely upon any allegation or material which was the subject matter of the order;

(b) draw such adverse inferences from the act of non-compliance as the circumstances justify;

(c) proceed to an award on the basis of such materials as have been properly provided to it;

(d) make such order as it thinks fit as to the payment of costs of the arbitration incurred in consequence of the non-compliance.

42.—Enforcement of peremptory orders of tribunal.

(1) Unless otherwise agreed by the parties, the court may make an order requiring a party to comply with a peremptory order made by the tribunal.

(2) An application for an order under this section may be made—

(a) by the tribunal (upon notice to the parties),

(b) by a party to the arbitral proceedings with the permission of the tribunal (and upon notice to the other parties), or

(c) where the parties have agreed that the powers of the court under this section shall be available.

(3) The court shall not act unless it is satisfied that the applicant has exhausted any available arbitral process in respect of failure to comply with the tribunal's order.

(4) No order shall be made under this section unless the court is satisfied that the person to whom the tribunal's order was directed has failed to comply with it within the time prescribed in the order or, if no time was prescribed, within a reasonable time.

(5) The leave of the court is required for any appeal from a decision of the court under this section.

43.—Securing the attendance of witnesses.

(1) A party to arbitral proceedings may use the same court procedures as are available in relation to legal proceedings to secure the attendance before the tribunal of a witness in order to give oral testimony or to produce documents or other material evidence.

(2) This may only be done with the permission of the tribunal or the agreement of the other parties.

(3)   The court procedures may only be used if—

(a)   the witness is in the United Kingdom, and

(b)   the arbitral proceedings are being conducted in England and Wales or, as the case may be, Northern Ireland.

(4)   A person shall not be compelled by virtue of this section to produce any document or other material evidence which he could not be compelled to produce in legal proceedings.

44.—Court powers exercisable in support of arbitral proceedings.

(1)   Unless otherwise agreed by the parties, the court has for the purposes of and in relation to arbitral proceedings the same power of making orders about the matters listed below as it has for the purposes of and in relation to legal proceedings.

(2)   Those matters are—

(a)   the taking of the evidence of witnesses;

(b)   the preservation of evidence;

(c)   making orders relating to property which is the subject of the proceedings or as to which any question arises in the proceedings—

(i)   for the inspection, photographing, preservation, custody or detention of the property, or

(ii)   ordering that samples be taken from, or any observation be made of or experiment conducted upon, the property; and for that purpose authorising any person to enter any premises in the possession or control of a party to the arbitration;

(d)   the sale of any goods the subject of the proceedings;

(e)   the granting of an interim injunction or the appointment of a receiver.

(3)   If the case is one of urgency, the court may, on the application of a party or proposed party to the arbitral proceedings, make such orders as it thinks necessary for the purpose of preserving evidence or assets.

(4)   If the case is not one of urgency, the court shall act only on the application of a party to the arbitral proceedings (upon notice to the other parties and to the tribunal) made with the permission of the tribunal or the agreement in writing of the other parties.

(5)   In any case the court shall act only if or to the extent that the arbitral tribunal, and any arbitral or other institution or person vested by the parties with power in that regard, has no power or is unable for the time being to act effectively.

(6)   If the court so orders, an order made by it under this section shall cease to have effect in whole or in part on the order of the tribunal or of any such arbitral or other institution or person having power to act in relation to the subject-matter of the order.

(7)   The leave of the court is required for any appeal from a decision of the court under this section.

45.—Determination of preliminary point of law.

(1)   Unless otherwise agreed by the parties, the court may on the application of a party to arbitral proceedings (upon notice to the other parties) determine any question of law arising in the course of the proceedings which the court is satisfied substantially affects the rights of one or more of the parties. An agreement to dispense with reasons for the tribunal's award shall be considered an agreement to exclude the court's jurisdiction under this section.

(2)   An application under this section shall not be considered unless—

    (a)   it is made with the agreement of all the other parties to the proceedings, or

    (b)   it is made with the permission of the tribunal and the court is satisfied—

        (i)   that the determination of the question is likely to produce substantial savings in costs, and

        (ii)   that the application was made without delay.

(3)   The application shall identify the question of law to be determined and, unless made with the agreement of all the other parties to the proceedings, shall state the grounds on which it is said that the question should be decided by the court.

(4)   Unless otherwise agreed by the parties, the arbitral tribunal may continue the arbitral proceedings and make an award while an application to the court under this section is pending.

(5)   Unless the court gives leave, no appeal lies from a decision of the court whether the conditions specified in subsection (2) are met.

(6)   The decision of the court on the question of law shall be treated as a judgment of the court for the purposes of an appeal. But no appeal lies without the leave of the court which shall not be given unless the court considers that the question is one of general importance, or is one which for some other special reason should be considered by the Court of Appeal.

46.—Rules applicable to substance of dispute.

(1) The arbitral tribunal shall decide the dispute—

    (a) in accordance with the law chosen by the parties as applicable to the substance of the dispute, or

    (b) if the parties so agree, in accordance with such other considerations as are agreed by them or determined by the tribunal.

(2) For this purpose the choice of the laws of a country shall be understood to refer to the substantive laws of that country and not its conflict of laws rules.

(3) If or to the extent that there is no such choice or agreement, the tribunal shall apply the law determined by the conflict of laws rules which it considers applicable.

47.—Awards on different issues, & c.

(1) Unless otherwise agreed by the parties, the tribunal may make more than one award at different times on different aspects of the matters to be determined.

(2) The tribunal may, in particular, make an award relating—

    (a) to an issue affecting the whole claim, or

    (b) to a part only of the claims or cross-claims submitted to it for decision.

(3) If the tribunal does so, it shall specify in its award the issue, or the claim or part of a claim, which is the subject matter of the award.

48.—Remedies.

(1) The parties are free to agree on the powers exercisable by the arbitral tribunal as regards remedies.

(2) Unless otherwise agreed by the parties, the tribunal has the following powers.

(3) The tribunal may make a declaration as to any matter to be determined in the proceedings.

(4) The tribunal may order the payment of a sum of money, in any currency.

(5) The tribunal has the same powers as the court—

    (a) to order a party to do or refrain from doing anything;

    (b) to order specific performance of a contract (other than a contract relating to land);

(c) to order the rectification, setting aside or cancellation of a deed or other document.

49.—Interest.

(1) The parties are free to agree on the powers of the tribunal as regards the award of interest.

(2) Unless otherwise agreed by the parties the following provisions apply.

(3) The tribunal may award simple or compound interest from such dates, at such rates and with such rests as it considers meets the justice of the case—

(a) on the whole or part of any amount awarded by the tribunal, in respect of any period up to the date of the award;

(b) on the whole or part of any amount claimed in the arbitration and outstanding at the commencement of the arbitral proceedings but paid before the award was made, in respect of any period up to the date of payment.

(4) The tribunal may award simple or compound interest from the date of the award (or any later date) until payment, at such rates and with such rests as it considers meets the justice of the case, on the outstanding amount of any award (including any award of interest under subsection (3) and any award as to costs).

(5) References in this section to an amount awarded by the tribunal include an amount payable in consequence of a declaratory award by the tribunal.

(6) The above provisions do not affect any other power of the tribunal to award interest.

50.—Extension of time for making award.

(1) Where the time for making an award is limited by or in pursuance of the arbitration agreement, then, unless otherwise agreed by the parties, the court may in accordance with the following provisions by order extend that time.

(2) An application for an order under this section may be made—

(a) by the tribunal (upon notice to the parties), or

(b) by any party to the proceedings (upon notice to the tribunal and the other parties), but only after exhausting any available arbitral process for obtaining an extension of time.

(3) The court shall only make an order if satisfied that a substantial injustice would otherwise be done.

(4)   The court may extend the time for such period and on such terms as it thinks fit, and may do so whether or not the time previously fixed (by or under the agreement or by a previous order) has expired.

(5)   The leave of the court is required for any appeal from a decision of the court under this section.

51.—Settlement.

(1)   If during arbitral proceedings the parties settle the dispute, the following provisions apply unless otherwise agreed by the parties.

(2)   The tribunal shall terminate the substantive proceedings and, if so requested by the parties and not objected to by the tribunal, shall record the settlement in the form of an agreed award.

(3)   An agreed award shall state that it is an award of the tribunal and shall have the same status and effect as any other award on the merits of the case.

(4)   The following provisions of this Part relating to awards (sections 52 to 58) apply to an agreed award.

(5)   Unless the parties have also settled the matter of the payment of the costs of the arbitration, the provisions of this Part relating to costs (sections 59 to 65) continue to apply.

52.—Form of award.

(1)   The parties are free to agree on the form of an award.

(2)   If or to the extent that there is no such agreement, the following provisions apply.

(3)   The award shall be in writing signed by all the arbitrators or all those assenting to the award.

(4)   The award shall contain the reasons for the award unless it is an agreed award or the parties have agreed to dispense with reasons.

(5)   The award shall state the seat of the arbitration and the date when the award is made.

53.—Place where award treated as made.

Unless otherwise agreed by the parties, where the seat of the arbitration is in England and Wales or Northern Ireland, any award in the proceedings shall be treated as made there, regardless of where it was signed, despatched or delivered to any of the parties.

54.—Date of award.

(1)   Unless otherwise agreed by the parties, the tribunal may decide what is to be taken to be the date on which the award was made.

(2) In the absence of any such decision, the date of the award shall be taken to be the date on which it is signed by the arbitrator or, where more than one arbitrator signs the award, by the last of them.

55.—Notification of award.

(1) The parties are free to agree on the requirements as to notification of the award to the parties.

(2) If there is no such agreement, the award shall be notified to the parties by service on them of copies of the award, which shall be done without delay after the award is made.

(3) Nothing in this section affects section 56 (power to withhold award in case of non-payment).

56.—Power to withhold award in case of non-payment.

(1) The tribunal may refuse to deliver an award to the parties except upon full payment of the fees and expenses of the arbitrators.

(2) If the tribunal refuses on that ground to deliver an award, a party to the arbitral proceedings may (upon notice to the other parties and the tribunal) apply to the court, which may order that—

    (a) the tribunal shall deliver the award on the payment into court by the applicant of the fees and expenses demanded, or such lesser amount as the court may specify,

    (b) the amount of the fees and expenses properly payable shall be determined by such means and upon such terms as the court may direct, and

    (c) out of the money paid into court there shall be paid out such fees and expenses as may be found to be properly payable and the balance of the money (if any) shall be paid out to the applicant.

(3) For this purpose the amount of fees and expenses properly payable is the amount the applicant is liable to pay under section 28 or any agreement relating to the payment of the arbitrators.

(4) No application to the court may be made where there is any available arbitral process for appeal or review of the amount of the fees or expenses demanded.

(5) References in this section to arbitrators include an arbitrator who has ceased to act and an umpire who has not replaced the other arbitrators.

(6) The above provisions of this section also apply in relation to any arbitral or other institution or person vested by the parties with powers in relation to the delivery of the tribunal's award. As they so apply, the references to the fees and expenses of the arbitrators shall be construed as including the fees and expenses of that institution or person.

(7) The leave of the court is required for any appeal from a decision of the court under this section.

(8) Nothing in this section shall be construed as excluding an application under section 28 where payment has been made to the arbitrators in order to obtain the award.

57.—Correction of award or additional award.

(1) The parties are free to agree on the powers of the tribunal to correct an award or make an additional award.

(2) If or to the extent there is no such agreement, the following provisions apply.

(3) The tribunal may on its own initiative or on the application of a party—

> (a) correct an award so as to remove any clerical mistake or error arising from an accidental slip or omission or clarify or remove any ambiguity in the award, or

> (b) make an additional award in respect of any claim (including a claim for interest or costs) which was presented to the tribunal but was not dealt with in the award. These powers shall not be exercised without first affording the other parties a reasonable opportunity to make representations to the tribunal.

(4) Any application for the exercise of those powers must be made within 28 days of the date of the award or such longer period as the parties may agree.

(5) Any correction of an award shall be made within 28 days of the date the application was received by the tribunal or, where the correction is made by the tribunal on its own initiative, within 28 days of the date of the award or, in either case, such longer period as the parties may agree.

(6) Any additional award shall be made within 56 days of the date of the original award or such longer period as the parties may agree.

(7) Any correction of an award shall form part of the award.

58.—Effect of award.

(1) Unless otherwise agreed by the parties, an award made by the tribunal pursuant to an arbitration agreement is final and binding both on the parties and on any persons claiming through or under them.

(2) This does not affect the right of a person to challenge the award by any available arbitral process of appeal or review or in accordance with the provisions of this Part.

59.—Costs of the arbitration.

(1)   References in this Part to the costs of the arbitration are to—

    (a)   the arbitrators' fees and expenses,

    (b)   the fees and expenses of any arbitral institution concerned, and

    (c)   the legal or other costs of the parties.

(2)   Any such reference includes the costs of or incidental to any proceedings to determine the amount of the recoverable costs of the arbitration (see section 63).

60. Agreement to pay costs in any event.

An agreement which has the effect that a party is to pay the whole or part of the costs of the arbitration in any event is only valid if made after the dispute in question has arisen.

61.—Award of costs.

(1)   The tribunal may make an award allocating the costs of the arbitration as between the parties, subject to any agreement of the parties.

(2)   Unless the parties otherwise agree, the tribunal shall award costs on the general principle that costs should follow the event except where it appears to the tribunal that in the circumstances this is not appropriate in relation to the whole or part of the costs.

62. Effect of agreement or award about costs.

Unless the parties otherwise agree, any obligation under an agreement between them as to how the costs of the arbitration are to be borne, or under an award allocating the costs of the arbitration, extends only to such costs as are recoverable.

63.—The recoverable costs of the arbitration.

(1)   The parties are free to agree what costs of the arbitration are recoverable.

(2)   If or to the extent there is no such agreement, the following provisions apply.

(3)   The tribunal may determine by award the recoverable costs of the arbitration on such basis as it thinks fit.

If it does so, it shall specify—

    (a)   the basis on which it has acted, and

    (b)   the items of recoverable costs and the amount referable to each.

(4)   If the tribunal does not determine the recoverable costs of the arbitration, any party to the arbitral proceedings may apply to the court (upon notice to the other parties) which may—

(a)   determine the recoverable costs of the arbitration on such basis as it thinks fit, or

(b)   order that they shall be determined by such means and upon such terms as it may specify.

(5)   Unless the tribunal or the court determines otherwise—

(a)   the recoverable costs of the arbitration shall be determined on the basis that there shall be allowed a reasonable amount in respect of all costs reasonably incurred, and

(b)   any doubt as to whether costs were reasonably incurred or were reasonable in amount shall be resolved in favour of the paying party.

(6)   The above provisions have effect subject to section 64 (recoverable fees and expenses of arbitrators).

(7)   Nothing in this section affects any right of the arbitrators, any expert, legal adviser or assessor appointed by the tribunal, or any arbitral institution, to payment of their fees and expenses.

64.—Recoverable fees and expenses of arbitrators.

(1)   Unless otherwise agreed by the parties, the recoverable costs of the arbitration shall include in respect of the fees and expenses of the arbitrators only such reasonable fees and expenses as are appropriate in the circumstances.

(2)   If there is any question as to what reasonable fees and expenses are appropriate in the circumstances, and the matter is not already before the court on an application under section 63(4), the court may on the application of any party (upon notice to the other parties)—

(a)   determine the matter, or

(b)   order that it be determined by such means and upon such terms as the court may specify.

(3)   Subsection (1) has effect subject to any order of the court under section 24(4) or 25(3)(b) (order as to entitlement to fees or expenses in case of removal or resignation of arbitrator).

(4)   Nothing in this section affects any right of the arbitrator to payment of his fees and expenses.

65.—Power to limit recoverable costs.

(1)   Unless otherwise agreed by the parties, the tribunal may direct that the recoverable costs of the arbitration, or of any part of the arbitral proceedings, shall be limited to a specified amount.

(2)   Any direction may be made or varied at any stage, but this must be done sufficiently in advance of the incurring of costs to which it relates, or

the taking of any steps in the proceedings which may be affected by it, for the limit to be taken into account.

66.—Enforcement of the award.

(1)   An award made by the tribunal pursuant to an arbitration agreement may, by leave of the court, be enforced in the same manner as a judgment or order of the court to the same effect.

(2)   Where leave is so given, judgment may be entered in terms of the award.

(3)   Leave to enforce an award shall not be given where, or to the extent that, the person against whom it is sought to be enforced shows that the tribunal lacked substantive jurisdiction to make the award. The right to raise such an objection may have been lost (see section 73).

(4)   Nothing in this section affects the recognition or enforcement of an award under any other enactment or rule of law, in particular under Part II of the Arbitration Act 1950 (enforcement of awards under Geneva Convention) or the provisions of Part III of this Act relating to the recognition and enforcement of awards under the New York Convention or by an action on the award.

67.—Challenging the award: substantive jurisdiction.

(1)   A party to arbitral proceedings may (upon notice to the other parties and to the tribunal) apply to the court—

   (a)   challenging any award of the arbitral tribunal as to its substantive jurisdiction; or

   (b)   for an order declaring an award made by the tribunal on the merits to be of no effect, in whole or in part, because the tribunal did not have substantive jurisdiction. A party may lose the right to object (see section 73) and the right to apply is subject to the restrictions in section 70(2) and (3).

(2)   The arbitral tribunal may continue the arbitral proceedings and make a further award while an application to the court under this section is pending in relation to an award as to jurisdiction.

(3)   On an application under this section challenging an award of the arbitral tribunal as to its substantive jurisdiction, the court may by order—

   (a)   confirm the award,

   (b)   vary the award, or

   (c)   set aside the award in whole or in part.

(4)   The leave of the court is required for any appeal from a decision of the court under this section.

68.—Challenging the award: serious irregularity.

(1) A party to arbitral proceedings may (upon notice to the other parties and to the tribunal) apply to the court challenging an award in the proceedings on the ground of serious irregularity affecting the tribunal, the proceedings or the award.

A party may lose the right to object (see section 73) and the right to apply is subject to the restrictions in section 70(2) and (3).

(2) Serious irregularity means an irregularity of one or more of the following kinds which the court considers has caused or will cause substantial injustice to the applicant—

- (a) failure by the tribunal to comply with section 33 (general duty of tribunal);

- (b) the tribunal exceeding its powers (otherwise than by exceeding its substantive jurisdiction: see section 67);

- (c) failure by the tribunal to conduct the proceedings in accordance with the procedure agreed by the parties;

- (d) failure by the tribunal to deal with all the issues that were put to it;

- (e) any arbitral or other institution or person vested by the parties with powers in relation to the proceedings or the award exceeding its powers;

- (f) uncertainty or ambiguity as to the effect of the award;

- (g) the award being obtained by fraud or the award or the way in which it was procured being contrary to public policy;

- (h) failure to comply with the requirements as to the form of the award; or

- (i) any irregularity in the conduct of the proceedings or in the award which is admitted by the tribunal or by any arbitral or other institution or person vested by the parties with powers in relation to the proceedings or the award.

(3) If there is shown to be serious irregularity affecting the tribunal, the proceedings or the award, the court may—

- (a) remit the award to the tribunal, in whole or in part, for reconsideration,

- (b) set the award aside in whole or in part, or

- (c) declare the award to be of no effect, in whole or in part.

The court shall not exercise its power to set aside or to declare an award to be of no effect, in whole or in part, unless it is satisfied that it would be inappropriate to remit the matters in question to the tribunal for reconsideration.

(4)   The leave of the court is required for any appeal from a decision of the court under this section.

69.—Appeal on point of law.

(1)   Unless otherwise agreed by the parties, a party to arbitral proceedings may (upon notice to the other parties and to the tribunal) appeal to the court on a question of law arising out of an award made in the proceedings.

An agreement to dispense with reasons for the tribunal's award shall be considered an agreement to exclude the court's jurisdiction under this section.

(2)   An appeal shall not be brought under this section except—

(a)   with the agreement of all the other parties to the proceedings, or

(b)   with the leave of the court.

The right to appeal is also subject to the restrictions in section 70(2) and (3).

(3)   Leave to appeal shall be given only if the court is satisfied—

(a)   that the determination of the question will substantially affect the rights of one or more of the parties,

(b)   that the question is one which the tribunal was asked to determine,

(c)   that, on the basis of the findings of fact in the award—

(i)   the decision of the tribunal on the question is obviously wrong, or

(ii)   the question is one of general public importance and the decision of the tribunal is at least open to serious doubt, and

(d)   that, despite the agreement of the parties to resolve the matter by arbitration, it is just and proper in all the circumstances for the court to determine the question.

(4)   An application for leave to appeal under this section shall identify the question of law to be determined and state the grounds on which it is alleged that leave to appeal should be granted.

(5)   The court shall determine an application for leave to appeal under this section without a hearing unless it appears to the court that a hearing is required.

(6)   The leave of the court is required for any appeal from a decision of the court under this section to grant or refuse leave to appeal.

(7)   On an appeal under this section the court may by order—

(a)   confirm the award,

(b)   vary the award,

(c)   remit the award to the tribunal, in whole or in part, for reconsideration in the light of the court's determination, or

(d)   set aside the award in whole or in part.

The court shall not exercise its power to set aside an award, in whole or in part, unless it is satisfied that it would be inappropriate to remit the matters in question to the tribunal for reconsideration.

(8)   The decision of the court on an appeal under this section shall be treated as a judgment of the court for the purposes of a further appeal. But no such appeal lies without the leave of the court which shall not be given unless the court considers that the question is one of general importance or is one which for some other special reason should be considered by the Court of Appeal.

70.—Challenge or appeal: supplementary provisions.

(1)   The following provisions apply to an application or appeal under section 67, 68 or 69.

(2)   An application or appeal may not be brought if the applicant or appellant has not first exhausted—

(a)   any available arbitral process of appeal or review, and

(b)   any available recourse under section 57 (correction of award or additional award).

(3)   Any application or appeal must be brought within 28 days of the date of the award or, if there has been any arbitral process of appeal or review, of the date when the applicant or appellant was notified of the result of that process.

(4)   If on an application or appeal it appears to the court that the award—

(a)   does not contain the tribunal's reasons, or

(b)   does not set out the tribunal's reasons in sufficient detail to enable the court properly to consider the application or appeal, the court may order the tribunal to state the reasons for its award in sufficient detail for that purpose.

(5)   Where the court makes an order under subsection (4), it may make such further order as it thinks fit with respect to any additional costs of the arbitration resulting from its order.

(6)   The court may order the applicant or appellant to provide security for the costs of the application or appeal, and may direct that the application

or appeal be dismissed if the order is not complied with. The power to order security for costs shall not be exercised on the ground that the applicant or appellant is—

(a) an individual ordinarily resident outside the United Kingdom, or

(b) a corporation or association incorporated or formed under the law of a country outside the United Kingdom, or whose central management and control is exercised outside the United Kingdom.

(7) The court may order that any money payable under the award shall be brought into court or otherwise secured pending the determination of the application or appeal, and may direct that the application or appeal be dismissed if the order is not complied with.

(8) The court may grant leave to appeal subject to conditions to the same or similar effect as an order under subsection (6) or (7). This does not affect the general discretion of the court to grant leave subject to conditions.

71.—Challenge or appeal: effect of order of court.

(1) The following provisions have effect where the court makes an order under section 67, 68 or 69 with respect to an award.

(2) Where the award is varied, the variation has effect as part of the tribunal's award.

(3) Where the award is remitted to the tribunal, in whole or in part, for reconsideration, the tribunal shall make a fresh award in respect of the matters remitted within three months of the date of the order for remission or such longer or shorter period as the court may direct.

(4) Where the award is set aside or declared to be of no effect, in whole or in part, the court may also order that any provision that an award is a condition precedent to the bringing of legal proceedings in respect of a matter to which the arbitration agreement applies, is of no effect as regards the subject matter of the award or, as the case may be, the relevant part of the award.

72.—Saving for rights of person who takes no part in proceedings.

(1) A person alleged to be a party to arbitral proceedings but who takes no part in the proceedings may question—

(a) whether there is a valid arbitration agreement,

(b) whether the tribunal is properly constituted, or

(c) what matters have been submitted to arbitration in accordance with the arbitration agreement, by proceedings in the court for a declaration or injunction or other appropriate relief.

(2)   He also has the same right as a party to the arbitral proceedings to challenge an award—

    (a) by an application under section 67 on the ground of lack of substantive jurisdiction in relation to him, or

    (b) by an application under section 68 on the ground of serious irregularity (within the meaning of that section affecting him; and section 70(2) (duty to exhaust arbitral procedures) does not apply in his case.

73.—Loss of right to object.

(1)   If a party to arbitral proceedings takes part, or continues to take part, in the proceedings without making, either forthwith or within such time as is allowed by the arbitration agreement or the tribunal or by any provision of this Part, any objection—

    (a) that the tribunal lacks substantive jurisdiction,

    (b) that the proceedings have been improperly conducted,

    (c) that there has been a failure to comply with the arbitration agreement or with any provision of this Part, or

    (d) that there has been any other irregularity affecting the tribunal or the proceedings, he may not raise that objection later, before the tribunal or the court, unless he shows that, at the time he took part or continued to take part in the proceedings, he did not know and could not with reasonable diligence have discovered the grounds for the objection.

(2)   Where the arbitral tribunal rules that it has substantive jurisdiction and a party to arbitral proceedings who could have questioned that ruling—

    (a) by any available arbitral process of appeal or review, or

    (b) by challenging the award, does not do so, or does not do so within the time allowed by the arbitration agreement or any provision of this Part, he may not object later to the tribunal's substantive jurisdiction on any ground which was the subject of that ruling.

74.—Immunity of arbitral institutions, & c.

(1)   An arbitral or other institution or person designated or requested by the parties to appoint or nominate an arbitrator is not liable for anything done or omitted in the discharge or purported discharge of that function unless the act or omission is shown to have been in bad faith.

(2)   An arbitral or other institution or person by whom an arbitrator is appointed or nominated is not liable, by reason of having appointed or nominated him, for anything done or omitted by the arbitrator (or his

employees or agents) in the discharge or purported discharge of his functions as arbitrator.

(3) The above provisions apply to an employee or agent of an arbitral or other institution or person as they apply to the institution or person himself.

75.—Charge to secure payment of solicitors' costs.

The powers of the court to make declarations and orders under section 73 of the Solicitors Act 1974 or Article 71H of the Solicitors (Northern Ireland) Order 1976 (power to charge property recovered in the proceedings with the payment of solicitors' costs) may be exercised in relation to arbitral proceedings as if those proceedings were proceedings in the court.

76.—Service of notices, & c.

(1) The parties are free to agree on the manner of service of any notice or other document required or authorised to be given or served in pursuance of the arbitration agreement or for the purposes of the arbitral proceedings.

(2) If or to the extent that there is no such agreement the following provisions apply.

(3) A notice or other document may be served on a person by any effective means.

(4) If a notice or other document is addressed, pre-paid and delivered by post—

    (a) to the addressee's last known principal residence or, if he is or has been carrying on a trade, profession or business, his last known principal business address, or

    (b) where the addressee is a body corporate, to the body's registered or principal office, it shall be treated as effectively served.

(5) This section does not apply to the service of documents for the purposes of legal proceedings, for which provision is made by rules of court.

(6) References in this Part to a notice or other document include any form of communication in writing and references to giving or serving a notice or other document shall be construed accordingly.

77.—Powers of court in relation to service of documents.

(1) This section applies where service of a document on a person in the manner agreed by the parties, or in accordance with provisions of section 76 having effect in default of agreement, is not reasonably practicable.

(2) Unless otherwise agreed by the parties, the court may make such order as it thinks fit—

    (a) for service in such manner as the court may direct, or

(b)   dispensing with service of the document.

(3)   Any party to the arbitration agreement may apply for an order, but only after exhausting any available arbitral process for resolving the matter.

(4)   The leave of the court is required for any appeal from a decision of the court under this section.

78.—Reckoning periods of time.

(1)   The parties are free to agree on the method of reckoning periods of time for the purposes of any provision agreed by them or any provision of this Part having effect in default of such agreement.

(2)   If or to the extent there is no such agreement, periods of time shall be reckoned in accordance with the following provisions.

(3)   Where the act is required to be done within a specified period after or from a specified date, the period begins immediately after that date.

(4)   Where the act is required to be done a specified number of clear days after a specified date, at least that number of days must intervene between the day on which the act is done and that date.

(5)   Where the period is a period of seven days or less which would include a Saturday, Sunday or a public holiday in the place where anything which has to be done within the period falls to be done, that day shall be excluded.

In relation to England and Wales or Northern Ireland, a "public holiday" means Christmas Day, Good Friday or a day which under the Banking and Financial Dealings Act 1971 is a bank holiday.

79.—Power of court to extend time limits relating to arbitral proceedings.

(1)   Unless the parties otherwise agree, the court may by order extend any time limit agreed by them in relation to any matter relating to the arbitral proceedings or specified in any provision of this Part having effect in default of such agreement. This section does not apply to a time limit to which section 12 applies (power of court to extend time for beginning arbitral proceedings, & c.).

(2)   An application for an order may be made—

(a)   by any party to the arbitral proceedings (upon notice to the other parties and to the tribunal), or

(b)   by the arbitral tribunal (upon notice to the parties).

(3) The court shall not exercise its power to extend a time limit unless it is satisfied—

(a) that any available recourse to the tribunal, or to any arbitral or other institution or person vested by the parties with power in that regard, has first been exhausted, and

(b) that a substantial injustice would otherwise be done.

(4) The court's power under this section may be exercised whether or not the time has already expired.

(5) An order under this section may be made on such terms as the court thinks fit.

(6) The leave of the court is required for any appeal from a decision of the court under this section.

80.—Notice and other requirements in connection with legal proceedings.

(1) References in this Part to an application, appeal or other step in relation to legal proceedings being taken "upon notice" to the other parties to the arbitral proceedings, or to the tribunal, are to such notice of the originating process as is required by rules of court and do not impose any separate requirement.

(2) Rules of court shall be made—

(a) requiring such notice to be given as indicated by any provision of this Part, and

(b) as to the manner, form and content of any such notice.

(3) Subject to any provision made by rules of court, a requirement to give notice to the tribunal of legal proceedings shall be construed—

(a) if there is more than one arbitrator, as a requirement to give notice to each of them; and

(b) if the tribunal is not fully constituted, as a requirement to give notice to any arbitrator who has been appointed.

(4) References in this Part to making an application or appeal to the court within a specified period are to the issue within that period of the appropriate originating process in accordance with rules of court.

(5) Where any provision of this Part requires an application or appeal to be made to the court within a specified time, the rules of court relating to the reckoning of periods, the extending or abridging of periods, and the consequences of not taking a step within the period prescribed by the rules, apply in relation to that requirement.

(6)   Provision may be made by rules of court amending the provisions of this Part—

(a)   with respect to the time within which any application or appeal to the court must be made,

(b)   so as to keep any provision made by this Part in relation to arbitral proceedings in step with the corresponding provision of rules of court applying in relation to proceedings in the court, or

(c)   so as to keep any provision made by this Part in relation to legal proceedings in step with the corresponding provision of rules of court applying generally in relation to proceedings in the court.

(7)   Nothing in this section affects the generality of the power to make rules of court.

81.—Saving for certain matters governed by common law.

(1)   Nothing in this Part shall be construed as excluding the operation of any rule of law consistent with the provisions of this Part, in particular, any rule of law as to—

(a)   matters which are not capable of settlement by arbitration;

(b)   the effect of an oral arbitration agreement; or

(c)   the refusal of recognition or enforcement of an arbitral award on grounds of public policy.

(2)   Nothing in this Act shall be construed as reviving any jurisdiction of the court to set aside or remit an award on the ground of errors of fact or law on the face of the award.

82.—Minor definitions.

(1)   In this Part—

"arbitrator", unless the context otherwise requires, includes an umpire;

"available arbitral process", in relation to any matter, includes any process of appeal to or review by an arbitral or other institution or person vested by the parties with powers in relation to that matter;

"claimant", unless the context otherwise requires, includes a counterclaimant, and related expressions shall be construed accordingly;

"dispute" includes any difference;

"enactment" includes an enactment contained in Northern Ireland legislation;

"legal proceedings" means civil proceedings [in England and Wales in the High Court or the county court or in Northern Ireland] in the High Court or a county court;

"peremptory order" means an order made under section 41(5) or made in exercise of any corresponding power conferred by the parties;

"premises" includes land, buildings, moveable structures, vehicles, vessels, aircraft and hovercraft;

"question of law" means—

(a) for a court in England and Wales, a question of the law of England and Wales, and

(b) for a court in Northern Ireland, a question of the law of Northern Ireland; "substantive jurisdiction", in relation to an arbitral tribunal, refers to the matters specified in section 30(1)(a) to (c), and references to the tribunal exceeding its substantive jurisdiction shall be construed accordingly.

(2) References in this Part to a party to an arbitration agreement include any person claiming under or through a party to the agreement.

83.—Index of defined expressions: Part I

In this Part the expressions listed below are defined or otherwise explained by the provisions indicated—

agreement, agree and agreed	section 5(1)
agreement in writing	section 5(2) to (5)
arbitration agreement	sections 6 and 5(1)
arbitrator	section 82(1)
available arbitral process	section 82(1)
claimant	section 82(1)
commencement (in relation to arbitral proceedings)	section 14
costs of the arbitration	section 59
the court	section 105
dispute	section 82(1)
enactment	section 82(1)
legal proceedings	section 82(1)
Limitation Acts	section 13(4)
notice (or other document)	section 76(6)
party—	
—in relation to an arbitration agreement	section 82(2)
—where section 106(2) or (3) applies	section 106(4)
peremptory order	section 82(1) (and see section 41(5))
premises	section 82(1)
question of law	section 82(1)

recoverable costs	sections 63 and 64
seat of the arbitration	section 3
serve and service (of notice or other document)	section 76(6)
substantive jurisdiction (in relation to an arbitral tribunal)	section 82(1) (and see section 30(1)(a) to (c))
upon notice (to the parties or the tribunal)	section 80
written and in writing	section 5(6)

84.—Transitional provisions.

(1) The provisions of this Part do not apply to arbitral proceedings commenced before the date on which this Part comes into force.

(2) They apply to arbitral proceedings commenced on or after that date under an arbitration agreement whenever made.

(3) The above provisions have effect subject to any transitional provision made by an order under section 109(2) (power to include transitional provisions in commencement order).

PART II

OTHER PROVISIONS RELATING TO ARBITRATION

85.—Modification of Part I in relation to domestic arbitration agreement.

(1) In the case of a domestic arbitration agreement the provisions of Part I are modified in accordance with the following sections.

(2) For this purpose a "domestic arbitration agreement" means an arbitration agreement to which none of the parties is—

(a) an individual who is a national of, or habitually resident in, a state other than the United Kingdom, or

(b) a body corporate which is incorporated in, or whose central control and management is exercised in, a state other than the United Kingdom, and under which the seat of the arbitration (if the seat has been designated or determined) is in the United Kingdom.

(3) In subsection (2) "arbitration agreement" and "seat of the arbitration" have the same meaning as in Part I (see sections 3, 5(1) and 6).

86.—Staying of legal proceedings.

(1) In section 9 (stay of legal proceedings), subsection (4) (stay unless the arbitration agreement is null and void, inoperative, or incapable of being performed) does not apply to a domestic arbitration agreement.

(2) On an application under that section in relation to a domestic arbitration agreement the court shall grant a stay unless satisfied—

(a) that the arbitration agreement is null and void, inoperative, or incapable of being performed, or

(b) that there are other sufficient grounds for not requiring the parties to abide by the arbitration agreement.

(3) The court may treat as a sufficient ground under subsection (2)(b) the fact that the applicant is or was at any material time not ready and willing to do all things necessary for the proper conduct of the arbitration or of any other dispute resolution procedures required to be exhausted before resorting to arbitration.

(4) For the purposes of this section the question whether an arbitration agreement is a domestic arbitration agreement shall be determined by reference to the facts at the time the legal proceedings are commenced.

87.—Effectiveness of agreement to exclude court's jurisdiction.

(1) In the case of a domestic arbitration agreement any agreement to exclude the jurisdiction of the court under—

(a) section 45 (determination of preliminary point of law), or

(b) section 69 (challenging the award: appeal on point of law), is not effective unless entered into after the commencement of the arbitral proceedings in which the question arises or the award is made.

(2) For this purpose the commencement of the arbitral proceedings has the same meaning as in Part I (see section 14).

(3) For the purposes of this section the question whether an arbitration agreement is a domestic arbitration agreement shall be determined by reference to the facts at the time the agreement is entered into.

88.—Power to repeal or amend sections 85 to 87.

(1) The Secretary of State may by order repeal or amend the provisions of sections 85 to 87.

(2) An order under this section may contain such supplementary, incidental and transitional provisions as appear to the Secretary of State to be appropriate.

(3) An order under this section shall be made by statutory instrument and no such order shall be made unless a draft of it has been laid before and approved by a resolution of each House of Parliament.

89.—Application of unfair terms regulations to consumer arbitration agreements.

(1) The following sections extend the application of the Unfair Terms in Consumer Contracts Regulations 1994 in relation to a term which constitutes an arbitration agreement. For this purpose "arbitration agreement" means an agreement to submit to arbitration present or future disputes or differences (whether or not contractual).

(2) In those sections "the Regulations" means those regulations and includes any regulations amending or replacing those regulations.

(3) Those sections apply whatever the law applicable to the arbitration agreement.

90.—Regulations apply where consumer is a legal person.

The Regulations apply where the consumer is a legal person as they apply where the consumer is a natural person.

91.—Arbitration agreement unfair where modest amount sought.

(1) A term which constitutes an arbitration agreement is unfair for the purposes of the Regulations so far as it relates to a claim for a pecuniary remedy which does not exceed the amount specified by order for the purposes of this section.

(2) Orders under this section may make different provision for different cases and for different purposes.

(3) The power to make orders under this section is exercisable—

  (a) for England and Wales, by the Secretary of State with the concurrence of the Lord Chancellor,

  (b) for Scotland, by the Secretary of State [. . .], and

  (c) for Northern Ireland, by the Department of Economic Development for Northern Ireland with the concurrence of the Lord Chancellor.

(4) Any such order for England and Wales or Scotland shall be made by statutory instrument which shall be subject to annulment in pursuance of a resolution of either House of Parliament.

(5) Any such order for Northern Ireland shall be a statutory rule for the purposes of the Statutory Rules (Northern Ireland) Order 1979 and shall be subject to negative resolution, within the meaning of section 41(6) of the Interpretation Act (Northern Ireland) 1954.

* * *

93.—Appointment of judges as arbitrators.

(1) A judge of the Commercial Court or an official referee may, if in all the circumstances he thinks fit, accept appointment as a sole arbitrator or as umpire by or by virtue of an arbitration agreement.

(2) A judge of the Commercial Court shall not do so unless the Lord Chief Justice has informed him that, having regard to the state of business in the High Court and the Crown Court, he can be made available.

(3) An official referee shall not do so unless the Lord Chief Justice has informed him that, having regard to the state of official referees' business, he can be made available.

(4) The fees payable for the services of a judge of the Commercial Court or official referee as arbitrator or umpire shall be taken in the High Court.

(5) In this section—"arbitration agreement" has the same meaning as in Part I; and "official referee" means a person nominated under [section 68(1)(a) of the Senior Courts Act 1981] to deal with official referees' business.

(6) The provisions of Part I of this Act apply to arbitration before a person appointed under this section with the modifications specified in Schedule 2.

94.—Application of Part I to statutory arbitrations.

(1) The provisions of Part I apply to every arbitration under an enactment (a "statutory arbitration"), whether the enactment was passed or made before or after the commencement of this Act, subject to the adaptations and exclusions specified in sections 95 to 98.

(2) The provisions of Part I do not apply to a statutory arbitration if or to the extent that their application—

    (a) is inconsistent with the provisions of the enactment concerned, with any rules or procedure authorised or recognised by it, or

    (b) is excluded by any other enactment.

(3) In this section and the following provisions of this Part "enactment"—

    (a) in England and Wales, includes an enactment contained in subordinate legislation within the meaning of the Interpretation Act 1978;

    (b) in Northern Ireland, means a statutory provision within the meaning of section 1(f) of the Interpretation Act (Northern Ireland) 1954.

95.—General adaptation of provisions in relation to statutory arbitrations.

(1) The provisions of Part I apply to a statutory arbitration—

   (a) as if the arbitration were pursuant to an arbitration agreement and as if the enactment were that agreement, and

   (b) as if the persons by and against whom a claim subject to arbitration in pursuance of the enactment may be or has been made were parties to that agreement.

(2) Every statutory arbitration shall be taken to have its seat in England and Wales or, as the case may be, in Northern Ireland.

96.—Specific adaptations of provisions in relation to statutory arbitrations.

(1) The following provisions of Part I apply to a statutory arbitration with the following adaptations.

(2) In section 30(1) (competence of tribunal to rule on its own jurisdiction), the reference in paragraph (a) to whether there is a valid arbitration agreement shall be construed as a reference to whether the enactment applies to the dispute or difference in question.

(3) Section 35 (consolidation of proceedings and concurrent hearings) applies only so as to authorise the consolidation of proceedings, or concurrent hearings in proceedings, under the same enactment.

(4) Section 46 (rules applicable to substance of dispute) applies with the omission of subsection (1)(b) (determination in accordance with considerations agreed by parties).

97. Provisions excluded from applying to statutory arbitrations.

The following provisions of Part I do not apply in relation to a statutory arbitration—

   (a) section 8 (whether agreement discharged by death of a party);

   (b) section 12 (power of court to extend agreed time limits);

   (c) sections 9(5), 10(2) and 71(4) (restrictions on effect of provision that award condition precedent to right to bring legal proceedings).

98.—Power to make further provision by regulations.

(1) The Secretary of State may make provision by regulations for adapting or excluding any provision of Part I in relation to statutory arbitrations in general or statutory arbitrations of any particular description.

(2) The power is exercisable whether the enactment concerned is passed or made before or after the commencement of this Act.

(3) Regulations under this section shall be made by statutory instrument which shall be subject to annulment in pursuance of a resolution of either House of Parliament.

PART III

RECOGNITION AND ENFORCEMENT OF CERTAIN FOREIGN AWARDS

Enforcement of Geneva Convention awards

99.—Continuation of Part II of the Arbitration Act 1950.

Part II of the Arbitration Act 1950 (enforcement of certain foreign awards) continues to apply in relation to foreign awards within the meaning of that Part which are not also New York Convention awards.

Recognition and enforcement of New York Convention awards

100.—New York Convention awards.

(1) In this Part a "New York Convention award" means an award made, in pursuance of an arbitration agreement, in the territory of a state (other than the United Kingdom) which is a party to the New York Convention.

(2) For the purposes of subsection (1) and of the provisions of this Part relating to such awards—

(a) "arbitration agreement" means an arbitration agreement in writing, and

(b) an award shall be treated as made at the seat of the arbitration, regardless of where it was signed, despatched or delivered to any of the parties.

In this subsection "agreement in writing" and "seat of the arbitration" have the same meaning as in Part I.

(3) If Her Majesty by Order in Council declares that a state specified in the Order is a party to the New York Convention, or is a party in respect of any territory so specified, the Order shall, while in force, be conclusive evidence of that fact.

In this section "the New York Convention" means the Convention on the Recognition and Enforcement of Foreign Arbitral Awards adopted by the United Nations Conference on International Commercial Arbitration on 10th June 1958.

101.—Recognition and enforcement of awards.

(1) A New York Convention award shall be recognised as binding on the persons as between whom it was made, and may accordingly be relied on by those persons by way of defence, set-off or otherwise in any legal proceedings in England and Wales or Northern Ireland.

(2) A New York Convention award may, by leave of the court, be enforced in the same manner as a judgment or order of the court to the same effect.

As to the meaning of "the court" see section 105.

(3) Where leave is so given, judgment may be entered in terms of the award.

102.—Evidence to be produced by party seeking recognition or enforcement.

(1) A party seeking the recognition or enforcement of a New York Convention award must produce—

(a) the duly authenticated original award or a duly certified copy of it, and

(b) the original arbitration agreement or a duly certified copy of it.

(2) If the award or agreement is in a foreign language, the party must also produce a translation of it certified by an official or sworn translator or by a diplomatic or consular agent.

103.—Refusal of recognition or enforcement.

(1) Recognition or enforcement of a New York Convention award shall not be refused except in the following cases.

(2) Recognition or enforcement of the award may be refused if the person against whom it is invoked proves—

(a) that a party to the arbitration agreement was (under the law applicable to him) under some incapacity;

(b) that the arbitration agreement was not valid under the law to which the parties subjected it or, failing any indication thereon, under the law of the country where the award was made;

(c) that he was not given proper notice of the appointment of the arbitrator or of the arbitration proceedings or was otherwise unable to present his case;

(d) that the award deals with a difference not contemplated by or not falling within the terms of the submission to arbitration or contains decisions on matters beyond the scope of the submission to arbitration (but see subsection (4));

(e) that the composition of the arbitral tribunal or the arbitral procedure was not in accordance with the agreement of the parties or, failing such agreement, with the law of the country in which the arbitration took place;

(f) that the award has not yet become binding on the parties, or has been set aside or suspended by a competent authority of the country in which, or under the law of which, it was made.

(3)   Recognition or enforcement of the award may also be refused if the award is in respect of a matter which is not capable of settlement by arbitration, or if it would be contrary to public policy to recognise or enforce the award.

(4)   An award which contains decisions on matters not submitted to arbitration may be recognised or enforced to the extent that it contains decisions on matters submitted to arbitration which can be separated from those on matters not so submitted.

(5)   Where an application for the setting aside or suspension of the award has been made to such a competent authority as is mentioned in subsection (2)(f), the court before which the award is sought to be relied upon may, if it considers it proper, adjourn the decision on the recognition or enforcement of the award.

It may also on the application of the party claiming recognition or enforcement of the award order the other party to give suitable security.

104.—Saving for other bases of recognition or enforcement.

Nothing in the preceding provisions of this Part affects any right to rely upon or enforce a New York Convention award at common law or under section 66.

PART IV
GENERAL PROVISIONS

105.—Meaning of "the court": jurisdiction of High Court and county court.

(1)   In this Act "the court" [in relation to England and Wales means the High Court or the county court and in relation to Northern Ireland] means the High Court or a county court, subject to the following provisions.

(2)   The Lord Chancellor may by order make provision—

   (a)   allocating proceedings under this Act to the High Court or to county courts; or

   (b)   specifying proceedings under this Act which may be commenced or taken only in the High Court or in a county court.

(3)   The Lord Chancellor may by order make provision requiring proceedings of any specified description under this Act in relation to which a county court has jurisdiction to be commenced or taken in one or more specified county courts. Any jurisdiction so exercisable by a specified county court is exercisable throughout England and Wales, or as the case may be, Northern Ireland.

(4) An order under this section—

(a) may differentiate between categories of proceedings by reference to such criteria as the Lord Chancellor sees fit to specify, and

(b) may make such incidental or transitional provision as the Lord Chancellor considers necessary or expedient.

(5) An order under this section for England and Wales shall be made by statutory instrument which shall be subject to annulment in pursuance of a resolution of either House of Parliament.

(6) An order under this section for Northern Ireland shall be a statutory rule for the purposes of the Statutory Rules (Northern Ireland) Order 1979 which shall be subject to negative resolution (within the meaning of section 41(6) of the Interpretation Act (Northern Ireland) 1954).

106.—Crown application.

(1) Part I of this Act applies to any arbitration agreement to which Her Majesty, either in right of the Crown or of the Duchy of Lancaster or otherwise, or the Duke of Cornwall, is a party.

(2) Where Her Majesty is party to an arbitration agreement otherwise than in right of the Crown, Her Majesty shall be represented for the purposes of any arbitral proceedings—

(a) where the agreement was entered into by Her Majesty in right of the Duchy of Lancaster, by the Chancellor of the Duchy or such person as he may appoint, and

(b) in any other case, by such person as Her Majesty may appoint in writing under the Royal Sign Manual.

(3) Where the Duke of Cornwall is party to an arbitration agreement, he shall be represented for the purposes of any arbitral proceedings by such person as he may appoint.

(4) References in Part I to a party or the parties to the arbitration agreement or to arbitral proceedings shall be construed, where subsection (2) or (3) applies, as references to the person representing Her Majesty or the Duke of Cornwall.

107.—Consequential amendments and repeals.

(1) The enactments specified in Schedule 3 are amended in accordance with that Schedule, the amendments being consequential on the provisions of this Act.

(2) The enactments specified in Schedule 4 are repealed to the extent specified.

108.—Extent.

(1) The provisions of this Act extend to England and Wales and, except as mentioned below, to Northern Ireland.

(2) The following provisions of Part II do not extend to Northern Ireland—section 92 (exclusion of Part I in relation to small claims arbitration in the county court), and section 93 and Schedule 2 (appointment of judges as arbitrators).

(3) Sections 89, 90 and 91 (consumer arbitration agreements) extend to Scotland and the provisions of Schedules 3 and 4 (consequential amendments and repeals) extend to Scotland so far as they relate to enactments which so extend, subject as follows.

(4) The repeal of the Arbitration Act 1975 extends only to England and Wales and Northern Ireland.

109.—Commencement.

(1) The provisions of this Act come into force on such day as the Secretary of State may appoint by order made by statutory instrument, and different days may be appointed for different purposes.

(2) An order under subsection (1) may contain such transitional provisions as appear to the Secretary of State to be appropriate.

110. Short title.

This Act may be cited as the Arbitration Act 1996.

E. INDIAN ARBITRATION AND CONCILIATION ACT OF 1996 (SELECTED PROVISIONS)*

PREAMBLE

WHEREAS the United Nations Commission on International Trade Law (UNCITRAL) has adopted the UNCITRAL Model Law on International Commercial Arbitration in 1985;

AND WHEREAS the General Assembly of the United Nations has recommended that all countries give due consideration to the said Model Law, in view of the desirability of uniformity of the law of arbitral procedures and the specific needs of international commercial arbitration practice;

AND WHEREAS the UNCITRAL has adopted the UNCITRAL Conciliation Rules in 1980;

---

*   Text is available on http://www.kluwerarbitration.com/default.aspx. [Follow the link for "Legislation".]

AND WHEREAS the General Assembly of the United Nations has recommended the use of the said Rules in cases where a dispute arises in the context of international commercial relations and the parties seek an amicable settlement of that dispute by recourse to conciliation;

AND WHEREAS the said Model Law and Rules make significant contribution to the establishment of a unified legal framework for the fair and efficient settlement of disputes arising in international commercial relations;

AND WHEREAS it is expedient to make law respecting arbitration and conciliation, taking into account the aforesaid Model law and Rules;

BE it enacted by Parliament in the forty seventh year of the Republic as follows:

PRELIMINARY

1. Short title, extent and Commencement.

(1) This Act may be called the Arbitration and Conciliation Act, 1996.

(2) It extends to the whole of India:

Provided that Parts I, III and IV shall extend to the State of Jammu and Kashmir only in so far as they relate to international commercial arbitration or, as the case may be, international commercial conciliation.

Explanation. In this sub-section, the expression "international commercial conciliation" shall have the same meaning as the expression "international commercial arbitration" in clause (f) of sub-section (1) of Section 2, subject to the modification that for the word "arbitration" occurring therein, the word "conciliation" shall be substituted.

(3) It shall be deemed to have came into force on the 25th day of January, 1996.

PART I

ARBITRATION

CHAPTER I

GENERAL PROVISIONS

2. Definitions.

(1) In this Part, unless the context otherwise requires

(a) "Arbitration" means any arbitration whether or not administered by permanent arbitral institution;

(b) "Arbitration agreement" means an agreement referred to in Section 7;

(c) "Arbitral award" includes an interim award;

(d) "Arbitral tribunal" means a sole arbitrator or a panel of arbitrators;

(e) "Court" means the Principal Civil Court of original jurisdiction in a district and includes the High Court in exercise of its ordinary original civil jurisdiction having jurisdiction to decide the questions forming the subject matter of the arbitration if the same had been the subject matter of a suit, but does not include any Civil Court of a grade inferior to such principal Civil Court or any Court of Small Causes;

(f) "International commercial arbitration" means an arbitration relating to disputes arising out of legal relationships, whether contractual or not, considered as commercial under the law in force in India and where at least one of the parties is

(i) an individual who is a national of, or habitually resident in, any country other than India; or

(ii) a body corporate which is incorporated in any country other than India; or

(iii) a company or an association or a body of individuals whose central management and control is exercised in any country other than India; or

(iv) the Government of a foreign country;

(g) "legal representative" means a person who in law represents the estate of a deceased person, and includes any person who intermeddles with the estate of the deceased and, where a party acts in a representative character, the person on whom the estate devolves on the death of the party so acting;

(h) "party" means a party to an arbitration agreement.

Scope

(2) This Part shall apply where the place of arbitration is in India.

(3) This Part shall not affect any other law for the time being in force by virtue of which certain disputes may not be submitted to arbitration.

(4) This Part except sub-section (1) of Section 40, Sections 41 and 43 shall apply to every arbitration under any other enactment for the time being in force, as if the arbitration were pursuant to an arbitration agreement and as if that other enactment were an arbitration agreement, except in so far as the provisions of this part are inconsistent with that other enactment or with any rules made thereunder.

(5) Subject to the provisions of sub-section (4), and save in so far as is otherwise provided by any law for the time being in-force or in any

agreement in force between India and any other country or countries, this part shall apply to all arbitrations and to all proceedings relating thereto.

Construction of References

* * *

(7) An arbitral award made under this part shall be considered as a domestic award.

* * *

CHAPTER VI

MAKING OF ARBITRAL AWARD & TERMINATION OF PROCEEDINGS

28. Rules applicable to substance of dispute.

(1) Where the place of arbitration is situate in India,

    (a) in an arbitration other than an international commercial arbitration, the arbitral tribunal shall decide the dispute submitted to arbitration in accordance with the substantive law for the time being in force in India;

    (b) in international commercial arbitration,

        (i) the arbitral tribunal shall decide the dispute in accordance with the rules of law designated by the parties as applicable to the substance of the dispute;

        (ii) any designation by the parties of the law or legal system of a given country shall be construed, unless otherwise expressed, as directly referring to the substantive law of that country and not to its conflict of laws rules;

        (iii) failing any designation of the law under sub-clause (ii) by the parties, the arbitral tribunal shall apply the rules of law it considers to the appropriate given all the circumstances surrounding the dispute.

(2) The arbitral tribunal shall decide *ex aequo et bono* or as *amiable compositeur* only if the parties have expressly authorized it to do so.

(3) In all cases, the arbitral tribunal shall decide in accordance with the terms of the contract and shall take into account the usages of the trade applicable to the transaction.

* * *

CHAPTER VII

RECOURSE AGAINST ARBITRAL AWARD

34. Application for setting aside arbitral award.

(1) Recourse to a Court against an arbitral award may be made only by an application for setting aside such award in accordance with sub-section (2) and sub-section (3).

(2) An arbitral award may be set aside by the Court only if—

    (a) the party making the application furnishes proof that—

        (i) a party was under some incapacity; or

        (ii) the arbitration agreement is not valid under the law to which the parties have subjected it or, failing any indication thereon, under the law for the time being in force; or

        (iii) the party making the application was not given proper notice of the appointment of an arbitrator or of the arbitral proceedings or was otherwise unable to present his case; or

        (iv) the arbitral award deals with a dispute not contemplated by or not falling within the terms of the submission to arbitration, or it contains decisions on matters beyond the scope of the submission to arbitrations: Provided that, if the decisions on matters submitted to arbitration can be separated from those not so submitted, only the part of the arbitral award which contains decisions on matters not submitted to arbitration may be set aside; or

        (v) the composition of the arbitral tribunal or the arbitral procedure was not in accordance with the agreement of the parties, unless such agreement was in conflict with a provision of this Part from which the parties cannot derogate, or failing such agreement, was not in accordance with this Part; or

    (b) the Court finds that—

        (i) the subject matter of the dispute is not capable of settlement by arbitration under the law for the time being in force; or

        (ii) the arbitral award is in conflict with the public policy of India.

Explanation.

Without prejudice to the generality of sub-clause (ii) of clause (b), it is hereby declared, for the avoidance of any doubt, that an award is in conflict with the public policy of India. If the making of the award was induced or affected by fraud or corruption or was in violation of Section 75 or Section 81.

(3) An application for setting aside may not be made after three months have elapsed from the date on which the party making that application had received that arbitral award or, if a request had been made under Section 33, from the date on which that request had been disposed of by the arbitral tribunal:

Provided that if the Court is satisfied that the applicant was prevented by sufficient cause from making the application within the said period of three months it may entertain the application within a further period of thirty days, but not thereafter.

(4) On receipt of an application under sub-section (1), the Court may, where it is appropriate and it is so requested by a party, adjourn the proceedings for a period of time determined by it in order to give the arbitral tribunal an opportunity to resume the arbitral proceedings or to take such other action as in the opinion of arbitral tribunal will eliminate the grounds for setting aside the arbitral award.

CHAPTER VIII

FINALITY & ENFORCEMENT OF ARBITRAL AWARDS

35. Finality of arbitral awards.

Subject to this Part an arbitral award shall be final and binding on the parties and person claiming under them respectively.

* * *

PART II

ENFORCEMENT OF CERTAIN FOREIGN AWARDS

CHAPTER I

New York Convention awards

44. Definition.

In this Chapter, unless the context otherwise requires, "foreign award" means an arbitral award on differences between persons arising out of legal relationships, whether contractual or not, considered as commercial under the law in force in India, made on or after the 11th day of October, 1960.

(a) in pursuance of an agreement in writing for arbitration to which the Convention set forth in the First Schedule applies, and

(b) in one of such territories as the Central Government, being satisfied that reciprocal provisions have been made may, by notification in the Official Gazette, declare to be territories to which the said Convention applies.

45. Power of judicial authority to refer parties to arbitration.

Notwithstanding anything contained in Part I or in the Code of Civil Procedure, 1908, a judicial authority, when seized of an action in a matter in respect of which the parties have made an agreement referred to in Section 44, shall, at the request of one of the parties or any person claiming through or under him, refer the parties to arbitration, unless it finds that the said agreement is null and void, inoperative or incapable of being performed.

46. When foreign award binding.

Any foreign award which would be enforceable under this Chapter shall be treated as binding for all purposes on the persons as between whom it was made, and may accordingly be relied on by any of those persons by way of defense, set off or otherwise in any legal proceedings in India and any references in this Chapter to enforcing a foreign award shall be construed as including references to relying on an award.

47. Evidence.

(1) The party applying for the enforcement of a foreign award shall, at the time of the application, produce before the Court—

- (a) the original award or a copy thereof, duly authenticated in the manner required by the law of the country in which it was made;
- (b) the original agreement for arbitration or a duly certified copy thereof; and
- (c) such evidence as may be necessary to prove that the award is a foreign award.

(2) If the award or agreement to be produced under sub-section (1) is in a foreign language, the party seeking to enforce the award shall produce a translation into English certified as correct by a diplomatic or consular agent of the country to which that party belongs or certified as correct in such other manner as may be sufficient according to the law in force in India.

Explanation.

In this section and all the following sections of this Chapter, "Court" means the principal Civil Court of original jurisdiction in a district, and includes the High Court in exercise of its ordinary original civil jurisdiction, having jurisdiction over the subject matter of the award if the same had been the subject matter of a suit, but does not include any civil court of a grade inferior to such principal Civil Court, or any court of Small Causes.

48. Conditions for enforcement of foreign awards.

(1)   Enforcement of a foreign award may be refused, at the request of the party against whom it is invoked, only if that party furnishes to the Court proof that—

(a)   the parties to the agreement referred to in Section 44 were, under the law applicable to them, under some incapacity, or the said agreement is not valid under the law to which the parties have subjected it or, failing any indication thereon, under the law of the country where the award was made; or

(b)   the party against whom the award is invoked was not given proper notice of the appointment of the arbitrator or of the arbitral proceedings or was otherwise unable to present his case; or

(c)   the award deals with a difference not contemplated by or not falling within the terms of the submission to arbitration, or it contains decisions on matters beyond the scope of the submission to arbitration: Provided that, if the decisions on matters submitted to arbitration can be separated from those not so submitted, that part of the award which contains decisions on matters submitted to arbitration may be enforced; or

(d)   the composition of the arbitral authority or the arbitral procedure was not in accordance with the agreement of the parties, or, failing such agreement, was not in accordance with the law of the country where the arbitration took place; or

(e)   the award has not yet become binding on the parties, or has been set aside or suspended by a competent authority of the country in which, or under the law of which, that award was made.

(2)   Enforcement of an arbitral award may also be refused if the Court finds that—

(a)   the subject-matter of the difference is not capable of settlement by arbitration under the law of India; or

(b)   the enforcement of the award would be contrary to the public policy of India.

Explanation.

Without prejudice to the generality of clause (b) of this section, it is hereby declared, for the avoidance of any doubt, that an award is in conflict with the public policy of India if the making of the award was induced or affected by fraud or corruption.

(3)   If an application for the setting aside or suspension of the award has been made to a competent authority referred to in clause (e) of sub-section (1) the Court may, if it considers it proper, adjourn the decision on the enforcement of the award and may also, on the application of the party

claiming enforcement of the award, order the other party to give suitable security.

49. Enforcement of foreign awards.

Where the court is satisfied that the foreign award is enforceable under this chapter, the award shall be deemed to be a decree of that court.

50. Appealable orders.

(1) An appeal shall lie from the order refusing to

(a) refer the parties to arbitration under Section 45;

(b) enforce a foreign award under Section 48, to the court authorised by law to hear appeals from such order.

(2) No second appeal shall lie from an order passed in appeal under this section, but nothing in this section shall affect or take away any right to appeal to the Supreme Court.

51. Saving.

Nothing in this Chapter shall prejudice any rights which any person would have had of enforcing in India of any award or of availing himself in India of any award if this Chapter had not been enacted.

* * *

F. JAPAN: ARBITRATION LAW*

(Law No.138 of 2003)

Chapter I: GENERAL PROVISIONS

Article 1.   (Purpose)

Arbitral proceedings where the place of arbitration is in the territory of Japan and court proceedings in connection with arbitral proceedings shall, in addition to the provisions of other laws, follow those of this Law.

Article 2.   (Definitions)

(1) For the purposes of this Law, "arbitration agreement" shall mean an agreement by the parties to submit to one or more arbitrators the resolution of all or certain civil disputes which have arisen or which may arise in respect of a defined legal relationship (whether contractual or not) and to abide by their award (hereinafter referred to as "arbitral award").

(2) For the purposes of this Law, "arbitral tribunal" shall mean a sole arbitrator or a panel of two or more arbitrators, who, based on an arbitration agreement, conduct proceedings and make an arbitral award in respect of civil disputes subject thereto.

---

*   The act can be found at http://www.jseinc.org/en/laws/new_arbitration_act.html.

(3)   For the purposes of this Law, "written statement" shall mean a document that a party prepares and submits to an arbitral tribunal in arbitral proceedings and which states the case of that party.

Article 3.   (Scope of Application)

(1)   The provisions of Chapters II through VII and Chapters IX and X, except the provisions specified in the following paragraph and article 8, apply only if the place of arbitration is in the territory of Japan.

(2)   The provisions of article 14, paragraph (1) and article 15 apply when the place of arbitration is in or outside the territory of Japan, or when the place of arbitration is not designated.

(3)   The provisions of Chapter VIII apply when the place of arbitration is in or outside the territory of Japan.

Article 4.   (Court Intervention)

With respect to arbitral proceedings, no court shall intervene except where so provided in this Law.

Article 5.   (Court Jurisdiction)

(1)   Only the following courts have jurisdiction over cases concerning court proceedings based on the provisions of this Law:

(i)   the district court designated by the agreement of the parties;

(ii)   the district court having jurisdiction over the place of arbitration (only when the designated place of arbitration falls within the jurisdiction of a single district court); or

(iii)   the district court having jurisdiction over the general forum of the counterparty in the relevant case.

(2)   In the event that two or more courts have jurisdiction based on the provisions of this Law, the court to which the request was first made shall have jurisdiction.

(3)   The court shall, upon determining that the whole or a part of a case concerning court proceedings based on the provisions of this Law does not fall under its jurisdiction, upon request or by its own authority, transfer such case to a court with jurisdiction.

Article 6.   (Voluntary Oral Hearing)

Any decision concerning court proceedings based on the provisions of this Law may be made without an oral hearing.

Article 7.   (Appeal against Court Decision)

Any party with an interest affected by the decision concerning court proceedings based on the provisions of this Law may, only if specifically provided for by this Law, file an immediate appeal against the decision within the peremptory term of two weeks from the day on which notice is given.

Article 8.   (Court Intervention in the Event that the Place of Arbitration Has Not Been Designated)

(1)   Even if the place of arbitration has not been designated, each of the court applications cited in the following items may be made when there is a possibility that the place of arbitration will be in the territory of Japan and the applicant or counterparty's general forum (excluding designations based on the last address) is in the territory of Japan. In such case, according to the classifications cited in the respective items, the respective provisions shall apply:

(i)   an article 16, paragraph (3) application: same article;

(ii)   an article 17, paragraphs (2) through (5) application: same article;

(iii) an article 19, paragraph (4) application: articles 18 and 19; or

(iv) an article 20 application: same article.

(2)   Notwithstanding the provisions of article 5, paragraph (1), only the district courts having jurisdiction over the general forum described in the preceding paragraph have jurisdiction over the case relating to the applications cited in each of the items in the preceding paragraph.

Article 9.   (Reading   of   Case   Records   Relating   to   Court Proceedings)

A party with an interest in any court proceedings based on the provisions of this Law may request any of the following from the court clerk:

(i)   a reading of or a copy of the case records;

(ii)   a copy of the records produced by electronic, magnetic or any other means unrecognizable by natural sensory function in the case records;

(iii) the delivery of an authenticated copy, transcript or extract thereof; or

(iv) the delivery of a certificate regarding matters relating to the case.

Article 10.   (Application of the Code of Civil Procedure to Court Proceedings)

Except as otherwise provided, the provisions of the Code of Civil Procedure [Law No. 109 of 1996] shall apply to any court proceedings based on the provisions of this Law.

Article 11.   (Supreme Court Rules)

In addition to those provided by this Law, particulars necessary in relation to court proceedings based on the provisions of this Law shall be as prescribed by the Rules of the Supreme Court.

Article 12.   (Written Notice)

(1)   Unless otherwise agreed by the parties, when notice in arbitral proceedings is given in writing, it is deemed to have been given at the time it is delivered to the addressee personally, or, at the time it is delivered to the addressee's domicile, habitual residence, place of business, office or delivery address (which hereafter in this article means the place stipulated by the addressee as the place for delivery of documents from the sender).

(2)   With respect to a written notice in arbitral proceedings, where it is possible for the notice to be delivered to the addressee's domicile, habitual residence, place of business, office or delivery address, whereas it is difficult for the sender to obtain materials to certify that the delivery has been made, if the court considers it necessary, it may upon request of the sender decide to serve the notice itself. The provisions of article 104 and articles 110 through 113 of the Code of Civil Procedure shall not apply with respect to service in such an event.

(3)   The provisions of the preceding paragraph shall not apply in the event the parties have agreed that the service described in the same paragraph shall not be made.

(4)   The case concerning the request described in paragraph (2) shall be, notwithstanding the provisions of article 5, paragraph (1), subject only to the jurisdiction of the courts cited in items (i) and (ii) of the same paragraph and the district court with jurisdiction over the addressee's domicile, habitual residence, place of business, office or delivery address.

(5)   When notice in arbitral proceedings is given in writing, if none of the addressee's domicile, habitual residence, place of business, office or delivery address can be found after making a reasonable inquiry, unless otherwise agreed by the parties, it will suffice if the sender sends its notice to the addressee's last-known domicile, habitual residence, place of business, office or delivery address by registered letter or any other means by which the attempt to deliver it can be certified. In such case, a written notice is deemed to have been given at the normally expected time of its arrival.

(6)   The provisions of paragraph (1) and the preceding paragraph shall not apply to notices in court proceedings based on the provisions of this Law.

Chapter II: ARBITRATION AGREEMENT

Article 13. (Effect of Arbitration Agreement)

(1) Unless otherwise provided by law, an arbitration agreement shall be valid only when its subject matter is a civil dispute that may be resolved by settlement between the parties (excluding that of divorce or separation).

(2) The arbitration agreement shall be in the form of a document signed by all the parties, letters or telegrams exchanged between the parties (including those sent by facsimile device or other communication device for parties at a distance which provides the recipient with a written record of the transmitted content), or other written instrument.

(3) When a written contract refers to a document that contains an arbitration clause and the reference is such as to make that clause part of the contract, the arbitration agreement shall be in writing.

(4) When an arbitration agreement is made by way of electromagnetic record (records produced by electronic, magnetic or any other means unrecognizable by natural sensory function and used for data-processing by a computer) recording its content, the arbitration agreement shall be in writing.

(5) When the parties to the arbitral proceedings exchange written statements in which the existence of an arbitration agreement is alleged by one party and not denied by another, the arbitration agreement shall be in writing.

(6) Even if in a particular contract containing an arbitration agreement, any or all of the contractual provisions, excluding the arbitration agreement, are found to be null and void, cancelled or for other reasons invalid, the validity of the arbitration agreement shall not necessarily be affected.

Article 14. (Arbitration Agreement and Substantive Claim before Court)

(1) A court before which an action is brought in respect of a civil dispute which is the subject of an arbitration agreement shall, if the defendant so requests, dismiss the action. Provided, this shall not apply in the following instances:

(i)   when the arbitration agreement is null and void, cancelled, or for other reasons invalid;

(ii) when arbitration proceedings are inoperative or incapable of being performed based on the arbitration agreement; or

(iii) when the request is made by the defendant subsequent to the presentation of its statement in the oral hearing or in the preparations for argument proceedings on the substance of the dispute.

(2) An arbitral tribunal may commence or continue arbitral proceedings and make an arbitral award even while the action referred to in the preceding paragraph is pending before the court.

Article 15. (Arbitration Agreement and Interim Measures by Court)

It is not incompatible with an arbitration agreement for a party to request, before or during arbitral proceedings, from a court an interim measure of protection and for a court to grant such measure in respect of any civil dispute which is the subject of the arbitration agreement.

Chapter III: ARBITRATOR

Article 16. (Number of Arbitrators)

(1) The parties are free to determine the number of arbitrators.

(2) Failing such determination as provided for in the preceding paragraph, when there are two parties in an arbitration, the number of arbitrators shall be three.

(3) Failing such determination as provided for in paragraph (1), when there are three or more parties in an arbitration, the court shall determine the number of arbitrators upon request of a party.

Article 17. (Appointment of Arbitrators)

(1) The parties are free to agree on a procedure of appointing the arbitrators. Provided, this shall not apply to the provisions of paragraphs (5) and (6).

(2) Failing such agreement as provided for in the preceding paragraph, when there are two parties in an arbitration with three arbitrators, each party shall appoint one arbitrator, and the two arbitrators thus appointed shall appoint the third arbitrator. In such case, if a party fails to appoint an arbitrator within thirty days of a request to do so by the other party who has appointed an arbitrator, the appointment shall be made by the court upon the request of that party, or if the two arbitrators appointed by the parties fail to agree on the third arbitrator within thirty days of their appointment, upon the request of a party.

(3) Failing such agreement as provided in paragraph (1) or any agreement on the appointment of arbitrators between the parties, when there are two parties in an arbitration with a sole arbitrator, the court shall appoint an arbitrator upon the request of a party.

(4) Failing such agreement as provided for in paragraph (1) when there are three or more parties, the court shall appoint arbitrators upon the request of a party.

(5) Where, under an appointment procedure for arbitrators agreed upon by the parties as provided for in paragraph (1), arbitrators cannot be

appointed due to a failure to act as requested under such procedure or for any other reason, a party may request of the court the appointment of arbitrators.

(6) The court, in appointing arbitrators based on the provisions contained in paragraphs (2) through (5), shall have due regard to the following items:

(i)   the qualifications required of the arbitrators by the agreement of the parties;

(ii) the impartiality and independence of the appointees; and

(iii) in the case of a sole arbitrator or in the case where the two arbitrators appointed by the parties are to appoint the third arbitrator, whether or not it would be appropriate to appoint an arbitrator of a nationality other than those of the parties.

Article 18.   (Grounds for Challenge)

(1)   A party may challenge an arbitrator:

(i)   if it does not possess the qualifications agreed to by the parties; or

(ii) if circumstances exist that give rise to justifiable doubts as to its impartiality or independence.

(2)   A party who appointed an arbitrator, or made recommendations with respect to the appointment of an arbitrator, or participated in any similar acts, may challenge that arbitrator only for reasons of which it becomes aware after the appointment has been made.

(3)   When a person is approached in connection with its possible appointment as an arbitrator, it shall fully disclose any circumstances likely to give rise to justifiable doubts as to its impartiality or independence.

(4)   An arbitrator, during the course of arbitral proceedings, shall without delay disclose any circumstances likely to give rise to justifiable doubts as to its impartiality or independence (unless the parties have already been informed of them by the arbitrator).

Article 19.   (Challenge Procedure)

(1)   The parties are free to agree on a procedure for challenging an arbitrator. Provided, this shall not apply to the provisions of paragraph (4).

(2)   Failing an agreement as provided for in the proceeding paragraph, upon request of a party, the arbitral tribunal shall decide on the challenge.

(3)   A party who intends to make a request as provided for in the preceding paragraph shall, within fifteen days of the later of either the day on which it became aware of the constitution of the arbitral tribunal or the day on which it became aware of any circumstance referred to in any item

of paragraph (1) of the preceding article, send a written request describing the reasons for the challenge to the arbitral tribunal. In such case, the arbitral tribunal shall decide that grounds for challenge exist when it finds that grounds for challenge exist with respect to the arbitrator.

(4) If a challenge of the arbitrator under the procedure for challenge prescribed in the preceding three paragraphs is not successful, the challenging party may request within thirty days after having received notice of the decision rejecting the challenge, the court to decide on the challenge. In such case, the court shall decide that grounds for challenge exist when it finds that grounds for challenge exist with respect to the arbitrator.

(5) While a case relating to a challenge as prescribed in paragraph (4) is pending before the court, the arbitral tribunal may commence or continue the arbitral proceedings and make an arbitral award.

Article 20.   (Request for Removal)

Any party may request the court to decide on the removal of an arbitrator if any of the following grounds exist. In such case, if the court finds that the grounds for the request exist, it shall decide to remove the said arbitrator:

(i)   if the arbitrator becomes de jure or de facto unable to perform its functions; or

(ii) for reasons other than those in the proceeding item, if the arbitrator fails to act without undue delay.

Article 21.   (Termination of an Arbitrator's Mandate)

(1) An arbitrator's mandate shall terminate upon the occurrence of any of the following:

(i)   the death of an arbitrator;

(ii) the resignation of an arbitrator;

(iii) the removal of an arbitrator upon the agreement of the parties;

(iv) a decision that grounds for challenge exist under the procedure for challenge described in the provisions of article 19, paragraphs (1) through (4); or

(v)   a decision to remove an arbitrator based on the provisions of the preceding article.

(2) If, during the course of procedure for challenge under the provisions of article 19, paragraphs (1) through (4), or removal proceedings under the provisions of the preceding article, an arbitrator withdraws from its office or is removed upon the agreement of the parties, this alone does not imply the existence of any ground referred to in the items in article 18,

paragraph (1) or the items in the preceding article with respect to the arbitrator.

Article 22.   (Appointment of Substitute Arbitrator)

Unless otherwise agreed by the parties, where the mandate of an arbitrator terminates under any of the grounds described in each item of paragraph (1) of the preceding article, a substitute arbitrator shall be appointed according to the rules that were applicable to the appointment of the arbitrator being replaced.

Chapter IV: SPECIAL JURISDICTION OF ARBITRAL TRIBUNAL

Article 23.   (Competence of Arbitral Tribunal to Rule on its Jurisdiction)

(1)   The arbitral tribunal may rule on assertions made in respect of the existence or validity of an arbitration agreement or its own jurisdiction (which hereafter in this article means its authority to conduct arbitral proceedings and to make arbitral awards).

(2)   A plea that the arbitral tribunal does not have jurisdiction shall be raised promptly in the case where the grounds for the assertion arise during the course of arbitral proceedings, or in other cases before the time at which the first written statement on the substance of the dispute is submitted to the arbitral tribunal (including the time at which initial assertions on the substance of the dispute are presented orally at an oral hearing). Provided, the arbitral tribunal may admit a later plea if it considers the delay justified.

(3)   A party may raise the plea prescribed in the preceding paragraph even if it has appointed an arbitrator, or made recommendations with respect to the appointment of an arbitrator, or participated in any similar acts.

(4)   The arbitral tribunal shall give the following ruling or arbitral award, as the case may be, on a plea raised in accordance with paragraph (2):

(i)   a preliminary independent ruling or an arbitral award, when it considers it has jurisdiction; or

(ii)   a ruling to terminate arbitral proceedings, when it considers it has no jurisdiction.

(5)   If the arbitral tribunal gives a preliminary independent ruling that it has jurisdiction, any party may, within thirty days of receipt of notice of such ruling, request the court to decide the matter. In such an event, while such a request is pending before the court, the arbitral tribunal may continue the arbitral proceedings and make an arbitral award.

Article 24.   (Interim Measures of Protection)

(1)   Unless otherwise agreed by the parties, the arbitral tribunal may, at the request of a party, order any party to take such interim measure of protection as the arbitral tribunal may consider necessary in respect of the subject matter of the dispute.

(2)   The arbitral tribunal may order any party to provide appropriate security in connection with such measure as prescribed in the preceding paragraph.

Chapter V: COMMENCEMENT AND CONDUCT OF ARBITRAL PROCEEDINGS

Article 25.   (Equal Treatment of Parties)

(1)   The parties shall be treated with equality in the arbitral proceedings.

(2)   Each party shall be given a full opportunity of presenting its case in the arbitral proceedings.

Article 26.   (Rules of Procedure)

(1)   The parties are free to agree on the procedure to be followed by the arbitral tribunal in conducting the arbitral proceedings. Provided, it shall not violate the provisions of this Law relating to public policy.

(2)   Failing such agreement as prescribed in the preceding paragraph, the arbitral tribunal may, subject to the provisions of this Law, conduct the arbitral proceedings in such manner as it considers appropriate.

(3)   Failing such agreement as prescribed in paragraph (1), the power conferred upon the arbitral tribunal includes the power to determine the admissibility, relevance, materiality and weight of any evidence.

Article 27.   (Waiver of right to object)

Unless otherwise agreed by the parties, as to arbitral proceedings, a party who knows that any provision of this Law or any arbitral proceedings rules agreed upon by the parties (to the extent that none of these relate to public policy) has not been complied with and yet fails to state its objection to such non-compliance without delay (if a time limit by which objections should be made is provided for, within such period of time), shall be deemed to have waived its right to object.

Article 28.   (Place of arbitration)

(1)   The parties are free to agree on the place of arbitration.

(2)   Failing such agreement as prescribed in the preceding paragraph, the place of arbitration shall be determined by the arbitral tribunal having regard to the circumstances of the case, including the convenience of the parties.

(3) Notwithstanding the place of arbitration determined in accordance with the provisions of the preceding two paragraphs, the arbitral tribunal may, unless otherwise agreed by the parties, carry out the following procedures at any place it considers appropriate:

(i)   consultation among the members of the arbitral tribunal;

(ii) hearing of parties, experts or witnesses; and

(iii) inspection of goods, other property or documents.

Article 29. (Commencement of arbitral proceedings and interruption of limitation)

(1) Unless otherwise agreed by the parties, the arbitral proceedings in respect of a particular civil dispute commence on the date on which one party gave the other party notice to refer that dispute to the arbitral proceedings.

(2) A claim made in arbitral proceedings shall give rise to an interruption of limitation. Provided, this shall not apply where the arbitral proceedings have been terminated for a reason other than the issuance of an arbitral award.

Article 30.   (Language)

(1) The parties are free to agree on the language or languages to be used in the arbitral proceedings and the proceedings to be conducted using that language or those languages.

(2) Failing such agreement as prescribed in the preceding paragraph, the arbitral tribunal shall determine the language or languages to be used in the arbitral proceedings and the proceedings to be conducted using that language or those languages.

(3) Failing any designation of proceedings to be conducted using the designated language or languages in the agreement prescribed in paragraph (1) or the determination prescribed in the preceding paragraph, the proceedings to be conducted using such language or languages are as follows:

(i)   any oral proceedings;

(ii) any statement or notice in writing by a party; or

(iii) any ruling (including an arbitral award) or notice in writing by the arbitral tribunal.

(4) The arbitral tribunal may order that any documentary evidence shall be accompanied by a translation into the language or languages designated in the agreement as prescribed in paragraph (1) or the determination prescribed in paragraph (2) (where designation has been

made as to the language or languages to be used for translation, such language or languages).

Article 31. (Time Restrictions on Parties' Statements)

(1) Within the period of time determined by the arbitral tribunal, the claimant (which hereinafter means the party that carried out the act to commence the arbitral proceedings) shall state the relief or remedy sought, the facts supporting its claim and the points at issue. In such case, the claimant may submit all documentary evidence it considers to be relevant or may add a reference to the documentary evidence or other evidence it will submit.

(2) Within the period of time determined by the arbitral tribunal, the respondent (which hereinafter means any party to the arbitral proceedings other than the claimant) shall state its defense in respect of the particulars stated according to the provisions of the preceding paragraph. In such case, the provisions of the latter part of the same paragraph shall apply.

(3) Any party may amend or supplement its statement during the course of the arbitral proceedings. Provided, the arbitral tribunal may refuse to allow such amendment or supplementation if made in delay.

(4) The preceding three paragraphs shall not apply when otherwise agreed by the parties.

Article 32.   (Procedure of the Hearing)

(1) The arbitral tribunal may hold oral hearings for the presentation of evidence or for oral argument by the parties. Provided, where a party makes an application for holding oral hearings, including the request in article 34, paragraph (3), the arbitral tribunal shall hold such oral hearings at an appropriate stage of the arbitral proceedings.

(2) The preceding paragraph shall not apply when otherwise agreed by the parties.

(3) When holding oral hearings for the purposes of oral argument or inspection of goods, other property or documents, the arbitral tribunal shall give sufficient advance notice to the parties of the time and place for such hearings.

(4) A party who supplied written statements, documentary evidence or any other records to the arbitral tribunal shall take necessary measures to ensure that the other party will be aware of their contents.

(5) The arbitral tribunal shall take necessary measures to ensure that all parties will be aware of the contents of any expert report or other evidence on which the arbitral tribunal may rely in making an arbitral award or other rulings.

Article 33. (Default of a Party)

(1) If the claimant violates the provisions of article 31, paragraph (1), the arbitral tribunal shall make a ruling to terminate the arbitral proceedings. Provided, this shall not apply in the case where there is sufficient cause for the violation.

(2) If the respondent violates the provisions of article 31, paragraph (2), the arbitral tribunal shall continue the arbitral proceedings without treating such violation in itself as an admission of the claimant's allegations.

(3) If any party fails to appear at an oral hearing or to produce documentary evidence, the arbitral tribunal may make the arbitral award on the evidence before it that has been collected up until such time. Provided, this shall not apply in the case where there is sufficient cause with respect to the failure to appear at an oral hearing or to produce documentary evidence.

(4) The preceding three paragraphs shall not apply when otherwise agreed by the parties.

Article 34. (Expert Appointed by Arbitral Tribunal)

(1) The arbitral tribunal may appoint one or more experts to appraise any necessary issues and to report their findings in writing or orally.

(2) In the case of the preceding paragraph, the arbitral tribunal may require a party to do the following acts:

(i) give the expert any relevant information; or

(ii) produce, or provide access to, any relevant documents, goods or other property to the expert for inspection.

(3) If a party so requests or if the arbitral tribunal considers it necessary, the expert shall, after delivery of its report described in paragraph (1), participate in an oral hearing.

(4) A party may carry out the following acts in the oral hearing described in the preceding paragraph:

(i) put questions to the expert; or

(ii) have experts whom it has personally appointed to testify on the points at issue.

(5) Each of the preceding paragraphs shall not apply when otherwise agreed by the parties.

Article 35. (Court Assistance in Taking Evidence)

(1) The arbitral tribunal or a party may apply to a court for assistance in taking evidence by any means that the arbitral tribunal considers necessary as entrustment of investigation, examination of witnesses,

expert testimony, investigation of documentary evidence (excluding documents that the parties may produce in person) or inspection (excluding that of objects the parties may produce in person) prescribed in the Code of Civil Procedure. Provided, this shall not apply in the case where the parties have agreed not to apply for all or some of these means.

(2)   In making the application described in the preceding paragraph, the party shall obtain the approval of the arbitral tribunal.

(3)   Notwithstanding the provisions of article 5, paragraph (1), only the following courts have jurisdiction over cases relating to the application described in paragraph (1):

(i)   the court described in article 5, paragraph (1), item (ii);

(ii)   the district court having jurisdiction over the domicile or place of residence of the person to be examined or the person holding the relevant documents, or the location of the object for inspection; or

(iii) the district court having jurisdiction over the general forum of the applicant or the counterparty (only if there is no court described in the preceding two items).

(4)   An immediate appeal may be made against the decision regarding the application in paragraph (1).

(5)   When the court carries out the examination of evidence based on the application in paragraph (1), the arbitrators may peruse the documents, inspect the objects and, with the approval of the presiding judge, put questions to the witness or expert (as prescribed in article 213 of the Code of Civil Procedure).

(6)   The court clerk shall enter in the record the matters concerning the examination of evidence carried out by the court following the application prescribed in paragraph (1).

Chapter VI: ARBITRAL AWARD AND TERMINATION OF ARBITRAL PROCEEDINGS

Article 36.   (Substantive Law to be Applied in Arbitral Award)

(1)   The arbitral tribunal shall decide the dispute in accordance with such rules of law as are agreed by the parties as applicable to the substance of the dispute. In such case, any designation of the law or legal system of a given State shall be construed, unless otherwise expressed, as directly referring to the substantive law of that State and not to its conflict of laws rules.

(2)   Failing agreement as provided in the preceding paragraph, the arbitral tribunal shall apply the substantive law of the State with which the civil dispute subject to the arbitral proceedings is most closely connected.

(3) Notwithstanding the provisions prescribed in the preceding two paragraphs, the arbitral tribunal shall decide ex aequo et bono only if the parties have expressly authorized it to do so.

(4) Where there is a contract relating to the civil dispute subject to the arbitral proceedings, the arbitral tribunal shall decide in accordance with the terms of such contract and shall take into account the usages, if any, that may apply to the civil dispute.

Article 37. (Proceedings by Panel of Arbitrators)

(1) An arbitral tribunal with more than one arbitrator shall elect a presiding arbitrator from among all its members.

(2) Any decision of the arbitral tribunal shall be made by a majority of all its members.

(3) Notwithstanding the provisions prescribed in the preceding paragraph, procedural matters in arbitral proceedings may be decided by the presiding arbitrator, if so authorized by the parties or all other members of the arbitral tribunal.

(4) The provisions of the preceding three paragraphs shall not apply when otherwise agreed by the parties.

Article 38. (Settlement)

(1) If, during arbitral proceedings, the parties settle the civil dispute subject to the arbitral proceedings and the parties so request, the arbitral tribunal may make a ruling on agreed terms.

(2) The ruling as provided for in the preceding paragraph shall have the same effect as an arbitral award.

(3) The ruling as provided for in paragraph (1) shall be made in writing in accordance with paragraphs (1) and (3) of the following article and shall state that it is an arbitral award.

(4) An arbitral tribunal or one or more arbitrators designated by it may attempt to settle the civil dispute subject to the arbitral proceedings, if consented to by the parties.

(5) Unless otherwise agreed by the parties, the consent provided for in the preceding paragraph or its withdrawal shall be made in writing.

Article 39. (Arbitral Award)

(1) The arbitral award shall be made in writing and shall be signed by the arbitrators who made it. Provided, in arbitral proceedings with more than one arbitrator, the signatures of the majority of all members of the arbitral tribunal shall suffice, if the reason for any omitted signature is stated.

(2) The arbitral award shall state the reasons upon which it is based. Provided, this shall not apply when otherwise agreed by the parties.

(3)   The arbitral award shall state its date and place of arbitration.

(4)   The arbitral award shall be deemed to have been made at the place of arbitration.

(5)   After the arbitral award is made, the arbitral tribunal shall notify each party of the arbitral award by sending a copy of the arbitral award signed by the arbitrators.

(6)   The proviso of paragraph (1) shall apply to the copy of the arbitral award described in the preceding paragraph.

Article 40.   (Termination of Arbitral Proceedings)

(1)   The arbitral proceedings are terminated by the arbitral award or by a ruling to terminate the arbitral proceedings.

(2)   Other than rulings based on the provisions of article 23, paragraph (4), item (ii) or article 33, paragraph (1), the arbitral tribunal shall issue a ruling to terminate arbitral proceedings in the case where any of the following grounds exists:

(i)   the claimant withdraws its claim. Provided, this shall not apply in the event that the respondent objects thereto and the arbitral tribunal recognizes a legitimate interest on its part in obtaining a settlement of the civil dispute subject to the arbitral proceedings;

(ii)   the parties agree to on termination of the arbitral proceedings;

(iii) the parties settle the civil dispute subject to the arbitral proceedings (excluding the case where a ruling under article 38, paragraph (1) is issued); or

(iv) other than the instances in the preceding three items, the arbitral tribunal finds that the continuation of the arbitral proceedings has become unnecessary or impossible.

(3)   The mandate of the arbitral tribunal terminates with the termination of the arbitral proceedings. Provided, the acts prescribed in the provisions of articles 41 through 43 may be made.

Article 41.   (Correction of Arbitral Award)

(1)   The arbitral tribunal may upon request of a party or by its own authority correct any errors in computation, any clerical or typographical errors or any errors of similar nature in the arbitral award.

(2)   Unless otherwise agreed by the parties, the request described in the preceding paragraph shall be made within thirty days of the receipt of the notice of the arbitral award.

(3)   When making the request described in paragraph (1), a party shall issue advance or simultaneous notice to the other party stating the content of the request.

(4)   The arbitral tribunal shall make a ruling with respect to the request described in paragraph (1) within thirty days of such request.

(5)   The arbitral tribunal may extend, if it considers it necessary, the period of time provided for in the preceding paragraph.

(6)   The provisions of article 39 shall apply to any ruling to correct the arbitral award or any ruling to dismiss the request in paragraph (1).

Article 42. (Interpretation of Arbitral Award by Arbitral Tribunal)

(1)   A party may request the arbitral tribunal to give an interpretation of a specific part of the arbitral award.

(2)   The request described in the preceding paragraph may be made only if so agreed by the parties.

(3)   The provisions of paragraphs (2) and (3) of the preceding article shall apply to the request described in paragraph (1) and the provisions of article 39 and paragraphs (4) and (5) of the preceding article shall apply to any rulings made with respect to the request described in paragraph (1).

Article 43.   (Additional Arbitral Award)

(1)   Unless otherwise agreed by the parties, a party may request the arbitral tribunal to make an arbitral award as to claims presented in the arbitral proceedings but omitted from the arbitral award. In such case, the provisions of article 41, paragraphs (2) and (3) shall apply.

(2)   The arbitral tribunal shall make a ruling with respect to the request described in the preceding paragraph within sixty days of such request. In such case, the provisions of article 41, paragraph (5) shall apply.

(3)   The provisions of article 39 shall apply to the ruling described in the preceding paragraph.

Chapter VII: SETTING ASIDE OF ARBITRAL AWARD

Article 44.

(1)   A party may apply to a court to set aside the arbitral award when any of the following grounds are present:

(i)   the arbitration agreement is not valid due to limits to a party's capacity;

(ii)   the arbitration agreement is not valid for a reason other than limits to a party's capacity under the law to which the parties have agreed to subject it (or failing any indication thereon, under the law of Japan);

(iii) the party making the application was not given notice as required by the provisions of the laws of Japan (or where the parties have otherwise reached an agreement on matters concerning the provisions of the law that do not relate to the public policy, such agreement) in the proceedings to appoint arbitrators or in the arbitral proceedings;

(iv) the party making the application was unable to present its case in the arbitral proceedings;

(v)   the arbitral award contains decisions on matters beyond the scope of the arbitration agreement or the claims in the arbitral proceedings;

(vi) the composition of the arbitral tribunal or the arbitral proceedings were not in accordance with the provisions of the laws of Japan (or where the parties have otherwise reached an agreement on matters concerning the provisions of the law that do not relate to the public policy, such agreement);

(vii) the claims in the arbitral proceedings relate to a dispute that cannot constitute the subject of an arbitration agreement under the laws of Japan; or

(viii) the content of the arbitral award is in conflict with the public policy or good morals of Japan.

(2)   The application described in the preceding paragraph may not be made after three months have elapsed from the date on which the party making the application had received the notice by the sending of a copy of the arbitral award (including the document constituting the ruling of the arbitral tribunal described in the provisions of articles 41 through 43), or after an enforcement decision under article 46 has become final and conclusive.

(3)   Even where the case for application described in paragraph (1) falls within its jurisdiction, a court may, upon request or by its own authority, if it finds it appropriate, transfer all or a part of said case to another competent court.

(4)   An immediate appeal may be filed against a decision made under the provisions of article 5, paragraph (3) or the preceding paragraph regarding the case for application described in paragraph (1).

(5)   A court may not make a decision with respect to the application described in paragraph (1), unless and until an oral hearing or oral proceeding at which the parties can attend was held.

(6)   Where an application is made under paragraph (1), an arbitral award may be set aside by the court in the event that it finds any of the grounds described in each of the items under the same paragraph to be present (with respect to the grounds described in items (i) through (vi) of the same paragraph, this shall be limited to where the party making the application has proved the existence of such grounds).

(7)   Where the ground described in paragraph (1), item (v) is present, and where the part relating to matters prescribed in the same item can be

separated from the arbitral award, only that part of the arbitral award may be set aside by the court.

(8)   An immediate appeal may be filed against the decision regarding the application in paragraph (1).

Chapter VIII: RECOGNITION AND ENFORCEMENT DECISION OF ARBITRAL AWARD

Article 45.   (Recognition of Arbitral Award)

(1)   An arbitral award (irrespective of whether or not the place of arbitration is in the territory of Japan; this shall apply throughout this chapter) shall have the same effect as a final and conclusive judgment. Provided, an enforcement based on the arbitral award shall be subject to an enforcement decision pursuant to the provisions of the following article.

(2)   The provisions of the preceding paragraph do not apply in the case where any of the following grounds are present (with respect to the grounds described in items (i) through (vii), this shall be limited to where either of the parties has proven the existence of the ground in question):

(i)   the arbitration agreement is not valid due to limits to a party's capacity;

(ii)   the arbitration agreement is not valid for a reason other than limits to a party's capacity under the law to which the parties have agreed to subject it (or failing any indication thereon, the law of the country under which the place of arbitration falls);

(iii) a party was not given notice as required by the provisions of the law of the country under which the place of arbitration falls (or where the parties have otherwise reached an agreement on matters concerning the provisions of the law that do not relate to public policy, such agreement) in the proceedings to appoint arbitrators or in the arbitral proceedings;

(iv)   a party was unable to present its case in the arbitral proceedings;

(v)   the arbitral award contains decisions on matters beyond the scope of the arbitration agreement or the claims in the arbitral proceedings;

(vi) the composition of an arbitral tribunal or the arbitral proceedings were not in accordance with the provisions of the law of the country under which the place of arbitration falls (or where the parties have otherwise reached an agreement on matters concerning the provisions of the law that do not relate to public policy, such agreement);

(vii)   according to the law of the country under which the place of arbitration falls (or where the law of a country other than the country under which the place of arbitration falls was applied to the arbitral proceedings, such country), the arbitral award has not yet become binding, or the arbitral award has been set aside or suspended by a court of such country;

(viii) the claims in the arbitral proceedings relate to a dispute that cannot constitute the subject of an arbitration agreement under the laws of Japan; or

(ix) the content of the arbitral award would be contrary to the public policy or good morals of Japan.

(3) Where the ground described in item (v) of the preceding paragraph is present, and where the part relating to matters described in the same item can be separated from the arbitral award, said part and any other parts in the arbitral award shall be deemed separate independent arbitral awards and the provisions of the preceding paragraph shall apply accordingly.

Article 46.   (Enforcement Decision of Arbitral Award)

(1) A party seeking enforcement based on the arbitral award may apply to a court for an enforcement decision (which hereinafter means a decision authorizing enforcement based on an arbitral award) against the debtor as counterparty.

(2) The party making the application described in the preceding paragraph shall supply a copy of the arbitral award, a document certifying that the content of said copy is identical to the arbitral award, and a Japanese translation of the arbitral award (except where made in Japanese).

(3) If an application for setting aside or suspension of an arbitral award has been made to the court as described in paragraph (2), item (vii) of the preceding article, the court where the application described in paragraph (1) has been made may, if it considers it necessary, suspend proceedings relating to the application described in paragraph (1). In such case, the court may, upon request of the party who made the application described in the same paragraph, order the other party to provide security.

(4) The case for application described in paragraph (1) shall be, notwithstanding the provisions of article 5, paragraph (1), subject only to the jurisdiction of the courts cited in each of the items of the same paragraph and a district court with jurisdiction over the location of the object of the claim or the debtor's seizable assets.

(5) Even where the case for application described in paragraph (1) falls within its jurisdiction, a court may, upon request or by its own authority, if it finds it appropriate, transfer all or a part of said case to another competent court.

(6) An immediate appeal may be filed against a decision made under the provisions of article 5, paragraph (3) or the preceding paragraph regarding the case for application described in paragraph (1).

(7) The court shall, except where it dismisses the application described in paragraph (1) pursuant to the provisions of the following paragraph or paragraph (9), issue an enforcement decision.

(8) The court may dismiss the application described in paragraph (1) only when it finds any of the grounds described in each of the items under paragraph (2) of the preceding article present (with respect to the grounds described in items (i) through (vii) of the same paragraph, this shall be limited to where the counterparty has proved the existence of the ground in question).

(9) The provisions of paragraph (3) of the preceding article shall apply with respect to the application of the provisions of the preceding paragraph in the event that the ground described in paragraph (2), item (v) of the same article is present.

(10) The provisions of article 44, paragraphs (5) and (8) shall apply with respect to decisions regarding the application described in paragraph (1).

Chapter IX: MISCELLANEOUS

Article 47. (Remuneration of Arbitrators)

(1) The arbitrators may receive remuneration in accordance with the agreement of the parties.

(2) Failing an agreement as described in the preceding paragraph, the arbitral tribunal shall determine the remuneration of the arbitrators. In such case, the remuneration shall be for an appropriate amount.

Article 48. (Deposit for the Costs of the Arbitral Proceedings)

(1) Unless otherwise agreed by the parties, the arbitral tribunal may order that the parties deposit an amount determined by the arbitral tribunal as the roughly estimated amount for costs of the arbitral proceedings within the appropriate period of time determined by the arbitral tribunal.

(2) Where such deposits, as ordered under the provisions of the preceding paragraph, have not been made, unless otherwise agreed by the parties, the arbitral tribunal may suspend or terminate the arbitral proceedings.

Article 49. (Apportionment of the Costs of the Arbitral Proceedings)

(1) The costs disbursed by the parties with respect to the arbitral proceedings shall be apportioned between the parties in accordance with the agreement of the parties.

(2) Failing an agreement as described in the preceding paragraph, each party shall bear the costs it has disbursed with respect to the arbitral proceedings.

(3) In accordance with the agreement of the parties, if any, the arbitral tribunal may, in an arbitral award or in an independent ruling, determine the apportionment between the parties of the costs disbursed by the parties with respect to the arbitral proceedings and the amount that one party should reimburse to the other party based thereon.

(4) If the matters described in the preceding paragraph have been determined in an independent ruling, such ruling shall have the same effect as an arbitral award.

(5) The provisions of article 39 shall apply to the ruling described in the preceding paragraph.

Chapter X: PENALTIES

Article 50. (Acceptance of Bribe; Acceptance with Request; Acceptance in Advance of Assumption of Office)

(1) An arbitrator who accepts, demands or promises to accept a bribe in relation to its duty shall be punished by imprisonment with labor for not more than five years. In such case, when the arbitrator agrees to do an act in response to a request, imprisonment with labor for not more than seven years shall be imposed.

(2) When a person to be appointed an arbitrator accepts, demands or promises to accept a bribe in relation to the duty to assume with agreement to do an act in response to a request, imprisonment with labor for not more than five years shall be imposed in the event of appointment.

Article 51.   (Bribe to Third Person)

When an arbitrator with agreement to do an act in response to a request, causes a bribe in relation to its duty to be given to a third person or demands or promises such bribe to be given to a third person, imprisonment with labor for not more than five years shall be imposed.

Article 52.   (Aggravated Acceptance; Acceptance after Resignation of Office)

(1) When an arbitrator commits a crime described in the preceding two articles and consequently acts illegally or refrains from acting in the exercise of its duty, imprisonment labor for a definite term of not less than one year shall be imposed.

(2) The provisions of the preceding paragraph shall apply when an arbitrator accepts, demands or promises to accept a bribe, or cause a bribe to be given to a third person or demands or promises a bribe to be given to a third person, in relation to having acted illegally or refrained from acting in the exercise of its duty.

(3) When a person who was an arbitrator accepts, demands or promises to accept a bribe in relation to having acted illegally or refrained

from acting in the exercise of its duty during its tenure as an arbitrator with agreement thereof in response to a request, imprisonment with labor for not more than five years shall be imposed.

Article 53. (Confiscation and Collection of Equivalent Value)

A bribe accepted by an offender or by a third person with such knowledge shall be confiscated. When the whole or a part of the bribe cannot be confiscated, a sum of money equivalent thereto shall be collected.

Article 54. (Giving a Bribe)

A person who gives, offers or promises to give a bribe as provided for in articles 50 through 52 shall be punished by imprisonment with labor for not more than three years or a fine of not more than two million five hundred thousand yen.

Article 55. (Crimes Committed Outside Japan)

(1) The provisions of articles 50 through 53 shall apply to an offender who commits any of the crimes described in articles 50 through 52 outside Japan.

(2) The crime described in the preceding article shall be treated in the same manner as provided in article 2 of the Criminal Code [Law No. 45 of 1907].

Supplementary Provisions

Article 1.   (Date of Enforcement)

This Law shall come into force from the date which shall be fixed by a Cabinet Order no later than nine months from the date of the promulgation of this Law.

Article 2.   (Transitory Measures Relating to Form of Arbitration Agreement)

The existing Law shall apply to the form for arbitration agreements which have been made prior to the enforcement of this Law.

Article 3.   (Exception Relating to Arbitration Agreements Concluded between Consumers and Businesses)

(1) For the time being until otherwise enacted, any arbitration agreements (excluding arbitration agreements described in the following article; hereafter in this article referred to as the "consumer arbitration agreement") concluded between consumers (which hereafter in this article shall mean consumers as described in article 2, paragraph (1) of the Consumer Contract Act [Law No. 61 of 2000]) and businesses (which hereafter in this article shall mean businesses as described in article 2, paragraph (2) of the same law) subsequent to the enforcement of this Law, the subject of which constitutes civil disputes that may arise between them

in the future, shall follow the provisions described in paragraphs (2) through (7).

(2) A consumer may cancel a consumer arbitration agreement. Provided, this shall not apply in the event that the consumer is a claimant in arbitral proceedings based on the consumer arbitration agreement.

(3) In the case where a business is the claimant in arbitral proceedings based on a consumer arbitration agreement, following the constitution of an arbitral tribunal the business shall request without delay that an oral hearing be conducted under the provisions of article 32, paragraph (1). In such case the arbitral tribunal shall make a ruling to carry out the oral hearing and notify the parties of the date, time and place therefor.

(4) The arbitral tribunal shall carry out the oral hearing described in the preceding paragraph prior to any other proceedings in the arbitral proceedings.

(5) Notice to the party who is a consumer based on the provisions of paragraph (3) shall be made by the sending of a document stating the following matters. In such case, the arbitral tribunal shall make every effort to use as simple an expression as possible with respect to matters described in items (ii) through (v):

(i)   date, time and place of the oral hearing;

(ii) that in the case where an arbitration agreement exists, the arbitral award with respect to the civil dispute constituting its subject shall have the same effect as a final and conclusive judgment of the court;

(iii) that in the case where an arbitration agreement exists, any suit filed with the court in respect of the civil dispute constituting its subject will be dismissed irrespective of the timing when the suit is filed before or after the arbitral award;

(iv) that the consumer may cancel the consumer arbitration agreement; and

(v) that in the event that the party who is the consumer fails to appear on the date of the oral hearing described in item (i), said party shall be deemed to have cancelled the consumer arbitration agreement.

(6) On the day of the oral hearing described in paragraph (3), the arbitral tribunal shall explain the matters described in items (ii) through (iv) of the preceding paragraph orally to the party who is a consumer. In such case, where the party does not express an intent to waive its right of cancellation described in paragraph (2), said party shall be deemed to have cancelled the consumer arbitration agreement.

(7)   In the event that the party who is a consumer fails to appear on the date of the oral hearing described in paragraph (3), said party shall be deemed to have cancelled the consumer arbitration agreement.

Article 4.   (Exception Relating to Arbitration Agreements Concerning Individual Labor-related Disputes)

For the time being until otherwise enacted, any arbitration agreements concluded following the enforcement of this Law, the subject of which constitutes individual labor-related disputes (which means individual labor-related disputes as described in article 1 of the Law on Promoting the Resolution of Individual Labor Disputes [Law No.112 of 2001]) that may arise in the future, shall be null and void.

Article 5.   (Transitional Measures Relating to Arbitral Proceedings)

Arbitral proceedings commenced prior to the enforcement of this Law and proceedings conducted by a court relating to such arbitral proceedings (excluding proceedings commenced after the issuance of an arbitral award) shall follow the existing Law.

Article 6.   (Transitional Measures Relating to Lawsuits for the Challenge against Arbitrators)

In addition to the provisions in the preceding article, the existing Law shall apply to suits for challenges against arbitrators brought prior to the enforcement of this Law.

Article 7.   (Transitional Measures Relating to the Request for the Challenge against Arbitrators to the Arbitral Tribunal)

In addition to the provisions of the preceding two articles, with respect to the request of the provisions of article 19, paragraph (3) in the case where the parties, prior to the enforcement of this Law, were aware of the fact that an arbitral tribunal had been formed and of the existence of any of the grounds referred to in any of the items of article 18, paragraph (1) for any arbitrator, the words "the later of either the day on which it became aware of the constitution of the arbitral tribunal or the day on which it became aware of any circumstance referred to in any item of paragraph (1) of the preceding article" in article 19, paragraph (3) shall be read as "the date on which this Law came into force".

Article 8.   (Transitional Measures Relating to the Force and Effect of Arbitral Awards)

In the case where an arbitral award had been issued prior to the enforcement of this Law, its deposit to a court, its force and effect, suits to set it aside, and enforcement based thereon, shall follow the existing Law.

Articles 9 through 22 [Omitted]

G. RUSSIAN ARBITRATION ACT OF JULY 7, 1993*

The present Act shall:

proceed from the recognition of the usefulness of arbitration (mediation) as a method widely applied in the settlement of disputes arising in international trade, and the need for complex regulation of international commercial arbitration in conformity with the law; take account of the provisions on such arbitration contained in the international treaties of the RF and in the Model Law on International Commercial Arbitration adopted in 1985 by the UN Commission on International Trade Law, and approved by the UN General Assembly, for possible use by states in their legislation.

Chapter I. GENERAL

Article 1. Scope of Application

1. The present Act shall apply to international commercial arbitration, if the place of arbitration is in the territory of the RF. However, the provisions of Articles 8, 9, 35 and 36 shall also apply in the cases in which the place of arbitration is abroad.

2. The following may be referred to international commercial arbitration pursuant to agreement between the parties: disputes arising from contractual and other civil-law relations in foreign-trade and other types of international economic relationships, where any of the parties has its place of business abroad, and also disputes between enterprises with foreign investments and international associations and organizations founded on RF territory, disputes between their participants, and disputes with other subjects of RF law.

3. For the purposes of Clause 2 of this Article:

if a party has more than one place of business, the place of business is that which has the closest relationship to the arbitration agreement;

if a party does not have a place of business, reference is to be made to his habitual residence.

4. The present Act shall not affect any other law of the RF by virtue of which certain disputes may not be submitted to arbitration or may be submitted to arbitration only according to provisions other than those of this Act.

---

*   A new draft is before Russian legislator and it is expected to come into force in 2016.

5.   Where an international treaty of the RF lays down rules other than those contained in RF arbitration law, the rules of the international treaty shall apply.

Article 2.   Definitions and Rules of Interpretation

For the purposes of this Act:

(a) "arbitration" means any arbitration whether or not administered by a permanent arbitral institution, notably, by the International Commercial Arbitration Court or by the Maritime Arbitration Commission under the RF Chamber of Commerce and Industry (Annexes I and II to this Act);

(b) "arbitral tribunal" (mediation) means a sole arbitrator or a panel of arbitrators;

(c) "court" means a body or organ of the judicial system of the state;

(d) where a provision of this Act, except Article 28, leaves the parties free to determine a certain issue, such freedom shall include the right of the parties to authorize a third party, including an institution, to make that determination;

(e) where a provision of this Act refers to the fact that the parties have agreed or that they may agree, or in any other way refers to an agreement of the parties, such agreement shall include any arbitration rules referred to in that agreement;

(f)   where a provision of this Act, other than Articles 25(a) and 32(2)(a) refers to a claim, it shall also apply to a counter-claim, and where it refers to a defense, it shall also apply to a defense to such counter-claim.

Article 3.   Receipt of Written Communications

1.   Unless otherwise agreed by the parties:

(a) any written communication shall be deemed to have been received if it is delivered to the addressee personally or if it is delivered at his place of business, habitual residence or mailing address; if none of these can be found after making a reasonable inquiry, a written communication shall be deemed to have been received if it is sent to the addressee's last-known place of business, habitual residence or mailing address by registered letter or any other means which provides a record of the attempt to deliver it;

(b) the communication shall be deemed to have been received on the day it is so delivered.

2.   The provisions of this Article shall not apply to communications in court proceedings.

Article 4.   Waiver of Right to Object

A party who knows that any provision of this Act from which the parties may derogate or any requirement under the arbitration agreement has not been complied with, and yet proceeds with the arbitration without stating his objection to such non-compliance without undue delay or, if a time limit is provided therefore, within such period of time, shall be deemed to have waived his right to object.

Article 5.   Extent of Court Intervention

In matters governed by this Act, no court shall intervene, except where such provision is contained in this Act.

Article 6.   Court or Other Authority for Certain Functions of Arbitration Assistance and Supervision

1.   The functions referred to in Articles 11(3), 11(4), 13(3) and 14 shall be performed by the President of the RF, Chamber of Commerce and Industry.

2.   The functions referred to in Articles 16(3) and 34(2) shall be performed by the Supreme Court of the republic within the RF. Territorial, regional or city court, the court of the autonomous region, and the court of the autonomous area in the place of arbitration.

Chapter II. ARBITRATION AGREEMENT

Article 7.   Definition and Form of Arbitration Agreement

1.   "Arbitration agreement" shall be an agreement by the parties to submit to arbitration all or certain disputes which have arisen or which may arise between them in respect of a defined legal relationship, whether contractual or not. An arbitration agreement may be in the form of an arbitration clause in a contract or in the form of a separate agreement.

2.   The arbitration agreement shall be in writing. An agreement is in writing if it is contained in a document signed by the parties or in an exchange of letters, telex, telegrams or other means of telecommunications which provide a record of the agreement, or in an exchange of statements of claim and defense in which the existence of an agreement is alleged by one party and not denied by another. A reference in the contract to a document containing an arbitration clause shall be an arbitration contract, provided the contract is in writing and the reference is such as to make that clause part of the contract.

Article 8.   Arbitration Agreement and Substantive Claim Before Court

1.   A court before which an action is brought in a matter which is the subject of an arbitration agreement shall, if a party so requests not later than when submitting his first statement on the substance of the dispute,

refer the parties to arbitration unless it finds that the agreement is null and void, inoperative and incapable of being performed.

2.   Where an action referred to in Paragraph 1 of this Article has been brought, arbitral proceedings may nevertheless be commenced or continued, and an award may be made, while the issue is pending before the court.

Article 9.   Arbitration Agreement and Interim Measures by Court

It shall not be incompatible with an arbitration agreement for a party to request, before or during arbitral proceedings, from a court an interim measure of protection, and for a court to grant such measure.

Chapter III.COMPOSITION OF ARBITRAL TRIBUNAL

Article 10.   Number of Arbitrators

1.   The parties shall be free to determine the number of arbitrators.

2.   Failing such determination, the number of arbitrators shall be three.

Article 11.   Appointment of Arbitrators

1.   No person shall be precluded by reason of his citizenship from acting as an arbitrator, unless otherwise agreed by the parties.

2.   The parties shall be free to agree on a procedure of appointing the arbitrator or arbitrators, subject to the provisions of Paragraphs 4 and 5 of this Article.

3.   Failing such agreement:

(a)   in an arbitration with three arbitrators, each party shall appoint one arbitrator, and the two arbitrators thus appointed shall appoint the third arbitrator; if a party fails to appoint the arbitrator within thirty days of receipt of a request to do so from the other party, or if the two arbitrators fail to agree on the third arbitrator within thirty days of their appointment, the appointment shall be made, upon request of a party, by the court or other authority specified in Article 6(1);

(b)   in an arbitration with a sole arbitrator, if the parties are unable to agree on the arbitrator, he shall be appointed, upon request of a party, by the court or other authority specified in Article 6(1).

4.   Where, under an appointment procedure agreed upon by the parties:

(a)   a party fails to act as required under such procedure, or

(b)   the parties or two arbitrators are unable to reach an agreement expected of them under such procedure, or

(c)   a third party, including an institution, fails to perform any function entrusted to it under such procedure,

any party may request a court or other authority specified in Article 6(1) to take the necessary measures, unless the agreement on the appointment procedure provides other means for securing the appointment.

5.   A decision on a matter entrusted by Paragraph 3 or 4 of this Article to the authority specified in Article 6(1) shall be subject to no appeal. This authority, in appointing an arbitrator, shall have due regard to any qualifications required of the arbitrator by the agreement of the parties and to such considerations as are likely to secure the appointment of an independent and impartial arbitrator and, in the case of a sole or third arbitrator, shall take into account as well the advisability of appointing an arbitrator of a citizenship other than those of the parties.

Article 12.   Grounds for Challenge

1.   When a person is approached in connection with his possible appointment as an arbitrator, he shall disclose any circumstances likely to give rise to justifiable doubts as to his impartiality or independence. An arbitrator, from the time of his appointment and throughout the arbitral proceedings, shall without delay disclose any such circumstances to the parties unless they have already been informed of them by him.

2.   An arbitrator may be challenged only if circumstances exist that give rise to justifiable doubts as to his impartiality or independence, or if he does not possess qualifications agreed to by the parties. A party may challenge an arbitrator appointed by him, or in whose appointment he has participated, only for reasons of which he becomes aware after the appointment has been made.

Article 13.   Challenge Procedure

1.   The parties shall be free to agree on a procedure for challenging an arbitrator, subject to the provisions of Paragraph 3 of this Article.

2.   Failing such agreement, a party who intends to challenge an arbitrator shall, within fifteen days after becoming aware of the constitution of the arbitral tribunal or after becoming aware of any circumstances referred to in Article 12(2), send a written statement of the reasons for the challenge to the arbitral tribunal. Unless the challenged arbitrator withdraws from his office or the other party agrees to the challenge, the arbitral tribunal shall decide on the challenge.

If a challenge under any procedure agreed upon by the parties or under the procedure of Paragraph 2 of this Article is not successful, the challenging party may request, within thirty days after having received notice of the decision rejecting the challenge, the authority specified in Article 6(1) to take a decision on the challenge, which decision shall be subject to no appeal; while such a request is pending, the arbitral tribunal, including the challenged arbitrator, may continue the arbitral proceedings and make an award.

Article 14.   Termination of Arbitrator's Mandate

1.   If an arbitrator becomes de jure or de facto unable to perform his functions or for other reasons fails to act without undue delay, his mandate terminates if he withdraws from his office or if the parties agree on the termination. Otherwise, if a controversy remains concerning any of these grounds, any party may request the authority specified in Article 6(1) to decide on the termination of the mandate, which decision shall be subject to no appeal.

2.   If, under this Article or Article 13(2), an arbitrator withdraws from his office or a party agrees to the termination of the mandate of an arbitrator, this shall not imply acceptance of the validity of any ground referred to in this Article or Article 12(2).

Article 15.   Appointment of Substitute Arbitrator

Where the mandate of an arbitrator terminates under Article 13 or 14, or because of his withdrawal from office for any other reason, or because of the revocation of his mandate by agreement of the parties, or in any other case of termination of his mandate, a substitute arbitrator shall be appointed according to the rules that were applicable to the appointment of the arbitrator being replaced.

Chapter IV. JURISDICTION OF ARBITRAL TRIBUNAL

Article 16.   Competence of Arbitral Tribunal to Rule on Its Jurisdiction

1.   The arbitral tribunal may rule on its own jurisdiction, including any objections with respect to the existence or validity of the arbitration agreement. For that purpose, an arbitration clause which forms part of a contract shall be treated as an agreement independent of the other terms of the contract. A decision by the arbitral tribunal that the contract is null and void shall not entail ipso jure the invalidity of the arbitration clause.

2.   A plea that the arbitral tribunal does not have jurisdiction shall be raised not later than the submission of the statement of defense. A party shall not be precluded from raising such a plea by the fact that he has appointed, or participated in the appointment of, an arbitrator. A plea that the arbitral tribunal is exceeding the scope of its authority shall be raised as soon as the matter alleged to be beyond the scope of its authority is raised during the arbitral proceedings. The arbitral tribunal may, in either case, admit a later plea if it considers the delay justified.

3.   The arbitral tribunal may rule on a plea referred to in Paragraph 2 of this Article either as a preliminary question or in an award on the merits. If the arbitral tribunal rules as a preliminary question that it has jurisdiction, any party may request, within thirty days after having received notice on that ruling, the court specified in Article 6(2) to decide

the matter, which decision shall be subject to no appeal; while such a request is pending, the arbitral tribunal may continue the arbitral proceedings and make an award.

Article 17.   Power of Arbitral Tribunal to Order Interim Measures

Unless otherwise agreed by the parties, the arbitral tribunal may, at the request of a party, order any party to take such interim measures of protection as the arbitral tribunal may consider necessary in respect of the subject-matter of the dispute. The arbitral tribunal may require any party to provide appropriate security in connection with such measures.

Chapter V.   CONDUCT OF ARBITRAL PROCEEDINGS

Article 18.   Equal Treatment of Parties

The parties shall be treated with equality and each party shall be given a full opportunity of presenting his case.

Article 19.   Determination of Rules of Procedure

1.   Subject to the provisions of this Act, the parties shall be free to agree on the procedure to be followed by the arbitral tribunal in conducting the proceedings.

2.   Failing such agreement, the arbitral tribunal may, subject to the provisions of this Act, conduct the arbitration in such manner as it considers appropriate. The powers conferred upon the arbitral tribunal shall include the power to determine the admissibility, relevance, materiality and weight of any evidence.

Article 20.   Place of Arbitration

1.   The parties shall be free to agree on the place of arbitration. Failing such agreement, the place of arbitration shall be determined by the arbitral tribunal having regard to the circumstances of the case, including the convenience of the parties.

2.   Notwithstanding the provisions of Paragraph 1 of this Article, the arbitral tribunal may, unless otherwise agreed by the parties, meet at any place it considers appropriate for consultation among its members, for hearing witnesses, experts or the parties, or for inspection of goods, other property or documents.

Article 21.   Commencement of Arbitral Proceedings

Unless otherwise agreed by the parties, the arbitral proceedings in respect of a particular dispute shall commence on the date on which a request for that dispute to be referred to arbitration is received by the respondent.

Article 22. Language

1.   The parties shall be free to agree on the language or languages to be used in the arbitral proceedings. Failing such agreement, the arbitral tribunal shall determine the language or languages to be used in the proceedings. This agreement or determination, unless otherwise specified therein, shall apply to any written statement by a party, any hearing and any award, decision or other communication by the arbitral tribunal.

2.   The arbitral tribunal may order that any documentary evidence shall be accompanied by a translation into the language or languages agreed upon by the parties or determined by the arbitral tribunal.

Article 23. Statements of Claim and Defense

1.   Within the period of time agreed by the parties or determined by the arbitral tribunal, the claimant shall state the facts supporting his claim, the points at issue, and the relief or remedy sought, and the respondent shall state his defense in respect of these particulars, unless the parties have otherwise agreed as to the required elements of such statements. The parties may submit with their statements all documents they consider to be relevant or may add a reference to the document or other evidence they will submit.

2.   Unless otherwise agreed by the parties, either party may amend or supplement his claim or defense during the course of the arbitral proceedings, unless the arbitral tribunal considers it inappropriate to allow such amendment, having regard to the delay in making it.

Article 24. Hearings and Written Proceedings

1.   Subject to any contrary agreement by the parties, the arbitral tribunal shall decide whether to hold oral hearings for the presentation of evidence or for oral argument, or whether the proceedings shall be conducted on the basis of documents and other materials. However, unless the parties have agreed that no hearings shall be held, the arbitral tribunal shall hold such hearings at an appropriate stage of the proceedings, if so requested by a party.

2.   The parties shall be given sufficient advance notice of any hearing and of any meeting of the arbitral tribunal for the purposes of inspection of goods, other property or documents.

3.   All statements, documents or other information supplied to the arbitral tribunal by one party shall be communicated to the other party. Any expert report or evidentiary document on which the arbitral tribunal may rely in making its decisions shall also be communicated to the parties.

Article 25. Default of a Party

Unless otherwise agreed by the parties, if, without showing sufficient cause:

(a) the claimant fails to communicate his statement of claim in accordance with Article 23(1), the arbitral tribunal shall terminate the proceedings;

(b) the respondent fails to communicate his statement of defense in accordance with Article 23(1), the arbitral tribunal shall continue the proceedings without treating such failure in itself as an admission of the claimant's allegations;

(c) any party fails to appear at a hearing or to produce documentary evidence, the arbitral tribunal may continue the proceedings and make the award on the evidence before it.

Article 26.   Expert Appointed by Arbitral Tribunal

1.   Unless otherwise agreed by the parties, the arbitral tribunal:

(a) may appoint one or more experts to report to it on specific issues to be determined by the arbitral tribunal;

(b) may require a party to give the expert any relevant information or to produce, or to provide access to, any relevant documents, goods or other property for his inspection.

2.   Unless otherwise agreed by the parties, if a party so requests or if the arbitral tribunal considers it necessary, the expert shall, after delivery of his written or oral report, participate in a hearing where the parties have the opportunity to put questions to him and to present expert witnesses in order to testify on the points at issue.

Article 27.   Court Assistance in Taking Evidence

The arbitral tribunal or a party with the approval of the arbitral tribunal may request assistance from a competent RF court in taking evidence. The court may execute the request within its competence and according to its rules on taking evidence.

Chapter VI. MAKING OF AWARD AND TERMINATION OF PROCEEDINGS

Article 28.   Rules Applicable to Substance of Dispute

1.   The arbitral tribunal shall decide the dispute in accordance with such rules of law as are chosen by the parties as applicable to the substance of the dispute. Any designation of the law or legal system of a given state shall be construed as directly referring to the substantive law and not to its conflict-of-laws rules.

2.   Failing any designation by the parties, the arbitral tribunal shall apply the law determined by the conflict-of-laws rules which it considers applicable.

3. In all cases, the arbitral tribunal shall decide in accordance with the terms of the contract and shall take into account the usages of the trade applicable to the transaction.

Article 29. Decision-Making by Panel of Arbitrators

In arbitral proceedings with more than one arbitrator, any decision of the arbitral tribunal shall be made, unless otherwise agreed by the parties, by a majority of all its members. However, questions of procedure may be decided by a presiding arbitrator, if so authorized by the parties or all members of the arbitral tribunal.

Article 30. Settlement

1. If, during arbitral proceedings, the parties settle the dispute, the arbitral tribunal shall terminate the proceeding and, if requested by the parties and not objected to by the arbitral tribunal, record the settlement in the form of an arbitral award on agreed terms.

2. An award on agreed terms shall be made in accordance with the provisions of Article 31 and shall state that it is an award. Such an award shall have the same status and effect as any other award on the merits of the case.

Article 31. Form and Content of Award

1. The award shall be made in writing and shall be signed by the arbitrator or arbitrators. In arbitral proceedings with more than one arbitrator, the signatures of the majority of all members of the arbitral tribunal shall suffice, provided that the reason for any omitted signature is stated.

2. The award shall state the reasons upon which it is based, the conclusion on satisfaction or denial of claim, the amount of arbitration charge, the arbitration costs, and their apportionment between the parties.

3. The award shall state its date and the place of arbitration, as determined in accordance with Article 20(1). The award shall be deemed to have been made at that place.

4. After the award is made, a copy signed by the arbitrators in accordance with Paragraph 1 of this Article shall be delivered to each party.

Article 32. Termination of Proceedings

1. The arbitral proceedings shall be terminated by the final award or by an order of the arbitral tribunal in accordance with Paragraph 2 of this Article.

2. The arbitral tribunal shall issue an order for the termination of the arbitral proceedings when:

(a) the claimant withdraws his claim, unless the respondent objects thereto and the arbitral tribunal recognizes a legitimate interest on his part in obtaining a final settlement of the dispute;

(b) the parties agree on the termination of the proceedings;

(c) the arbitral tribunal finds that the continuation of the proceedings has for any other reasons become unnecessary or impossible.

3. The mandate of the arbitral tribunal shall terminate with the termination of the arbitral proceedings, subject to the provisions of Article 33 and 34(4).

Article 33. Correction and Interpretation of Award. Additional Award

1. Within thirty days of receipt of the award, unless another period of time has been agreed upon by the parties:

(a) a party, with notice to the other party, may request the arbitral tribunal to correct in the award any errors in computation, any clerical or typographical errors, or any errors of similar nature;

(b) if so agreed by the parties, a party, with notice to the other party, may request the arbitral tribunal to give an interpretation of a specific point or part of the award.

If the arbitral tribunal considers the request to be justified, it shall make the correction or give the interpretation within thirty days of receipt of the request. The interpretation shall form part of the award.

2. The arbitral tribunal may correct any error of the type referred to in Paragraph 1(a) of this Article on its own initiative within thirty days of the date of the award.

3. Unless otherwise agreed by the parties, a party, with notice to the other party, may request, within thirty days of receipt of the award, the arbitral tribunal to make an additional award as to claims presented in the arbitral proceedings but omitted from the award. If the arbitral tribunal considers the request to be justified, it shall make the additional award within sixty days.

4. The arbitral tribunal may extend, if necessary, the period of time within which it shall make a correction, interpretation or additional award under Paragraph 1 or 3 of this Article.

5. The provisions of Article 31 shall apply to a correction or interpretation of the award or to an additional award.

Chapter VII.   RECOURSE AGAINST AWARD

Article 34. Application for Setting Aside as Exclusive Recourse Against Arbitral Award

1. Recourse to a court against an arbitral award may be made only by an application for setting aside in accordance with Paragraphs 2 and 3 of this Article.

2. An arbitral award may be set aside by the court specified in Article 6(2), only if:

(a) the party making the application furnishes proof that:

(i) a party to the arbitration agreement referred to in Article 7 was under some incapacity; or the said agreement is not valid under the law to which the parties have subjected it, or, failing any indication thereon, under RF law; or

(ii) the party making the application was not given proper notice of the appointment of an arbitrator or of the arbitral proceedings, or was otherwise unable to present his case; or

(iii) the award deals with a dispute not contemplated by or not falling within the terms of the submission to arbitration, or contains decisions on matters beyond the scope of the submission to arbitration, provided that, if the decisions on matters submitted to arbitration can be separated from those not so submitted, only that part of the award which contains decisions on matters not submitted to arbitration may be set aside; or

(iv) the composition of the arbitral tribunal or the arbitral procedure was not in accordance with the agreement of the parties, unless such agreement was in conflict with a provision of this Act from which the parties cannot derogate, or, failing such agreement, was not in accordance with this Act; or

(b) the court finds that:

(i) the subject-matter of the dispute is not capable of settlement by arbitration under RF law; or

(ii) the award is in conflict with the public policy of the RF.

3. An application for setting aside may not be made after three months have elapsed from the date on which the party making that application received the award or, if a request was made under Article 33, from the date on which that request was disposed of by the arbitral tribunal.

4. The court, when asked to set aside an award, may, where appropriate and so requested by a party, suspend the setting-aside proceedings for a period of time determined by it in order to give the

arbitral tribunal an opportunity to resume the arbitral proceedings or to take such other action as, in the arbitral tribunal's opinion, will eliminate the grounds for setting aside.

Chapter VIII.   RECOGNITION AND ENFORCEMENT OF AWARDS

Article 35.   Recognition and Enforcement

1.   An arbitral award, irrespective of the country in which it was made, shall be recognized as binding and, upon application in writing to the competent court, shall be enforced, subject to the provisions of this Article and of Article 36.

2.   The party relying on an award or applying for its enforcement shall supply the duly authenticated original award or a duly certified copy thereof, and the original arbitration agreement referred to in Article 7 or a duly certified copy thereof. If the award or agreement is made in a foreign language, the party shall supply a duly certified translation thereof into the Russian language.

Article 36.   Grounds for Refusing Recognition or Enforcement

1.   Recognition or enforcement of an arbitral award, irrespective of the country in which it was made, may be refused only:

(a)   at the request of the party against whom it is invoked, if that party furnished to the competent court where recognition or enforcement is sought proof that:

(i)   a party to the arbitration agreement referred to in Article 7 was under some incapacity; or the said agreement is not valid under the law to which the parties have subjected it, or, failing any indication thereon, under the law of the country where the award was made; or

(ii)   the party against whom the award is invoked was not given proper notice of the appointment of an arbitrator or of the arbitral proceedings, or was otherwise unable to present his case; or

(iii) the award deals with a dispute not contemplated by or not falling within the terms of the submission to arbitration, or it contains decisions on matters beyond the scope of the submission to arbitration, provided that, if the decisions on matters submitted to arbitration can be separated from those not so submitted, that part of the award which contains decisions on matters submitted to arbitration may be recognized and enforced; or

(iv) the composition of the arbitral tribunal or the arbitral procedure was not in accordance with the agreement of the parties or, failing such agreement, was not in accordance with the law of the country where the arbitration took place; or

(v)   the award has not yet become binding on the parties or has been set aside or suspended by a court of the country in which, or under the law of which, that award was made; or

(b)   if the court finds that:

(i)   the subject-matter of the dispute is not capable of settlement by arbitration under RF law; or

(ii)   the recognition or enforcement of the award would be contrary to the public policy of the RF.

2.   If an application for setting aside or suspension of an award has been made to a court referred to in Paragraph 1(a)(v) of this Article, the court where recognition or enforcement is sought may, if it considers it proper, adjourn its decision, and may also, on the application of the party claiming recognition or enforcement of the award, order the other party to provide appropriate security.

H. GERMAN ARBITRATION LAW 1998*

Act on the Reform of the Law relating to Arbitral Proceedings

The following provisions have entered into force on

Book Ten of the Code of Civil Procedure[1]

1 January 1998

Arbitration Procedure
Sections 1025–1066

Chapter I
General provisions

Section 1025
Scope of application

(1)   The provisions of this Book apply if the place of arbitration as referred to in section 1043 subs. 1 is situated in Germany.

(2)   The provisions of sections 1032, 1033 and 1050 also apply if the place of arbitration is situated outside Germany or has not yet been determined.

(3)   If the place of arbitration has not yet been determined, the German courts are competent to perform the court functions specified in

---

*   Unofficial translation by the German Institution of Arbitration (DIS) and the German Federal Ministry of Justice. Reprinted with the kind permission of German Institution of Arbitration.

[1]   Completely revised by Article 1, No. 7 of the Act on the Reform of the Law relating to Arbitral Proceedings of 22 December 1997, Bundesgesetzblatt (Federal Law Gazette) 1997 Part I page 3224. The Act entered into force on 1 January 1998.

sections 1034, 1035, 1037 and 1038 if the respondent or the claimant has his place of business or habitual residence in Germany.

(4)   Sections 1061 to 1065 apply to the recognition and enforcement of foreign arbitral awards.

Section 1026
Extent of court intervention

In matters governed by sections 1025 to 1061, no court shall intervene except where so provided in this Book.

Section 1027
Loss of right to object

A party who knows that any provision of this Book from which the parties may derogate or any agreed requirement under the arbitral procedure has not been complied with and yet proceeds with the arbitration without stating his objection to such non-compliance without undue delay or, if a time-limit is provided therefor, within such period of time, may not raise that objection later.

Section 1028
Receipt of written communications in case of
unknown whereabouts

(1)   Unless otherwise agreed by the parties, if the whereabouts of a party or of a person entitled to receive communications on his behalf are not known, any written communication shall be deemed to have been received on the day on which it could have been received at the addressee's last-known mailing address, place of business or habitual residence after proper transmission by registered mail/return receipt requested or any other means which provides a record of the attempt to deliver it there.

(2)   Subsection 1 does not apply to communications in court proceedings.

Chapter II
Arbitration agreement

Section 1029
Definition

(1)   "Arbitration agreement" is an agreement by the parties to submit to arbitration all or certain disputes which have arisen or which may arise between them in respect of a defined legal relationship, whether contractual or not.

(2)   An arbitration agreement may be in the form of a separate agreement ("separate arbitration agreement") or in the form of a clause in a contract ("arbitration clause").

Section 1030
Arbitrability

(1)   Any claim involving an economic interest ("vermögensrechtlicher Anspruch") can be the subject of an arbitration agreement. An arbitration agreement concerning claims not involving an economic interest shall have legal effect to the extent that the parties are entitled to conclude a settlement on the issue in dispute.

(2)   An arbitration agreement relating to disputes on the existence of a lease of residential accommodation within Germany shall be null and void. This does not apply to residential accommodation as specified in section 549 subs. 1 to 3[2] of the Civil Code.

(3)   Statutory provisions outside this Book by virtue of which certain disputes may not be submitted to arbitration, or may be submitted to arbitration only under certain conditions, remain unaffected.

Section 1031
Form of arbitration agreement

(1)   The arbitration agreement shall be contained either in a document signed by the parties or in an exchange of letters, telefaxes, telegrams or other means of telecommunication which provide a record of the agreement.

(2)   The form requirement of subsection 1 shall be deemed to have been complied with if the arbitration agreement is contained in a document transmitted from one party to the other party or by a third party to both parties and—if no objection was raised in good time—the contents of such document are considered to be part of the contract in accordance with common usage.

(3)   The reference in a contract complying with the form requirements of subsection 1 or 2 to a document containing an arbitration clause constitutes an arbitration agreement provided that the reference is such as to make that clause part of the contract.

(4)   [abolished].[3]

(5)   Arbitration agreements to which a consumer[4] is a party must be contained in a document which has been personally signed by the parties.

---

[2]   Section 1030 subs. 2, sentence 2 was amended by Article 3 of the Act on the Reform of the Rent Law of 19 June 2001, Bundesgesetzblatt (Federal Law Gazette) 2001 Part I, p. 1149, in force as of 1 September 2001.

[3]   Section 1031 subs. 4 was abolished by the Law for the reform of maritime trade law, 20 April 2012 (BGBl. I 831). The abolished section stated: "An arbitration agreement is also concluded by the issuance of a bill of lading, if the latter contains an express reference to an arbitration clause in a charter party."

[4]   A consumer is any natural person who concludes a transaction for a purpose which can be regarded as being outside his trade or self-employed profession ("gewerbliche oder selbständige

The written form pursuant to subsection 1 may be substituted by electronic form pursuant to section 126 a of the Civil Code ("Bürgerliches Gesetzbuch-BGB").[5] No agreements other than those referring to the arbitral proceedings may be contained in such a document or electronic document; this shall not apply in the case of a notarial certification.[6]

(6)   Any non-compliance with the form requirements is cured by entering into argument on the substance of the dispute in the arbitral proceedings.

<h3 style="text-align:center">Section 1032
Arbitration agreement and substantive claim before court</h3>

(1)   A court before which an action is brought in a matter which is the subject of an arbitration agreement shall, if the respondent raises an objection prior to the beginning of the oral hearing on the substance of the dispute, reject the action as inadmissible unless the court finds that the arbitration agreement is null and void, inoperative or incapable of being performed.

(2)   Prior to the constitution of the arbitral tribunal, an application may be made to the court to determine whether or not arbitration is admissible.

(3)   Where an action or application referred to in subsection 1 or 2 has been brought, arbitral proceedings may nevertheless be commenced or continued, and an arbitral award may be made, while the issue is pending before the court.

---

berufliche Tätigkeit")—section 13 Civil Law Code. Section 13 Civil Law Code was newly introduced by Art. 2 subs. 1 of the Act of 27 June 2000. By the same Act, section 1031 subs. 5, 3rd sentence was deleted.

  [5]   Section 126a Civil Code ("BGB") [Electronic form]: (1) If the statutory written form is to be substituted by electronic form, the author of the statement must add his name to the statement and append a qualified electronic signature pursuant to the Signature Act.

  (2) In the case of a contract, the parties must each electronically sign a document identical in wording in the manner prescribed in subsection 1.

  Section 126a Civil Code was newly introduced by Art. 1 of the Act of 13 July 2001 (Bundesgesetzblatt Part I, p. 1542).

  Section 2 Signature Act ("Signaturgesetz-SigG") [Qualified electronic form]: For the purpose of this Act,

    1. "electronic signature" means data in electronic form which are attached to or logically associated with other electronic data and which serve as a method of authentication;

    2. "advanced electronic signature" means an electronic signature pursuant to No. 1 which a) is uniquely linked to the signatory, b) is capable of identifying the signatory, c) is created using means that the signatory can maintain under his sole control, and d) is linked to the data to which it relates in such a manner that any subsequent change of the data is detectable;

    3. "qualified electronic signature" means an electronic signature pursuant to No. 2 which a) is based on a qualified certificate valid at the time of the signature's creation, and b) is created with a secure signature-creation device; . . . —Act of 16 May 2001 (Signature Act), Bundesgesetzblatt Part I, p. 876.

  [6]   Sentence 2 and 3 of section 1031 subs. 5 were amended by Art. 2 of the Act of 14 December 2001 (Electronic Commerce Act), Bundesgesetzblatt Part I, p. 3721.

Section 1033
Arbitration agreement and interim measures by court

It is not incompatible with an arbitration agreement for a court to grant, before or during arbitral proceedings, an interim measure of protection relating to the subject-matter of the arbitration upon request of a party.

Chapter III
Constitution of arbitral tribunal

Section 1034
Composition of arbitral tribunal

(1) The parties are free to determine the number of arbitrators. Failing such determination, the number of arbitrators shall be three.

(2) If the arbitration agreement grants preponderant rights to one party with regard to the composition of the arbitral tribunal which place the other party at a disadvantage, that other party may request the court to appoint the arbitrator or arbitrators in deviation from the nomination made, or from the agreed nomination procedure. The request must be submitted at the latest within two weeks of the party becoming aware of the constitution of the arbitral tribunal. Section 1032 subs. 3 applies mutatis mutandis.

Section 1035
Appointment of arbitrators

(1) The parties are free to agree on a procedure of appointing the arbitrator or arbitrators.

(2) Unless otherwise agreed by the parties, a party shall be bound by his appointment of an arbitrator as soon as the other party has received notice of the appointment.

(3) Failing an agreement between the parties on the appointment of the arbitrators, a sole arbitrator shall, if the parties are unable to agree on his appointment, be appointed, upon request of a party, by the court. In an arbitration with three arbitrators, each party shall appoint one arbitrator, and the two arbitrators thus appointed shall appoint the third arbitrator who shall act as chairman of the arbitral tribunal. If a party fails to appoint the arbitrator within one month of receipt of a request to do so from the other party, or if the two arbitrators fail to agree on the third arbitrator within one month of their appointment, the appointment shall be made, upon request of a party, by the court.

(4) Where, under an appointment procedure agreed upon by the parties, a party fails to act as required under such procedure, or if the parties, or two arbitrators, are unable to reach an agreement expected of them under such procedure, or a third party fails to perform any function

entrusted to it under such procedure, any party may request the court to take the necessary measure, unless the agreement on the appointment procedure provides other means for securing the appointment.

(5) The court, in appointing an arbitrator, shall have due regard to any qualifications required of the arbitrator by the agreement of the parties and to such considerations as are likely to secure the appointment of an independent and impartial arbitrator. In the case of a sole or third arbitrator, the court shall take into account as well the advisability of appointing an arbitrator of a nationality other than those of the parties.

Section 1036
Challenge of an arbitrator

(1) When a person is approached in connection with his possible appointment as an arbitrator, he shall disclose any circumstances likely to give rise to justifiable doubts as to his impartiality or independence. An arbitrator, from the time of his appointment and throughout the arbitral proceedings, shall without delay disclose any such circumstances to the parties unless they have already been informed of them by him.

(2) An arbitrator may be challenged only if circumstances exist that give rise to justifiable doubts as to his impartiality or independence, or if he does not possess qualifications agreed to by the parties. A party may challenge an arbitrator appointed by him, or in whose appointment he has participated, only for reasons of which he becomes aware after the appointment has been made.

Section 1037
Challenge procedure

(1) The parties are free to agree on a procedure for challenging an arbitrator, subject to the provisions of subsection 3 of this section.

(2) Failing such agreement, a party who intends to challenge an arbitrator shall, within two weeks after becoming aware of the constitution of the arbitral tribunal or after becoming aware of any circumstance referred to in section 1036 subs. 2, send a written statement of the reasons for the challenge to the arbitral tribunal. Unless the challenged arbitrator withdraws from his office or the other party agrees to the challenge, the arbitral tribunal shall decide on the challenge.

(3) If a challenge under any procedure agreed upon by the parties or under the procedure of subsection 2 of this section is not successful, the challenging party may request, within one month after having received notice of the decision rejecting the challenge, the court to decide on the challenge; the parties may agree on a different time-limit. While such a request is pending, the arbitral tribunal, including the challenged arbitrator, may continue the arbitral proceedings and make an award.

Section 1038
Failure or impossibility to act

(1)   If an arbitrator becomes de jure or de facto unable to perform his functions or for other reasons fails to act without undue delay, his mandate terminates if he withdraws from his office or if the parties agree on the termination. If the arbitrator does not withdraw from his office or if the parties cannot agree on the termination, any party may request the court to decide on the termination of the mandate.

(2)   If, under subsection 1 of this section or section 1037 subs. 2, an arbitrator withdraws from his office or a party agrees to the termination of the mandate of an arbitrator, this does not imply acceptance of the validity of any ground for withdrawal referred to in subsection 1 of this section or section 1036 subs. 2.

Section 1039
Appointment of substitute arbitrator

(1)   Where the mandate of an arbitrator terminates under section 1037 or 1038 or because of his withdrawal from office for any other reason or because of the revocation of his mandate by agreement of the parties, a substitute arbitrator shall be appointed according to the rules that were applicable to the appointment of the arbitrator being replaced.

(2)   The parties are free to agree on another procedure.

Chapter IV
Jurisdiction of arbitral tribunal

Section 1040
Competence of arbitral tribunal to rule on its jurisdiction

(1)   The arbitral tribunal may rule on its own jurisdiction and in this connection on the existence or validity of the arbitration agreement. For that purpose, an arbitration clause which forms part of a contract shall be treated as an agreement independent of the other terms of the contract.

(2)   A plea that the arbitral tribunal does not have jurisdiction shall be raised not later than the submission of the statement of defense. A party is not precluded from raising such a plea by the fact that he has appointed, or participated in the appointment of, an arbitrator. A plea that the arbitral tribunal is exceeding the scope of its authority shall be raised as soon as the matter alleged to be beyond the scope of its authority is raised during the arbitral proceedings. The arbitral tribunal may, in either case, admit a later plea if it considers that the party has justified the delay.

(3)   If the arbitral tribunal considers that it has jurisdiction, it rules on a plea referred to in subsection 2 of this section in general by means of a preliminary ruling. In this case, any party may request, within one month after having received written notice of that ruling, the court to decide the

matter. While such a request is pending, the arbitral tribunal may continue the arbitral proceedings and make an award.

Section 1041
Interim measures of protection

(1)   Unless otherwise agreed by the parties, the arbitral tribunal may, at the request of a party, order such interim measures of protection as the arbitral tribunal may consider necessary in respect of the subject-matter of the dispute. The arbitral tribunal may require any party to provide appropriate security in connection with such measure.

(2)   The court may, at the request of a party, permit enforcement of a measure referred to in subsection 1, unless application for a corresponding interim measure has already been made to a court. It may recast such an order if necessary for the purpose of enforcing the measure.

(3)   The court may, upon request, repeal or amend the decision referred to in subsection 2.

(4)   If a measure ordered under subsection 1 proves to have been unjustified from the outset, the party who obtained its enforcement is obliged to compensate the other party for damage resulting from the enforcement of such measure or from his providing security in order to avoid enforcement. This claim may be put forward in the pending arbitral proceedings.

Chapter V
Conduct of arbitral proceedings

Section 1042
General rules of procedure

(1)   The parties shall be treated with equality and each party shall be given a full opportunity of presenting his case.

(2)   Counsel may not be excluded from acting as authorized representatives.

(3)   Otherwise, subject to the mandatory provisions of this Book, the parties are free to determine the procedure themselves or by reference to a set of arbitration rules.

(4)   Failing an agreement by the parties, and in the absence of provisions in this Book, the arbitral tribunal shall conduct the arbitration in such manner as it considers appropriate. The arbitral tribunal is empowered to determine the admissibility of taking evidence, take evidence and assess freely such evidence.

Section 1043
Place of arbitration

(1)   The parties are free to agree on the place of arbitration. Failing such agreement, the place of arbitration shall be determined by the arbitral tribunal having regard to the circumstances of the case, including the convenience of the parties.

(2)   Notwithstanding the provisions of subsection 1 of this section, the arbitral tribunal may, unless otherwise agreed by the parties, meet at any place it considers appropriate for an oral hearing, for hearing witnesses, experts or the parties, for consultation among its members or for inspection of property or documents.

Section 1044
Commencement of arbitral proceedings

Unless otherwise agreed by the parties, the arbitral proceedings in respect of a particular dispute commence on the date on which a request for that dispute to be referred to arbitration is received by the respondent. The request shall state the names of the parties, the subject-matter of the dispute and contain a reference to the arbitration agreement.

Section 1045
Language of proceedings

(1)   The parties are free to agree on the language or languages to be used in the arbitral proceedings. Failing such agreement, the arbitral tribunal shall determine the language or languages to be used in the proceedings. This agreement or determination, unless otherwise specified therein, shall apply to any written statement by a party, any hearing and any award, decision or other communication by the arbitral tribunal.

(2)   The arbitral tribunal may order that any documentary evidence shall be accompanied by a translation into the language or languages agreed upon by the parties or determined by the arbitral tribunal.

Section 1046
Statements of claim and defense

(1)   Within the period of time agreed by the parties or determined by the arbitral tribunal, the claimant shall state his claim and the facts supporting the claim, and the respondent shall state his defense in respect of these particulars. The parties may submit with their statements all documents they consider to be relevant or may add a reference to other evidence they will submit.

(2)   Unless otherwise agreed by the parties, either party may amend or supplement his claim or defense during the course of the arbitral proceedings, unless the arbitral tribunal considers it inappropriate to allow

such amendment having regard to the delay in making it without sufficient justification.

(3)   Subsections 1 and 2 apply mutatis mutandis to counter-claims.

Section 1047
Oral hearings and written proceedings

(1)   Subject to agreement by the parties, the arbitral tribunal shall decide whether to hold oral hearings or whether the proceedings shall be conducted on the basis of documents and other materials. Unless the parties have agreed that no hearings shall be held, the arbitral tribunal shall hold such hearings at an appropriate stage of the proceedings, if so requested by a party.

(2)   The parties shall be given sufficient advance notice of any hearing and of any meeting of the arbitral tribunal for the purpose of taking evidence.

(3)   All statements, documents or other information supplied to the arbitral tribunal by one party shall be communicated to the other party. Also, any expert report or evidentiary document on which the arbitral tribunal may rely in making its decision shall be communicated to both parties.

Section 1048
Default of a party

(1)   If the claimant fails to communicate his statement of claim in accordance with section 1046 subs. 1, the arbitral tribunal shall terminate the proceedings.

(2)   If the respondent fails to communicate his statement of defense in accordance with section 1046 subs. 1, the arbitral tribunal shall continue the proceedings without treating such failure in itself as an admission of the claimant's allegations.

(3)   If any party fails to appear at an oral hearing or to produce documentary evidence within a set time-limit, the arbitral tribunal may continue the proceedings and make the award on the evidence before it.

(4)   Any default which has been justified to the tribunal's satisfaction will be disregarded. Apart from that, the parties may agree otherwise on the consequences of default.

Section 1049
Expert appointed by arbitral tribunal

(1)   Unless otherwise agreed by the parties, the arbitral tribunal may appoint one or more experts to report to it on specific issues to be determined by the arbitral tribunal. It may also require a party to give the

expert any relevant information or to produce, or to provide access to, any relevant documents or property for his inspection.

(2)   Unless otherwise agreed by the parties, if a party so requests or if the arbitral tribunal considers it necessary, the expert shall, after delivery of his written or oral report, participate in an oral hearing where the parties have the opportunity to put questions to him and to present expert witnesses in order to testify on the points at issue.

(3)   Sections 1036 and 1037 subs. 1 and 2 apply mutatis mutandis to an expert appointed by the arbitral tribunal.

Section 1050
Court assistance in taking evidence and other judicial acts

The arbitral tribunal or a party with the approval of the arbitral tribunal may request from a court assistance in taking evidence or performance of other judicial acts which the arbitral tribunal is not empowered to carry out. Unless it regards the application as inadmissible, the court shall execute the request according to its rules on taking evidence or other judicial acts. The arbitrators are entitled to participate in any judicial taking of evidence and to ask questions.

Chapter VI
Making of award and termination of proceedings

Section 1051
Rules applicable to substance of dispute

(1)   The arbitral tribunal shall decide the dispute in accordance with such rules of law as are chosen by the parties as applicable to the substance of the dispute. Any designation of the law or legal system of a given State shall be construed, unless otherwise expressed, as directly referring to the substantive law of that State and not to its conflict of laws rules.

(2)   Failing any designation by the parties, the arbitral tribunal shall apply the law of the State with which the subject-matter of the proceedings is most closely connected.

(3)   The arbitral tribunal shall decide ex aequo et bono or as amiable compositeur only if the parties have expressly authorized it to do so. The parties may so authorize the arbitral tribunal up to the time of its decision.

(4)   In all cases, the arbitral tribunal shall decide in accordance with the terms of the contract and shall take into account the usages of the trade applicable to the transaction.

Section 1052
Decision making by panel of arbitrators

(1) In arbitral proceedings with more than one arbitrator, any decision of the arbitral tribunal shall be made, unless otherwise agreed by the parties, by a majority of all its members.

(2) If an arbitrator refuses to take part in the vote on a decision, the other arbitrators may take the decision without him, unless otherwise agreed by the parties. The parties shall be given advance notice of the intention to make an award without the arbitrator refusing to participate in the vote. In the case of other decisions, the parties shall subsequent to the decision be informed of the refusal to participate in the vote.

(3) Individual questions of procedure may be decided by a presiding arbitrator alone if so authorized by the parties or all members of the arbitral tribunal.

Section 1053
Settlement

(1) If, during arbitral proceedings, the parties settle the dispute, the arbitral tribunal shall terminate the proceedings. If requested by the parties, it shall record the settlement in the form of an arbitral award on agreed terms, unless the contents are in violation of public policy (ordre public).

(2) An award on agreed terms shall be made in accordance with section 1054 and shall state that it is an award. Such an award has the same effect as any other award on the merits of the case.

(3) If notarial certification is required for a declaration to be effective, it will be substituted, in the case of an arbitral award on agreed terms, by recording the declaration of the parties in the award.

(4) An award on agreed terms may, upon agreement between the parties, also be declared enforceable by a notary whose notarial office is in the district of the court competent for the declaration of enforceability according to section 1062 subs. 1, no. 2. The notary shall refuse the declaration of enforceability, if the requirements of subsection 1, sentence 2 are not complied with.

Section 1054
Form and contents of award

(1) The award shall be made in writing and shall be signed by the arbitrator or arbitrators. In arbitral proceedings with more than one arbitrator, the signatures of the majority of all members of the arbitral tribunal shall suffice, provided that the reason for any omitted signature is stated.

(2)   The award shall state the reasons upon which it is based, unless the parties have agreed that no reasons are to be given or the award is an award on agreed terms under section 1053.

(3)   The award shall state its date and the place of arbitration as determined in accordance with section 1043 subs. 1. The award shall be deemed to have been made on that date and at that place.

(4)   A copy of the award signed by the arbitrators shall be delivered to each party.

Section 1055
Effect of arbitral award

The arbitral award has the same effect between the parties as a final and binding court judgment.

Section 1056
Termination of proceedings

(1)   The arbitral proceedings are terminated by the final award or by an order of the arbitral tribunal in accordance with subsection 2 of this section.

(2)   The arbitral tribunal shall issue an order for the termination of the arbitral proceedings when

1.   the claimant:

a.   fails to state his claim according to section 1046 subs. 1 and section 1048 subs. 4 does not apply, or

b.   withdraws his claim, unless the respondent objects thereto and the arbitral tribunal recognizes a legitimate interest on his part in obtaining a final settlement of the dispute, or

2.   the parties agree on the termination of the proceedings, or

3.   the parties fail to pursue the arbitral proceedings in spite of being so requested by the arbitral tribunal or when the continuation of the proceedings has for any other reason become impossible.

(3)   The mandate of the arbitral tribunal terminates with the termination of the arbitral proceedings, subject to the provisions of sections 1057 subs. 2, 1058 and 1059 subs. 4.

Section 1057
Decision on costs

(1)   Unless the parties agree otherwise, the arbitral tribunal shall allocate, by means of an arbitral award, the costs of the arbitration as between the parties, including those incurred by the parties necessary for the proper pursuit of their claim or defense. It shall do so at its discretion

and take into consideration the circumstances of the case, in particular the outcome of the proceedings.

(2) To the extent that the costs of the arbitral proceedings have been fixed, the arbitral tribunal shall also decide on the amount to be borne by each party. If the costs have not been fixed or if they can only be fixed once the arbitral proceedings have been terminated, the decision shall be taken by means of a separate award.

Section 1058
Correction and interpretation of award; additional award

(1) Any party may request the arbitral tribunal

1. to correct in the award any errors in computation, any clerical or typographical errors or any errors of similar nature,

2. to give an interpretation of specific parts of the award,

3. to make an additional award as to claims presented in the arbitral proceedings but omitted from the award.

(2) Unless otherwise agreed by the parties, the request shall be made within one month of receipt of the award.

(3) The arbitral tribunal shall make the correction or give the interpretation within one month and make an additional award within two months.

(4) The arbitral tribunal may make a correction of the award on its own initiative.

(5) Section 1054 shall apply to a correction or interpretation of the award or to an additional award.

Chapter VII
Recourse against award

Section 1059
Application for setting aside

(1) Recourse to a court against an arbitral award may be made only by an application for setting aside in accordance with subsections 2 and 3 of this section.

(2) An arbitral award may be set aside only if:

1. the applicant shows sufficient cause that:
    a) a party to the arbitration agreement referred to in sections 1029 and 1031 was under some incapacity pursuant to the law applicable to him; or the said agreement is not valid under the law to which the parties have subjected it or, failing any indication thereon, under German law; or

b) he was not given proper notice of the appointment of an arbitrator or of the arbitral proceedings or was otherwise unable to present his case; or

c) the award deals with a dispute not contemplated by or not falling within the terms of the submission to arbitration, or contains decisions on matters beyond the scope of the submission to arbitration; provided that, if the decisions on matters submitted to arbitration can be separated from those not so submitted, only that part of the award which contains decisions on matters not submitted to arbitration may be set aside; or

d) the composition of the arbitral tribunal or the arbitral procedure was not in accordance with a provision of this Book or with an admissible agreement of the parties and this presumably affected the award; or

2. the court finds that

a) the subject-matter of the dispute is not capable of settlement by arbitration under German law; or

b) recognition or enforcement of the award leads to a result which is in conflict with public policy (ordre public).

(3) Unless the parties have agreed otherwise, an application for setting aside to the court may not be made after three months have elapsed. The period of time shall commence on the date on which the party making the application had received the award. If a request had been made under section 1058, the time-limit shall be extended by not more than one month from receipt of the decision on the request. No application for setting aside the award may be made once the award has been declared enforceable by a German court.

(4) The court, when asked to set aside an award, may, where appropriate, set aside the award and remit the case to the arbitral tribunal.

(5) Setting aside the arbitral award shall, in the absence of any indication to the contrary, result in the arbitration agreement becoming operative again in respect of the subject-matter of the dispute.

Chapter VIII
Recognition and enforcement of awards

Section 1060
Domestic awards

(1) Enforcement of the award takes place if it has been declared enforceable.

(2) An application for a declaration of enforceability shall be refused and the award set aside if one of the grounds for setting aside under section

1059 subs. 2 exists. Grounds for setting aside shall not be taken into account, if at the time when the application for a declaration of enforceability is served, an application for setting aside based on such grounds has been finally rejected. Grounds for setting aside under section 1059 subs. 2, no. 1 shall also not be taken into account if the time-limits set by section 1059 subs. 3 have expired without the party opposing the application having made an application for setting aside the award.

Section 1061
Foreign awards

(1) Recognition and enforcement of foreign arbitral awards shall be granted in accordance with the Convention on the Recognition and Enforcement of Foreign Arbitral Awards of 10 June 1958 (Bundesgesetzblatt [BGBl.] 1961 Part II p. 121). The provisions of other treaties on the recognition and enforcement of arbitral awards shall remain unaffected.

(2) If the declaration of enforceability is to be refused, the court shall rule that the arbitral award is not to be recognized in Germany.

(3) If the award is set aside abroad after having been declared enforceable, application for setting aside the declaration of enforceability may be made.

Chapter IX
Court proceedings

Section 1062
Competence

(1) The Higher Regional Court ("Oberlandesgericht") designated in the arbitration agreement or, failing such designation, the Higher Regional Court in whose district the place of arbitration is situated, is competent for decisions on applications relating to

1.   the appointment of an arbitrator (sections 1034 and 1035), the challenge of an arbitrator (section 1037) or the termination of an arbitrator's mandate (section 1038);

2.   the determination of the admissibility or inadmissibility of arbitration (section 1032) or the decision of an arbitral tribunal confirming its competence in a preliminary ruling (section 1040);

3.   the enforcement, setting aside or amendment of an order for interim measures of protection by the arbitral tribunal (section 1041);

4.   the setting aside (section 1059) or the declaration of enforceability of the award (section 1060 et seq.) or the setting aside of the declaration of enforceability (section 1061).

(2)   If the place of arbitration in the cases referred to in subsection 1, no. 2, first alternative, nos. 3 and 4 is not in Germany, competence lies with the Higher Regional Court ("Oberlandesgericht") where the party opposing the application has his place of business or place of habitual residence, or where assets of that party or the property in dispute or affected by the measure is located, failing which the Berlin Higher Regional Court ("Kammergericht") shall be competent.

(3)   In the cases referred to in section 1025 subs. 3, the Higher Regional Court ("Oberlandesgericht") in whose district the claimant or the respondent has his place of business or place of habitual residence is competent.

(4)   For assistance in the taking of evidence and other judicial acts (section 1050), the Local Court ("Amtsgericht"), in whose district the judicial act is to be carried out, is competent.

(5)   Where there are several Higher Regional Courts ("Oberlandesgerichte") in one Land, the Government of that Land may transfer by ordinance competence to one Higher Regional Court, or, where existent, to the highest Regional Court ("Oberstes Landesgericht"); the Land Government may transfer such authority to the Department of Justice of the Land concerned by ordinance. Several Länder may agree on cross-border competence of a single Higher Regional Court.

Section 1063
General provisions

(1)   The court shall decide by means of an order.[7] The party opposing the application shall be given an opportunity to comment before a decision is taken.

(2)   The court shall order an oral hearing to be held, if the setting aside of the award has been requested or if, in an application for recognition or declaration of enforceability of the award, grounds for setting aside in terms of section 1059 subs. 2 are to be considered.

(3)   The presiding judge of the civil court senate ("Zivilsenat") may issue, without prior hearing of the party opposing the application, an order to the effect that, until a decision on the request has been reached, the applicant may pursue enforcement of the award or enforce the interim measure of protection of the arbitration court pursuant to section 1041. In the case of an award, enforcement of the award may not go beyond measures of protection. The party opposing the application may prevent

---

[7]   Amended by Art. 2 subs. 1 no. 104 of the Act of 27 July 2001 (Civil Procedure Reform Act), Bundesgesetzblatt Part I, p. 1887. Cf. section 128 CCP [Principle of Oral Presentation]: (4) Unless provided otherwise, decisions of the court which do not constitute judgments can be rendered without oral hearing.

enforcement by providing as security an amount corresponding to the amount that may be enforced by the applicant.

(4) As long as no oral hearing is ordered, applications and declarations may be put on record at the court registry.

Section 1064
Particularities regarding the enforcement of awards

(1) At the time of the application for a declaration of enforceability of an arbitral award the award or a certified copy of the award shall be supplied. The certification may also be made by counsel authorized to represent the party in the judicial proceedings.

(2) The order declaring the award enforceable shall be declared provisionally enforceable.

(3) Unless otherwise provided in treaties, subsections 1 and 2 shall apply to foreign awards.

Section 1065
Legal remedies[8]

(1) A complaint on a point of law is available against the decisions mentioned under section 1062 subs. 1, nos. 2 and 4. No recourse against other decisions in the proceedings specified in section 1062 subs. 1 may be made.

(2) The complaint on a point of law can also be based on the ground that the decision is based on a violation of a treaty. Sections 707 and 717 apply mutatis mutandis.

Chapter X
Arbitral tribunals not established by agreement

Section 1066
Mutatis mutandis application of the provisions of the Tenth Book

The provisions of this Book apply mutatis mutandis to arbitral tribunals established lawfully by disposition on death or other dispositions not based on an agreement.

Article 2 of the Arbitral Proceedings Reform Act:

Section 19
Amendment to the Act on Restraints of Competition

Section 91 of the Act on Restraints of Competition (Gesetz gegen Wettbewerbsbeschränkungen) as promulgated on 20 February 1990 (Bundesgesetzblatt Part I p.235), last amended by section 2 subs. 20 of the Act of 17 December 1997 (Bundesgesetzblatt Part I p. 3108), is repealed.

---

[8]   Amended by Art. 2 subs. 1 no. 105 of the Act of 27 July 2001 (Civil Procedure Reform Act), Bundesgesetzblatt Part I, p. 1887.

Note:

The repeal of section 91 of the Act on Restraints of Competition is of great relevance for economic arbitration, since the restrictions on the arbitrability of cartel disputes are thereby abolished. The arbitrability of cartel disputes is now determined solely according to the general provisions on arbitrability contained in section 1030 of the Code of Civil Procedure.

Section 91 of the Act on Restraints of Competition had provided that arbitration agreements on *future* legal disputes arising out of effective cartel agreements or decisions, which do not grant each party the right to choose between proceedings before an arbitral tribunal or a state court, are null and void.

Article 4 of the Arbitral Proceedings Reform Act:

Transitional provisions
Section 1. Arbitral proceedings

(1) The effectiveness of arbitration agreements that have been concluded prior to the entry into force of this Act, shall be determined according to the law previously in force.

(2) Arbitral proceedings that are pending but not terminated upon the entry into force of this Act are governed by the law previously in force provided that the arbitral settlement ("schiedsrichterlicher Vergleich") is substituted by the award on agreed terms. The parties may agree to apply the new law.

(3) Court proceedings pending upon the entry into force of this Act remain subject to the law previously in force.

(4) Arbitral settlements that have been concluded and declared enforceable prior to the entry into force of this Act are subject to enforcement provided that the decision on their enforceability has become final and binding or has been declared provisionally enforceable.

. . .

I. SWEDISH ARBITRATION ACT OF 1999
(SFS 1999:116)*

The Arbitration Agreement

Section 1

Disputes concerning matters in respect of which the parties may reach a settlement may, by agreement, be referred to one or several arbitrators for resolution. Such an agreement may relate to future disputes pertaining to a legal relationship specified in the agreement. The dispute may concern

---

*   Available at http://www.sccinstitute.com/about-the-scc/legal-resources/legislation/.

the existence of a particular fact. In addition to interpreting agreements, the filling of gaps in contracts can also be referred to arbitrators. Arbitrators may rule on the civil law effects of competition law as between the parties.

Section 2

The arbitrators may rule on their own jurisdiction to decide the dispute. The aforesaid shall not prevent a court from determining such a question at the request of a party. The arbitrators may continue the arbitral proceedings pending the determination by the court. Notwithstanding that the arbitrators have, in a decision during the proceedings, determined that they possess jurisdiction to resolve the dispute, such decision is not binding. The provisions of sections 34 and 36 shall apply in respect of an action to challenge an arbitration award which entails a decision in respect of jurisdiction.

Section 3

Where the validity of an arbitration agreement which constitutes part of another agreement must be determined in conjunction with a determination of the jurisdiction of the arbitrators, the arbitration agreement shall be deemed to constitute a separate agreement.

Section 4

A court may not, over an objection of a party, rule on an issue which, pursuant to an arbitration agreement, shall be decided by arbitrators. A party must invoke an arbitration agreement on the first occasion that a party pleads his case on the merits in the court. The invocation of an arbitration agreement raised on a later occasion shall have no effect unless the party had a legal excuse and invoked such as soon as the excuse ceased to exist. The invocation of an arbitration agreement shall be considered notwithstanding that the party who invoked the agreement has allowed an issue which is covered by the arbitration agreement to be determined by the Debt Enforcement Authority in a case concerning expedited collection procedures. During the pendency of a dispute before arbitrators or prior thereto, a court may, irrespective of the arbitration agreement, issue such decisions in respect of security measures as the court has jurisdiction to issue.

Section 5

A party shall forfeit his right to invoke the arbitration agreement as a bar to court proceedings where the party:

1. has opposed a request for arbitration;

2. failed to appoint an arbitrator in due time; or

3. fails, within due time, to provide his share of the requested security for compensation to the arbitrators.

Section 6

Where a dispute between a business enterprise and a consumer concerns goods, services, or any other products supplied principally for private use, an arbitration agreement may not be invoked where such was entered into prior to the dispute. However, such agreements shall apply with respect to rental or lease relationships where, through the agreement, a regional rent tribunal or a regional tenancies tribunal is appointed as an arbitral tribunal and the provisions of Chapter 8, section 28 or Chapter 12, section 66 of the Real Estate Code do not prescribe otherwise. The first paragraph shall not apply where the dispute concerns an agreement between an insurer and a policy-holder concerning insurance based on a collective agreement or group agreement and handled by representatives of the group. Nor shall the first paragraph apply where Sweden's international obligations provide to the contrary.

The Arbitrators Section 7

Any person who possesses full legal capacity in regard to his actions and his property may act as an arbitrator.

Section 8

An arbitrator shall be impartial. If a party so requests, an arbitrator shall be discharged if there exists any circumstance which may diminish confidence in the arbitrator's impartiality. Such a circumstance shall always be deemed to exist:

1.   where the arbitrator or a person closely associated to him is a party, or otherwise may expect benefit or detriment worth attention, as a result of the outcome of the dispute;

2.   where the arbitrator or a person closely associated to him is the director of a company or any other association which is a party, or otherwise represents a party or any other person who may expect benefit or detriment worth attention as a result of the outcome of the dispute;

3.   where the arbitrator has taken a position in the dispute, as an expert or otherwise, or has assisted a party in the preparation or conduct of his case in the dispute; or

4.   where the arbitrator has received or demanded compensation in violation of section 39, second paragraph.

Section 9

A person who is asked to accept an appointment as arbitrator shall immediately disclose all circumstances which, pursuant to sections 7 or 8, might be considered to prevent him from serving as arbitrator. An arbitrator shall inform the parties and the other arbitrators of such circumstances as soon as all arbitrators have been appointed and thereafter in the course of the arbitral proceedings as soon as he has learned of any new circumstance.

Section 10

A challenge of an arbitrator on account of a circumstance set forth in section 8 shall be presented within fifteen days commencing on the date on which the party became aware both of the appointment of the arbitrator and of the existence of the circumstance. The challenge shall be adjudicated by the arbitrators, unless the parties have decided that it shall be determined by another party. If the challenge is successful, the decision shall be subject to no appeal. A party who is dissatisfied with a decision denying a motion or dismissing a motion on the grounds that the motion was not timely filed may file an application with the District Court that the arbitrator be removed from his post. The application must be submitted within thirty days commencing on the date on which the party receives the decision. The arbitrators may continue with the arbitral proceedings pending the determination of the District Court.

Section 11

The parties may agree that a motion as referred to in section 10, first paragraph shall be conclusively determined by an arbitration institution.

Section 12

The parties may determine the number of arbitrators and the manner in which they shall be appointed. Sections 13–16 shall apply unless the parties have agreed otherwise. Where the parties have so agreed, and any of the parties so requests, the District Court shall appoint arbitrators also in situations other than those stated in sections 14–17.

Section 13

The arbitrators shall be three in number. Each party shall appoint one arbitrator, and the arbitrators so appointed shall appoint the third.

Section 14

Where each party is required to appoint an arbitrator and one party has notified the opposing party of his choice of arbitrator in a request for arbitration pursuant to section 19, the opposing party must, within thirty days of receipt of the notice, notify the first party in writing in respect of his choice of arbitrator. A party who, in this manner, has notified the opposing party of his choice of arbitrator may not revoke the appointment without the consent of the other party. If the opposing party fails to appoint an arbitrator within the stipulated time, the District Court shall appoint an arbitrator upon request by the first party.

Section 15

Where an arbitrator shall be appointed by other arbitrators, but they fail to do so within thirty days commencing on the date on which the last arbitrator was appointed, the District Court shall appoint the arbitrator upon request by a party. Where an arbitrator shall be appointed by someone other than a party or arbitrators, but such is not done within thirty days of the date on which a party desiring the appointment of an arbitrator requested that the person responsible for the appointment make such appointment, the District Court shall, upon the request by a party, appoint the arbitrator. The same shall apply where an arbitrator shall be appointed by the parties jointly, but they have failed to agree within thirty days commencing on the date on which the question was raised through receipt by one party of notice from the opposing party.

Section 16

Where an arbitrator resigns or is discharged, the District Court shall, upon request by a party, appoint a new arbitrator. Where the arbitrator cannot fulfil his duties due to circumstances which arise after his appointment, the person who originally was required to make the appointment shall, instead, appoint a new arbitrator. Sections 14 and 15 shall apply in conjunction with such an appointment. The period of time within which a new arbitrator shall be appointed, even for the party who requested the arbitration, is thirty days calculated, with respect to all parties, from the date on which the person who shall appoint the arbitrator became aware thereof.

Section 17

Where an arbitrator has delayed the proceedings, the District Court shall, upon request by a party, discharge the arbitrator and appoint another arbitrator. The parties may decide that such a request shall, instead, be conclusively determined by an arbitration institution.

Section 18

Where a party has requested that the District Court appoint an arbitrator pursuant to section 12, third paragraph or sections 14–17, the Court may reject the request on the grounds that the arbitration is not legally permissible only where such is manifest.

The Proceedings Section 19

Unless otherwise agreed by the parties, the arbitral proceedings are initiated when a party receives a request for arbitration in accordance with the second paragraph hereof. A request for arbitration must be in writing and include:

1.   an express and unconditional request for arbitration;

2.   a statement of the issue which is covered by the arbitration agreement and which is to be resolved by the arbitrators; and

3.   a statement of the party's choice of arbitrator where the party is required to appoint an arbitrator.

Section 20

Where the arbitral tribunal is composed of more than one arbitrator, one of them shall be appointed chairman. Unless the parties or the arbitrators have decided otherwise, the chairman shall be the arbitrator appointed by the other arbitrators or the District Court, in their stead.

Section 21

The arbitrators shall handle the dispute in an impartial, practical, and speedy manner. They shall thereupon act in accordance with the decisions of the parties insofar as there is no impediment to so doing.

Section 22

The parties shall determine the place of arbitration. Where this is not the case, the arbitrators shall determine the place of arbitration. The arbitrators may hold hearings and other meetings elsewhere in Sweden, or abroad, unless otherwise agreed by the parties.

Section 23

Within the period of time determined by the arbitrators, the claimant shall state his claims in respect of the issue stated in the request for arbitration, as well as the circumstances invoked by the party in support thereof. Thereafter, within the period of time determined by the arbitrators, the respondent shall state his position in relation to the claims, and the circumstances invoked by the respondent in support thereof. The claimant may submit new claims, and the respondent his own claims, provided that the claims fall within the scope of the arbitration agreement and, taking into consideration the time at which they are submitted or other circumstances, the arbitrators do not consider it inappropriate to adjudicate such claims. Subject to the same conditions, during the proceedings, each party may amend or supplement previously presented claims and may invoke new circumstances in support of his case. The first and second paragraphs hereof shall not apply where the parties have decided otherwise.

Section 24

The arbitrators shall afford the parties, to the extent necessary, an opportunity to present their respective cases in writing or orally. Where a party so requests, and provided that the parties have not otherwise agreed, an oral hearing shall be held prior to the determination of an issue referred to the arbitrators for resolution. A party shall be given an opportunity to review all documents and all other materials pertaining to the dispute which are supplied to the arbitrators by the opposing party or another person. Where one of the parties, without valid cause, fails to appear at a hearing or otherwise fails to comply with an order of the arbitrators, such failure shall not prevent a continuation of the proceedings and a resolution of the dispute on the basis of the existing materials.

Section 25

The parties shall supply the evidence. However, the arbitrators may appoint experts, unless both parties are opposed thereto. The arbitrators may refuse to admit evidence which is offered where such evidence is manifestly irrelevant to the case or where such refusal is justified having regard to the time at which the evidence is offered. The arbitrators may not administer oaths or truth affirmations. Nor may they impose conditional fines or otherwise use compulsory measures in order to obtain requested evidence. Unless the parties have agreed otherwise, the arbitrators may, at the request of a party, decide that, during the proceedings, the opposing party must undertake a certain interim measure to secure the claim which is to be adjudicated by the arbitrators. The arbitrators may prescribe that the party requesting the interim measure must provide reasonable security for the damage which may be incurred by the opposing party as a result of the interim measure.

Section 26

Where a party wishes a witness or an expert to testify under oath, or a party to be examined under truth affirmation, the party may, after obtaining the consent of the arbitrators, submit an application to such effect to the District Court. The aforementioned shall apply where a party wishes that a party or other person be ordered to produce as evidence a document or an object. If the arbitrators consider that the measure is justified having regard to the evidence in the case, they shall approve the request. Where the measure may lawfully be taken, the District Court shall grant the application. The provisions of the Code of Judicial Procedure shall apply with respect to a measure as referred to in the first paragraph. The arbitrators shall be summoned to hear the testimony of a witness, an expert, or a party, and be afforded the opportunity to ask questions. The absence of an arbitrator from the giving of testimony shall not prevent the hearing from taking place.

The Award Section 27

The issues which have been referred to the arbitrators shall be decided in an award. Where the arbitrators terminate the arbitral proceedings without deciding such issues, such shall also take place through an award. Where the parties enter into a settlement agreement, the arbitrators may, at the request of the parties, confirm it in an award.

Other determinations, which are not embodied in an award, are designated as decisions. The mandate of the arbitrators shall be deemed to be completed when they have delivered a final award, unless otherwise provided in sections 32 or 35.

Section 28

Where a party withdraws a claim, the arbitrators shall dismiss that part of the dispute, unless the opposing party requests that the arbitrators rule on the claim.

Section 29

A part of the dispute, or a certain issue which is of significance to the resolution of the dispute, may be decided through a separate award, unless opposed by both parties. However, a claim invoked as a defense by way of set off shall be adjudicated in the same award as the main claim. Where a party has admitted a claim, in whole or in part, a separate award may be rendered in respect of that which has been admitted.

Section 30

Where an arbitrator fails, without valid cause, to participate in the determination of an issue by the arbitral tribunal, such failure will not prevent the other arbitrators from ruling on the matter. Unless the parties have decided otherwise, the opinion agreed upon by the majority of the arbitrators participating in the determination shall prevail. If no majority is attained for any opinion, the opinion of the chairman shall prevail.

Section 31

An award shall be made in writing, signed by the arbitrators. It suffices that the award is signed by a majority of the arbitrators, provided that the reason why all of the arbitrators have not signed the award is noted therein. The parties may decide that the chairman of the arbitral tribunal alone shall sign the award. The award shall state the place of arbitration and the date when the award is made. The award shall be delivered to the parties immediately.

Section 32

If the arbitrators find that an award contains any obvious inaccuracy as a consequence of a typographical, computational, or other similar mistake by the arbitrators or any another person, or if the arbitrators by oversight have failed to decide an issue which should have been dealt with in the award, they may, within thirty days of the date of the announcement of the award, decide to correct or supplement the award. They may also correct or supplement an award, or interpret the decision in an award, where any of the parties so requests within thirty days of receipt of the award by that party. Where, upon request by any of the parties, the arbitrators decide to correct an award or interpret the decision in an award, such shall take place within thirty days from the date of receipt by the arbitrators of the party's request. Where the arbitrators decide to supplement the award, such shall take place within sixty days. Before any decision is made pursuant to this section, the parties should be afforded an opportunity to express their views with respect to the measure.

Invalidity of Awards and Setting Aside Awards Section 33

An award is invalid:

1.   if it includes determination of an issue which, in accordance with Swedish law, may not be decided by arbitrators;

2.   if the award, or the manner in which the award arose, is clearly incompatible with the basic principles of the Swedish legal system; or

3.   if the award does not fulfil the requirements with regard to the written form and signature in accordance with section 31, first paragraph. The invalidity may apply to a certain part of the award.

Section 34

An award which may not be challenged in accordance with section 36 shall, following an application, be wholly or partially set aside upon motion of a party:

1.   if it is not covered by a valid arbitration agreement between the parties;

2.   if the arbitrators have made the award after the expiration of the period decided on by the parties, or where the arbitrators have otherwise exceeded their mandate;

3.   if arbitral proceedings, according to section 47, should not have taken place in Sweden;

4.   if an arbitrator has been appointed contrary to the agreement between the parties or this Act;

5.   if an arbitrator was unauthorized due to any circumstance set forth in sections 7 or 8; or

6.   if, without fault of the party, there otherwise occurred an irregularity in the course of the proceedings which probably influenced the outcome of the case.

A party shall not be entitled to rely upon a circumstance which, through participation in the proceedings without objection, or in any other manner, he may be deemed to have waived. A party shall not be regarded as having accepted the arbitrators' jurisdiction to determine the issue referred to arbitration solely by having appointed an arbitrator. Pursuant to sections 10 and 11, a party may lose the right in accordance with the first paragraph, sub-section 5 to rely upon a circumstance as set forth in section 8. An action must be brought within three months from the date upon which the party received the award or, where correction, supplementation, or interpretation has taken place pursuant to section 32, within a period of three months from the date when the party received the award in its final wording. Following the expiration of the time limit, a party may not invoke a new ground of objection in support of his claim.

Section 35

A court may stay proceedings concerning the invalidity or setting aside of an award for a certain period of time in order to provide the arbitrators with an opportunity to resume the arbitral proceedings or to take some other measure which, in the opinion of the arbitrators, will eliminate the ground for the invalidity or setting aside:

1. provided the court holds that the claim in the case shall be accepted and either of the parties requests a stay; or

2. both parties request a stay. Where the arbitrators make a new award, a party may, within the period of time determined by the court and without issuing a writ of summons, challenge the award insofar as it was based upon the resumed arbitral proceedings or an amendment to the first award. Notwithstanding Chapter 43, section 11, second paragraph of the Code of Judicial Procedure, a trial may continue even where the period of the stay exceeds fifteen days.

Section 36

An award whereby the arbitrators concluded the proceedings without ruling on the issues submitted to them for resolution may be amended, in whole or in part, upon the application of a party. An action must be brought within three months from the date upon which the party received the award or, where correction, supplementation, or interpretation has taken place in accordance with section 32, within a period of three months from the date upon which the party received the award in its final wording. The award shall contain clear instructions as to what must be done by a party who wishes to challenge the award. An action in accordance with the first paragraph which only concerns an issue as referred to in section 42 is permissible where the award means that the arbitrators have considered themselves to lack jurisdiction to determine the dispute. Where the award entails another matter, a party who desires to challenge the award may do so in accordance with the provisions of section 34.

Costs of Arbitration Section 37

The parties shall be jointly and severally liable to pay reasonable compensation to the arbitrators for work and expenses. However, where the arbitrators have stated in the award that they lack jurisdiction to determine the dispute, the party that did not request arbitration shall be liable to make payment only insofar as required due to special circumstances. In a final award, the arbitrators may order the parties to pay compensation to them, together with interest from the date occurring one month following the date of the announcement of the award. The compensation shall be stated separately for each arbitrator.

Section 38

The arbitrators may request security for the compensation. They may fix separate security for individual claims. Where a party fails to provide its share of the requested security within the period specified by the arbitrators, the opposing party may provide the entire security. Where the requested security is not provided, the arbitrators may terminate the proceedings, in whole or in part. During the proceedings, the arbitrators may decide to realise security in order to cover expenses. Following the determination of the arbitrators' compensation in a final award and where the award in that respect has become enforceable, the arbitrators may realise their payment from the security, in the event the parties fail to fulfil their payment obligations in accordance with the award. The right to security also includes income from the property.

Section 39

The provisions of sections 37 and 38 shall apply unless otherwise jointly decided by the parties in a manner that is binding upon the arbitrators. An agreement regarding compensation to the arbitrators that is not entered into with the parties jointly is void. Where one of the parties has provided the entire security, such party may, however, solely consent to the realization of the security by the arbitrators in order to cover the compensation for work expended.

Section 40

The arbitrators may not withhold the award pending the payment of compensation.

Section 41

A party or an arbitrator may bring an action in the District Court against the award regarding the payment of compensation to the arbitrators. Such action must be brought within three months from the date upon which the party received the award and, in the case of an arbitrator, within the same period from the announcement of the award. Where correction, supplementation, or interpretation has taken place in accordance with section 32, the action must be brought by a party within three months from the date upon which the party received the award in its final wording and, in the case of an arbitrator, within the same period from the date when the award was announced in its final wording. The award shall contain clear instructions as to what must be done by a party who wishes to bring an action against the award in this respect. A judgment pursuant to which the compensation to an arbitrator is reduced shall also apply to the party who did not bring the action.

Section 42

Unless otherwise agreed by the parties, the arbitrators may, upon request by a party, order the opposing party to pay compensation for the party's costs and determine the manner in which the compensation to the arbitrators shall be finally allocated between the parties. The arbitrators' order may also include interest, if a party has so requested.

Forum and Limitation Periods Section 43

An action against an award pursuant to sections 33, 34, and 36 shall be considered by the Court of Appeal within the jurisdiction where the arbitral proceedings were held. Where the place of arbitration is not stated in the award, the action may be brought before the Svea Court of Appeal. The determination of the Court of Appeal may not be appealed. However, the Court of Appeal may grant leave to appeal the determination where it is of importance as a matter of precedent that the appeal be considered by the Supreme Court. An action regarding compensation to an arbitrator shall be considered by the District Court at the place of arbitration. Where the place of arbitration is not stated in the award, the action may be brought before the Stockholm District Court.

Section 44

Applications to appoint or discharge an arbitrator shall be considered by the District Court at the place where one of the parties is domiciled or by the District Court at the place of arbitration. The application may also be considered by the Stockholm District Court. Where possible the opposing party shall be afforded the opportunity to express his opinion upon the application before it is granted. Where the application concerns the removal of an arbitrator, the arbitrator should also be heard. Applications concerning the taking of evidence in accordance with section 26 shall be considered by the District Court determined by the arbitrators. In the absence of such decision, the application shall be considered by the Stockholm District Court. Where the District Court has granted an application to appoint or remove an arbitrator, such decision may not appealed. Nor may a determination of the District Court in accordance with section 10, third paragraph otherwise be appealed.

Section 45

Where, according to law or by agreement, an action by a party must be brought within a certain period, but the action is covered by an arbitration agreement, the party must request arbitration in accordance with section 19 within the stated period. Where arbitration has been requested in due time but the arbitral proceedings are terminated without a legal determination of the issue which was submitted to the arbitrators, and this is not due to the negligence of the party, the action shall be deemed to have been instituted in due time where a party requests arbitration or institutes court proceedings within thirty days of receipt of the award, or where the award has been set aside or declared invalid or an action against the award in accordance with section 36 has been dismissed, from the time that this decision becomes final.

International Matters Section 46

This Act shall apply to arbitral proceedings which take place in Sweden notwithstanding that the dispute has an international connection.

Section 47

Arbitral proceedings in accordance with this Act may be commenced in Sweden, where the arbitration agreement provides that the proceedings shall take place in Sweden, or where the arbitrators or an arbitration institution pursuant to the agreement have determined that the proceedings shall take place in Sweden, or the opposing party otherwise consents thereto. Arbitral proceedings in accordance with this Act may also be commenced in Sweden against a party which is domiciled in Sweden or is otherwise subject to the jurisdiction of the Swedish courts with regard to the matter in dispute, unless the arbitration agreement provides that the proceedings shall take place abroad. In other cases, arbitral proceedings in accordance with this Act may not take place in Sweden.

Section 48

Where an arbitration agreement has an international connection, the agreement shall be governed by the law agreed upon by the parties. Where the parties have not reached such an agreement, the arbitration agreement shall be governed by the law of the country in which, by virtue of the agreement, the proceedings have taken place or shall take place. The first paragraph shall not apply to the issue of whether a party was authorized to enter into an arbitration agreement or was duly represented.

Section 49

Where foreign law is applicable to the arbitration agreement, section 4 shall apply to issues which are covered by the agreement, except when:

1.   in accordance with the applicable law, the agreement is invalid, inoperative, or incapable of being performed; or

2.   in accordance with Swedish law, the dispute may not be determined by arbitrators. The jurisdiction of a court to issue such decisions regarding security measures as the court is entitled to issue in accordance with law, notwithstanding the arbitration agreement, is set forth in section 4, third paragraph.

Section 50

The provisions of sections 26 and 44 regarding the taking of evidence during the arbitral proceedings in Sweden shall also apply in respect of arbitral proceedings which take place abroad, where the proceedings are based upon an arbitration agreement and, pursuant to Swedish law, the issues which are referred to the arbitrators may be resolved by arbitrators.

Section 51

Where none of the parties is domiciled or has its place of business in Sweden, such parties may in a commercial relationship through an express written agreement exclude or limit the application of the grounds for setting aside an award as are set forth in section 34. An award which is subject to such an agreement shall be recognized and enforced in Sweden in accordance with the rules applicable to a foreign award.

Recognition and Enforcement of Foreign Awards, etc. Section 52

An award made abroad shall be deemed to be a foreign award. In conjunction with the application of this Act, an award shall be deemed to have been made in the country in which the place of arbitration is situated.

Section 53

Unless otherwise stated in sections 54–60, a foreign award which is based on an arbitration agreement shall be recognized and enforced in Sweden.

Section 54

A foreign award shall not be recognized and enforced in Sweden where the party against whom the award is invoked proves:

1.   that the parties to the arbitration agreement, pursuant to the law applicable to them, lacked capacity to enter into the agreement or were not properly represented, or that the arbitration agreement was not valid under the law to which the parties have subjected it or, failing any indication thereon, under the law of the country where the award was made;

2.   that the party against whom the award is invoked was not given proper notice of the appointment of the arbitrator or of the arbitration proceedings, or was otherwise unable to present his case;

3.   that the award deals with a dispute not contemplated by, or not falling within, the terms of the submission to arbitration, or contains decisions on matters which are beyond the scope of the arbitration agreement, provided that, if the decision on a matter which falls within

the mandate can be separated from those which fall outside the mandate, that part of the award which contains decisions on matters falling within the mandate may be recognized and enforced;

4.   that the composition of the arbitral tribunal, or the arbitral procedure, was not in accordance with the agreement of the parties or, failing such agreement, was not in accordance with the law of the country where the arbitration took place; or

5.   that the award has not yet become binding on the parties, or has been set aside or suspended by a competent authority of the country in which, or under the law of which, the award was made.

Section 55

Recognition and enforcement of a foreign award shall also be refused where a court finds:

1.   that the award includes determination of an issue which, in accordance with Swedish law, may not be decided by arbitrators; or

2.   that it would be clearly incompatible with the basic principles of the Swedish legal system to recognize and enforce the award.

Section 56

An application for the enforcement of a foreign award shall be lodged with the Svea Court of Appeal. The original award or a certified copy of the award must be appended to the application. Unless the Court of Appeal decides otherwise, a certified translation into the Swedish language of the entire award must also be submitted.

Section 57

An application for enforcement shall not be granted unless the opposing party has been afforded an opportunity to express his opinion upon the application.

Section 58

Where the opposing party objects that an arbitration agreement was not entered into, the applicant must submit the arbitration agreement in an original or a certified copy and, unless otherwise decided by the Court of Appeal, must submit a certified translation into the Swedish language, or in some other manner prove that an arbitration agreement was entered into. Where the opposing party objects that a petition has been lodged to set aside the award or a motion for a stay of execution has been submitted to the competent authority as referred to in section 54, sub-section 5, the Court of Appeal may postpone its decision and, upon request by the applicant, order the opposing party to provide reasonable security in default of which enforcement might otherwise be ordered.

Section 59

Where the Court of Appeal grants the application, the award shall be enforced as a final judgment of a Swedish court, unless otherwise determined by the Supreme Court following an appeal of the Court of Appeal's decision.

Section 60

Where a security measure has been granted in accordance with Chapter 15 of the Code of Judicial Procedure, in conjunction with the application of section 7 of the same Chapter, a request for arbitration abroad which might result in an award which is recognized and may be enforced in Sweden shall be equated with the commencement of an action. Where an application for the enforcement of a foreign award has been lodged, the Court of Appeal shall examine a request for a security measure or a request to set aside such decision.

1.   This Act shall enter into force on 1 April 1999, at which time the Arbitration Act (SFS 1929:145) and the Foreign Arbitration Agreements and Awards Act (SFS 1929:147) shall be repealed.

2.   The previous Act shall apply to arbitral proceedings which have been commenced prior to the entry into force or, with respect to enforcement of a foreign award, when the application for enforcement was lodged prior to the entry into force.

3.   Where an arbitration agreement has been concluded prior to the entry into force, the provisions of section 18, second paragraph, section 21, first paragraph, sub-section 1, and section 26, second and third paragraphs of the Arbitration Act (SFS 1929:145) shall apply, with respect to the period within which the award shall be rendered, to proceedings that are commenced within two years from the date of the entry into force of the new Act.

4.   In the circumstances set forth in sub-sections 2 and 3, the parties may agree that only the new Act shall apply.

5.   References in statutes or other legislation to the Arbitration Act (SFS 1929:145) shall refer instead to the new Act.

J. ARBITRATION LEGISLATION OF THE PEOPLE'S REPUBLIC OF CHINA

J.1. ARBITRATION LAW OF THE PEOPLE'S REPUBLIC OF CHINA OF 1994*

(Adopted at the Ninth Meeting of the Standing Committee of the Eighth National People's Congress on August 31, 1994 and promulgated by Order No.31 of the President of the People's Republic of China on August 31, 1994)

Chapter I

General Provisions

Article 1

This Law is formulated in order to ensure the impartial and prompt arbitration of economic disputes, to protect the legitimate rights and interests of the parties and to safeguard the sound development of the socialist market economy.

Article 2

Contractual disputes and other disputes over rights and interests in property between citizens, legal persons and other organizations that are equal subjects may be arbitrated.

Article 3

The following disputes may not be arbitrated:

(1) marital, adoption, guardianship, support and succession disputes;
(2) administrative disputes that shall be handled by administrative organs as prescribed by law.

Article 4

The parties' submission to arbitration to resolve their dispute shall be on the basis of both parties' free will and an arbitration agreement reached between them. If a party applies for arbitration in the absence of an arbitration agreement, the arbitration commission shall not accept the case.

---

* Official translation by the National People's Congress, available at http://www.npc.gov.cn/englishnpc/Law/Integrated_index.html.

Article 5

If the parties have concluded an arbitration agreement and one party institutes an action in a people's court, the people's court shall not accept the case, unless the arbitration agreement is null and void[1].

Article 6

The arbitration commission shall be selected by the parties through agreement. In arbitration, there shall be no jurisdiction by level and no territorial jurisdiction.[2]

Article 7

In arbitration, disputes shall be resolved on the basis of facts, in compliance with the law and in an equitable and reasonable manner.

Article 8

Arbitration shall be carried out independently according to law and shall be free from interference of administrative organs, social organizations or individuals.

Article 9

A system of a single and final award shall be practised for arbitration. If a party applies for arbitration to an arbitration commission or institutes an action in a people's court regarding the same dispute after an arbitration award has been made, the arbitration commission or the people's court shall not accept the case.

If an arbitration award is set aside or its enforcement is disallowed by the people's court in accordance with the law, a party may apply for arbitration on the basis of a new arbitration agreement reached between the parties, or institute an action in the people's court, regarding the same dispute.

Chapter II

Arbitration Commissions and the Arbitration Association

Article 10

Arbitration commissions may be established in municipalities directly under the Central Government and in cities that are the seats of the people's governments of provinces or autonomous regions. They may also be established in other cities divided into districts, according to need.[3]

---

[1]   Here, "invalid" may be a better translation than "null and void" (comments to the Act are provided by Frank Zhang).

[2]   The second sentence of this article means that venue provisions in *PRC Civil Procedure Law* do not apply to arbitration commissions (F.Zhang).

[3]   A better translation for this sentence may be, "They may also be established in other cities, which have districts thereunder, according to need" (F.Zhang).

Arbitration commissions shall not be established at each level of the administrative divisions.

People's governments of the cities referred to in the preceding paragraph shall arrange for the relevant departments and chambers of commerce to organize arbitration commissions in a unified manner.

The establishment of an arbitration commission shall be registered with the administrative department of justice of the relevant province, autonomous region or municipality directly under the Central Government.

Article 11

An arbitration commission shall meet the conditions set forth below:

   (1) to have its own name, domicile and charter;

   (2) to have the necessary property;

   (3) to have the personnel that are to form the commission; and

   (4) to have appointed[4] arbitrators.

The charter of an arbitration commission shall be formulated in accordance with this Law.

Article 12

An arbitration commission shall be composed of one chairman, two to four vice chairmen and seven to eleven members.

The offices of chairman, vice chairman and members of an arbitration commission shall be held by experts in the field of law, economy and trade and persons with practical working experience. Experts in the field of law, economy and trade shall account for at least two thirds of the people forming an arbitration commission.

Article 13

An arbitration commission shall appoint[5] its arbitrators from among righteous and upright persons.

An arbitrator shall meet one of the conditions set forth below:

   (1) to have been engaged in arbitration work for at least eight years;

   (2) to have worked as a lawyer for at least eight years;

   (3) to have served as a judge for at least eight years;

   (4) to have been engaged in legal research or legal education, possessing a senior professional title; or

---

[4]   Here, "engaged" may be a better translation than "appointed" (F.Zhang).

[5]   Here, "engage" may be a better translation than "appoint" (F.Zhang).

(5) to have acquired the knowledge of law, engaged in the professional work in the field of economy and trade, etc., possessing a senior professional title or having an equivalent professional level.

An arbitration commission shall have a register of arbitrators in different specializations.

Article 14

Arbitration commissions shall be independent from administrative organs and there shall be no subordinate relationships between arbitration commissions and administrative organs. There shall also be no subordinate relationships between arbitration commissions.

Article 15

China Arbitration Association is a social organization with the status of a legal person. Arbitration commissions are members of China Arbitration Association. The charter of China Arbitration Association shall be formulated by its national congress of members.

China Arbitration Association is a self-disciplined organization of arbitration commissions. It shall, in accordance with its charter, supervise arbitration commissions and their members and arbitrators as to whether or not they breach discipline.

China Arbitration Association shall formulate rules of arbitration in accordance with this Law and the relevant provisions of the Civil Procedure Law.

Chapter III

Arbitration Agreement

Article 16

An arbitration agreement shall include arbitration clauses stipulated in the contract and agreements of submission to arbitration that are concluded in other written forms before or after disputes arise.

An arbitration agreement shall contain the following particulars:

(1) an expression of intention to apply for arbitration;

(2) matters for arbitration; and

(3) a designated arbitration commission.

Article 17

An arbitration agreement shall be null and void[6] under one of the following circumstances:

---

6 Here, "invalid" may be a better translation than "null and void" (F.Zhang).

(1) the agreed matters for arbitration exceed the range of arbitrable matters as specified by law;

(2) one party that concluded the arbitration agreement has no capacity for civil conducts or has limited capacity for civil conducts; or

(3) one party coerced the other party into concluding the arbitration agreement.

Article 18

If an arbitration agreement contains no or unclear provisions concerning the matters for arbitration or the arbitration commission, the parties may reach a supplementary agreement. If no such supplementary agreement can be reached, the arbitration agreement shall be null and void[7].

Article 19

An arbitration agreement shall exist independently. The amendment, rescission, termination or invalidity of a contract shall not affect the validity of the arbitration agreement.

The arbitration tribunal shall have the power to affirm[8] the validity of a contract.

Article 20

If a party challenges the validity of the arbitration agreement, he may request the arbitration commission to make a decision or apply to the people's court for a ruling. If one party requests the arbitration commission to make a decision and the other party applies to the people's court for a ruling, the people's court shall give a ruling.

A party's challenge of the validity of the arbitration agreement shall be raised prior to the arbitration tribunal's first hearing.

Chapter IV

Arbitration Proceedings

Section 1

Application and Acceptance

Article 21

A party's application for arbitration shall meet the following requirements:

(1) there is an arbitration agreement;

(2) there is a specific arbitration claim and there are facts and reasons therefore; and

---

[7] Here, "invalid" may be a better translation than "null and void" (F.Zhang).
[8] Here, "determine" may be a better translation than "affirm" (F.Zhang).

    (3) the application is within the scope of the arbitration commission's acceptability.

Article 22

To apply for arbitration, a party shall submit to the arbitration commission the written arbitration agreement and a written application for arbitration together with copies thereof.

Article 23

A written application for arbitration shall specify the following particulars:

    (1) the name, sex, age, occupation, work unit and domicile of each party, or the name and domicile of legal persons or other organizations and the names and positions of their legal representatives or chief responsible persons;

    (2) the arbitration claim and the facts and reasons on which it is based; and

    (3) the evidence, the source of the evidence and the names and domiciles of witnesses.

Article 24

When an arbitration commission receives a written application for arbitration and considers that the application complies with the conditions for acceptance, it shall accept the application and notify the party within five days from the date of receipt. If the arbitration commission considers that the application does not comply with the conditions for acceptance, it shall inform the party in writing of its rejection of the application and explain the reasons for rejection within five days from the date of receipt.

Article 25

After an arbitration commission accepts an application for arbitration, it shall, within the time limit specified in the rules of arbitration, deliver a copy of the rules of arbitration and the register of arbitrators to the claimant, and serve one copy of the application for arbitration together with the rules of arbitration and the register of arbitrators on the respondent.

After receiving the copy of the application for arbitration, the respondent shall submit a written defense to the arbitration commission within the time limit specified in the rules of arbitration. After receiving the written defense, the arbitration commission shall serve a copy thereof on the claimant within the time limit specified in the rules of arbitration. Failure on the part of the respondent to submit a written defense shall not affect the progress of the arbitration proceedings.

Article 26

If the parties have concluded an arbitration agreement and one party has instituted an action in a people's court without declaring the existence of the arbitration agreement and, after the people's court has accepted the case, the other party submits the arbitration agreement prior to the first hearing, the people's court shall dismiss the case unless the arbitration agreement is null and void[9]. If, prior to the first hearing, the other party has not raised an objection to the people's court's acceptance of the case, he shall be deemed to have renounced the arbitration agreement and the people's court shall continue to try the case.

Article 27

The claimant may renounce or amend its arbitration claim. The respondent may accept or refuse an arbitration claim and shall have the right to make a counter-claim.

Article 28

A party may apply for property preservation if it may become impossible or difficult for the party to implement the award due to an act of the other party or other causes.

If a party applies for property preservation, the arbitration commission shall submit the party's application to the people's court in accordance with the relevant provisions of the Civil Procedure Law.

If an application for property preservation has been wrongfully made, the applicant shall compensate the person against whom the application has been made for any loss incurred from property preservation.

Article 29

A party or statutory agent may appoint a lawyer or other agent to carry out arbitration activities. To appoint a lawyer or other agent to carry out arbitration activities, a power of attorney shall be submitted to the arbitration commission.

Section 2

Formation of Arbitration Tribunal

Article 30

An arbitration tribunal may be composed of either three arbitrators or one arbitrator. An arbitration tribunal composed of three arbitrators shall have a presiding arbitrator.

---

[9] Here, "invalid" may be a better translation than "null and void" (F.Zhang).

Article 31

If the parties agree that the arbitration tribunal shall be composed of three arbitrators, they shall each appoint or entrust the chairman of the arbitration commission to appoint one arbitrator. The parties shall jointly select or jointly entrust the chairman of the arbitration commission to appoint the third arbitrator who shall be the presiding arbitrator.

If the parties agree that the arbitration tribunal shall be composed of one arbitrator, they shall jointly appoint or jointly entrust the chairman of the arbitration commission to appoint the arbitrator.

Article 32

If the parties fail to agree on the method of formation of the arbitration tribunal or to select the arbitrators within the time limit specified in the rules of arbitration, the arbitrators shall be appointed by the chairman of the arbitration commission.

Article 33

After the arbitration tribunal has been formed, the arbitration commission shall notify the parties in writing of the tribunal's formation.

Article 34

In one of the following circumstances, the arbitrator must withdraw, and the parties shall also have the right to challenge the arbitrator for a withdrawal:

    (1)   the arbitrator is a party in the case or a close relative of a party or of an agent in the case;

    (2)   the arbitrator has a personal interest in the case;

    (3)   the arbitrator has other relationship with a party or his agent in the case which may affect the impartiality of arbitration; or

    (4)   the arbitrator has privately met with a party or agent or accepted an invitation to entertainment or gift from a party or agent.

Article 35

If a party challenges an arbitrator, he shall submit his challenge, with a statement of the reasons therefore, prior to the first hearing. If the matter giving rise to the challenge became known after the first hearing, the challenge may be made before the conclusion of the final hearing of the case.

Article 36

The decision as to whether or not the arbitrator should withdraw shall be made by the chairman of the arbitration commission. If the chairman of the arbitration commission serves as an arbitrator, the decision shall be made collectively by the arbitration commission.

Article 37

If an arbitrator cannot perform his duties due to his withdrawal or for other reasons, a substitute arbitrator shall be selected or appointed in accordance with this Law.

After a substitute arbitrator has been selected or appointed on account of an arbitrator's withdrawal, a party may request that the arbitration proceedings already carried out should be carried out anew. The decision as to whether to approve it or not shall be made by the arbitration tribunal. The arbitration tribunal may also make a decision of its own motion as to whether or not the arbitration proceedings already carried out should be carried out anew.

Article 38

If an arbitrator is involved in the circumstances described in item (4) of Article 34 of this Law and the circumstances are serious or involved in the circumstances described in item (6) of Article 58 of this Law, he shall assume legal liability according to law and the arbitration commission shall remove his name from the register of arbitrators.

Section 3

Hearing and Award

Article 39

Arbitration shall be conducted by means of oral hearings. If the parties agree to arbitration without oral hearings, the arbitration tribunal may render an arbitration award on the basis of the written application for arbitration, the written defense and other material.

Article 40

Arbitration shall be conducted in camera.[10] If the parties agree to public arbitration, the arbitration may be public unless State secrets are involved.

Article 41

The arbitration commission shall notify the parties of the date of the hearing within the time limit specified in the rules of arbitration. A party may, within the time limit specified in the rules of arbitration, request a postponement of the hearing if he has justified reasons therefore. The arbitration tribunal shall decide whether or not to postpone the hearing.

Article 42

If the claimant fails to appear before the arbitration tribunal without justified reasons after having been notified in writing or leaves the hearing

---

[10] A better translation for this sentence may be, "Arbitration shall not be conducted openly" (F.Zhang).

prior to its conclusion without the permission of the arbitration tribunal, he may be deemed to have withdrawn his application for arbitration.

If the respondent fails to appear before the arbitration tribunal without justified reasons after having been notified in writing or leaves the hearing prior to its conclusion without the permission of the arbitration tribunal, a default award may be made.

Article 43

Parties shall provide evidences in support of their own arguments.

The arbitration tribunal may, as it considers necessary, collect evidences on its own.

Article 44

If the arbitration tribunal considers that a special issue requires appraisal, it may refer the issue for appraisal to an appraisal department agreed on by the parties or to an appraisal department designated by the arbitration tribunal.

If requested by a party or required by the arbitration tribunal, the appraisal department shall send its appraiser to attend the hearing. Subject to the permission of the arbitration tribunal, the parties may question the appraiser.

Article 45

The evidence shall be presented during the hearings and may be examined by the parties.

Article 46

Under circumstances where the evidence may be destroyed or lost or difficult to obtain at a later time, a party may apply for preservation of the evidence. If a party applies for preservation of the evidence, the arbitration commission shall submit his application to the basic people's court[11] in the place where the evidence is located.

Article 47

The parties shall have the right to carry on debate in the course of arbitration. At the end of the debate, the presiding arbitrator or the sole arbitrator shall solicit final opinions from the parties.

Article 48

The arbitration tribunal shall make records of the hearings in writing. The parties and other participants in the arbitration shall have the right to apply for supplementation or correction of the record of their own statements if they consider that such record contains omissions or errors.

---

[11] Here, "people's court at the basic level" may be a better translation than "basic people's court" (F.Zhang).

If no supplementation or corrections are to be made, their application therefore shall be recorded.

The record shall be signed or sealed by the arbitrators, the recordist, the parties and other participants in the arbitration.

Article 49

After an application for arbitration has been made, the parties may settle their dispute on their own. If the parties have reached a settlement agreement, they may request the arbitration tribunal to make an arbitration award in accordance with the settlement agreement; alternatively, they may withdraw their application for arbitration.

Article 50

If a party repudiates the settlement agreement after the application for arbitration has been withdrawn, he may apply for arbitration again in accordance with the arbitration agreement.

Article 51

The arbitration tribunal may carry out conciliation prior to giving an arbitration award. The arbitration tribunal shall conduct conciliation if both parties voluntarily seek conciliation. If conciliation is unsuccessful, an arbitration award shall be made promptly.

If conciliation leads to a settlement agreement, the arbitration tribunal shall make a written conciliation statement or make an arbitration award in accordance with the result of the settlement agreement. A written conciliation statement and an arbitration award shall have equal legal effect.

Article 52

A written conciliation statement shall specify the arbitration claim and the results of the settlement agreed upon between the parties. The written conciliation statement shall be signed by the arbitrators, sealed by the arbitration commission, and then served on both parties.

The written conciliation statement shall become legally effective immediately after both parties have signed for receipt thereof.

If the written conciliation statement is repudiated by a party before he signs for receipt thereof, the arbitration tribunal shall promptly make an arbitration award.

Article 53

The arbitration award shall be made in accordance with the opinion of the majority of the arbitrators. The opinion of the minority of the arbitrators may be entered in the record. If the arbitration tribunal is unable to form a majority opinion, the arbitration award shall be made in accordance with the opinion of the presiding arbitrator.

Article 54

An arbitration award shall specify the arbitration claim, the facts of the dispute, the reasons for the decision, the results of the award, the allocation of arbitration fees and the date of the award. If the parties agree that they do not wish the facts of the dispute and the reasons for the decision to be specified in the arbitration award, the same may be omitted. The arbitration award shall be signed by the arbitrators and sealed by the arbitration commission. An arbitrator with dissenting opinions as to the arbitration award may sign the award or choose not to sign it.

Article 55

In arbitration proceedings, if a part of the facts involved has already become clear, the arbitration tribunal may first make an award in respect of such part of the facts.

Article 56

If there are literal or calculation errors in the arbitration award, or if the matters which have been decided by the arbitration tribunal are omitted in the arbitration award, the arbitration tribunal shall make due corrections or supplementation. The parties may, within 30 days from the date of receipt of the award, request the arbitration tribunal to make such corrections or supplementation.

Article 57

The arbitration award shall be legally effective as of the date on which it is made.

Chapter V

Application for Setting Aside Arbitration Award

Article 58

A party may apply for setting aside an arbitration award to the intermediate people's court in the place where the arbitration commission is located if he can produce evidence which proves that the arbitration award involves one of the following circumstances:

(1) there is no arbitration agreement;

(2) the matters decided in the award exceed the scope of the arbitration agreement or are beyond the arbitral authority of the arbitration commission;

(3) the formation of the arbitration tribunal or the arbitration procedure was not in conformity with the statutory procedure[12];

(4) the evidence on which the award is based was forged;

(5) the other party has withheld the evidence which is sufficient to affect the impartiality of the arbitration;[13] or

(6) the arbitrators have committed embezzlement, accepted bribes or done malpractices for personal benefits or perverted the law in the arbitration of the case.

The people's court shall rule to set aside the arbitration award if a collegial panel formed by the people's court verifies upon examination that the award involves one of the circumstances set forth in the preceding paragraph.

If the people's court determines that the arbitration award violates the public interest, it shall rule to set aside the award.

Article 59

A party that wishes to apply for setting aside the arbitration award shall submit such application within six months from the date of receipt of the award.

Article 60

The people's court shall, within two months from the date of accepting an application for setting aside an arbitration award, rule to set aside the award or to reject the application.

Article 61

If, after accepting an application for setting aside an arbitration award, the people's court considers that the case may be re-arbitrated by the arbitration tribunal, it shall notify the tribunal that it shall re-arbitrate the case within a certain time limit and shall rule to stay the setting-aside procedure. If the arbitration tribunal refuses to re-arbitrate the case, the people's court shall rule to resume the setting-aside procedure.

Chapter VI

Enforcement

Article 62

The parties shall perform the arbitration award. If a party fails to perform the arbitration award, the other party may apply to the people's court for enforcement in accordance with the relevant provisions of the Civil

---

[12] Here, "procedure provided by law" may be a better translation than "statutory procedure" (F.Zhang).

[13] A better translation for this sentence may be, "The opposing party has concealed evidences that may sufficiently affect the just finding of the case" (F.Zhang).

Procedure Law. The people's court to which the application has been made shall enforce the award.

Article 63

If the party against whom the enforcement is sought presents evidence which proves that the arbitration award involves one of the circumstances set forth in the second paragraph of Article 217 of the Civil Procedure Law,[14] the people's court shall, after examination and verification by a collegial panel formed by the people's court, rule to disallow the award.

Article 64

If one party applies for enforcement of the arbitration award and the other party applies for setting aside the arbitration award, the people's court shall rule to suspend the procedure of enforcement.

If the people's court rules to set aside the arbitration award, it shall rule to terminate the enforcement procedure. If the people's court rules to reject the application for setting aside the arbitration award, it shall rule to resume the enforcement procedure.

Chapter VII

Special Provisions for Arbitration Involving Foreign Elements

Article 65

The provisions of this Chapter shall apply to the arbitration of disputes arising from economic, trade, transportation and maritime activities involving a foreign element. For matters not covered in this Chapter, the other relevant provisions of this Law shall apply.

Article 66

Foreign-related arbitration commissions may be organized and established by the China Chamber of International Commerce.

A foreign-related arbitration commission shall be composed of one chairman, a certain number of vice chairmen and members.

The chairman, vice chairmen and members of a foreign-related arbitration commission may be appointed by the China Chamber of International Commerce.

Article 67

A foreign-related arbitration commission may appoint[15] arbitrators from among foreigners with special knowledge in the fields of law, economy and trade, science and technology, etc.

---

[14] After the *Civil Procedure Law*'s amendment in 2007, the clause being referred to here is Article 213, Paragraph 2 (F.Zhang).

[15] Here, "engaged" may be a better translation than "appointed" (F.Zhang).

Article 68

If a party to a foreign-related arbitration applies for preservation of the evidence, the foreign-related arbitration commission shall submit his application to the intermediate people's court in the place where the evidence is located.

Article 69

A foreign-related arbitration tribunal may enter the details of the hearings in written records or make written minutes thereof. The written minutes may be signed or sealed by the parties and other participants in the arbitration.

Article 70

If a party presents evidence which proves that a foreign-related arbitration award involves one of the circumstances set forth in the first paragraph of Article 260 of the Civil Procedure Law, the people's court shall, after examination and verification by a collegial panel formed by the people's court, rule to set aside the award.

Article 71

If the party against whom the enforcement is sought presents evidence which proves that the foreign-related arbitration award involves one of the circumstances set forth in the first paragraph of Article 260 of the Civil Procedure Law,[16] the people's court shall, after examination and verification by a collegial panel formed by the people's court, rule to disallow the enforcement.

Article 72

If a party applies for enforcement of a legally effective arbitration award made by a foreign-related arbitration commission and if the party against whom the enforcement is sought or such party's property is not within the territory of the People's Republic of China, he shall directly apply to a competent foreign court for recognition and enforcement of the award.

Article 73

Foreign-related arbitration rules may be formulated by the China Chamber of International Commerce in accordance with this Law and the relevant provisions of the Civil Procedure Law.

---

[16] After the *Civil Procedure Law*'s amendment in 2007, the clause being referred to here is Article 258 (F.Zhang).

Chapter VIII

Supplementary Provisions

Article 74

If prescription for arbitration is provided by law, such provisions shall apply. In the absence of such provisions, the prescription for litigation shall apply to arbitration.[17]

Article 75

Prior to the formulation of rules of arbitration by China Arbitration Association, arbitration commissions may formulate provisional rules of arbitration in accordance with this Law and the relevant provisions of the Civil Procedure Law.

Article 76

Parties shall pay arbitration fees according to regulations.[18]

Measures[19] for charging arbitration fees shall be submitted to the price control authorities for examination and approval.

Article 77

Regulations concerning arbitration of labor disputes and agricultural contractor's contract disputes arising within the agricultural collective economic organizations shall be formulated separately.[20]

Article 78

If regulations governing arbitration promulgated prior to the implementation of this Law contravene the provisions of this Law, the provisions of this Law shall prevail.

Article 79

Arbitration institutions established prior to the implementation of this Law in the municipalities directly under the Central Government, in the cities that are the seats of the people's governments of provinces or autonomous regions and in other cities divided into districts[21] shall be reorganized in accordance with this Law. Those of such arbitration

---

[17] A better translation for this article may be, "Where the law provides a statute of limitation for arbitration, such provisions shall apply. Where the law does not provide any statute of limitation for arbitration, the statute of limitation for litigation shall apply" (F.Zhang).

[18] A better translation for this article may be, "Parties shall pay arbitration fees according to relevant provisions" (F.Zhang).

[19] Here, "Schedules" may be a better translation than "Measures" (F.Zhang).

[20] A better translation for this article may be, "Arbitration of labor disputes and disputes arising from agricultural contracting contracts within agricultural collective economic organizations shall be subject to other regulations" (F.Zhang).

[21] Here, "cities, which have districts thereunder" may be a better translation than "cities divided into districts" (F.Zhang).

institutions that have not been reorganized shall terminate upon the end of one year from the date of the implementation of this Law.

Other arbitration institutions established prior to the implementation of this Law that do not comply with the provisions of this Law shall terminate on the date of the implementation of this Law.

Article 80

This Law shall go into effect as of September 1, 1995.

J.2. CIVIL PROCEDURE LAW OF THE PEOPLE'S REPUBLIC OF CHINA* (SELECTED PROVISIONS)

Chapter XX

Application for Execution[22] and Referral

Article 237

If a party fails to comply with an award of an arbitral organ[23] established according to the law, the other party may apply for execution[24] to the people's court which has jurisdiction over the case. The people's court applied to shall enforce the award.

If the party against whom the application is made furnishes proof that the arbitral award involves any of the following circumstances, the people's court shall, after examination and verification by a collegial panel, make a written order not to allow the enforcement:

(1) the parties have had no arbitration clause in their contract, nor have subsequently reached a written agreement on arbitration;

(2) the matters dealt with by the award fall outside the scope of the arbitration agreement or are matters which the arbitral organ[25] has no power to arbitrate;

(3) the composition of the arbitration tribunal or the procedure for arbitration contradicts the procedure prescribed by the law.

(4) the evidence based on which the arbitral award is made is falsified;

(5) the other parties conceal the evidence from the arbitral organ and is sufficient to affect the impartiality of the arbitral award; or

---

* Official translation by the National People's Congress, available at Certain textual adjustments were made and numeric has been changed by Yue Ma (CEU S.J.D. Candidate) in order to reflect the law's amendments made in 2012.

[22] Here, "enforcement" may be a better translation than "execution" (F.Zhang).

[23] Here, "arbitration institution" may be a better translation than "arbitral organ" (F.Zhang).

[24] Here, "enforcement" may be a better translation than "execution" (F.Zhang).

[25] Here, "arbitration institution" may be a better translation than "arbitral organ" (F.Zhang).

(6)   the arbitrators have committed embezzlement, accepted bribes or done malpractice for personal benefits or perverted the law in the arbitration of the case.

If the people's court determines that the execution[26] of the arbitral award is against the social and public interest, it shall make an order not to allow the execution[27].

The above-mentioned written order shall be served on both parties and the arbitral organ[28].

If the execution[29] of an arbitral award is disallowed by a written order of the people's court, the parties may, in accordance with a written agreement on arbitration reached between them, apply for arbitration again; they may also bring an action in a people's court.

Chapter XXVI

Arbitration

Article 271

In the case of a dispute arising from the foreign economic, trade, transport or maritime activities of China, if the parties have had an arbitration clause in the contract concerned or have subsequently reached a written arbitration agreement stipulating the submission of the dispute for arbitration to an arbitral organ[30] in the People's Republic of China handling cases involving foreign element, or to any other arbitral body, they may not bring an action in a people's court.

If the parties have not had an arbitration clause in the contract concerned or have not subsequently reached a written arbitration agreement, they may bring an action in a people's court.

Article 272

If a party has applied for the adoption of preservation measure, the arbitral organ[31] of the People's Republic of China handling cases involving foreign element shall refer the party's application for a decision to the intermediate people's court of the place where the party against whom the application is made has his domicile or where his property is located.

---

[26]   Here, "enforcement" may be a better translation than "execution" (F.Zhang).

[27]   *Id.*

[28]   Here, "arbitration institution" may be a better translation than "arbitral organ" (F.Zhang).

[29]   Here, "enforcement" may be a better translation than "execution" (F.Zhang).

[30]   Here, "arbitration institution" may be a better translation than "arbitral organ" (F.Zhang).

[31]   *Id.*

Article 273

In a case in which an award has been made by an arbitral organ[32] of the People's Republic of China handling cases involving foreign element, the parties may not bring an action in a people's court. If one party fails to comply with the arbitral award, the other party may apply for its enforcement to the intermediate people's court of the place where the party against whom the application for enforcement is made has his domicile or where his property is located.

Article 274

A people's court shall, after examination and verification by a collegial panel of the court, make a written order not to allow the enforcement of the award rendered by an arbitral organ[33] of the People's Republic of China handling cases involving foreign element, if the party against whom the application for enforcement is made furnishes proof that:

(1) the parties have not had an arbitration clause in the contract or have not subsequently reached a written arbitration agreement;

(2) the party against whom the application for enforcement is made was not given notice for the appointment of an arbitrator or for the inception of the arbitration proceedings or was unable to present his case due to causes for which he is not responsible;

(3) the composition of the arbitration tribunal or the procedure for arbitration was not in conformity with the rules of arbitration; or

(4) the matters dealt with by the award fall outside the scope of the arbitration agreement or which the arbitral organ[34] was not empowered to arbitrate.

If the people's court determines that the enforcement of the award goes against the social and public interest of the country, the people's court shall make a written order not to allow the enforcement of the arbitral award.

Article 275

If the enforcement of an arbitral award is disallowed by a written order of a people's court, the parties may, in accordance with a written arbitration agreement reached between them, apply for arbitration again; they may also bring an action in a people's court.

---

[32] *Id.*

[33] *Id.*

[34] *Id.*

Chapter XXVII
Judicial Assistance

Article 282

In the case of an application or request for recognition and enforcement of a legally effective judgment or written order of a foreign court, the people's court shall, after examining it in accordance with the international treaties concluded or acceded to by the People's Republic of China or with the principle of reciprocity and arriving at the conclusion that it does not contradict the basic principles of the law of the People's Republic of China nor violates State sovereignty, security and social and public interest of the country, recognize the validity of the judgment or written order, and, if required, issue a writ of execution to enforce it in accordance with the relevant provisions of this Law; if the application or request contradicts the basic principles of the law of the People's Republic of China or violates State sovereignty, security and social and public interest of the country, the people's court shall not recognize and enforce it.

Article 283

If an award made by a foreign arbitral organ[35] requires the recognition and enforcement by a people's court of the People's Republic of China, the party concerned shall directly apply to the intermediate people's court of the place where the party subjected to enforcement has his domicile or where his property is located. The people's court shall deal with the matter in accordance with the international treaties concluded or acceded to by the People's Republic of China or with the principle of reciprocity.

J.3. THE SUPREME PEOPLE'S COURT'S INTERPRETATION ON CERTAIN ISSUES CONCERNING THE APPLICATION OF THE "ARBITRATION LAW OF THE PEOPLE'S REPUBLIC OF CHINA"*

(Adopted at No. 1375 Meeting of the Adjudication
Committee of the Supreme People's Court on
December 26, 2005, Fa Shi (2006) No.7)

In accordance with the "Arbitration Law of the People's Republic of China", the "Civil Procedure Law of the People's Republic of China" and other laws, the following interpretation is made concerning certain issues relating to the application of law in arbitration cases heard by the people's courts:

---

[35] *Id.*

*   English translation prepared by Tietie (Frank) Zhang of Cornell Law School.

Article 1

Arbitration agreements in "other writing forms" as provided in Article 16 of the Arbitration Law include agreements calling for arbitration reached in forms of contract, letter, data message (including telegraph, telex, facsimile, electronic data interchange, and e-mail) and other forms.

Article 2

Where parties agree in general that subject matters for arbitration are contract disputes, disputes arising from the establishment, validity, amendment, transfer, performance, liability for breach, interpretation and rescission of a contract may all be found as subject matters for arbitration.

Article 3

Where the name of the arbitration institution agreed in an arbitration agreement is inaccurate, but a specific arbitration institution could be ascertained, it should be found that the arbitration institution has been chosen.

Article 4

Where the arbitration agreement only agrees on the applicable arbitration rules for the dispute, it shall be deemed that no arbitration institution has been agreed, except that the parties reach a supplementary agreement or the arbitration institution could be ascertained according to the agreed arbitration rules.

Article 5

Where two or more arbitration institutions are agreed in an arbitration agreement, the parties may agree to choose one of the arbitration institutions and apply for arbitration; where the parties cannot reach an agreement on the choice of arbitration institution, the arbitration agreement is invalid.

Article 6

Where it is agreed in an arbitration agreement to arbitrate in the arbitration institution at a certain place, if there is only one arbitration institution at such place, then this arbitration institution is deemed as the agreed arbitration institution. If there are two or more arbitration institutions at such place, the parties may agree to choose one of the arbitration institutions and apply for arbitration; if the parties cannot reach an agreement on the choice of arbitration institution, the arbitration agreement is invalid.

Article 7

Where the parties agree that they may either apply for arbitration to an arbitration institution or file a lawsuit to a people's court to resolve their dispute, the arbitration agreement is invalid, except that one party applies for arbitration to an arbitration institution and the other party does not raise any dispute within the time limit provided in Article 20, Paragraph 2 of the Arbitration law.

Article 8

Where a party merges with others or separates itself after concluding an arbitration agreement, the arbitration agreement is binding upon the successor to its rights and obligations.

Where a party deceases after concluding an arbitration agreement, the arbitration agreement is binding upon the heir inheriting the party's rights and obligations of the subject matters for arbitration.

Situations provided in the two preceding paragraphs shall not apply if the parties agree otherwise when concluding the arbitration agreement.

Article 9

Where rights and obligations are transferred in parts or in whole, the arbitration agreement is binding upon the transferee, except that parties agree otherwise, or that the transferee opposes it when accepting the rights and obligations, or that the transferee does not know the existence of a separate arbitration agreement.

Article 10

Where the contract does not take effect after being established, or is cancelled, Article 19, Paragraph 1 of the Arbitration Law shall apply when finding the validity of the arbitration agreement.

Where the parties reach an arbitration agreement when concluding a contract, the failure to establish the contract does not affect the validity of the arbitration agreement.

Article 11

Where it is agreed in a contract that a valid arbitration clause in another contract or document shall apply to the settlement of disputes, when contractual disputes arise, the parties shall call for arbitration according to such arbitration clause.

Where there are arbitration provisions in a relevant international convention which shall apply to a foreign-related contract, when contractual disputes arise, the parties shall call for arbitration according to the arbitration provisions in the international convention.

Article 12

Cases in which a party applies to the people's court to confirm the validity of an arbitration agreement shall fall into the jurisdiction of the intermediate people's court at the place where the arbitration institution agreed in the arbitration agreement resides; if the arbitration institution agreed in the arbitration agreement is not clear, the case shall fall into the jurisdiction of the intermediate people's court at the place where the arbitration agreement is concluded, or where the respondent domiciles.

Cases in which a party applies to confirm the validity of a foreign-related arbitration agreement shall fall into the jurisdiction of the intermediate people's court at the place where the arbitration institution agreed in the arbitration agreement resides, where the arbitration agreement is concluded, or where the applicant or the respondent domiciles.

Cases relating to the validity of an arbitration agreement in admiralty or maritime disputes shall fall into the jurisdiction of the maritime court at the place where the arbitration institution agreed in the arbitration agreement resides, where the arbitration agreement is concluded, or where the applicant or the respondent domiciles; if there is no maritime court at the above places, the case shall fall into the jurisdiction of the nearest maritime court.

Article 13

According to Article 20, Paragraph 2 of the Arbitration Law, where a party does not raise any dispute concerning the validity of the arbitration agreement before the first hearing is held by the arbitration tribunal, but subsequently applies to the people's court to confirm the arbitration agreement is invalid, the people's court shall not accept the case.

After an arbitration institution has made a decision on the validity of an arbitration agreement, if a party applies to the people's court to confirm the validity of the arbitration agreement or to set aside the arbitration institution's decision, the people's court shall not accept the case.

Article 14

The "first hearing" provided in Article 26 of the Arbitration Law refers to the first trial hearing organized by the people's court after the defense period expires, excluding all kinds of activities in the pre-trial proceedings.

Article 15

When hearing cases concerning confirmation of the validity of an arbitration agreement, the people's court shall form a collegial panel to conduct examination, and to inquire the parties.

Article 16

When reviewing the validity of a foreign-related arbitration agreement, the law chosen by the parties shall apply; where the parties failed to agree on the applicable law, but did agree on the place of arbitration, the law at the place of arbitration shall apply; where the parties agreed on neither the applicable law nor the place of arbitration, or otherwise the place of arbitration agreed on is not clear, the law at the place of the court shall apply.

Article 17

Where a party applies to set aside an arbitration award basing upon reasons other than those provided in Article 58 of the Arbitration Law or Article 260[36] of the Civil Procedure Law, the people's court shall not sustain such application.

Article 18

The phrase "there is no arbitration agreement" provided in Article 58, Paragraph 1, Item (1) of the Arbitration Law refers to the situation where the parties did not reach an arbitration agreement. Where an arbitration agreement is found to be invalid or cancelled, it shall be treated as if there is no arbitration agreement.

Article 19

Where a party applies to set aside an arbitration award basing on the reason that matters decided in the award fall outside the scope of the arbitration agreement, if it has been found true after review, the people's court shall set aside the part of the arbitration award that is outside the scope. However, if the part outside the scope is not severable from other matters in the award, the people's court shall set aside the arbitration award.

Article 20

The "in violation of procedures provided by law" provided in Article 58 of the Arbitration Law refers to situations in violation of the arbitration proceeding provided in Arbitration Law and the arbitration rules chosen by the parties, that may affect the correct decision on the case.

Article 21

Where the case in which a party applies for setting aside a domestic award falls into to one of the situations mentioned below, the people's court may, according to Article 61 of the Arbitration Law, notify the arbitration tribunal to re-arbitrate within a certain period:

(1) The evidences on which the award is based are forged;

(2) The opposing party has concealed evidences that may sufficiently affect the just finding of the case.

The people's court shall specify its detailed reason for requiring re-arbitration within the notification.

Article 22

Where an arbitration tribunal starts to re-arbitrate within the time limit specified by the people's court, the people's court shall rule to terminate the

---

[36] Now Article 274 (after 2012 amendments). Numeric update made by Yue Ma (CEU S.J.D. Candidate).

procedure for setting aside; where the re-arbitration is not started, the people's court shall rule to resume the procedure for setting aside.

Article 23

Where a party does not agree with the re-arbitration award, it may apply to the people's court according to Article 58 of the Arbitration Law for setting aside within 6 months after the service of the re-arbitration award.

Article 24

In cases in which a party applies for setting aside an arbitration award, the people's court shall form a collegial panel to hear the case and to question the parties.

Article 25

After the people's court accepts a party's application for setting aside an arbitration award, where the other party applies for enforcing the same arbitration award, the people's court accepting the application for enforcement shall rule to stay the enforcement after accepting the case.

Article 26

After a party's application for setting aside an arbitration award is overruled, where it also raises, in the enforcement procedure, defense opinions not to enforce the award on the same reasons, such opinions shall not be sustained by the people's court.

Article 27

Where a party did not dispute the validity of the arbitration agreement in the arbitration proceeding, after the arbitration award is rendered, however, it moves to set aside the arbitration award or puts forward defense opinion not to enforce the arbitration award basing upon the invalidity of the arbitration agreement, it shall not be supported by the people's court.

Where a party disputed the validity of the arbitration agreement in the arbitration proceeding, and after the arbitration award is rendered, it further moves to set aside the arbitration award or puts forward defense opinion not to enforce the arbitration award basing upon the same reason, after review, if it is in accordance with provisions of Article 58 of the Arbitration Law, Article 217 or Article 260[37] of the Civil Procedure Law, it shall be supported by the people's court.

---

[37] Now Article 237 or 274 (after 2012 amendments). Numeric update made by Yue Ma (CEU S.J.D. Candidate).

Article 28

Where a party applies for not enforcing a written conciliation statement or an arbitration award rendered basing upon the settlement agreement between the parties, it shall not be supported by the people's court.

Article 29

The case in which a party applies for enforcing an arbitration award shall fall into the jurisdiction of the intermediate people's court at the place where the party subject to enforcement domiciles or where the property subject to enforcement locates.

Article 30

Basing upon actual needs in hearing cases concerning setting aside and enforcing arbitration awards, the people's court may require statement from arbitration institutions or request to review the case files of relevant arbitration institutions.

The rulings issued by the people's court in conducting cases relating to arbitration may also be sent to relevant arbitration institutions.

Article 31

This Interpretation will be implemented as from the date of promulgation.

Where judicial interpretations issued by this Court previously are inconsistent with this Interpretation, this Interpretation shall prevail.

CHAPTER IV

ARBITRATION RULES

■ ■ ■

A. INTERNATIONAL CHAMBER OF COMMERCE 2012 ARBITRATION RULES*

RULES OF ARBITRATION OF THE INTERNATIONAL CHAMBER OF COMMERCE

In force as from 1 January 2012
Costs scales effective as of 1 January 2012

INTRODUCTORY PROVISIONS

Article 1: International Court of Arbitration

1

The International Court of Arbitration (the "Court") of the International Chamber of Commerce (the "ICC") is the independent arbitration body of the ICC. The statutes of the Court are set forth in Appendix I.

2

The Court does not itself resolve disputes. It administers the resolution of disputes by arbitral tribunals, in accordance with the Rules of Arbitration of the ICC (the "Rules"). The Court is the only body authorized to administer arbitrations under the Rules, including the scrutiny and approval of awards rendered in accordance with the Rules. It draws up its own internal rules, which are set forth in Appendix II (the "Internal Rules").

3

The President of the Court (the "President") or, in the President's absence or otherwise at the President's request, one of its Vice-Presidents shall have the power to take urgent decisions on behalf of the Court, provided that any such decision is reported to the Court at its next session.

4

As provided for in the Internal Rules, the Court may delegate to one or more committees composed of its members the power to take certain decisions, provided that any such decision is reported to the Court at its next session.

5

The Court is assisted in its work by the Secretariat of the Court (the "Secretariat") under the direction of its Secretary General (the "Secretary General").

Article 2: Definitions

In the Rules:

"arbitral tribunal" includes one or more arbitrators;

"claimant" includes one or more claimants, "respondent" includes one or more respondents, and "additional party" includes one or more additional parties;

"party" or "parties" include claimants, respondents or additional parties; "claim" or "claims" include any claim by any party against any other party;

"award" includes, *inter alia*, an interim, partial or final award.

Article 3: Written Notifications or Communications; Time Limits

1

All pleadings and other written communications submitted by any party, as well as all documents annexed thereto, shall be supplied in a number of copies sufficient to provide one copy for each party, plus one for each arbitrator, and one for the Secretariat. A copy of any notification or communication from the arbitral tribunal to the parties shall be sent to the Secretariat.

2

All notifications or communications from the Secretariat and the arbitral tribunal shall be made to the last address of the party or its representative for whom the same are intended, as notified either by the party in question or by the other party. Such notification or communication may be made by delivery against receipt, registered post, courier, email, or any other means of telecommunication that provides a record of the sending thereof.

3

A notification or communication shall be deemed to have been made on the day it was received by the party itself or by its representative, or would have been received if made in accordance with Article 3(2).

4

Periods of time specified in or fixed under the Rules shall start to run on the day following the date a notification or communication is deemed to have been made in accordance with Article 3(3). When the day next following such date is an official holiday, or a non-business day in the country where the notification or communication is deemed to have been made, the period of time shall commence on the first following business day. Official holidays and non-business days are included in the calculation of the period of time. If the last day of the relevant period of time granted is an official holiday or a non-business day in the country where the notification or communication is deemed to have been made, the period of time shall expire at the end of the first following business day.

COMMENCING THE ARBITRATION

Article 4: Request for Arbitration

1

A party wishing to have recourse to arbitration under the Rules shall submit its Request for Arbitration (the "Request") to the Secretariat at any of the offices specified in the Internal Rules. The Secretariat shall notify the claimant and respondent of the receipt of the Request and the date of such receipt.

2

The date on which the Request is received by the Secretariat shall, for all purposes, be deemed to be the date of the commencement of the arbitration.

3

The Request shall contain the following information:

     a)   the name in full, description, address and other contact details of each of the parties;

     b)   the name in full, address and other contact details of any person(s) representing the claimant in the arbitration;

     c)   a description of the nature and circumstances of the dispute giving rise to the claims and of the basis upon which the claims are made;

     d)   a statement of the relief sought, together with the amounts of any quantified claims and, to the extent possible, an estimate of the monetary value of any other claims;

     e)   any relevant agreements and, in particular, the arbitration agreement(s);

     f)   where claims are made under more than one arbitration agreement, an indication of the arbitration agreement under which each claim is made;

g) all relevant particulars and any observations or proposals concerning the number of arbitrators and their choice in accordance with the provisions of Articles 12 and 13, and any nomination of an arbitrator required thereby; and

h) all relevant particulars and any observations or proposals as to the place of the arbitration, the applicable rules of law and the language of the arbitration.

The claimant may submit such other documents or information with the Request as it considers appropriate or as may contribute to the efficient resolution of the dispute.

4

Together with the Request, the claimant shall:

a) submit the number of copies thereof required by Article 3(1); and

b) make payment of the filing fee required by Appendix III ("Arbitration Costs and Fees") in force on the date the Request is submitted.

In the event that the claimant fails to comply with either of these requirements, the Secretariat may fix a time limit within which the claimant must comply, failing which the file shall be closed without prejudice to the claimant's right to submit the same claims at a later date in another Request.

5

The Secretariat shall transmit a copy of the Request and the documents annexed thereto to the respondent for its Answer to the Request once the Secretariat has sufficient copies of the Request and the required filing fee.

Article 5: Answer to the Request; Counterclaims

1

Within 30 days from the receipt of the Request from the Secretariat, the respondent shall submit an Answer (the "Answer") which shall contain the following information:

a) its name in full, description, address and other contact details;

b) the name in full, address and other contact details of any person(s) representing the respondent in the arbitration;

c) its comments as to the nature and circumstances of the dispute giving rise to the claims and the basis upon which the claims are made;

d) its response to the relief sought;

e) any observations or proposals concerning the number of arbitrators and their choice in light of the claimant's proposals and in accordance with the provisions of Articles 12 and 13, and any nomination of an arbitrator required thereby; and

f)   any observations or proposals as to the place of the arbitration, the applicable rules of law and the language of the arbitration.

The respondent may submit such other documents or information with the Answer as it considers appropriate or as may contribute to the efficient resolution of the dispute.

2

The Secretariat may grant the respondent an extension of the time for submitting the Answer, provided the application for such an extension contains the respondent's observations or proposals concerning the number of arbitrators and their choice and, where required by Articles 12 and 13, the nomination of an arbitrator. If the respondent fails to do so, the Court shall proceed in accordance with the Rules.

3

The Answer shall be submitted to the Secretariat in the number of copies specified by Article 3(1).

4

The Secretariat shall communicate the Answer and the documents annexed thereto to all other parties.

5

Any counterclaims made by the respondent shall be submitted with the Answer and shall provide:

a)   a description of the nature and circumstances of the dispute giving rise to the counterclaims and of the basis upon which the counterclaims are made;

b)   a statement of the relief sought together with the amounts of any quantified counterclaims and, to the extent possible, an estimate of the monetary value of any other counterclaims; c) any relevant agreements and, in particular, the arbitration agreement(s); and

d)   where counterclaims are made under more than one arbitration agreement, an indication of the arbitration agreement under which each counterclaim is made.

The respondent may submit such other documents or information with the counterclaims as it considers appropriate or as may contribute to the efficient resolution of the dispute.

6

The claimant shall submit a reply to any counterclaim within 30 days from the date of receipt of the counterclaims communicated by the Secretariat.

Prior to the transmission of the file to the arbitral tribunal, the Secretariat may grant the claimant an extension of time for submitting the reply.

Article 6: Effect of the Arbitration Agreement

1

Where the parties have agreed to submit to arbitration under the Rules, they shall be deemed to have submitted *ipso facto* to the Rules in effect on the date of commencement of the arbitration, unless they have agreed to submit to the Rules in effect on the date of their arbitration agreement.

2

By agreeing to arbitration under the Rules, the parties have accepted that the arbitration shall be administered by the Court.

3

If any party against which a claim has been made does not submit an answer, or raises one or more pleas concerning the existence, validity or scope of the arbitration agreement or concerning whether all of the claims made in the arbitration may be determined together in a single arbitration, the arbitration shall proceed and any question of jurisdiction or of whether the claims may be determined together in that arbitration shall be decided directly by the arbitral tribunal, unless the Secretary General refers the matter to the Court for its decision pursuant to Article 6(4).

4

In all cases referred to the Court under Article 6(3), the Court shall decide whether and to what extent the arbitration shall proceed. The arbitration shall proceed if and to the extent that the Court is *prima facie* satisfied that an arbitration agreement under the Rules may exist. In particular:

(i) where there are more than two parties to the arbitration, the arbitration shall proceed between those of the parties, including any additional parties joined pursuant to Article 7, with respect to which the Court is *prima facie* satisfied that an arbitration agreement under the Rules that binds them all may exist; and

(ii) where claims pursuant to Article 9 are made under more than one arbitration agreement, the arbitration shall proceed as to those claims with respect to which the Court is *prima facie* satisfied (a) that the arbitration agreements under which those claims are made may be compatible, and (b) that all parties to the arbitration may have agreed that those claims can be determined together in a single arbitration.

The Court's decision pursuant to Article 6(4) is without prejudice to the admissibility or merits of any party's plea or pleas.

5

In all matters decided by the Court under Article 6(4), any decision as to the jurisdiction of the arbitral tribunal, except as to parties or claims with respect to which the Court decides that the arbitration cannot proceed, shall then be taken by the arbitral tribunal itself.

6

Where the parties are notified of the Court's decision pursuant to Article 6(4) that the arbitration cannot proceed in respect of some or all of them, any party retains the right to ask any court having jurisdiction whether or not, and in respect of which of them, there is a binding arbitration agreement.

7

Where the Court has decided pursuant to Article 6(4) that the arbitration cannot proceed in respect of any of the claims, such decision shall not prevent a party from reintroducing the same claim at a later date in other proceedings.

8

If any of the parties refuses or fails to take part in the arbitration or any stage thereof, the arbitration shall proceed notwithstanding such refusal or failure.

9

Unless otherwise agreed, the arbitral tribunal shall not cease to have jurisdiction by reason of any allegation that the contract is non-existent or null and void, provided that the arbitral tribunal upholds the validity of the arbitration agreement. The arbitral tribunal shall continue to have jurisdiction to determine the parties' respective rights and to decide their claims and pleas even though the contract itself may be non-existent or null and void.

MULTIPLE PARTIES, MULTIPLE CONTRACTS
AND CONSOLIDATION

Article 7: Joinder of Additional Parties

1

A party wishing to join an additional party to the arbitration shall submit its request for arbitration against the additional party (the "Request for Joinder") to the Secretariat. The date on which the Request for Joinder is received by the Secretariat shall, for all purposes, be deemed to be the date of the commencement of arbitration against the additional party. Any such joinder shall be subject to the provisions of Articles 6(3)–6(7) and 9. No additional party may be joined after the confirmation or appointment of any arbitrator, unless all parties, including the additional party, otherwise agree. The Secretariat may fix a time limit for the submission of a Request for Joinder.

2

The Request for Joinder shall contain the following information:

    a)   the case reference of the existing arbitration;

    b)   the name in full, description, address and other contact details of each of the parties, including the additional party; and

    c)   the information specified in Article 4(3) subparagraphs c), d), e) and f).

The party filing the Request for Joinder may submit therewith such other documents or information as it considers appropriate or as may contribute to the efficient resolution of the dispute.

3

The provisions of Articles 4(4) and 4(5) shall apply, *mutatis mutandis,* to the Request for Joinder.

4

The additional party shall submit an Answer in accordance, *mutatis mutandis*, with the provisions of Articles 5(1)–5(4). The additional party may make claims against any other party in accordance with the provisions of Article 8.

Article 8: Claims Between Multiple Parties

1

In an arbitration with multiple parties, claims may be made by any party against any other party, subject to the provisions of Articles 6(3)–6(7) and 9 and provided that no new claims may be made after the Terms of Reference are signed or approved by the Court without the authorization of the arbitral tribunal pursuant to Article 23(4).

2

Any party making a claim pursuant to Article 8(1) shall provide the information specified in Article 4(3) subparagraphs c), d), e) and f).

3

Before the Secretariat transmits the file to the arbitral tribunal in accordance with Article 16, the following provisions shall apply, *mutatis mutandis*, to any claim made: Article 4(4) subparagraph a); Article 4(5); Article 5(1) except for subparagraphs a), b), e) and f); Article 5(2); Article 5(3) and Article 5(4). Thereafter, the arbitral tribunal shall determine the procedure for making a claim.

Article 9: Multiple Contracts

Subject to the provisions of Articles 6(3)–6(7) and 23(4), claims arising out of or in connection with more than one contract may be made in a single arbitration, irrespective of whether such claims are made under one or more than one arbitration agreement under the Rules.

Article 10: Consolidation of Arbitrations

The Court may, at the request of a party, consolidate two or more arbitrations pending under the Rules into a single arbitration, where:

a)   the parties have agreed to consolidation; or

b)   all of the claims in the arbitrations are made under the same arbitration agreement; or

c)   where the claims in the arbitrations are made under more than one arbitration agreement, the arbitrations are between the same parties, the disputes in the arbitrations arise in connection with the same legal relationship, and the Court finds the arbitration agreements to be compatible.

In deciding whether to consolidate, the Court may take into account any circumstances it considers to be relevant, including whether one or more arbitrators have been confirmed or appointed in more than one of the arbitrations and, if so, whether the same or different persons have been confirmed or appointed.

When arbitrations are consolidated, they shall be consolidated into the arbitration that commenced first, unless otherwise agreed by all parties.

THE ARBITRAL TRIBUNAL

Article 11: General Provisions

1

Every arbitrator must be and remain impartial and independent of the parties involved in the arbitration.

2

Before appointment or confirmation, a prospective arbitrator shall sign a statement of acceptance, availability, impartiality and independence. The prospective arbitrator shall disclose in writing to the Secretariat any facts or circumstances which might be of such a nature as to call into question the arbitrator's independence in the eyes of the parties, as well as any circumstances that could give rise to reasonable doubts as to the arbitrator's impartiality. The Secretariat shall provide such information to the parties in writing and fix a time limit for any comments from them.

3

An arbitrator shall immediately disclose in writing to the Secretariat and to the parties any facts or circumstances of a similar nature to those referred to in Article 11(2) concerning the arbitrator's impartiality or independence which may arise during the arbitration.

4

The decisions of the Court as to the appointment, confirmation, challenge or replacement of an arbitrator shall be final, and the reasons for such decisions shall not be communicated.

5

By accepting to serve, arbitrators undertake to carry out their responsibilities in accordance with the Rules.

6

Insofar as the parties have not provided otherwise, the arbitral tribunal shall be constituted in accordance with the provisions of Articles 12 and 13.

Article 12: Constitution of the Arbitral Tribunal

Number of Arbitrators

1

The disputes shall be decided by a sole arbitrator or by three arbitrators.

2

Where the parties have not agreed upon the number of arbitrators, the Court shall appoint a sole arbitrator, save where it appears to the Court that the dispute is such as to warrant the appointment of three arbitrators. In such case, the claimant shall nominate an arbitrator within a period of 15 days from the receipt of the notification of the decision of the Court, and the respondent shall nominate an arbitrator within a period of 15 days from the receipt of the notification of the nomination made by the claimant. If a party fails to nominate an arbitrator, the appointment shall be made by the Court.

Sole Arbitrator

3

Where the parties have agreed that the dispute shall be resolved by a sole arbitrator, they may, by agreement, nominate the sole arbitrator for confirmation. If the parties fail to nominate a sole arbitrator within 30 days from the date when the claimant's Request for Arbitration has been received by the other party, or within such additional time as may be allowed by the Secretariat, the sole arbitrator shall be appointed by the Court.

Three Arbitrators

4

Where the parties have agreed that the dispute shall be resolved by three arbitrators, each party shall nominate in the Request and the Answer, respectively, one arbitrator for confirmation. If a party fails to nominate an arbitrator, the appointment shall be made by the Court.

5

Where the dispute is to be referred to three arbitrators, the third arbitrator, who will act as president of the arbitral tribunal, shall be appointed by the Court, unless the parties have agreed upon another procedure for such appointment, in which case the nomination will be subject to confirmation pursuant to Article 13. Should such procedure not result in a nomination within 30 days from the confirmation or appointment of the co-arbitrators or any other time limit agreed by the parties or fixed by the Court, the third arbitrator shall be appointed by the Court.

6

Where there are multiple claimants or multiple respondents, and where the dispute is to be referred to three arbitrators, the multiple claimants, jointly, and the multiple respondents, jointly, shall nominate an arbitrator for confirmation pursuant to Article 13.

7

Where an additional party has been joined, and where the dispute is to be referred to three arbitrators, the additional party may, jointly with the claimant(s) or with the respondent(s), nominate an arbitrator for confirmation pursuant to Article 13.

8

In the absence of a joint nomination pursuant to Articles 12(6) or 12(7) and where all parties are unable to agree to a method for the constitution of the arbitral tribunal, the Court may appoint each member of the arbitral tribunal and shall designate one of them to act as president. In such case, the Court shall be at liberty to choose any person it regards as suitable to act as arbitrator, applying Article 13 when it considers this appropriate.

Article 13: Appointment and Confirmation of the Arbitrators

1

In confirming or appointing arbitrators, the Court shall consider the prospective arbitrator's nationality, residence and other relationships with the countries of which the parties or the other arbitrators are nationals and the prospective arbitrator's availability and ability to conduct the arbitration in accordance with the Rules. The same shall apply where the Secretary General confirms arbitrators pursuant to Article 13(2).

2

The Secretary General may confirm as co-arbitrators, sole arbitrators and presidents of arbitral tribunals persons nominated by the parties or pursuant to their particular agreements, provided that the statement they have submitted contains no qualification regarding impartiality or independence or that a qualified statement regarding impartiality or independence has not given rise to objections. Such confirmation shall be reported to the Court at its next session. If the Secretary General considers that a co-arbitrator, sole arbitrator or president of an arbitral tribunal should not be confirmed, the matter shall be submitted to the Court.

3

Where the Court is to appoint an arbitrator, it shall make the appointment upon proposal of a National Committee or Group of the ICC that it considers to be appropriate. If the Court does not accept the proposal made, or if the National Committee or Group fails to make the proposal requested within the time limit fixed by the Court, the Court may repeat its request, request a proposal from another National Committee or Group that it considers to be appropriate, or appoint directly any person whom it regards as suitable.

4

The Court may also appoint directly to act as arbitrator any person whom it regards as suitable where:

a)   one or more of the parties is a state or claims to be a state entity; or

b)   the Court considers that it would be appropriate to appoint an arbitrator from a country or territory where there is no National Committee or Group; or

c)   the President certifies to the Court that circumstances exist which, in the President's opinion, make a direct appointment necessary and appropriate.

5

The sole arbitrator or the president of the arbitral tribunal shall be of a nationality other than those of the parties. However, in suitable circumstances and provided that none of the parties objects within the time limit fixed by the Court, the sole arbitrator or the president of the arbitral tribunal may be chosen from a country of which any of the parties is a national.

Article 14: Challenge of Arbitrators

1

A challenge of an arbitrator, whether for an alleged lack of impartiality or independence, or otherwise, shall be made by the submission to the Secretariat of a written statement specifying the facts and circumstances on which the challenge is based.

2

For a challenge to be admissible, it must be submitted by a party either within 30 days from receipt by that party of the notification of the appointment or confirmation of the arbitrator, or within 30 days from the date when the party making the challenge was informed of the facts and circumstances on which the challenge is based if such date is subsequent to the receipt of such notification.

3

The Court shall decide on the admissibility and, at the same time, if necessary, on the merits of a challenge after the Secretariat has afforded an opportunity for the arbitrator concerned, the other party or parties and any other members of the arbitral tribunal to comment in writing within a suitable period of time. Such comments shall be communicated to the parties and to the arbitrators.

Article 15: Replacement of Arbitrators

1

An arbitrator shall be replaced upon death, upon acceptance by the Court of the arbitrator's resignation, upon acceptance by the Court of a challenge, or upon acceptance by the Court of a request of all the parties.

2

An arbitrator shall also be replaced on the Court's own initiative when it decides that the arbitrator is prevented *de jure* or *de facto* from fulfilling the arbitrator's functions, or that the arbitrator is not fulfilling those functions in accordance with the Rules or within the prescribed time limits.

3

When, on the basis of information that has come to its attention, the Court considers applying Article 15(2), it shall decide on the matter after the arbitrator concerned, the parties and any other members of the arbitral tribunal have had an opportunity to comment in writing within a suitable period of time. Such comments shall be communicated to the parties and to the arbitrators.

4

When an arbitrator is to be replaced, the Court has discretion to decide whether or not to follow the original nominating process. Once reconstituted, and after having invited the parties to comment, the arbitral tribunal shall determine if and to what extent prior proceedings shall be repeated before the reconstituted arbitral tribunal.

5

Subsequent to the closing of the proceedings, instead of replacing an arbitrator who has died or been removed by the Court pursuant to Articles 15(1) or 15(2), the Court may decide, when it considers it appropriate, that the remaining arbitrators shall continue the arbitration. In making such determination, the Court shall take into account the views of the remaining arbitrators and of the parties and such other matters that it considers appropriate in the circumstances.

THE ARBITRAL PROCEEDINGS

Article 16: Transmission of the File to the Arbitral Tribunal

The Secretariat shall transmit the file to the arbitral tribunal as soon as it has been constituted, provided the advance on costs requested by the Secretariat at this stage has been paid.

Article 17: Proof of Authority

At any time after the commencement of the arbitration, the arbitral tribunal or the Secretariat may require proof of the authority of any party representatives.

Article 18: Place of the Arbitration

1

The place of the arbitration shall be fixed by the Court, unless agreed upon by the parties.

2

The arbitral tribunal may, after consultation with the parties, conduct hearings and meetings at any location it considers appropriate, unless otherwise agreed by the parties.

3

The arbitral tribunal may deliberate at any location it considers appropriate.

Article 19: Rules Governing the Proceedings

The proceedings before the arbitral tribunal shall be governed by the Rules and, where the Rules are silent, by any rules which the parties or, failing them, the arbitral tribunal may settle on, whether or not reference is thereby made to the rules of procedure of a national law to be applied to the arbitration.

Article 20: Language of the Arbitration

In the absence of an agreement by the parties, the arbitral tribunal shall determine the language or languages of the arbitration, due regard being given to all relevant circumstances, including the language of the contract.

Article 21: Applicable Rules of Law

1

The parties shall be free to agree upon the rules of law to be applied by the arbitral tribunal to the merits of the dispute. In the absence of any such agreement, the arbitral tribunal shall apply the rules of law which it determines to be appropriate.

2

The arbitral tribunal shall take account of the provisions of the contract, if any, between the parties and of any relevant trade usages.

3

The arbitral tribunal shall assume the powers of an *amiable compositeur* or decide *ex aequo et bono* only if the parties have agreed to give it such powers.

Article 22: Conduct of the Arbitration

1

The arbitral tribunal and the parties shall make every effort to conduct the arbitration in an expeditious and cost-effective manner, having regard to the complexity and value of the dispute.

2

In order to ensure effective case management, the arbitral tribunal, after consulting the parties, may adopt such procedural measures as it considers appropriate, provided that they are not contrary to any agreement of the parties.

3

Upon the request of any party, the arbitral tribunal may make orders concerning the confidentiality of the arbitration proceedings or of any other matters in connection with the arbitration and may take measures for protecting trade secrets and confidential information.

4

In all cases, the arbitral tribunal shall act fairly and impartially and ensure that each party has a reasonable opportunity to present its case.

5

The parties undertake to comply with any order made by the arbitral tribunal.

Article 23: Terms of Reference

1

As soon as it has received the file from the Secretariat, the arbitral tribunal shall draw up, on the basis of documents or in the presence of the parties and in the light of their most recent submissions, a document defining its Terms of Reference. This document shall include the following particulars:

a)   the names in full, description, address and other contact details of each of the parties and of any person(s) representing a party in the arbitration;

b)   the addresses to which notifications and communications arising in the course of the arbitration may be made;

c)   a summary of the parties' respective claims and of the relief sought by each party, together with the amounts of any quantified claims and, to the extent possible, an estimate of the monetary value of any other claims;

d)   unless the arbitral tribunal considers it inappropriate, a list of issues to be determined;

e)   the names in full, address and other contact details of each of the arbitrators;

f)   the place of the arbitration; and

g)   particulars of the applicable procedural rules and, if such is the case, reference to the power conferred upon the arbitral tribunal to act as *amiable compositeur* or to decide *ex aequo et bono*.

2

The Terms of Reference shall be signed by the parties and the arbitral tribunal. Within two months of the date on which the file has been transmitted to it, the arbitral tribunal shall transmit to the Court the Terms of Reference signed by it and by the parties. The Court may extend this time limit pursuant to a reasoned request from the arbitral tribunal or on its own initiative if it decides it is necessary to do so.

3

If any of the parties refuses to take part in the drawing up of the Terms of Reference or to sign the same, they shall be submitted to the Court for approval. When the Terms of Reference have been signed in accordance with Article 23(2) or approved by the Court, the arbitration shall proceed.

4

After the Terms of Reference have been signed or approved by the Court, no party shall make new claims which fall outside the limits of the Terms of Reference unless it has been authorized to do so by the arbitral tribunal, which shall consider the nature of such new claims, the stage of the arbitration and other relevant circumstances.

Article 24: Case Management Conference and Procedural Timetable

1

When drawing up the Terms of Reference or as soon as possible thereafter, the arbitral tribunal shall convene a case management conference to consult the parties on procedural measures that may be adopted pursuant to Article 22(2). Such measures may include one or more of the case management techniques described in Appendix IV.

2

During or following such conference, the arbitral tribunal shall establish the procedural timetable that it intends to follow for the conduct of the arbitration. The procedural timetable and any modifications thereto shall be communicated to the Court and the parties.

3

To ensure continued effective case management, the arbitral tribunal, after consulting the parties by means of a further case management conference or otherwise, may adopt further procedural measures or modify the procedural timetable.

4

Case management conferences may be conducted through a meeting in person, by video conference, telephone or similar means of communication. In the absence of an agreement of the parties, the arbitral tribunal shall determine the means by which the conference will be conducted. The arbitral tribunal may request the parties to submit case management proposals in advance of a case management conference and may request the attendance at any case management conference of the parties in person or through an internal representative.

Article 25: Establishing the Facts of the Case

1

The arbitral tribunal shall proceed within as short a time as possible to establish the facts of the case by all appropriate means.

2

After studying the written submissions of the parties and all documents relied upon, the arbitral tribunal shall hear the parties together in person if any of them so requests or, failing such a request, it may of its own motion decide to hear them.

3

The arbitral tribunal may decide to hear witnesses, experts appointed by the parties or any other person, in the presence of the parties, or in their absence provided they have been duly summoned.

4

The arbitral tribunal, after having consulted the parties, may appoint one or more experts, define their terms of reference and receive their reports. At the request of a party, the parties shall be given the opportunity to question at a hearing any such expert.

5

At any time during the proceedings, the arbitral tribunal may summon any party to provide additional evidence.

6

The arbitral tribunal may decide the case solely on the documents submitted by the parties unless any of the parties requests a hearing.

Article 26: Hearings

1

When a hearing is to be held, the arbitral tribunal, giving reasonable notice, shall summon the parties to appear before it on the day and at the place fixed by it.

2

If any of the parties, although duly summoned, fails to appear without valid excuse, the arbitral tribunal shall have the power to proceed with the hearing.

3

The arbitral tribunal shall be in full charge of the hearings, at which all the parties shall be entitled to be present. Save with the approval of the arbitral tribunal and the parties, persons not involved in the proceedings shall not be admitted.

4

The parties may appear in person or through duly authorized representatives. In addition, they may be assisted by advisers.

Article 27: Closing of the Proceedings and Date for Submission of Draft Awards

As soon as possible after the last hearing concerning matters to be decided in an award or the filing of the last authorized submissions concerning such matters, whichever is later, the arbitral tribunal shall:

a)   declare the proceedings closed with respect to the matters to be decided in the award; and

b)   inform the Secretariat and the parties of the date by which it expects to submit its draft award to the Court for approval pursuant to Article 33.

After the proceedings are closed, no further submission or argument may be made, or evidence produced, with respect to the matters to be decided in the award, unless requested or authorized by the arbitral tribunal.

Article 28: Conservatory and Interim Measures

1

Unless the parties have otherwise agreed, as soon as the file has been transmitted to it, the arbitral tribunal may, at the request of a party, order any interim or conservatory measure it deems appropriate. The arbitral tribunal may make the granting of any such measure subject to appropriate security being furnished by the requesting party. Any such measure shall take the form of an order, giving reasons, or of an award, as the arbitral tribunal considers appropriate.

2

Before the file is transmitted to the arbitral tribunal, and in appropriate circumstances even thereafter, the parties may apply to any competent judicial authority for interim or conservatory measures. The application of a party to a judicial authority for such measures or for the implementation of any such measures ordered by an arbitral tribunal shall not be deemed to be an infringement or a waiver of the arbitration agreement and shall not affect the relevant powers reserved to the arbitral tribunal. Any such application and any measures taken by the judicial authority must be notified without delay to the Secretariat. The Secretariat shall inform the arbitral tribunal thereof.

Article 29: Emergency Arbitrator

1

A party that needs urgent interim or conservatory measures that cannot await the constitution of an arbitral tribunal ("Emergency Measures") may make an application for such measures pursuant to the Emergency Arbitrator Rules in Appendix V. Any such application shall be accepted only if it is received by the Secretariat prior to the transmission of the file to the arbitral tribunal pursuant to Article 16 and irrespective of whether the party making the application has already submitted its Request for Arbitration.

2

The emergency arbitrator's decision shall take the form of an order. The parties undertake to comply with any order made by the emergency arbitrator.

3

The emergency arbitrator's order shall not bind the arbitral tribunal with respect to any question, issue or dispute determined in the order. The arbitral tribunal may modify, terminate or annul the order or any modification thereto made by the emergency arbitrator.

4

The arbitral tribunal shall decide upon any party's requests or claims related to the emergency arbitrator proceedings, including the reallocation of the costs of such proceedings and any claims arising out of or in connection with the compliance or non-compliance with the order.

5

Articles 29(1)–29(4) and the Emergency Arbitrator Rules set forth in Appendix V (collectively the "Emergency Arbitrator Provisions") shall apply only to parties that are either signatories of the arbitration agreement under the Rules that is relied upon for the application or successors to such signatories.

6

The Emergency Arbitrator Provisions shall not apply if:

the arbitration agreement under the Rules was concluded before the date on which the Rules came into force;

the parties have agreed to opt out of the Emergency Arbitrator Provisions; or

the parties have agreed to another pre-arbitral procedure that provides for the granting of conservatory, interim or similar measures.

7

The Emergency Arbitrator Provisions are not intended to prevent any party from seeking urgent interim or conservatory measures from a competent judicial authority at any time prior to making an application for such measures, and in appropriate circumstances even thereafter, pursuant to the Rules. Any application for such measures from a competent judicial authority shall not be deemed to be an infringement or a waiver of the arbitration agreement. Any such application and any measures taken by the judicial authority must be notified without delay to the Secretariat.

AWARDS

Article 30: Time Limit for the Final Award

1

The time limit within which the arbitral tribunal must render its final award is six months. Such time limit shall start to run from the date of the last signature by the arbitral tribunal or by the parties of the Terms of Reference or, in the case of application of Article 23(3), the date of the notification to the arbitral tribunal by the Secretariat of the approval of the Terms of Reference by the Court. The Court may fix a different time limit based upon the procedural timetable established pursuant to Article 24(2).

2

The Court may extend the time limit pursuant to a reasoned request from the arbitral tribunal or on its own initiative if it decides it is necessary to do so.

Article 31: Making of the Award

1

When the arbitral tribunal is composed of more than one arbitrator, an award is made by a majority decision. If there is no majority, the award shall be made by the president of the arbitral tribunal alone.

2

The award shall state the reasons upon which it is based.

3

The award shall be deemed to be made at the place of the arbitration and on the date stated therein.

Article 32: Award by Consent

If the parties reach a settlement after the file has been transmitted to the arbitral tribunal in accordance with Article 16, the settlement shall be recorded in the form of an award made by consent of the parties, if so requested by the parties and if the arbitral tribunal agrees to do so.

Article 33: Scrutiny of the Award by the Court

Before signing any award, the arbitral tribunal shall submit it in draft form to the Court. The Court may lay down modifications as to the form of the award and, without affecting the arbitral tribunal's liberty of decision, may also draw its attention to points of substance. No award shall be rendered by the arbitral tribunal until it has been approved by the Court as to its form.

Article 34: Notification, Deposit and Enforceability of the Award

1

Once an award has been made, the Secretariat shall notify to the parties the text signed by the arbitral tribunal, provided always that the costs of the arbitration have been fully paid to the ICC by the parties or by one of them.

2

Additional copies certified true by the Secretary General shall be made available on request and at any time to the parties, but to no one else.

3

By virtue of the notification made in accordance with Article 34(1), the parties waive any other form of notification or deposit on the part of the arbitral tribunal.

4

An original of each award made in accordance with the Rules shall be deposited with the Secretariat.

5

The arbitral tribunal and the Secretariat shall assist the parties in complying with whatever further formalities may be necessary.

6

Every award shall be binding on the parties. By submitting the dispute to arbitration under the Rules, the parties undertake to carry out any award without delay and shall be deemed to have waived their right to any form of recourse insofar as such waiver can validly be made.

Article 35: Correction and Interpretation of the Award; Remission of Awards

1

On its own initiative, the arbitral tribunal may correct a clerical, computational or typographical error, or any errors of similar nature contained in an award, provided such correction is submitted for approval to the Court within 30 days of the date of such award.

2

Any application of a party for the correction of an error of the kind referred to in Article 35(1), or for the interpretation of an award, must be made to the Secretariat within 30 days of the receipt of the award by such party, in a number of copies as stated in Article 3(1). After transmittal of the application to the arbitral tribunal, the latter shall grant the other party a short time limit, normally not exceeding 30 days, from the receipt of the application by that party, to submit any comments thereon. The arbitral tribunal shall submit its decision on the application in draft form to the Court not later than 30 days following the expiration of the time limit for the receipt of any comments from the other party or within such other period as the Court may decide.

3

A decision to correct or to interpret the award shall take the form of an addendum and shall constitute part of the award. The provisions of Articles 31, 33 and 34 shall apply *mutatis mutandis.*

4

Where a court remits an award to the arbitral tribunal, the provisions of Articles 31, 33, 34 and this Article 35 shall apply *mutatis mutandis* to any addendum or award made pursuant to the terms of such remission. The Court may take any steps as may be necessary to enable the arbitral tribunal to comply with the terms of such remission and may fix an advance to cover any additional fees and expenses of the arbitral tribunal and any additional ICC administrative expenses.

COSTS

Article 36: Advance to Cover the Costs of the Arbitration

1

After receipt of the Request, the Secretary General may request the claimant to pay a provisional advance in an amount intended to cover the costs of the arbitration until the Terms of Reference have been drawn up. Any provisional advance paid will be considered as a partial payment by the claimant of any advance on costs fixed by the Court pursuant to this Article 36.

2

As soon as practicable, the Court shall fix the advance on costs in an amount likely to cover the fees and expenses of the arbitrators and the ICC administrative expenses for the claims which have been referred to it by the parties, unless any claims are made under Article 7 or 8 in which case Article 36(4) shall apply. The advance on costs fixed by the Court pursuant to this Article 36(2) shall be payable in equal shares by the claimant and the respondent.

3

Where counterclaims are submitted by the respondent under Article 5 or otherwise, the Court may fix separate advances on costs for the claims and the counterclaims. When the Court has fixed separate advances on costs, each of the parties shall pay the advance on costs corresponding to its claims.

4

Where claims are made under Article 7 or 8, the Court shall fix one or more advances on costs that shall be payable by the parties as decided by the Court. Where the Court has previously fixed any advance on costs pursuant to this Article 36, any such advance shall be replaced by the advance(s) fixed pursuant to this Article 36(4), and the amount of any advance previously paid by any party will be considered as a partial payment by such party of its share of the advance(s) on costs as fixed by the Court pursuant to this Article 36(4).

5

The amount of any advance on costs fixed by the Court pursuant to this Article 36 may be subject to readjustment at any time during the arbitration. In all cases, any party shall be free to pay any other party's share of any advance on costs should such other party fail to pay its share.

6

When a request for an advance on costs has not been complied with, and after consultation with the arbitral tribunal, the Secretary General may direct the arbitral tribunal to suspend its work and set a time limit, which must be not less than 15 days, on the expiry of which the relevant claims shall be considered as withdrawn. Should the party in question wish to object to this measure, it must make a request within the aforementioned period for the matter to be decided by the Court. Such party shall not be prevented, on the ground of such withdrawal, from reintroducing the same claims at a later date in another proceeding.

7

If one of the parties claims a right to a set-off with regard to any claim, such set-off shall be taken into account in determining the advance to cover the costs of the arbitration in the same way as a separate claim insofar as it may require the arbitral tribunal to consider additional matters.

Article 37: Decision as to the Costs of the Arbitration

1

The costs of the arbitration shall include the fees and expenses of the arbitrators and the ICC administrative expenses fixed by the Court, in accordance with the scale in force at the time of the commencement of the arbitration, as well as the fees and expenses of any experts appointed by the arbitral tribunal and the reasonable legal and other costs incurred by the parties for the arbitration.

2

The Court may fix the fees of the arbitrators at a figure higher or lower than that which would result from the application of the relevant scale should this be deemed necessary due to the exceptional circumstances of the case.

3

At any time during the arbitral proceedings, the arbitral tribunal may make decisions on costs, other than those to be fixed by the Court, and order payment.

4

The final award shall fix the costs of the arbitration and decide which of the parties shall bear them or in what proportion they shall be borne by the parties.

5

In making decisions as to costs, the arbitral tribunal may take into account such circumstances as it considers relevant, including the extent to which each party has conducted the arbitration in an expeditious and cost-effective manner.

6

In the event of the withdrawal of all claims or the termination of the arbitration before the rendering of a final award, the Court shall fix the fees and expenses of the arbitrators and the ICC administrative expenses. If the parties have not agreed upon the allocation of the costs of the arbitration or other relevant issues with respect to costs, such matters shall be decided by the arbitral tribunal. If the arbitral tribunal has not been constituted at the time of such withdrawal or termination, any party may request the Court to proceed with the constitution of the arbitral tribunal in accordance with the Rules so that the arbitral tribunal may make decisions as to costs.

MISCELLANEOUS

Article 38: Modified Time Limits

1

The parties may agree to shorten the various time limits set out in the Rules. Any such agreement entered into subsequent to the constitution of an arbitral tribunal shall become effective only upon the approval of the arbitral tribunal.

2

The Court, on its own initiative, may extend any time limit which has been modified pursuant to Article 38(1) if it decides that it is necessary to do so in order that the arbitral tribunal and the Court may fulfil their responsibilities in accordance with the Rules.

Article 39: Waiver

A party which proceeds with the arbitration without raising its objection to a failure to comply with any provision of the Rules, or of any other rules applicable to the proceedings, any direction given by the arbitral tribunal, or any requirement under the arbitration agreement relating to the constitution of the arbitral tribunal or the conduct of the proceedings, shall be deemed to have waived its right to object.

Article 40: Limitation of Liability

The arbitrators, any person appointed by the arbitral tribunal, the emergency arbitrator, the Court and its members, the ICC and its employees, and the ICC National Committees and Groups and their employees and representatives shall not be liable to any person for any act or omission in connection with the arbitration, except to the extent such limitation of liability is prohibited by applicable law.

Article 41: General Rule

In all matters not expressly provided for in the Rules, the Court and the arbitral tribunal shall act in the spirit of the Rules and shall make every effort to make sure that the award is enforceable at law.

APPENDIX I: STATUTES OF THE INTERNATIONAL COURT OF ARBITRATION

Article 1: Function

1

The function of the International Court of Arbitration of the International Chamber of Commerce (the "Court") is to ensure the application of the Rules of Arbitration of the International Chamber of Commerce, and it has all the necessary powers for that purpose.

2

As an autonomous body, it carries out these functions in complete independence from the ICC and its organs.

3

Its members are independent from the ICC National Committees and Groups.

Article 2: Composition of the Court

The Court shall consist of a President,[1] Vice-Presidents,[2] and members and alternate members (collectively designated as members). In its work it is assisted by its Secretariat (Secretariat of the Court).

Article 3: Appointment

1

The President is elected by the ICC World Council upon the recommendation of the Executive Board of the ICC.

2

The ICC World Council appoints the Vice-Presidents of the Court from among the members of the Court or otherwise.

3

Its members are appointed by the ICC World Council on the proposal of National Committees or Groups, one member for each National Committee or Group.

4

On the proposal of the President of the Court, the World Council may appoint alternate members.

5

The term of office of all members, including, for the purposes of this paragraph, the President and Vice-Presidents, is three years. If a member is no longer in a position to exercise the member's functions, a successor is appointed by the World Council for the remainder of the term. Upon the recommendation of the Executive Board, the duration of the term of office of any member may be extended beyond three years if the World Council so decides.

Article 4: Plenary Session of the Court

The Plenary Sessions of the Court are presided over by the President or, in the President's absence, by one of the Vice-Presidents designated by the President. The deliberations shall be valid when at least six members are present. Decisions are taken by a majority vote, the President or Vice-President, as the case may be, having a casting vote in the event of a tie.

---

[1] Referred to as "Chairman of the International Court of Arbitration" in the Constitution of the International Chamber of Commerce.

[2] Referred to as "Vice-Chairmen of the International Court of Arbitration" in the Constitution of the International Chamber of Commerce.

Article 5: Committees

The Court may set up one or more Committees and establish the functions and organization of such Committees.

Article 6: Confidentiality

The work of the Court is of a confidential nature which must be respected by everyone who participates in that work in whatever capacity. The Court lays down the rules regarding the persons who can attend the meetings of the Court and its Committees and who are entitled to have access to materials related to the work of the Court and its Secretariat.

Article 7: Modification of the Rules of Arbitration

Any proposal of the Court for a modification of the Rules is laid before the Commission on Arbitration before submission to the Executive Board of the ICC for approval, provided, however, that the Court, in order to take account of developments in information technology, may propose to modify or supplement the provisions of Article 3 of the Rules or any related provisions in the Rules without laying any such proposal before the Commission.

APPENDIX II: INTERNAL RULES OF THE INTERNATIONAL COURT OF ARBITRATION

Article 1: Confidential Character of the Work of the International Court of Arbitration

1

For the purposes of this Appendix, members of the Court include the President and Vice-Presidents of the Court.

2

The sessions of the Court, whether plenary or those of a Committee of the Court, are open only to its members and to the Secretariat.

3

However, in exceptional circumstances, the President of the Court may invite other persons to attend. Such persons must respect the confidential nature of the work of the Court.

4

The documents submitted to the Court, or drawn up by it or the Secretariat in the course of the Court's proceedings, are communicated only to the members of the Court and to the Secretariat and to persons authorized by the President to attend Court sessions.

5

The President or the Secretary General of the Court may authorize researchers undertaking work of an academic nature to acquaint themselves with awards and other documents of general interest, with the exception of memoranda, notes, statements and documents remitted by the parties within the framework of arbitration proceedings.

6

Such authorization shall not be given unless the beneficiary has undertaken to respect the confidential character of the documents made available and to refrain from publishing anything based upon information contained therein without having previously submitted the text for approval to the Secretary General of the Court.

7

The Secretariat will in each case submitted to arbitration under the Rules retain in the archives of the Court all awards, Terms of Reference and decisions of the Court, as well as copies of the pertinent correspondence of the Secretariat.

8

Any documents, communications or correspondence submitted by the parties or the arbitrators may be destroyed unless a party or an arbitrator requests in writing within a period fixed by the Secretariat the return of such documents, communications or correspondence. All related costs and expenses for the return of those documents shall be paid by such party or arbitrator.

Article 2: Participation of Members of the International Court of Arbitration in ICC Arbitration

1

The President and the members of the Secretariat of the Court may not act as arbitrators or as counsel in cases submitted to ICC arbitration.

2

The Court shall not appoint Vice-Presidents or members of the Court as arbitrators. They may, however, be proposed for such duties by one or more of the parties, or pursuant to any other procedure agreed upon by the parties, subject to confirmation.

3

When the President, a Vice-President or a member of the Court or of the Secretariat is involved in any capacity whatsoever in proceedings pending before the Court, such person must inform the Secretary General of the Court upon becoming aware of such involvement.

4

Such person must be absent from the Court session whenever the matter is considered by the Court and shall not participate in the discussions or in the decisions of the Court.

5

Such person will not receive any material documentation or information pertaining to such proceedings.

Article 3: Relations between the Members of the Court and the ICC National Committees and Groups

1

By virtue of their capacity, the members of the Court are independent of the ICC National Committees and Groups which proposed them for appointment by the ICC World Council.

2

Furthermore, they must regard as confidential, vis-à-vis the said National Committees and Groups, any information concerning individual cases with which they have become acquainted in their capacity as members of the Court, except when they have been requested by the President of the Court, by a Vice-President of the Court authorized by the President of the Court, or by the Court's Secretary General to communicate specific information to their respective National Committees or Groups.

Article 4: Committee of the Court

1

In accordance with the provisions of Article 1(4) of the Rules and Article 5 of its statutes (Appendix I), the Court hereby establishes a Committee of the Court.

2

The members of the Committee consist of a president and at least two other members. The President of the Court acts as the president of the Committee. In the President's absence or otherwise at the President's request, a Vice-President of the Court or, in exceptional circumstances, another member of the Court may act as president of the Committee.

3

The other two members of the Committee are appointed by the Court from among the Vice-presidents or the other members of the Court. At each Plenary Session the Court appoints the members who are to attend the meetings of the Committee to be held before the next Plenary Session.

4

The Committee meets when convened by its president. Two members constitute a quorum.

5

(a) The Court shall determine the decisions that may be taken by the Committee.

(b) The decisions of the Committee are taken unanimously.

(c) When the Committee cannot reach a decision or deems it preferable to abstain, it transfers the case to the next Plenary Session, making any suggestions it deems appropriate.

(d) The Committee's decisions are brought to the notice of the Court at its next Plenary Session.

Article 5: Court Secretariat

1

In the Secretary General's absence or otherwise at the Secretary General's request, the Deputy Secretary General and/or the General Counsel shall have the authority to refer matters to the Court, confirm arbitrators, certify true copies of Awards and request the payment of a provisional advance, respectively provided for in Articles 6(3), 13(2), 34 (2) and 36(1) of the Rules.

2

The Secretariat may, with the approval of the Court, issue notes and other documents for the information of the parties and the arbitrators, or as necessary for the proper conduct of the arbitral proceedings.

3

Offices of the Secretariat may be established outside the headquarters of the ICC. The Secretariat shall keep a list of offices designated by the Secretary General. Requests for Arbitration may be submitted to the Secretariat at any of its offices, and the Secretariat's functions under the Rules may be carried out from any of its offices, as instructed by the Secretary General, Deputy Secretary General or General Counsel.

Article 6: Scrutiny of Arbitral Awards

When the Court scrutinizes draft awards in accordance with Article 33 of the Rules, it considers, to the extent practicable, the requirements of mandatory law at the place of the arbitration.

APPENDIX III: ARBITRATION COSTS AND FEES
Article 1: Advance on Costs

1

Each request to commence an arbitration pursuant to the Rules must be accompanied by a filing fee of US$3,000. Such payment is non-refundable and shall be credited to the claimant's portion of the advance on costs.

2

The provisional advance fixed by the Secretary General according to Article 36(1) of the Rules shall normally not exceed the amount obtained by adding together the ICC administrative expenses, the minimum of the fees (as set out in the scale hereinafter) based upon the amount of the claim and the expected reimbursable expenses of the arbitral tribunal incurred with respect to the drafting of the Terms of Reference. If such amount is not quantified, the provisional advance shall be fixed at the discretion of the Secretary General. Payment by the claimant shall be credited to its share of the advance on costs fixed by the Court.

3

In general, after the Terms of Reference have been signed or approved by the Court and the procedural timetable has been established, the arbitral tribunal shall, in accordance with Article 36(6) of the Rules, proceed only with respect to those claims or counterclaims in regard to which the whole of the advance on costs has been paid.

4

The advance on costs fixed by the Court according to Articles 36(2) or 36(4) of the Rules comprises the fees of the arbitrator or arbitrators (hereinafter referred to as "arbitrator"), any arbitration-related expenses of the arbitrator and the ICC administrative expenses.

5

Each party shall pay its share of the total advance on costs in cash. However, if a party's share of the advance on costs is greater than US$500,000 (the "Threshold Amount"), such party may post a bank guarantee for any amount above the Threshold Amount. The Court may modify the Threshold Amount at any time at its discretion.

6

The Court may authorize the payment of advances on costs, or any party's share thereof, in instalments, subject to such conditions as the Court thinks fit, including the payment of additional ICC administrative expenses.

7

A party that has already paid in full its share of the advance on costs fixed by the Court may, in accordance with Article 36(5) of the Rules, pay the unpaid portion of the advance owed by the defaulting party by posting a bank guarantee.

8

When the Court has fixed separate advances on costs pursuant to Article 36(3) of the Rules, the Secretariat shall invite each party to pay the amount of the advance corresponding to its respective claim(s).

9

When, as a result of the fixing of separate advances on costs, the separate advance fixed for the claim of either party exceeds one half of such global advance as was previously fixed (in respect of the same claims and counterclaims that are the subject of separate advances), a bank guarantee may be posted to cover any such excess amount. In the event that the amount of the separate advance is subsequently increased, at least one half of the increase shall be paid in cash.

10

The Secretariat shall establish the terms governing all bank guarantees which the parties may post pursuant to the above provisions.

11

As provided in Article 36(5) of the Rules, the advance on costs may be subject to readjustment at any time during the arbitration, in particular to take into account fluctuations in the amount in dispute, changes in the amount of the estimated expenses of the arbitrator, or the evolving difficulty or complexity of arbitration proceedings.

12

Before any expertise ordered by the arbitral tribunal can be commenced, the parties, or one of them, shall pay an advance on costs fixed by the arbitral tribunal sufficient to cover the expected fees and expenses of the expert as determined by the arbitral tribunal. The arbitral tribunal shall be responsible for ensuring the payment by the parties of such fees and expenses.

13

The amounts paid as advances on costs do not yield interest for the parties or the arbitrator.

Article 2: Costs and Fees

1

Subject to Article 37(2) of the Rules, the Court shall fix the fees of the arbitrator in accordance with the scale hereinafter set out or, where the amount in dispute is not stated, at its discretion.

2

In setting the arbitrator's fees, the Court shall take into consideration the diligence and efficiency of the arbitrator, the time spent, the rapidity of the proceedings, the complexity of the dispute and the timeliness of the submission of the draft award, so as to arrive at a figure within the limits specified or, in exceptional circumstances (Article 37(2) of the Rules), at a figure higher or lower than those limits.

3

When a case is submitted to more than one arbitrator, the Court, at its discretion, shall have the right to increase the total fees up to a maximum which shall normally not exceed three times the fees of one arbitrator.

4

The arbitrator's fees and expenses shall be fixed exclusively by the Court as required by the Rules. Separate fee arrangements between the parties and the arbitrator are contrary to the Rules.

5

The Court shall fix the ICC administrative expenses of each arbitration in accordance with the scale hereinafter set out or, where the amount in dispute is not stated, at its discretion. In exceptional circumstances, the Court may fix the ICC administrative expenses at a lower or higher figure than that which would result from the application of such scale, provided that such expenses shall normally not exceed the maximum amount of the scale.

6

At any time during the arbitration, the Court may fix as payable a portion of the ICC administrative expenses corresponding to services that have already been performed by the Court and the Secretariat.

7

The Court may require the payment of administrative expenses in addition to those provided in the scale of administrative expenses as a condition for holding an arbitration in abeyance at the request of the parties or of one of them with the acquiescence of the other.

8

If an arbitration terminates before the rendering of a final award, the Court shall fix the fees and expenses of the arbitrators and the ICC administrative expenses at its discretion, taking into account the stage attained by the arbitral proceedings and any other relevant circumstances.

9

Any amount paid by the parties as an advance on costs exceeding the costs of the arbitration fixed by the Court shall be reimbursed to the parties having regard to the amounts paid.

10

In the case of an application under Article 35(2) of the Rules or of a remission pursuant to Article 35(4) of the Rules, the Court may fix an advance to cover additional fees and expenses of the arbitral tribunal and additional ICC administrative expenses and may make the transmission of such application to the arbitral tribunal subject to the prior cash payment in full to the ICC of such advance. The Court shall fix at its discretion the costs of the procedure following an application or a remission, which shall include any possible fees of the arbitrator and ICC administrative expenses, when approving the decision of the arbitral tribunal.

11

The Secretariat may require the payment of administrative expenses in addition to those provided in the scale of administrative expenses for any expenses arising in relation to a request pursuant to Article 34(5) of the Rules.

12

When an arbitration is preceded by an attempt at amicable resolution pursuant to the ICC ADR Rules, one half of the ICC administrative expenses paid for such ADR proceedings shall be credited to the ICC administrative expenses of the arbitration.

13

Amounts paid to the arbitrator do not include any possible value added tax (VAT) or other taxes or charges and imposts applicable to the arbitrator's fees. Parties have a duty to pay any such taxes or charges; however, the recovery of any such charges or taxes is a matter solely between the arbitrator and the parties.

14

Any ICC administrative expenses may be subject to value added tax (VAT) or charges of a similar nature at the prevailing rate.

Article 3: ICC as Appointing Authority

Any request received for an authority of the ICC to act as appointing authority will be treated in accordance with the Rules of ICC as Appointing Authority in UNCITRAL or Other *Ad Hoc* Arbitration Proceedings and shall be accompanied by a non-refundable filing fee of US$3,000. No request shall be processed unless accompanied by the said filing fee. For additional services, ICC may at its discretion fix ICC administrative expenses, which shall be commensurate with the services provided and shall normally not exceed the maximum amount of US$10,000.

Article 4: Scales of Administrative Expenses and Arbitrator's Fees

1

The Scales of Administrative Expenses and Arbitrator's Fees set forth below shall be effective as of 1 January 2012 in respect of all arbitrations commenced on or after such date, irrespective of the version of the Rules applying to such arbitrations.

2

To calculate the ICC administrative expenses and the arbitrator's fees, the amounts calculated for each successive tranche of the amount in dispute must be added together, except that where the amount in dispute is over US$500 million, a flat amount of US$113,215 shall constitute the entirety of the ICC administrative expenses.

3

All amounts fixed by the Court or pursuant to any of the appendices to the Rules are payable in US$ except where prohibited by law, in which case the ICC may apply a different scale and fee arrangement in another currency.

A. ADMINISTRATIVE EXPENSES			
Amount in dispute (in US Dollars)			Administrative expenses(*)
up to		50,000	$3,000
from	50,001	to 100,000	4.73%
from	100,001	to 200,000	2.53%
from	200,001	to 500,000	2.09%
from	500,001	to 1,000,000	1.51%
from	1,000,001	to 2,000,000	0.95%
from	2,000,001	to 5,000,000	0.46%
from	5,000,001	to 10,000,000	0.25%

from	10,000,001	to	30,000,000	0.10%
from	30,000,001	to	50,000,000	0.09%
from	50,000,001	to	80,000,000	0.01%
from	80,000,001	to	500,000,000	0.0035%
over	500,000,000			$113,215

(*) For illustrative purposes only, the table on the following page indicates the resulting administrative expenses in US$ when the proper calculations have been made.

B. ARBITRATOR'S FEES

Amount in dispute (in US Dollars)			Fees (**)	
			minimum	maximum
up to	50,000		$3,000	18.0200%
from	50,001	to 100,000	2.6500%	13.5680%
from	100,001	to 200,000	1.4310%	7.6850%
from	200,001	to 500,000	1.3670%	6.8370%
from	500,001	to 1,000,000	0.9540%	4.0280%
from	1,000,001	to 2,000,000	0.6890%	3.6040%
from	2,000,001	to 5,000,000	0.3750%	1.3910%
from	5,000,001	to 10,000,000	0.1280%	0.9100%
from	10,000,001	to 30,000,000	0.0640%	0.2410%
from	30,000,001	to 50,000,000	0.0590%	0.2280%
from	50,000,001	to 80,000,000	0.0330%	0.1570%
from	80,000,001	to 100,000,000	0.0210%	0.1150%
from	100,000,001	to 500,000,000	0.0110%	0.0580%
over	500,000,000		0.0100%	0.0400%

(**) For illustrative purposes only, the table on the following page indicates the resulting range of fees in US$ when the proper calculations have been made.

AMOUNT IN DISPUTE (in US Dollars)			A. ADMINISTRATIVE EXPENSES (*) (in US Dollars)			
up to	50,000		3,000			
from 50,001	to 100,000		3,000	+ 4.73%	of amt. over	50,000
from 100,001	to 200,000		5,365	+ 2.53%	of amt. over	100,000
from 200,001	to 500,000		7,895	+ 2.09%	of amt. over	200,000
from 500,001	to 1,000,000		14,165	+ 1.51%	of amt. over	500,000

			base		of amt. over	
from	1,000,001	to 2,000,000	21,715	+ 0.95%	of amt. over	1,000,000
from	2,000,001	to 5,000,000	31,215	+ 0.46%	of amt. over	2,000,000
from	5,000,001	to 10,000,000	45,015	+ 0.25%	of amt. over	5,000,000
from	10,000,001	to 30,000,000	57,515	+ 0.10%	of amt. over	10,000,000
from	30,000,001	to 50,000,000	77,515	+ 0.09%	of amt. over	30,000,000
from	50,000,001	to 80,000,000	95,515	+ 0.01%	of amt. over	50,000,000
from	80,000,001	to 100,000,000	98,515	+ 0.0035%	of amt. over	80,000,000
from	100,000,001	to 500,000,000	99,215	+ 0.0035%	of amt. over	100,000,000
over	500,000,000		113,215			

AMOUNT IN DISPUTE (in US Dollars)		B. ARBITRATOR'S FEES (**) (in US Dollars)					
		Minimum			Maximum		
up to		3,000			18.0200% of amount in dispute		
from 50,001	to 50,000	3,000	+2.6500% of amt. over	50,000	9,010	+ 13.5680% of amt. over	50,000
from 100,001	to 100,000	4,325	+1.4310% of amt. over	100,000	15,794	+ 7.6850% of amt. over	100,000
from 200,001	to 200,000	5,756	+1.3670% of amt. over	200,000	23,479	+ 6.8370% of amt. over	200,000
from 500,001	to 500,000	9,857	+0.9540% of amt. over	500,000	43,990	+ 4.0280% of amt. over	500,000
from 1,000,001	to 1,000,000	14,627	+0.6890% of amt. over	1,000,000	64,130	+ 3.6040% of amt. over	1,000,000
from 2,000,001	to 2,000,000	21,517	+0.3750% of amt. over	2,000,000	100,170	+ 1.3910% of amt. over	2,000,000
from 5,000,001	to 5,000,000	32,767	+0.1280% of amt. over	5,000,000	141,900	+ 0.9100% of amt. over	5,000,000
from 10,000,001	to 10,000,000	39,167	+0.0640% of amt. over	10,000,000	187,400	+ 0.2410% of amt. over	10,000,000
from 30,000,001	to 30,000,000	51,967	+0.0590% of amt. over	30,000,000	235,600	+ 0.2280% of amt. over	30,000,000
from 50,000,001	to 50,000,000	63,767	+0.0330% of amt. over	50,000,000	281,200	+ 0.1570% of amt. over	50,000,000
from 80,000,001	to 80,000,000	73,667	+0.0210% of amt. over	80,000,000	328,300	+ 0.1150% of amt. over	80,000,000
from 100,000,001	to 100,000,000	77,867	+0.0110% of amt. over	100,000,000	351,300	+ 0.0580% of amt. over	100,000,000
over 500,000,000	500,000,000	121,867	+0.0100% of amt. over	500,000,000	583,300	+ 0.0400% of amt. over	500,000,000

(*)(**) See preceding page

B. RULES OF ICC AS APPOINTING AUTHORITY IN UNCITRAL OR OTHER *AD HOC* ARBITRATION PROCEEDINGS*

Effective as of 1 January 2004, the Rules of ICC as Appointing Authority chiefly cover the appointment and challenge of arbitrators in proceedings conducted under the UNCITRAL Arbitration Rules and in other *ad hoc* proceedings.

Foreword

One of the key steps in any arbitration is the constitution of the arbitral tribunal. Whilst this gives the parties the opportunity to designate arbitrators of their choice, especial care is required to ensure the independence and competence of the persons chosen, particularly in international proceedings. For this reason, parties may prefer to leave the task to a specialized institution, such as ICC.

During more than eighty years of administering international arbitrations, ICC has acquired exceptional experience in appointing arbitrators. In addition, it enjoys the support of a worldwide network of national committees able to identify arbitrators with appropriate qualifications of many different nationalities and from various spheres of activity.

The present rules supersede the rules ICC as Appointing Authority under the UNCITRAL Arbitration Rules, which have been in force for some twenty years and applied only to cases conducted under the UNCITRAL Arbitration Rules. The scope of the new rules extends also to ad hoc proceedings not conducted under the UNCITRAL Arbitration Rules. In both cases, in addition to making appointments, the ICC International Court of Arbitration may be given other powers, including the power to decide upon challenges of arbitrators, whether or not appointed by ICC.

Article 1 ICC as Appointing Authority in UNCITRAL or Other *Ad Hoc* Arbitration Proceedings

1

If so empowered by an arbitration clause, a subsequent agreement of the parties, a designation by the Secretary-General of the Permanent Court of Arbitration in The Hague, or otherwise, the International Chamber of Commerce ('ICC') shall act as appointing authority in accordance with the parties' agreement and/or the UNCITRAL Arbitration Rules.

2

The present Rules shall also apply where an authority within ICC[1] is requested to act as appointing authority in accordance with the parties' agreement or is designated by the Secretary-General of the Permanent Court of Arbitration in The Hague. References to ICC in these Rules include such other authorities.

3

Where ICC is empowered or requested to act as appointing authority under Articles 1(1) or 1(2), the function shall be carried out by the ICC International Court of Arbitration (the 'Court'). To fulfil this role, the Court

---

[1]   Such as the Chairman or Secretary General of ICC or the Chairman or Secretary General of the ICC International Court of Arbitration.

shall create a special committee (the 'Special Committee') consisting of the Chairman of the Court and two other members of the Court. The Chairman may designate a Vice-Chairman of the Court to replace him at a meeting of the Special Committee. Unless otherwise provided, the Special Committee shall carry out the functions of the Court under these Rules. The Special Committee's decisions shall be taken unanimously. In the event that a unanimous decision cannot be reached, the matter shall be referred to the Court sitting as a special plenary session (the 'Special Plenary Session'). When making decisions upon challenges pursuant to these Rules, the Court shall do so at a Special Plenary Session.

Article 2 Request for ICC to Act as Appointing Authority

1

In cases referred to in Article 1 of these Rules, a party wishing ICC to act as appointing authority shall submit a request (the 'Request') to the Secretariat of the Court (the 'Secretariat'), which shall notify the other party or parties of the receipt of the Request and the date of such receipt.

2

The Request shall contain all the information that the requesting party deems appropriate to allow the Court to make the requested appointment.

3

The Request and all documents annexed thereto shall be supplied in a sufficient number of copies to provide one for each party and one for the Secretariat. When submitting its Request, the requesting party shall make the payment required by Article 6 of these Rules. Should the requesting party fail to comply with either of these requirements, the Secretariat may set a time limit for compliance. Failing compliance within the time limit, the file shall be closed without prejudice to the right of the requesting party to resubmit its Request at a later date.

Article 3 The Court Acting as Appointing Authority under the UNCITRAL Arbitration Rules

1

When acting as the appointing authority for the purpose of appointing a sole or presiding (third) arbitrator pursuant to Articles 6(2) and 7(3) of the UNCITRAL Arbitration Rules, the Court shall follow the list-procedure set forth in Article 6(3) of the UNCITRAL Arbitration Rules, unless all parties agree that the list-procedure should not be used or the Court determines in its discretion that the use of the list-procedure is not appropriate for the case.

2

When following the list-procedure, the Court shall prepare a list of at least three candidates which shall be communicated to the parties by the Secretariat. Within 15 days of receiving this list, each party may return the list to the Secretariat after deleting the name or names to which it objects and numbering the remaining names on the list in the order of its preference. After expiration of the aforementioned 15-day time limit, the Court shall appoint the sole or presiding arbitrator from among the names approved on the list returned to the Secretariat and in accordance with the order of preference indicated by the parties. If for any reason the appointment cannot be made according to this procedure, the Court may exercise its discretion in appointing the sole or presiding arbitrator.

3

In accordance with Article 6(4) of the UNCITRAL Arbitration Rules, when making the appointment, the Court shall have regard to such considerations as are likely to secure the appointment of an independent and impartial arbitrator and shall take into account as well the advisability of appointing an arbitrator of a nationality other than that of the parties.

4

When appointing an arbitrator on behalf of a party in default under Article 7 of the UNCITRAL Arbitration Rules, the Court may exercise its discretion in making the appointment.

5

When making decisions upon challenges submitted by any party under Article 12 of the UNCITRAL Arbitration Rules, the Court will do so at a Special Plenary Session after the Secretariat has afforded an opportunity for the arbitrator concerned, the other party or parties and any other members of the arbitral tribunal to comment in writing within a suitable period of time. Such comments shall be communicated to the parties and to the arbitrators, before being submitted to the Court.

6

When appointing a substitute arbitrator under Articles 12(2) and 13 of the UNCITRAL Arbitration Rules, the Court shall follow the procedure set forth in the preceding paragraphs.

7

At the request of any party and pursuant to Article 39(4) of the UNCITRAL Arbitration Rules, the Court may, on a consultative basis, provide a statement concerning the fees of the arbitrators, taking into account the ICC Scale of Arbitrator's Fees for cases conducted under the ICC Rules of Arbitration.

8

At the request of any party and pursuant to Article 41(3) of the UNCITRAL Arbitration Rules, the Court may, on a consultative basis, give the arbitral tribunal any comments it deems appropriate concerning the amount of any deposit or supplementary deposit to be made under Article 41 of the UNCITRAL Arbitration Rules.

Article 4 The Court Acting as Appointing Authority in *Ad Hoc*, Non-UNCITRAL Arbitration Proceedings

1

Where the parties have agreed or where an applicable text provides that ICC shall act as appointing authority in ad hoc, non-UNCITRAL (hereafter, non-UNCITRAL) arbitral proceedings, the Court, exercising its discretion within the limits fixed by the parties in their agreement(s), or the limits contained in the applicable text, shall appoint an arbitrator independent of the parties involved in the arbitration.

2

The parties to non-UNCITRAL arbitral proceedings may agree that the Court, as appointing authority, shall have the power to decide upon a challenge made by any of the parties against any member of the arbitral tribunal. A challenge shall be made by submitting to the Secretariat a written statement specifying the facts and circumstances on which the challenge is based.

3

The Court shall decide on the challenge at a Special Plenary Session after the Secretariat has afforded an opportunity for the arbitrator concerned, the other party or parties and any other members of the arbitral tribunal to comment in writing within a suitable period of time. Such comments shall be communicated to the parties and to the arbitrators, before being submitted to the Court.

Article 5 General Provisions

1

When requested to act under these Rules, the Court shall proceed if it is satisfied that an agreement authorizing it to act as appointing authority may exist.

2

If so empowered by an arbitration clause, a subsequent agreement of the parties, or otherwise, the Court shall consider providing services, besides those specifically indicated in these Rules, in accordance with the parties' agreement.

3

Before appointment in cases provided for under Articles 3 and 4 of these Rules, a prospective arbitrator shall sign a declaration of acceptance and a statement of independence and disclose in writing to the Secretariat any facts or circumstances which might be of such a nature as to call into question the arbitrator's independence in the eyes of the parties.

4

The reasons for the decisions taken by the Court under these Rules shall not be communicated.

5

Neither the Court and its members, nor the International Chamber of Commerce and its employees shall be liable to any person for any act or omission in connection with the activities performed under these Rules.

Article 6 ICC Costs for Services Rendered as Appointing Authority

1

Each Request submitted to the Secretariat must be accompanied by payment to ICC of a non-refundable sum, the amount of which shall be determined according to the Appendix to these Rules.

2

For services provided pursuant to Article 5(2) of these Rules, the Court may fix administrative expenses commensurate with these services, which shall be paid by the requesting party or parties.

APPENDIX ICC COSTS FOR SERVICES RENDERED AS APPOINTING AUTHORITY

Article 1

The non-refundable amount referred to in Article 6(1) of these Rules is US$3,000. The non-refundable amount is payable by the party or parties submitting the Request. No Request shall be processed unless accompanied by the requisite payment.

Article 2

The administrative expenses of ICC for the services rendered pursuant to Article 5(2) of these Rules shall be fixed at ICC's discretion depending on the tasks carried out by ICC. Such administrative expenses shall be commensurate with said services and shall not exceed the maximum sum of US$10,000.

C. AMERICAN ARBITRATION ASSOCIATION INTERNATIONAL RULES OF 2014[*]

International Dispute Resolution Procedures (Including Mediation and Arbitration Rules)

Rules Amended and Effective June 1, 2014
Fee Schedule Amended and Effective June 1, 2014

Introduction

These Procedures are designed to provide a complete dispute resolution framework for disputing parties, their counsel, arbitrators, and mediators. They provide a balance between the autonomy of the parties to agree to the dispute resolution process they want and the need for process management by mediators and arbitrators.

The International Centre for Dispute Resolution® ("ICDR®") is the international division of the American Arbitration Association® ("AAA®"). The ICDR provides dispute resolution services around the world in locations chosen by the parties. ICDR arbitrations and mediations may be conducted in any language chosen by the parties. The ICDR Procedures reflect best international practices that are designed to deliver efficient, economic, and fair proceedings.

International Arbitration

A dispute can be submitted to an arbitral tribunal for a final and binding decision. In ICDR arbitration, each party is given the opportunity to make a case presentation following the process provided by these Rules and the tribunal.

Parties can provide for arbitration of future disputes by inserting the following clause into their contracts:

Any controversy or claim arising out of or relating to this contract, or the breach thereof, shall be determined by arbitration administered by the International Centre for Dispute Resolution in accordance with its International Arbitration Rules.

The parties should consider adding:

a.   *The number of arbitrators shall be (one or three);*

b.   *The place of arbitration shall be [city, (province or state), country]; and*

c.   *The language(s) of the arbitration shall be _____.*

For more complete clause-drafting guidance, please refer to the ***ICDR Guide to Drafting International Dispute Resolution Clauses*** on the

---

[*]   Reprinted by permission of the American Arbitration Association.

Clause Drafting page at www.icdr.org. When writing a clause or agreement for dispute resolution, the parties may choose to confer with the ICDR on useful options. Please see the contact information provided in **How to File a Case with the ICDR**.

INTERNATIONAL ARBITRATION RULES

Article 1: Scope of These Rules

1.   Where parties have agreed to arbitrate disputes under these International Arbitration Rules ("Rules"), or have provided for arbitration of an international dispute by the International Centre for Dispute Resolution (ICDR) or the American Arbitration Association (AAA) without designating particular rules, the arbitration shall take place in accordance with these Rules as in effect at the date of commencement of the arbitration, subject to modifications that the parties may adopt in writing. The ICDR is the Administrator of these Rules.

2.   These Rules govern the arbitration, except that, where any such rule is in conflict with any provision of the law applicable to the arbitration from which the parties cannot derogate, that provision shall prevail.

3.   When parties agree to arbitrate under these Rules, or when they provide for arbitration of an international dispute by the ICDR or the AAA without designating particular rules, they thereby authorize the ICDR to administer the arbitration. These Rules specify the duties and responsibilities of the ICDR, a division of the AAA, as the Administrator. The Administrator may provide services through any of the ICDR's case management offices or through the facilities of the AAA or arbitral institutions with which the ICDR or the AAA has agreements of cooperation. Arbitrations administered under these Rules shall be administered only by the ICDR or by an individual or organization authorized by the ICDR to do so.

4.   Unless the parties agree or the Administrator determines otherwise, the International Expedited Procedures shall apply in any case in which no disclosed claim or counterclaim exceeds USD $250,000 exclusive of interest and the costs of arbitration. The parties may also agree to use the International Expedited Procedures in other cases. The International Expedited Procedures shall be applied as described in Articles E–1 through E–10 of these Rules, in addition to any other portion of these Rules that is not in conflict with the Expedited Procedures. Where no party's claim or counterclaim exceeds USD $100,000 exclusive of interest, attorneys' fees, and other arbitration costs, the dispute shall be resolved by written submissions only unless the arbitrator determines that an oral hearing is necessary.

Commencing the Arbitration
Article 2: Notice of Arbitration

1.   The party initiating arbitration ("Claimant") shall, in compliance with Article 10, give written Notice of Arbitration to the Administrator and at the same time to the party against whom a claim is being made ("Respondent"). The Claimant may also initiate the arbitration through the Administrator's online filing system located at www.icdr.org.

2.   The arbitration shall be deemed to commence on the date on which the Administrator receives the Notice of Arbitration.

3.   The Notice of Arbitration shall contain the following information:

a.   a demand that the dispute be referred to arbitration;

b.   the names, addresses, telephone numbers, fax numbers, and email addresses of the parties and, if known, of their representatives;

c.   a copy of the entire arbitration clause or agreement being invoked, and, where claims are made under more than one arbitration agreement, a copy of the arbitration agreement under which each claim is made;

d.   a reference to any contract out of or in relation to which the dispute arises;

e.   a description of the claim and of the facts supporting it;

f.   the relief or remedy sought and any amount claimed; and

g.   optionally, proposals, consistent with any prior agreement between or among the parties, as to the means of designating the arbitrators, the number of arbitrators, the place of arbitration, the language(s) of the arbitration, and any interest in mediating the dispute.

4.   The Notice of Arbitration shall be accompanied by the appropriate filing fee.

5.   Upon receipt of the Notice of Arbitration, the Administrator shall communicate with all parties with respect to the arbitration and shall acknowledge the commencement of the arbitration.

Article 3: Answer and Counterclaim

1.   Within 30 days after the commencement of the arbitration, Respondent shall submit to Claimant, to any other parties, and to the Administrator a written Answer to the Notice of Arbitration.

2.   At the time Respondent submits its Answer, Respondent may make any counterclaims covered by the agreement to arbitrate or assert any setoffs and Claimant shall within 30 days submit to Respondent, to

any other parties, and to the Administrator a written Answer to the counterclaim or setoffs.

3.   A counterclaim or setoff shall contain the same information required of a Notice of Arbitration under Article 2(3) and shall be accompanied by the appropriate filing fee.

4.   Respondent shall within 30 days after the commencement of the arbitration submit to Claimant, to any other parties, and to the Administrator a response to any proposals by Claimant not previously agreed upon, or submit its own proposals, consistent with any prior agreement between or among the parties, as to the means of designating the arbitrators, the number of arbitrators, the place of the arbitration, the language(s) of the arbitration, and any interest in mediating the dispute.

5.   The arbitral tribunal, or the Administrator if the tribunal has not yet been constituted, may extend any of the time limits established in this Article if it considers such an extension justified.

6.   Failure of Respondent to submit an Answer shall not preclude the arbitration from proceeding.

7.   In arbitrations with multiple parties, Respondent may make claims or assert setoffs against another Respondent and Claimant may make claims or assert setoffs against another Claimant in accordance with the provisions of this Article 3.

Article 4: Administrative Conference

The Administrator may conduct an administrative conference before the arbitral tribunal is constituted to facilitate party discussion and agreement on issues such as arbitrator selection, mediating the dispute, process efficiencies, and any other administrative matters.

Article 5: Mediation

Following the time for submission of an Answer, the Administrator may invite the parties to mediate in accordance with the ICDR's International Mediation Rules. At any stage of the proceedings, the parties may agree to mediate in accordance with the ICDR's International Mediation Rules. Unless the parties agree otherwise, the mediation shall proceed concurrently with arbitration and the mediator shall not be an arbitrator appointed to the case.

Article 6: Emergency Measures of Protection

1.   A party may apply for emergency relief before the constitution of the arbitral tribunal by submitting a written notice to the Administrator and to all other parties setting forth the nature of the relief sought, the reasons why such relief is required on an emergency basis, and the reasons why the party is entitled to such relief. The notice shall be submitted concurrent with or following the submission of a Notice of Arbitration. Such

notice may be given by email, or as otherwise permitted by Article 10, and must include a statement certifying that all parties have been notified or an explanation of the steps taken in good faith to notify all parties.

2.   Within one business day of receipt of the notice as provided in Article 6(1), the Administrator shall appoint a single emergency arbitrator. Prior to accepting appointment, a prospective emergency arbitrator shall, in accordance with Article 13, disclose to the Administrator any circumstances that may give rise to justifiable doubts as to the arbitrator's impartiality or independence. Any challenge to the appointment of the emergency arbitrator must be made within one business day of the communication by the Administrator to the parties of the appointment of the emergency arbitrator and the circumstances disclosed.

3.   The emergency arbitrator shall as soon as possible, and in any event within two business days of appointment, establish a schedule for consideration of the application for emergency relief. Such schedule shall provide a reasonable opportunity to all parties to be heard and may provide for proceedings by telephone, video, written submissions, or other suitable means, as alternatives to an in-person hearing. The emergency arbitrator shall have the authority vested in the arbitral tribunal under Article 19, including the authority to rule on her/his own jurisdiction, and shall resolve any disputes over the applicability of this Article.

4.   The emergency arbitrator shall have the power to order or award any interim or conservancy measures that the emergency arbitrator deems necessary, including injunctive relief and measures for the protection or conservation of property. Any such measures may take the form of an interim award or of an order. The emergency arbitrator shall give reasons in either case. The emergency arbitrator may modify or vacate the interim award or order. Any interim award or order shall have the same effect as an interim measure made pursuant to Article 24 and shall be binding on the parties when rendered. The parties shall undertake to comply with such an interim award or order without delay.

5.   The emergency arbitrator shall have no further power to act after the arbitral tribunal is constituted. Once the tribunal has been constituted, the tribunal may reconsider, modify, or vacate the interim award or order of emergency relief issued by the emergency arbitrator. The emergency arbitrator may not serve as a member of the tribunal unless the parties agree otherwise.

6.   Any interim award or order of emergency relief may be conditioned on provision of appropriate security by the party seeking such relief.

7.   A request for interim measures addressed by a party to a judicial authority shall not be deemed incompatible with this Article 6 or with the agreement to arbitrate or a waiver of the right to arbitrate.

8.   The costs associated with applications for emergency relief shall be addressed by the emergency arbitrator, subject to the power of the arbitral tribunal to determine finally the allocation of such costs.

Article 7: Joinder

1.   A party wishing to join an additional party to the arbitration shall submit to the Administrator a Notice of Arbitration against the additional party. No additional party may be joined after the appointment of any arbitrator, unless all parties, including the additional party, otherwise agree. The party wishing to join the additional party shall, at that same time, submit the Notice of Arbitration to the additional party and all other parties. The date on which such Notice of Arbitration is received by the Administrator shall be deemed to be the date of the commencement of arbitration against the additional party. Any joinder shall be subject to the provisions of Articles 12 and 19.

2.   The request for joinder shall contain the same information required of a Notice of Arbitration under Article 2(3) and shall be accompanied by the appropriate filing fee.

3.   The additional party shall submit an Answer in accordance with the provisions of Article 3.

4.   The additional party may make claims, counterclaims, or assert setoffs against any other party in accordance with the provisions of Article 3.

Article 8: Consolidation

1.   At the request of a party, the Administrator may appoint a consolidation arbitrator, who will have the power to consolidate two or more arbitrations pending under these Rules, or these and other arbitration rules administered by the AAA or ICDR, into a single arbitration where:

a.   the parties have expressly agreed to consolidation; or

b.   all of the claims and counterclaims in the arbitrations are made under the same arbitration agreement; or

c.   the claims, counterclaims, or setoffs in the arbitrations are made under more than one arbitration agreement; the arbitrations involve the same parties; the disputes in the arbitrations arise in connection with the same legal relationship; and the consolidation arbitrator finds the arbitration agreements to be compatible.

2.   A consolidation arbitrator shall be appointed as follows:

a.   The Administrator shall notify the parties in writing of its intention to appoint a consolidation arbitrator and invite the parties to agree upon a procedure for the appointment of a consolidation arbitrator.

b.   If the parties have not within 15 days of such notice agreed upon a procedure for appointment of a consolidation arbitrator, the Administrator shall appoint the consolidation arbitrator.

c.   Absent the agreement of all parties, the consolidation arbitrator shall not be an arbitrator who is appointed to any pending arbitration subject to potential consolidation under this Article.

d.   The provisions of Articles 13–15 of these Rules shall apply to the appointment of the consolidation arbitrator.

3.   In deciding whether to consolidate, the consolidation arbitrator shall consult the parties and may consult the arbitral tribunal(s) and may take into account all relevant circumstances, including:

a.   applicable law;

b.   whether one or more arbitrators have been appointed in more than one of the arbitrations and, if so, whether the same or different persons have been appointed;

c.   the progress already made in the arbitrations;

d.   whether the arbitrations raise common issues of law and/or facts; and

e.   whether the consolidation of the arbitrations would serve the interests of justice and efficiency.

4.   The consolidation arbitrator may order that any or all arbitrations subject to potential consolidation be stayed pending a ruling on a request for consolidation.

5.   When arbitrations are consolidated, they shall be consolidated into the arbitration that commenced first, unless otherwise agreed by all parties or the consolidation arbitrator finds otherwise.

6.   Where the consolidation arbitrator decides to consolidate an arbitration with one or more other arbitrations, each party in those arbitrations shall be deemed to have waived its right to appoint an arbitrator. The consolidation arbitrator may revoke the appointment of any arbitrators and may select one of the previously-appointed tribunals to serve in the consolidated proceeding. The Administrator shall, as necessary, complete the appointment of the tribunal in the consolidated proceeding. Absent the agreement of all parties, the consolidation arbitrator shall not be appointed in the consolidated proceeding.

7.   The decision as to consolidation, which need not include a statement of reasons, shall be rendered within 15 days of the date for final submissions on consolidation.

Article 9: Amendment or Supplement of Claim, Counterclaim, or Defense

Any party may amend or supplement its claim, counterclaim, setoff, or defense unless the arbitral tribunal considers it inappropriate to allow such amendment or supplement because of the party's delay in making it, prejudice to the other parties, or any other circumstances. A party may not amend or supplement a claim or counterclaim if the amendment or supplement would fall outside the scope of the agreement to arbitrate. The tribunal may permit an amendment or supplement subject to an award of costs and/or the payment of filing fees as determined by the Administrator.

Article 10: Notices

1.   Unless otherwise agreed by the parties or ordered by the arbitral tribunal, all notices and written communications may be transmitted by any means of communication that allows for a record of its transmission including mail, courier, fax, or other written forms of electronic communication addressed to the party or its representative at its last-known address, or by personal service.

2.   For the purpose of calculating a period of time under these Rules, such period shall begin to run on the day following the day when a notice is made. If the last day of such period is an official holiday at the place received, the period is extended until the first business day that follows. Official holidays occurring during the running of the period of time are included in calculating the period.

The Tribunal

Article 11: Number of Arbitrators

If the parties have not agreed on the number of arbitrators, one arbitrator shall be appointed unless the Administrator determines in its discretion that three arbitrators are appropriate because of the size, complexity, or other circumstances of the case.

Article 12: Appointment of Arbitrators

1.   The parties may agree upon any procedure for appointing arbitrators and shall inform the Administrator as to such procedure. In the absence of party agreement as to the method of appointment, the Administrator may use the ICDR list method as provided in Article 12(6).

2.   The parties may agree to select arbitrators, with or without the assistance of the Administrator. When such selections are made, the parties shall take into account the arbitrators' availability to serve and shall notify the Administrator so that a Notice of Appointment can be communicated to the arbitrators, together with a copy of these Rules.

3.   If within 45 days after the commencement of the arbitration, all parties have not agreed on a procedure for appointing the arbitrator(s) or

have not agreed on the selection of the arbitrator(s), the Administrator shall, at the written request of any party, appoint the arbitrator(s). Where the parties have agreed upon a procedure for selecting the arbitrator(s), but all appointments have not been made within the time limits provided by that procedure, the Administrator shall, at the written request of any party, perform all functions provided for in that procedure that remain to be performed.

4.   In making appointments, the Administrator shall, after inviting consultation with the parties, endeavor to appoint suitable arbitrators, taking into account their availability to serve. At the request of any party or on its own initiative, the Administrator may appoint nationals of a country other than that of any of the parties.

5.   If there are more than two parties to the arbitration, the Administrator may appoint all arbitrators unless the parties have agreed otherwise no later than 45 days after the commencement of the arbitration.

6.   If the parties have not selected an arbitrator(s) and have not agreed upon any other method of appointment, the Administrator, at its discretion, may appoint the arbitrator(s) in the following manner using the ICDR list method. The Administrator shall send simultaneously to each party an identical list of names of persons for consideration as arbitrator(s). The parties are encouraged to agree to an arbitrator(s) from the submitted list and shall advise the Administrator of their agreement. If, after receipt of the list, the parties are unable to agree upon an arbitrator(s), each party shall have 15 days from the transmittal date in which to strike names objected to, number the remaining names in order of preference, and return the list to the Administrator. The parties are not required to exchange selection lists. If a party does not return the list within the time specified, all persons named therein shall be deemed acceptable. From among the persons who have been approved on the parties' lists, and in accordance with the designated order of mutual preference, the Administrator shall invite an arbitrator(s) to serve. If the parties fail to agree on any of the persons listed, or if acceptable arbitrators are unable or unavailable to act, or if for any other reason the appointment cannot be made from the submitted lists, the Administrator shall have the power to make the appointment without the submission of additional lists. The Administrator shall, if necessary, designate the presiding arbitrator in consultation with the tribunal.

7.   The appointment of an arbitrator is effective upon receipt by the Administrator of the Administrator's Notice of Appointment completed and signed by the arbitrator.

Article 13: Impartiality and Independence of Arbitrator

1.   Arbitrators acting under these Rules shall be impartial and independent and shall act in accordance with the terms of the Notice of Appointment provided by the Administrator.

2.   Upon accepting appointment, an arbitrator shall sign the Notice of Appointment provided by the Administrator affirming that the arbitrator is available to serve and is independent and impartial. The arbitrator shall disclose any circumstances that may give rise to justifiable doubts as to the arbitrator's impartiality or independence and any other relevant facts the arbitrator wishes to bring to the attention of the parties.

3.   If, at any stage during the arbitration, circumstances arise that may give rise to such doubts, an arbitrator or party shall promptly disclose such information to all parties and to the Administrator. Upon receipt of such information from an arbitrator or a party, the Administrator shall communicate it to all parties and to the tribunal.

4.   Disclosure by an arbitrator or party does not necessarily indicate belief by the arbitrator or party that the disclosed information gives rise to justifiable doubts as to the arbitrator's impartiality or independence.

5.   Failure of a party to disclose any circumstances that may give rise to justifiable doubts as to an arbitrator's impartiality or independence within a reasonable period after the party becomes aware of such information constitutes a waiver of the right to challenge an arbitrator based on those circumstances.

6.   No party or anyone acting on its behalf shall have any *ex parte* communication relating to the case with any arbitrator, or with any candidate for party-appointed arbitrator, except to advise the candidate of the general nature of the controversy and of the anticipated proceedings and to discuss the candidate's qualifications, availability, or impartiality and independence in relation to the parties, or to discuss the suitability of candidates for selection as a presiding arbitrator where the parties or party-appointed arbitrators are to participate in that selection. No party or anyone acting on its behalf shall have any *ex parte* communication relating to the case with any candidate for presiding arbitrator.

Article 14: Challenge of an Arbitrator

1.   A party may challenge an arbitrator whenever circumstances exist that give rise to justifiable doubts as to the arbitrator's impartiality or independence. A party shall send a written notice of the challenge to the Administrator within 15 days after being notified of the appointment of the arbitrator or within 15 days after the circumstances giving rise to the challenge become known to that party. The challenge shall state in writing the reasons for the challenge. The party shall not send this notice to any member of the arbitral tribunal.

2.   Upon receipt of such a challenge, the Administrator shall notify the other party of the challenge and give such party an opportunity to respond. The Administrator shall not send the notice of challenge to any member of the tribunal but shall notify the tribunal that a challenge has been received, without identifying the party challenging. The Administrator may advise the challenged arbitrator of the challenge and request information from the challenged arbitrator relating to the challenge. When an arbitrator has been challenged by a party, the other party may agree to the acceptance of the challenge and, if there is agreement, the arbitrator shall withdraw. The challenged arbitrator, after consultation with the Administrator, also may withdraw in the absence of such agreement. In neither case does withdrawal imply acceptance of the validity of the grounds for the challenge.

3.   If the other party does not agree to the challenge or the challenged arbitrator does not withdraw, the Administrator in its sole discretion shall make the decision on the challenge.

4.   The Administrator, on its own initiative, may remove an arbitrator for failing to perform his or her duties.

Article 15: Replacement of an Arbitrator

1.   If an arbitrator resigns, is incapable of performing the duties of an arbitrator, or is removed for any reason and the office becomes vacant, a substitute arbitrator shall be appointed pursuant to the provisions of Article 12, unless the parties otherwise agree.

2.   If a substitute arbitrator is appointed under this Article, unless the parties otherwise agree the arbitral tribunal shall determine at its sole discretion whether all or part of the case shall be repeated.

3.   If an arbitrator on a three-person arbitral tribunal fails to participate in the arbitration for reasons other than those identified in Article 15(1), the two other arbitrators shall have the power in their sole discretion to continue the arbitration and to make any decision, ruling, order, or award, notwithstanding the failure of the third arbitrator to participate. In determining whether to continue the arbitration or to render any decision, ruling, order, or award without the participation of an arbitrator, the two other arbitrators shall take into account the stage of the arbitration, the reason, if any, expressed by the third arbitrator for such non-participation and such other matters as they consider appropriate in the circumstances of the case. In the event that the two other arbitrators determine not to continue the arbitration without the participation of the third arbitrator, the Administrator on proof satisfactory to it shall declare the office vacant, and a substitute arbitrator shall be appointed pursuant to the provisions of Article 12, unless the parties otherwise agree.

General Conditions

Article 16: Party Representation

Any party may be represented in the arbitration. The names, addresses, telephone numbers, fax numbers, and email addresses of representatives shall be communicated in writing to the other party and to the Administrator. Unless instructed otherwise by the Administrator, once the arbitral tribunal has been established, the parties or their representatives may communicate in writing directly with the tribunal with simultaneous copies to the other party and, unless otherwise instructed by the Administrator, to the Administrator. The conduct of party representatives shall be in accordance with such guidelines as the ICDR may issue on the subject.

Article 17: Place of Arbitration

1.   If the parties do not agree on the place of arbitration by a date established by the Administrator, the Administrator may initially determine the place of arbitration, subject to the power of the arbitral tribunal to determine finally the place of arbitration within 45 days after its constitution.

2.   The tribunal may meet at any place it deems appropriate for any purpose, including to conduct hearings, hold conferences, hear witnesses, inspect property or documents, or deliberate, and, if done elsewhere than the place of arbitration, the arbitration shall be deemed conducted at the place of arbitration and any award shall be deemed made at the place of arbitration.

Article 18: Language of Arbitration

If the parties have not agreed otherwise, the language(s) of the arbitration shall be the language(s) of the documents containing the arbitration agreement, subject to the power of the arbitral tribunal to determine otherwise. The tribunal may order that any documents delivered in another language shall be accompanied by a translation into the language(s) of the arbitration.

Article 19: Arbitral Jurisdiction

1.   The arbitral tribunal shall have the power to rule on its own jurisdiction, including any objections with respect to the existence, scope, or validity of the arbitration agreement(s), or with respect to whether all of the claims, counterclaims, and setoffs made in the arbitration may be determined in a single arbitration.

2.   The tribunal shall have the power to determine the existence or validity of a contract of which an arbitration clause forms a part. Such an arbitration clause shall be treated as an agreement independent of the other terms of the contract. A decision by the tribunal that the contract is

null and void shall not for that reason alone render invalid the arbitration clause.

3.   A party must object to the jurisdiction of the tribunal or to arbitral jurisdiction respecting the admissibility of a claim, counterclaim, or setoff no later than the filing of the Answer, as provided in Article 3, to the claim, counterclaim, or setoff that gives rise to the objection. The tribunal may extend such time limit and may rule on any objection under this Article as a preliminary matter or as part of the final award.

4.   Issues regarding arbitral jurisdiction raised prior to the constitution of the tribunal shall not preclude the Administrator from proceeding with administration and shall be referred to the tribunal for determination once constituted.

Article 20: Conduct of Proceedings

1.   Subject to these Rules, the arbitral tribunal may conduct the arbitration in whatever manner it considers appropriate, provided that the parties are treated with equality and that each party has the right to be heard and is given a fair opportunity to present its case.

2.   The tribunal shall conduct the proceedings with a view to expediting the resolution of the dispute. The tribunal may, promptly after being constituted, conduct a preparatory conference with the parties for the purpose of organizing, scheduling, and agreeing to procedures, including the setting of deadlines for any submissions by the parties. In establishing procedures for the case, the tribunal and the parties may consider how technology, including electronic communications, could be used to increase the efficiency and economy of the proceedings.

3.   The tribunal may decide preliminary issues, bifurcate proceedings, direct the order of proof, exclude cumulative or irrelevant testimony or other evidence, and direct the parties to focus their presentations on issues whose resolution could dispose of all or part of the case.

4.   At any time during the proceedings, the tribunal may order the parties to produce documents, exhibits, or other evidence it deems necessary or appropriate. Unless the parties agree otherwise in writing, the tribunal shall apply Article 21.

5.   Documents or information submitted to the tribunal by one party shall at the same time be transmitted by that party to all parties and, unless instructed otherwise by the Administrator, to the Administrator.

6.   The tribunal shall determine the admissibility, relevance, materiality, and weight of the evidence.

7.   The parties shall make every effort to avoid unnecessary delay and expense in the arbitration. The arbitral tribunal may allocate costs,

draw adverse inferences, and take such additional steps as are necessary to protect the efficiency and integrity of the arbitration.

Article 21: Exchange of Information

1.   The arbitral tribunal shall manage the exchange of information between the parties with a view to maintaining efficiency and economy. The tribunal and the parties should endeavor to avoid unnecessary delay and expense while at the same time avoiding surprise, assuring equality of treatment, and safeguarding each party's opportunity to present its claims and defenses fairly.

2.   The parties may provide the tribunal with their views on the appropriate level of information exchange for each case, but the tribunal retains final authority. To the extent that the parties wish to depart from this Article, they may do so only by written agreement and in consultation with the tribunal.

3.   The parties shall exchange all documents upon which each intends to rely on a schedule set by the tribunal.

4.   The tribunal may, upon application, require a party to make available to another party documents in that party's possession not otherwise available to the party seeking the documents, that are reasonably believed to exist and to be relevant and material to the outcome of the case. Requests for documents shall contain a description of specific documents or classes of documents, along with an explanation of their relevance and materiality to the outcome of the case.

5.   The tribunal may condition any exchange of information subject to claims of commercial or technical confidentiality on appropriate measures to protect such confidentiality.

6.   When documents to be exchanged are maintained in electronic form, the party in possession of such documents may make them available in the form (which may be paper copies) most convenient and economical for it, unless the tribunal determines, on application, that there is a compelling need for access to the documents in a different form. Requests for documents maintained in electronic form should be narrowly focused and structured to make searching for them as economical as possible. The tribunal may direct testing or other means of focusing and limiting any search.

7.   The tribunal may, on application, require a party to permit inspection on reasonable notice of relevant premises or objects.

8.   In resolving any dispute about pre-hearing exchanges of information, the tribunal shall require a requesting party to justify the time and expense that its request may involve and may condition granting such a request on the payment of part or all of the cost by the party seeking

the information. The tribunal may also allocate the costs of providing information among the parties, either in an interim order or in an award.

9.   In the event a party fails to comply with an order for information exchange, the tribunal may draw adverse inferences and may take such failure into account in allocating costs.

10.   Depositions, interrogatories, and requests to admit as developed for use in U.S. court procedures generally are not appropriate procedures for obtaining information in an arbitration under these Rules.

Article 22: Privilege

The arbitral tribunal shall take into account applicable principles of privilege, such as those involving the confidentiality of communications between a lawyer and client. When the parties, their counsel, or their documents would be subject under applicable law to different rules, the tribunal should, to the extent possible, apply the same rule to all parties, giving preference to the rule that provides the highest level of protection.

Article 23: Hearing

1.   The arbitral tribunal shall give the parties reasonable notice of the date, time, and place of any oral hearing.

2.   At least 15 days before the hearings, each party shall give the tribunal and the other parties the names and addresses of any witnesses it intends to present, the subject of their testimony, and the languages in which such witnesses will give their testimony.

3.   The tribunal shall determine the manner in which witnesses are examined and who shall be present during witness examination.

4.   Unless otherwise agreed by the parties or directed by the tribunal, evidence of witnesses may be presented in the form of written statements signed by them. In accordance with a schedule set by the tribunal, each party shall notify the tribunal and the other parties of the names of any witnesses who have presented a witness statement whom it requests to examine. The tribunal may require any witness to appear at a hearing. If a witness whose appearance has been requested fails to appear without valid excuse as determined by the tribunal, the tribunal may disregard any written statement by that witness.

5.   The tribunal may direct that witnesses be examined through means that do not require their physical presence.

6.   Hearings are private unless the parties agree otherwise or the law provides to the contrary.

Article 24: Interim Measures

1.   At the request of any party, the arbitral tribunal may order or award any interim or conservatory measures it deems necessary, including

injunctive relief and measures for the protection or conservation of property.

2. Such interim measures may take the form of an interim order or award, and the tribunal may require security for the costs of such measures.

3. A request for interim measures addressed by a party to a judicial authority shall not be deemed incompatible with the agreement to arbitrate or a waiver of the right to arbitrate.

4. The arbitral tribunal may in its discretion allocate costs associated with applications for interim relief in any interim order or award or in the final award.

5. An application for emergency relief prior to the constitution of the arbitral tribunal may be made as provided for in Article 6.

Article 25: Tribunal-Appointed Expert

1. The arbitral tribunal, after consultation with the parties, may appoint one or more independent experts to report to it, in writing, on issues designated by the tribunal and communicated to the parties.

2. The parties shall provide such an expert with any relevant information or produce for inspection any relevant documents or goods that the expert may require. Any dispute between a party and the expert as to the relevance of the requested information or goods shall be referred to the tribunal for decision.

3. Upon receipt of an expert's report, the tribunal shall send a copy of the report to all parties and shall give the parties an opportunity to express, in writing, their opinion of the report. A party may examine any document on which the expert has relied in such a report.

4. At the request of any party, the tribunal shall give the parties an opportunity to question the expert at a hearing. At this hearing, parties may present expert witnesses to testify on the points at issue.

Article 26: Default

1. If a party fails to submit an Answer in accordance with Article 3, the arbitral tribunal may proceed with the arbitration.

2. If a party, duly notified under these Rules, fails to appear at a hearing without showing sufficient cause for such failure, the tribunal may proceed with the hearing.

3. If a party, duly invited to produce evidence or take any other steps in the proceedings, fails to do so within the time established by the tribunal without showing sufficient cause for such failure, the tribunal may make the award on the evidence before it.

Article 27: Closure of Hearing

1.   The arbitral tribunal may ask the parties if they have any further submissions and upon receiving negative replies or if satisfied that the record is complete, the tribunal may declare the arbitral hearing closed.

2.   The tribunal in its discretion, on its own motion, or upon application of a party, may reopen the arbitral hearing at any time before the award is made.

Article 28: Waiver

A party who knows of any non-compliance with any provision or requirement of the Rules or the arbitration agreement, and proceeds with the arbitration without promptly stating an objection in writing, waives the right to object.

Article 29: Awards, Orders, Decisions and Rulings

1.   In addition to making a final award, the arbitral tribunal may make interim, interlocutory, or partial awards, orders, decisions, and rulings.

2.   When there is more than one arbitrator, any award, order, decision, or ruling of the tribunal shall be made by a majority of the arbitrators.

3.   When the parties or the tribunal so authorize, the presiding arbitrator may make orders, decisions, or rulings on questions of procedure, including exchanges of information, subject to revision by the tribunal.

Article 30: Time, Form, and Effect of Award

1.   Awards shall be made in writing by the arbitral tribunal and shall be final and binding on the parties. The tribunal shall make every effort to deliberate and prepare the award as quickly as possible after the hearing. Unless otherwise agreed by the parties, specified by law, or determined by the Administrator, the final award shall be made no later than 60 days from the date of the closing of the hearing. The parties shall carry out any such award without delay and, absent agreement otherwise, waive irrevocably their right to any form of appeal, review, or recourse to any court or other judicial authority, insofar as such waiver can validly be made. The tribunal shall state the reasons upon which an award is based, unless the parties have agreed that no reasons need be given.

2.   An award shall be signed by the arbitrator(s) and shall state the date on which the award was made and the place of arbitration pursuant to Article 17. Where there is more than one arbitrator and any of them fails to sign an award, the award shall include or be accompanied by a statement of the reason for the absence of such signature.

3.   An award may be made public only with the consent of all parties or as required by law, except that the Administrator may publish or otherwise make publicly available selected awards, orders, decisions, and rulings that have become public in the course of enforcement or otherwise and, unless otherwise agreed by the parties, may publish selected awards, orders, decisions, and rulings that have been edited to conceal the names of the parties and other identifying details.

4.   The award shall be transmitted in draft form by the tribunal to the Administrator. The award shall be communicated to the parties by the Administrator.

5.   If applicable law requires an award to be filed or registered, the tribunal shall cause such requirement to be satisfied. It is the responsibility of the parties to bring such requirements or any other procedural requirements of the place of arbitration to the attention of the tribunal.

Article 31: Applicable Laws and Remedies

1.   The arbitral tribunal shall apply the substantive law(s) or rules of law agreed by the parties as applicable to the dispute. Failing such an agreement by the parties, the tribunal shall apply such law(s) or rules of law as it determines to be appropriate.

2.   In arbitrations involving the application of contracts, the tribunal shall decide in accordance with the terms of the contract and shall take into account usages of the trade applicable to the contract.

3.   The tribunal shall not decide as *amiable compositeur* or *ex aequo et bono* unless the parties have expressly authorized it to do so.

4.   A monetary award shall be in the currency or currencies of the contract unless the tribunal considers another currency more appropriate, and the tribunal may award such pre-award and post-award interest, simple or compound, as it considers appropriate, taking into consideration the contract and applicable law(s).

5.   Unless the parties agree otherwise, the parties expressly waive and forego any right to punitive, exemplary, or similar damages unless any applicable law(s) requires that compensatory damages be increased in a specified manner. This provision shall not apply to an award of arbitration costs to a party to compensate for misconduct in the arbitration.

Article 32: Settlement or Other Reasons for Termination

1.   If the parties settle the dispute before a final award is made, the arbitral tribunal shall terminate the arbitration and, if requested by all parties, may record the settlement in the form of a consent award on agreed terms. The tribunal is not obliged to give reasons for such an award.

2.   If continuation of the arbitration becomes unnecessary or impossible due to the non-payment of deposits required by the Administrator, the arbitration may be suspended or terminated as provided in Article 36(3).

3.   If continuation of the arbitration becomes unnecessary or impossible for any reason other than as stated in Sections 1 and 2 of this Article, the tribunal shall inform the parties of its intention to terminate the arbitration. The tribunal shall thereafter issue an order terminating the arbitration, unless a party raises justifiable grounds for objection.

Article 33: Interpretation and Correction of Award

1.   Within 30 days after the receipt of an award, any party, with notice to the other party, may request the arbitral tribunal to interpret the award or correct any clerical, typographical, or computational errors or make an additional award as to claims, counterclaims, or setoffs presented but omitted from the award.

2.   If the tribunal considers such a request justified after considering the contentions of the parties, it shall comply with such a request within 30 days after receipt of the parties' last submissions respecting the requested interpretation, correction, or additional award. Any interpretation, correction, or additional award made by the tribunal shall contain reasoning and shall form part of the award.

3.   The tribunal on its own initiative may, within 30 days of the date of the award, correct any clerical, typographical, or computational errors or make an additional award as to claims presented but omitted from the award.

4.   The parties shall be responsible for all costs associated with any request for interpretation, correction, or an additional award, and the tribunal may allocate such costs.

Article 34: Costs of Arbitration

The arbitral tribunal shall fix the costs of arbitration in its award(s). The tribunal may allocate such costs among the parties if it determines that allocation is reasonable, taking into account the circumstances of the case.

Such costs may include:

a.   the fees and expenses of the arbitrators;

b.   the costs of assistance required by the tribunal, including its experts;

c.   the fees and expenses of the Administrator;

d.   the reasonable legal and other costs incurred by the parties;

e.   any costs incurred in connection with a notice for interim or emergency relief pursuant to Articles 6 or 24;

f.   any costs incurred in connection with a request for consolidation pursuant to Article 8; and

g.   any costs associated with information exchange pursuant to Article 21.

Article 35: Fees and Expenses of Arbitral Tribunal

1.   The fees and expenses of the arbitrators shall be reasonable in amount, taking into account the time spent by the arbitrators, the size and complexity of the case, and any other relevant circumstances.

2.   As soon as practicable after the commencement of the arbitration, the Administrator shall designate an appropriate daily or hourly rate of compensation in consultation with the parties and all arbitrators, taking into account the arbitrators' stated rate of compensation and the size and complexity of the case.

3.   Any dispute regarding the fees and expenses of the arbitrators shall be determined by the Administrator.

Article 36: Deposits

1.   The Administrator may request that the parties deposit appropriate amounts as an advance for the costs referred to in Article 34.

2.   During the course of the arbitration, the Administrator may request supplementary deposits from the parties.

3.   If the deposits requested are not paid promptly and in full, the Administrator shall so inform the parties in order that one or more of them may make the required payment. If such payment is not made, the arbitral tribunal may order the suspension or termination of the proceedings. If the tribunal has not yet been appointed, the Administrator may suspend or terminate the proceedings.

4.   Failure of a party asserting a claim or counterclaim to pay the required deposits shall be deemed a withdrawal of the claim or counterclaim.

5.   After the final award has been made, the Administrator shall render an accounting to the parties of the deposits received and return any unexpended balance to the parties.

Article 37: Confidentiality

1.   Confidential information disclosed during the arbitration by the parties or by witnesses shall not be divulged by an arbitrator or by the Administrator. Except as provided in Article 30, unless otherwise agreed by the parties or required by applicable law, the members of the arbitral

tribunal and the Administrator shall keep confidential all matters relating to the arbitration or the award.

2.   Unless the parties agree otherwise, the tribunal may make orders concerning the confidentiality of the arbitration or any matters in connection with the arbitration and may take measures for protecting trade secrets and confidential information.

Article 38: Exclusion of Liability

The members of the arbitral tribunal, any emergency arbitrator appointed under Article 6, any consolidation arbitrator appointed under Article 8, and the Administrator shall not be liable to any party for any act or omission in connection with any arbitration under these Rules, except to the extent that such a limitation of liability is prohibited by applicable law. The parties agree that no arbitrator, emergency arbitrator, or consolidation arbitrator, nor the Administrator shall be under any obligation to make any statement about the arbitration, and no party shall seek to make any of these persons a party or witness in any judicial or other proceedings relating to the arbitration.

Article 39: Interpretation of Rules

The arbitral tribunal, any emergency arbitrator appointed under Article 6, and any consolidation arbitrator appointed under Article 8, shall interpret and apply these Rules insofar as they relate to their powers and duties. The Administrator shall interpret and apply all other Rules.

ADMINISTRATIVE FEES

Administrative Fee Schedules (Standard and Flexible Fee)

The ICDR has two administrative fee options for parties filing claims or counterclaims: the Standard Fee Schedule and the Flexible Fee Schedule. The Standard Fee Schedule has a two-payment schedule, and the Flexible Fee Schedule has a three-payment schedule that offers lower initial filing fees but potentially higher total administrative fees of approximately 12% to 19% for cases that proceed to a hearing. The administrative fees of the ICDR are based on the amount of the claim or counterclaim. Arbitrator compensation is not included in this schedule. Unless the parties agree otherwise, arbitrator compensation and administrative fees are subject to allocation by the arbitrator in the award.

Fees for incomplete or deficient filings: Where the applicable arbitration agreement does not reference the ICDR or the AAA, the ICDR will attempt to obtain the agreement of the other parties to the dispute to have the arbitration administered by the ICDR. However, where the ICDR is unable to obtain the agreement of the parties to have the ICDR administer the arbitration, the ICDR will administratively close the case and will not proceed with the administration of the arbitration. In these cases, the ICDR will return the filing fees to the filing party, less the amount specified in the fee schedule below for deficient filings.

Parties that file demands for arbitration that are incomplete or otherwise do not meet the filing requirements contained in these Rules shall also be charged the amount specified below for deficient filings if they fail or are unable to respond to the ICDR's request to correct the deficiency.

Fees for additional services: The ICDR reserves the right to assess additional administrative fees for services performed by the ICDR beyond those provided for in these Rules, which may be required by the parties' agreement or stipulation.

Suspension for Nonpayment: If arbitrator compensation or administrative charges have not been paid in full, the administrator may so inform the parties in order that one of them may advance the required payment. If such payment is not made, the tribunal may order the suspension or termination of the proceedings. If no arbitrator has yet been appointed, the ICDR may suspend or terminate the proceedings.

Standard Fee Schedule

An Initial Filing Fee is payable in full by a filing party when a claim, counterclaim, setoff or additional claim, counterclaim, or setoff is filed. A Final Fee will be incurred for all cases that proceed to their first hearing. This fee will be payable in advance at the time that the first hearing is scheduled. This fee will be refunded at the conclusion of the case if no hearings have occurred. However, if the Administrator is not notified at least 24 hours before the time of the scheduled hearing, the Final Fee will remain due and will not be refunded.

These fees will be billed in accordance with the following schedule:

Amount of Claim	Initial Filing Fee	Final Fee
Above $0 to $10,000	$775	$200
Above $10,000 to $75,000	$975	$300
Above $75,000 to $150,000	$1,850	$750
Above $150,000 to $300,000	$2,800	$1,250
Above $300,000 to $500,000	$4,350	$1,750
Above $500,000 to $1,000,000	$6,200	$2,500
Above $1,000,000 to $5,000,000	$8,200	$3,250
Above $5,000,000 to $10,000,000	$10,200	$4,000
Above $10,000,000	Base fee of $12,800 plus .01% of the amount of claim above $10,000,000	$6,000

	Fee Capped at $65,000	
Nonmonetary Claims[1]	$3,350	$1,250
Deficient Claim Filing[2]	$350	
Additional Services[3]		

[1]   *This fee is applicable when a claim or counterclaim is not for a monetary amount. Where a monetary claim amount is not known, parties will be required to state a range of claims or be subject to a filing fee of $10,200.*

[2]   *The Deficient Claim Filing Fee shall not be charged in cases filed by a consumer in an arbitration governed by the Supplementary Procedures for the Resolution of Consumer-Related Disputes or in cases filed by an Employee who is submitting a dispute to arbitration pursuant to an employer-promulgated plan.*

[3]   *The ICDR may assess additional fees where procedures or services outside the Rules sections are required under the parties' agreement or by stipulation.*

Fees are subject to increase if the amount of a claim or counterclaim is modified after the initial filing date. Fees are subject to decrease if the amount of a claim or counterclaim is modified before the first hearing.

The minimum fees for any case having three or more arbitrators are $2,800 for the filing fee, plus a $1,250 Case Service Fee.

Each party on cases filed under either the Flexible Fee Schedule or the Standard Fee Schedule that are held in abeyance for one year will be assessed an annual abeyance fee of $300. If a party refuses to pay the assessed fee, the other party or parties may pay the entire fee on behalf of all parties, failing which the matter will be administratively closed.

For more information, please contact the ICDR at +1.212.484.4181.

Refund Schedule for Standard Fee Schedule

The ICDR offers a refund schedule on filing fees connected with the Standard Fee Schedule. For cases with claims up to $75,000, a minimum filing fee of $350 will not be refunded. For all other cases, a minimum fee of $600 will not be refunded. Subject to the minimum fee requirements, refunds will be calculated as follows:

- 100% of the filing fee, above the minimum fee, will be refunded if the case is settled or withdrawn within five calendar days of filing.

- 50% of the filing fee will be refunded if the case is settled or withdrawn between six and 30 calendar days of filing.

- 25% of the filing fee will be refunded if the case is settled or withdrawn between 31 and 60 calendar days of filing.

No refund will be made once an arbitrator has been appointed (this includes one arbitrator on a three-arbitrator panel). No refunds will be granted on awarded cases.

Note: The date of receipt of the demand for arbitration with the ICDR will be used to calculate refunds of filing fees for both claims and counterclaims.

Flexible Fee Schedule

A non-refundable Initial Filing Fee is payable in full by a filing party when a claim, counterclaim, or additional claim is filed. Upon receipt of the Demand for Arbitration, the ICDR will promptly initiate the case and notify all parties as well as establish the due date for filing of an Answer, which may include a Counterclaim. In order to proceed with the further administration of the arbitration and appointment of the arbitrator(s), the appropriate, non-refundable Proceed Fee outlined below must be paid.

If a Proceed Fee is not submitted within 90 days of the filing of the Claimant's Demand for Arbitration, the ICDR will administratively close the file and notify all parties.

No refunds or refund schedule will apply to the Filing or Proceed Fees once received.

The Flexible Fee Schedule below also may be utilized for the filing of counterclaims. However, as with the Claimant's claim, the counterclaim will not be presented to the arbitrator until the Proceed Fee is paid.

A Final Fee will be incurred for all claims and/or counterclaims that proceed to their first hearing. This fee will be payable in advance when the first hearing is scheduled but will be refunded at the conclusion of the case if no hearings have occurred. However, if the administrator is not notified of a cancellation at least 24 hours before the time of the scheduled hearing, the Final Fee will remain due and will not be refunded.

All fees will be billed in accordance with the following schedule:

Amount of Claim	Initial Filing Fee	Proceed Fee	Final Fee
Above $0 to $10,000	$400	$475	$200
Above $10,000 to $75,000	$625	$500	$300
Above $75,000 to $150,000	$850	$1,250	$750
Above $150,000 to $300,000	$1,000	$2,125	$1,250
Above $300,000 to $500,000	$1,500	$3,400	$1,750
Above $500,000 to $1,000,000	$2,500	$4,500	$2,500
Above $1,000,000 to $5,000,000	$2,500	$6,700	$3,250
Above $5,000,000 to $10,000,000	$3,500	$8,200	$4,000

Above $10,000,000	$4,500	$10,300 plus .01% of claim amount over $10,000,000 up to $65,000	$6,000
Nonmonetary Claims[1]	$2,000	$2,000	$1,250
Deficient Claim Filing Fee	$350		
Additional Services[2]			

[1]   *This fee is applicable when a claim or counterclaim is not for a monetary amount. Where a monetary claim amount is not known, parties will be required to state a range of claims or be subject to a filing fee of $3,500 and a proceed fee of $8,200.*

[2]   *The ICDR reserves the right to assess additional administrative fees for services performed by the ICDR beyond those provided for in these Rules and which may be required by the parties' agreement or stipulation.*

All fees are subject to increase if the amount of a claim or counterclaim is modified after the initial filing date. Fees are subject to decrease if the amount of a claim or counterclaim is modified before the first hearing.

The minimum fees for any case having three or more arbitrators are $1,000 for the Initial Filing Fee; $2,125 for the Proceed Fee; and $1,250 for the Final Fee.

Under the Flexible Fee Schedule, a party's obligation to pay the Proceed Fee shall remain in effect regardless of any agreement of the parties to stay, postpone, or otherwise modify the arbitration proceedings. Parties that, through mutual agreement, have held their case in abeyance for one year will be assessed an annual abeyance fee of $300. If a party refuses to pay the assessed fee, the other party or parties may pay the entire fee on behalf of all parties, otherwise the matter will be administratively closed.

Note: The date of receipt by the ICDR of the demand/notice for arbitration will be used to calculate the 90-day time limit for payment of the Proceed Fee.

For more information, please contact the ICDR at +1.212.484.4181.

There is no Refund Schedule in the Flexible Fee Schedule.

Hearing Room Rental

The fees described above do not cover the cost of hearing rooms, which are available on a rental basis. Check with the ICDR for availability and rates.

D. ARBITRATION RULES OF THE LONDON COURT OF INTERNATIONAL ARBITRATION OF 2014

LCIA Arbitration Rules*

(effective 1 October 2014)

Preamble

Where any agreement, submission or reference howsoever made or evidenced in writing (whether signed or not) provides in whatsoever manner for arbitration under the rules of or by the LCIA, the London Court of International Arbitration, the London Court of Arbitration or the London Court, the parties thereto shall be taken to have agreed in writing that any arbitration between them shall be conducted in accordance with the LCIA Rules or such amended rules as the LCIA may have adopted hereafter to take effect before the commencement of the arbitration and that such LCIA Rules form part of their agreement (collectively, the "Arbitration Agreement"). These LCIA Rules comprise this Preamble, the Articles and the Index, together with the Annex to the LCIA Rules and the Schedule of Costs as both from time to time may be separately amended by the LCIA (the "LCIA Rules").

Article 1 Request for Arbitration

1.1 Any party wishing to commence an arbitration under the LCIA Rules (the "Claimant") shall deliver to the Registrar of the LCIA Court (the "Registrar") a written request for arbitration (the "Request"), containing or accompanied by:

(i) the full name and all contact details (including postal address, e-mail address, telephone and facsimile numbers) of the Claimant for the purpose of receiving delivery of all documentation in the arbitration; and the same particulars of the Claimant's legal representatives (if any) and of all other parties to the arbitration;

(ii) the full terms of the Arbitration Agreement (excepting the LCIA Rules) invoked by the Claimant to support its claim, together with a copy of any contractual or other documentation in which those terms are contained and to which the Claimant's claim relates;

(iii) a statement briefly summarising the nature and circumstances of the dispute, its estimated monetary amount or value, the transaction(s) at issue and the claim advanced by the Claimant against any other party to the arbitration (each such other party being here separately described as a "Respondent");

---

*   The LCIA Rules can be found at the LCIA Website at http://www.lcia.org/. Reprinted by permission of the LCIA.

(iv) a statement of any procedural matters for the arbitration (such as the arbitral seat, the language(s) of the arbitration, the number of arbitrators, their qualifications and identities) upon which the parties have already agreed in writing or in respect of which the Claimant makes any proposal under the Arbitration Agreement;

(v) if the Arbitration Agreement (or any other written agreement) howsoever calls for any form of party nomination of arbitrators, the full name, postal address, e-mail address, telephone and facsimile numbers of the Claimant's nominee;

(vi) confirmation that the registration fee prescribed in the Schedule of Costs has been or is being paid to the LCIA, without which actual receipt of such payment the Request shall be treated by the Registrar as not having been delivered and the arbitration as not having been commenced under the Arbitration Agreement; and

(vii) confirmation that copies of the Request (including all accompanying documents) have been or are being delivered to all other parties to the arbitration by one or more means to be identified specifically in such confirmation, to be supported then or as soon as possible thereafter by documentary proof satisfactory to the LCIA Court of actual delivery (including the date of delivery) or, if actual delivery is demonstrated to be impossible to the LCIA Court's satisfaction, sufficient information as to any other effective form of notification.

1.2 The Request (including all accompanying documents) may be submitted to the Registrar in electronic form (as e-mail attachments) or in paper form or in both forms. If submitted in paper form, the Request shall be submitted in two copies where a sole arbitrator is to be appointed, or, if the parties have agreed or the Claimant proposes that three arbitrators are to be appointed, in four copies.

1.3 The Claimant may use, but is not required to do so, the standard electronic form available on-line from the LCIA's website for LCIA Requests.

1.4 The date of receipt by the Registrar of the Request shall be treated as the date upon which the arbitration has commenced for all purposes (the "Commencement Date"), subject to the LCIA's actual receipt of the registration fee.

1.5 There may be one or more Claimants (whether or not jointly represented); and in such event, where appropriate, the term "Claimant" shall be so interpreted under the Arbitration Agreement.

Article 2 Response

2.1 Within 28 days of the Commencement Date, or such lesser or greater period to be determined by the LCIA Court upon application by any party or upon its own initiative (pursuant to Article 22.5), the Respondent shall deliver to the Registrar a written response to the Request (the "Response"), containing or accompanied by:

(i) the Respondent's full name and all contact details (including postal address, e-mail address, telephone and facsimile numbers) for the purpose of receiving delivery of all documentation in the arbitration and the same particulars of its legal representatives (if any);

(ii) confirmation or denial of all or part of the claim advanced by the Claimant in the Request, including the Claimant's invocation of the Arbitration Agreement in support of its claim;

(iii) if not full confirmation, a statement briefly summarising the nature and circumstances of the dispute, its estimated monetary amount or value, the transaction(s) at issue and the defence advanced by the Respondent, and also indicating whether any cross-claim will be advanced by the Respondent against any other party to the arbitration (such cross-claim to include any counterclaim against any Claimant and any other cross-claim against any Respondent);

(iv) a response to any procedural statement for the arbitration contained in the Request under Article 1.1(iv), including the Respondent's own statement relating to the arbitral seat, the language(s) of the arbitration, the number of arbitrators, their qualifications and identities and any other procedural matter upon which the parties have already agreed in writing or in respect of which the Respondent makes any proposal under the Arbitration Agreement;

(v) if the Arbitration Agreement (or any other written agreement) howsoever calls for party nomination of arbitrators, the full name, postal address, e-mail address, telephone and facsimile numbers of the Respondent's nominee; and

(vi) confirmation that copies of the Response (including all accompanying documents) have been or are being delivered to all other parties to the arbitration by one or more means of delivery to be identified specifically in such confirmation, to be supported then or as soon as possible thereafter by documentary proof satisfactory to the LCIA Court of actual delivery (including the date of delivery) or, if actual delivery is demonstrated to be impossible to the LCIA Court's satisfaction, sufficient information as to any other effective form of notification.

2.2 The Response (including all accompanying documents) may be submitted to the Registrar in electronic form (as e-mail attachments) or in paper form or in both forms. If submitted in paper form, the Response shall be submitted in two copies where a sole arbitrator is to be appointed, or, if the parties have agreed or the Respondent proposes that three arbitrators are to be appointed, in four copies.

2.3 The Respondent may use, but is not required to do so, the standard electronic form available on-line from the LCIA's website for LCIA Responses.

2.4 Failure to deliver a Response within time shall constitute an irrevocable waiver of that party's opportunity to nominate or propose any arbitral candidate. Failure to deliver any or any part of a Response within time or at all shall not (by itself) preclude the Respondent from denying any claim or from advancing any defence or cross-claim in the arbitration.

2.5 There may be one or more Respondents (whether or not jointly represented); and in such event, where appropriate, the term "Respondent" shall be so interpreted under the Arbitration Agreement.

Article 3 LCIA Court and Registrar

3.1 The functions of the LCIA Court under the Arbitration Agreement shall be performed in its name by the President of the LCIA Court (or any of its Vice-Presidents, Honorary Vice-Presidents or former Vice-Presidents) or by a division of three or more members of the LCIA Court appointed by its President or any Vice-President (the "LCIA Court").

3.2 The functions of the Registrar under the Arbitration Agreement shall be performed under the supervision of the LCIA Court by the Registrar or any deputy Registrar.

3.3 All communications in the arbitration to the LCIA Court from any party, arbitrator or expert to the Arbitral Tribunal shall be addressed to the Registrar.

Article 4 Written Communications and Periods of Time

4.1 Any written communication by the LCIA Court, the Registrar or any party may be delivered personally or by registered postal or courier service or (subject to Article 4.3) by facsimile, e-mail or any other electronic means of telecommunication that provides a record of its transmission, or in any other manner ordered by the Arbitral Tribunal.

4.2 Unless otherwise ordered by the Arbitral Tribunal, if an address has been agreed or designated by a party for the purpose of receiving any communication in regard to the Arbitration Agreement or (in the absence of such agreement or designation) has been regularly used in the parties' previous dealings, any written communication (including the Request and Response) may be delivered to such party at that address, and if so delivered, shall be treated as having been received by such party.

4.3 Delivery by electronic means (including e-mail and facsimile) may only be effected to an address agreed or designated by the receiving party for that purpose or ordered by the Arbitral Tribunal.

4.4 For the purpose of determining the commencement of any time-limit, a written communication shall be treated as having been received by a party on the day it is delivered or, in the case of electronic means, transmitted in accordance with Articles 4.1 to 4.3 (such time to be determined by reference to the recipient's time-zone).

4.5   For the purpose of determining compliance with a time-limit, a written communication shall be treated as having been sent by a party if made or transmitted in accordance with Articles 4.1 to 4.3 prior to or on the date of the expiration of the time-limit.

4.6   For the purpose of calculating a period of time, such period shall begin to run on the day following the day when a written communication is received by the addressee. If the last day of such period is an official holiday or non-business day at the place of that addressee (or the place of the party against whom the calculation of time applies), the period shall be extended until the first business day which follows that last day. Official holidays and non-business days occurring during the running of the period of time shall be included in calculating that period.

Article 5 Formation of Arbitral Tribunal

5.1   The formation of the Arbitral Tribunal by the LCIA Court shall not be impeded by any controversy between the parties relating to the sufficiency of the Request or the Response. The LCIA Court may also proceed with the arbitration notwithstanding that the Request is incomplete or the Response is missing, late or incomplete.

5.2   The expression the "Arbitral Tribunal" includes a sole arbitrator or all the arbitrators where more than one.

5.3   All arbitrators shall be and remain at all times impartial and independent of the parties; and none shall act in the arbitration as advocate for or representative of any party. No arbitrator shall advise any party on the parties' dispute or the outcome of the arbitration.

5.4   Before appointment by the LCIA Court, each arbitral candidate shall furnish to the Registrar (upon the latter's request) a brief written summary of his or her qualifications and professional positions (past and present); the candidate shall also agree in writing fee-rates conforming to the Schedule of Costs; the candidate shall sign a written declaration stating: (i) whether there are any circumstances currently known to the candidate which are likely to give rise in the mind of any party to any justifiable doubts as to his or her impartiality or independence and, if so, specifying in full such circumstances in the declaration; and (ii) whether the candidate is ready, willing and able to devote sufficient time, diligence and industry to ensure the expeditious and efficient conduct of the arbitration. The candidate shall furnish promptly such agreement and declaration to the Registrar.

5.5   If appointed, each arbitral candidate shall thereby assume a continuing duty as an arbitrator, until the arbitration is finally concluded, forthwith to disclose in writing any circumstances becoming known to that arbitrator after the date of his or her written declaration (under Article 5.4) which are likely to give rise in the mind of any party to any justifiable doubts as to his or her impartiality or independence, to be delivered to the LCIA Court, any other members of the Arbitral Tribunal and all parties in the arbitration.

5.6 The LCIA Court shall appoint the Arbitral Tribunal promptly after receipt by the Registrar of the Response or, if no Response is received, after 35 days from the Commencement Date (or such other lesser or greater period to be determined by the LCIA Court pursuant to Article 22.5).

5.7 No party or third person may appoint any arbitrator under the Arbitration Agreement: the LCIA Court alone is empowered to appoint arbitrators (albeit taking into account any written agreement or joint nomination by the parties).

5.8 A sole arbitrator shall be appointed unless the parties have agreed in writing otherwise or if the LCIA Court determines that in the circumstances a three-member tribunal is appropriate (or, exceptionally, more than three).

5.9 The LCIA Court shall appoint arbitrators with due regard for any particular method or criteria of selection agreed in writing by the parties. The LCIA Court shall also take into account the transaction(s) at issue, the nature and circumstances of the dispute, its monetary amount or value, the location and languages of the parties, the number of parties and all other factors which it may consider relevant in the circumstances.

5.10 The President of the LCIA Court shall only be eligible to be appointed as an arbitrator if the parties agree in writing to nominate him or her as the sole or presiding arbitrator; and the Vice Presidents of the LCIA Court and the Chairman of the LCIA Board of Directors (the latter being ex officio a member of the LCIA Court) shall only be eligible to be appointed as arbitrators if nominated in writing by a party or parties—provided that no such nominee shall have taken or shall take thereafter any part in any function of the LCIA Court or LCIA relating to such arbitration.

Article 6 Nationality of Arbitrators

6.1 Where the parties are of different nationalities, a sole arbitrator or the presiding arbitrator shall not have the same nationality as any party unless the parties who are not of the same nationality as the arbitral candidate all agree in writing otherwise.

6.2 The nationality of a party shall be understood to include those of its controlling shareholders or interests.

6.3 A person who is a citizen of two or more States shall be treated as a national of each State; citizens of the European Union shall be treated as nationals of its different Member States and shall not be treated as having the same nationality; a citizen of a State's overseas territory shall be treated as a national of that territory and not of that State; and a legal person incorporated in a State's overseas territory shall be treated as such and not (by such fact alone) as a national of or a legal person incorporated in that State.

Article 7 Party and Other Nominations

7.1 If the parties have agreed howsoever that any arbitrator is to be appointed by one or more of them or by any third person (other than the LCIA Court), that agreement shall be treated under the Arbitration Agreement as an agreement to nominate an arbitrator for all purposes. Such nominee may only be appointed by the LCIA Court as arbitrator subject to that nominee's compliance with Articles 5.3 to 5.5; and the LCIA Court shall refuse to appoint any nominee if it determines that the nominee is not so compliant or is otherwise unsuitable.

7.2 Where the parties have howsoever agreed that the Claimant or the Respondent or any third person (other than the LCIA Court) is to nominate an arbitrator and such nomination is not made within time or at all (in the Request, Response or otherwise), the LCIA Court may appoint an arbitrator notwithstanding any absent or late nomination.

7.3 In the absence of written agreement between the Parties, no party may unilaterally nominate a sole arbitrator or presiding arbitrator.

Article 8 Three or More Parties

8.1 Where the Arbitration Agreement entitles each party howsoever to nominate an arbitrator, the parties to the dispute number more than two and such parties have not all agreed in writing that the disputant parties represent collectively two separate "sides" for the formation of the Arbitral Tribunal (as Claimants on one side and Respondents on the other side, each side nominating a single arbitrator), the LCIA Court shall appoint the Arbitral Tribunal without regard to any party's entitlement or nomination.

8.2 In such circumstances, the Arbitration Agreement shall be treated for all purposes as a written agreement by the parties for the nomination and appointment of the Arbitral Tribunal by the LCIA Court alone.

Article 9A Expedited Formation of Arbitral Tribunal

9.1 In the case of exceptional urgency, any party may apply to the LCIA Court for the expedited formation of the Arbitral Tribunal under Article 5.

9.2 Such an application shall be made to the Registrar in writing (preferably by electronic means), together with a copy of the Request (if made by a Claimant) or a copy of the Response (if made by a Respondent), delivered or notified to all other parties to the arbitration. The application shall set out the specific grounds for exceptional urgency requiring the expedited formation of the Arbitral Tribunal.

9.3 The LCIA Court shall determine the application as expeditiously as possible in the circumstances. If the application is granted, for the purpose of forming the Arbitral Tribunal the LCIA Court may abridge any period of time under the Arbitration Agreement or other agreement of the parties (pursuant to Article 22.5).

Article 9B Emergency Arbitrator

9.4 Subject always to Article 9.14 below, in the case of emergency at any time prior to the formation or expedited formation of the Arbitral Tribunal (under Articles 5 or 9A), any party may apply to the LCIA Court for the immediate appointment of a temporary sole arbitrator to conduct emergency proceedings pending the formation or expedited formation of the Arbitral Tribunal (the "Emergency Arbitrator").

9.5 Such an application shall be made to the Registrar in writing (preferably by electronic means), together with a copy of the Request (if made by a Claimant) or a copy of the Response (if made by a Respondent), delivered or notified to all other parties to the arbitration. The application shall set out, together with all relevant documentation: (i) the specific grounds for requiring, as an emergency, the appointment of an Emergency Arbitrator; and (ii) the specific claim, with reasons, for emergency relief. The application shall be accompanied by the applicant's written confirmation that the applicant has paid or is paying to the LCIA the Special Fee under Article 9B, without which actual receipt of such payment the application shall be dismissed by the LCIA Court. The Special Fee shall be subject to the terms of the Schedule of Costs. Its amount is prescribed in the Schedule, covering the fees and expenses of the Emergency Arbitrator and the administrative fees and expenses of the LCIA, with additional charges (if any) of the LCIA Court. After the appointment of the Emergency Arbitrator, the amount of the Special Fee payable by the applicant may be increased by the LCIA Court in accordance with the Schedule. Article 24 shall not apply to any Special Fee paid to the LCIA.

9.6 The LCIA Court shall determine the application as soon as possible in the circumstances. If the application is granted, an Emergency Arbitrator shall be appointed by the LCIA Court within three days of the Registrar's receipt of the application (or as soon as possible thereafter). Articles 5.1, 5.7, 5.9, 5.10, 6, 9C, 10 and 16.2 (last sentence) shall apply to such appointment. The Emergency Arbitrator shall comply with the requirements of Articles 5.3, 5.4 and (until the emergency proceedings are finally concluded) Article 5.5.

9.7 The Emergency Arbitrator may conduct the emergency proceedings in any manner determined by the Emergency Arbitrator to be appropriate in the circumstances, taking account of the nature of such emergency proceedings, the need to afford to each party, if possible, an opportunity to be consulted on the claim for emergency relief (whether or not it avails itself of such opportunity), the claim and reasons for emergency relief and the parties' further submissions (if any). The Emergency Arbitrator is not required to hold any hearing with the parties (whether in person, by telephone or otherwise) and may decide the claim for emergency relief on available documentation. In the event of a hearing, Articles 16.3, 19.2, 19.3 and 19.4 shall apply.

9.8 The Emergency Arbitrator shall decide the claim for emergency relief as soon as possible, but no later than 14 days following the Emergency Arbitrator's appointment. This deadline may only be extended by the LCIA Court in exceptional circumstances (pursuant to Article 22.5) or by the written agreement of all parties to the emergency proceedings. The Emergency Arbitrator may make any order or award which the Arbitral Tribunal could make under the Arbitration Agreement (excepting Arbitration and Legal Costs under Articles 28.2 and 28.3); and, in addition, make any order adjourning the consideration of all or any part of the claim for emergency relief to the proceedings conducted by the Arbitral Tribunal (when formed).

9.9 An order of the Emergency Arbitrator shall be made in writing, with reasons. An award of the Emergency Arbitrator shall comply with Article 26.2 and, when made, take effect as an award under Article 26.8 (subject to Article 9.11). The Emergency Arbitrator shall be responsible for delivering any order or award to the Registrar, who shall transmit the same promptly to the parties by electronic means, in addition to paper form (if so requested by any party). In the event of any disparity between electronic and paper forms, the electronic form shall prevail.

9.10 The Special Fee paid shall form a part of the Arbitration Costs under Article 28.2 determined by the LCIA Court (as to the amount of Arbitration Costs) and decided by the Arbitral Tribunal (as to the proportions in which the parties shall bear Arbitration Costs). Any legal or other expenses incurred by any party during the emergency proceedings shall form a part of the Legal Costs under Article 28.3 decided by the Arbitral Tribunal (as to amount and as to payment between the parties of Legal Costs).

9.11 Any order or award of the Emergency Arbitrator (apart from any order adjourning to the Arbitral Tribunal, when formed, any part of the claim for emergency relief) may be confirmed, varied, discharged or revoked, in whole or in part, by order or award made by the Arbitral Tribunal upon application by any party or upon its own initiative.

9.12 Article 9B shall not prejudice any party's right to apply to a state court or other legal authority for any interim or conservatory measures before the formation of the Arbitration Tribunal; and it shall not be treated as an alternative to or substitute for the exercise of such right. During the emergency proceedings, any application to and any order by such court or authority shall be communicated promptly in writing to the Emergency Arbitrator, the Registrar and all other parties.

9.13 Articles 3.3, 13.1–13.4, 14.4, 14.5, 16, 17, 18, 22.3, 22.4, 23, 28, 29, 30, 31 and 32 and the Annex shall apply to emergency proceedings. In addition to the provisions expressly set out there and in Article 9B above, the Emergency Arbitrator and the parties to the emergency proceedings shall also be guided by other provisions of the Arbitration Agreement, whilst recognising that several such provisions may not be fully applicable or appropriate to emergency proceedings. Wherever relevant, the LCIA Court may abridge under any such provisions any period of time (pursuant to Article 22.5).

9.14 Article 9B shall not apply if either: (i) the parties have concluded their arbitration agreement before 1 October 2014 and the parties have not agreed in writing to 'opt in' to Article 9B; or (ii) the parties have agreed in writing at any time to 'opt out' of Article 9B.

Article 9C Expedited Appointment of Replacement Arbitrator

9.15 Any party may apply to the LCIA Court for the expedited appointment of a replacement arbitrator under Article 11.

9.16 Such an application shall be made in writing to the Registrar (preferably by electronic means), delivered (or notified) to all other parties to the arbitration; and it shall set out the specific grounds requiring the expedited appointment of the replacement arbitrator.

9.17 The LCIA Court shall determine the application as expeditiously as possible in the circumstances. If the application is granted, for the purpose of expediting the appointment of the replacement arbitrator the LCIA Court may abridge any period of time in the Arbitration Agreement or any other agreement of the parties (pursuant to Article 22.5).

Article 10 Revocation and Challenges

10.1 The LCIA Court may revoke any arbitrator's appointment upon its own initiative, at the written request of all other members of the Arbitral Tribunal or upon a written challenge by any party if: (i) that arbitrator gives written notice to the LCIA Court of his or her intent to resign as arbitrator, to be copied to all parties and all other members of the Arbitral Tribunal (if any); (ii) that arbitrator falls seriously ill, refuses or becomes unable or unfit to act; or (iii) circumstances exist that give rise to justifiable doubts as to that arbitrator's impartiality or independence.

10.2 The LCIA Court may determine that an arbitrator is unfit to act under Article 10.1 if that arbitrator: (i) acts in deliberate violation of the Arbitration Agreement; (ii) does not act fairly or impartially as between the parties; or (iii) does not conduct or participate in the arbitration with reasonable efficiency, diligence and industry.

10.3 A party challenging an arbitrator under Article 10.1 shall, within 14 days of the formation of the Arbitral Tribunal or (if later) within 14 days of becoming aware of any grounds described in Article 10.1 or 10.2, deliver a written statement of the reasons for its challenge to the LCIA Court, the Arbitral Tribunal and all other parties. A party may challenge an arbitrator whom it has nominated, or in whose appointment it has participated, only for reasons of which it becomes aware after the appointment has been made by the LCIA Court.

10.4 The LCIA Court shall provide to those other parties and the challenged arbitrator a reasonable opportunity to comment on the challenging party's written statement. The LCIA Court may require at any time further information and materials from the challenging party, the challenged arbitrator, other parties and other members of the Arbitral Tribunal (if any).

10.5 If all other parties agree in writing to the challenge within 14 days of receipt of the written statement, the LCIA Court shall revoke that arbitrator's appointment (without reasons).

10.6 Unless the parties so agree or the challenged arbitrator resigns in writing within 14 days of receipt of the written statement, the LCIA Court shall decide the challenge and, if upheld, shall revoke that arbitrator's appointment. The LCIA Court's decision shall be made in writing, with reasons; and a copy shall be transmitted by the Registrar to the parties, the challenged arbitrator and other members of the Arbitral Tribunal (if any). A challenged arbitrator who resigns in writing prior to the LCIA Court's decision shall not be considered as having admitted any part of the written statement.

10.7 The LCIA Court shall determine the amount of fees and expenses (if any) to be paid for the former arbitrator's services, as it may consider appropriate in the circumstances. The LCIA Court may also determine whether, in what amount and to whom any party should pay forthwith the costs of the challenge; and the LCIA Court may also refer all or any part of such costs to the later decision of the Arbitral Tribunal and/or the LCIA Court under Article 28.

Article 11 Nomination and Replacement

11.1 In the event that the LCIA Court determines that justifiable doubts exist as to any arbitral candidate's suitability, independence or impartiality, or if a nominee declines appointment as arbitrator, or if an arbitrator is to be replaced for any reason, the LCIA Court may determine whether or not to follow the original nominating process for such arbitral appointment.

11.2 The LCIA Court may determine that any opportunity given to a party to make any re-nomination (under the Arbitration Agreement or otherwise) shall be waived if not exercised within 14 days (or such lesser or greater time as the LCIA Court may determine), after which the LCIA Court shall appoint the replacement arbitrator without such re-nomination.

Article 12 Majority Power to Continue Deliberations

12.1 In exceptional circumstances, where an arbitrator without good cause refuses or persistently fails to participate in the deliberations of an Arbitral Tribunal, the remaining arbitrators jointly may decide (after their written notice of such refusal or failure to the LCIA Court, the parties and the absent arbitrator) to continue the arbitration (including the making of any award) notwithstanding the absence of that other arbitrator, subject to the written approval of the LCIA Court.

12.2 In deciding whether to continue the arbitration, the remaining arbitrators shall take into account the stage of the arbitration, any explanation made by or on behalf of the absent arbitrator for his or her refusal or non-participation, the likely effect upon the legal recognition or enforceability of any award at the seat of the arbitration and such other matters as they consider appropriate in the circumstances. The reasons for such decision shall be stated in any award made by the remaining arbitrators without the participation of the absent arbitrator.

12.3 In the event that the remaining arbitrators decide at any time thereafter not to continue the arbitration without the participation of the absent arbitrator, the remaining arbitrators shall notify in writing the parties and the LCIA Court of such decision; and, in that event, the remaining arbitrators or any party may refer the matter to the LCIA Court for the revocation of the absent arbitrator's appointment and the appointment of a replacement arbitrator under Articles 10 and 11.

Article 13 Communications between Parties and Arbitral Tribunal

13.1 Following the formation of the Arbitral Tribunal, all communications shall take place directly between the Arbitral Tribunal and the parties (to be copied to the Registrar), unless the Arbitral Tribunal decides that communications should continue to be made through the Registrar.

13.2 Where the Registrar sends any written communication to one party on behalf of the Arbitral Tribunal or the LCIA Court, he or she shall send a copy to each of the other parties.

13.3 Where any party delivers to the Arbitral Tribunal any communication (including statements and documents under Article 15), whether by electronic means or otherwise, it shall deliver a copy to each arbitrator, all other parties and the Registrar; and it shall confirm to the Arbitral Tribunal in writing that it has done or is doing so.

13.4 During the arbitration from the Arbitral Tribunal's formation onwards, no party shall deliberately initiate or attempt to initiate any unilateral contact relating to the arbitration or the parties' dispute with any member of the Arbitral Tribunal or any member of the LCIA Court exercising any function in regard to the arbitration (but not including the Registrar), which has not been disclosed in writing prior to or shortly after the time of such contact to all other parties, all members of the Arbitral Tribunal (if comprised of more than one arbitrator) and the Registrar.

13.5 Prior to the Arbitral Tribunal's formation, unless the parties agree otherwise in writing, any arbitrator, candidate or nominee who is required to participate in the selection of a presiding arbitrator may consult any party in order to obtain the views of that party as to the suitability of any candidate or nominee as presiding arbitrator, provided that such arbitrator, candidate or nominee informs the Registrar of such consultation.

Article 14 Conduct of Proceedings

14.1 The parties and the Arbitral Tribunal are encouraged to make contact (whether by a hearing in person, telephone conference-call, video conference or exchange of correspondence) as soon as practicable but no later than 21 days from receipt of the Registrar's written notification of the formation of the Arbitral Tribunal.

14.2 The parties may agree on joint proposals for the conduct of their arbitration for consideration by the Arbitral Tribunal. They are encouraged to do so in consultation with the Arbitral Tribunal and consistent with the Arbitral Tribunal's general duties under the Arbitration Agreement.

14.3 Such agreed proposals shall be made by the parties in writing or recorded in writing by the Arbitral Tribunal at the parties' request and with their authority.

14.4 Under the Arbitration Agreement, the Arbitral Tribunal's general duties at all times during the arbitration shall include:

(i) a duty to act fairly and impartially as between all parties, giving each a reasonable opportunity of putting its case and dealing with that of its opponent(s); and

(ii) a duty to adopt procedures suitable to the circumstances of the arbitration, avoiding unnecessary delay and expense, so as to provide a fair, efficient and expeditious means for the final resolution of the parties' dispute.

14.5 The Arbitral Tribunal shall have the widest discretion to discharge these general duties, subject to such mandatory law(s) or rules of law as the Arbitral Tribunal may decide to be applicable; and at all times the parties shall do everything necessary in good faith for the fair, efficient and expeditious conduct of the arbitration, including the Arbitral Tribunal's discharge of its general duties.

14.6 In the case of an Arbitral Tribunal other than a sole arbitrator, the presiding arbitrator, with the prior agreement of its other members and all parties, may make procedural orders alone.

Article 15 Written Statements

15.1 Unless the parties have agreed or jointly proposed in writing otherwise or the Arbitral Tribunal should decide differently, the written stage of the arbitration and its procedural time-table shall be as set out in this Article 15.

15.2 Within 28 days of receipt of the Registrar's written notification of the Arbitral Tribunal's formation, the Claimant shall deliver to the Arbitral Tribunal and all other parties either: (i) its written election to have its Request treated as its Statement of Case complying with this Article 15.2; or (ii) its written Statement of Case setting out in sufficient detail the relevant facts and legal submissions on which it relies, together with the relief claimed against all other parties, and all essential documents.

15.3 Within 28 days of receipt of the Claimant's Statement of Case or the Claimant's election to treat the Request as its Statement of Case, the Respondent shall deliver to the Arbitral Tribunal and all other parties either: (i) its written election to have its Response treated as its Statement of Defence and (if applicable) Cross-claim complying with this Article 15.3; or (ii) its written Statement of Defence and (if applicable) Statement of Cross-claim setting out in sufficient detail the relevant facts and legal submissions on which it relies, together with the relief claimed against all other parties, and all essential documents.

15.4 Within 28 days of receipt of the Respondent's Statement of Defence and (if applicable) Statement of Cross-claim or the Respondent's election to treat the Response as its Statement of Defence and (if applicable) Cross-claim, the Claimant shall deliver to the Arbitral Tribunal and all other parties a written Statement of Reply which, where there are any cross-claims, shall also include a Statement of Defence to Cross-claim in the same manner required for a Statement of Defence, together with all essential documents.

15.5 If the Statement of Reply contains a Statement of Defence to Cross-claim, within 28 days of its receipt the Respondent shall deliver to the Arbitral Tribunal and all other parties its written Statement of Reply to the Defence to Cross-claim, together with all essential documents.

15.6 The Arbitral Tribunal may provide additional directions as to any part of the written stage of the arbitration (including witness statements, submissions and evidence), particularly where there are multiple claimants, multiple respondents or any cross-claim between two or more respondents or between two or more claimants.

15.7 No party may submit any further written statement following the last of these Statements, unless otherwise ordered by the Arbitral Tribunal.

15.8 If the Respondent fails to submit a Statement of Defence or the Claimant a Statement of Defence to Cross-claim, or if at any time any party fails to avail itself of the opportunity to present its written case in the manner required under this Article 15 or otherwise by order of the Arbitral Tribunal, the Arbitral Tribunal may nevertheless proceed with the arbitration (with or without a hearing) and make one or more awards.

15.9 As soon as practicable following this written stage of the arbitration, the Arbitral Tribunal shall proceed in such manner as has been agreed in writing by the parties or pursuant to its authority under the Arbitration Agreement.

15.10 In any event, the Arbitral Tribunal shall seek to make its final award as soon as reasonably possible following the last submission from the parties (whether made orally or in writing), in accordance with a timetable notified to the parties and the Registrar as soon as practicable (if necessary, as revised and re-notified from time to time). When the Arbitral Tribunal (not being a sole arbitrator) establishes a time for what it contemplates shall be the last submission from the parties (whether written or oral), it shall set aside adequate time for deliberations as soon as possible after that last submission and notify the parties of the time it has set aside.

Article 16 Seat(s) of Arbitration and Place(s) of Hearing

16.1 The parties may agree in writing the seat (or legal place) of their arbitration at any time before the formation of the Arbitral Tribunal and, after such formation, with the prior written consent of the Arbitral Tribunal.

16.2 In default of any such agreement, the seat of the arbitration shall be London (England), unless and until the Arbitral Tribunal orders, in view of the circumstances and after having given the parties a reasonable opportunity to make written comments to the Arbitral Tribunal, that another arbitral seat is more appropriate. Such default seat shall not be considered as a relevant circumstance by the LCIA Court in appointing any arbitrators under Articles 5, 9A, 9B, 9C and 11.

16.3 The Arbitral Tribunal may hold any hearing at any convenient geographical place in consultation with the parties and hold its deliberations at any geographical place of its own choice; and if such place(s) should be elsewhere than the seat of the arbitration, the arbitration shall nonetheless be treated for all purposes as an arbitration conducted at the arbitral seat and any order or award as having been made at that seat.

16.4 The law applicable to the Arbitration Agreement and the arbitration shall be the law applicable at the seat of the arbitration, unless and to the extent that the parties have agreed in writing on the application of other laws or rules of law and such agreement is not prohibited by the law applicable at the arbitral seat.

Article 17 Language(s) of Arbitration

17.1 The initial language of the arbitration (until the formation of the Arbitral Tribunal) shall be the language or prevailing language of the Arbitration Agreement, unless the parties have agreed in writing otherwise.

17.2 In the event that the Arbitration Agreement is written in more than one language of equal standing, the LCIA Court may, unless the Arbitration Agreement provides that the arbitration proceedings shall be conducted from the outset in more than one language, determine which of those languages shall be the initial language of the arbitration.

17.3 A non-participating or defaulting party shall have no cause for complaint if communications to and from the LCIA Court and Registrar are conducted in the initial language(s) of the arbitration or of the arbitral seat.

17.4 Following the formation of the Arbitral Tribunal, unless the parties have agreed upon the language or languages of the arbitration, the Arbitral Tribunal shall decide upon the language(s) of the arbitration after giving the parties a reasonable opportunity to make written comments and taking into account the initial language(s) of the arbitration and any other matter it may consider appropriate in the circumstances.

17.5 If any document is expressed in a language other than the language(s) of the arbitration and no translation of such document is submitted by the party relying upon the document, the Arbitral Tribunal may order or (if the Arbitral Tribunal has not been formed) the Registrar may request that party to submit a translation of all or any part of that document in any language(s) of the arbitration or of the arbitral seat.

Article 18 Legal Representatives

18.1 Any party may be represented in the arbitration by one or more authorised legal representatives appearing by name before the Arbitral Tribunal.

18.2 Until the Arbitral Tribunal's formation, the Registrar may request from any party: (i) written proof of the authority granted by that party to any legal representative designated in its Request or Response; and (ii) written confirmation of the names and addresses of all such party's legal representatives in the arbitration. After its formation, at any time, the Arbitral Tribunal may order any party to provide similar proof or confirmation in any form it considers appropriate.

18.3 Following the Arbitral Tribunal's formation, any intended change or addition by a party to its legal representatives shall be notified promptly in writing to all other parties, the Arbitral Tribunal and the Registrar; and any such intended change or addition shall only take effect in the arbitration subject to the approval of the Arbitral Tribunal.

18.4 The Arbitral Tribunal may withhold approval of any intended change or addition to a party's legal representatives where such change or addition could compromise the composition of the Arbitral Tribunal or the finality of any award (on the grounds of possible conflict or other like impediment). In deciding whether to grant or withhold such approval, the Arbitral Tribunal shall have regard to the circumstances, including: the general principle that a party may be represented by a legal representative chosen by that party, the stage which the arbitration has reached, the efficiency resulting from maintaining the composition of the Arbitral Tribunal (as constituted throughout the arbitration) and any likely wasted costs or loss of time resulting from such change or addition.

18.5 Each party shall ensure that all its legal representatives appearing by name before the Arbitral Tribunal have agreed to comply with the general guidelines contained in the Annex to the LCIA Rules, as a condition of such representation. In permitting any legal representative so to appear, a party shall thereby represent that the legal representative has agreed to such compliance.

18.6 In the event of a complaint by one party against another party's legal representative appearing by name before the Arbitral Tribunal (or of such complaint by the Arbitral Tribunal upon its own initiative), the Arbitral Tribunal may decide, after consulting the parties and granting that legal representative a reasonable opportunity to answer the complaint, whether or not the legal representative has violated the general guidelines. If such violation is found by the Arbitral Tribunal, the Arbitral Tribunal may order any or all of the following sanctions against the legal representative: (i) a written reprimand; (ii) a written caution as to future conduct in the arbitration; and (iii) any other measure necessary to fulfil within the arbitration the general duties required of the Arbitral Tribunal under Articles 14.4(i) and (ii).

Article 19 Oral Hearing(s)

19.1 Any party has the right to a hearing before the Arbitral Tribunal on the parties' dispute at any appropriate stage of the arbitration (as decided by the Arbitral Tribunal), unless the parties have agreed in writing upon a documents-only arbitration. For this purpose, a hearing may consist of several part-hearings (as decided by the Arbitral Tribunal).

19.2 The Arbitral Tribunal shall organise the conduct of any hearing in advance, in consultation with the parties. The Arbitral Tribunal shall have the fullest authority under the Arbitration Agreement to establish the conduct of a hearing, including its date, form, content, procedure, time-limits and geographical place. As to form, a hearing may take place by video or telephone conference or in person (or a combination of all three). As to content, the Arbitral Tribunal may require the parties to address a list of specific questions or issues arising from the parties' dispute.

19.3 The Arbitral Tribunal shall give to the parties reasonable notice in writing of any hearing.

19.4 All hearings shall be held in private, unless the parties agree otherwise in writing.

Article 20 Witness(es)

20.1 Before any hearing, the Arbitral Tribunal may order any party to give written notice of the identity of each witness that party wishes to call (including rebuttal witnesses), as well as the subject-matter of that witness's testimony, its content and its relevance to the issues in the arbitration.

20.2 Subject to any order otherwise by the Arbitral Tribunal, the testimony of a witness may be presented by a party in written form, either as a signed statement or like document.

20.3 The Arbitral Tribunal may decide the time, manner and form in which these written materials shall be exchanged between the parties and presented to the Arbitral Tribunal; and it may allow, refuse or limit the written and oral testimony of witnesses (whether witnesses of fact or expert witnesses).

20.4 The Arbitral Tribunal and any party may request that a witness, on whose written testimony another party relies, should attend for oral questioning at a hearing before the Arbitral Tribunal. If the Arbitral Tribunal orders that other party to secure the attendance of that witness and the witness refuses or fails to attend the hearing without good cause, the Arbitral Tribunal may place such weight on the written testimony or exclude all or any part thereof altogether as it considers appropriate in the circumstances.

20.5 Subject to the mandatory provisions of any applicable law, rules of law and any order of the Arbitral Tribunal otherwise, it shall not be improper for any party or its legal representatives to interview any potential witness for the purpose of presenting his or her testimony in written form to the Arbitral Tribunal or producing such person as an oral witness at any hearing.

20.6 Subject to any order by the Arbitral Tribunal otherwise, any individual intending to testify to the Arbitral Tribunal may be treated as a witness notwithstanding that the individual is a party to the arbitration or was, remains or has become an officer, employee, owner or shareholder of any party or is otherwise identified with any party.

20.7 Subject to the mandatory provisions of any applicable law, the Arbitral Tribunal shall be entitled (but not required) to administer any appropriate oath to any witness at any hearing, prior to the oral testimony of that witness.

20.8 Any witness who gives oral testimony at a hearing before the Arbitral Tribunal may be questioned by each of the parties under the control of the Arbitral Tribunal. The Arbitral Tribunal may put questions at any stage of such testimony.

Article 21 Expert(s) to Arbitral Tribunal

21.1 The Arbitral Tribunal, after consultation with the parties, may appoint one or more experts to report in writing to the Arbitral Tribunal and the parties on specific issues in the arbitration, as identified by the Arbitral Tribunal.

21.2 Any such expert shall be and remain impartial and independent of the parties; and he or she shall sign a written declaration to such effect, delivered to the Arbitral Tribunal and copied to all parties.

21.3 The Arbitral Tribunal may require any party at any time to give to such expert any relevant information or to provide access to any relevant documents, goods, samples, property, site or thing for inspection under that party's control on such terms as the Arbitral Tribunal thinks appropriate in the circumstances.

21.4 If any party so requests or the Arbitral Tribunal considers it necessary, the Arbitral Tribunal may order the expert, after delivery of the expert's written report, to participate in a hearing at which the parties shall have a reasonable opportunity to question the expert on the report and to present witnesses in order to testify on relevant issues arising from the report.

21.5 The fees and expenses of any expert appointed by the Arbitral Tribunal under this Article 21 may be paid out of the deposits payable by the parties under Article 24 and shall form part of the Arbitration Costs under Article 28.

Article 22 Additional Powers

22.1 The Arbitral Tribunal shall have the power, upon the application of any party or (save for sub-paragraphs (viii), (ix) and (x) below) upon its own initiative, but in either case only after giving the parties a reasonable opportunity to state their views and upon such terms (as to costs and otherwise) as the Arbitral Tribunal may decide:

(i)   to allow a party to supplement, modify or amend any claim, defence, cross-claim, defence to cross-claim and reply, including a Request, Response and any other written statement, submitted by such party;

(ii) to abridge or extend (even where the period of time has expired) any period of time prescribed under the Arbitration Agreement, any other agreement of the parties or any order made by the Arbitral Tribunal;

(iii) to conduct such enquiries as may appear to the Arbitral Tribunal to be necessary or expedient, including whether and to what extent the Arbitral Tribunal should itself take the initiative in identifying relevant issues and ascertaining relevant facts and the law(s) or rules of law applicable to the Arbitration Agreement, the arbitration and the merits of the parties' dispute;

(iv) to order any party to make any documents, goods, samples, property, site or thing under its control available for inspection by the Arbitral Tribunal, any other party, any expert to such party and any expert to the Tribunal;

(v)   to order any party to produce to the Arbitral Tribunal and to other parties documents or copies of documents in their possession, custody or power which the Arbitral Tribunal decides to be relevant;

(vi) to decide whether or not to apply any strict rules of evidence (or any other rules) as to the admissibility, relevance or weight of any material tendered by a party on any issue of fact or expert opinion; and to decide the time, manner and form in which such material should be exchanged between the parties and presented to the Arbitral Tribunal;

(vii) to order compliance with any legal obligation, payment of compensation for breach of any legal obligation and specific performance of any agreement (including any arbitration agreement or any contract relating to land);

(viii) to allow one or more third persons to be joined in the arbitration as a party provided any such third person and the applicant party have consented to such joinder in writing following the Commencement Date or (if earlier) in the Arbitration Agreement; and thereafter to make a single final award, or separate awards, in respect of all parties so implicated in the arbitration;

(ix) to order, with the approval of the LCIA Court, the consolidation of the arbitration with one or more other arbitrations into a single arbitration subject to the LCIA Rules where all the parties to the arbitrations to be consolidated so agree in writing;

(x) to order, with the approval of the LCIA Court, the consolidation of the arbitration with one or more other arbitrations subject to the LCIA Rules commenced under the same arbitration agreement or any compatible arbitration agreement(s) between the same disputing parties, provided that no arbitral tribunal has yet been formed by the LCIA Court for such other arbitration(s) or, if already formed, that such tribunal(s) is(are) composed of the same arbitrators; and

(xi) to order the discontinuance of the arbitration if it appears to the Arbitral Tribunal that the arbitration has been abandoned by the parties or all claims and any cross-claims withdrawn by the parties, provided that, after fixing a reasonable period of time within which the parties shall be invited to agree or to object to such discontinuance, no party has stated its written objection to the Arbitral Tribunal to such discontinuance upon the expiry of such period of time.

22.2 By agreeing to arbitration under the Arbitration Agreement, the parties shall be treated as having agreed not to apply to any state court or other legal authority for any order available from the Arbitral Tribunal (if formed) under Article 22.1, except with the agreement in writing of all parties.

22.3 The Arbitral Tribunal shall decide the parties' dispute in accordance with the law(s) or rules of law chosen by the parties as applicable to the merits of their dispute. If and to the extent that the Arbitral Tribunal decides that the parties have made no such choice, the Arbitral Tribunal shall apply the law(s) or rules of law which it considers appropriate.

22.4 The Arbitral Tribunal shall only apply to the merits of the dispute principles deriving from "ex aequo et bono", "amiable composition" or "honourable engagement" where the parties have so agreed in writing.

22.5 Subject to any order of the Arbitral Tribunal under Article 22.1(ii), the LCIA Court may also abridge or extend any period of time under the Arbitration Agreement or other agreement of the parties (even where the period of time has expired).

22.6 Without prejudice to the generality of Articles 22.1(ix) and (x), the LCIA Court may determine, after giving the parties a reasonable opportunity to state their views, that two or more arbitrations, subject to the LCIA Rules and commenced under the same arbitration agreement between the same disputing parties, shall be consolidated to form one single arbitration subject to the LCIA Rules, provided that no arbitral tribunal has yet been formed by the LCIA Court for any of the arbitrations to be consolidated.

Article 23 Jurisdiction and Authority

23.1 The Arbitral Tribunal shall have the power to rule upon its own jurisdiction and authority, including any objection to the initial or continuing existence, validity, effectiveness or scope of the Arbitration Agreement.

23.2 For that purpose, an arbitration clause which forms or was intended to form part of another agreement shall be treated as an arbitration agreement independent of that other agreement. A decision by the Arbitral Tribunal that such other agreement is non-existent, invalid or ineffective shall not entail (of itself) the non-existence, invalidity or ineffectiveness of the arbitration clause.

23.3 An objection by a Respondent that the Arbitral Tribunal does not have jurisdiction shall be raised as soon as possible but not later than the time for its Statement of Defence; and a like objection by any party responding to a cross-claiming party shall be raised as soon as possible but not later than the time for its Statement of Defence to Cross-claim. An objection that the Arbitral Tribunal is exceeding the scope of its authority shall be raised promptly after the Arbitral Tribunal has indicated its intention to act upon the matter alleged to lie beyond its authority. The Arbitral Tribunal may nevertheless admit an untimely objection as to its jurisdiction or authority if it considers the delay justified in the circumstances.

23.4 The Arbitral Tribunal may decide the objection to its jurisdiction or authority in an award as to jurisdiction or authority or later in an award on the merits, as it considers appropriate in the circumstances.

23.5 By agreeing to arbitration under the Arbitration Agreement, after the formation of the Arbitral Tribunal the parties shall be treated as having agreed not to apply to any state court or other legal authority for any relief regarding the Arbitral Tribunal's jurisdiction or authority, except (i) with the prior agreement in writing of all parties to the arbitration, or (ii) the prior authorisation of the Arbitral Tribunal, or (iii) following the latter's award on the objection to its jurisdiction or authority.

Article 24 Deposits

24.1 The LCIA Court may direct the parties, in such proportions and at such times as it thinks appropriate, to make one or more payments to the LCIA on account of the Arbitration Costs. Such payments deposited by the parties may be applied by the LCIA Court to pay any item of such Arbitration Costs (including the LCIA's own fees and expenses) in accordance with the LCIA Rules.

24.2 All payments made by parties on account of the Arbitration Costs shall be held by the LCIA in trust under English law in England, to be disbursed or otherwise applied by the LCIA in accordance with the LCIA Rules and invested having regard also to the interests of the LCIA. Each payment made by a party shall be credited by the LCIA with interest at the rate from time to time credited to an overnight deposit of that amount with the bank(s) engaged by the LCIA to manage deposits from time to time; and any surplus income (beyond such interest) shall accrue for the sole benefit of the LCIA. In the event that payments (with such interest) exceed the total amount of the Arbitration Costs at the conclusion of the arbitration, the excess amount shall be returned by the LCIA to the parties as the ultimate default beneficiaries of the trust.

24.3 Save for exceptional circumstances, the Arbitral Tribunal should not proceed with the arbitration without having ascertained from the Registrar that the LCIA is or will be in requisite funds as regards outstanding and future Arbitration Costs.

24.4 In the event that a party fails or refuses to make any payment on account of the Arbitration Costs as directed by the LCIA Court, the LCIA Court may direct the other party or parties to effect a substitute payment to allow the arbitration to proceed (subject to any order or award on Arbitration Costs).

24.5 In such circumstances, the party effecting the substitute payment may request the Arbitral Tribunal to make an order or award in order to recover that amount as a debt immediately due and payable to that party by the defaulting party, together with any interest.

24.6 Failure by a claiming or cross-claiming party to make promptly and in full any required payment on account of Arbitration Costs may be treated by the Arbitral Tribunal as a withdrawal from the arbitration of the claim or cross-claim respectively, thereby removing such claim or cross-claim (as the case may be) from the scope of the Arbitral Tribunal's jurisdiction under the Arbitration Agreement, subject to any terms decided by the Arbitral Tribunal as to the reinstatement of the claim or cross-claim in the event of subsequent payment by the claiming or cross-claiming party. Such a withdrawal shall not preclude the claiming or cross-claiming party from defending as a respondent any claim or cross-claim made by another party.

Article 25 Interim and Conservatory Measures

25.1 The Arbitral Tribunal shall have the power upon the application of any party, after giving all other parties a reasonable opportunity to respond to such application and upon such terms as the Arbitral Tribunal considers appropriate in the circumstances:

(i) to order any respondent party to a claim or cross-claim to provide security for all or part of the amount in dispute, by way of deposit or bank guarantee or in any other manner;

(ii) to order the preservation, storage, sale or other disposal of any documents, goods, samples, property, site or thing under the control of any party and relating to the subject-matter of the arbitration; and

(iii) to order on a provisional basis, subject to a final decision in an award, any relief which the Arbitral Tribunal would have power to grant in an award, including the payment of money or the disposition of property as between any parties.

Such terms may include the provision by the applicant party of a cross-indemnity, secured in such manner as the Arbitral Tribunal considers appropriate, for any costs or losses incurred by the respondent party in complying with the Arbitral Tribunal's order. Any amount payable under such cross-indemnity and any consequential relief may be decided by the Arbitral Tribunal by one or more awards in the arbitration.

25.2 The Arbitral Tribunal shall have the power upon the application of a party, after giving all other parties a reasonable opportunity to respond to such application, to order any claiming or cross-claiming party to provide or procure security for Legal Costs and Arbitration Costs by way of deposit or bank guarantee or in any other manner and upon such terms as the Arbitral Tribunal considers appropriate in the circumstances. Such terms may include the provision by that other party of a cross-indemnity, itself secured in such manner as the Arbitral Tribunal considers appropriate, for any costs and losses incurred by such claimant or cross-claimant in complying with the Arbitral Tribunal's order. Any amount payable under such cross-indemnity and any consequential relief may be decided by the Arbitral Tribunal by one or more awards in the arbitration. In the event that a claiming or cross-claiming party does not comply with any order to provide security, the Arbitral Tribunal may stay that party's claims or cross-claims or dismiss them by an award.

25.3 The power of the Arbitral Tribunal under Article 25.1 shall not prejudice any party's right to apply to a state court or other legal authority for interim or conservatory measures to similar effect: (i) before the formation of the Arbitral Tribunal; and (ii) after the formation of the Arbitral Tribunal, in exceptional cases and with the Arbitral Tribunal's authorisation, until the final award. After the Commencement Date, any application and any order for such measures before the formation of the Arbitral Tribunal shall be communicated promptly in writing by the applicant party to the Registrar; after its formation, also to the Arbitral Tribunal; and in both cases also to all other parties.

25.4 By agreeing to arbitration under the Arbitration Agreement, the parties shall be taken to have agreed not to apply to any state court or other legal authority for any order for security for Legal Costs or Arbitration Costs.

Article 26 Award(s)

26.1 The Arbitral Tribunal may make separate awards on different issues at different times, including interim payments on account of any claim or cross-claim (including Legal and Arbitration Costs). Such awards shall have the same status as any other award made by the Arbitral Tribunal.

26.2 The Arbitral Tribunal shall make any award in writing and, unless all parties agree in writing otherwise, shall state the reasons upon which such award is based. The award shall also state the date when the award is made and the seat of the arbitration; and it shall be signed by the Arbitral Tribunal or those of its members assenting to it.

26.3 An award may be expressed in any currency, unless the parties have agreed otherwise.

26.4 Unless the parties have agreed otherwise, the Arbitral Tribunal may order that simple or compound interest shall be paid by any party on any sum awarded at such rates as the Arbitral Tribunal decides to be appropriate (without being bound by rates of interest practised by any state court or other legal authority) in respect of any period which the Arbitral Tribunal decides to be appropriate ending not later than the date upon which the award is complied with.

26.5 Where there is more than one arbitrator and the Arbitral Tribunal fails to agree on any issue, the arbitrators shall decide that issue by a majority. Failing a majority decision on any issue, the presiding arbitrator shall decide that issue.

26.6 If any arbitrator refuses or fails to sign the award, the signatures of the majority or (failing a majority) of the presiding arbitrator shall be sufficient, provided that the reason for the omitted signature is stated in the award by the majority or by the presiding arbitrator.

26.7 The sole or presiding arbitrator shall be responsible for delivering the award to the LCIA Court, which shall transmit to the parties the award authenticated by the Registrar as an LCIA award, provided that all Arbitration Costs have been paid in full to the LCIA in accordance with Articles 24 and 28. Such transmission may be made by any electronic means, in addition to paper form (if so requested by any party). In the event of any disparity between electronic and paper forms, the paper form shall prevail.

26.8 Every award (including reasons for such award) shall be final and binding on the parties. The parties undertake to carry out any award immediately and without any delay (subject only to Article 27); and the parties also waive irrevocably their right to any form of appeal, review or recourse to any state court or other legal authority, insofar as such waiver shall not be prohibited under any applicable law.

26.9 In the event of any final settlement of the parties' dispute, the Arbitral Tribunal may decide to make an award recording the settlement if the parties jointly so request in writing (a "Consent Award"), provided always that such Consent Award shall contain an express statement on its face that it is an award made at the parties' joint request and with their consent. A Consent Award need not contain reasons. If the parties do not jointly request a Consent Award, on written confirmation by the parties to the LCIA Court that a final settlement has been reached, the Arbitral Tribunal shall be discharged and the arbitration proceedings concluded by the LCIA Court, subject to payment by the parties of any outstanding Arbitration Costs in accordance with Articles 24 and 28.

Article 27 Correction of Award(s) and Additional Award(s)

27.1 Within 28 days of receipt of any award, a party may by written notice to the Registrar (copied to all other parties) request the Arbitral Tribunal to correct in the award any error in computation, any clerical or typographical error, any ambiguity or any mistake of a similar nature. If the Arbitral Tribunal considers the request to be justified, after consulting the parties, it shall make the correction within 28 days of receipt of the request. Any correction shall take the form of a memorandum by the Arbitral Tribunal.

27.2 The Arbitral Tribunal may also correct any error (including any error in computation, any clerical or typographical error or any error of a similar nature) upon its own initiative in the form of a memorandum within 28 days of the date of the award, after consulting the parties.

27.3 Within 28 days of receipt of the final award, a party may by written notice to the Registrar (copied to all other parties), request the Arbitral Tribunal to make an additional award as to any claim or cross-claim presented in the arbitration but not decided in any award. If the Arbitral Tribunal considers the request to be justified, after consulting the parties, it shall make the additional award within 56 days of receipt of the request.

27.4 As to any claim or cross-claim presented in the arbitration but not decided in any award, the Arbitral Tribunal may also make an additional award upon its own initiative within 28 days of the date of the award, after consulting the parties.

27.5 The provisions of Article 26.2 to 26.7 shall apply to any memorandum or additional award made hereunder. A memorandum shall be treated as part of the award.

Article 28 Arbitration Costs and Legal Costs

28.1 The costs of the arbitration other than the legal or other expenses incurred by the parties themselves (the "Arbitration Costs") shall be determined by the LCIA Court in accordance with the Schedule of Costs. The parties shall be jointly and severally liable to the LCIA and the Arbitral Tribunal for such Arbitration Costs.

28.2 The Arbitral Tribunal shall specify by an award the amount of the Arbitration Costs determined by the LCIA Court (in the absence of a final settlement of the parties' dispute regarding liability for such costs). The Arbitral Tribunal shall decide the proportions in which the parties shall bear such Arbitration Costs. If the Arbitral Tribunal has decided that all or any part of the Arbitration Costs shall be borne by a party other than a party which has already covered such costs by way of a payment to the LCIA under Article 24, the latter party shall have the right to recover the appropriate amount of Arbitration Costs from the former party.

28.3 The Arbitral Tribunal shall also have the power to decide by an award that all or part of the legal or other expenses incurred by a party (the "Legal Costs") be paid by another party. The Arbitral Tribunal shall decide the amount of such Legal Costs on such reasonable basis as it thinks appropriate. The Arbitral Tribunal shall not be required to apply the rates or procedures for assessing such costs practised by any state court or other legal authority.

28.4 The Arbitral Tribunal shall make its decisions on both Arbitration Costs and Legal Costs on the general principle that costs should reflect the parties' relative success and failure in the award or arbitration or under different issues, except where it appears to the Arbitral Tribunal that in the circumstances the application of such a general principle would be inappropriate under the Arbitration Agreement or otherwise. The Arbitral Tribunal may also take into account the parties' conduct in the arbitration, including any co-operation in facilitating the proceedings as to time and cost and any non-co-operation resulting in undue delay and unnecessary expense. Any decision on costs by the Arbitral Tribunal shall be made with reasons in the award containing such decision.

28.5 In the event that the parties have howsoever agreed before their dispute that one or more parties shall pay the whole or any part of the Arbitration Costs or Legal Costs whatever the result of any dispute, arbitration or award, such agreement (in order to be effective) shall be confirmed by the parties in writing after the Commencement Date.

28.6 If the arbitration is abandoned, suspended, withdrawn or concluded, by agreement or otherwise, before the final award is made, the parties shall remain jointly and severally liable to pay to the LCIA and the Arbitral Tribunal the Arbitration Costs determined by the LCIA Court.

28.7 In the event that the Arbitration Costs are less than the deposits received by the LCIA under Article 24, there shall be a refund by the LCIA to the parties in such proportions as the parties may agree in writing, or failing such agreement, in the same proportions and to the same payers as the deposits were paid to the LCIA.

Article 29 Determinations and Decisions by LCIA Court

29.1 The determinations of the LCIA Court with respect to all matters relating to the arbitration shall be conclusive and binding upon the parties and the Arbitral Tribunal, unless otherwise directed by the LCIA Court. Save for reasoned decisions on arbitral challenges under Article 10, such determinations are to be treated as administrative in nature; and the LCIA Court shall not be required to give reasons for any such determination.

29.2 To the extent permitted by any applicable law, the parties shall be taken to have waived any right of appeal or review in respect of any determination and decision of the LCIA Court to any state court or other legal authority. If such appeal or review takes place due to mandatory provisions of any applicable law or otherwise, the LCIA Court may determine whether or not the arbitration should continue, notwithstanding such appeal or review.

Article 30 Confidentiality

30.1 The parties undertake as a general principle to keep confidential all awards in the arbitration, together with all materials in the arbitration created for the purpose of the arbitration and all other documents produced by another party in the proceedings not otherwise in the public domain, save and to the extent that disclosure may be required of a party by legal duty, to protect or pursue a legal right, or to enforce or challenge an award in legal proceedings before a state court or other legal authority.

30.2 The deliberations of the Arbitral Tribunal shall remain confidential to its members, save as required by any applicable law and to the extent that disclosure of an arbitrator's refusal to participate in the arbitration is required of the other members of the Arbitral Tribunal under Articles 10, 12, 26 and 27.

30.3 The LCIA does not publish any award or any part of an award without the prior written consent of all parties and the Arbitral Tribunal.

Article 31 Limitation of Liability

31.1 None of the LCIA (including its officers, members and employees), the LCIA Court (including its President, Vice-Presidents, Honourary Vice-Presidents and members), the Registrar (including any deputy Registrar), any arbitrator, any Emergency Arbitrator and any expert to the Arbitral Tribunal shall be liable to any party howsoever for any act or omission in connection with any arbitration, save: (i) where the act or omission is shown by that party to constitute conscious and deliberate wrongdoing committed by the body or person alleged to be liable to that party; or (ii) to the extent that any part of this provision is shown to be prohibited by any applicable law.

31.2 After the award has been made and all possibilities of any memorandum or additional award under Article 27 have lapsed or been exhausted, neither the LCIA (including its officers, members and employees), the LCIA Court (including its President, Vice-Presidents, Honourary Vice-Presidents and members), the Registrar (including any deputy Registrar), any arbitrator, any Emergency Arbitrator or any expert to the Arbitral Tribunal shall be under any legal obligation to make any statement to any person about any matter concerning the arbitration; nor shall any party seek to make any of these bodies or persons a witness in any legal or other proceedings arising out of the arbitration.

Article 32 General Rules

32.1 A party who knows that any provision of the Arbitration Agreement has not been complied with and yet proceeds with the arbitration without promptly stating its objection as to such non-compliance to the Registrar (before the formation of the Arbitral Tribunal) or the Arbitral Tribunal (after its formation), shall be treated as having irrevocably waived its right to object for all purposes.

32.2 For all matters not expressly provided in the Arbitration Agreement, the LCIA Court, the LCIA, the Registrar, the Arbitral Tribunal and each of the parties shall act at all times in good faith, respecting the spirit of the Arbitration Agreement, and shall make every reasonable effort to ensure that any award is legally recognised and enforceable at the arbitral seat.

32.3 If and to the extent that any part of the Arbitration Agreement is decided by the Arbitral Tribunal, the Emergency Arbitrator, or any court or other legal authority of competent jurisdiction to be invalid, ineffective or unenforceable, such decision shall not, of itself, adversely affect any order or award by the Arbitral Tribunal or the Emergency Arbitrator or any other part of the Arbitration Agreement which shall remain in full force and effect, unless prohibited by any applicable law.

Index (in alphabetical order)

Statement of Case   see Article 15.2;
Statement of Defence   see Article 15.3;
Statement of Cross-claim   see Article 15.3;
Statement of Defence to Cross-claim   see Article 15.4; and
Statement of Reply   see Article 15.4.

(N.B. This Index comprises both defined and other undefined terms. All references to any person or party include both masculine and feminine).

ANNEX TO THE LCIA RULES

General Guidelines for the Parties' Legal Representatives (Articles 18.5 and 18.6 of the LCIA Rules)

Paragraph 1: These general guidelines are intended to promote the good and equal conduct of the parties' legal representatives appearing by name within the arbitration. Nothing in these guidelines is intended to derogate from the Arbitration Agreement or to undermine any legal representative's primary duty of loyalty to the party represented in the arbitration or the obligation to present that party's case effectively to the Arbitral Tribunal. Nor shall these guidelines derogate from any mandatory laws, rules of law, professional rules or codes of conduct if and to the extent that any are shown to apply to a legal representative appearing in the arbitration.

Paragraph 2: A legal representative should not engage in activities intended unfairly to obstruct the arbitration or to jeopardise the finality of any award, including repeated challenges to an arbitrator's appointment or to the jurisdiction or authority of the Arbitral Tribunal known to be unfounded by that legal representative.

Paragraph 3: A legal representative should not knowingly make any false statement to the Arbitral Tribunal or the LCIA Court.

Paragraph 4: A legal representative should not knowingly procure or assist in the preparation of or rely upon any false evidence presented to the Arbitral Tribunal or the LCIA Court.

Paragraph 5: A legal representative should not knowingly conceal or assist in the concealment of any document (or any part thereof) which is ordered to be produced by the Arbitral Tribunal.

Paragraph 6: During the arbitration proceedings, a legal representative should not deliberately initiate or attempt to initiate with any member of the Arbitral Tribunal or with any member of the LCIA Court making any determination or decision in regard to the arbitration (but not including the Registrar) any unilateral contact relating to the arbitration or the parties' dispute, which has not been disclosed in writing prior to or shortly after the time of such contact to all other parties, all members of the Arbitral Tribunal (if comprised of more than one arbitrator) and the Registrar in accordance with Article 13.4.

Paragraph 7: In accordance with Articles 18.5 and 18.6, the Arbitral Tribunal may decide whether a legal representative has violated these general guidelines and, if so, how to exercise its discretion to impose any or all of the sanctions listed in Article 18.6.

Schedule of Arbitration Costs (LCIA)

(effective 1 October 2014)

For arbitrations conducted under the LCIA arbitration rules (the Rules).

This schedule of arbitration costs (the Schedule), as amended from time to time by the LCIA, forms part of the Rules, and will apply in all current and future arbitrations as from its effective date.

1.   Administrative charges

1(i)   Registration Fee (payable in advance with the Request for Arbitration: non-refundable). £1,750

1(ii)   Time spent* by the Secretariat of the LCIA in the administration of the arbitration.**

Registrar / Deputy Registrar £250 per hour

Counsel £225 per hour

Case administrators £175 per hour

Casework accounting functions £150 per hour

1(iii)   Time spent by members of the LCIA Court in carrying out their functions in deciding any challenge brought under the Rules.**

at hourly rates advised by members of the LCIA Court

1(iv)   A sum equivalent to 5% of the fees of the Tribunal (excluding expenses) in respect of the LCIA's general overhead.**

1(v)   Expenses incurred by the Secretariat and by members of the LCIA Court, in connection with the arbitration (such as postage, telephone, facsimile, travel etc.), and additional arbitration support services, whether provided by the Secretariat or by the members of the LCIA Court from their own resources or otherwise.**

1(vi)   The LCIA's charges will be invoiced in sterling, but may be paid in other convertible currencies, at rates prevailing at the time of payment.

1(vii)   Charges may be subject to Value Added Tax at the prevailing rate.

2.   Fees and expenses of the Tribunal

2(i)   The Tribunal's fees will be calculated by reference to work done by its members in connection with the arbitration and will be charged at rates appropriate to the particular circumstances of the case, including its complexity and the special qualifications of the arbitrators. The Tribunal shall agree in writing upon fee rates conforming to the Schedule prior to its appointment by the LCIA Court. The rates will be advised by the Registrar to the parties at the time of the appointment of the Tribunal, but may be reviewed if the duration or a change in the circumstances of the arbitration requires.

Fees shall be at hourly rates not exceeding £450.

However, in exceptional cases, the rate may be higher, provided that, in such cases, (i) the fees of the Tribunal shall be fixed by the LCIA Court on the recommendation of the Registrar, following consultations with the arbitrator(s), and (ii) the fees shall be agreed expressly by all parties.

2(ii)   The Tribunal's fees may include a charge for time spent travelling.

2(iii)   The Tribunal's fees may also include a charge for time reserved but not used as a result of late postponement or cancellation of hearings, provided that the basis for such charge shall be advised in writing to, and approved by, the LCIA Court and that the parties have been informed in advance.

2(iv)   The Tribunal may also recover such expenses as are reasonably incurred in connection with the arbitration, and as are reasonable in amount, provided that claims for expenses should be supported by invoices or receipts.

2(v)   The Tribunal's fees shall be invoiced in the currency of account between the Tribunal and the parties.

2(vi)   In the event of the revocation of the appointment of any arbitrator, pursuant to the provisions of Article 10 of the Rules, the LCIA Court shall, in accordance with Article 10.7, determine the amount of fees and expenses (if any) to be paid for the former arbitrator's services as it may consider appropriate in all the circumstances. 2(vii) Charges may be subject to Value Added Tax at the prevailing rate.

3.   Deposits

3(i)   The LCIA Court may direct the parties, in such proportions and at such times as it thinks appropriate, to make one or more payments to the LCIA on account of the costs of the arbitration, other than the legal or other expenses incurred by the parties themselves (the Arbitration Costs). Such payments deposited by the parties may be applied by the LCIA Court to pay any item of such Arbitration Costs (including the LCIA's own fees and expenses) in accordance with the LCIA Rules.

3(ii)   All payments made by parties on account of the Arbitration Costs shall be held by the LCIA in trust under English law in England, to be disbursed or otherwise applied by the LCIA in accordance with the LCIA Rules and invested having regard also to the interests of the LCIA. Each payment made by a party shall be credited by the LCIA with interest at the rate from time to time credited to an overnight deposit of that amount with the bank(s) engaged by the LCIA to manage deposits from time to time; and any surplus income (beyond such interest) shall accrue for the sole benefit of the LCIA. In the event that payments (with such interest) exceed the total amount of the Arbitration Costs at the conclusion of the arbitration, the excess amount shall be returned by the LCIA to the parties as the ultimate default beneficiaries of the trust.

3(iii)   Save for exceptional circumstances, the Arbitral Tribunal should not proceed with the arbitration without having ascertained from the Registrar that the LCIA is or will be in requisite funds as regards outstanding and future Arbitration Costs.

3(iv)   In the event that a party fails or refuses to make any payment on account of the Arbitration Costs as directed by the LCIA Court, the LCIA Court may direct the other party or parties to effect a substitute payment to allow the arbitration to proceed (subject to any order or award on Arbitration Costs).

3(v)   In such circumstances, the party effecting the substitute payment may request the Arbitral Tribunal to make an order or award in order to recover that amount as a debt immediately due and payable to that party by the defaulting party, together with any interest.

4.   Interim payments

When interim payments are required to cover any part of the Arbitration Costs, including the LCIA's administrative charges; the fees or expenses of members of the LCIA Court, the Tribunal's fees or expenses, including the fees or expenses of any expert appointed by the Tribunal, the fees or expenses of any Secretary to the Tribunal; or charges for hearing rooms and other support services, such payments may be made against the invoices for any of the above from funds held on deposit. If no or insufficient funds are held at the time the interim payment is required, the invoices for any of the above may be submitted for payment direct by the parties.

5.   Registrar's authority

5(i)   For the purposes of sections 3(i) and 3(iv) above, and of Articles 24.1 and 24.4 of the Rules, the Registrar has the authority of the LCIA Court to make the directions referred to, under the supervision of the Court.

5(ii)   For the purposes of section 4 above, and of Article 24.1 of the Rules, the Registrar has the authority of the LCIA Court to approve the payments referred to.

5(iii)   Any request by an arbitrator for payment on account of his fees shall be supported by a fee note, which shall include, or be accompanied by, a detailed breakdown of the time spent at the rates that have been advised to the parties by the LCIA, and the fee note will be forwarded to the parties prior to settlement of the account.

5(iv)   Any dispute regarding the LCIA's administrative charges, or the fees and expenses of the Tribunal shall be determined by the LCIA Court.

6.   Arbitration costs

6(i)   The parties shall be jointly and severally liable to the Tribunal and the LCIA for the costs of the arbitration (other than the legal or other costs incurred by the parties themselves).

6(ii)   Any bank charges incurred on any transfer of funds by the parties to the LCIA shall be borne exclusively by the party or parties transferring the funds. 6(iii) In accordance with Article 26.7 of the Rules, the Tribunal's Award(s) shall be transmitted to the parties by the LCIA Court provided that the costs of the arbitration have been paid to the LCIA in accordance with Article 28 of the Rules.

7.   Emergency Arbitrator

7(i)   Application fee (payable with the application for the appointment of an Emergency Arbitrator under Article 9B of the Rules: non-refundable).

£8,000

7(ii)   Emergency Arbitrator's fee, to cover time charges and expenses (payable with the application for the appointment of an Emergency Arbitrator: non-refundable if the LCIA Court appoints an Emergency Arbitrator).

£20,000

7(iii)   The Emergency Arbitrator's fee may be increased by the LCIA Court on the recommendation of the Registrar at any time during the emergency proceedings if the particular circumstances of the case are deemed to warrant a higher fee.

7(iv)   In the event of a challenge by any party to the Emergency Arbitrator, the party that applied for the appointment of the Emergency Arbitrator shall pay forthwith to the LCIA such further sum as may be directed by the LCIA Court in respect of the fees and expenses of the individual or division appointed to decide the challenge.

7(v)   If the LCIA refuses an application for the appointment of an Emergency Arbitrator, the Emergency Arbitrator's fee shall be treated as a deposit lodged by the applicant party on account of the Arbitration Costs in accordance with Article 24 of the Rules and the Schedule.

*   Minimum unit of time in all cases: 15 minutes.

**   Items 1(ii), 1(iii), 1(iv) and 1(v) above, are payable on interim invoice; with the award, or as directed by the LCIA Court under Article 24.1 of the Rules.

E. CHINA INTERNATIONAL ECONOMIC AND TRADE ARBITRATION COMMISSION (CIETAC) RULES OF 2015*

ARBITRATION RULES

(Revised and adopted by the China Council for the Promotion of International Trade/China Chamber of International Commerce on November 4, 2014. Effective as of January 1, 2015.)

Chapter I General Provisions

Article 1 The Arbitration Commission

1. The China International Economic and Trade Arbitration Commission ("CIETAC"), originally named the Foreign Trade Arbitration Commission of the China Council for the Promotion of International Trade and later renamed the Foreign Economic and Trade Arbitration Commission of the China Council for the Promotion of International Trade, concurrently uses as its name the "Arbitration Institute of the China Chamber of International Commerce".

2. Where an arbitration agreement provides for arbitration by the China Council for the Promotion of International Trade/China Chamber of International Commerce, or by the Arbitration Commission or the Arbitration Institute of the China Council for the Promotion of International Trade/China Chamber of International Commerce, or refers to CIETAC's previous names, it shall be deemed that the parties have agreed to arbitration by CIETAC.

Article 2 Structure and Duties

1. The Chairman of CIETAC shall perform the functions and duties vested in him/her by these Rules while a Vice Chairman may perform the Chairman's functions and duties with the Chairman's authorization.

2. CIETAC has an Arbitration Court (the "Arbitration Court"), which performs its functions in accordance with these Rules under the direction of the authorized Vice Chairman and the President of the Arbitration Court.

3. CIETAC is based in Beijing. It has sub-commissions or arbitration centers (Appendix I). The sub-commissions/arbitration centers are CIETAC's branches, which accept arbitration applications and administer arbitration cases with CIETAC's authorization.

4. A sub-commission/arbitration center has an arbitration court, which performs the functions of the Arbitration Court in accordance with

---

* The CIETAC Rules can be found at http://www.cietac.org/index.cms. Reprinted with permission from CIETAC.

these Rules under the direction of the president of the arbitration court of the sub-commission/arbitration center.

5.   Where a case is administered by a sub-commission/arbitration center, the functions and duties vested in the President of the Arbitration Court under these Rules may, by his/her authorization, be performed by the president of the arbitration court of the relevant sub-commission/arbitration center.

6.   The parties may agree to submit their disputes to CIETAC or a sub-commission/arbitration center of CIETAC for arbitration. Where the parties have agreed to arbitration by CIETAC, the Arbitration Court shall accept the arbitration application and administer the case. Where the parties have agreed to arbitration by a sub-commission/arbitration center, the arbitration court of the sub-commission/arbitration center agreed upon by the parties shall accept the arbitration application and administer the case. Where the sub-commission/arbitration center agreed upon by the parties does not exist or its authorization has been terminated, or where the agreement is ambiguous, the Arbitration Court shall accept the arbitration application and administer the case. In the event of any dispute, a decision shall be made by CIETAC.

Article 3 Jurisdiction

1.   CIETAC accepts cases involving economic, trade and other disputes of a contractual or non-contractual nature, based on an agreement of the parties.

2.   The cases referred to in the preceding paragraph include:

(a)   international or foreign-related disputes;

(b)   disputes related to the Hong Kong Special Administrative Region, the Macao Special Administrative Region and the Taiwan region; and

(c)   domestic disputes.

Article 4 Scope of Application

1.   These Rules uniformly apply to CIETAC and its sub-commissions/arbitration centers.

2.   Where the parties have agreed to refer their dispute to CIETAC for arbitration, they shall be deemed to have agreed to arbitration in accordance with these Rules.

3.   Where the parties agree to refer their dispute to CIETAC for arbitration but have agreed on a modification of these Rules or have agreed on the application of other arbitration rules, the parties' agreement shall prevail unless such agreement is inoperative or in conflict with a mandatory provision of the law applicable to the arbitral proceedings.

Where the parties have agreed on the application of other arbitration rules, CIETAC shall perform the relevant administrative duties.

4.   Where the parties agree to refer their dispute to arbitration under these Rules without providing the name of the arbitration institution, they shall be deemed to have agreed to refer the dispute to arbitration by CIETAC.

5.   Where the parties agree to refer their dispute to arbitration under CIETAC's customized arbitration rules for a specific trade or profession, the parties' agreement shall prevail. However, if the dispute falls outside the scope of the specific rules, these Rules shall apply.

Article 5 Arbitration Agreement

1.   An arbitration agreement means an arbitration clause in a contract or any other form of a written agreement concluded between the parties providing for the settlement of disputes by arbitration.

2.   The arbitration agreement shall be in writing. An arbitration agreement is in writing if it is contained in the tangible form of a document such as a contract, letter, telegram, telex, fax, electronic data interchange, or email. An arbitration agreement shall be deemed to exist where its existence is asserted by one party and not denied by the other during the exchange of the Request for Arbitration and the Statement of Defense.

3.   Where the law applicable to an arbitration agreement has different provisions as to the form and validity of the arbitration agreement, those provisions shall prevail.

4.   An arbitration clause contained in a contract shall be treated as a clause independent and separate from all other clauses of the contract, and an arbitration agreement attached to a contract shall also be treated as independent and separate from all other clauses of the contract. The validity of an arbitration clause or an arbitration agreement shall not be affected by any modification, cancellation, termination, transfer, expiry, invalidity, ineffectiveness, rescission or non-existence of the contract.

Article 6 Objection to Arbitration Agreement and/or Jurisdiction

1.   CIETAC has the power to determine the existence and validity of an arbitration agreement and its jurisdiction over an arbitration case. CIETAC may, where necessary, delegate such power to the arbitral tribunal.

2.   Where CIETAC is satisfied by prima facie evidence that a valid arbitration agreement exists, it may make a decision based on such evidence that it has jurisdiction over the arbitration case, and the arbitration shall proceed. Such a decision shall not prevent CIETAC from making a new decision on jurisdiction based on facts and/or evidence found

by the arbitral tribunal during the arbitral proceedings that are inconsistent with the prima facie evidence.

3.   Where CIETAC has delegated the power to determine jurisdiction to the arbitral tribunal, the arbitral tribunal may either make a separate decision on jurisdiction during the arbitral proceedings or incorporate the decision in the final arbitral award.

4.   Any objection to an arbitration agreement and/or the jurisdiction over an arbitration case shall be raised in writing before the first oral hearing held by the arbitral tribunal. Where a case is to be decided on the basis of documents only, such an objection shall be raised before the submission of the first substantive defense.

5.   The arbitration shall proceed notwithstanding an objection to the arbitration agreement and/or jurisdiction over the arbitration case.

6.   The aforesaid objections to and/or decisions on jurisdiction by CIETAC shall include 6. The aforesaid objections to and/or decisions on jurisdiction by CIETAC shall include objections to and/or decisions on a party's standing to participate in the arbitration.

7.   CIETAC or its authorized arbitral tribunal shall decide to dismiss the case upon finding that CIETAC has no jurisdiction over an arbitration case. Where a case is to be dismissed before the formation of the arbitral tribunal, the decision shall be made by the President of the Arbitration Court. Where the case is to be dismissed after the formation of the arbitral tribunal, the decision shall be made by the arbitral tribunal.

Article 7 Place of Arbitration

1.   Where the parties have agreed on the place of arbitration, the parties' agreement shall prevail.

2.   Where the parties have not agreed on the place of arbitration or their agreement is ambiguous, the place of arbitration shall be the domicile of CIETAC or its sub-commission/arbitration center administering the case. CIETAC may also determine the place of arbitration to be another location having regard to the circumstances of the case.

3.   The arbitral award shall be deemed as having been made at the place of arbitration.

Article 8 Service of Documents and Periods of Time

1.   All documents, notices and written materials in relation to the arbitration may be delivered in person or sent by registered mail or express mail, fax, or by any other means considered proper by the Arbitration Court or the arbitral tribunal.

2.   The arbitration documents referred to in the preceding Paragraph 1 shall be sent to the address provided by the party itself or by its

representative(s), or to an address agreed by the parties. Where a party or its representative(s) has not provided an address or the parties have not agreed on an address, the arbitration documents shall be sent to such party's address as provided by the other party or its representative(s).

3. Any arbitration correspondence to a party or its representative(s) shall be deemed to have been properly served on the party if delivered to the addressee or sent to the addressee's place of business, place of registration, domicile, habitual residence or mailing address, or where, after reasonable inquiries by the other party, none of the aforesaid addresses can be found, the arbitration correspondence is sent by the Arbitration Court to the addressee's last known place of business, place of registration, domicile, habitual residence or mailing address by registered or express mail, or by any other means that can provide a record of the attempt at delivery, including but not limited to service by public notary, entrustment or retention.

4. The periods of time specified in these Rules shall begin on the day following the day when the party receives or should have received the arbitration correspondence, notices or written materials sent by the Arbitration Court.

Article 9 Good Faith

Arbitration participants shall proceed with the arbitration in good faith.

Article 10 Waiver of Right to Object

A party shall be deemed to have waived its right to object where it knows or should have known that any provision of, or requirement under, these Rules has not been complied with and yet participates in or proceeds with the arbitral proceedings without promptly and explicitly submitting its objection in writing to such non-compliance.

Chapter II Arbitral Proceedings

Section 1 Request for Arbitration, Defense and Counterclaim

Article 11 Commencement of Arbitration

The arbitral proceedings shall commence on the day on which the Arbitration Court receives a Request for Arbitration.

Article 12 Application for Arbitration

A party applying for arbitration under these Rules shall:

1. Submit a Request for Arbitration in writing signed and/or sealed by the Claimant or its authorized representative(s), which shall, inter alia, include:

(a) the names and addresses of the Claimant and the Respondent, including the zip code, telephone, fax, email, or any other means of electronic telecommunications;

(b) a reference to the arbitration agreement that is invoked;

(c) a statement of the facts of the case and the main issues in dispute;

(d) the claim of the Claimant; and

(e) the facts and grounds on which the claim is based.

2.   Attach to the Request for Arbitration the relevant documentary and other evidence on which the Claimant's claim is based.

3.   Pay the arbitration fee in advance to CIETAC in accordance with its Arbitration Fee Schedule.

Article 13 Acceptance of a Case

1.   Upon the written application of a party, CIETAC shall accept a case in accordance with an arbitration agreement concluded between the parties either before or after the occurrence of the dispute, in which it is provided that disputes are to be referred to arbitration by CIETAC.

2.   Upon receipt of a Request for Arbitration and its attachments, where after examination the Arbitration Court finds the formalities required for arbitration application to be complete, it shall send a Notice of Arbitration to both parties together with one copy each of these Rules and CIETAC's Panel of Arbitrators. The Request for Arbitration and its attachments submitted by the Claimant shall be sent to the Respondent under the same cover.

3.   Where after examination the Arbitration Court finds the formalities required for the arbitration application to be incomplete, it may request the Claimant to complete them within a specified time period. The Claimant shall be deemed not to have submitted a Request for Arbitration if it fails to complete the required formalities within the specified time period. In such a case, the Claimant's Request for Arbitration and its attachments shall not be kept on file by the Arbitration Court.

4.   After CIETAC accepts a case, the Arbitration Court shall designate a case manager to assist with the procedural administration of the case.

Article 14 Multiple Contracts

The Claimant may initiate a single arbitration concerning disputes arising out of or in connection with multiple contracts, provided that:

(a) such contracts consist of a principal contract and its ancillary contract(s), or such contracts involve the same parties as well as legal relationships of the same nature;

(b) the disputes arise out of the same transaction or the same series of transactions; and

(c) the arbitration agreements in such contracts are identical or compatible.

Article 15 Statement of Defense

1. The Respondent shall file a Statement of Defense in writing within forty-five (45) days from the date of its receipt of the Notice of Arbitration. If the Respondent has justified reasons to request an extension of the time period, the arbitral tribunal shall decide whether to grant an extension. Where the arbitral tribunal has not yet been formed, the decision on whether to grant the extension of the time period shall be made by the Arbitration Court.

2. The Statement of Defense shall be signed and/or sealed by the Respondent or its authorized representative(s), and shall, inter alia, include the following contents and attachments:

(a) the name and address of the Respondent, including the zip code, telephone, fax, email, or any other means of electronic telecommunications;

(b) the defense to the Request for Arbitration setting forth the facts and grounds on which the defense is based; and

(c) the relevant documentary and other evidence on which the defense is based.

3. The arbitral tribunal has the power to decide whether to accept a Statement of Defense submitted after the expiration of the above time period.

4. Failure by the Respondent to file a Statement of Defense shall not affect the conduct of the arbitral proceedings.

Article 16 Counterclaim

1. The Respondent shall file a counterclaim, if any, in writing within forty-five (45) days from the date of its receipt of the Notice of Arbitration. If the Respondent has justified reasons to request an extension of the time period, the arbitral tribunal shall decide whether to grant an extension. Where the arbitral tribunal has not yet been formed, the decision on whether to grant the extension of the time period shall be made by the Arbitration Court.

2. When filing the counterclaim, the Respondent shall specify the counterclaim in its Statement of Counterclaim and state the facts and grounds on which the counterclaim is based with the relevant documentary and other evidence attached thereto.

3. When filing the counterclaim, the Respondent shall pay an arbitration fee in advance in accordance with the Arbitration Fee Schedule of CIETAC within a specified time period, failing which the Respondent shall be deemed not to have filed any counterclaim.

4. Where the formalities required for filing a counterclaim are found to be complete, the Arbitration Court shall send a Notice of Acceptance of Counterclaim to the parties. The Claimant shall submit its Statement of Defense in writing within thirty (30) days from the date of its receipt of the Notice. If the Claimant has justified reasons to request an extension of the time period, the arbitral tribunal shall decide whether to grant such an extension. Where the arbitral tribunal has not yet been formed, the decision on whether to grant the extension of the time period shall be made by the Arbitration Court.

5. The arbitral tribunal has the power to decide whether to accept a counterclaim or a Statement of Defense submitted after the expiration of the above time period.

6. Failure of the Claimant to file a Statement of Defense to the Respondent's counterclaim shall not affect the conduct of the arbitral proceedings.

Article 17 Amendment to Claim or Counterclaim

The Claimant may apply to amend its claim and the Respondent may apply to amend its counterclaim. However, the arbitral tribunal may refuse any such amendment if it considers that the amendment is too late and may delay the arbitral proceedings.

Article 18 Joinder of Additional Parties

1. During the arbitral proceedings, a party wishing to join an additional party to the arbitration may file the Request for Joinder with CIETAC, based on the arbitration agreement invoked in the arbitration that prima facie binds the additional party. Where the Request for Joinder is filed after the formation of the arbitral tribunal, a decision shall be made by CIETAC after the arbitral tribunal hears from all parties including the additional party if the arbitral tribunal considers the joinder necessary. The date on which the Arbitration Court receives the Request for Joinder shall be deemed to be the date of the commencement of arbitration against the additional party.

2. The Request for Joinder shall contain the case number of the existing arbitration; the name, address and other means of communication of each of the parties, including the additional party; the arbitration agreement invoked to join the additional party as well as the facts and grounds the request relies upon; and the claim. The relevant documentary and other evidence on which the request is based shall be attached to the Request for Joinder.

3.   Where any party objects to the arbitration agreement and/or jurisdiction over the arbitration with respect to the joinder proceedings, CIETAC has the power to decide on its jurisdiction based on the arbitration agreement and relevant evidence.

4.   After the joinder proceedings commence, the conduct of the arbitral proceedings shall be decided by the Arbitration Court if the arbitral tribunal is not formed, or shall be decided by the arbitral tribunal if it has been formed.

5.   Where the joinder takes place prior to the formation of the arbitral tribunal, the relevant provisions on party's nominating or entrusting of the Chairman of CIETAC to appoint arbitrator under these Rules shall apply to the additional party. The arbitral tribunal shall be formed in accordance with Article 29 of these Rules.

Where the joinder takes place after the formation of the arbitral tribunal, the arbitral tribunal shall hear from the additional party of its comments on the past arbitral proceedings including the formation of the arbitral tribunal. If the additional party requests to nominate or entrust the Chairman of CIETAC to appoint an arbitrator, both parties shall nominate or entrust the Chairman of CIETAC to appoint arbitrators again. The arbitral tribunal shall be formed in accordance with Article 29 of these Rules.

6.   The relevant provisions on the submission of the Statement of Defense and the Statement of Counterclaim under these Rules shall apply to the additional party. The time period for the additional party to submit its Statement of Defense and Statement of Counterclaim shall start counting from the date of its receipt of the Notice of Joinder.

7.   CIETAC shall have the power to decide not to join an additional party where the additional party is prima facie not bound by the arbitration agreement invoked in the arbitration, or where any other circumstance exists that makes the joinder inappropriate.

Article 19 Consolidation of Arbitrations

1.   At the request of a party, CIETAC may consolidate two or more arbitrations pending under these Rules into a single arbitration if:

(a)   all of the claims in the arbitrations are made under the same arbitration agreement;

(b)   the claims in the arbitrations are made under multiple arbitration agreements that are identical or compatible and the arbitrations involve the same parties as well as legal relationships of the same nature;

(c)   the claims in the arbitrations are made under multiple arbitration agreements that are identical or compatible and the multiple contracts involved consist of a principle contract and its ancillary contract(s); or

(d)   all the parties to the arbitrations have agreed to consolidation.

2.   In deciding whether to consolidate the arbitrations in accordance with the preceding Paragraph 1, CIETAC shall take into account the opinions of all parties and other relevant factors such as the correlation between the arbitrations concerned, including the nomination and appointment of arbitrators in the separate arbitrations.

3.   Unless otherwise agreed by all the parties, the arbitrations shall be consolidated into the arbitration that was first commenced.

4.   After the consolidation of arbitrations, the conduct of the arbitral proceedings shall be decided by the Arbitration Court if the arbitral tribunal is not formed, or shall be decided by the arbitral tribunal if it has been formed.

Article 20 Submission and Exchange of Arbitration Documents

1.   All arbitration documents from the parties shall be submitted to the Arbitration Court.

2.   All arbitration documents to be exchanged during the arbitral proceedings shall be exchanged among the arbitral tribunal and the parties by the Arbitration Court unless otherwise agreed by the parties and with the consent of the arbitral tribunal or otherwise decided by the arbitral tribunal.

Article 21 Copies of Arbitration Documents

When submitting the Request for Arbitration, the Statement of Defense, the Statement of Counterclaim, evidence, and other arbitration documents, the parties shall make their submissions in quintuplicate. Where there are multiple parties, additional copies shall be provided accordingly. Where the party applies for preservation of property or protection of evidence, it shall also provide additional copies accordingly. Where the arbitral tribunal is composed of a sole arbitrator, the number of copies submitted may be reduced by two.

Article 22 Representation

A party may be represented by its authorized Chinese and/or foreign representative(s) in handling matters relating to the arbitration. In such a case, a Power of Attorney shall be forwarded to the Arbitration Court by the party or its authorized representative(s).

Article 23 Conservatory and Interim Measures

1.   Where a party applies for conservatory measures pursuant to the laws of the People's Republic of China, CIETAC shall forward the party's

application to the competent court designated by that party in accordance with the law.

2.   In accordance with the applicable law or the agreement of the parties, a party may apply to the Arbitration Court for emergency relief pursuant to the CIETAC Emergency Arbitrator Procedures (Appendix III). The emergency arbitrator may decide to order or award necessary or appropriate emergency measures. The decision of the emergency arbitrator shall be binding upon both parties.

3.   At the request of a party, the arbitral tribunal may decide to order or award any interim measure it deems necessary or proper in accordance with the applicable law or the agreement of the parties and may require the requesting party to provide appropriate security in connection with the measure.

Section 2 Arbitrators and the Arbitral Tribunal

Article 24 Duties of Arbitrator

An arbitrator shall not represent either party, and shall be and remain independent of the parties and treat them equally.

Article 25 Number of Arbitrators

1.   The arbitral tribunal shall be composed of one or three arbitrators.

2.   Unless otherwise agreed by the parties or provided by these Rules, the arbitral tribunal shall be composed of three arbitrators.

Article 26 Nomination or Appointment of Arbitrator

1.   CIETAC maintains a Panel of Arbitrators which uniformly applies to itself and all its sub-commissions/arbitration centers. The parties shall nominate arbitrators from the Panel of Arbitrators provided by CIETAC.

2.   Where the parties have agreed to nominate arbitrators from outside CIETAC's Panel of Arbitrators, an arbitrator so nominated by the parties or nominated according to the agreement of the parties may act as arbitrator subject to the confirmation by the Chairman of CIETAC.

Article 27 Three-Arbitrator Tribunal

1.   Within fifteen (15) days from the date of receipt of the Notice of Arbitration, the Claimant and the Respondent shall each nominate, or entrust the Chairman of CIETAC to appoint, an arbitrator, failing which the arbitrator shall be appointed by the Chairman of CIETAC.

2.   Within fifteen (15) days from the date of the Respondent's receipt of the Notice of Arbitration, the parties shall jointly nominate, or entrust the Chairman of CIETAC to appoint, the third arbitrator, who shall act as the presiding arbitrator.

3.   The parties may each recommend one to five arbitrators as candidates for the presiding arbitrator and shall each submit a list of recommended candidates within the time period specified in the preceding Paragraph 2. Where there is only one common candidate on the lists, such candidate shall be the presiding arbitrator jointly nominated by the parties. Where there is more than one common candidate on the lists, the Chairman of CIETAC shall choose the presiding arbitrator from among the common candidates having regard to the circumstances of the case, and he/she shall act as the presiding arbitrator jointly nominated by the parties. Where there is no common candidate on the lists, the presiding arbitrator shall be appointed by the Chairman of CIETAC.

4.   Where the parties have failed to jointly nominate the presiding arbitrator according to the above provisions, the presiding arbitrator shall be appointed by the Chairman of CIETAC.

Article 28 Sole-Arbitrator Tribunal

Where the arbitral tribunal is composed of one arbitrator, the sole arbitrator shall be nominated pursuant to the procedures stipulated in Paragraphs 2, 3 and 4 of Article 27 of these Rules.

Article 29 Multiple-Party Tribunal

1.   Where the arbitral tribunal is composed of one arbitrator, the sole arbitrator shall be nominated pursuant to the procedures stipulated in Paragraphs 2, 3 and 4 of Article 27 of these Rules.

2.   The presiding arbitrator or the sole arbitrator shall be nominated in accordance with the procedures stipulated in Paragraphs 2, 3 and 4 of Article 27 of these Rules. When making such nomination pursuant to Paragraph 3 of Article 27 of these Rules, the Claimant side and/or the Respondent side, following discussion, shall each submit a list of their jointly agreed candidates.

3.   Where either the Claimant side or the Respondent side fails to jointly nominate or jointly entrust the Chairman of CIETAC to appoint one arbitrator within fifteen (15) days from the date of its receipt of the Notice of Arbitration, the Chairman of CIETAC shall appoint all three members of the arbitral tribunal and designate one of them to act as the presiding arbitrator.

Article 30 Considerations in Appointing Arbitrators

When appointing arbitrators pursuant to these Rules, the Chairman of CIETAC shall take into consideration the law applicable to the dispute, the place of arbitration, the language of arbitration, the nationalities of the parties, and any other factor(s) the Chairman considers relevant.

Article 31 Disclosure

1.   An arbitrator nominated by the parties or appointed by the Chairman of CIETAC shall sign a Declaration and disclose any facts or circumstances likely to give rise to justifiable doubts as to his/her impartiality or independence.

2.   If circumstances that need to be disclosed arise during the arbitral proceedings, the arbitrator shall promptly disclose such circumstances in writing.

3.   The Declaration and/or the disclosure of the arbitrator shall be submitted to the Arbitration Court to be forwarded to the parties.

Article 32 Challenge to Arbitrator

1.   Upon receipt of the Declaration and/or the written disclosure of an arbitrator, a party wishing to challenge the arbitrator on the grounds of the disclosed facts or circumstances shall forward the challenge in writing within ten (10) days from the date of such receipt. If a party fails to file a challenge within the above time period, it may not subsequently challenge the arbitrator on the basis of the matters disclosed by the arbitrator.

2.   A party having justifiable doubts as to the impartiality or independence of an arbitrator may challenge that arbitrator in writing and shall state the facts and reasons on which the challenge is based with supporting evidence.

3.   A party may challenge an arbitrator in writing within fifteen (15) days from the date it receives the Notice of Formation of the Arbitral Tribunal. Where a party becomes aware of a reason for a challenge after such receipt, the party may challenge the arbitrator in writing within fifteen (15) days after such reason has become known to it, but no later than the conclusion of the last oral hearing.

4.   The challenge by one party shall be promptly communicated to the other party, the arbitrator being challenged and the other members of the arbitral tribunal.

5.   Where an arbitrator is challenged by one party and the other party agrees to the challenge, or the arbitrator being challenged voluntarily withdraws from his/her office, such arbitrator shall no longer be a member of the arbitral tribunal. However, in neither case shall it be implied that the reasons for the challenge are sustained.

6.   In circumstances other than those specified in the preceding Paragraph 5, the Chairman of CIETAC shall make a final decision on the challenge with or without stating the reasons.

7.   An arbitrator who has been challenged shall continue to serve on the arbitral tribunal until a final decision on the challenge has been made by the Chairman of CIETAC.

Article 33 Replacement of Arbitrator

1.   In the event that an arbitrator is prevented de jure or de facto from fulfilling his/her functions, or fails to fulfill his/her functions in accordance with the requirements of these Rules or within the time period specified in these Rules, the Chairman of CIETAC shall have the power to replace the arbitrator. Such arbitrator may also voluntarily withdraw from his/her office.

2.   The Chairman of CIETAC shall make a final decision on whether or not an arbitrator should be replaced with or without stating the reasons.

3.   In the event that an arbitrator is unable to fulfill his/her functions due to challenge or replacement, a substitute arbitrator shall be nominated or appointed within the time period specified by the Arbitration Court according to the same procedure that applied to the nomination or appointment of the arbitrator being challenged or replaced. If a party fails to nominate or appoint a substitute arbitrator accordingly, the substitute arbitrator shall be appointed by the Chairman of CIETAC.

4.   After the replacement of an arbitrator, the arbitral tribunal shall decide whether and to what extent the previous proceedings in the case shall be repeated.

Article 34 Continuation of Arbitration by Majority

After the conclusion of the last oral hearing, if an arbitrator on a three-member tribunal is unable to participate in the deliberations and/or to render the award owing to his/her demise or to his/her removal from CIETAC's Panel of Arbitrators, or for any other reason, the other two arbitrators may request the Chairman of CIETAC to replace that arbitrator pursuant to Article 33 of these Rules. After consulting with the parties and upon the approval of the Chairman of CIETAC, the other two arbitrators may also continue the arbitral proceedings and make decisions, rulings, or render the award. The Arbitration Court shall notify the parties of the above circumstances.

Section 3 Hearing

Article 35 Conduct of Hearing

1.   The arbitral tribunal shall examine the case in any way it deems appropriate unless otherwise agreed by the parties. Under all circumstances, the arbitral tribunal shall act impartially and fairly and shall afford a reasonable opportunity to both parties to present their case.

2.   The arbitral tribunal shall hold oral hearings when examining the case. However, the arbitral tribunal may examine the case on the basis of documents only if the parties so agree and the arbitral tribunal consents or the arbitral tribunal deems that oral hearings are unnecessary and the parties so agree.

3.   Unless otherwise agreed by the parties, the arbitral tribunal may adopt an inquisitorial or adversarial approach in hearing the case having regard to the circumstances of the case.

4.   The arbitral tribunal may hold deliberations at any place or in any manner that it considers appropriate.

5.   Unless otherwise agreed by the parties, the arbitral tribunal may, if it considers it necessary, issue procedural orders or question lists, produce terms of reference, or hold pre-hearing conferences, etc. With the authorization of the other members of the arbitral tribunal, the presiding arbitrator may decide on the procedural arrangements for the arbitral proceedings at his/her own discretion.

Article 36 Place of Oral Hearing

1.   Where the parties have agreed on the place of an oral hearing, the case shall be heard at that agreed place except in the circumstances stipulated in Paragraph 3 of Article 82 of these Rules.

2.   Unless otherwise agreed by the parties, the place of oral hearings shall be in Beijing for a case administered by the Arbitration Court or at the domicile of the sub-commission/arbitration center administering the case, or if the arbitral tribunal considers it necessary and with the approval of the President of the Arbitration Court, at another location.

Article 37 Notice of Oral Hearing

1.   Where a case is to be examined by way of an oral hearing, the parties shall be notified of the date of the first oral hearing at least twenty (20) days in advance of the oral hearing. A party having justified reasons may request a postponement of the oral hearing. However, the party shall communicate such request in writing to the arbitral tribunal within five (5) days of its receipt of the notice of the oral hearing. The arbitral tribunal shall decide whether or not to postpone the oral hearing.

2.   Where a party has justified reasons for its failure to submit a request for a postponement of the oral hearing in accordance with the preceding Paragraph 1, the arbitral tribunal shall decide whether or not to accept the request.

3.   A notice of a subsequent oral hearing, a notice of a postponed oral hearing, as well as a request for postponement of such an oral hearing, shall not be subject to the time periods specified in the preceding Paragraph 1.

Article 38 Confidentiality

1.   Hearings shall be held in camera. Where both parties request an open hearing, the arbitral tribunal shall make a decision.

2.   For cases heard in camera, the parties and their representatives, the arbitrators, the witnesses, the interpreters, the experts consulted by the arbitral tribunal, the appraisers appointed by the arbitral tribunal and other relevant persons shall not disclose to any outsider any substantive or procedural matters relating to the case.

Article 39 Default

1.   If the Claimant fails to appear at an oral hearing without showing sufficient cause, or withdraws from an on-going oral hearing without the permission of the arbitral tribunal, the Claimant may be deemed to have withdrawn its application for arbitration. In such a case, if the Respondent has filed a counterclaim, the arbitral tribunal shall proceed with the hearing of the counterclaim and make a default award.

2.   If the Respondent fails to appear at an oral hearing without showing sufficient cause, or withdraws from an on-going oral hearing without the permission of the arbitral tribunal, the arbitral tribunal may proceed with the arbitration and make a default award. In such a case, if the Respondent has filed a counterclaim, the Respondent may be deemed to have withdrawn its counterclaim.

Article 40 Record of Oral Hearing

1.   The arbitral tribunal may arrange for a written and/or an audio-visual record to be made of an oral hearing. The arbitral tribunal may, if it considers it necessary, take minutes of the oral hearing and request the parties and/or their representatives, witnesses and/or other persons involved to sign and/or affix their seals to the written record or the minutes.

2.   The written record, the minutes and the audio-visual record of an oral hearing shall be available for use and reference by the arbitral tribunal.

3.   At the request of a party, the Arbitration Court may, having regard to the specific circumstances of the arbitration, decide to engage a stenographer to make a stenographic record of an oral hearing, the cost of which shall be advanced by the parties.

Article 41 Evidence

1.   Each party shall bear the burden of proving the facts on which it relies to support its claim, defense or counterclaim and provide the basis for its opinions, arguments and counter-arguments.

2.   The arbitral tribunal may specify a time period for the parties to produce evidence and the parties shall produce evidence within the specified time period. The arbitral tribunal may refuse to admit any evidence produced after that time period. If a party experiences difficulties in producing evidence within the specified time period, it may apply for an

extension before the end of the period. The arbitral tribunal shall decide whether or not to extend the time period.

3. If a party bearing the burden of proof fails to produce evidence within the specified time period, or if the produced evidence is not sufficient to support its claim or counterclaim, it shall bear the consequences thereof.

Article 42 Examination of Evidence

1. Where a case is examined by way of an oral hearing, the evidence shall be produced at the oral hearing and may be examined by the parties.

2. Where a case is to be decided on the basis of documents only, or where the evidence is submitted after the hearing and both parties have agreed to examine the evidence by means of writing, the parties may examine the evidence in writing. In such circumstances, the parties shall submit their written opinions on the evidence within the time period specified by the arbitral tribunal.

Article 43 Investigation and Evidence Collection by the Arbitral Tribunal

1. The arbitral tribunal may undertake investigation and collect evidence as it considers necessary.

2. When investigating and collecting evidence, the arbitral tribunal may notify the parties to be present. In the event that one or both parties fail to be present after being notified, the investigation and collection of evidence shall proceed without being affected.

3. Evidence collected by the arbitral tribunal through its investigation shall be forwarded to the parties for their comments.

Article 44 Expert's Report and Appraiser's Report

1. The arbitral tribunal may consult experts or appoint appraisers for clarification on specific issues of the case. Such an expert or appraiser may be a Chinese or foreign institution or natural person.

2. The arbitral tribunal has the power to request the parties, and the parties are also obliged, to deliver or produce to the expert or appraiser any relevant materials, documents, property, or physical objects for examination, inspection or appraisal by the expert or appraiser.

3. Copies of the expert's report and the appraiser's report shall be forwarded to the parties for their comments. At the request of either party and with the approval of the arbitral tribunal, the expert or appraiser shall participate in an oral hearing and give explanations on the report when the arbitral tribunal considers it necessary.

Article 45 Suspension of the Arbitral Proceedings

1.   Where the parties jointly or separately request a suspension of the arbitral proceedings, or under circumstances where such suspension is necessary, the arbitral proceedings may be suspended.

2.   The arbitral proceedings shall resume as soon as the reason for the suspension disappears or the suspension period ends.

3.   The arbitral tribunal shall decide whether to suspend or resume the arbitral proceedings. Where the arbitral tribunal has not yet been formed, the decision shall be made by the President of the Arbitration Court.

Article 46 Withdrawal and Dismissal

1.   A party may withdraw its claim or counterclaim in its entirety. In the event that the Claimant withdraws its claim in its entirety, the arbitral tribunal may proceed with its examination of the counterclaim and render an arbitral award thereon. In the event that the Respondent withdraws its counterclaim in its entirety, the arbitral tribunal may proceed with the examination of the claim and render an arbitral award thereon.

2.   A party may be deemed to have withdrawn its claim or counterclaim if the arbitral proceedings cannot proceed for reasons attributable to that party.

3.   A case may be dismissed if the claim and counterclaim have been withdrawn in their entirety. Where a case is to be dismissed prior to the formation of the arbitral tribunal, the President of the Arbitration Court shall make a decision on the dismissal. Where a case is to be dismissed after the formation of the arbitral tribunal, the arbitral tribunal shall make the decision.

4.   The seal of CIETAC shall be affixed to the Dismissal Decision referred to in the preceding Paragraph 3 and Paragraph 7 of Article 6 of these Rules.

Article 47 Combination of Conciliation with Arbitration

1.   Where both parties wish to conciliate, or where one party wishes to conciliate and the other party's consent has been obtained by the arbitral tribunal, the arbitral tribunal may conciliate the dispute during the arbitral proceedings. The parties may also settle their dispute by themselves.

2.   With the consents of both parties, the arbitral tribunal may conciliate the case in a manner it considers appropriate.

3.   During the process of conciliation, the arbitral tribunal shall terminate the conciliation proceedings if either party so requests or if the arbitral tribunal considers that further conciliation efforts will be futile.

4.   The parties shall sign a settlement agreement where they have reached settlement through conciliation by the arbitral tribunal or by themselves.

5.   Where the parties have reached a settlement agreement through conciliation by the arbitral tribunal or by themselves, they may withdraw their claim or counterclaim, or request the arbitral tribunal to render an arbitral award or a conciliation statement in accordance with the terms of the settlement agreement.

6.   Where the parties request for a conciliation statement, the conciliation statement shall clearly set forth the claims of the parties and the terms of the settlement agreement. It shall be signed by the arbitrators, sealed by CIETAC, and served upon both parties.

7.   Where conciliation is not successful, the arbitral tribunal shall resume the arbitral proceedings and render an arbitral award.

8.   Where the parties wish to conciliate their dispute but do not wish to have conciliation conducted by the arbitral tribunal, CIETAC may, with the consents of both parties, assist the parties to conciliate the dispute in a manner and procedure it considers appropriate.

9.   Where conciliation is not successful, neither party may invoke any opinion, view or statement, and any proposal or proposition expressing acceptance or opposition by either party or by the arbitral tribunal in the process of conciliation as grounds for any claim, defense or counterclaim in the subsequent arbitral proceedings, judicial proceedings, or any other proceedings.

10.   Where the parties have reached a settlement agreement by themselves through negotiation or conciliation before the commencement of an arbitration, either party may, based on an arbitration agreement concluded between them that provides for arbitration by CIETAC and the settlement agreement, request CIETAC to constitute an arbitral tribunal to render an arbitral award in accordance with the terms of the settlement agreement. Unless otherwise agreed by the parties, the Chairman of CIETAC shall appoint a sole arbitrator to form such an arbitral tribunal, which shall examine the case in a procedure it considers appropriate and render an award in due course. The specific procedure and time period for rendering the award shall not be subject to other provisions of these Rules.

Chapter III Arbitral Award

Article 48 Time Period for Rendering Award

1.   The arbitral tribunal shall render an arbitral award within six (6) months from the date on which the arbitral tribunal is formed.

2.   Upon the request of the arbitral tribunal, the President of the Arbitration Court may extend the time period if he/she considers it truly necessary and the reasons for the extension truly justified.

3.   Any suspension period shall be excluded when calculating the time period in the preceding Paragraph 1.

Article 49 Making of Award

1.   The arbitral tribunal shall independently and impartially render a fair and reasonable arbitral award based on the facts of the case and the terms of the contract, in accordance with the law, and with reference to international practices.

2.   Where the parties have agreed on the law applicable to the merits of their dispute, the parties' agreement shall prevail. In the absence of such an agreement or where such agreement is in conflict with a mandatory provision of the law, the arbitral tribunal shall determine the law applicable to the merits of the dispute.

3.   The arbitral tribunal shall state in the award the claims, the facts of the dispute, the reasons on which the award is based, the result of the award, the allocation of the arbitration costs, and the date on which and the place at which the award is made. The facts of the dispute and the reasons on which the award is based may not be stated in the award if the parties have so agreed, or if the award is made in accordance with the terms of a settlement agreement between the parties. The arbitral tribunal has the power to fix in the award the specific time period for the parties to perform the award and the liabilities for failure to do so within the specified time period.

4.   The seal of CIETAC shall be affixed to the arbitral award.

5.   Where a case is examined by an arbitral tribunal composed of three arbitrators, the award shall be rendered by all three arbitrators or a majority of the arbitrators. A written dissenting opinion shall be kept with the file and may be appended to the award. Such dissenting opinion shall not form a part of the award.

6.   Where the arbitral tribunal cannot reach a majority opinion, the arbitral award shall be rendered in accordance with the presiding arbitrator's opinion. The written opinions of the other arbitrators shall be kept with the file and may be appended to the award. Such written opinions shall not form a part of the award.

7.   Unless the arbitral award is made in accordance with the opinion of the presiding arbitrator or the sole arbitrator and signed by the same, the arbitral award shall be signed by a majority of the arbitrators. An arbitrator who has a dissenting opinion may or may not sign his/her name on the award.

8.   The date on which the award is made shall be the date on which the award comes into legal effect.

9.   The arbitral award is final and binding upon both parties. Neither party may bring a lawsuit before a court or make a request to any other organization for revision of the award.

Article 50 Partial Award

1.   Where the arbitral tribunal considers it necessary, or where a party so requests and the arbitral tribunal agrees, the arbitral tribunal may first render a partial award on any part of the claim before rendering the final award. A partial award is final and binding upon both parties.

2.   Failure of either party to perform a partial award shall neither affect the arbitral proceedings nor prevent the arbitral tribunal from making the final award.

Article 51 Scrutiny of Draft Award

The arbitral tribunal shall submit its draft award to CIETAC for scrutiny before signing the award. CIETAC may bring to the attention of the arbitral tribunal issues addressed in the award on the condition that the arbitral tribunal's independence in rendering the award is not affected.

Article 52 Allocation of Fees

1.   The arbitral tribunal has the power to determine in the arbitral award the arbitration fees and other expenses to be paid by the parties to CIETAC.

2.   The arbitral tribunal has the power to decide in the arbitral award, having regard to the circumstances of the case, that the losing party shall compensate the winning party for the expenses reasonably incurred by it in pursuing the case. In deciding whether or not the winning party's expenses incurred in pursuing the case are reasonable, the arbitral tribunal shall take into consideration various factors such as the outcome and complexity of the case, the workload of the winning party and/or its representative(s), the amount in dispute, etc.

Article 53 Correction of Award

1.   Within a reasonable time after the award is made, the arbitral tribunal may, on its own initiative, make corrections in writing of any clerical, typographical or calculation errors, or any errors of a similar nature contained in the award.

2.   Within thirty (30) days from its receipt of the arbitral award, either party may request the arbitral tribunal in writing for a correction of any clerical, typographical or calculation errors, or any errors of a similar nature contained in the award. If such an error does exist in the award, the

arbitral tribunal shall make the correction in writing within thirty (30) days of its receipt of the written request for the correction.

3.　　The above written correction shall form a part of the arbitral award and shall be subject to the provisions in Paragraphs 4 to 9 of Article 49 of these Rules.

Article 54 Additional Award

1.　　Where any matter which should have been decided by the arbitral tribunal was omitted from the arbitral award, the arbitral tribunal may, on its own initiative, make an additional award within a reasonable time after the award is made.

2.　　Either party may, within thirty (30) days from its receipt of the arbitral award, request the arbitral tribunal in writing for an additional award on any claim or counterclaim which was advanced in the arbitral proceedings but was omitted from the award. If such an omission does exist, the arbitral tribunal shall make an additional award within thirty (30) days of its receipt of the written request.

3.　　Such additional award shall form a part of the arbitral award and shall be subject to the provisions in Paragraphs 4 to 9 of Article 49 of these Rules.

Article 55 Performance of Award

1.　　The parties shall perform the arbitral award within the time period specified in the award. If no time period is specified in the award, the parties shall perform the award immediately.

2.　　Where one party fails to perform the award, the other party may apply to a competent court for enforcement of the award in accordance with the law.

Chapter IV Summary Procedure

Article 56 Application

1.　　The Summary Procedure shall apply to any case where the amount in dispute does not exceed RMB 5,000,000 unless otherwise agreed by the parties; or where the amount in dispute exceeds RMB 5,000,000, yet one party applies for arbitration under the Summary Procedure and the other party agrees in writing; or where both parties have agreed to apply the Summary Procedure.

2.　　Where there is no monetary claim or the amount in dispute is not clear, CIETAC shall determine whether or not to apply the Summary Procedure after full consideration of relevant factors, including but not limited to the complexity of the case and the interests involved.

Article 57 Notice of Arbitration

Where after examination the Claimant's arbitration application is accepted for arbitration under the Summary Procedure, the Arbitration Court shall send a Notice of Arbitration to both parties.

Article 58 Formation of the Arbitral Tribunal

Unless otherwise agreed by the parties, a sole-arbitrator tribunal shall be formed in accordance with Article 28 of these Rules to hear a case under the Summary Procedure.

Article 59 Defense and Counterclaim

1. The Respondent shall submit its Statement of Defense, evidence and other supporting documents within twenty (20) days of its receipt of the Notice of Arbitration. Counterclaim, if any, shall also be filed with evidence and supporting documents within such time period.

2. The Claimant shall file its Statement of Defense to the Respondent's counterclaim within twenty (20) days of its receipt of the counterclaim and its attachments.

3. If a party has justified reasons to request an extension of the time period, the arbitral tribunal shall decide whether to grant such extension. Where the arbitral tribunal has not yet been formed, such decision shall be made by the Arbitration Court.

Article 60 Conduct of Hearing

The arbitral tribunal may examine the case in the manner it considers appropriate. The arbitral tribunal may decide whether to examine the case solely on the basis of the written materials and evidence submitted by the parties or to hold an oral hearing after hearing from the parties of their opinions.

Article 61 Notice of Oral Hearing

1. For a case examined by way of an oral hearing, after the arbitral tribunal has fixed a date for the first oral hearing, the parties shall be notified of the date at least fifteen (15) days in advance of the oral hearing. A party having justified reasons may request a postponement of the oral hearing. However, the party shall communicate such request in writing to the arbitral tribunal within three (3) days of its receipt of the notice of the oral hearing. The arbitral tribunal shall decide whether or not to postpone the oral hearing.

2. If a party has justified reasons for failure to submit a request for a postponement of the oral hearing in accordance with the preceding Paragraph 1, the arbitral tribunal shall decide whether to accept such a request.

3.   A notice of a subsequent oral hearing, a notice of a postponed oral hearing, as well as a request for postponement of such oral hearing, shall not be subject to the time periods specified in the preceding Paragraph 1.

Article 62 Time Period for Rendering Award

1.   The arbitral tribunal shall render an arbitral award within three (3) months from the date on which the arbitral tribunal is formed.

2.   Upon the request of the arbitral tribunal, the President of the Arbitration Court may extend the time period if he/she considers it truly necessary and the reasons for the extension truly justified.

3.   Any suspension period shall be excluded when calculating the time period in the preceding Paragraph 1.

Article 63 Change of Procedure

The Summary Procedure shall not be affected by any amendment to the claim or by the filing of a counterclaim. Where the amount in dispute of the amended claim or that of the counterclaim exceeds RMB 5,000,000, the Summary Procedure shall continue to apply unless the parties agree or the arbitral tribunal decides that a change to the general procedure is necessary.

Article 64 Context Reference

The relevant provisions in the other Chapters of these Rules shall apply to matters not covered in this Chapter.

Chapter V Special Provisions for Domestic Arbitration

Article 65 Application

1.   The provisions of this Chapter shall apply to domestic arbitration cases.

2.   The provisions of the Summary Procedure in Chapter IV shall apply if a domestic arbitration case falls within the scope of Article 56 of these Rules.

Article 66 Acceptance of a Case

1.   Upon receipt of a Request for Arbitration, where the Arbitration Court finds the Request to meet the requirements specified in Article 12 of these Rules, the Arbitration Court shall notify the parties accordingly within five (5) days from its receipt of the Request. Where a Request for Arbitration is found not to be in conformity with the requirements, the Arbitration Court shall notify the party in writing of its refusal of acceptance with reasons stated.

2.   Upon receipt of a Request for Arbitration, where after examination, the Arbitration Court finds the Request not to be in conformity with the formality requirements specified in Article 12 of these

Rules, it may request the Claimant to comply with the requirements within a specified time period.

Article 67 Formation of the Arbitral Tribunal

The arbitral tribunal shall be formed in accordance with the provisions of Articles 25, 26, 27, 28, 29 and 30 of these Rules.

Article 68 Defense and Counterclaim

1.   Within twenty (20) days from the date of its receipt of the Notice of Arbitration, the Respondent shall submit its Statement of Defense, evidence and other supporting documents. Counterclaim, if any, shall also be filed with evidence and other supporting documents within the time period.

2.   The Claimant shall file its Statement of Defense to the Respondent's counterclaim within twenty (20) days from the date of its receipt of the counterclaim and its attachments.

3.   If a party has justified reasons to request an extension of the time period, the arbitral tribunal shall decide whether to grant such extension. Where the arbitral tribunal has not yet been formed, such decision shall be made by the Arbitration Court.

Article 69 Notice of Oral Hearing

1.   For a case examined by way of an oral hearing, after the arbitral tribunal has fixed a date for the first oral hearing, the parties shall be notified of the date at least fifteen (15) days in advance of the oral hearing. A party having justified reason may request a postponement of the oral hearing. However, the party shall communicate such request in writing to the arbitral tribunal within three (3) days of its receipt of the notice of the oral hearing. The arbitral tribunal shall decide whether or not to postpone the oral hearing.

2.   If a party has justified reasons for failure to submit a request for a postponement of the oral hearing in accordance with the preceding Paragraph 1, the arbitral tribunal shall decide whether to accept such a request.

3.   A notice of a subsequent oral hearing, a notice of a postponed oral hearing, as well as a request for postponement of such oral hearing, shall not be subject to the time periods specified in the preceding Paragraph 1.

Article 70 Record of Oral Hearing

1.   The arbitral tribunal shall make a written record of the oral hearing. Any party or participant in the arbitration may apply for a correction upon finding any omission or mistake in the record regarding its own statements. If the application is refused by the arbitral tribunal, it shall nevertheless be recorded and kept with the file.

2.   The written record shall be signed or sealed by the arbitrator(s), the recorder, the parties, and any other participant in the arbitration.

Article 71 Time Period for Rendering Award

1.   The arbitral tribunal shall render an arbitral award within four (4) months from the date on which the arbitral tribunal is formed.

2.   Upon the request of the arbitral tribunal, the President of the Arbitration Court may extend the time period if he/she considers it truly necessary and the reasons for the extension truly justified.

3.   Any suspension period shall be excluded when calculating the time period in the preceding Paragraph 1.

Article 72 Context Reference

The relevant provisions in the other Chapters of these Rules, with the exception of Chapter VI, shall apply to matters not covered in this Chapter.

Chapter VI Special Provisions for Hong Kong Arbitration

Article 73 Application

1.   CIETAC has established the CIETAC Hong Kong Arbitration Center in the Hong Kong Special Administrative Region. The provisions of this Chapter shall apply to arbitration cases accepted and administered by the CIETAC Hong Kong Arbitration Center.

2.   Where the parties have agreed to submit their disputes to the CIETAC Hong Kong Arbitration Center for arbitration or to CIETAC for arbitration in Hong Kong, the CIETAC Hong Kong Arbitration Center shall accept the arbitration application and administer the case.

Article 74 Place of Arbitration and Law Applicable to the Arbitral Proceedings

Unless otherwise agreed by the parties, for an arbitration administered by the CIETAC Hong Kong Arbitration Center, the place of arbitration shall be Hong Kong, the law applicable to the arbitral proceedings shall be the arbitration law of Hong Kong, and the arbitral award shall be a Hong Kong award.

Article 75 Decision on Jurisdiction

Any objection to an arbitration agreement and/or the jurisdiction over an arbitration case shall be raised in writing no later than the submission of the first substantive defense.

The arbitral tribunal shall have the power to determine the existence and validity of the arbitration agreement and its jurisdiction over the arbitration case.

Article 76 Nomination or Appointment of Arbitrator

The CIETAC Panel of Arbitrators in effect shall be recommended in arbitration cases administered by the CIETAC Hong Kong Arbitration Center. The parties may nominate arbitrators from outside the CIETAC's Panel of Arbitrators. An arbitrator so nominated shall be subject to the confirmation of the Chairman of CIETAC.

Article 77 Interim Measures and Emergency Relief

1. Unless otherwise agreed by the parties, the arbitral tribunal has the power to order appropriate interim measures at the request of a party.

2. Where the arbitral tribunal has not yet been formed, a party may apply for emergency relief pursuant to the CIETAC Emergency Arbitrator Procedures (Appendix III).

Article 78 Seal on Award

The seal of the CIETAC Hong Kong Arbitration Center shall be affixed to the arbitral award.

Article 79 Arbitration Fees

The CIETAC Arbitration Fee Schedule III (Appendix II) shall apply to the arbitration cases accepted and administered in accordance with this Chapter.

Article 80 Context Reference

The relevant provisions in the other Chapters of these Rules, with the exception of Chapter V, shall apply to matters not covered in this Chapter.

Chapter VII Supplementary Provisions

Article 81 Language

1. Where the parties have agreed on the language of arbitration, their agreement shall prevail. In the absence of such agreement, the language of arbitration to be used in the proceedings shall be Chinese. CIETAC may also designate another language as the language of arbitration having regard to the circumstances of the case.

2. If a party or its representative(s) or witness(es) requires interpretation at an oral hearing, an interpreter may be provided either by the Arbitration Court or by the party.

3. The arbitral tribunal or the Arbitration Court may, if it considers it necessary, require the parties to submit a corresponding translation of their documents and evidence into Chinese or other languages.

Article 82 Arbitration Fees and Costs

1. Apart from the arbitration fees charged in accordance with its Arbitration Fee Schedule, CIETAC may charge the parties for any other

additional and reasonable actual costs, including but not limited to arbitrators' special remuneration, their travel and accommodation expenses incurred in dealing with the case, engagement fees of stenographers, as well as the costs and expenses of experts, appraisers or interpreters appointed by the arbitral tribunal. The Arbitration Court shall, after hearing from the arbitrator and the party concerned, determine the arbitrator's special remuneration with reference to the standards of arbitrators' fees and expenses set forth in the CIETAC Arbitration Fee Schedule III (Appendix II).

2.   Where a party has nominated an arbitrator but fails to advance a deposit for such actual costs as the special remuneration, travel and accommodation expenses of the nominated arbitrator within the time period specified by CIETAC, the party shall be deemed not to have nominated the arbitrator.

3.   Where the parties have agreed to hold an oral hearing at a place other than the domicile of CIETAC or its relevant sub-commission/arbitration center, they shall advance a deposit for the actual costs such as travel and accommodation expenses incurred thereby. In the event that the parties fail to do so within the time period specified by CIETAC, the oral hearing shall be held at the domicile of CIETAC or its relevant sub-commission/arbitration center.

4.   Where the parties have agreed to use two or more than two languages as the languages of arbitration, or where the parties have agreed on a three-arbitrator tribunal in a case where the Summary Procedure shall apply in accordance with Article 56 of these Rules, CIETAC may charge the parties for any additional and reasonable costs.

Article 83 Interpretation

1.   The headings of the articles in these Rules shall not be construed as interpretations of the contents of the provisions contained therein.

2.   These Rules shall be interpreted by CIETAC.

Article 84 Coming into Force

These Rules shall be effective as of January 1, 2015. For cases administered by CIETAC or its sub-commissions/arbitration centers before these Rules come into force, the Arbitration Rules effective at the time of acceptance shall apply, or where both parties agree, these Rules shall apply.

Appendix I

Directory of China International Economic and Trade Arbitration Commission and its Sub-commissions/Arbitration Centers

China International Economic and Trade Arbitration Commission (CIETAC)

Add: 6/F, CCOIC Building, No.2 Huapichang Hutong,

Xicheng District, Beijing, 10035, P.R. China

Tel: 86 10 82217788

Fax: 86 10 82217766/64643500

E-mail: info@cietac.org

Website: http://www.cietac.org

CIETAC South China Sub-Commission

Add: 14A01, Anlian Plaza, No.4018, Jintian Road, Futian District, Shenzhen 518026, Guangdong Province, P.R.China

Tel: 86 755 82796739

Fax: 86 755 23964130

E-mail: infosz@cietac.org

Website: http://www.cietac.org

CIETAC Shanghai Sub-Commission

Add: 18/F, Tomson Commercial Building, 710 Dongfang Road,

Pudong New Area, Shanghai 200122 P.R.China

Tel: 86 21 60137688

Fax: 86 21 60137689

E-Mail: infosh@cietac.org

Website: http://www.cietac.org

CIETAC Tianjin International Economic and Financial Arbitration Center

(Tianjin Sub-commission)

Add: 4/F, E2–ABC, Financial Street, No.20 Guangchangdong Road,

Tianjin Economic-Technological Development Zone,

Tianjin 300457, P.R.China

Tel: 86 22 66285688

Fax: 86 22 66285678

Email: tianjin@cietac.org

Website: http://www.cietac-tj.org

CIETAC Southwest Sub-Commission

Add: 1/F, Bld B, Caifu 3, Caifu Garden, Cai fu Zhongxin, Yubei, Chongqing 401121, China

Tel: 86 23 86871307

Fax: 86 23 86871190

Email: cietac-sw@cietac.org

Website: http://www.cietac-sw.org

CIETAC Hong Kong Arbitration Center

Add: Unit 4705, 47th Floor, Far East Finance Center, No.16 Harcourt Road, Hong Kong.

Tel: 852 25298066

Fax: 852 25298266

Email: hk@cietac.org

Website: http://www.cietachk.org

Appendix II

China International Economic and Trade Arbitration Commission

Arbitration Fee Schedule I

(This fee schedule applies to arbitration cases accepted under Item (a) and (b), Paragraph 2 of Article 3 of the Arbitration Rules)

Amount in Dispute (RMB)	Arbitration Fee (RMB)
Up to 1,000,000	4% of the amount, minimum 10,000
From 1,000,001 to 2,000,000	40,000 + 3.5% of the amount over 1,000,000
From 2,000,001 to 5,000,000	75,000 + 2.5% of the amount over 2,000,000
From 5,000,001 to 10,000,000	225,000 + 1% of the amount over 10,000,000
From 10,000,001 to 50,000,000	225,000 + 1% of the amount over 10,000,000
From 50,000,001 to 100,000,000	625,000 + 0.5% of the amount over 50,000,000
From 100,000,001 to 500,000,000	875,000 + 0.48% of the amount over 100,000,000
From 500,000,001 to 1,000,000,000	2,795,000 + 0.47% of the amount over 500,000,000

| From 1,000,000,001 to 2,000,000,000 | 5,145,000 + 0.46% of the amount over 1,000,000,000 |
| Over 2,000,000,001 | 9,745,000 + 0.45% of the amount over 2,000,000,000, maximum 15,000,000 |

When a case is accepted, an additional amount of RMB 10,000 shall be charged as the registration fee, which shall include the expenses for examining the application for arbitration, initiating the arbitral proceedings, computerizing management and filing documents.

The amount in dispute referred to in this Schedule shall be based on the sum of money claimed by the Claimant. If the amount claimed is different from the actual amount in dispute, the actual amount in dispute shall be the basis for calculation.

Where the amount in dispute is not ascertained at the time of applying for arbitration, or where special circumstances exist, the amount of the arbitration fee shall be determined by CIETAC.

Where the arbitration fee is to be charged in a foreign currency, the amount in the foreign currency shall be equivalent to the corresponding amount in RMB as specified in this Schedule.

Apart from charging the arbitration fee according to this Schedule, CIETAC may also collect other additional and reasonable actual expenses pursuant to the relevant provisions of the Arbitration Rules.

China International Economic and Trade Arbitration Commission

Arbitration Fee Schedule II

(This fee schedule applies to arbitration cases accepted under Item (c), Paragraph 2 of Article 3 of the Arbitration Rules)

I.   Registration Fee

Amount in Dispute (RMB)	Registration Fee (RMB)
Up to 1,000	Minimum 100
From 1,001 to 50,000	100 + 5% of the amount over 1,000
From 50,001 to 100,000	2,550 + 4% of the amount over 50,000
From 100,001 to 200,000	4,550 + 3% of the amount over 100,000
From 200,001 to 500,000	7,550 + 2% of the amount over 200,000
From 500,001 to 1,000,000	13,550 + 1% of the amount over 500,000
Over 1,000,001	18,550 + 0.5% of the amount over 1,000,000

II. Handling Fee

Amount in Dispute (RMB)	Handling Fee (RMB)
Up to 200,000	Minimum 6,000
From 200,001 to 500,000	6,000 + 2% of the amount over 200,000
From 500,001 to 1,000,000	12,000 + 1.5% of the amount over 500,000
From 1,000,001 to 2,000,000	19,500 + 0.5% of the amount over 1,000,000
From 2,000,001 to 5,000,000	24,500 + 0.45% of the amount over 2,000,000
From 5,000,001 to 10,000,000	38,000 + 0.4% of the amount over 5,000,000
From 10,000,001 to 20,000,000	58,000 + 0.3% of the amount over 10,000,000
From 20,000,001 to 40,000,000	88,000 + 0.2% of the amount over 20,000,000
From 40,000,001 to 100,000,000	128,000 + 0.15% of the amount over 40,000,000
From 100,000,001 to 500,000,000	218,000 + 0.13% of the amount over 100,000,00
Over 500,000,000	738,000 + 0.12% of the amount over 500,000,000

The amount in dispute referred to in this Schedule shall be based on the sum of money claimed by the Claimant. If the amount claimed is different from the actual amount in dispute, the actual amount in dispute shall be the basis for calculation.

Where the amount in dispute is not ascertained at the time of applying for arbitration, or where special circumstances exist, the amount of the arbitration fee deposit shall be determined by CIETAC in consideration of the specific rights and interests involved in the dispute.

Apart from charging the arbitration fee according to this Schedule, CIETAC may also collect other additional and reasonable actual expenses pursuant to the relevant provisions of the Arbitration Rules.

China International Economic and Trade Arbitration Commission

Arbitration Fee Schedule III

(This fee schedule applies to arbitration cases administered by the CIETAC Hong Kong Arbitration Center under Chapter VI of the Arbitration Rules)

I. Registration Fee

When submitting a Request for Arbitration to the CIETAC Hong Kong Arbitration Center, the Claimant shall pay a registration fee of HKD 8,000, which shall include the expenses for examining the application for arbitration, initiating the arbitral proceedings, computerizing management, filing documents and labor costs. The registration fee is not refundable.

II. Administrative Fee

1. Administrative Fee Table

Amount in Dispute (HKD)	Administrative Fee (HKD)
Up to 500,000	16,000
From 500,000 to 1,000,000	16,000 + 0.78% of the amount over 500,000
From 1,000,001 to 5,000,000	19,900 + 0.65% of the amount over 1,000,000
From 5,000,001 to 10,000,000	45,900 + 0.38% of the amount over 5,000,000
From 10,000,001 to 20,000,000	64,900 + 0.22% of the amount over 10,000,000
From 20,000,001 to 40,000,000	86,900 + 0.15% of the amount over 20,000,000
From 40,000,001 to 80,000,000	116,900 + 0.08% of the amount over 40,000,000
From 80,000,001 to 200,000,000	148,900 + 0.052% of the amount over 80,000,000
From 200,000,001 to 400,000,000	211,300 + 0.04% of the amount over 200,000,000
Over 400,000,001	291,300

2.   The administrative fee includes the remuneration of the case manager and the costs of using oral hearing rooms of CIETAC and/or its sub-commissions/arbitration centers.

3.   Claims and counterclaims are aggregated for the determination of the amount in dispute. Where the amount in dispute is not ascertained at the time of applying for arbitration, or where special circumstances exist, the amount of the administrative fee shall be determined by CIETAC taking into account the circumstances of the case.

4.   Apart from charging the administrative fee according to this Table, the CIETAC Hong Kong Arbitration Center may also collect other additional and reasonable actual expenses pursuant to the relevant provisions of the Arbitration Rules, including but not limited to translation fees, written record fees, and the costs of using oral hearing rooms other than those of CIETAC and/or its sub-commissions/arbitration centers.

5.   Where the registration fee and the administrative fee are to be charged in a currency other than HKD, the CIETAC Hong Kong Arbitration Center shall charge an amount of the foreign currency equivalent to the corresponding amount in HKD as specified in this Table.

II. Arbitrator's Fees and Expenses

A. Arbitrator's Fees and Expenses (Based on the Amount in Dispute)

1. Arbitrator's Fees Table

Amount in Dispute (HKD)	Arbitrator's Fees (HKD, per arbitrator)	
	Minimum	Maximum
Up to 500,000	15,000	60,000
From 500,001 to 1,000,000	15,000 + 2.30% of the amount over 500,000	60,000 + 8.50% of the amount over 500,000
From 1,000,001 to 5,000,000	26,500 + 0.80% of the amount over 1,000,000	102,500 + 4.3% of the amount over 1,000,00044
From 5,000,001 to 10,000,000	58,500 + 0.60% of the amount over 5,000,000	274,500 + 2.30% of the amount over 5,000,000
From 10,000,001 to 20,000,000	88,500 + 0.35% of the amount over 10,000,000	389,500 + 1.00% of the amount over 10,000,000
From 20,000,001 to 40,000,000	123,500 + 0.20% of the amount over 20,000,000	489,500 + 0.65% of the amount over 20,000,000
From 40,000,001 to 80,000.000	163,500 + 0.07% of the amount over 40,000,000	619,500 + 0.35% of the amount over 40,000,000
From 80,000,001 to 200,000,000	191,500 + 0.05% of the amount over 80,000,000	759,500 + 0.25% of the amount over 80,000,000
From 200,000,001 to 400,000,000	251,500 + 0.03% of the amount over 200,000,000	1,059,500 + 0.15% of the amount over 200,000,000
From 400,000,001 to 600,000,000	311,500 + 0.02% of the amount over 400,000,000	1,359,500 + 0.12% of the amount over 400,000,000

| From 600,000,001 to 750,000,000 | 351,500 + 0.01% of the amount over 600,000,000 | 1,599,500 + 0.10% of the amount over 600,000,000 |
| Over 750,000,000 | 366,500 + 0.008% of the amount over 750,000,000 | 1,749,500 + 0.06% of the amount over 750,000,000 |

2.   Unless otherwise stipulated in this Schedule, the arbitrator's fees shall be determined by CIETAC in accordance with the above Table taking into account the circumstances of the case. The arbitrator's expenses shall include all reasonable actual expenses incurred from the arbitrator's arbitration activities.

3.   The arbitrator's fees may exceed the corresponding maximum amount listed in the Table provided that the parties so agree in writing or CIETAC so determines under exceptional circumstances.

4.   The parties shall advance the payment of the arbitrator's fees and expenses determined by CIETAC to the CIETAC Hong Kong Arbitration Center. Subject to the approval of the CIETAC Hong Kong Arbitration Center, the parties may pay the arbitrator's fees and expenses in installments. The parties shall be jointly and severally liable for the payment of the arbitrator's fees and expenses.

5.   Claims and counterclaims are aggregated for the determination of the amount in dispute. Where the amount in dispute is not ascertainable, or where special circumstances exist, the amount of the arbitrator's fees shall be determined by CIETAC taking into account the circumstances of the case.

B.   Arbitrator's Fees and Expenses (Based on an Hourly Rate)

1.   Where the parties have agreed in writing that the arbitrator's fees and expenses are to be based on an hourly rate, their agreement shall prevail. The arbitrator is entitled to fees based on an hourly rate for all the reasonable efforts devoted in the arbitration. The arbitrator's expenses shall include all reasonable actual expenses incurred from the arbitrator's arbitration activities.

2.   Where a party applies for the Emergency Arbitrator Procedures, the emergency arbitrator's fees shall be based on an hourly rate.

3.   The hourly rate for each co-arbitrator shall be the rate agreed upon by that co-arbitrator and the nominating party. The hourly rate for a sole or presiding arbitrator shall be the rate agreed upon by that arbitrator and both parties. Where the hourly rate cannot be agreed upon, or the arbitrator is appointed by the Chairman of CIETAC, the hourly rate of the arbitrator shall be determined by CIETAC. The hourly rate for the emergency arbitrator shall be determined by CIETAC.

4.   An agreed or determined hourly rate shall not exceed the maximum rate fixed by CIETAC as provided on the website of the CIETAC Hong Kong Arbitration Center on the date of the submission of the Request for Arbitration. The arbitrator's fees may exceed the fixed maximum rate provided that the parties so agree in writing or CIETAC so determines under exceptional circumstances.

5.   The parties shall advance the payment of the arbitrator's fees and expenses to the CIETAC Hong Kong Arbitration Center, which amount shall be fixed by the latter. The parties shall be jointly and severally liable for the payment of the arbitrator's fees and expenses.

C.   Miscellaneous

1.   In accordance with the decision of the arbitral tribunal, the CIETAC Hong Kong Arbitration Center shall have a lien over the award rendered by the tribunal so as to secure the payment of the outstanding fees for the arbitrators and all the expenses due. After all such fees and expenses have been paid in full jointly or by one of the parties, the CIETAC Hong Kong Arbitration Center shall release such award to the parties according to the decision of the arbitral tribunal.

2.   Where the arbitrator's fees and expenses are to be charged in a currency other than HKD, the CIETAC Hong Kong Arbitration Center shall charge an amount of the foreign currency equivalent to the corresponding amount in HKD as specified in this Schedule.

Appendix III

China International Economic and Trade Arbitration Commission Emergency Arbitrator Procedures

Article 1 Application for the Emergency Arbitrator Procedures

1.   A party requiring emergency relief may apply for the Emergency Arbitrator Procedures based upon the applicable law or the agreement of the parties.

2.   The party applying for the Emergency Arbitrator Procedures (the "Applicant") shall submit its Application for the Emergency Arbitrator Procedures to the Arbitration Court or the arbitration court of the relevant sub-commission/arbitration center of CIETAC administering the case prior to the formation of the arbitral tribunal.

3.   The Application for the Emergency Arbitrator Procedures shall include the following information:

   (a)   the names and other basic information of the parties involved in the Application;

   (b)   a description of the underlying dispute giving rise to the Application and the reasons why emergency relief is required;

(c) a statement of the emergency measures sought and the reasons why the applicant is entitled to such emergency relief;

(d) other necessary information required to apply for the emergency relief; and

(e) comments on the applicable law and the language of the Emergency Arbitrator Procedures.

When submitting its Application, the Applicant shall attach the relevant documentary and other evidence on which the Application is based, including but not limited to the arbitration agreement and any other agreements giving rise to the underlying dispute. The Application, evidence and other documents shall be submitted in triplicate. Where there are multiple parties, additional copies shall be provided accordingly.

4.   The Applicant shall advance the costs for the Emergency Arbitrator Procedures.

5.   Where the parties have agreed on the language of arbitration, such language shall be the language of the Emergency Arbitrator Procedures. In the absence of such agreement, the language of the Procedures shall be determined by the Arbitration Court.

Article 2 Acceptance of Application and Appointment of the Emergency Arbitrator

1.   After a preliminary review on the basis of the Application, the arbitration agreement and relevant evidence submitted by the Applicant, the Arbitration Court shall decide whether the Emergency Arbitrator Procedures shall apply. If the Arbitration Court decides to apply the Emergency Arbitrator Procedures, the President of the Arbitration Court shall appoint an emergency arbitrator within one (1) day from his/her receipt of both the Application and the advance payment of the costs for the Emergency Arbitrator Procedures.

2.   Once the emergency arbitrator has been appointed by the President of the Arbitration Court, the Arbitration Court shall promptly transmit the Notice of Acceptance and the Applicant's application file to the appointed emergency arbitrator and the party against whom the emergency measures are sought, meanwhile copying the Notice of Acceptance to each of the other parties to the arbitration and the Chairman of CIETAC.

Article 3 Disclosure and Challenge of the Emergency Arbitrator

1.   An emergency arbitrator shall not represent either party, and shall be and remain independent of the parties and treat them equally.

2.   Upon acceptance of the appointment, an emergency arbitrator shall sign a Declaration and disclose to the Arbitration Court any facts or circumstances likely to give rise to justifiable doubts as to his/her impartiality or independence. If circumstances that need to be disclosed

arise during the Emergency Arbitrator Procedures, the emergency arbitrator shall promptly disclose such circumstances in writing.

3.   The Declaration and/or the disclosure of the emergency arbitrator shall be communicated to the parties by the Arbitration Court.

4.   Upon receipt of the Declaration and/or the written disclosure of an emergency arbitrator, a party wishing to challenge the arbitrator on the grounds of the facts or circumstances disclosed by the emergency arbitrator shall forward the challenge in writing within two (2) days from the date of such receipt. If a party fails to file a challenge within the above time period, it may not subsequently challenge the emergency arbitrator on the basis of the matters disclosed by the emergency arbitrator.

5.   A party which has justifiable doubts as to the impartiality or independence of the appointed emergency arbitrator may challenge that emergency arbitrator in writing and shall state the facts and reasons on which the challenge is based with supporting evidence.

6.   A party may challenge an emergency arbitrator in writing within two (2) days from the date of its receipt of the Notice of Acceptance. Where a party becomes aware of a reason for a challenge after such receipt, the party may challenge the emergency arbitrator in writing within two (2) days after such reason has become known, but no later than the formation of the arbitral tribunal.

7.   The President of the Arbitration Court shall make a final decision on the challenge of the emergency arbitrator. If the challenge is accepted, the President of the Arbitration Court shall reappoint an emergency arbitrator within one (1) day from the date of the decision confirming the challenge, and copy the decision to the Chairman of CIETAC. The emergency arbitrator who has been challenged shall continue to perform his/her functions until a final decision on the challenge has been made.

The disclosure and challenge proceedings shall apply equally to the reappointed emergency arbitrator.

8.   Unless otherwise agreed by the parties, the emergency arbitrator shall not accept nomination or appointment to act as a member of the arbitral tribunal in any arbitration relating to the underlying dispute.

Article 4 Place of the Emergency Arbitrator Proceedings

Unless otherwise agreed by the parties, the place of the emergency arbitrator proceedings shall be the place of arbitration, which is determined in accordance with Article 7 of the Arbitration Rules.

Article 5 The Emergency Arbitrator Proceedings

1.   The emergency arbitrator shall establish a procedural timetable for the emergency arbitrator proceedings within a time as short as possible, best within two (2) days from his/her acceptance of the appointment. The

emergency arbitrator shall conduct the proceedings in the manner the emergency arbitrator considers to be appropriate, taking into account the nature and the urgency of the emergency relief, and shall ensure that each party has a reasonable opportunity to present its case.

2.   The emergency arbitrator may order the provision of appropriate security by the party seeking the emergency relief as the precondition of taking emergency measures.

3.   The power of the emergency arbitrator and the emergency arbitrator proceedings shall cease on the date of the formation of the arbitral tribunal.

4.   The emergency arbitrator proceedings shall not affect the right of the parties to seek interim measures from a competent court pursuant to the applicable law.

Article 6 Order of the Emergency Arbitrator

1.   The emergency arbitrator has the power to make a decision to order or award necessary emergency relief, and shall make every reasonable effort to ensure that the decision is valid.

2.   The decision of the emergency arbitrator shall be made within fifteen (15) days from the date of that arbitrator's acceptance of the appointment. The President of the Arbitration Court may extend the time period upon the request of the emergency arbitrator only if the President of the Arbitration Court considers it reasonable.

3.   The decision of the emergency arbitrator shall state the reasons for taking the emergency measures, be signed by the emergency arbitrator and stamped with the seal of the Arbitration Court or the arbitration court of its relevant sub-commission/arbitration center.

4.   The decision of the emergency arbitrator shall be binding upon both parties. A party may seek enforcement of the decision from a competent court pursuant to the relevant law provisions of the enforcing state or region. Upon a reasoned request of a party, the emergency arbitrator or the arbitral tribunal to be formed may modify, suspend or terminate the decision.

5.   The emergency arbitrator may decide to dismiss the application of the Applicant and terminate the emergency arbitrator proceedings, if that arbitrator considers that circumstances exist where emergency measures are unnecessary or unable to be taken for various reasons.

6.   The decision of the emergency arbitrator shall cease to be binding:

   (a) if the emergency arbitrator or the arbitral tribunal terminates the decision of the emergency arbitrator;

   (b) if the President of the Arbitration Court decides to accept a challenge against the emergency arbitrator;

(c) upon the rendering of a final award by the arbitral tribunal, unless the arbitral tribunal decides that the decision of the emergency arbitrator shall continue to be effective;

(d) upon the Applicant's withdrawal of all claims before the rendering of a final award;

(e) if the arbitral tribunal is not formed within ninety (90) days from the date of the decision of the emergency arbitrator. This period of time may be extended by agreement of the parties or by the Arbitration Court under circumstances it considers appropriate; or

(f) if the arbitration proceedings have been suspended for sixty (60) consecutive days after the formation of the arbitral tribunal.

Article 7 Costs of the Emergency Arbitrator Proceedings

1. The Applicant shall advance an amount of RMB 30,000 as the costs of the emergency arbitrator proceedings, consisting of the remuneration of the emergency arbitrator and the administrative fee of CIETAC. The Arbitration Court may require the Applicant to advance any other additional and reasonable actual costs.

A party applying to the CIETAC Hong Kong Arbitration Center for emergency relief shall advance the costs of the emergency arbitrator proceedings in accordance with the CIETAC Arbitration Fee Schedule III (Appendix II).

2. The emergency arbitrator shall determine in its decision in what proportion the costs of the emergency arbitrator proceedings shall be borne by the parties, subject to the power of the arbitral tribunal to finally determine the allocation of such costs at the request of a party.

3. The Arbitration Court may fix the amount of the costs of the emergency arbitrator proceedings refundable to the Applicant if such proceedings terminate before the emergency arbitrator has made a decision.

Article 8 Miscellaneous

These rules for the Emergency Arbitrator Procedures shall be interpreted by CIETAC.

F. SWISS RULES OF INTERNATIONAL ARBITRATION (SWISS RULES 2012)* (EFFECTIVE, JUNE, 2012)

Swiss Chambers' Arbitration Institution

The Swiss Chambers Of Commerce Association for Arbitration and Mediation

Chamber of Commerce of

Basel

Bern

Geneva

Neuchâtel

Ticino

Vaud

Zurich

Swiss Rules of International Arbitration (Swiss Rules)

MODEL ARBITRATION CLAUSE

Any dispute, controversy, or claim arising out of, or in relation to, this contract, including the validity, invalidity, breach, or termination thereof, shall be resolved by arbitration in accordance with the Swiss Rules of International Arbitration of the Swiss Chambers' Arbitration Institution in force on the date on which the Notice of Arbitration is submitted in accordance with these Rules.

The number of arbitrators shall be . . . ("one", "three", "one or three");

The seat of the arbitration shall be . . . (name of city in Switzerland, unless the parties agree on a city in another country);

The arbitral proceedings shall be conducted in . . . (insert desired language).

Introduction

(a)   In order to harmonise their rules of arbitration the Chambers of Commerce and Industry of Basel, Bern, Geneva, Neuchâtel, Ticino, Vaud and Zurich in 2004 replaced their former rules by the Swiss Rules of International Arbitration (hereinafter the "Swiss Rules" or the "Rules").

(b)   For the purpose of providing arbitration services, the Chambers founded the Swiss Chambers' Arbitration Institution. In order to

---

*   The Swiss Rules can be found at https://www.swissarbitration.org/sa/en/. Copyright © (2012). Reprinted with permission of Swiss Chambers' Arbitration Institution.

administer arbitrations under the Swiss Rules, the Swiss Chambers' Arbitration Institution has established the Arbitration Court (hereinafter the "Court"), which is comprised of experienced international arbitration practitioners. The Court shall render decisions as provided for under these Rules. It may delegate to one or more members or committees the power to take certain decisions pursuant to its Internal Rules[1]. The Court is assisted in its work by the Secretariat of the Court (hereinafter the "Secretariat").

(c) The Swiss Chambers' Arbitration Institution provides domestic and international arbitration services, as well as other dispute resolution services, under any applicable law, in Switzerland or in any other country.

Section I.   Introductory Rules

Article 1

Scope of Application

1.   These Rules shall govern arbitrations where an agreement to arbitrate refers to these Rules or to the arbitration rules of the Chambers of Commerce and Industry of Basel, Bern, Geneva, Neuchâtel, Ticino, Vaud, Zurich, or any further Chamber of Commerce and Industry that may adhere to these Rules.

2.   The seat of arbitration designated by the parties may be in Switzerland or in any other country.

3.   This version of the Rules shall come into force on 1 June 2012 and, unless the parties have agreed otherwise, shall apply to all arbitral proceedings in which the Notice of Arbitration is submitted on or after that date.

4.   By submitting their dispute to arbitration under these Rules, the parties confer on the Court, to the fullest extent permitted under the law applicable to the arbitration, all of the powers required for the purpose of supervising the arbitral proceedings otherwise vested in the competent judicial authority, including the power to extend the term of office of the arbitral tribunal and to decide on the challenge of an arbitrator on grounds not provided for in these Rules.

5.   These Rules shall govern the arbitration, except if one of them is in conflict with a provision of the law applicable to the arbitration from which the parties cannot derogate, in which case that provision shall prevail.

Article 2

Notice, Calculation of Periods of Time

1.   For the purposes of these Rules, any notice, including a notification, communication, or proposal, is deemed to have been received

---

[1]   The Internal Rules are available on the website www.swissarbitration.org.

if it is delivered to the addressee, or to its habitual residence, place of business, postal or electronic address, or, if none of these can be identified after making a reasonable inquiry, to the addressee's last-known residence or place of business. A notice shall be deemed to have been received on the day it is delivered.

2.   A period of time under these Rules shall begin to run on the day following the day when a notice, notification, communication, or proposal is received. If the last day of such a period is an official holiday or a non-business day at the residence or place of business of the addressee, the period is extended until the first business day which follows. Official holidays or non-business days are included in the calculation of a period of time.

3.   If the circumstances so justify, the Court may extend or shorten any time-limit it has fixed or has the authority to fix or amend.

Article 3

Notice of Arbitration and Answer to the Notice of Arbitration

1.   The party initiating arbitration (hereinafter called the "Claimant" or, where applicable, the "Claimants") shall submit a Notice of Arbitration to the Secretariat at any of the addresses listed in Appendix A.

2.   Arbitral proceedings shall be deemed to commence on the date on which the Notice of Arbitration is received by the Secretariat.

3.   The Notice of Arbitration shall be submitted in as many copies as there are other parties (hereinafter called the "Respondent" or, where applicable, the "Respondents"), together with an additional copy for each arbitrator and one copy for the Secretariat, and shall include the following:

(a)   A demand that the dispute be referred to arbitration;

(b)   The names, addresses, telephone and fax numbers, and e-mail addresses (if any) of the parties and of their representative(s);

(c)   A copy of the arbitration clause or the separate arbitration agreement that is invoked;

(d)   A reference to the contract or other legal instrument(s) out of, or in relation to, which the dispute arises;

(e)   The general nature of the claim and an indication of the amount involved, if any;

(f)   The relief or remedy sought;

(g)   A proposal as to the number of arbitrators (i.e. one or three), the language, and the seat of the arbitration, if the parties have not previously agreed thereon;

(h)   The Claimant's designation of one or more arbitrators, if the parties' agreement so requires;

(i) Confirmation of payment by check or transfer to the relevant account listed in Appendix A of the Registration Fee as required by Appendix B (Schedule of Costs) in force on the date the Notice of Arbitration is submitted.

4. The Notice of Arbitration may also include:

(a) The Claimant's proposal for the appointment of a sole arbitrator referred to in Article 7;

(b) The Statement of Claim referred to in Article 18.

5. If the Notice of Arbitration is incomplete, if the required number of copies or attachments are not submitted, or if the Registration Fee is not paid, the Secretariat may request the Claimant to remedy the defect within an appropriate period of time. The Secretariat may also request the Claimant to submit a translation of the Notice of Arbitration within the same period of time if it is not submitted in English, German, French, or Italian. If the Claimant complies with such directions within the applicable time-limit, the Notice of Arbitration shall be deemed to have been validly filed on the date on which the initial version was received by the Secretariat.

6. The Secretariat shall provide, without delay, a copy of the Notice of Arbitration together with any exhibits to the Respondent.

7. Within thirty days from the date of receipt of the Notice of Arbitration, the Respondent shall submit to the Secretariat an Answer to the Notice of Arbitration. The Answer to the Notice of Arbitration shall be submitted in as many copies as there are other parties, together with an additional copy for each arbitrator and one copy for the Secretariat, and shall, to the extent possible, include the following:

(a) The name, address, telephone and fax numbers, and e-mail address of the Respondent and of its representative(s);

(b) Any plea that an arbitral tribunal constituted under these Rules lacks jurisdiction;

(c) The Respondent's comments on the particulars set forth in the Notice of Arbitration referred to in Article 3(3)(e);

(d) The Respondent's answer to the relief or remedy sought in the Notice of Arbitration referred to in Article 3(3)(f);

(e) The Respondent's proposal as to the number of arbitrators (i.e. one or three), the language, and the seat of the arbitration referred to in Article 3(3)(g);

(f) The Respondent's designation of one or more arbitrators if the parties' agreement so requires.

8.   The Answer to the Notice of Arbitration may also include:

(a)   The Respondent's proposal for the appointment of a sole arbitrator referred to in Article 7;

(b)   The Statement of Defence referred to in Article 19.

9.   Articles 3(5) and (6) are applicable to the Answer to the Notice of Arbitration.

10.   Any counterclaim or set-off defence shall in principle be raised with the Answer to the Notice of Arbitration. Article 3(3) is applicable to the counterclaim or set-off defence.

11.   If no counterclaim or set-off defence is raised with the Answer to the Notice of Arbitration, or if there is no indication of the amount of the counterclaim or set-off defence, the Court may rely exclusively on the Notice of Arbitration in order to determine the possible application of Article 42(2) (Expedited Procedure).

12.   If the Respondent neither submits an Answer to the Notice of Arbitration nor raises an objection to the arbitration being administered under these Rules, the Court shall administer the case, unless there is manifestly no agreement to arbitrate referring to these Rules.

Article 4

Consolidation and Joinder

1.   Where a Notice of Arbitration is submitted between parties already involved in other arbitral proceedings pending under these Rules, the Court may decide, after consulting with the parties and any confirmed arbitrator in all proceedings, that the new case shall be consolidated with the pending arbitral proceedings. The Court may proceed in the same way where a Notice of Arbitration is submitted between parties that are not identical to the parties in the pending arbitral proceedings. When rendering its decision, the Court shall take into account all relevant circumstances, including the links between the cases and the progress already made in the pending arbitral proceedings. Where the Court decides to consolidate the new case with the pending arbitral proceedings, the parties to all proceedings shall be deemed to have waived their right to designate an arbitrator, and the Court may revoke the appointment and confirmation of arbitrators and apply the provisions of Section II (Composition of the Arbitral Tribunal).

2.   Where one or more third persons request to participate in arbitral proceedings already pending under these Rules or where a party to pending arbitral proceedings under these Rules requests that one or more third persons participate in the arbitration, the arbitral tribunal shall decide on such request, after consulting with all of the parties, including the person or persons to be joined, taking into account all relevant circumstances.

Section II. Composition of the Arbitral Tribunal

Article 5

Confirmation Of Arbitrators

1.   All designations of an arbitrator made by the parties or the arbitrators are subject to confirmation by the Court, upon which the appointments shall become effective. The Court has no obligation to give reasons when it does not confirm an arbitrator.

2.   Where a designation is not confirmed, the Court may either:

(a)   invite the party or parties concerned, or, as the case may be, the arbitrators, to make a new designation within a reasonable time-limit; or

(b)   in exceptional circumstances, proceed directly with the appointment.

3.   In the event of any failure in the constitution of the arbitral tribunal under these Rules, the Court shall have all powers to address such failure and may, in particular, revoke any appointment made, appoint or reappoint any of the arbitrators and designate one of them as the presiding arbitrator.

4.   If, before the arbitral tribunal is constituted, the parties agree on a settlement of the dispute, or the continuation of the arbitral proceedings becomes unnecessary or impossible for other reasons, the Secretariat shall give advance notice to the parties that the Court may terminate the proceedings. Any party may request that the Court proceed with the constitution of the arbitral tribunal in accordance with these Rules in order that the arbitral tribunal determine and apportion the costs not agreed upon by the parties.

5.   Once the Registration Fee and any Provisional Deposit have been paid in accordance with Appendix B (Schedule of Costs) and all arbitrators have been confirmed, the Secretariat shall transmit the file to the arbitral tribunal without delay.

Article 6

Number of Arbitrators

1.   If the parties have not agreed upon the number of arbitrators, the Court shall decide whether the case shall be referred to a sole arbitrator or to a three-member arbitral tribunal, taking into account all relevant circumstances.

2.   As a rule, the Court shall refer the case to a sole arbitrator, unless the complexity of the subject matter and/or the amount in dispute justify that the case be referred to a three-member arbitral tribunal.

3.   If the arbitration agreement provides for an arbitral tribunal composed of more than one arbitrator, and this appears inappropriate in view of the amount in dispute or of other circumstances, the Court shall invite the parties to agree to refer the case to a sole arbitrator.

4.   Where the amount in dispute does not exceed CHF 1'000'000 (one million Swiss francs), Article 42(2) (Expedited Procedure) shall apply.

Article 7

Appointment of a Sole Arbitrator

1.   Where the parties have agreed that the dispute shall be referred to a sole arbitrator, they shall jointly designate the sole arbitrator within thirty days from the date on which the Notice of Arbitration was received by the Respondent(s), unless the parties' agreement provides otherwise.

2.   Where the parties have not agreed upon the number of arbitrators, they shall jointly designate the sole arbitrator within thirty days from the date of receipt of the Court's decision that the dispute shall be referred to a sole arbitrator.

3.   If the parties fail to designate the sole arbitrator within the applicable time-limit, the Court shall proceed with the appointment.

Article 8

Appointment of Arbitrators In Bi-Party or Multi-Party Proceedings

1.   Where a dispute between two parties is referred to a three-member arbitral tribunal, each party shall designate one arbitrator, unless the parties have agreed otherwise.

2.   If a party fails to designate an arbitrator within the time-limit set by the Court or resulting from the arbitration agreement, the Court shall appoint the arbitrator. Unless the parties' agreement provides otherwise, the two arbitrators so appointed shall designate, within thirty days from the confirmation of the second arbitrator, a third arbitrator who shall act as the presiding arbitrator of the arbitral tribunal. Failing such designation, the Court shall appoint the presiding arbitrator.

3.   In multi-party proceedings, the arbitral tribunal shall be constituted in accordance with the parties' agreement.

4.   If the parties have not agreed upon a procedure for the constitution of the arbitral tribunal in multi-party proceedings, the Court shall set an initial thirty-day time-limit for the Claimant or group of Claimants to designate an arbitrator, and set a subsequent thirty-day time-limit for the Respondent or group of Respondents to designate an arbitrator. If the party or group(s) of parties have each designated an

arbitrator, Article 8(2) shall apply to the designation of the presiding arbitrator.

    5.   Where a party or group of parties fails to designate an arbitrator in multi-party proceedings, the Court may appoint all of the arbitrators, and shall specify the presiding arbitrator.

Article 9

Independence and Challenge of Arbitrators

    1.   Any arbitrator conducting an arbitration under these Rules shall be and shall remain at all times impartial and independent of the parties.

    2.   Prospective arbitrators shall disclose to those who approach them in connection with a possible appointment any circumstances likely to give rise to justifiable doubts as to their impartiality or independence. An arbitrator, once designated or appointed, shall disclose such circumstances to the parties, unless they have already been so informed.

Article 10

    1.   Any arbitrator may be challenged if circumstances exist that give rise to justifiable doubts as to the arbitrator's impartiality or independence.

    2.   A party may challenge the arbitrator designated by it only for reasons of which it becomes aware after the appointment has been made.

Article 11

    1.   A party intending to challenge an arbitrator shall send a notice of challenge to the Secretariat within 15 days after the circumstances giving rise to the challenge became known to that party.

    2.   If, within 15 days from the date of the notice of challenge, all of the parties do not agree to the challenge, or the challenged arbitrator does not withdraw, the Court shall decide on the challenge.

    3.   The decision of the Court is final and the Court has no obligation to give reasons.

Article 12

Removal of an Arbitrator

    1.   If an arbitrator fails to perform his or her functions despite a written warning from the other arbitrators or from the Court, the Court may revoke the appointment of that arbitrator.

    2.   The arbitrator shall first have an opportunity to present his or her position to the Court. The decision of the Court is final and the Court has no obligation to give reasons.

Article 13

Replacement of an Arbitrator

1.   Subject to Article 13(2), in all instances in which an arbitrator has to be replaced, a replacement arbitrator shall be designated or appointed pursuant to the procedure provided for in Articles 7 and 8 within the time-limit set by the Court. Such procedure shall apply even if a party or the arbitrators had failed to make the required designation during the initial appointment process.

2.   In exceptional circumstances, the Court may, after consulting with the parties and any remaining arbitrators:

(a)   directly appoint the replacement arbitrator; or

(b)   after the closure of the proceedings, authorise the remaining arbitrator(s) to proceed with the arbitration and make any decision or award.

Article 14

If an arbitrator is replaced, the proceedings shall, as a rule, resume at the stage reached when the arbitrator who was replaced ceased to perform his or her functions, unless the arbitral tribunal decides otherwise.

Section III. Arbitral Proceedings

Article 15

General Provisions

1.   Subject to these Rules, the arbitral tribunal may conduct the arbitration in such manner as it considers appropriate, provided that it ensures equal treatment of the parties and their right to be heard.

2.   At any stage of the proceedings, the arbitral tribunal may hold hearings for the presentation of evidence by witnesses, including expert witnesses, or for oral argument. After consulting with the parties, the arbitral tribunal may also decide to conduct the proceedings on the basis of documents and other materials.

3.   At an early stage of the arbitral proceedings, and in consultation with the parties, the arbitral tribunal shall prepare a provisional timetable for the arbitral proceedings, which shall be provided to the parties and, for information, to the Secretariat.

4.   All documents or information provided to the arbitral tribunal by one party shall at the same time be communicated by that party to the other parties.

5.   The arbitral tribunal may, after consulting with the parties, appoint a secretary. Articles 9 to 11 shall apply to the secretary.

6.   The parties may be represented or assisted by persons of their choice.

7.   All participants in the arbitral proceedings shall act in good faith, and make every effort to contribute to the efficient conduct of the proceedings and to avoid unnecessary costs and delays. The parties undertake to comply with any award or order made by the arbitral tribunal or emergency arbitrator without delay.

8.   With the agreement of each of the parties, the arbitral tribunal may take steps to facilitate the settlement of the dispute before it. Any such agreement by a party shall constitute a waiver of its right to challenge an arbitrator's impartiality based on the arbitrator's participation and knowledge acquired in taking the agreed steps.

Article 16

Seat of the Arbitration

1.   If the parties have not determined the seat of the arbitration, or if the designation of the seat is unclear or incomplete, the Court shall determine the seat of the arbitration, taking into account all relevant circumstances, or shall request the arbitral tribunal to determine it.

2.   Without prejudice to the determination of the seat of the arbitration, the arbitral tribunal may decide where the proceedings shall be conducted. In particular, it may hear witnesses and hold meetings for consultation among its members at any place it deems appropriate, having regard to the circumstances of the arbitration.

3.   The arbitral tribunal may meet at any place it deems appropriate for the inspection of goods, other property, or documents. The parties shall be given sufficient notice to enable them to be present at such an inspection.

4.   The award shall be deemed to be made at the seat of the arbitration.

Article 17

Language

1.   Subject to an agreement of the parties, the arbitral tribunal shall, promptly after its appointment, determine the language or languages to be used in the proceedings. This determination shall apply to the Statement of Claim, the Statement of Defence, any further written statements, and to any oral hearings.

2.   The arbitral tribunal may order that any documents annexed to the Statement of Claim or Statement of Defence, and any supplementary documents or exhibits submitted in the course of the proceedings in a language other than the language or languages agreed upon by the parties

or determined by the arbitral tribunal shall be accompanied by a translation into such language or languages.

Article 18

Statement of Claim

1. Within a period of time to be determined by the arbitral tribunal, and unless the Statement of Claim was contained in the Notice of Arbitration, the Claimant shall communicate its Statement of Claim in writing to the Respondent and to each of the arbitrators. A copy of the contract, and, if it is not contained in the contract, of the arbitration agreement, shall be annexed to the Statement of Claim.

2. The Statement of Claim shall include the following particulars:

(a) The names and addresses of the parties;

(b) A statement of the facts supporting the claim;

(c) The points at issue;

(d) The relief or remedy sought.

3. As a rule, the Claimant shall annex to its Statement of Claim all documents and other evidence on which it relies.

Article 19

Statement of Defence

1. Within a period of time to be determined by the arbitral tribunal, and unless the Statement of Defence was contained in the Answer to the Notice of Arbitration, the Respondent shall communicate its Statement of Defence in writing to the Claimant and to each of the arbitrators.

2. The Statement of Defence shall reply to the particulars of the Statement of Claim set out in Articles 18(2)(b) to (d). If the Respondent raises an objection to the jurisdiction or to the proper constitution of the arbitral tribunal, the Statement of Defence shall contain the factual and legal basis of such objection. As a rule, the Respondent shall annex to its Statement of Defence all documents and other evidence on which it relies.

3. Articles 18(2)(b) to (d) shall apply to a counterclaim and a claim relied on for the purpose of a set-off.

Article 20

Amendments to the Claim or Defence

1. During the course of the arbitral proceedings, a party may amend or supplement its claim or defence, unless the arbitral tribunal considers it inappropriate to allow such amendment having regard to the delay in making it, the prejudice to the other parties, or any other circumstances. However, a claim may not be amended in such a manner that the amended

claim falls outside the scope of the arbitration clause or separate arbitration agreement.

2.   The arbitral tribunal may adjust the costs of the arbitration if a party amends or supplements its claims, counterclaims, or defences.

Article 21

Objections To The Jurisdiction of The Arbitral Tribunal

1.   The arbitral tribunal shall have the power to rule on any objections to its jurisdiction, including any objection with respect to the existence or validity of the arbitration clause or of the separate arbitration agreement.

2.   The arbitral tribunal shall have the power to determine the existence or the validity of the contract of which an arbitration clause forms part. For the purposes of Article 21, an arbitration clause which forms part of a contract and which provides for arbitration under these Rules shall be treated as an agreement independent of the other terms of the contract. A decision by the arbitral tribunal that the contract is null and void shall not entail *ipso jure* the invalidity of the arbitration clause.

3.   As a rule, any objection to the jurisdiction of the arbitral tribunal shall be raised in the Answer to the Notice of Arbitration, and in no event later than in the Statement of Defence referred to in Article 19, or, with respect to a counterclaim, in the reply to the counterclaim.

4.   In general, the arbitral tribunal should rule on any objection to its jurisdiction as a preliminary question. However, the arbitral tribunal may proceed with the arbitration and rule on such an objection in an award on the merits.

5.   The arbitral tribunal shall have jurisdiction to hear a set-off defence even if the relationship out of which the defence is said to arise is not within the scope of the arbitration clause, or falls within the scope of another arbitration agreement or forum-selection clause.

Article 22

Further Written Statements

The arbitral tribunal shall decide which further written statements, in addition to the Statement of Claim and the Statement of Defence, shall be required from the parties or may be presented by them and shall set the periods of time for communicating such statements.

Article 23

Periods of Time

The periods of time set by the arbitral tribunal for the communication of written statements (including the Statement of Claim and Statement of

Defence) should not exceed forty-five days. However, the arbitral tribunal may extend the time-limits if it considers that an extension is justified.

Article 24

Evidence and Hearings

1.   Each party shall have the burden of proving the facts relied on to support its claim or defence.

2.   The arbitral tribunal shall determine the admissibility, relevance, materiality, and weight of the evidence.

3.   At any time during the arbitral proceedings, the arbitral tribunal may require the parties to produce documents, exhibits, or other evidence within a period of time determined by the arbitral tribunal.

Article 25

1.   The arbitral tribunal shall give the parties adequate advance notice of the date, time, and place of any oral hearing.

2.   Any person may be a witness or an expert witness in the arbitration. It is not improper for a party, its officers, employees, legal advisors, or counsel to interview witnesses, potential witnesses, or expert witnesses.

3.   Prior to a hearing and within a period of time determined by the arbitral tribunal, the evidence of witnesses and expert witnesses may be presented in the form of written statements or reports signed by them.

4.   At the hearing, witnesses and expert witnesses may be heard and examined in the manner set by the arbitral tribunal. The arbitral tribunal may direct that witnesses or expert witnesses be examined through means that do not require their physical presence at the hearing (including by videoconference).

5.   Arrangements shall be made for the translation of oral statements made at a hearing and for a record of the hearing to be provided if this is deemed necessary by the arbitral tribunal having regard to the circumstances of the case, or if the parties so agree.

6.   Hearings shall be held *in camera* unless the parties agree otherwise. The arbitral tribunal may order witnesses or expert witnesses to retire during the testimony of other witnesses or expert witnesses.

Article 26

Interim Measures of Protection

1.   At the request of a party, the arbitral tribunal may grant any interim measures it deems necessary or appropriate. Upon the application of any party or, in exceptional circumstances and with prior notice to the

parties, on its own initiative, the arbitral tribunal may also modify, suspend or terminate any interim measures granted.

2.   Interim measures may be granted in the form of an interim award. The arbitral tribunal shall be entitled to order the provision of appropriate security.

3.   In exceptional circumstances, the arbitral tribunal may rule on a request for interim measures by way of a preliminary order before the request has been communicated to any other party, provided that such communication is made at the latest together with the preliminary order and that the other parties are immediately granted an opportunity to be heard.

4.   The arbitral tribunal may rule on claims for compensation for any damage caused by an unjustified interim measure or preliminary order.

5.   By submitting their dispute to arbitration under these Rules, the parties do not waive any right that they may have under the applicable laws to submit a request for interim measures to a judicial authority. A request for interim measures addressed by any party to a judicial authority shall not be deemed to be incompatible with the agreement to arbitrate, or to constitute a waiver of that agreement.

6.   The arbitral tribunal shall have discretion to apportion the costs relating to a request for interim measures in an interim award or in the final award.

Article 27

Tribunal-Appointed Experts

1.   The arbitral tribunal, after consulting with the parties, may appoint one or more experts to report to it, in writing, on specific issues to be determined by the arbitral tribunal. A copy of the expert's terms of reference, established by the arbitral tribunal, shall be communicated to the parties.

2.   The parties shall give the expert any relevant information or produce for the expert's inspection any relevant documents or goods that the expert may require of them. Any dispute between a party and the expert as to the relevance of the required information, documents or goods shall be referred to the arbitral tribunal.

3.   Upon receipt of the expert's report, the arbitral tribunal shall communicate a copy of the report to the parties, which shall be given the opportunity to express, in writing, their opinion on the report. A party shall be entitled to examine any document on which the expert has relied in the report.

4.   At the request of any party, the expert, after delivery of the report, may be heard at a hearing during which the parties shall have the

opportunity to be present and to examine the expert. At this hearing, any party may present expert witnesses in order to testify on the points at issue. Article 25 shall be applicable to such proceedings.

5.   Articles 9 to 11 shall apply to any expert appointed by the arbitral tribunal.

Article 28

Default

1.   If, within the period of time set by the arbitral tribunal, the Claimant has failed to communicate its claim without showing sufficient cause for such failure, the arbitral tribunal shall issue an order for the termination of the arbitral proceedings. If, within the period of time set by the arbitral tribunal, the Respondent has failed to communicate its Statement of Defence without showing sufficient cause for such failure, the arbitral tribunal shall order that the proceedings continue.

2.   If one of the parties, duly notified under these Rules, fails to appear at a hearing, without showing sufficient cause for such failure, the arbitral tribunal may proceed with the arbitration.

3.   If one of the parties, duly invited to produce documentary or other evidence, fails to do so within the period of time determined by the arbitral tribunal, without showing sufficient cause for such failure, the arbitral tribunal may make the award on the evidence before it.

Article 29

Closure of Proceedings

1.   When it is satisfied that the parties have had a reasonable opportunity to present their respective cases on matters to be decided in an award, the arbitral tribunal may declare the proceedings closed with regard to such matters.

2.   The arbitral tribunal may, if it considers it necessary owing to exceptional circumstances, decide, on its own initiative or upon the application of a party, to reopen the proceedings on the matters with regard to which the proceedings were closed pursuant to Article 29(1) at any time before the award on such matters is made.

Article 30

Waiver of Rules

If a party knows that any provision of, or requirement under, these Rules or any other applicable procedural rule has not been complied with and yet proceeds with the arbitration without promptly stating its objection to such non-compliance, it shall be deemed to have waived its right to raise an objection.

Section IV. The Award

Article 31

Decisions

1.   If the arbitral tribunal is composed of more than one arbitrator, any award or other decision of the arbitral tribunal shall be made by a majority of the arbitrators. If there is no majority, the award shall be made by the presiding arbitrator alone.

2.   If authorized by the arbitral tribunal, the presiding arbitrator may decide on questions of procedure, subject to revision by the arbitral tribunal.

Article 32

Form and Effect of The Award

1.   In addition to making a final award, the arbitral tribunal may make interim, interlocutory, or partial awards. If appropriate, the arbitral tribunal may also award costs in awards that are not final.

2.   The award shall be made in writing and shall be final and binding on the parties.

3.   The arbitral tribunal shall state the reasons upon which the award is based, unless the parties have agreed that no reasons are to be given.

4.   An award shall be signed by the arbitrators and it shall specify the seat of the arbitration and the date on which the award was made. Where the arbitral tribunal is composed of more than one arbitrator and any of them fails to sign, the award shall state the reason for the absence of the signature.

5.   The publication of the award is governed by Article 44.

6.   Originals of the award signed by the arbitrators shall be communicated by the arbitral tribunal to the parties and to the Secretariat. The Secretariat shall retain a copy of the award.

Article 33

Applicable Law, Amiable Compositeur

1.   The arbitral tribunal shall decide the case in accordance with the rules of law agreed upon by the parties or, in the absence of a choice of law, by applying the rules of law with which the dispute has the closest connection.

2.   The arbitral tribunal shall decide as *amiable compositeur* or *ex aequo et bono* only if the parties have expressly authorised the arbitral tribunal to do so.

3.   In all cases, the arbitral tribunal shall decide in accordance with the terms of the contract and shall take into account the trade usages applicable to the transaction.

Article 34

Settlement or Other Grounds for Termination

1.   If, before the award is made, the parties agree on a settlement of the dispute, the arbitral tribunal shall either issue an order for the termination of the arbitral proceedings or, if requested by the parties and accepted by the arbitral tribunal, record the settlement in the form of an arbitral award on agreed terms. The arbitral tribunal is not obliged to give reasons for such an award.

2.   If, before the award is made, the continuation of the arbitral proceedings becomes unnecessary or impossible for any reason not mentioned in Article 34(1), the arbitral tribunal shall give advance notice to the parties that it may issue an order for the termination of the proceedings. The arbitral tribunal shall have the power to issue such an order, unless a party raises justifiable grounds for objection.

3.   Copies of the order for termination of the arbitral proceedings or of the arbitral award on agreed terms, signed by the arbitrators, shall be communicated by the arbitral tribunal to the parties and to the Secretariat. Where an arbitral award on agreed terms is made, Articles 32(2) and (4) to (6) shall apply.

Article 35

Interpretation of The Award

1.   Within thirty days after the receipt of the award, a party, with notice to the Secretariat and to the other parties, may request that the arbitral tribunal give an interpretation of the award. The arbitral tribunal may set a time-limit, as a rule not exceeding thirty days, for the other parties to comment on the request.

2.   The interpretation shall be given in writing within forty-five days after the receipt of the request. The Court may extend this time limit. The interpretation shall form part of the award and Articles 32(2) to (6) shall apply.

Article 36

Correction of The Award

1.   Within thirty days after the receipt of the award, a party, with notice to the Secretariat and to the other parties, may request the arbitral tribunal to correct in the award any errors in computation, any clerical or typographical errors, or any errors of similar nature. The arbitral tribunal

may set a time-limit, as a rule not exceeding thirty days, for the other parties to comment on the request.

2.   The arbitral tribunal may within thirty days after the communication of the award make such corrections on its own initiative.

3.   Such corrections shall be in writing, and Articles 32(2) to (6) shall apply.

Article 37

Additional Award

1.   Within thirty days after the receipt of the award, a party, with notice to the Secretariat and the other parties, may request the arbitral tribunal to make an additional award as to claims presented in the arbitral proceedings but omitted from the award. The arbitral tribunal may set a time-limit, as a rule not exceeding thirty days, for the other parties to comment on the request.

2.   If the arbitral tribunal considers the request for an additional award to be justified and considers that the omission can be rectified without any further hearings or evidence, it shall complete its award within sixty days after the receipt of the request. The Court may extend this time-limit.

3.   Articles 32(2) to (6) shall apply to any additional award.

Article 38

Costs

The award shall contain a determination of the costs of the arbitration. The term "costs" includes only:

(a)   The fees of the arbitral tribunal, to be stated separately as to each arbitrator and any secretary, and to be determined by the arbitral tribunal itself in accordance with Articles 39 and 40(3) to (5);

(b)   The travel and other expenses incurred by the arbitral tribunal and any secretary;

(c)   The costs of expert advice and of other assistance required by the arbitral tribunal;

(d)   The travel and other expenses of witnesses, to the extent such expenses are approved by the arbitral tribunal;

(e)   The costs for legal representation and assistance, if such costs were claimed during the arbitral proceedings, and only to the extent that the arbitral tribunal determines that the amount of such costs is reasonable;

(f)   The Registration Fee and the Administrative Costs in accordance with Appendix B (Schedule of Costs);

(g) The Registration Fee, the fees and expenses of any emergency arbitrator, and the costs of expert advice and of other assistance required by such emergency arbitrator, determined in accordance with Article 43(9).

Article 39

1.   The fees and expenses of the arbitral tribunal shall be reasonable in amount, taking into account the amount in dispute, the complexity of the subject-matter of the arbitration, the time spent and any other relevant circumstances of the case, including the discontinuation of the arbitral proceedings in case of settlement. In the event of a discontinuation of the arbitral proceedings, the fees of the arbitral tribunal may be less than the minimum amount resulting from Appendix B (Schedule of the Costs of Arbitration).

2.   The fees and expenses of the arbitral tribunal shall be determined in accordance with Appendix B (Schedule of Costs).

3.   The arbitral tribunal shall decide on the allocation of its fees among its members. As a rule, the presiding arbitrator shall receive between 40% and 50% and each co-arbitrator between 25% and 30% of the total fees, in view of the time and efforts spent by each arbitrator.

Article 40

1.   Except as provided in Article 40(2), the costs of the arbitration shall in principle be borne by the unsuccessful party. However, the arbitral tribunal may apportion any of the costs of the arbitration among the parties if it determines that such apportionment is reasonable, taking into account the circumstances of the case.

2.   With respect to the costs of legal representation and assistance referred to in Article 38(e), the arbitral tribunal, taking into account the circumstances of the case, shall be free to determine which party shall bear such costs or may apportion such costs among the parties if it determines that an apportionment is reasonable.

3.   If the arbitral tribunal issues an order for the termination of the arbitral proceedings or makes an award on agreed terms, it shall determine the costs of the arbitration referred to in Articles 38 and 39 in the order or award.

4.   Before rendering an award, termination order, or decision on a request under Articles 35 to 37, the arbitral tribunal shall submit to the Secretariat a draft thereof for approval or adjustment by the Court of the determination on costs made pursuant to Articles 38(a) to (c) and (f) and Article 39. Any such approval or adjustment shall be binding upon the arbitral tribunal.

5.   No additional costs may be charged by an arbitral tribunal for interpretation, correction, or completion of its award under Articles 35 to 37, unless they are justified by the circumstances.

Article 41

Deposit of Costs

1.   The arbitral tribunal, once constituted, and after consulting with the Court, shall request each party to deposit an equal amount as an advance for the costs referred to in Articles 38(a) to (c) and the Administrative Costs referred to in Art. 38(f). Any Provisional Deposit paid by a party in accordance with Appendix B (Schedule of Costs) shall be considered as a partial payment of its deposit. The arbitral tribunal shall provide a copy of such request to the Secretariat.

2.   Where a Respondent submits a counterclaim, or it otherwise appears appropriate in the circumstances, the arbitral tribunal may in its discretion establish separate deposits.

3.   During the course of the arbitral proceedings, the arbitral tribunal may, after consulting with the Court, request supplementary deposits from the parties. The arbitral tribunal shall provide a copy of any such request to the Secretariat.

4.   If the required deposits are not paid in full within fifteen days after the receipt of the request, the arbitral tribunal shall notify the parties in order that one or more of them may make the required payment. If such payment is not made, the arbitral tribunal may order the suspension or termination of the arbitral proceedings.

5.   In its final award, the arbitral tribunal shall issue to the parties a statement of account of the deposits received. Any unused amount shall be returned to the parties.

Section V.   Other Provisions

Article 42

Expedited Procedure

1.   If the parties so agree, or if Article 42(2) is applicable, the arbitral proceedings shall be conducted in accordance with an Expedited Procedure based upon the foregoing provisions of these Rules, subject to the following changes:

(a) The file shall be transmitted to the arbitral tribunal only upon payment of the Provisional Deposit as required by Section 1.4 of Appendix B (Schedule of Costs);

(b) After the submission of the Answer to the Notice of Arbitration, the parties shall, as a rule, be entitled to submit only a Statement of

Claim, a Statement of Defence (and counterclaim) and, where applicable, a Statement of Defence in reply to the counterclaim;

(c)   Unless the parties agree that the dispute shall be decided on the basis of documentary evidence only, the arbitral tribunal shall hold a single hearing for the examination of the witnesses and expert witnesses, as well as for oral argument;

(d)   The award shall be made within six months from the date on which the Secretariat transmitted the file to the arbitral tribunal. In exceptional circumstances, the Court may extend this time-limit;

(e)   The arbitral tribunal shall state the reasons upon which the award is based in summary form, unless the parties have agreed that no reasons are to be given.

2.   The following provisions shall apply to all cases in which the amount in dispute, representing the aggregate of the claim and the counterclaim (or any set-off defence), does not exceed CHF 1'000'000 (one million Swiss francs), unless the Court decides otherwise, taking into account all relevant circumstances:

(a)   The arbitral proceedings shall be conducted in accordance with the Expedited Procedure set forth in Article 42(1);

(b)   The case shall be referred to a sole arbitrator, unless the arbitration agreement provides for more than one arbitrator;

(c)   If the arbitration agreement provides for an arbitral tribunal composed of more than one arbitrator, the Secretariat shall invite the parties to agree to refer the case to a sole arbitrator. If the parties do not agree to refer the case to a sole arbitrator, the fees of the arbitrators shall be determined in accordance with Appendix B (Schedule of Costs), but shall in no event be less than the fees resulting from the hourly rate set out in Section 2.8 of Appendix B.

Article 43

Emergency Relief

1.   Unless the parties have agreed otherwise, a party requiring urgent interim measures pursuant to Article 26 before the arbitral tribunal is constituted may submit to the Secretariat an application for emergency relief proceedings (hereinafter the "Application"). In addition to the particulars set out in Articles 3(3)(b) to (e), the Application shall include:

(a)   A statement of the interim measure(s) sought and the reasons therefor, in particular the reason for the purported urgency;

(b)   Comments on the language, the seat of arbitration, and the applicable law;

(c)   Confirmation of payment by check or transfer to the relevant account listed in Appendix A of the Registration Fee and of the deposit for emergency relief proceedings as required by Section 1.6 of Appendix B (Schedule of Costs).

2.   As soon as possible after receipt of the Application, the Registration Fee, and the deposit for emergency relief proceedings, the Court shall appoint and transmit the file to a sole emergency arbitrator, unless

(a) there is manifestly no agreement to arbitrate referring to these Rules, or

(b) it appears more appropriate to proceed with the constitution of the arbitral tribunal and refer the Application to it.

3.   If the Application is submitted before the Notice of Arbitration, the Court shall terminate the emergency relief proceedings if the Notice of Arbitration is not submitted within ten days from the receipt of the Application. In exceptional circumstances, the Court may extend this time-limit.

4.   Articles 9 to 12 shall apply to the emergency arbitrator, except that the time-limits set out in Articles 11(1) and (2) are shortened to three days.

5.   If the parties have not determined the seat of the arbitration, or if the designation of the seat is unclear or incomplete, the seat of the arbitration for the emergency relief proceedings shall be determined by the Court without prejudice to the determination of the seat of the arbitration pursuant to Article 16(1).

6.   The emergency arbitrator may conduct the emergency relief proceedings in such a manner as the emergency arbitrator considers appropriate, taking into account the urgency inherent in such proceedings and ensuring that each party has a reasonable opportunity to be heard on the Application.

7.   The decision on the Application shall be made within fifteen days from the date on which the Secretariat transmitted the file to the emergency arbitrator. This period of time may be extended by agreement of the parties or, in appropriate circumstances, by the Court. The decision on the Application may be made even if in the meantime the file has been transmitted to the arbitral tribunal.

8.   A decision of the emergency arbitrator shall have the same effects as a decision pursuant to Article 26. Any interim measure granted by the emergency arbitrator may be modified, suspended or terminated by the emergency arbitrator or, after transmission of the file to it, by the arbitral tribunal.

9.   The decision on the Application shall include a determination of costs as referred to in Article 38(g). Before rendering the decision on the

Application, the emergency arbitrator shall submit to the Secretariat a draft thereof for approval or adjustment by the Court of the determination of costs. The costs shall be payable out of the deposit for emergency relief proceedings. The determination of costs pursuant to Article 38(d) and (e) and the apportionment of all costs among the parties shall be decided by the arbitral tribunal. If no arbitral tribunal is constituted, the determination of costs pursuant to Article 38(d) and (e) and the apportionment of all costs shall be decided by the emergency arbitrator in a separate award.

10. Any measure granted by the emergency arbitrator ceases to be binding on the parties either upon the termination of the emergency relief proceedings pursuant to Article 43(3), upon the termination of the arbitral proceedings, or upon the rendering of a final award, unless the arbitral tribunal expressly decides otherwise in the final award.

11. The emergency arbitrator may not serve as arbitrator in any arbitration relating to the dispute in respect of which the emergency arbitrator has acted, unless otherwise agreed by the parties.

Article 44

Confidentiality

1. Unless the parties expressly agree in writing to the contrary, the parties undertake to keep confidential all awards and orders as well as all materials submitted by another party in the framework of the arbitral proceedings not already in the public domain, except and to the extent that a disclosure may be required of a party by a legal duty, to protect or pursue a legal right, or to enforce or challenge an award in legal proceedings before a judicial authority. This undertaking also applies to the arbitrators, the tribunal-appointed experts, the secretary of the arbitral tribunal, the members of the board of directors of the Swiss Chambers' Arbitration Institution, the members of the Court and the Secretariat, and the staff of the individual Chambers.

2. The deliberations of the arbitral tribunal are confidential.

3. An award or order may be published, whether in its entirety or in the form of excerpts or a summary, only under the following conditions:

(a) A request for publication is addressed to the Secretariat;

(b) All references to the parties' names are deleted; and

(c) No party objects to such publication within the time-limit fixed for that purpose by the Secretariat.

Article 45

Exclusion of Liability

1.   Neither the members of the board of directors of the Swiss Chambers' Arbitration Institution, the members of the Court and the Secretariat, the individual Chambers or their staff, the arbitrators, the tribunal-appointed experts, nor the secretary of the arbitral tribunal shall be liable for any act or omission in connection with an arbitration conducted under these Rules, except if the act or omission is shown to constitute intentional wrongdoing or gross negligence.

2.   After the award or termination order has been made and the possibilities of correction, interpretation and additional awards referred to in Articles 35 to 37 have lapsed or have been exhausted, neither the members of the board of the Swiss Chambers' Arbitration Institution, the members of the Court and the Secretariat, the individual Chambers or their staff, the arbitrators, the tribunal-appointed experts, nor the secretary of the arbitral tribunal shall be under an obligation to make statements to any person about any matter concerning the arbitration. No party shall seek to make any of these persons a witness in any legal or other proceedings arising out of the arbitration.

Appendix A. Offices of the Secretariat of the Arbitration Court

Swiss Chambers' Arbitration Institution

Arbitration Court

Secretariat

c/o Basel Chamber of Commerce

Aeschenvorstadt 67

P.O. Box

CH–4010 Basel

Telephone: +41 61 270 60 50

Fax: +41 61 270 60 05

E-mail: basel@swissarbitration.org

Bank details: UBS AG, CH–4002 Basel

Account No: 292–10157720.0

Clearing No: 292

Swift Code: UBSWCHZH80A

Iban: CH98 0029 2292 10157720 0

c/o Chamber of Commerce and Industry of Bern

Kramgasse 2

P.O. Box 5464

CH–3001 Bern

Telephone: +41 31 388 87 87

Fax: +41 31 388 87 88

E-mail: bern@swissarbitration.org

Bank details: BEKB

Account No: KK 16 166.151.0.44 HIV Kanton Bern

Clearing No: 790

Swift Code: KBBECH22

Iban: CH35 0079 0016 1661 5104 4

c/o Geneva Chamber of Commerce, Industry and Services

4, Boulevard du Théâtre

P.O. Box 5039

CH–1211 Geneva 11

Telephone: +41 22 819 91 11

Fax: +41 22 819 91 36

E-mail: geneva@swissarbitration.org

Bank details: UBS SA, Rue du Rhône 8, 1204 Genève

Account No: 279–HU108533.1

Clearing No: 279

Swift code: UBSWCHZH80A

Iban: CH13 0027 9279 HU1085331

c/o Neuchatel Chamber of Commerce and Industry

4, rue de la Serre

P.O. Box 2012

CH–2001 Neuchâtel

Telephone: +41 32 722 15 22

Fax: +41 32 722 15 20

E-mail: neuchatel@swissarbitration.org

Bank: BCN, Neuchâtel

Account No.: C0029.20.09

Clearing Nr: 766

Swift code: BCNNCH22

Iban: CH69 0076 6000 C002 9200 9

c/o Chamber of Commerce and Industry of Ticino

Corso Elvezia 16

P.O. Box 5399

CH–6901 Lugano

Telephone: +41 91 911 51 11

Fax: +41 91 911 51 12

E-mail: lugano@swissarbitration.org

Bank details: Banca della Svizzera Italiana (BSI), Via Magatti 2, CH–6901 Lugano

Account No: A201021A

Clearing No: 8465

Swift code: BSILCH22

Iban: CH64 0846 5000 0A20 1021 A

c/o Chamber of Commerce and Industry of Vaud

Avenue d'Ouchy 47

P.O. Box 315

CH–1001 Lausanne

Telephone: +41 21 613 35 31

Fax: +41 21 613 35 05

E-mail: lausanne@swissarbitration.org

Bank details: Banque Cantonale Vaudoise, 1001 Lausanne

Account No: CO 5284.78.17

Clearing No: 767

Swift Code: BCVLCH2LXX

Iban: CH44 0076 7000 U528 4781 7

c/o Zurich Chamber of Commerce

Selnaustrasse 32

P.O. Box 3058

CH–8022 Zurich

Telephone: +41 44 217 40 50

Fax: +41 44 217 40 51

E-mail: zurich@swissarbitration.org

Bank details: Credit Suisse, CH–8070 Zurich

Account No: 497380–01

Clearing No: 4835

Swift Code: CRESCHZZ80A

Iban: CH62 0483 5049 7380 0100 0

Appendix B. Schedule of Costs (effective as of 1 June 2012)

(All amounts in this Appendix B are in Swiss francs, hereinafter "CHF")

1. Registration Fee and Deposits

1.1 When submitting a Notice of Arbitration, the Claimant shall pay a non-refundable Registration Fee of

- CHF 4'500 for arbitrations where the amount in dispute does not exceed CHF 2'000'000;
- CHF 6'000 for arbitrations where the amount in dispute is between CHF 2'000'001 and CHF 10'000'000;
- CHF 8'000 for arbitrations where the amount in dispute exceeds CHF10'000'000.

1.2 If the amount in dispute is not quantified, the Claimant shall pay a non-refundable Registration Fee of CHF 6'000.

1.3 The above provisions shall apply to any counterclaim.

1.4 Under the Expedited Procedure, upon receipt of the Notice of Arbitration, the Court shall request the Claimant to pay a Provisional Deposit of CHF 5'000.

1.5 If the Registration Fee or any Provisional Deposit is not paid, the arbitration shall not proceed with respect to the related claim(s) or counterclaim(s).

1.6 A party applying for Emergency Relief shall pay a non-refundable Registration Fee of CHF 4'500 and a deposit as an advance for the costs of the emergency relief proceedings of CHF 20'000 together with the Application. If the Registration Fee and the deposit are not paid, the Court shall not proceed with the emergency relief proceedings.

1.7 In case of a request for the correction or interpretation of the award or for an additional award made pursuant to Articles 35, 36 or 37, or where a judicial authority remits an award to the arbitral tribunal, the arbitral tribunal may request a supplementary deposit with prior approval of the Court.

2. Fees and Administrative Costs

2.1 The fees referred to in Articles 38(a) and (g) shall cover the activities of the arbitral tribunal and the emergency arbitrator, respectively, from the moment the file is transmitted until the final award, termination order, or decision in emergency relief proceedings.

2.2 Where the amount in dispute exceeds the threshold specified in Section 6 of this Appendix B, Administrative Costs[2] shall be payable to the Swiss Chambers' Arbitration Institution, in addition to the Registration Fee.

2.3 As a rule, and except for emergency relief proceedings, the fees of the arbitral tribunal and the Administrative Costs shall be computed on the basis of the scale in Section 6 of this Appendix B, taking into account the criteria of Article 39(1). The fees of the arbitral tribunal, the deposits requested pursuant to Article 41, as well as the Administrative Costs may exceed the amounts set out in the scale only in exceptional circumstances and with prior approval of the Court.

2.4 Claims and counterclaims are added for the determination of the amount in dispute. The same rule applies to set-off defences, unless the arbitral tribunal, after consulting with the parties, concludes that such set-off defences will not require significant additional work.

2.5 Interest claims shall not be taken into account for the calculation of the amount in dispute. However, when the interest claims exceed the amount claimed as principal, the interest claims alone shall be taken into account for the calculation of the amount in dispute.

2.6 Amounts in currencies other than the Swiss franc shall be converted into Swiss francs at the rate of exchange applicable at the time the Notice of Arbitration is received by the Secretariat or at the time any new claim, counterclaim, set-off defence or amendment to a claim or defence is filed.

2.7 If the amount in dispute is not quantified, the fees of the arbitral tribunal and the Administrative Costs shall be determined by the arbitral tribunal, taking into account all relevant circumstances.

2.8 Where the parties do not agree to refer the case to a sole arbitrator as provided for by Article 42(2) (Expedited Procedure), the fees of the arbitrators shall be determined in accordance with the scale in Section 6 of this Appendix B, but shall not be less than the fees resulting from the application of an hourly rate of CHF 350 (three hundred fifty Swiss francs) for the arbitrators.

---

[2] This is a contribution, in the maximum amount of CHF 50,000, to the Administrative Costs of the Swiss Chambers' Arbitration Institution, in addition to the Registration Fee. In the event of a discontinuation of the arbitral proceedings (Article 39(1)), the Swiss Chambers' Arbitration Institution may, in its discretion, decide not to charge all or part of the Administrative Costs.

2.9 The fees of the emergency arbitrator shall range from CHF 2'000 to CHF 20'000. They may exceed CHF 20'000 only in exceptional circumstances and with the approval of the Court.

3. Expenses

The expenses of the arbitral tribunal and the emergency arbitrator shall cover their reasonable disbursements for the arbitration, such as expenses for travel, accommodation, meals, and any other costs related to the conduct of the proceedings. The Court shall issue general guidelines for the accounting of such expenses[3].

4. Administration of Deposits

4.1 The Secretariat or, if so requested by the Secretariat, the arbitral tribunal, is to hold the deposits to be paid by the parties in a separate bank account which is solely used for, and clearly identified as relating to, the arbitral proceedings in question.

4.2 With the approval of the Court, part of the deposits may from time to time be released to each member of the arbitral tribunal as an advance on costs, as the arbitration progresses.

5. Taxes and Charges Applicable to Fees

Amounts payable to the arbitral tribunal or emergency arbitrator do not include any possible value added taxes (VAT) or other taxes or charges that may be applicable to the fees of a member of the arbitral tribunal or emergency arbitrator. Parties have a duty to pay any such taxes or charges. The recovery of any such taxes or charges is a matter solely between each member of the arbitral tribunal, or the emergency arbitrator, on the one hand, and the parties, on the other.

6. Scale of Arbitrator's Fees and Administrative Costs

6.1 Sole Arbitrator

Amount in dispute (in Swiss francs)	Administrative costs	Sole Arbitrator	
		Minimum	Maximum
0–300'000	–	4% of amount	12% of amount
300'001–600'000	–	12'000 + 2% of amount over 300'000	36'000 + 8% of amount over 300'000

---

[3]   The guidelines are available at www.swissarbitration.org.

600'001– 1'000'000	–	18'000 + 1.5% of amount over 600'000	60'000 + 6% of amount over 600'000
1'000'001– 2'000'000	–	24'000 + 0.6% of amount over 1'000'000	84'000 + 3.6% of amount over 1'000'000
2'000'001– 10'000'000	4'000 + 0.2% of amount over 2'000'000	30'000 + 0.38% of amount over 2'000'000	120'000 + 1.5% of amount over 2'000'000
10'000'001– 20'000'000	20'000 + 0.1% of amount over 10'000'000	60'400 + 0.3% of amount over 10'000'000	240'000 + 0.6% of amount over 10'000'000
20'000'001– 50'000'000	30'000 + 0.05% of amount over 20'000'000	90'400 + 0.1% of amount over 20'000'000	300'000 + 0.2% of amount over 20'000'000
50'000'001– 100'000'000	45'000 + 0.01% of amount over 50'000'000	120'400 + 0.06% of amount over 50'000'000	360'000 + 0.18% of amount over 50'000'000
100'000'001– 250'000'000	50'000	150'400 + 0.02% of amount over 100'000'000	450'000 + 0,1% of amount over 100'000'000
> 250'000'000	50'000	180'400 + 0.01% of amount over 250'000'000	600'000 + 0.06% of amount over 250'000'000

6.2 Three Arbitrators[4]

Amount in dispute (in Swiss francs)	Administrative costs	Three-member arbitral tribunal	
		Minimum	Maximum
0–300'000	–	10% of amount	30% of amount
300'001– 600'000	–	30'000 + 5% of amount over 300'000	90'000 + 20% of amount over 300'000

---

[4]   The fees of an arbitral tribunal consisting of more than one arbitrator represent those of a sole arbitrator plus 75% for each additional arbitrator, i.e. 250% of the fees of a sole arbitrator for a three-member tribunal.

600'001–1'000'000	–	45'000 + 3.75% of amount over 600'000	150'000 + 15% of amount over 600'000
1'000'001–2'000'000	–	60'000 + 1.5% of amount over 1'000'000	210'000 + 9% of amount over 1'000'000
2'000'001–10'000'000	4'000 + 0.2% of amount over 2'000'000	75'000 + 0.95% of amount over 2'000'000	300'000 + 3.75% of amount over 2'000'000
10'000'001–20'000'000	20'000 + 0.1% of amount over 10'000'000	151'000 + 0.75% of amount over 10'000'000	600'000 + 1.5% of amount over 10'000'000
20'000'001–50'000'000	30'000 + 0.05% of amount over 20'000'000	226'000 + 0.25% of amount over 20'000'000	750'000 + 0.5% of amount over 20'000'000
50'000'001–100'000'000	45'000 + 0.01% of amount over 50'000'000	301'000 + 0.15% of amount over 50'000'000	900'000 + 0.45% of amount over 50'000'000
100'000'001–250'000'000	50'000	376'000 + 0.05% of amount over 100'000'000	1'125'000 + 0,25% of amount over 100'000'000
> 250'000'000	50'000	451'000 + 0.025% of amount over 250'000'000	1'500'000 + 0.15% of amount over 250'000'000

Chapter V

Specialized Arbitration Rules

∎ ∎ ∎

A. STOCKHOLM RULES FOR EXPEDITED ARBITRATIONS

RULES FOR EXPEDITED ARBITRATIONS OF THE STOCKHOLM CHAMBER OF COMMERCE[*]

(Adopted by the Stockholm Chamber of Commerce
and in force as of 1 January 2010)

Article 1 About the SCC

The Arbitration Institute of the Stockholm Chamber of Commerce (the "SCC") is the body responsible for the administration of disputes in accordance with the "SCC Rules"; the Arbitration Rules of the Arbitration Institute of the Stockholm Chamber of Commerce (the "Arbitration Rules") and the Rules for Expedited Arbitrations of the Stockholm Chamber of Commerce (the "Rules for Expedited Arbitrations"), and other procedures or rules agreed upon by the parties. The SCC is composed of a board of directors (the "Board") and a secretariat (the "Secretariat"). Detailed provisions regarding the organisation of the SCC are set out in Appendix I.

Commencement of proceedings

Article 2 Request for Arbitration

A Request for Arbitration shall include:

(i)   a statement of the names, addresses, telephone and facsimile numbers and e-mail addresses of the parties and their counsel;

(ii)   a summary of the dispute;

(iii) a preliminary statement of the relief sought by the Claimant;

(iv) a copy or description of the arbitration agreement or clause under which the dispute is to be settled; and

(v)   comments on the seat of arbitration.

---

[*]   Available   at: http://www.sccinstitute.com/dispute-resolution/expedited-arbitration/.
Reprinted with permission of the Arbitration Institute of the Stockholm Chamber of Commerce.

Article 3 Registration Fee

(1)   Upon filing the Request for Arbitration, the Claimant shall pay a Registration Fee. The amount of the Registration Fee shall be determined in accordance with the Schedule of Costs (Appendix III) in force on the date when the Request for Arbitration is filed.

(2)   If the Registration Fee is not paid upon filing the Request for Arbitration, the Secretariat shall set a time period within which the Claimant shall pay the Registration Fee. If the Registration Fee is not paid within this time period, the Secretariat shall dismiss the Request for Arbitration.

Article 4 Commencement of arbitration

Arbitration is commenced on the date when the SCC receives the Request for Arbitration.

Article 5 Answer

(1)   The Secretariat shall send a copy of the Request for Arbitration and the documents attached thereto to the Respondent. The Secretariat shall set a time period within which the Respondent shall submit an Answer to the SCC. The Answer shall include:

> (i)   any objections concerning the existence, validity or applicability of the arbitration agreement; however, failure to raise any objections shall not preclude the Respondent from subsequently raising such objections at any time up to and including the submission of the Statement of Defence;

> (ii)   an admission or denial of the relief sought in the Request for Arbitration;

> (iii) a preliminary statement of any counterclaims or set-offs; and

> (iv) comments on the seat of arbitration.

(2)   The Secretariat shall send a copy of the Answer to the Claimant. The Claimant shall be given an opportunity to submit comments on the Answer.

(3)   Failure by the Respondent to submit an Answer shall not prevent the arbitration from proceeding.

Article 6 Request for further details

The Board may request further details from either party regarding any of their written submissions to the SCC. If the Claimant fails to comply with a request for further details, the Board may dismiss the case. If the Respondent fails to comply with a request for further details regarding its counterclaim or set-off, the Board may dismiss the counterclaim or set-off. Failure by the Respondent to otherwise comply with a request for further details shall not prevent the arbitration from proceeding.

Article 7 Time periods

The Board may, on application by either party or on its own motion, extend any time period which has been set for a party to comply with a particular direction.

Article 8 Notices

(1)   Any notice or other communication from the Secretariat or the Board shall be delivered to the last known address of the addressee.

(2)   Any notice or other communication shall be delivered by courier or registered mail, facsimile transmission, e-mail or any other means of communication that provides a record of the sending thereof.

(3)   A notice or communication sent in accordance with paragraph (2) shall be deemed to have been received by the addressee on the date it would normally have been received given the chosen means of communication.

Article 9 Decisions by the Board

When necessary the Board shall:

   (i)   decide whether the SCC manifestly lacks jurisdiction over the dispute pursuant to Article 10 (i);

   (ii)   decide whether to consolidate cases pursuant to Article 11;

   (iii) make any appointment of arbitrator pursuant to Article 13;

   (iv)   decide the seat of arbitration pursuant to Article 20; and

   (v)   determine the Advance on Costs pursuant to Article 44.

Article 10 Dismissal

The Board shall dismiss a case, in whole or in part, if:

   (i)   the SCC manifestly lacks jurisdiction over the dispute; or

   (ii)   the Advance on Costs is not paid pursuant to Article 44.

Article 11 Consolidation

If arbitration is commenced concerning a legal relationship in respect of which an arbitration between the same parties is already pending under these Rules, the Board may, at the request of a party, decide to consolidate the new claims with the pending proceedings. Such decision may only be made after consulting the parties and the Arbitrator.

The Arbitrator

Article 12 Number of Arbitrators

The arbitration shall be decided by a sole Arbitrator.

Article 13 Appointment of Arbitrator

(1)   The parties may agree on a different procedure for appointment of the Arbitrator than as provided under this Article. In such cases, if the Arbitrator has not been appointed within the time period agreed by the parties or, where the parties have not agreed on a time period, within the time period set by the Board, the appointment shall be made pursuant to paragraphs (2)–(4).

(2)   The parties shall be given 10 days within which to jointly appoint the Arbitrator. If the parties fail to make the appointment within this time period, the Arbitrator shall be appointed by the Board.

(3)   If the parties are of different nationalities, the Arbitrator shall be of a different nationality than the parties, unless the parties have agreed otherwise or unless otherwise deemed appropriate by the Board.

(4)   When appointing Arbitrator, the Board shall consider the nature and circumstances of the dispute, the applicable law, the seat and language of the arbitration and the nationality of the parties.

Article 14 Impartiality and independence

(1)   The Arbitrator must be impartial and independent.

(2)   Before being appointed as Arbitrator, a person shall disclose any circumstances which may give rise to justifiable doubts as to his/her impartiality or independence. If the person is appointed as Arbitrator, he/she shall submit to the Secretariat a signed statement of impartiality and independence disclosing any circumstances which may give rise to justifiable doubts as to that person's impartiality or independence. The Secretariat shall send a copy of the statement of impartiality and independence to the parties.

(3)   The Arbitrator shall immediately inform the parties in writing where any circumstances referred to in paragraph (2) arise during the course of the arbitration.

Article 15 Challenge to Arbitrator

(1)   A party may challenge the Arbitrator if circumstances exist which give rise to justifiable doubts as to the Arbitrator's impartiality or independence or if he/she does not possess qualifications agreed by the parties.

(2)   A challenge to the Arbitrator shall be made by submitting a written statement to the Secretariat setting forth the reasons for the challenge within 15 days from when the circumstances giving rise to the challenge became known to the party. Failure by a party to challenge the Arbitrator within the stipulated time period constitutes a waiver of the right to make the challenge.

(3) The Secretariat shall notify the parties and the Arbitrator of the challenge and give them an opportunity to submit comments on the challenge.

(4) If the other party agrees to the challenge, the Arbitrator shall resign. In all other cases, the Board shall make the final decision on the challenge.

Article 16 Release from appointment

(1) The Board shall release the Arbitrator from appointment where:

    (i) the Board accepts the resignation of the Arbitrator;

    (ii) a challenge to the Arbitrator under Article 15 is sustained; or

    (iii) the Arbitrator is otherwise prevented from fulfilling his/her duties or fails to perform his/her functions in an adequate manner.

(2) Before the Board releases an arbitrator, the Secretariat may give the parties and the Arbitrator an opportunity to submit comments.

Article 17 Replacement of Arbitrator

(1) The Board shall appoint a new Arbitrator where the Arbitrator has been released from his/her appointment pursuant to Article 16, or where the Arbitrator has died.

(2) Where the Arbitrator has been replaced, the new Arbitrator shall decide whether and to what extent the proceedings are to be repeated.

The proceedings before the Arbitrator

Article 18 Referral to the Arbitrator

When the Arbitrator has been appointed and the Advance on Costs has been paid, the Secretariat shall refer the case to the Arbitrator.

Article 19 Conduct of the arbitration

(1) Subject to these Rules and any agreement between the parties, the Arbitrator may conduct the arbitration in such manner as the Arbitrator considers appropriate.

(2) In all cases, the Arbitrator shall conduct the arbitration in an impartial, practical and expeditious manner, giving each party an equal and reasonable opportunity to present its case.

(3) The following shall apply to the proceedings, unless the Arbitrator, for special reasons, decides otherwise:

    (i) in addition to the Statement of Claim and the Statement of Defence, the parties each may only submit one written statement, including statements of evidence;

    (ii) the statements must be brief; and

(iii) the time limits within which the documents shall be submitted may not exceed 10 working days.

(4)   The Arbitrator may order a party to finally state its claims for relief and the facts relied on as grounds thereof, and the evidence on which the party relies. At the expiration of the time period for such statement, the party may not amend its claim for relief nor adduce additional facts or evidence, unless the Arbitrator, for special reasons, so permits.

Article 20 Seat of arbitration

(1)   Unless agreed upon by the parties, the Board shall decide the seat of arbitration.

(2)   The Arbitrator may, after consultation with the parties, conduct hearings at any place which the Arbitrator considers appropriate. If any hearing or meeting is held elsewhere than at the seat of arbitration, the arbitration shall be deemed to have taken place at the seat of arbitration.

(3)   The award shall be deemed to have been made at the seat of arbitration.

Article 21 Language

(1)   Unless agreed upon by the parties, the Arbitrator shall determine the language(s) of the arbitration. In so determining, the Arbitrator shall have due regard to all relevant circumstances and shall give the parties an opportunity to submit comments.

(2)   The Arbitrator may request that any documents submitted in languages other than the language(s) of the arbitration be accompanied by a translation into the language(s) of the arbitration.

Article 22 Applicable law

(1)   The Arbitrator shall decide the merits of the dispute on the basis of the law(s) or rules of law agreed upon by the parties. In the absence of such agreement, the Arbitrator shall apply the law or rules of law which the Arbitrator considers to be most appropriate.

(2)   Any designation made by the parties of the law of a given state shall be deemed to refer to the substantive law of that state and not to its conflict of laws rules.

(3)   The Arbitrator shall decide the dispute *ex aequo et bono* or as *amiable compositeur* only if the parties have expressly authorised the Arbitrator to do so.

Article 23 Timetable

After the referral of the case to the Arbitrator, the Arbitrator shall promptly establish a timetable for the conduct of the arbitration. The

Arbitrator shall send a copy of the timetable to the parties and to the Secretariat.

Article 24 Written submissions

(1) The Claimant shall, within the period of time determined by the Arbitrator, submit a Statement of Claim which shall include, unless previously submitted:

> (i)   the specific relief sought;
>
> (ii) the material circumstances on which the Claimant relies; and
>
> (iii) the documents on which the Claimant relies.

(2) The Respondent shall, within the period of time determined by the Arbitrator, submit a Statement of Defence which shall include, unless previously submitted:

> (i)   any objections concerning the existence, validity or applicability of the arbitration agreement;
>
> (ii) a statement whether, and to what extent, the Respondent admits or denies the relief sought by the Claimant;
>
> (iii) the material circumstances on which the Respondent relies;
>
> (iv) any counterclaim or set-off and the grounds on which it is based; and
>
> (v)   the documents on which the Respondent relies.

(3) The Arbitrator may order the parties to submit additional written submissions.

Article 25 Amendments

At any time prior to the close of proceedings pursuant to Article 34, a party may amend or supplement its claim, counterclaim, defence or set-off provided its case, as amended or supplemented, is still comprised by the arbitration agreement, unless the Arbitrator considers it inappropriate to allow such amendment or supplement having regard to the delay in making it, the prejudice to the other party or any other circumstances.

Article 26 Evidence

(1) The admissibility, relevance, materiality and weight of evidence shall be for the Arbitrator to determine.

(2) The Arbitrator may order a party to identify the documentary evidence it intends to rely on and specify the circumstances intended to be proved by such evidence.

(3) At the request of a party, the Arbitrator may order a party to produce any documents or other evidence which may be relevant to the outcome of the case.

Article 27 Hearings

(1) A hearing shall be held if requested by a party and if deemed necessary by the Arbitrator.

(2) The Arbitrator shall, in consultation with the parties, determine the date, time and location of any hearing and shall provide the parties with reasonable notice thereof.

(3) Unless otherwise agreed by the parties, hearings will be held in private.

Article 28 Witnesses

(1) In advance of any hearing, the Arbitrator may order the parties to identify each witness or expert they intend to call and specify the circumstances intended to be proved by each testimony.

(2) The testimony of witnesses or party-appointed experts may be submitted in the form of signed statements.

(3) Any witness or expert, on whose testimony a party seeks to rely, shall attend a hearing for examination, unless otherwise agreed by the parties.

Article 29 Experts appointed by the Arbitrator

(1) After consultation with the parties, the Arbitrator may appoint one or more experts to report to the Arbitrator on specific issues set out by the Arbitrator in writing.

(2) Upon receipt of a report from an expert appointed by the Arbitrator, the Arbitrator shall send a copy of the report to the parties and shall give the parties an opportunity to submit written comments on the report.

(3) Upon the request of a party, the parties shall be given an opportunity to examine any expert appointed by the Arbitrator at a hearing.

Article 30 Default

(1) If the Claimant, without showing good cause, fails to submit a Statement of Claim in accordance with Article 24, the Arbitrator shall terminate the proceedings provided the Respondent has not filed a counterclaim.

(2) If a party, without showing good cause, fails to submit a Statement of Defence or other written statement in accordance with Article 24, or fails to appear at a hearing, or otherwise fails to avail itself of the opportunity to present its case, the Arbitrator may proceed with the arbitration and make an award.

(3) If a party without good cause fails to comply with any provision of, or requirement under, these Rules or any procedural order given by the Arbitrator, the Arbitrator may draw such inferences as it considers appropriate.

Article 31 Waiver

A party, who during the arbitration fails to object without delay to any failure to comply with the arbitration agreement, these Rules or other rules applicable to the proceedings, shall be deemed to have waived the right to object to such failure.

Article 32 Interim measures

(1) The Arbitrator may, at the request of a party, grant any interim measures the Arbitrator deems appropriate.

(2) The Arbitrator may order the party requesting an interim measure to provide appropriate security in connection with the measure.

(3) An interim measure shall take the form of an order or an award.

(4) Provisions with respect to interim measures requested before arbitration has been commenced or a case has been referred to an Arbitrator are set out in Appendix II.

(5) A request for interim measures made by a party to a judicial authority is not incompatible with the arbitration agreement or with these Rules.

Article 33 Communications from the Arbitrator

Article 8 shall apply to communications from the Arbitrator.

Article 34 Close of proceedings

The Arbitrator shall declare the proceedings closed when the Arbitrator is satisfied that the parties have had a reasonable opportunity to present their cases. In exceptional circumstances, prior to the making of the final award, the Arbitrator may reopen the proceedings on the Arbitrator's own motion, or upon the application of a party.

Awards and decisions

Article 35 Making of awards

(1) The Arbitrator shall make the award in writing and sign the award. A party may request a reasoned award no later than at the closing statement.

(2) An award shall include the date of the award and the seat of arbitration in accordance with Article 20.

(3) The Arbitrator shall deliver a copy of the award to each of the parties and to the SCC without delay.

Article 36 Time limit for final award

The final award shall be made not later than three months from the date upon which the arbitration was referred to the Arbitrator pursuant to Article 18. The Board may extend this time limit upon a reasoned request from the Arbitrator, or if otherwise deemed necessary.

Article 37 Separate award

The Arbitrator may decide a separate issue or part of the dispute in a separate award.

Article 38 Settlement or other grounds for termination of the arbitration

(1) If the parties reach a settlement before the final award is made, the Arbitrator may, upon the request of both parties, record the settlement in the form of a consent award.

(2) If the arbitration for any other reason is terminated before the final award is made, the Arbitrator shall issue an award recording the termination.

Article 39 Effect of an award

An award shall be final and binding on the parties when rendered. By agreeing to arbitration under these Rules, the parties undertake to carry out any award without delay.

Article 40 Correction and interpretation of an award

(1) Within 30 days of receiving an award, a party may, upon notice to the other party, request that the Arbitrator correct any clerical, typographical or computational errors in the award, or provide an interpretation of a specific point or part of the award. If the Arbitrator considers the request justified, the Arbitrator shall make the correction or provide the interpretation within 30 days of receiving the request.

(2) The Arbitrator may correct any error of the type referred to in paragraph (1) above on the Arbitrator's own motion within 30 days of the date of an award.

(3) Any correction or interpretation of an award shall be in writing and shall comply with the requirements of Article 35.

Article 41 Additional award

Within 30 days of receiving an award, a party may, upon notice to the other party, request the Arbitrator to make an additional award on claims presented in the arbitration but not determined in the award. If the Arbitrator considers the request justified, the Arbitrator shall make the additional award within 30 days of receipt of the request. When deemed necessary, the Board may extend this 30 day time limit.

Costs of the Arbitration

Article 42 Costs of the Arbitration

(1) The Costs of the Arbitration consist of:

(i)   the Fee of the Arbitrator;

(ii) the Administrative Fee; and

(iii) the expenses of the Arbitrator and the SCC.

(2)   Before making the final award, the Arbitrator shall request the Board to finally determine the Costs of the Arbitration. The Board shall finally determine the Costs of the Arbitration in accordance with the Schedule of Costs (Appendix III) in force on the date of commencement of the arbitration pursuant to Article 4.

(3)   If the arbitration is terminated before the final award is made pursuant to Article 38, the Board shall finally determine the Costs of the Arbitration having regard to when the arbitration terminates, the work performed by the Arbitrator and other relevant circumstances. The Arbitrator shall include in the final award the Costs of the Arbitration as finally determined by the Board and specify the fees and expenses of the Arbitrator and the SCC.

(4)   Unless otherwise agreed by the parties, the Arbitrator shall, at the request of a party, apportion the Costs of the Arbitration between the parties, having regard to the outcome of the case and other relevant circumstances.

(5)   The parties are jointly and severally liable to the Arbitrator and to the SCC for the Costs of the Arbitration.

Article 43 Costs incurred by a party

Unless otherwise agreed by the parties, the Arbitrator may in the final award, upon the request of a party, order one party to pay any reasonable costs incurred by another party, including costs for legal representation, having regard to the outcome of the case and other relevant circumstances.

Article 44 Advance on Costs

(1)   The Board shall determine an amount to be paid by the parties as an Advance on Costs.

(2)   The Advance on Costs shall correspond to the estimated amount of the Costs of Arbitration pursuant to Article 42 (1).

(3)   Each party shall pay half of the Advance on Costs, unless separate advances are determined. Where counterclaims or set-offs are submitted, the Board may decide that each of the parties shall pay the advances on costs corresponding to its claim. Upon a request from the Arbitrator or if otherwise deemed necessary, the Board may order parties to pay additional advances during the course of the arbitration.

(4)   If a party fails to make a required payment, the Secretariat shall give the other party an opportunity to do so within a specified period of time. If the required payment is not made, the Board shall dismiss the case in whole or in part. If the other party makes the required payment, the

Arbitrator may, at the request of such party, make a separate award for reimbursement of the payment.

(5)   At any stage during the arbitration or after the Award has been made, the Board may draw on the Advance on Costs to cover the Costs of the Arbitration.

(6)   The Board may decide that part of the Advance on Costs may be provided in the form of a bank guarantee or other form of security.

General rules

Article 45 Confidentiality

Unless otherwise agreed by the parties, the SCC and the Arbitrator shall maintain the confidentiality of the arbitration and the award.

Article 46 Enforcement

In all matters not expressly provided for in these Rules, the SCC, the Arbitrator and the parties shall act in the spirit of these Rules and shall make every reasonable effort to ensure that all awards are legally enforceable.

Article 47 Exclusion of liability

Neither the SCC nor the arbitrator are liable to any party for any act or omission in connection with the arbitration unless such act or omission constitutes willful misconduct or gross negligence.

APPENDIX I
ORGANISATION

Article 1 About the SCC

The Arbitration Institute of the Stockholm Chamber of Commerce (the "SCC") is a body providing administrative services in relation to the settlement of disputes. The SCC is part of the Stockholm Chamber of Commerce, but is independent in exercising its functions in the administration of disputes. The SCC is composed of a board of directors (the "Board") and a secretariat (the "Secretariat").

Article 2 Function of the SCC

The SCC does not itself decide disputes. The function of the SCC is to:

(i)   administer domestic and international disputes in accordance with the SCC Rules and other procedures or rules agreed upon by the parties; and

(ii) provide information concerning arbitration and mediation matters.

Article 3 The Board

The Board shall be composed of one chairperson, a maximum of three vice-chairpersons and a maximum of 12 additional members. The Board includes both Swedish and non-Swedish nationals.

Article 4 Appointment of the Board

The Board shall be appointed by the Board of Directors of the Stockholm Chamber of Commerce (the "Board of Directors"). The members of the Board shall be appointed for a period of three years and are eligible for re-appointment in their respective capacities for one further three year period only, unless exceptional circumstances apply.

Article 5 Removal of a member of the Board

In exceptional circumstances, the Board of Directors may remove a member of the Board. If a member resigns or is removed during a term of office, the Board of Directors shall appoint a new member for the remainder of the term.

Article 6 Function of the Board

The function of the Board is to take the decisions required of the SCC in administering disputes under the SCC Rules and any other rules or procedures agreed upon by the parties. Such decisions include decisions on the jurisdiction of the SCC, determination of advances on costs, appointment of arbitrators, decisions upon challenges to arbitrators, removal of arbitrators and the fixing of arbitration costs.

Article 7 Decisions by the Board

Two members of the Board form a quorum. If a majority is not attained, the Chairperson has the casting vote. The Chairperson or a Vice Chairperson may take decisions on behalf of the Board in urgent matters. A committee of the Board may be appointed to take certain decisions on behalf of the Board. The Board may delegate decisions to the Secretariat, including decisions on advances on costs, extension of time for rendering an award, dismissal for non-payment of registration fee, release of arbitrators and fixing of arbitration costs. Decisions by the Board are final.

Article 8 The Secretariat

The Secretariat acts under the direction of a Secretary General. The Secretariat carries out the functions assigned to it under the SCC Rules. The Secretariat may also take decisions delegated to it by the Board.

Article 9 Procedures

The SCC shall maintain the confidentiality of the arbitration and the award and shall deal with the arbitration in an impartial, practical and expeditious manner.

APPENDIX II
EMERGENCY ARBITRATOR

Article 1 Emergency Arbitrator

(1) A party may apply for the appointment of an Emergency Arbitrator until the case has been referred to the Arbitrator pursuant to Article 18 of the Rules for Expedited Arbitrations.

(2) The powers of the Emergency Arbitrator shall be those set out in Article 32 (1)–(3) of the Rules for Expedited Arbitrations. Such powers terminate when the case has been referred to the Arbitrator pursuant to Article 18 of the Rules for Expedited Arbitrations or when an emergency decision ceases to be binding according to Article 9 (4) of this Appendix.

Article 2 Application for the appointment of an Emergency Arbitrator

An application for the appointment of an Emergency Arbitrator shall include:

(i)   a statement of the names and addresses, telephone and facsimile numbers and e-mail addresses of the parties and their counsel;

(ii) a summary of the dispute;

(iii) a statement of the interim relief sought and the reasons therefor;

(iv) a copy or description of the arbitration agreement or clause on the basis of which the dispute is to be settled;

(v)   comments on the seat of the emergency proceedings, the applicable law(s) and the language(s) of the proceedings; and

(vi) proof of payment of the costs for the emergency proceedings pursuant to Article 10 (1)–(2) of this Appendix.

Article 3 Notice

As soon as an application for the appointment of an Emergency Arbitrator has been received, the Secretariat shall send the application to the other party.

Article 4 Appointment of the Emergency Arbitrator

(1) The Board shall seek to appoint an Emergency Arbitrator within 24 hours of receipt of the application for the appointment of an Emergency Arbitrator.

(2) An Emergency Arbitrator shall not be appointed if the SCC manifestly lacks jurisdiction over the dispute.

(3) Article 15 of the Rules for Expedited Arbitrations applies except that a challenge must be made within 24 hours from when the circumstances

giving rise to the challenge of an Emergency Arbitrator became known to the party.

(4) An Emergency Arbitrator may not act as an arbitrator in any future arbitration relating to the dispute, unless otherwise agreed by the parties.

Article 5 Seat of the emergency proceedings

The seat of the emergency proceedings shall be that which has been agreed upon by the parties as the seat of the arbitration. If the seat of the arbitration has not been agreed by the parties, the Board shall determine the seat of the emergency proceedings.

Article 6 Referral to the Emergency Arbitrator

Once an Emergency Arbitrator has been appointed, the Secretariat shall promptly refer the application to the Emergency Arbitrator.

Article 7 Conduct of the emergency proceedings

Article 19 of the Rules for Expedited Arbitrations shall apply to the emergency proceedings, taking into account the urgency inherent in such proceedings.

Article 8 Emergency decisions on interim measures

(1) Any emergency decision on interim measures shall be made not later than 5 days from the date upon which the application was referred to the Emergency Arbitrator pursuant to Article 6 of this Appendix. The Board may extend this time limit upon a reasoned request from the Emergency Arbitrator, or if otherwise deemed necessary.

(2) Any emergency decision on interim measures shall:

(i) be made in writing;

(ii) state the date when it was made, the seat of the emergency proceedings and the reasons upon which the decision is based; and

(iii) be signed by the Emergency Arbitrator.

(3) The Emergency Arbitrator shall promptly deliver a copy of the emergency decision to each of the parties and to the SCC.

Article 9 Binding effect of emergency decisions

(1) An emergency decision shall be binding on the parties when rendered.

(2) The emergency decision may be amended or revoked by the Emergency Arbitrator upon a reasoned request by a party.

(3) By agreeing to arbitration under the Rules for Expedited Arbitrations, the parties undertake to comply with any emergency decision without delay.

(4) The emergency decision ceases to be binding if:

(i)   the Emergency Arbitrator or an Arbitrator so decides;

(ii) an Arbitrator makes a final award;

(iii) arbitration is not commenced within 30 days from the date of the emergency decision; or

(iv) the case is not referred to an Arbitrator within 90 days from the date of the emergency decision.

(5) An Arbitrator is not bound by the decision(s) and reasons of the Emergency Arbitrator.

Article 10 Costs of the emergency proceedings

(1) The party applying for the appointment of an Emergency Arbitrator shall pay the costs of the emergency proceedings upon filing the application.

(2) The costs of the emergency proceedings include:

(i)   the fee of the Emergency Arbitrator which amounts to EUR 6,000; and

(ii) the application fee which amounts to EUR 1,500.

(3) Upon a request from the Emergency Arbitrator or if otherwise deemed appropriate, the Board may decide to increase or reduce the costs having regard to the nature of the case, the work performed by the Emergency Arbitrator and the SCC, and other relevant circumstances.

(4) If payment of the costs of the emergency proceedings is not made in due time, the Secretariat shall dismiss the application.

(5) At the request of a party, the costs of the emergency proceedings may be apportioned between the parties by an Arbitrator in a final award.

APPENDIX III
SCHEDULE OF COSTS*
ARBITRATION COSTS

Article 1 Registration Fee

(1) The Registration Fee referred to in Article 3 of the Rules for Expedited Arbitrations amounts to EUR 1 500.

(2) The Registration Fee is non-refundable and constitutes a part of the Administrative Fee in Article 3 below. The Registration Fee shall be credited to the Advance on Costs to be paid by the Claimant pursuant to Article 44 of the Rules for Expedited Arbitrations.

---

*   Revised and in force as of 1 January 2015.

Article 2 Fee of the Arbitrator

(1) The Board shall determine the Fee of the Arbitrator based on the amount in dispute in accordance with the table below.

(2) The amount in dispute shall be the aggregate value of all claims, counterclaims and set-offs. Where the amount in dispute cannot be ascertained, the Board shall determine the Fee of the Arbitrator taking all relevant circumstances into account.

(3) In exceptional circumstances, the Board may deviate from the amounts set out in the table.

Article 3 Administrative Fee

(1) The Administrative Fee shall be determined in accordance with the table below.

(2) The amount in dispute shall be the aggregate value of all claims, counterclaims and set-offs. Where the amount in dispute cannot be ascertained, the Board shall determine the Administrative Fee taking all relevant circumstances into account.

(3) In exceptional circumstances, the Board may deviate from the amounts set out in the table.

Article 4 Expenses

In addition to the Fee of the Arbitrator and the Administrative Fee, the Board shall fix an amount to cover any reasonable expenses incurred by the Arbitrator and the SCC. The expenses of the Arbitrator may include the fee and expenses of any expert appointed by the Arbitrator pursuant to Article 29 of the Rules for Expedited Arbitrations.

ARBITRATORS' FEES

Amount in dispute	Arbitrator's Fee	
(EUR)	Minimum (EUR)	Maximum (EUR)
to 25 000	4 000	6 000
from 25 001 to 50 000	4 000 + 2% of the amount above 25 000	6 000 + 6% of the amount above 25 000
from 50 001 to 100 000	4 500 + 0,01% of the amount above 50 000	7 500 + 6% of the amount above 50 000
from 100 001 to 500 000	4 505 + 1,5% of the amount above 100 000	9 500 + 1% of the amount above 100 000
from 500 001 to 1 000 000	10 505 + 0,8% of the amount above 500 000	13 500 + 2,2% of the amount above 500 000

from 1 000 001 to 2 000 000	14 505 + 0,3% of the amount above 1 000 000	24 500 + 1,4% of the amount above 1 000 000
from 2 000 001 to 5 000 000	17 505 + 0,05% of the amount above 2 000 000	38 500 + 0,1% of the amount above 2 000 000
from 5 000 001 to 10 000 000	19 005 + 0,07% of the amount above 5 000 000	41 500 + 0,3% of the amount above 5 000 000
from 10 000 001 to 50 000 000	22 505 + 0,03% of the amount above 10 000 000	56 500 + 0,02% of the amount above 10 000 000
from 50 000 001 to 75 000 000	34 505 + 0,03% of the amount above 50 000 000	64 500 + 0,02% of the amount above 50 000 000
from 75 000 001	42 005 + 0,02% of the amount above 75 000 000	69 500 + 0,02% of the amount above 75 000 000

ADMINISTRATIVE FEE

Amount in dispute (EUR)	Administrative Fee (EUR)
to 25 000	1 500
from 25 001 to 50 000	1 500 + 2% of the amount above 25 000
from 50 001 to 100 000	2 000 + 1,5% of the amount above 50 000
from 100 001 to 500 000	2 750 + 0,75% of the amount above 100 000
from 500 001 to 1 000 000	5 750 + 0,5% of the amount above 500 000
from 1 000 001 to 2 000 000	8 250 + 0,25% of the amount above 1 000 000
from 2 000 001 to 5 000 000	10 750 + 0,12% of the amount above 2 000 000
from 5 000 001 to 10 000 000	14 350 + 0,06% of the amount above 5 000 000

from 10 000 001 to 50 000 000	17 350 + 0,01% of the amount above 10 000 000
	Maximum 35 000

* * *

B. ICC EXPERTS RULES

ICC RULES FOR THE ADMINISTRATION OF EXPERT PROCEEDINGS*

(In force as of 1 February 2015)

Preamble

The ICC Rules for the Administration of Expert Proceedings (the "Rules") are administered by the ICC International Centre for ADR (the "Centre"), which is a separate administrative body within the International Chamber of Commerce (the "ICC"). In administering the Rules, the Centre is assisted by a Standing Committee, the statutes of which are set forth in Appendix I.

When disputes or differences arise, parties may wish to have recourse to an expert who can provide findings on specified issues through expert proceedings administered by the ICC. Such issues may concern specialist areas such as accounting, finance, engineering, information technology, construction, energy and law. The expert may be a physical person or a legal person, such as a company or a partnership.

In the absence of an agreement of the parties to the contrary, the expert's findings shall be non-binding and can be used by the parties as a basis for negotiations with a view to reaching a settlement of their dispute or differences. However, the parties may agree, subject to applicable law, that the expert's findings shall constitute a contractually binding expert determination. In all cases, an expert appointed under the Rules is not an arbitrator, and the expert's findings are not enforceable like an arbitral award. Unless otherwise agreed by the parties, the expert's report shall be admissible in any judicial or arbitral proceedings between the same parties.

The Centre will administer expert proceedings pursuant to the Rules when all of the parties have agreed to refer a dispute to the Rules or where the Centre is otherwise satisfied that there is a sufficient basis for administering expert proceedings under the Rules. In administering the

---

*   © International Chamber of Commerce (ICC). Reproduced with permission of the ICC. The text reproduced here is valid at the time of publication. As amendments may from time to time be made to the text, please refer to the website www.iccadr.org for the latest version and for more information on this ICC dispute resolution service. Also available in the ICC Dispute Resolution Library at www.iccdrl.com.

proceedings, the Centre appoints the expert in the absence of a joint nomination by the parties, coordinates between the parties and the expert, initiates the appropriate steps to encourage the expeditious completion of the expert proceedings, supervises the financial aspects of the proceedings and scrutinizes the expert's report.

Article 1

Recourse to the Centre

1

Any request for the administration of expert proceedings (the "Request") shall be submitted to the Centre. Any Request shall be processed by the Centre only when it is based upon an agreement for the administration of expert proceedings by the Centre or when the Centre is otherwise satisfied that there is a sufficient basis for administering expert proceedings.

2

The Request shall include:

a) the names, addresses, telephone numbers, email addresses and any other contact details of the parties to the dispute and any person(s) representing the parties in the proceedings;

b) if applicable, the name and contact details of any person or entity relevant for checking potential conflicts of interest of the expert;

c) a description of the dispute including, if possible, an assessment of its value;

d) a description of the field of activity of the expert to be appointed;

e) any desired attributes of the expert, including but not limited to education, qualifications, language skills and professional experience;

f) any undesired attributes of the expert and a description of any matters that would disqualify a potential expert;

g) a detailed description of the work to be carried out by the expert, including whether site visits will be required;

h) the desired time frame for completing such work;

i) any agreement as to the location of any physical meetings between the expert and the parties or, in the absence thereof, any proposal as to such location;

j) any agreement as to the language(s) of the proceedings or, in the absence thereof, any proposal as to such language(s);

k) any agreement that the findings of the expert shall be contractually binding on the parties or, in the absence thereof, any proposal to that effect; and

l) a copy of any agreement for the administration of expert proceedings by the Centre and/or of any other elements which form the basis of the Request.

3

Together with the Request, the party or parties filing the Request shall pay the non-refundable amount specified in Article 1 of Appendix II.

4

The Centre shall acknowledge receipt of the Request and of the filing fee in writing to the party or parties that filed the Request.

5

The Centre shall notify the other party or parties in writing of the Request once the Centre has sufficient copies of the Request and has received the filing fee required under Article 12.

6

The date on which the Request is received by the Centre shall, for all purposes, be deemed to be the date of the commencement of the expert proceedings.

Article 2

Written Notifications or Communications

1

All written communications submitted to the Centre by any party to the expert proceedings, as well as all documents annexed thereto, shall be supplied in a number of copies sufficient to provide one copy for the Centre, one copy for each party and one copy for each expert.

2

All notifications or communications from the Centre and the expert shall be made to the last address of the party or its representative for whom the same are intended, as notified either by the party in question or by the other party. Such notification or communication may be made by delivery against receipt, registered post, courier, email or any other means of telecommunication that provides a record of the sending thereof.

3

A notification or communication shall be deemed to have been made on the day it was received by the party itself or by its representative, or would have been received if made in accordance with the preceding paragraph.

Article 3

Selection of the Expert

1

The parties may jointly nominate an expert for confirmation by the Centre.

2

In the absence of a joint nomination of an expert by the parties, the Centre shall appoint an expert.

3

Before appointment or confirmation, a prospective expert shall sign a statement of acceptance, availability, impartiality and independence. The prospective expert shall disclose in writing to the Centre any facts or circumstances which might be of such a nature as to call into question the expert's independence in the eyes of the parties, as well as any circumstances that could give rise to reasonable doubts as to the expert's impartiality. The Centre shall provide such information to the parties in writing and shall fix a time limit for any comments from them.

4

In confirming or appointing an expert, the Centre shall consider the prospective expert's nationality, residence, training and experience, and the prospective expert's availability and ability to conduct the expert proceedings in accordance with the Rules.

5

Where the Centre appoints an expert, it shall do so either on the basis of a proposal by an ICC National Committee or Group, or otherwise. The Centre shall make all reasonable efforts to appoint an expert having the attributes, if any, that have been agreed upon by all of the parties. If, despite such efforts, the Centre is not able to identify an expert having all of the attributes agreed upon by all parties, the Centre may ask the parties whether they wish the Centre to appoint more than one expert (who between them have the requested attributes), or whether the attributes agreed upon by the parties may be modified.

6

Upon agreement of all of the parties, the parties may nominate more than one expert or request the Centre to appoint more than one expert, in accordance with the provisions of the Rules. In appropriate circumstances, the Centre may propose to the parties that there be more than one expert.

7

The Centre may terminate the administered expert proceedings by notifying the parties that, in the judgment of the Centre, there has been a failure to nominate an expert or that it has not been reasonably possible to appoint an expert.

Article 4

Continued Impartiality and Independence of the Expert— Replacement of the Expert

1

Every expert must be and remain impartial and independent of the parties involved in the expert proceedings, unless otherwise agreed in writing by such parties.

2

An expert shall immediately disclose in writing to the Centre and to the parties any facts or circumstances of a similar nature to those referred to in Article 3(3) concerning the expert's impartiality or independence which may arise during the expert proceedings.

3

An expert confirmed or appointed by the Centre, who has died or resigned or is unable to carry out the expert's functions, shall be replaced.

4

An expert confirmed or appointed by the Centre shall be replaced upon acceptance by the Centre of a written request of all of the parties.

5

If any party files a written objection with the Centre asserting that the expert does not have the necessary attributes, is not fulfilling the expert's functions in accordance with the Rules or in a timely fashion, or is not independent or impartial, the Centre may replace the expert after having considered the observations of the expert and the other party or parties.

6

When an expert is to be replaced, the Centre has discretion to decide whether or not to follow the original appointing process.

Article 5

Location and Language(s) of the Expert Proceedings

1

In the absence of an agreement of the parties, the expert, after consulting the parties, shall determine the location of any physical meeting of the expert and the parties.

2

In the absence of an agreement of the parties, the expert, after consulting the parties, shall determine the language(s) in which the expert proceedings shall be conducted.

Article 6

The Expert's Mission

1

The expert and the parties shall make every effort to conduct the expert proceedings in an expeditious and cost-effective manner, having regard to the complexity and value of the findings to be made in the expert's report.

2

As soon as the expert has received the file from the Centre, the expert, after having consulted the parties, shall set out the expert's mission in a written document. That document shall be consistent with the Rules and any agreement of all of the parties. It shall be communicated to the parties and to the Centre and shall include:

a)   the names in full, descriptions, addresses and other contact details of the expert, of each of the parties and of any person(s) representing a party in the administered expert proceedings;

b)   addresses to which notifications and communications arising in the course of the administered expert proceedings may be made;

c)   a list of the issues on which the expert shall make findings in the expert's report;

d)   the procedure to be followed by the expert; and

e)   the location of any physical meeting of the expert and the parties and the language(s) in which the administered expert proceedings will be conducted.

3

Modifications to the expert's mission may be made by the expert, in writing, only after consultation with the parties. Any such written modifications shall be communicated to the parties and to the Centre.

4

In the event of a disagreement between the parties as to the scope of the expert's mandate, the expert may continue with the administered expert proceedings to the extent the expert considers that the issues set out in the expert's mission fall within the scope of the expert's mandate. Unless otherwise agreed by all of the parties, the expert shall give reasons for such considerations. The continuation of the administered expert proceedings shall be without prejudice to any determination by an arbitral tribunal or a competent judicial authority as to the scope of the expert's mandate.

Article 7

Procedural Timetable

Upon preparing the document setting out the expert's mission or as soon as possible thereafter, the expert, after having consulted the parties, shall prepare a procedural timetable for the conduct of the administered expert proceedings. The procedural timetable shall be communicated to the parties and to the Centre. Any subsequent modifications to the provisional timetable shall be promptly communicated to the parties and to the Centre.

Article 8

The Expert's Report

1

The expert's main task is to make findings in a written expert's report within the limits set by the expert's mission after giving each party a reasonable opportunity to present its case. Unless otherwise agreed by all of the parties, the expert's report shall give reasons for the findings made.

2

The findings of the expert shall not be binding on the parties, unless all of the parties expressly agree in writing that such findings shall be contractually binding upon them.

3

Unless otherwise agreed by all of the parties, the expert's report shall be admissible in any judicial or arbitral proceedings in which all of the parties thereto were parties to the administered expert proceedings in which such report was prepared.

Article 9

Scrutiny of the Expert's Report by the Centre

1

The expert's report shall be submitted in draft form to the Centre before it is signed. The Centre may lay down modifications as to the form of the report and, without affecting the expert's liberty of decision, may also draw the expert's attention to points of substance. No report shall be communicated to the parties by the expert. No report shall be signed by the expert prior to the Centre's approval of such report.

2

The Centre may waive the requirements laid down in Article 9(1) if expressly requested to do so in writing by all the parties and if the Centre considers that such a waiver is appropriate under the circumstances of the case.

Article 10

Notification of the Expert's Report and Termination of the Administered Expert Proceedings

The expert's report, once signed by the expert, shall be sent to the Centre in as many copies as there are parties plus one for the Centre. Thereafter, the Centre shall notify the expert's report to the party or parties and declare in writing that the administered expert proceedings have been terminated.

Article 11

Duties and Responsibilities of the Parties and the Expert

1

The non-participation of a party in the administered expert proceedings does not deprive the expert of the power to make findings and render the expert's report, provided that such party has been given the opportunity to participate.

2

In agreeing to the application of the Rules, the parties shall provide the expert with all necessary means to implement the expert's mission and, in particular, make available all documents the expert may consider necessary and also grant the expert free access to any place where the expert may be required to go for the proper completion of the expert's mission. The expert shall give each party the opportunity to comment on any information or documents provided by any other party.

3

Any information or documents given to the expert by the Centre or any party in connection with the administered expert proceedings shall be used by the expert only for the purposes of such proceedings and shall be treated by the expert as confidential.

Article 12

Fees and Costs

1

Each Request must be accompanied by the non-refundable filing fee specified in Article 1 of Appendix II. This amount will be credited to the requesting party's or parties' portion of the deposit pursuant to Article 12(2). No Request shall be processed unless accompanied by the filing fee.

2

Following the receipt of a Request, the Centre shall request the parties to pay one or more deposits in an amount likely to cover the administrative costs of the Centre and the fees and expenses of the expert for the administered expert proceedings, as set out in Articles 2 and 3 of Appendix II. The Centre may stay such proceedings until payment of such deposit has been received by the Centre, or the Centre may set a time limit on the expiry of which the administered expert proceedings may be considered withdrawn.

3

Each written objection pursuant to Article 4(5) of the Rules must be accompanied by the non-refundable amount specified in Article 1 of Appendix II. No objection shall be processed unless accompanied by the requisite payment.

4

Upon the termination of administered expert proceedings, the Centre shall fix the total costs of the proceedings and shall, as the case may be, reimburse the party or parties for any excess payment or bill the party or parties for any balance required pursuant to the Rules. The balance, if any, shall be payable before the notification of the final expert's report to the party or parties.

5

All above deposits and costs shall be borne in equal shares by the parties, unless they agree otherwise in writing. However, any party shall be free to pay the unpaid balance of such deposits and costs should the other party or parties fail to pay its or their share.

6

A party's other expenditure shall remain the responsibility of that party, unless otherwise agreed by the parties.

Article 13

Waiver

A party that proceeds with the administered expert proceedings without raising an objection to a failure to comply with any provision of the Rules, any direction given by the Centre or by the expert, any requirement of the expert's mission, or any requirement relating to the appointment of an expert or to the conduct of the administered expert proceedings, shall be deemed to have waived its right to object.

Article 14

General Provisions

1

An expert appointed under the Rules may be a physical person or a legal person, such as a company or a partnership. The term "expert" as used in the Rules applies mutatis mutandis to both physical and legal persons.

2

Where, prior to the date of the entry into force of the Rules, the parties have agreed to refer their dispute to the administration of expertise proceedings pursuant to the Rules for Expertise of the ICC, they shall be deemed to have referred to the ICC Rules for the Administration of Expert Proceedings, unless any of the parties objects thereto, in which case the Rules for Expertise of the ICC shall apply.

3

The expert, the Centre, the ICC and its employees, and the ICC National Committees and Groups and their employees and representatives shall not be liable to any person for any act or omission in connection with the administration of expert proceedings, except to the extent such limitation of liability is prohibited by applicable law.

4

In all matters not expressly provided for in the Rules, the Centre and the expert shall act in the spirit of the Rules.

ICC RULES FOR THE ADMINISTRATION OF EXPERT PROCEEDINGS

APPENDIX I—STATUTES OF THE STANDING COMMITTEE

Article 1

Composition of the Standing Committee

The Standing Committee is composed of a maximum of fifteen members (a president, three vice-presidents and up to eleven members) appointed by the ICC for a three-year renewable term.

Article 2

Meetings

A meeting of the Standing Committee shall be convened by its president whenever necessary.

Article 3

Function and Duties of the Standing Committee

1

The Standing Committee shall advise the Centre concerning all aspects of the proceedings, in order to help ensure the quality of the services carried out by the Centre. It shall assist the Centre in reviewing the attributes of the experts to be confirmed or appointed and in scrutinizing the expert's report pursuant to the Rules.

2

The president shall make the final decision on the confirmation or appointment of experts.

3

The Standing Committee shall be informed of the death or resignation of any expert, of any objection by a party or parties or the Centre concerning an expert, or of any other matter requiring the replacement of an expert. It shall provide recommendations to the president as to whether there is any reason not to comply with a request of all of the parties pursuant to Article 4(4) of the Rules and as to whether the objection of a party pursuant to Article 4(5) of the Rules is justified.

4

The president will make the final decision on whether the objection is justified and on the manner in which a replacement will be made.

5

Upon the termination of administered expert proceedings, the president shall fix the expert's fees and expenses in accordance with the Rules.

6

In the absence of the president, or otherwise at the president's request, one of the three vice-presidents shall be authorized by the Centre to fulfil the tasks of the president, including taking decisions pursuant to these statutes.

Article 4

Confidentiality

The work of the Standing Committee and the Centre is of a confidential nature, which must be respected by everyone who participates in that work in whatever capacity.

APPENDIX II—COSTS

Article 1

Filing Fee

Each Request pursuant to the Rules must be accompanied by a filing fee of US$3,000. The filing fee is non-refundable and shall be credited towards the deposit of the party or parties having filed the Request. No Request shall be processed unless accompanied by the requisite payment.

Article 2

Administrative Expenses

1

The administrative expenses of the ICC for the administration of expert proceedings shall be fixed at the Centre's discretion depending on the tasks carried out by the Centre. The administrative expenses are added to the filing fee; they shall normally not be less than US$2,500 and they shall not exceed the following:

- US$10,000, for amounts in dispute up to and including US$200,000;
- US$15,000, for amounts in dispute between US$200,001 and US$2,000,000;
- US$20,000, for amounts in dispute between US$2,000,001 and US$10,000,000;
- US$30,000, for amounts in dispute between US$10,000,001 and US$50,000,000;
- US$40,000, for amounts in dispute between US$50,000,001 and US$100,000,000;
- US$50,000, for amounts in dispute over US$100,000,000.

2

Where the amount in dispute is not stated, the administrative expenses may be fixed by the Centre at its discretion, taking into account all the circumstances of the case, including indications regarding the value of the dispute, but they shall not exceed US$50,000.

3

In exceptional circumstances, the Centre may fix the administrative expenses at a higher figure than that which would result from the application of the above scale, provided that such expenses shall normally not exceed the maximum amount of the scale.

4

The Centre may require the payment of administrative expenses in addition to those provided in the scale described in Article 2(1) of this Appendix as a condition for holding the proceedings in abeyance at the request of the parties or of one of them with the acquiescence of the other. Such abeyance fee shall normally not exceed US$2,000 per party per year.

Article 3

Expert's Fees and Expenses

1

The fees of the expert shall be calculated on the basis of the time reasonably spent by the expert in the administered expert proceedings, taking into account the diligence and efficiency of the expert and any other relevant circumstances. These fees shall be based on an hourly rate fixed by the Centre when appointing or confirming the expert and after having consulted the expert and the parties. The hourly rate shall be reasonable in amount and shall be determined in light of the complexity of the work to be performed by the expert.

2

The amount of reasonable expenses of the expert shall be fixed by the Centre.

3

The expert's fees and expenses shall be fixed exclusively by the Centre as required by the Rules. Separate fee arrangements between the parties and the expert are not permitted by the Rules.

Article 4

Additional Costs for Objection and Replacement

Each written objection to the appointment of an expert by the Centre pursuant to Article 4(5) of the Rules shall be accompanied by a non-refundable amount of US$3,000. The amount is to be paid by the party or parties filing the objection. No objection shall be processed unless accompanied by the requisite payment.

Article 5

Early Termination

If administered expert proceedings terminate before the notification of the expert's report, the Centre shall fix the costs of the administered expert proceedings, including the fees and expenses of the expert and the ICC administrative expenses, at its discretion, taking into account the stage attained in the administered expert proceedings and any other relevant circumstances.

Article 6

Currency, VAT and Scope

1

All amounts fixed by the Centre or pursuant to any Appendix to the Rules are payable in US dollars except where prohibited by law, in which case the ICC may apply a different scale and fee arrangement in another currency.

2

Amounts paid to the expert do not include any possible value added tax (VAT) or other taxes or charges and imposts applicable to the expert's fees. Parties have a duty to pay any such taxes or charges; however, the recovery of any such taxes or charges is a matter solely between the expert and the parties.

3

Any ICC administrative expenses may be subject to value added tax (VAT) or charges of a similar nature at the prevailing rate.

4

The above provisions on the costs of the administration of expert proceedings shall be effective as of 1 February 2015 in respect of all proceedings commenced on or after such date under the present Rules and in respect of the administration of any expertise proceedings commenced on or after such date under the Rules for Expertise of the ICC.

C. VIENNA CONCILIATION RULES

RULES OF ARBITRATION OF VIENNA INTERNATIONAL ARBITRAL CENTRE/VIENNA RULES*

Official English version adopted by the Extended Presiding Committee of the Austrian Federal Economic Chamber on 8 May 2013, with effect from 1 July 2013

* * *

Conciliation Rules

Annex 5

(1) Where VIAC has jurisdiction over the subject matter, conciliation proceedings may be conducted at the request of a party. A valid arbitration agreement is not required.

(2) The request for the initiation of conciliation proceedings shall be filed with the Secretariat. The latter shall invite the opposing party or parties to comment within 30 days of service of the request. If a party refuses to participate in the conciliation proceedings or does not reply by the applicable deadline, the conciliation shall be considered unsuccessful.

(3) When the opposing party or parties accept(s) recourse to conciliation, the Board shall nominate one of its members or another qualified person to act as conciliator. The parties may also agree on the conciliator. The latter shall study the documents submitted by the parties, convene a hearing to discuss the dispute and then submit proposals for the amicable resolution of the dispute.

(4) If agreement is reached, a transcript thereof shall be drafted and signed by the parties and the conciliator. Upon request of all parties, and

---

    *   Reprinted with kind permission of the International Arbitral Centre of the Austrian Federal Economic Chamber.

if a valid arbitration agreement exists, the Board shall appoint the conciliator as sole arbitrator. The sole arbitrator shall record the agreement in the form of an arbitral settlement or, if the parties so request, render an arbitral award on agreed terms.

(5) If no agreement is reached, the conciliation shall be deemed unsuccessful. Parties shall not, in any subsequent arbitration be bound by statements made in the course of conciliation proceedings. The conciliator may not be appointed as an arbitrator in a subsequent arbitration except under the conditions in Article 4 of this Annex.

(6) The costs of the conciliation proceedings and services rendered by the conciliator under the conditions outlined in Article 4 of this Annex shall be determined by the Secretary General at an appropriate share of the fees applicable for arbitration on the basis of the corresponding amount in dispute (Article 44 Vienna Rules). The same shall apply to the advance on costs to be fixed by the Secretary General (Article 42 Vienna Rules).

CHAPTER VI

CODES OF ETHICS

■ ■ ■

A. AAA/ABA CODE OF ETHICS FOR ARBITRATORS IN COMMERCIAL DISPUTES*

Effective March 1, 2004

The Code of Ethics for Arbitrators in Commercial Disputes was originally prepared in 1977 by a joint committee consisting of a special committee of the American Arbitration Association and a special committee of the American Bar Association. The Code was revised in 2003 by an ABA Task Force and special committee of the AAA.

PREAMBLE

The use of arbitration to resolve a wide variety of disputes has grown extensively and forms a significant part of the system of justice on which our society relies for a fair determination of legal rights. Persons who act as arbitrators therefore undertake serious responsibilities to the public, as well as to the parties. Those responsibilities include important ethical obligations.

Few cases of unethical behavior by commercial arbitrators have arisen. Nevertheless, this Code sets forth generally accepted standards of ethical conduct for the guidance of arbitrators and parties in commercial disputes, in the hope of contributing to the maintenance of high standards and continued confidence in the process of arbitration.

This Code provides ethical guidelines for many types of arbitration but does not apply to labor arbitration, which is generally conducted under the Code of Professional Responsibility for Arbitrators of Labor-Management Disputes.

There are many different types of commercial arbitration. Some proceedings are conducted under arbitration rules established by various organizations and trade associations, while others are conducted without such rules. Although most proceedings are arbitrated pursuant to voluntary agreement of the parties, certain types of disputes are submitted to arbitration by reason of particular laws. This Code is intended to apply to all such proceedings in which disputes or claims are submitted for

---

*   The text can be found at https://www.adr.org/aaa/ShowProperty?nodeId=/UCM/ADRSTG_003867. Reprinted with permission of the American Arbitration Association.

decision to one or more arbitrators appointed in a manner provided by an agreement of the parties, by applicable arbitration rules, or by law. In all such cases, the persons who have the power to decide should observe fundamental standards of ethical conduct. In this Code, all such persons are called "arbitrators," although in some types of proceeding they might be called "umpires," "referees," "neutrals," or have some other title.

Arbitrators, like judges, have the power to decide cases. However, unlike full-time judges, arbitrators are usually engaged in other occupations before, during, and after the time that they serve as arbitrators. Often, arbitrators are purposely chosen from the same trade or industry as the parties in order to bring special knowledge to the task of deciding. This Code recognizes these fundamental differences between arbitrators and judges.

In those instances where this Code has been approved and recommended by organizations that provide, coordinate, or administer services of arbitrators, it provides ethical standards for the members of their respective panels of arbitrators. However, this Code does not form a part of the arbitration rules of any such organization unless its rules so provide.

Note on Neutrality

In some types of commercial arbitration, the parties or the administering institution provide for three or more arbitrators. In some such proceedings, it is the practice for each party, acting alone, to appoint one arbitrator (a "party-appointed arbitrator") and for one additional arbitrator to be designated by the party-appointed arbitrators, or by the parties, or by an independent institution or individual. The sponsors of this Code believe that it is preferable for all arbitrators including any party-appointed arbitrators to be neutral, that is, independent and impartial, and to comply with the same ethical standards. This expectation generally is essential in arbitrations where the parties, the nature of the dispute, or the enforcement of any resulting award may have international aspects. However, parties in certain domestic arbitrations in the United States may prefer that party-appointed arbitrators be non-neutral and governed by special ethical considerations. These special ethical considerations appear in Canon X of this Code.

This Code establishes a presumption of neutrality for all arbitrators, including party-appointed arbitrators, which applies unless the parties' agreement, the arbitration rules agreed to by the parties or applicable laws provide otherwise. This Code requires all party-appointed arbitrators, whether neutral or not, to make pre-appointment disclosures of any facts which might affect their neutrality, independence, or impartiality. This Code also requires all party-appointed arbitrators to ascertain and disclose as soon as practicable whether the parties intended for them to serve as neutral or not. If any doubt or uncertainty exists, the party-appointed arbitrators should serve as neutrals unless and until such doubt or uncertainty is resolved in accordance with Canon IX. This Code expects all arbitrators, including those serving under Canon X, to preserve the integrity and fairness of the process.

Note on Construction

Various aspects of the conduct of arbitrators, including some matters covered by this Code, may also be governed by agreements of the parties, arbitration rules to which the parties have agreed, applicable law, or other applicable ethics rules, all of which should be consulted by the arbitrators. This Code does not take the place of or supersede such laws, agreements, or arbitration rules to which the parties have agreed and should be read in conjunction with other rules of ethics. It does not establish new or additional grounds for judicial review of arbitration awards.

All provisions of this Code should therefore be read as subject to contrary provisions of applicable law and arbitration rules. They should also be read as subject to contrary agreements of the parties. Nevertheless, this Code imposes no obligation on any arbitrator to act in a manner inconsistent with the arbitrator's fundamental duty to preserve the integrity and fairness of the arbitral process.

Canons I through VIII of this Code apply to all arbitrators. Canon IX applies to all party-appointed arbitrators, except that certain party-appointed arbitrators are exempted by Canon X from compliance with certain provisions of Canons I–IX related to impartiality and independence, as specified in Canon X.

CANON I.

AN ARBITRATOR SHOULD UPHOLD THE INTEGRITY AND FAIRNESS OF THE ARBITRATION PROCESS

A. An arbitrator has a responsibility not only to the parties but also to the process of arbitration itself, and must observe high standards of conduct so that the integrity and fairness of the process will be preserved. Accordingly, an arbitrator should recognize a responsibility to the public, to the parties whose rights will be decided, and to all other participants in the proceeding. This responsibility may include pro bono service as an arbitrator where appropriate.

B. One should accept appointment as an arbitrator only if fully satisfied:

(1) that he or she can serve impartially;

(2) that he or she can serve independently from the parties, potential witnesses, and the other arbitrators;

(3) that he or she is competent to serve; and

(4) that he or she can be available to commence the arbitration in accordance with the requirements of the proceeding and thereafter to devote the time and attention to its completion that the parties are reasonably entitled to expect.

C.   After accepting appointment and while serving as an arbitrator, a person should avoid entering into any business, professional, or personal relationship, or acquiring any financial or personal interest, which is likely to affect impartiality or which might reasonably create the appearance of partiality. For a reasonable period of time after the decision of a case, persons who have served as arbitrators should avoid entering into any such relationship, or acquiring any such interest, in circumstances which might reasonably create the appearance that they had been influenced in the arbitration by the anticipation or expectation of the relationship or interest. Existence of any of the matters or circumstances described in this paragraph C does not render it unethical for one to serve as an arbitrator where the parties have consented to the arbitrator's appointment or continued services following full disclosure of the relevant facts in accordance with Canon II.

D.   Arbitrators should conduct themselves in a way that is fair to all parties and should not be swayed by outside pressure, public clamor, and fear of criticism or self-interest. They should avoid conduct and statements that give the appearance of partiality toward or against any party.

E.   When an arbitrator's authority is derived from the agreement of the parties, an arbitrator should neither exceed that authority nor do less than is required to exercise that authority completely. Where the agreement of the parties sets forth procedures to be followed in conducting the arbitration or refers to rules to be followed, it is the obligation of the arbitrator to comply with such procedures or rules. An arbitrator has no ethical obligation to comply with any agreement, procedures or rules that are unlawful or that, in the arbitrator's judgment, would be inconsistent with this Code.

F.   An arbitrator should conduct the arbitration process so as to advance the fair and efficient resolution of the matters submitted for decision. An arbitrator should make all reasonable efforts to prevent delaying tactics, harassment of parties or other participants, or other abuse or disruption of the arbitration process.

G.   The ethical obligations of an arbitrator begin upon acceptance of the appointment and continue throughout all stages of the proceeding. In addition, as set forth in this Code, certain ethical obligations begin as soon as a person is requested to serve as an arbitrator and certain ethical obligations continue after the decision in the proceeding has been given to the parties.

H.   Once an arbitrator has accepted an appointment, the arbitrator should not withdraw or abandon the appointment unless compelled to do so by unanticipated circumstances that would render it impossible or impracticable to continue. When an arbitrator is to be compensated for his or her services, the arbitrator may withdraw if the parties fail or refuse to provide for payment of the compensation as agreed.

I.   An arbitrator who withdraws prior to the completion of the arbitration, whether upon the arbitrator's initiative or upon the request of one or more of the parties, should take reasonable steps to protect the interests of the parties in the arbitration, including return of evidentiary materials and protection of confidentiality.

Comment to Canon I

A prospective arbitrator is not necessarily partial or prejudiced by having acquired knowledge of the parties, the applicable law or the customs and practices of the business involved. Arbitrators may also have special experience or expertise in the areas of business, commerce, or technology which are involved in the arbitration. Arbitrators do not contravene this Canon if, by virtue of such experience or expertise, they have views on certain general issues likely to arise in the arbitration, but an arbitrator may not have prejudged any of the specific factual or legal determinations to be addressed during the arbitration.

During an arbitration, the arbitrator may engage in discourse with the parties or their counsel, draw out arguments or contentions, comment on the law or evidence, make interim rulings, and otherwise control or direct the arbitration. These activities are integral parts of an arbitration. Paragraph D of Canon I is not intended to preclude or limit either full discussion of the issues during the course of the arbitration or the arbitrator's management of the proceeding.

CANON II.

AN ARBITRATOR SHOULD DISCLOSE ANY INTEREST OR RELATIONSHIP LIKELY TO AFFECT IMPARTIALITY OR WHICH MIGHT CREATE AN APPEARANCE OF PARTIALITY

A.   Persons who are requested to serve as arbitrators should, before accepting, disclose:

(1)   any known direct or indirect financial or personal interest in the outcome of the arbitration;

(2)   any known existing or past financial, business, professional or personal relationships which might reasonably affect impartiality or lack of independence in the eyes of any of the parties. For example, prospective arbitrators should disclose any such relationships which

they personally have with any party or its lawyer, with any co-arbitrator, or with any individual whom they have been told will be a witness. They should also disclose any such relationships involving their families or household members or their current employers, partners, or professional or business associates that can be ascertained by reasonable efforts;

(3)   the nature and extent of any prior knowledge they may have of the dispute; and

(4)   any other matters, relationships, or interests which they are obligated to disclose by the agreement of the parties, the rules or practices of an institution, or applicable law regulating arbitrator disclosure.

B.   Persons who are requested to accept appointment as arbitrators should make a reasonable effort to inform themselves of any interests or relationships described in paragraph A.

C.   The obligation to disclose interests or relationships described in paragraph A is a continuing duty which requires a person who accepts appointment as an arbitrator to disclose, as soon as practicable, at any stage of the arbitration, any such interests or relationships which may arise, or which are recalled or discovered.

D.   Any doubt as to whether or not disclosure is to be made should be resolved in favor of disclosure.

E.   Disclosure should be made to all parties unless other procedures for disclosure are provided in the agreement of the parties, applicable rules or practices of an institution, or by law. Where more than one arbitrator has been appointed, each should inform the others of all matters disclosed.

F.   When parties, with knowledge of a person's interests and relationships, nevertheless desire that person to serve as an arbitrator, that person may properly serve.

G.   If an arbitrator is requested by all parties to withdraw, the arbitrator must do so. If an arbitrator is requested to withdraw by less than all of the parties because of alleged partiality, the arbitrator should withdraw unless either of the following circumstances exists:

(1)   An agreement of the parties, or arbitration rules agreed to by the parties, or applicable law establishes procedures for determining challenges to arbitrators, in which case those procedures should be followed; or

(2)   In the absence of applicable procedures, if the arbitrator, after carefully considering the matter, determines that the reason for the challenge is not substantial, and that he or she can nevertheless act and decide the case impartially and fairly.

H. If compliance by a prospective arbitrator with any provision of this Code would require disclosure of confidential or privileged information, the prospective arbitrator should either:

(1) Secure the consent to the disclosure from the person who furnished the information or the holder of the privilege; or

(2) Withdraw.

CANON III.

AN ARBITRATOR SHOULD AVOID IMPROPRIETY OR THE APPEARANCE OF IMPROPRIETY IN COMMUNICATING WITH PARTIES

A. If an agreement of the parties or applicable arbitration rules establishes the manner or content of communications between the arbitrator and the parties, the arbitrator should follow those procedures notwithstanding any contrary provision of paragraphs B and C.

B. An arbitrator or prospective arbitrator should not discuss a proceeding with any party in the absence of any other party, except in any of the following circumstances:

(1) When the appointment of a prospective arbitrator is being considered, the prospective arbitrator:

(a) may ask about the identities of the parties, counsel, or witnesses and the general nature of the case; and

(b) may respond to inquiries from a party or its counsel designed to determine his or her suitability and availability for the appointment. In any such dialogue, the prospective arbitrator may receive information from a party or its counsel disclosing the general nature of the dispute but should not permit them to discuss the merits of the case.

(2) In an arbitration in which the two party-appointed arbitrators are expected to appoint the third arbitrator, each party-appointed arbitrator may consult with the party who appointed the arbitrator concerning the choice of the third arbitrator;

(3) In an arbitration involving party-appointed arbitrators, each party-appointed arbitrator may consult with the party who appointed the arbitrator concerning arrangements for any compensation to be paid to the party-appointed arbitrator. Submission of routine written requests for payment of compensation and expenses in accordance with such arrangements and written communications pertaining solely to such requests need not be sent to the other party;

(4) In an arbitration involving party-appointed arbitrators, each party-appointed arbitrator may consult with the party who appointed

the arbitrator concerning the status of the arbitrator (i.e., neutral or non-neutral), as contemplated by paragraph C of Canon IX;

(5)   Discussions may be had with a party concerning such logistical matters as setting the time and place of hearings or making other arrangements for the conduct of the proceedings. However, the arbitrator should promptly inform each other party of the discussion and should not make any final determination concerning the matter discussed before giving each absent party an opportunity to express the party's views; or

(6)   If a party fails to be present at a hearing after having been given due notice, or if all parties expressly consent, the arbitrator may discuss the case with any party who is present.

C.   Unless otherwise provided in this Canon, in applicable arbitration rules or in an agreement of the parties, whenever an arbitrator communicates in writing with one party, the arbitrator should at the same time send a copy of the communication to every other party, and whenever the arbitrator receives any written communication concerning the case from one party which has not already been sent to every other party, the arbitrator should send or cause it to be sent to the other parties.

CANON IV.

AN ARBITRATOR SHOULD CONDUCT THE PROCEEDINGS FAIRLY AND DILIGENTLY

A.   An arbitrator should conduct the proceedings in an even-handed manner. The arbitrator should be patient and courteous to the parties, their representatives, and the witnesses and should encourage similar conduct by all participants.

B.   The arbitrator should afford to all parties the right to be heard and due notice of the time and place of any hearing. The arbitrator should allow each party a fair opportunity to present its evidence and arguments.

C.   The arbitrator should not deny any party the opportunity to be represented by counsel or by any other person chosen by the party.

D.   If a party fails to appear after due notice, the arbitrator should proceed with the arbitration when authorized to do so, but only after receiving assurance that appropriate notice has been given to the absent party.

E.   When the arbitrator determines that more information than has been presented by the parties is required to decide the case, it is not improper for the arbitrator to ask questions, call witnesses, and request documents or other evidence, including expert testimony.

F.   Although it is not improper for an arbitrator to suggest to the parties that they discuss the possibility of settlement or the use of mediation, or other dispute resolution processes, an arbitrator should not exert pressure on any party to settle or to utilize other dispute resolution processes. An arbitrator should not be present or otherwise participate in settlement discussions or act as a mediator unless requested to do so by all parties.

G.   Co-arbitrators should afford each other full opportunity to participate in all aspects of the proceedings.

Comment to paragraph G

Paragraph G of Canon IV is not intended to preclude one arbitrator from acting in limited circumstances (e.g., ruling on discovery issues) where authorized by the agreement of the parties, applicable rules or law, nor does it preclude a majority of the arbitrators from proceeding with any aspect of the arbitration if an arbitrator is unable or unwilling to participate and such action is authorized by the agreement of the parties or applicable rules or law. It also does not preclude ex parte requests for interim relief.

CANON V.

AN ARBITRATOR SHOULD MAKE DECISIONS IN A JUST, INDEPENDENT AND DELIBERATE MANNER

A.   The arbitrator should, after careful deliberation, decide all issues submitted for determination. An arbitrator should decide no other issues.

B.   An arbitrator should decide all matters justly, exercising independent judgment, and should not permit outside pressure to affect the decision.

C.   An arbitrator should not delegate the duty to decide to any other person.

D.   In the event that all parties agree upon a settlement of issues in dispute and request the arbitrator to embody that agreement in an award, the arbitrator may do so, but is not required to do so unless satisfied with the propriety of the terms of settlement. Whenever an arbitrator embodies a settlement by the parties in an award, the arbitrator should state in the award that it is based on an agreement of the parties.

CANON VI.

AN ARBITRATOR SHOULD BE FAITHFUL TO THE RELATIONSHIP OF TRUST AND CONFIDENTIALITY INHERENT IN THAT OFFICE

A.   An arbitrator is in a relationship of trust to the parties and should not, at any time, use confidential information acquired during the arbitration proceeding to gain personal advantage or advantage for others, or to affect adversely the interest of another.

B.   The arbitrator should keep confidential all matters relating to the arbitration proceedings and decision. An arbitrator may obtain help from an associate, a research assistant or other persons in connection with reaching his or her decision if the arbitrator informs the parties of the use of such assistance and such persons agree to be bound by the provisions of this Canon.

C.   It is not proper at any time for an arbitrator to inform anyone of any decision in advance of the time it is given to all parties. In a proceeding in which there is more than one arbitrator, it is not proper at any time for an arbitrator to inform anyone about the substance of the deliberations of the arbitrators. After an arbitration award has been made, it is not proper for an arbitrator to assist in proceedings to enforce or challenge the award.

D.   Unless the parties so request, an arbitrator should not appoint himself or herself to a separate office related to the subject matter of the dispute, such as receiver or trustee, nor should a panel of arbitrators appoint one of their number to such an office.

CANON VII.

AN ARBITRATOR SHOULD ADHERE TO STANDARDS OF INTEGRITY AND FAIRNESS WHEN MAKING ARRANGEMENTS FOR COMPENSATION AND REIMBURSEMENT OF EXPENSES

A.   Arbitrators who are to be compensated for their services or reimbursed for their expenses shall adhere to standards of integrity and fairness in making arrangements for such payments.

B.   Certain practices relating to payments are generally recognized as tending to preserve the integrity and fairness of the arbitration process. These practices include:

(1)   Before the arbitrator finally accepts appointment, the basis of payment, including any cancellation fee, compensation in the event of withdrawal and compensation for study and preparation time, and all other charges, should be established. Except for arrangements for the compensation of party-appointed arbitrators, all parties should be informed in writing of the terms established;

(2)   In proceedings conducted under the rules or administration of an institution that is available to assist in making arrangements for payments, communication related to compensation should be made through the institution. In proceedings where no institution has been engaged by the parties to administer the arbitration, any communication with arbitrators (other than party appointed arbitrators) concerning payments should be in the presence of all parties; and

(3) Arbitrators should not, absent extraordinary circumstances, request increases in the basis of their compensation during the course of a proceeding.

CANON VIII.

AN ARBITRATOR MAY ENGAGE IN ADVERTISING OR PROMOTION OF ARBITRAL SERVICES WHICH IS TRUTHFUL AND ACCURATE

A. Advertising or promotion of an individual's willingness or availability to serve as an arbitrator must be accurate and unlikely to mislead. Any statements about the quality of the arbitrator's work or the success of the arbitrator's practice must be truthful.

B. Advertising and promotion must not imply any willingness to accept an appointment otherwise than in accordance with this Code.

Comment to Canon VIII

This Canon does not preclude an arbitrator from printing, publishing, or disseminating advertisements conforming to these standards in any electronic or print medium, from making personal presentations to prospective users of arbitral services conforming to such standards or from responding to inquiries concerning the arbitrator's availability, qualifications, experience, or fee arrangements.

CANON IX.

ARBITRATORS APPOINTED BY ONE PARTY HAVE A DUTY TO DETERMINE AND DISCLOSE THEIR STATUS AND TO COMPLY WITH THIS CODE, EXCEPT AS EXEMPTED BY CANON X

A. In some types of arbitration in which there are three arbitrators, it is customary for each party, acting alone, to appoint one arbitrator. The third arbitrator is then appointed by agreement either of the parties or of the two arbitrators, or failing such agreement, by an independent institution or individual. In tripartite arbitrations to which this Code applies, all three arbitrators are presumed to be neutral and are expected to observe the same standards as the third arbitrator.

B. Notwithstanding this presumption, there are certain types of tripartite arbitration in which it is expected by all parties that the two arbitrators appointed by the parties may be predisposed toward the party appointing them. Those arbitrators, referred to in this Code as "Canon X arbitrators," are not to be held to the standards of neutrality and independence applicable to other arbitrators. Canon X describes the special ethical obligations of party-appointed arbitrators who are not expected to meet the standard of neutrality.

C. A party-appointed arbitrator has an obligation to ascertain, as early as possible but not later than the first meeting of the arbitrators and parties, whether the parties have agreed that the party-appointed arbitrators will serve as neutrals or whether they shall be subject to Canon X, and to provide a timely report of their conclusions to the parties and other arbitrators:

(1) Party-appointed arbitrators should review the agreement of the parties, the applicable rules and any applicable law bearing upon arbitrator neutrality. In reviewing the agreement of the parties, party-appointed arbitrators should consult any relevant express terms of the written or oral arbitration agreement. It may also be appropriate for them to inquire into agreements that have not been expressly set forth, but which may be implied from an established course of dealings of the parties or well-recognized custom and usage in their trade or profession;

(2) Where party-appointed arbitrators conclude that the parties intended for the party-appointed arbitrators not to serve as neutrals, they should so inform the parties and the other arbitrators. The arbitrators may then act as provided in Canon X unless or until a different determination of their status is made by the parties, any administering institution or the arbitral panel; and

(3) Until party-appointed arbitrators conclude that the party-appointed arbitrators were not intended by the parties to serve as neutrals, or if the party-appointed arbitrators are unable to form a reasonable belief of their status from the foregoing sources and no decision in this regard has yet been made by the parties, any administering institution, or the arbitral panel, they should observe all of the obligations of neutral arbitrators set forth in this Code.

D. Party-appointed arbitrators not governed by Canon X shall observe all of the obligations of Canons I through VIII unless otherwise required by agreement of the parties, any applicable rules, or applicable law.

CANON X.

EXEMPTIONS FOR ARBITRATORS APPOINTED BY ONE PARTY WHO ARE NOT SUBJECT TO RULES OF NEUTRALITY

Canon X arbitrators are expected to observe all of the ethical obligations prescribed by this Code except those from which they are specifically excused by Canon X.

A. *Obligations under Canon I*

Canon X arbitrators should observe all of the obligations of Canon I subject only to the following provisions:

(1) Canon X arbitrators may be predisposed toward the party who appointed them but in all other respects are obligated to act in good faith and with integrity and fairness. For example, Canon X arbitrators should not engage in delaying tactics or harassment of any party or witness and should not knowingly make untrue or misleading statements to the other arbitrators; and

(2) The provisions of subparagraphs B(1), B(2), and paragraphs C and D of Canon I, insofar as they relate to partiality, relationships, and interests are not applicable to Canon X arbitrators.

B. *Obligations under Canon II*

(1) Canon X arbitrators should disclose to all parties, and to the other arbitrators, all interests and relationships which Canon II requires be disclosed. Disclosure as required by Canon II is for the benefit not only of the party who appointed the arbitrator, but also for the benefit of the other parties and arbitrators so that they may know of any partiality which may exist or appear to exist; and

(2) Canon X arbitrators are not obliged to withdraw under paragraph G of Canon II if requested to do so only by the party who did not appoint them.

C. *Obligations under Canon III*

Canon X arbitrators should observe all of the obligations of Canon III subject only to the following provisions:

(1) Like neutral party-appointed arbitrators, Canon X arbitrators may consult with the party who appointed them to the extent permitted in paragraph B of Canon III;

(2) Canon X arbitrators shall, at the earliest practicable time, disclose to the other arbitrators and to the parties whether or not they intend to communicate with their appointing parties. If they have disclosed the intention to engage in such communications, they may thereafter communicate with their appointing parties concerning any other aspect of the case, except as provided in paragraph (3);

(3) If such communication occurred prior to the time they were appointed as arbitrators, or prior to the first hearing or other meeting of the parties with the arbitrators, the Canon X arbitrator should, at or before the first hearing or meeting of the arbitrators with the parties, disclose the fact that such communication has taken place. In complying with the provisions of this subparagraph, it is sufficient that there be disclosure of the fact that such communication has

occurred without disclosing the content of the communication. A single timely disclosure of the Canon X arbitrator's intention to participate in such communications in the future is sufficient;

(4) Canon X arbitrators may not at any time during the arbitration:

(a) disclose any deliberations by the arbitrators on any matter or issue submitted to them for decision;

(b) communicate with the parties that appointed them concerning any matter or issue taken under consideration by the panel after the record is closed or such matter or issue has been submitted for decision; or

(c) disclose any final decision or interim decision in advance of the time that it is disclosed to all parties.

(5) Unless otherwise agreed by the arbitrators and the parties, a Canon X arbitrator may not communicate orally with the neutral arbitrator concerning any matter or issue arising or expected to arise in the arbitration in the absence of the other Canon X arbitrator. If a Canon X arbitrator communicates in writing with the neutral arbitrator, he or she shall simultaneously provide a copy of the written communication to the other Canon X arbitrator;

(6) When Canon X arbitrators communicate orally with the parties that appointed them concerning any matter on which communication is permitted under this Code, they are not obligated to disclose the contents of such oral communications to any other party or arbitrator; and

(7) When Canon X arbitrators communicate in writing with the party who appointed them concerning any matter on which communication is permitted under this Code, they are not required to send copies of any such written communication to any other party or arbitrator.

D. *Obligations under Canon IV*

Canon X arbitrators should observe all of the obligations of Canon IV.

E. *Obligations under Canon V*

Canon X arbitrators should observe all of the obligations of Canon V, except that they may be predisposed toward deciding in favor of the party who appointed them.

F. *Obligations under Canon VI*

Canon X arbitrators should observe all of the obligations of Canon VI.

G. *Obligations under Canon VII*

Canon X arbitrators should observe all of the obligations of Canon VII.

H. *Obligations under Canon VIII*

Canon X arbitrators should observe all of the obligations of Canon VIII.

I. *Obligations under Canon IX*

The provisions of paragraph D of Canon IX are inapplicable to Canon X arbitrators, except insofar as the obligations are also set forth in this Canon.

* * *

B. IBA RULES OF ETHICS FOR INTERNATIONAL ARBITRATORS*

Adopted by International Bar Association in 1986.

Introductory Note

International arbitrators should be impartial, independent, competent, diligent and discreet. These rules seek to establish the manner in which these abstract qualities may be assessed in practice. Rather than rigid rules, they reflect internationally acceptable guidelines developed by practicing lawyers from all continents. They will attain their objectives only if they are applied in good faith. The rules cannot be directly binding either on arbitrators, or on the parties themselves, unless they are adopted by agreement. Whilst the International Bar Association hopes that they will be taken into account in the context of challenges to arbitrators, it is emphasised that these guidelines are not intended to create grounds for the setting aside of awards by national courts.

If parties wish to adopt the rules they may add the following to their arbitration clause or arbitration agreement:

> "The parties agree that the rules of Ethics for International Arbitrators established by the International Bar Association, in force at the date of the commencement of any arbitration under this clause, shall be applicable to the arbitrators appointed in respect of such arbitration."

The International Bar Association takes the position that (whatever may be the case in domestic arbitration) international arbitrators should in principle be granted immunity from suit under national laws, except in extreme cases of willful or reckless disregard of their legal obligations. Accordingly, the International Bar Association wishes to make it clear that it is not the intention of these rules to create opportunities for aggrieved parties to sue international arbitrators in national courts. The normal

---

*   The IBA Rules of Ethics for International Arbitrators, reprinted with kind permission from the International Bar Association, London, UK. © International Bar Association.

sanction for breach of an ethical duty is removal from office, with consequent loss of entitlement to remuneration. The International Bar Association also emphasises that these rules do not affect, and are intended to be consistent with, the International Code of Ethics for lawyers, adopted at Oslo on 25th July 1956, and amended by the General Meeting of the International Bar Association at Mexico City on 24th July 1964.

1. Fundamental Rule

Arbitrators shall proceed diligently and efficiently to provide the parties with a just and effective resolution of their disputes, and shall be and shall remain free from bias.

2. Acceptance of Appointment

2.1 A prospective arbitrator shall accept an appointment only if he is fully satisfied that he is able to discharge his duties without bias.

2.2 A prospective arbitrator shall accept an appointment only if he is fully satisfied that he is competent to determine the issues in dispute, and has an adequate knowledge of the language of the arbitration.

2.3 A prospective arbitrator should accept an appointment only if he is able to give to the arbitration the time and attention which the parties are reasonably entitled to expect.

2.4 It is inappropriate to contact parties in order to solicit appointment as arbitrator.

3. Elements of Bias

3.1 The criteria for assessing questions relating to bias are impartiality and independence. Partiality arises where an arbitrator favours one of the parties, or where he is prejudiced in relation to the subject-matter of the dispute. Dependence arises from relationships between an arbitrator and one of the parties, or with someone closely connected with one of the parties.

3.2 Facts which might lead a reasonable person, not knowing the arbitrator's true state of mind, to consider that he is dependent on a party create an appearance of bias. The same is true if an arbitrator has a material interest in the outcome of the dispute, or if he has already taken a position in relation to it. The appearance of bias is best overcome by full disclosure as described in Article 4 below.

3.3 Any current direct or indirect business relationship between an arbitrator and a party, or with a person who is known to be a potentially important witness, will normally give rise to justifiable doubts as to a prospective arbitrator's impartiality or independence. He should decline to accept an appointment in such circumstances unless the parties agree in writing that he may proceed. Examples of indirect relationships are where a member of the prospective arbitrator's family, his firm, or any business partner has a business relationship with one of the parties.

3.4 Past business relationships will not operate as an absolute bar to acceptance of appointment, unless they are of such magnitude or nature as to be likely to affect a prospective arbitrator's judgment.

3.5 Continuous and substantial social or professional relationships between a prospective arbitrator and a party, or with a person who is known to be a potentially important witness in the arbitration, will normally give rise to justifiable doubts as to the impartiality or independence of a prospective arbitrator.

4. Duty of Disclosure

4.1 A prospective arbitrator should disclose all facts or circumstances that may give rise to justifiable doubts as to his impartiality or independence. Failure to make such disclosure creates an appearance of bias, and may of itself be a ground for disqualification even though the non-disclosed facts or circumstances would not of themselves justify disqualification.

4.2 A prospective arbitrator should disclose:

(a) any past or present business relationship, whether direct or indirect as illustrated in Article 3.3, including prior appointment as arbitrator, with any party to the dispute, or any representative of a party, or any person known to be a potentially important witness in the arbitration. With regard to present relationships, the duty of disclosure applies irrespective of their magnitude, but with regard to past relationships only if they were of more than a trivial nature in relation to the arbitrator's professional or business affairs. Non-disclosure of an indirect relationship unknown to a prospective arbitrator will not be a ground for disqualification unless it could have been ascertained by making reasonable enquiries;

(b) the nature and duration of any substantial social relationships with any party or any person known to be likely to be an important witness in the arbitration;

(c) the nature of any previous relationship with any fellow arbitrator (including prior joint service as an arbitrator);

(d) the extent of any prior knowledge he may have of the dispute;

(e) the extent of any commitments which may affect his availability to perform his duties as arbitrator as may be reasonably anticipated.

4.3 The duty of disclosure continues throughout the arbitral proceedings as regards new facts or circumstances.

4.4 Disclosure should be made in writing and communicated to all parties and arbitrators. When an arbitrator has been appointed, any previous disclosure made to the parties should be communicated to the other arbitrators.

5.   Communications with Parties

5.1 When approached with a view to appointment, a prospective arbitrator should make sufficient enquiries in order to inform himself whether there may be any justifiable doubts regarding his impartiality or independence; whether he is competent to determine the issues in dispute; and whether he is able to give the arbitration the time and attention required. He may also respond to enquiries from those approaching him, provided that such enquiries are designed to determine his suitability and availability for the appointment and provided that the merits of the case are not discussed. In the event that a prospective sole arbitrator or presiding arbitrator is approached by one party alone, or by one arbitrator chosen unilaterally by a party (a "party-nominated" arbitrator), he should ascertain that the other party or parties, or the other arbitrator, has consented to the manner in which he has been approached. In such circumstances he should, in writing or orally, inform the other party or parties, or the other arbitrator, of the substance of the initial conversation.

5.2 If a party-nominated arbitrator is required to participate in the selection of a third or presiding arbitrator, it is acceptable for him (although he is not so required) to obtain the views of the party who nominated him as to the acceptability of candidates being considered.

5.3 Throughout the arbitral proceedings, an arbitrator should avoid any unilateral communications regarding the case with any party, or its representatives. If such communication should occur, the arbitrator should inform the other party or parties and arbitrators of its substance.

5.4 If an arbitrator becomes aware that a fellow arbitrator has been in improper communication with a party, he may inform the remaining arbitrators and they should together determine what action should be taken. Normally, the appropriate initial course of action is for the offending arbitrator to be requested to refrain from making any further improper communications with the party. Where the offending arbitrator fails or refuses to refrain from improper communications, the remaining arbitrators may inform the innocent party in order that he may consider what action he should take. An arbitrator may act unilaterally to inform a party of the conduct of another arbitrator in order to allow the said party to consider a challenge of the offending arbitrator only in extreme circumstances, and after communicating his intention to his fellow arbitrators in writing.

5.5 No arbitrator should accept any gift or substantial hospitality, directly or indirectly, from any party to the arbitration. Sole arbitrators and presiding arbitrators should be particularly meticulous in avoiding significant social or professional contacts with any party to the arbitration other than in the presence of the other parties.

6.   Fees

Unless the parties agree otherwise or a party defaults, an arbitrator shall make no unilateral arrangements for fees or expenses.

7.   Duty of Diligence

All arbitrators should devote such time and attention as the parties may reasonably require having regard to all the circumstances of the case, and shall do their best to conduct the arbitration in such a manner that costs do not rise to an unreasonable proportion of the interests at stake.

8.   Involvement in Settlement Proposals

Where the parties have so requested, or consented to a suggestion to this effect by the arbitral tribunal, the tribunal as a whole (or the presiding arbitrator where appropriate), may make proposals for settlement to both parties simultaneously, and preferably in the presence of each other. Although any procedure is possible with the agreement of the parties, the arbitral tribunal should point out to the parties that it is undesirable that any arbitrator should discuss settlement terms with a party in the absence of the other parties since this will normally have the result that any arbitrator involved in such discussions will become disqualified from any future participation in the arbitration.

9.   Confidentiality of the Deliberations

The deliberations of the arbitral tribunal, and the contents of the award itself, remain confidential in perpetuity unless the parties release the arbitrators from this obligation. An arbitrator should not participate in, or give any information for the purpose of assistance in, any proceedings to consider the award unless, exceptionally, he considers it his duty to disclose any material misconduct or fraud on the part of his fellow arbitrators.

C. IBA GUIDELINES ON CONFLICTS OF INTEREST IN INTERNATIONAL ARBITRATION*

Adopted by resolution of the IBA Council on Thursday
23 October 2014

Introduction

1.   Arbitrators and party representatives are often unsure about the scope of their disclosure obligations. The growth of international business,

---

including larger corporate groups and international law firms, has generated more disclosures and resulted in increased complexity in the analysis of disclosure and conflict of interest issues. Parties have more opportunities to use challenges of arbitrators to delay arbitrations, or to deny the opposing party the arbitrator of its choice. Disclosure of any relationship, no matter how minor or serious, may lead to unwarranted or frivolous challenges. At the same time, it is important that more information be made available to the parties, so as to protect awards against challenges based upon alleged failures to disclose, and to promote a level playing field among parties and among counsel engaged in international arbitration.

2.   Parties, arbitrators, institutions and courts face complex decisions about the information that arbitrators should disclose and the standards to apply to disclosure. In addition, institutions and courts face difficult decisions when an objection or a challenge is made after a disclosure. There is a tension between, on the one hand, the parties' right to disclosure of circumstances that may call into question an arbitrator's impartiality or independence in order to protect the parties' right to a fair hearing, and, on the other hand, the need to avoid unnecessary challenges against arbitrators in order to protect the parties' ability to select arbitrators of their choosing.

3.   It is in the interest of the international arbitration community that arbitration proceedings are not hindered by ill-founded challenges against arbitrators and that the legitimacy of the process is not affected by uncertainty and a lack of uniformity in the applicable standards for disclosures, objections and challenges. The 2004 Guidelines reflected the view that the standards existing at the time lacked sufficient clarity and uniformity in their application. The Guidelines, therefore, set forth some 'General Standards and Explanatory Notes on the Standards'. Moreover, in order to promote greater consistency and to avoid unnecessary challenges and arbitrator withdrawals and removals, the Guidelines list specific situations indicating whether they warrant disclosure or disqualification of an arbitrator. Such lists, designated 'Red', 'Orange' and 'Green' (the 'Application Lists'), have been updated and appear at the end of these revised Guidelines.

4.   The Guidelines reflect the understanding of the IBA Arbitration Committee as to the best current international practice, firmly rooted in the principles expressed in the General Standards below. The General Standards and the Application Lists are based upon statutes and case law in a cross-section of jurisdictions, and upon the judgement and experience of practitioners involved in international arbitration. In reviewing the 2004 Guidelines, the IBA Arbitration Committee updated its analysis of the laws and practices in a number of jurisdictions. The Guidelines seek to balance the various interests of parties, representatives, arbitrators and

arbitration institutions, all of whom have a responsibility for ensuring the integrity, reputation and efficiency of international arbitration. Both the 2004 Working Group and the Subcommittee in 2012/2014 have sought and considered the views of leading arbitration institutions, corporate counsel and other persons involved in international arbitration through public consultations at IBA annual meetings, and at meetings with arbitrators and practitioners. The comments received were reviewed in detail and many were adopted. The IBA Arbitration Committee is grateful for the serious consideration given to its proposals by so many institutions and individuals.

5.   The Guidelines apply to international commercial arbitration and investment arbitration, whether the representation of the parties is carried out by lawyers or non-lawyers, and irrespective of whether or not non-legal professionals serve as arbitrators.

6.   These Guidelines are not legal provisions and do not override any applicable national law or arbitral rules chosen by the parties. However, it is hoped that, as was the case for the 2004 Guidelines and other sets of rules and guidelines of the IBA Arbitration Committee, the revised Guidelines will find broad acceptance within the international arbitration community, and that they will assist parties, practitioners, arbitrators, institutions and courts in dealing with these important questions of impartiality and independence. The IBA Arbitration Committee trusts that the Guidelines will be applied with robust common sense and without unduly formalistic interpretation.

7.   The Application Lists cover many of the varied situations that commonly arise in practice, but they do not purport to be exhaustive, nor could they be. Nevertheless, the IBA Arbitration Committee is confident that the Application Lists provide concrete guidance that is useful in applying the General Standards. The IBA Arbitration Committee will continue to study the actual use of the Guidelines with a view to furthering their improvement.

8.   In 1987, the IBA published Rules of Ethics for International Arbitrators. Those Rules cover more topics than these Guidelines, and they remain in effect as to subjects that are not discussed in the Guidelines. The Guidelines supersede the Rules of Ethics as to the matters treated here.

Part I:

**General Standards Regarding Impartiality,
Independence and Disclosure**

(1) General Principle

Every arbitrator shall be impartial and independent of the parties at the time of accepting an appointment to serve and shall remain so until the final award has been rendered or the proceedings have otherwise finally terminated.

Explanation to General Standard 1:

A fundamental principle underlying these Guidelines is that each arbitrator must be impartial and independent of the parties at the time he or she accepts an appointment to act as arbitrator, and must remain so during the entire course of the arbitration proceeding, including the time period for the correction or interpretation of a final award under the relevant rules, assuming such time period is known or readily ascertainable. The question has arisen as to whether this obligation should extend to the period during which the award may be challenged before the relevant courts. The decision taken is that this obligation should not extend in this manner, unless the final award may be referred back to the original Arbitral Tribunal under the relevant applicable law or relevant institutional rules. Thus, the arbitrator's obligation in this regard ends when the Arbitral Tribunal has rendered the final award, and any correction or interpretation as may be permitted under the relevant rules has been issued, or the time for seeking the same has elapsed, the proceedings have been finally terminated (for example, because of a settlement), or the arbitrator otherwise no longer has jurisdiction. If, after setting aside or other proceedings, the dispute is referred back to the same Arbitral Tribunal, a fresh round of disclosure and review of potential conflicts of interests may be necessary.

(2) Conflicts of Interest

  (a) *An arbitrator shall decline to accept an appointment or, if the arbitration has already been commenced, refuse to continue to act as an arbitrator, if he or she has any doubt as to his or her ability to be impartial or independent.*

  (b) *The same principle applies if facts or circumstances exist, or have arisen since the appointment, which, from the point of view of a reasonable third person having knowledge of the relevant facts and circumstances, would give rise to justifiable doubts as to the arbitrator's impartiality or independence, unless the parties have accepted the arbitrator in accordance with the requirements set out in General Standard 4.*

  (c) *Doubts are justifiable if a reasonable third person, having knowledge of the relevant facts and circumstances, would reach the conclusion that there is a likelihood that the arbitrator may be influenced by factors other than the merits of the case as presented by the parties in reaching his or her decision.*

(d) Justifiable doubts necessarily exist as to the arbitrator's impartiality or independence in any of the situations described in the Non-Waivable Red List.

Explanation to General Standard 2:

(a)   If the arbitrator has doubts as to his or her ability to be impartial and independent, the arbitrator must decline the appointment. This standard should apply regardless of the stage of the proceedings. This is a basic principle that is spelled out in these Guidelines in order to avoid confusion and to foster confidence in the arbitral process.

(b)   In order for standards to be applied as consistently as possible, the test for disqualification is an objective one. The wording 'impartiality or independence' derives from the widely adopted Article 12 of the United Nations Commission on International Trade Law (UNCITRAL) Model Law, and the use of an appearance test based on justifiable doubts as to the impartiality or independence of the arbitrator, as provided in Article 12(2) of the UNCITRAL Model Law, is to be applied objectively (a 'reasonable third person test'). Again, as described in the Explanation to General Standard 3(e), this standard applies regardless of the stage of the proceedings.

(c)   Laws and rules that rely on the standard of justifiable doubts often do not define that standard. This General Standard is intended to provide some context for making this determination.

(d)   The Non-Waivable Red List describes circumstances that necessarily raise justifiable doubts as to the arbitrator's impartiality or independence. For example, because no one is allowed to be his or her own judge, there cannot be identity between an arbitrator and a party. The parties, therefore, cannot waive the conflict of interest arising in such a situation.

(3) Disclosure by the Arbitrator

(a)   If facts or circumstances exist that may, in the eyes of the parties, give rise to doubts as to the arbitrator's impartiality or independence, the arbitrator shall disclose such facts or circumstances to the parties, the arbitration institution or other appointing authority (if any, and if so required by the applicable institutional rules) and the co-arbitrators, if any, prior to accepting his or her appointment or, if thereafter, as soon as he or she learns of them.

(b)   An advance declaration or waiver in relation to possible conflicts of interest arising from facts and circumstances that may arise in the future does not discharge the arbitrator's ongoing duty of disclosure under General Standard 3(a).

(c)   *It follows from General Standards 1 and 2(a) that an arbitrator who has made a disclosure considers himself or herself to be impartial and independent of the parties, despite the disclosed facts, and, therefore, capable of performing his or her duties as arbitrator. Otherwise, he or she would have declined the nomination or appointment at the outset, or resigned.*

(d)   *Any doubt as to whether an arbitrator should disclose certain facts or circumstances should be resolved in favour of disclosure.*

(e)   *When considering whether facts or circumstances exist that should be disclosed, the arbitrator shall not take into account whether the arbitration is at the beginning or at a later stage.*

Explanation to General Standard 3:

(a)   The arbitrator's duty to disclose under General Standard 3(a) rests on the principle that the parties have an interest in being fully informed of any facts or circumstances that may be relevant in their view. Accordingly, General Standard 3(d) provides that any doubt as to whether certain facts or circumstances should be disclosed should be resolved in favour of disclosure. However, situations that, such as those set out in the Green List, could never lead to disqualification under the objective test set out in General Standard 2, need not be disclosed. As reflected in General Standard 3(c), a disclosure does not imply that the disclosed facts are such as to disqualify the arbitrator under General Standard 2. The duty of disclosure under General Standard 3(a) is ongoing in nature.

(b)   The IBA Arbitration Committee has considered the increasing use by prospective arbitrators of declarations in respect of facts or circumstances that may arise in the future, and the possible conflicts of interest that may result, sometimes referred to as 'advance waivers'. Such declarations do not discharge the arbitrator's ongoing duty of disclosure under General Standard 3(a). The Guidelines, however, do not otherwise take a position as to the validity and effect of advance declarations or waivers, because the validity and effect of any advance declaration or waiver must be assessed in view of the specific text of the advance declaration or waiver, the particular circumstances at hand and the applicable law.

(c)   A disclosure does not imply the existence of a conflict of interest. An arbitrator who has made a disclosure to the parties considers himself or herself to be impartial and independent of the parties, despite the disclosed facts, or else he or she would have declined the nomination, or resigned. An arbitrator making a disclosure thus feels capable of performing his or her duties. It is the purpose of disclosure to allow the parties to judge whether they agree with the evaluation of the arbitrator and, if they so wish, to explore the situation further. It is hoped that the promulgation of this General Standard will eliminate the misconception that disclosure itself implies doubts sufficient to disqualify the arbitrator, or even creates a presumption in favour of disqualification. Instead, any challenge should only be successful if an objective test, as set forth in General Standard 2 above, is met. Under Comment 5 of the Practical Application of the General Standards, a failure to disclose certain facts and circumstances that may, in the eyes of the parties, give rise to doubts as to the arbitrator's impartiality or independence, does not necessarily mean that a conflict of interest exists, or that a disqualification should ensue.

(d)   In determining which facts should be disclosed, an arbitrator should take into account all circumstances known to him or her. If the arbitrator finds that he or she should make a disclosure, but that professional secrecy rules or other rules of practice or professional conduct prevent such disclosure, he or she should not accept the appointment, or should resign.

(e)   Disclosure or disqualification (as set out in General Standards 2 and 3) should not depend on the particular stage of the arbitration. In order to determine whether the arbitrator should disclose, decline the appointment or refuse to continue to act, the facts and circumstances alone are relevant, not the current stage of the proceedings, or the consequences of the withdrawal. As a practical matter, arbitration institutions may make a distinction depending on the stage of the arbitration. Courts may likewise apply different standards. Nevertheless, no distinction is made by these Guidelines depending on the stage of the arbitral proceedings. While there are practical concerns, if an arbitrator must withdraw after the arbitration has commenced, a distinction based on the stage of the arbitration would be inconsistent with the General Standards.

(4) Waiver by the Parties

(a) *If, within 30 days after the receipt of any disclosure by the arbitrator, or after a party otherwise learns of facts or circumstances that could constitute a potential conflict of interest for an arbitrator, a party does not raise an express objection with regard to that arbitrator, subject to paragraphs (b) and (c) of this General Standard, the party is deemed to have waived any potential conflict of interest in respect of the arbitrator based on such facts or circumstances and may not raise any objection based on such facts or circumstances at a later stage.*

(b) *However, if facts or circumstances exist as described in the Non-Waivable Red List, any waiver by a party (including any declaration or advance waiver, such as that contemplated in General Standard 3(b)), or any agreement by the parties to have such a person serve as arbitrator, shall be regarded as invalid.*

(c) *A person should not serve as an arbitrator when a conflict of interest, such as those exemplified in the Waivable Red List, exists. Nevertheless, such a person may accept appointment as arbitrator, or continue to act as an arbitrator, if the following conditions are met:*

> *(i)   all parties, all arbitrators and the arbitration institution, or other appointing authority (if any), have full knowledge of the conflict of interest; and*

> *(ii) all parties expressly agree that such a person may serve as arbitrator, despite the conflict of interest.*

(d)   An arbitrator may assist the parties in reaching a settlement of the dispute, through conciliation, mediation or otherwise, at any stage of the proceedings. However, before doing so, the arbitrator should receive an express agreement by the parties that acting in such a manner shall not disqualify the arbitrator from continuing to serve as arbitrator. Such express agreement shall be considered to be an effective waiver of any potential conflict of interest that may arise from the arbitrator's participation in such a process, or from information that the arbitrator may learn in the process. If the assistance by the arbitrator does not lead to the final settlement of the case, the parties remain bound by their waiver. However, consistent with General Standard 2(a) and notwithstanding such agreement, the arbitrator shall resign if, as a consequence of his or her involvement in the settlement process, the arbitrator develops doubts as to his or her ability to remain impartial or independent in the future course of the arbitration.

Explanation to General Standard 4:

(a)   Under General Standard 4(a), a party is deemed to have waived any potential conflict of interest, if such party has not raised an objection in respect of such conflict of interest within 30 days. This time limit should run from the date on which the party learns of the relevant facts or circumstances, including through the disclosure process.

(b)   General Standard 4(b) serves to exclude from the scope of General Standard 4(a) the facts and circumstances described in the Non-Waivable Red List. Some arbitrators make declarations that seek waivers from the parties with respect to facts or circumstances that may arise in the future. Irrespective of any such waiver sought by the arbitrator, as provided in General Standard 3(b), facts and circumstances arising in the course of the arbitration should be disclosed to the parties by virtue of the arbitrator's ongoing duty of disclosure.

(c)   Notwithstanding a serious conflict of interest, such as those that are described by way of example in the Waivable Red List, the parties may wish to engage such a person as an arbitrator. Here, party autonomy and the desire to have only impartial and independent arbitrators must be balanced. Persons with a serious conflict of interest, such as those that are described by way of example in the Waivable Red List, may serve as arbitrators only if the parties make fully informed, explicit waivers.

(d) The concept of the Arbitral Tribunal assisting the parties in reaching a settlement of their dispute in the course of the arbitration proceedings is well-established in some jurisdictions, but not in others. Informed consent by the parties to such a process prior to its beginning should be regarded as an effective waiver of a potential conflict of interest. Certain jurisdictions may require such consent to be in writing and signed by the parties. Subject to any requirements of applicable law, express consent may be sufficient and may be given at a hearing and reflected in the minutes or transcript of the proceeding. In addition, in order to avoid parties using an arbitrator as mediator as a means of disqualifying the arbitrator, the General Standard makes clear that the waiver should remain effective, if the mediation is unsuccessful. In giving their express consent, the parties should realise the consequences of the arbitrator assisting them in a settlement process, including the risk of the resignation of the arbitrator.

(5) Scope

> (a) *These Guidelines apply equally to tribunal chairs, sole arbitrators and co-arbitrators, howsoever appointed.*
>
> (b) *Arbitral or administrative secretaries and assistants, to an individual arbitrator or the Arbitral Tribunal, are bound by the same duty of independence and impartiality as arbitrators, and it is the responsibility of the Arbitral Tribunal to ensure that such duty is respected at all stages of the arbitration.*

Explanation to General Standard 5:

(a) Because each member of an Arbitral Tribunal has an obligation to be impartial and independent, the General Standards do not distinguish between sole arbitrators, tribunal chairs, party-appointed arbitrators or arbitrators appointed by an institution.

(b) Some arbitration institutions require arbitral or administrative secretaries and assistants to sign a declaration of independence and impartiality. Whether or not such a requirement exists, arbitral or administrative secretaries and assistants to the Arbitral Tribunal are bound by the same duty of independence and impartiality (including the duty of disclosure) as arbitrators, and it is the responsibility of the Arbitral Tribunal to ensure that such duty is respected at all stages of the arbitration. Furthermore, this duty applies to arbitral or administrative secretaries and assistants to either the Arbitral Tribunal or individual members of the Arbitral Tribunal.

(6) Relationships

>   *(a) The arbitrator is in principle considered to bear the identity of his or her law firm, but when considering the relevance of facts or circumstances to determine whether a potential conflict of interest exists, or whether disclosure should be made, the activities of an arbitrator's law firm, if any, and the relationship of the arbitrator with the law firm, should be considered in each individual case. The fact that the activities of the arbitrator's firm involve one of the parties shall not necessarily constitute a source of such conflict, or a reason for disclosure. Similarly, if one of the parties is a member of a group with which the arbitrator's firm has a relationship, such fact should be considered in each individual case, but shall not necessarily constitute by itself a source of a conflict of interest, or a reason for disclosure.*

>   *(b) If one of the parties is a legal entity, any legal or physical person having a controlling influence on the legal entity, or a direct economic interest in, or a duty to indemnify a party for, the award to be rendered in the arbitration, may be considered to bear the identity of such party.*

Explanation to General Standard 6:

(a) The growing size of law firms should be taken into account as part of today's reality in international arbitration. There is a need to balance the interests of a party to appoint the arbitrator of its choice, who may be a partner at a large law firm, and the importance of maintaining confidence in the impartiality and independence of international arbitrators. The arbitrator must, in principle, be considered to bear the identity of his or her law firm, but the activities of the arbitrator's firm should not automatically create a conflict of interest. The relevance of the activities of the arbitrator's firm, such as the nature, timing and scope of the work by the law firm, and the relationship of the arbitrator with the law firm, should be considered in each case. General Standard 6(a) uses the term 'involve' rather than 'acting for' because the relevant connections with a party may include activities other than representation on a legal matter. Although barristers' chambers should not be equated with law firms for the purposes of conflicts, and no general standard is proffered for barristers' chambers, disclosure may be warranted in view of the relationships among barristers, parties or counsel. When a party to an arbitration is a member of a group of companies, special questions regarding conflicts of interest arise. Because individual corporate structure arrangements vary widely, a catch-all rule is not appropriate. Instead, the particular circumstances of an affiliation with another entity within the same group of companies, and the relationship of that entity with the arbitrator's law firm, should be considered in each individual case.

(b)   When a party in international arbitration is a legal entity, other legal and physical persons may have a controlling influence on this legal entity, or a direct economic interest in, or a duty to indemnify a party for, the award to be rendered in the arbitration. Each situation should be assessed individually, and General Standard 6(b) clarifies that such legal persons and individuals may be considered effectively to be that party. Third-party funders and insurers in relation to the dispute may have a direct economic interest in the award, and as such may be considered to be the equivalent of the party. For these purposes, the terms 'third-party funder' and 'insurer' refer to any person or entity that is contributing funds, or other material support, to the prosecution or defence of the case and that has a direct economic interest in, or a duty to indemnify a party for, the award to be rendered in the arbitration.

(7) Duty of the Parties and the Arbitrator

(a)   *A party shall inform an arbitrator, the Arbitral Tribunal, the other parties and the arbitration institution or other appointing authority (if any) of any relationship, direct or indirect, between the arbitrator and the party (or another company of the same group of companies, or an individual having a controlling influence on the party in the arbitration), or between the arbitrator and any person or entity with a direct economic interest in, or a duty to indemnify a party for, the award to be rendered in the arbitration. The party shall do so on its own initiative at the earliest opportunity.*

(b)   *A party shall inform an arbitrator, the Arbitral Tribunal, the other parties and the arbitration institution or other appointing authority (if any) of the identity of its counsel appearing in the arbitration, as well as of any relationship, including membership of the same barristers' chambers, between its counsel and the arbitrator. The party shall do so on its own initiative at the earliest opportunity, and upon any change in its counsel team.*

(c)   *In order to comply with General Standard 7(a), a party shall perform reasonable enquiries and provide any relevant information available to it.*

(d)   *An arbitrator is under a duty to make reasonable enquiries to identify any conflict of interest, as well as any facts or circumstances that may reasonably give rise to doubts as to his or her impartiality or independence. Failure to disclose a conflict is not excused by lack of knowledge, if the arbitrator does not perform such reasonable enquiries.*

Explanation to General Standard 7:

(a) The parties are required to disclose any relationship with the arbitrator. Disclosure of such relationships should reduce the risk of an unmeritorious challenge of an arbitrator's impartiality or independence based on information learned after the appointment. The parties' duty of disclosure of any relationship, direct or indirect, between the arbitrator and the party (or another company of the same group of companies, or an individual having a controlling influence on the party in the arbitration) has been extended to relationships with persons or entities having a direct economic interest in the award to be rendered in the arbitration, such as an entity providing funding for the arbitration, or having a duty to indemnify a party for the award.

(b) Counsel appearing in the arbitration, namely the persons involved in the representation of the parties in the arbitration, must be identified by the parties at the earliest opportunity. A party's duty to disclose the identity of counsel appearing in the arbitration extends to all members of that party's counsel team and arises from the outset of the proceedings.

(c) In order to satisfy their duty of disclosure, the parties are required to investigate any relevant information that is reasonably available to them. In addition, any party to an arbitration is required, at the outset and on an ongoing basis during the entirety of the proceedings, to make a reasonable effort to ascertain and to disclose available information that, applying the general standard, might affect the arbitrator's impartiality or independence.

(d) In order to satisfy their duty of disclosure under the Guidelines, arbitrators are required to investigate any relevant information that is reasonably available to them.

Part II: Practical Application of the General Standards

1. If the Guidelines are to have an important practical influence, they should address situations that are likely to occur in today's arbitration practice and should provide specific guidance to arbitrators, parties, institutions and courts as to which situations do or do not constitute conflicts of interest, or should or should not be disclosed. For this purpose, the Guidelines categorise situations that may occur in the following Application Lists. These lists cannot cover every situation. In all cases, the General Standards should control the outcome.

2. The Red List consists of two parts: 'a Non-Waivable Red List' (see General Standards 2(d) and 4(b)); and 'a Waivable Red List' (see General Standard 4(c)). These lists are non-exhaustive and detail specific situations that, depending on the facts of a given case, give rise to justifiable doubts as to the arbitrator's impartiality and independence. That is, in these circumstances, an objective conflict of interest exists from the point of view

of a reasonable third person having knowledge of the relevant facts and circumstances (see General Standard 2(b)). The Non-Waivable Red List includes situations deriving from the overriding principle that no person can be his or her own judge. Therefore, acceptance of such a situation cannot cure the conflict. The Waivable Red List covers situations that are serious but not as severe. Because of their seriousness, unlike circumstances described in the Orange List, these situations should be considered waivable, but only if and when the parties, being aware of the conflict of interest situation, expressly state their willingness to have such a person act as arbitrator, as set forth in General Standard 4(c).

3.   The Orange List is a non-exhaustive list of specific situations that, depending on the facts of a given case, may, in the eyes of the parties, give rise to doubts as to the arbitrator's impartiality or independence. The Orange List thus reflects situations that would fall under General Standard 3(a), with the consequence that the arbitrator has a duty to disclose such situations. In all these situations, the parties are deemed to have accepted the arbitrator if, after disclosure, no timely objection is made, as established in General Standard 4(a).

4.   Disclosure does not imply the existence of a conflict of interest; nor should it by itself result either in a disqualification of the arbitrator, or in a presumption regarding disqualification. The purpose of the disclosure is to inform the parties of a situation that they may wish to explore further in order to determine whether objectively—that is, from the point of view of a reasonable third person having knowledge of the relevant facts and circumstances—there are justifiable doubts as to the arbitrator's impartiality or independence. If the conclusion is that there are no justifiable doubts, the arbitrator can act. Apart from the situations covered by the Non-Waivable Red List, he or she can also act if there is no timely objection by the parties or, in situations covered by the Waivable Red List, if there is a specific acceptance by the parties in accordance with General Standard 4(c). If a party challenges the arbitrator, he or she can nevertheless act, if the authority that rules on the challenge decides that the challenge does not meet the objective test for disqualification.

5.   A later challenge based on the fact that an arbitrator did not disclose such facts or circumstances should not result automatically in non-appointment, later disqualification or a successful challenge to any award. Nondisclosure cannot by itself make an arbitrator partial or lacking independence: only the facts or circumstances that he or she failed to disclose can do so.

6.   Situations not listed in the Orange List or falling outside the time limits used in some of the Orange List situations are generally not subject to disclosure. However, an arbitrator needs to assess on a case-by-case basis whether a given situation, even though not mentioned in the Orange

List, is nevertheless such as to give rise to justifiable doubts as to his or her impartiality or independence. Because the Orange List is a non-exhaustive list of examples, there may be situations not mentioned, which, depending on the circumstances, may need to be disclosed by an arbitrator. Such may be the case, for example, in the event of repeat past appointments by the same party or the same counsel beyond the three-year period provided for in the Orange List, or when an arbitrator concurrently acts as counsel in an unrelated case in which similar issues of law are raised. Likewise, an appointment made by the same party or the same counsel appearing before an arbitrator, while the case is ongoing, may also have to be disclosed, depending on the circumstances. While the Guidelines do not require disclosure of the fact that an arbitrator concurrently serves, or has in the past served, on the same Arbitral Tribunal with another member of the tribunal, or with one of the counsel in the current proceedings, an arbitrator should assess on a case-by-case basis whether the fact of having frequently served as counsel with, or as an arbitrator on, Arbitral Tribunals with another member of the tribunal may create a perceived imbalance within the tribunal. If the conclusion is 'yes', the arbitrator should consider a disclosure.

7.   The Green List is a non-exhaustive list of specific situations where no appearance and no actual conflict of interest exists from an objective point of view. Thus, the arbitrator has no duty to disclose situations falling within the Green List. As stated in the Explanation to General Standard 3(a), there should be a limit to disclosure, based on reasonableness; in some situations, an objective test should prevail over the purely subjective test of 'the eyes' of the parties.

8.   The borderline between the categories that comprise the Lists can be thin. It can be debated whether a certain situation should be on one List instead of another. Also, the Lists contain, for various situations, general terms such as 'significant' and 'relevant'. The Lists reflect international principles and best practices to the extent possible. Further definition of the norms, which are to be interpreted reasonably in light of the facts and circumstances in each case, would be counterproductive.

1.   Non-Waivable Red List

1.1 There is an identity between a party and the arbitrator, or the arbitrator is a legal representative or employee of an entity that is a party in the arbitration.

1.2 The arbitrator is a manager, director or member of the supervisory board, or has a controlling influence on one of the parties or an entity that has a direct economic interest in the award to be rendered in the arbitration.

1.3 The arbitrator has a significant financial or personal interest in one of the parties, or the outcome of the case.

1.4 The arbitrator or his or her firm regularly advises the party, or an affiliate of the party, and the arbitrator or his or her firm derives significant financial income therefrom.

2. Waivable Red List

2.1 Relationship of the arbitrator to the dispute

>   2.1.1   The arbitrator has given legal advice, or provided an expert opinion, on the dispute to a party or an affiliate of one of the parties.

>   2.1.2   The arbitrator had a prior involvement in the dispute.

2.2 Arbitrator's direct or indirect interest in the dispute

>   2.2.1   The arbitrator holds shares, either directly or indirectly, in one of the parties, or an affiliate of one of the parties, this party or an affiliate being privately held.

>   2.2.2   A close family member[3] of the arbitrator has a significant financial interest in the outcome of the dispute.

>   2.2.3   The arbitrator, or a close family member of the arbitrator, has a close relationship with a non-party who may be liable to recourse on the part of the unsuccessful party in the dispute.

2.3 Arbitrator's relationship with the parties or counsel

>   2.3.1   The arbitrator currently represents or advises one of the parties, or an affiliate of one of the parties.

>   2.3.2   The arbitrator currently represents or advises the lawyer or law firm acting as counsel for one of the parties.

>   2.3.3   The arbitrator is a lawyer in the same law firm as the counsel to one of the parties.

>   2.3.4   The arbitrator is a manager, director or member of the supervisory board, or has a controlling influence in an affiliate[4] of one of the parties, if the affiliate is directly involved in the matters in dispute in the arbitration.

>   2.3.5   The arbitrator's law firm had a previous but terminated involvement in the case without the arbitrator being involved himself or herself.

>   2.3.6   The arbitrator's law firm currently has a significant commercial relationship with one of the parties, or an affiliate of one of the parties.

---

[3]   Throughout the Application Lists, the term 'close family member' refers to a: spouse, sibling, child, parent or life partner, in addition to any other family member with whom a close relationship exists.

[4]   Throughout the Application Lists, the term 'affiliate' encompasses all companies in a group of companies, including the parent company.

2.3.7   The arbitrator regularly advises one of the parties, or an affiliate of one of the parties, but neither the arbitrator nor his or her firm derives a significant financial income therefrom.

2.3.8   The arbitrator has a close family relationship with one of the parties, or with a manager, director or member of the supervisory board, or any person having a controlling influence in one of the parties, or an affiliate of one of the parties, or with a counsel representing a party.

2.3.9   A close family member of the arbitrator has a significant financial or personal interest in one of the parties, or an affiliate of one of the parties.

3.   Orange List

3.1   Previous services for one of the parties or other involvement in the case

3.1.1   The arbitrator has, within the past three years, served as counsel for one of the parties, or an affiliate of one of the parties, or has previously advised or been consulted by the party, or an affiliate of the party, making the appointment in an unrelated matter, but the arbitrator and the party, or the affiliate of the party, have no ongoing relationship.

3.1.2   The arbitrator has, within the past three years, served as counsel against one of the parties, or an affiliate of one of the parties, in an unrelated matter.

3.1.3   The arbitrator has, within the past three years, been appointed as arbitrator on two or more occasions by one of the parties, or an affiliate of one of the parties.[5]

3.1.4   The arbitrator's law firm has, within the past three years, acted for or against one of the parties, or an affiliate of one of the parties, in an unrelated matter without the involvement of the arbitrator.

3.1.5   The arbitrator currently serves, or has served within the past three years, as arbitrator in another arbitration involving one of the parties, or an affiliate of one of the parties.

3.2   Current services for one of the parties

3.2.1   The arbitrator's law firm is currently rendering services to one of the parties, or to an affiliate of one of the parties, without

---

[5] It may be the practice in certain types of arbitration, such as maritime, sports or commodities arbitration, to draw arbitrators from a smaller or specialised pool of individuals. If in such fields it is the custom and practice for parties to frequently appoint the same arbitrator in different cases, no disclosure of this fact is required, where all parties in the arbitration should be familiar with such custom and practice.

creating a significant commercial relationship for the law firm and without the involvement of the arbitrator.

3.2.2   A law firm or other legal organisation that shares significant fees or other revenues with the arbitrator's law firm renders services to one of the parties, or an affiliate of one of the parties, before the Arbitral Tribunal.

3.3.3   The arbitrator or his or her firm represents a party, or an affiliate of one of the parties to the arbitration, on a regular basis, but such representation does not concern the current dispute.

3.3 Relationship between an arbitrator and another arbitrator or counsel

3.3.1   The arbitrator and another arbitrator are lawyers in the same law firm.

3.3.2   The arbitrator and another arbitrator, or the counsel for one of the parties, are members of the same barristers' chambers.

3.3.3   The arbitrator was, within the past three years, a partner of, or otherwise affiliated with, another arbitrator or any of the counsel in the arbitration.

3.3.4   A lawyer in the arbitrator's law firm is an arbitrator in another dispute involving the same party or parties, or an affiliate of one of the parties.

3.3.5   A close family member of the arbitrator is a partner or employee of the law firm representing one of the parties, but is not assisting with the dispute.

3.3.6   A close personal friendship exists between an arbitrator and a counsel of a party.

3.3.7   Enmity exists between an arbitrator and counsel appearing in the arbitration.

3.3.8   The arbitrator has, within the past three years, been appointed on more than three occasions by the same counsel, or the same law firm.

3.3.9   The arbitrator and another arbitrator, or counsel for one of the parties in the arbitration, currently act or have acted together within the past three years as co-counsel.

3.4 Relationship between arbitrator and party and others involved in the arbitration

3.4.1   The arbitrator's law firm is currently acting adversely to one of the parties, or an affiliate of one of the parties.

3.4.2   The arbitrator has been associated with a party, or an affiliate of one of the parties, in a professional capacity, such as a former employee or partner.

3.4.3   A close personal friendship exists between an arbitrator and a manager or director or a member of the supervisory board of: a party; an entity that has a direct economic interest in the award to be rendered in the arbitration; or any person having a controlling influence, such as a controlling shareholder interest, on one of the parties or an affiliate of one of the parties or a witness or expert.

3.4.4   Enmity exists between an arbitrator and a manager or director or a member of the supervisory board of: a party; an entity that has a direct economic interest in the award; or any person having a controlling influence in one of the parties or an affiliate of one of the parties or a witness or expert.

3.4.5   If the arbitrator is a former judge, he or she has, within the past three years, heard a significant case involving one of the parties, or an affiliate of one of the parties.

3.5   Other circumstances

3.5.1   The arbitrator holds shares, either directly or indirectly, that by reason of number or denomination constitute a material holding in one of the parties, or an affiliate of one of the parties, this party or affiliate being publicly listed.

3.5.2   The arbitrator has publicly advocated a position on the case, whether in a published paper, or speech, or otherwise.

3.5.3   The arbitrator holds a position with the appointing authority with respect to the dispute.

3.5.4   The arbitrator is a manager, director or member of the supervisory board, or has a controlling influence on an affiliate of one of the parties, where the affiliate is not directly involved in the matters in dispute in the arbitration.

4.   Green List

4.1   Previously expressed legal opinions

4.1.1   The arbitrator has previously expressed a legal opinion (such as in a law review article or public lecture) concerning an issue that also arises in the arbitration (but this opinion is not focused on the case).

4.2   Current services for one of the parties

4.2.1   A firm, in association or in alliance with the arbitrator's law firm, but that does not share significant fees or other revenues with the arbitrator's law firm, renders services to one of the parties, or an affiliate of one of the parties, in an unrelated matter.

4.3   Contacts with another arbitrator, or with counsel for one of the parties

4.3.1   The arbitrator has a relationship with another arbitrator, or with the counsel for one of the parties, through membership in the same professional association, or social or charitable organisation, or through a social media network.

4.3.2   The arbitrator and counsel for one of the parties have previously served together as arbitrators.

4.3.3   The arbitrator teaches in the same faculty or school as another arbitrator or counsel to one of the parties, or serves as an officer of a professional association or social or charitable organisation with another arbitrator or counsel for one of the parties.

4.3.4   The arbitrator was a speaker, moderator or organiser in one or more conferences, or participated in seminars or working parties of a professional, social or charitable organisation, with another arbitrator or counsel to the parties.

4.4   Contacts between the arbitrator and one of the parties

4.4.1   The arbitrator has had an initial contact with a party, or an affiliate of a party (or their counsel) prior to appointment, if this contact is limited to the arbitrator's availability and qualifications to serve, or to the names of possible candidates for a chairperson, and did not address the merits or procedural aspects of the dispute, other than to provide the arbitrator with a basic understanding of the case.

4.4.2   The arbitrator holds an insignificant amount of shares in one of the parties, or an affiliate of one of the parties, which is publicly listed.

4.4.3   The arbitrator and a manager, director or member of the supervisory board, or any person having a controlling influence on one of the parties, or an affiliate of one of the parties, have worked together as joint experts, or in another professional capacity, including as arbitrators in the same case.

4.4.4   The arbitrator has a relationship with one of the parties or its affiliates through a social media network.

D. IBA GUIDELINES ON PARTY REPRESENTATION IN INTERNATIONAL ARBITRATION*

Adopted by a resolution of the IBA Council 25 May 2013
International Bar Association

Preamble

The IBA Arbitration Committee established the Task Force on Counsel Conduct in International Arbitration (the 'Task Force') in 2008.

The mandate of the Task Force was to focus on issues of counsel conduct and party representation in international arbitration that are subject to, or informed by, diverse and potentially conflicting rules and norms. As an initial inquiry, the Task Force undertook to determine whether such differing norms and practises may undermine the fundamental fairness and integrity of international arbitral proceedings and whether international guidelines on party representation in international arbitration may assist parties, counsel and arbitrators. In 2010, the Task Force commissioned a survey (the 'Survey') in order to examine these issues. Respondents to the Survey expressed support for the development of international guidelines for party representation.

The Task Force proposed draft guidelines to the IBA Arbitration Committee's officers in October 2012. The Committee then reviewed the draft guidelines and consulted with experienced arbitration practitioners, arbitrators and arbitral institutions. The draft guidelines were then submitted to all members of the IBA Arbitration Committee for consideration.

Unlike in domestic judicial settings, in which counsel are familiar with, and subject, to a single set of professional conduct rules, party representatives in international arbitration may be subject to diverse and potentially conflicting bodies of domestic rules and norms. The range of rules and norms applicable to the representation of parties in international arbitration may include those of the party representative's home jurisdiction, the arbitral seat, and the place where hearings physically take place. The Survey revealed a high degree of uncertainty among respondents regarding what rules govern party representation in international arbitration. The potential for confusion may be aggravated when individual counsel working collectively, either within a firm or through a co-counsel relationship, are themselves admitted to practise in multiple jurisdictions that have conflicting rules and norms.

In addition to the potential for uncertainty, rules and norms developed for domestic judicial litigation may be ill-adapted to international arbitral

---

proceedings. Indeed, specialised practises and procedures have been developed in international arbitration to accommodate the legal and cultural differences among participants and the complex, multinational nature of the disputes. Domestic professional conduct rules and norms, by contrast, are developed to apply in specific legal cultures consistent with established national procedures.

The IBA Guidelines on Party Representation in International Arbitration (the 'Guidelines') are inspired by the principle that party representatives should act with integrity and honesty and should not engage in activities designed to produce unnecessary delay or expense, including tactics aimed at obstructing the arbitration proceedings.

As with the International Principles on Conduct for the Legal Profession, adopted by the IBA on 28 May 2011, the Guidelines are not intended to displace otherwise applicable mandatory laws, professional or disciplinary rules, or agreed arbitration rules that may be relevant or applicable to matters of party representation. They are also not intended to vest arbitral tribunals with powers otherwise reserved to bars or other professional bodies.

The use of the term guidelines rather than rules is intended to highlight their contractual nature. The parties may thus adopt the Guidelines or a portion thereof by agreement. Arbitral tribunals may also apply the Guidelines in their discretion, subject to any applicable mandatory rules, if they determine that they have the authority to do so.

The Guidelines are not intended to limit the flexibility that is inherent in, and a considerable advantage of, international arbitration, and parties and arbitral tribunals may adapt them to the particular circumstances of each arbitration.

Definitions

In the IBA Guidelines on Party Representation in International Arbitration:

'Arbitral Tribunal' or 'Tribunal' means a sole Arbitrator or a panel of Arbitrators in the arbitration;

'Arbitrator' means an arbitrator in the arbitration;

'Document' means a writing, communication, picture, drawing, program or data of any kind, whether recorded or maintained on paper or by electronic, audio, visual or any other means;

'Domestic Bar' or 'Bar' means the national or local authority or authorities responsible for the regulation of the professional conduct of lawyers;

'Evidence' means documentary evidence and written and oral testimony.

'Ex Parte Communications' means oral or written communications between a Party Representative and an Arbitrator or prospective Arbitrator without the presence or knowledge of the opposing Party or Parties;

'Expert' means a person or organisation appearing before an Arbitral Tribunal to provide expert analysis and opinion on specific issues determined by a Party or by the Arbitral Tribunal;

'Expert Report' means a written statement by an Expert;

'Guidelines' mean these IBA Guidelines on Party Representation in International Arbitration, as they may be revised or amended from time to time;

'Knowingly' means with actual knowledge of the fact in question;

'Misconduct' means a breach of the present Guidelines or any other conduct that the Arbitral Tribunal determines to be contrary to the duties of a Party Representative;

'Party' means a party to the arbitration;

'Party-Nominated Arbitrator' means an Arbitrator who is nominated or appointed by one or more Parties;

'Party Representative' or 'Representative' means any person, including a Party's employee, who appears in an arbitration on behalf of a Party and makes submissions, arguments or representations to the Arbitral Tribunal on behalf of such Party, other than in the capacity as a Witness or Expert, and whether or not legally qualified or admitted to a Domestic Bar;

'Presiding Arbitrator' means an arbitrator who is either a sole Arbitrator or the chairperson of the Arbitral Tribunal;

'Request to Produce' means a written request by a Party that another Party produce Documents;

'Witness' means a person appearing before an Arbitral Tribunal to provide testimony of fact;

'Witness Statement' means a written statement by a Witness recording testimony.

Application of Guidelines

1.   The Guidelines shall apply where and to the extent that the Parties have so agreed, or the Arbitral Tribunal, after consultation with the Parties, wishes to rely upon them after having determined that it has the authority to rule on matters of Party representation to ensure the integrity and fairness of the arbitral proceedings.

2.   In the event of any dispute regarding the meaning of the Guidelines, the Arbitral Tribunal should interpret them in accordance with their

overall purpose and in the manner most appropriate for the particular arbitration.

3.   The Guidelines are not intended to displace otherwise applicable mandatory laws, professional or disciplinary rules, or agreed arbitration rules, in matters of Party representation. The Guidelines are also not intended to derogate from the arbitration agreement or to undermine either a Party representative's primary duty of loyalty to the party whom he or she represents or a Party representative's paramount obligation to present such Party's case to the Arbitral Tribunal.

Comments to Guidelines 1–3

As explained in the Preamble, the Parties and Arbitral Tribunals may benefit from guidance in matters of Party Representation, in particular in order to address instances where differing norms and expectations may threaten the integrity and fairness of the arbitral proceedings.

By virtue of these Guidelines, Arbitral Tribunals need not, in dealing with such issues, and subject to applicable mandatory laws, be limited by a choice-of-law rule or private international law analysis to choosing among national or domestic professional conduct rules. Instead, these Guidelines offer an approach designed to account for the multi-faceted nature of international arbitral proceedings.

These Guidelines shall apply where and to the extent that the Parties have so agreed. Parties may adopt these Guidelines, in whole or in part, in their arbitration agreement or at any time subsequently.

An Arbitral Tribunal may also apply, or draw inspiration from, the Guidelines, after having determined that it has the authority to rule on matters of Party representation in order to ensure the integrity and fairness of the arbitral proceedings. Before making such determination, the Arbitral Tribunal should give the Parties an opportunity to express their views.

These Guidelines do not state whether Arbitral Tribunals have the authority to rule on matters of Party representation and to apply the Guidelines in the absence of an agreement by the Parties to that effect. The Guidelines neither recognise nor exclude the existence of such authority. It remains for the Tribunal to make a determination as to whether it has the authority to rule on matters of Party representation and to apply the Guidelines.

A Party Representative, acting within the authority granted to it, acts on behalf of the Party whom he or she represents. It follows therefore that an obligation or duty bearing on a Party Representative is an obligation or duty of the represented Party, who may ultimately bear the consequences of the misconduct of its Representative.

Party Representation

4.   Party Representatives should identify themselves to the other Party or Parties and the Arbitral Tribunal at the earliest opportunity. A Party should promptly inform the Arbitral Tribunal and the other Party or Parties of any change in such representation.

5.   Once the Arbitral Tribunal has been constituted, a person should not accept representation of a Party in the arbitration when a relationship exists between the person and an Arbitrator that would create a conflict of interest, unless none of the Parties objects after proper disclosure.

6.   The Arbitral Tribunal may, in case of breach of Guideline 5, take measures appropriate to safeguard the integrity of the proceedings, including the exclusion of the new Party Representative from participating in all or part of the arbitral proceedings.

Comments to Guidelines 4–6

Changes in Party representation in the course of the arbitration may, because of conflicts of interest between a newly-appointed Party Representative and one or more of the Arbitrators, threaten the integrity of the proceedings. In such case, the Arbitral Tribunal may, if compelling circumstances so justify, and where it has found that it has the requisite authority, consider excluding the new Representative from participating in all or part of the arbitral proceedings. In assessing whether any such conflict of interest exists, the Arbitral Tribunal may rely on the IBA Guidelines on Conflicts of Interest in International Arbitration.

Before resorting to such measure, it is important that the Arbitral Tribunal give the Parties an opportunity to express their views about the existence of a conflict, the extent of the Tribunal's authority to act in relation to such conflict, and the consequences of the measure that the Tribunal is contemplating.

Communications with Arbitrators

7.   Unless agreed otherwise by the Parties, and subject to the exceptions below, a Party Representative should not engage in any Ex Parte Communications with an Arbitrator concerning the arbitration.

8.   It is not improper for a Party Representative to have Ex Parte Communications in the following circumstances:

    (a) A Party Representative may communicate with a prospective Party-Nominated Arbitrator to determine his or her expertise, experience, ability, availability, willingness and the existence of potential conflicts of interest.

    (b) A Party Representative may communicate with a prospective or appointed Party-Nominated Arbitrator for the purpose of the selection of the Presiding Arbitrator.

(c)   A Party Representative may, if the Parties are in agreement that such a communication is permissible, communicate with a prospective Presiding Arbitrator to determine his or her expertise, experience, ability, availability, willingness and the existence of potential conflicts of interest.

(d) While communications with a prospective Party-Nominated Arbitrator or Presiding Arbitrator may include a general description of the dispute, a Party Representative should not seek the views of the prospective Party-Nominated Arbitrator or Presiding Arbitrator on the substance of the dispute.

Comments to Guidelines 7–8

Guidelines 7–8 deal with communications between a Party Representative and an Arbitrator or potential Arbitrator concerning the arbitration.

The Guidelines seek to reflect best international practices and, as such, may depart from potentially diverging domestic arbitration practices that are more restrictive or, to the contrary, permit broader Ex Parte Communications.

Ex Parte Communications, as defined in these Guidelines, may occur only in defined circumstances, and a Party Representative should otherwise refrain from any such communication. The Guidelines do not seek to define when the relevant period begins or ends. Any communication that takes place in the context of, or in relation to, the constitution of the Arbitral Tribunal is covered.

Ex Parte Communications with a prospective Arbitrator (Party-Nominated or Presiding Arbitrator) should be limited to providing a general description of the dispute and obtaining information regarding the suitability of the potential Arbitrator, as described in further detail below. A Party Representative should not take the opportunity to seek the prospective Arbitrator's views on the substance of the dispute.

The following discussion topics are appropriate in pre-appointment communications in order to assess the prospective Arbitrator's expertise, experience, ability, availability, willingness and the existence of potential conflicts of interest:

(a)   the prospective Arbitrator's publications, including books, articles and conference papers or engagements;

(b)   any activities of the prospective Arbitrator and his or her law firm or organisation within which he or she operates, that may raise justifiable doubts as to the prospective Arbitrator's independence or impartiality;

(c)   a description of the general nature of the dispute;

(d) the terms of the arbitration agreement, and in particular any agreement as to the seat, language, applicable law and rules of the arbitration; (e) the identities of the Parties, Party Representatives, Witnesses, Experts and interested parties; and (f) the anticipated timetable and general conduct of the proceedings.

Applications to the Arbitral Tribunal without the presence or knowledge of the opposing Party or Parties may be permitted in certain circumstances, if the parties so agreed, or as permitted by applicable law. Such may be the case, in particular, for interim measures.

Finally, a Party Representative may communicate with the Arbitral Tribunal if the other Party or Parties fail to participate in a hearing or proceedings and are not represented.

Submissions to the Arbitral Tribunal

9. A Party Representative should not make any knowingly false submission of fact to the Arbitral Tribunal.

10. In the event that a Party Representative learns that he or she previously made a false submission of fact to the Arbitral Tribunal, the Party Representative should, subject to countervailing considerations of confidentiality and privilege, promptly correct such submission.

11. A Party Representative should not submit Witness or Expert evidence that he or she knows to be false. If a Witness or Expert intends to present or presents evidence that a Party Representative knows or later discovers to be false, such Party Representative should promptly advise the Party whom he or she represents of the necessity of taking remedial measures and of the consequences of failing to do so. Depending upon the circumstances, and subject to countervailing considerations of confidentiality and privilege, the Party Representative should promptly take remedial measures, which may include one or more of the following:

(a) advise the Witness or Expert to testify truthfully;

(b) take reasonable steps to deter the Witness or Expert from submitting false evidence;

(c) urge the Witness or Expert to correct or withdraw the false evidence;

(d) correct or withdraw the false evidence;

(e) withdraw as Party Representative if the circumstances so warrant.

Comments to Guidelines 9–11

Guidelines 9–11 concern the responsibility of a Party Representative when making submissions and tendering evidence to the Arbitral Tribunal. This principle is sometimes referred to as the duty of candour or honesty owed to the Tribunal.

The Guidelines identify two aspects of the responsibility of a Party Representative: the first relates to submissions of fact made by a Party Representative (Guidelines 9 and 10), and the second concerns the evidence given by a Witness or Expert (Guideline 11).

With respect to submissions to the Arbitral Tribunal, these Guidelines contain two limitations to the principles set out for Party Representatives. First, Guidelines 9 and 10 are restricted to false submissions of fact. Secondly, the Party Representative must have actual knowledge of the false nature of the submission, which may be inferred from the circumstances.

Under Guideline 10, a Party Representative should promptly correct any false submissions of fact previously made to the Tribunal, unless prevented from doing so by countervailing considerations of confidentiality and privilege. Such principle also applies, in case of a change in representation, to a newly-appointed Party Representative who becomes aware that his or her predecessor made a false submission.

With respect to legal submissions to the Tribunal, a Party Representative may argue any construction of a law, a contract, a treaty or any authority that he or she believes is reasonable.

Guideline 11 addresses the presentation of evidence to the Tribunal that a Party Representative knows to be false. A Party Representative should not offer knowingly false evidence or testimony. A Party Representative therefore should not assist a Witness or Expert or seek to influence a Witness or Expert to give false evidence to the Tribunal in oral testimony or written Witness Statements or Expert Reports.

The considerations outlined for Guidelines 9 and 10 apply equally to Guideline 11. Guideline 11 is more specific in terms of the remedial measures that a Party Representative may take in the event that the Witness or Expert intends to present or presents evidence that the Party Representative knows or later discovers to be false. The list of remedial measures provided in Guideline 11 is not exhaustive. Such remedial measures may extend to the Party Representative's withdrawal from the case, if the circumstances so warrant. Guideline 11 acknowledges, by using the term 'may', that certain remedial measures, such as correcting or withdrawing false Witness or Expert evidence may not be compatible with the ethical rules bearing on counsel in some jurisdictions.

Information Exchange and Disclosure

12. When the arbitral proceedings involve or are likely to involve Document production, a Party Representative should inform the client of the need to preserve, so far as reasonably possible, Documents, including

electronic Documents that would otherwise be deleted in accordance with a Document retention policy or in the ordinary course of business, which are potentially relevant to the arbitration.

13. A Party Representative should not make any Request to Produce, or any objection to a Request to Produce, for an improper purpose, such as to harass or cause unnecessary delay.

14. A Party Representative should explain to the Party whom he or she represents the necessity of producing, and potential consequences of failing to produce, any Document that the Party or Parties have undertaken, or been ordered, to produce.

15. A Party Representative should advise the Party whom he or she represents to take, and assist such Party in taking, reasonable steps to ensure that: (i) a reasonable search is made for Documents that a Party has undertaken, or been ordered, to produce; and (ii) all non-privileged, responsive Documents are produced.

16. A Party Representative should not suppress or conceal, or advise a Party to suppress or conceal, Documents that have been requested by another Party or that the Party whom he or she represents has undertaken, or been ordered, to produce.

17. If, during the course of an arbitration, a Party Representative becomes aware of the existence of a Document that should have been produced, but was not produced, such Party Representative should advise the Party whom he or she represents of the necessity of producing the Document and the consequences of failing to do so.

Comments to Guidelines 12–17

The IBA addressed the scope of Document production in the IBA Rules on the Taking of Evidence in International Arbitration (see Articles 3 and 9). Guidelines 12–17 concern the conduct of Party Representatives in connection with Document production.

Party Representatives are often unsure whether and to what extent their respective domestic standards of professional conduct apply to the process of preserving, collecting and producing documents in international arbitration. It is common for Party Representatives in the same arbitration proceeding to apply different standards. For example, one Party Representative may consider him-or her-self obligated to ensure that the Party whom he or she represents undertakes a reasonable search for, and produces, all responsive, non-privileged Documents, while another Party Representative may view Document production as the sole responsibility of the Party whom he or she represents. In these circumstances, the disparity in access to information or evidence may undermine the integrity and fairness of the arbitral proceedings.

The Guidelines are intended to address these difficulties by suggesting standards of conduct in international arbitration. They may not be necessary in cases where Party Representatives share similar expectations with respect to their role in relation to Document production or in cases where Document production is not done or is minimal.

The Guidelines are intended to foster the taking of objectively reasonable steps to preserve, search for and produce Documents that a Party has an obligation to disclose.

Under Guidelines 12–17, a Party Representative should, under the given circumstances, advise the Party whom he or she represents to: (i) identify those persons within the Party's control who might possess Documents potentially relevant to the arbitration, including electronic Documents; (ii) notify such persons of the need to preserve and not destroy any such Documents; and (iii) suspend or otherwise make arrangements to override any Document retention or other policies/practises whereby potentially relevant Documents might be destroyed in the ordinary course of business.

Under Guidelines 12–17, a Party Representative should, under the given circumstances, advise the Party whom he or she represents to, and assist such Party to: (i) put in place a reasonable and proportionate system for collecting and reviewing Documents within the possession of persons within the Party's control in order to identify Documents that are relevant to the arbitration or that have been requested by another Party; and (ii) ensure that the Party Representative is provided with copies of, or access to, all such Documents.

While Article 3 of the IBA Rules on the Taking of Evidence in International Arbitration requires the production of Documents relevant to the case and material to its outcome, Guideline 12 refers only to potentially relevant Documents because its purpose is different: when a Party Representative advises the Party whom he or she represents to preserve evidence, such Party Representative is typically not at that stage in a position to assess materiality, and the test for preserving and collecting Documents therefore should be potential relevance to the case at hand.

Finally, a Party Representative should not make a Request to Produce, or object to a Request to Produce, when such request or objection is only aimed at harassing, obtaining documents for purposes extraneous to the arbitration, or causing unnecessary delay (Guideline 13).

Witnesses and Experts

18. Before seeking any information from a potential Witness or Expert, a Party Representative should identify himself or herself, as well as the Party he or she represents, and the reason for which the information is sought.

19. A Party Representative should make any potential Witness aware that he or she has the right to inform or instruct his or her own counsel about the contact and to discontinue the communication with the Party Representative.

20. A Party Representative may assist Witnesses in the preparation of Witness Statements and Experts in the preparation of Expert Reports.

21. A Party Representative should seek to ensure that a Witness Statement reflects the Witness's own account of relevant facts, events and circumstances.

22. A Party Representative should seek to ensure that an Expert Report reflects the Expert's own analysis and opinion.

23. A Party Representative should not invite or encourage a Witness to give false evidence.

24. A Party Representative may, consistent with the principle that the evidence given should reflect the Witness's own account of relevant facts, events or circumstances, or the Expert's own analysis or opinion, meet or interact with Witnesses and Experts in order to discuss and prepare their prospective testimony.

25. A Party Representative may pay, offer to pay, or acquiesce in the payment of:

(a) expenses reasonably incurred by a Witness or Expert in preparing to testify or testifying at a hearing;

(b) reasonable compensation for the loss of time incurred by a Witness in testifying and preparing to testify; and

(c) reasonable fees for the professional services of a Party-appointed Expert.

Comments to Guidelines 18–25

Guidelines 18–25 are concerned with interactions between Party Representatives and Witnesses and Experts. The interaction between Party Representatives and Witnesses is also addressed in Guidelines 9–11 concerning Submissions to the Arbitral Tribunal.

Many international arbitration practitioners desire more transparent and predictable standards of conduct with respect to relations with Witnesses and Experts in order to promote the principle of equal treatment among Parties. Disparate practises among jurisdictions may create inequality and threaten the integrity of the arbitral proceedings.

The Guidelines are intended to reflect best international arbitration practise with respect to the preparation of Witness and Expert testimony.

When a Party Representative contacts a potential Witness, he or she should disclose his or her identity and the reason for the contact before seeking any information from the potential Witness (Guideline 18). A Party Representative should also make the potential Witness aware of his or her right to inform or instruct counsel about this contact and involve such counsel in any further communication (Guideline 19).

Domestic professional conduct norms in some jurisdictions require higher standards with respect to contacts with potential Witnesses who are known to be represented by counsel. For example, some common law jurisdictions maintain a prohibition against contact by counsel with any potential Witness whom counsel knows to be represented in respect of the particular arbitration.

If a Party Representative determines that he or she is subject to a higher standard than the standard prescribed in these Guidelines, he or she may address the situation with the other Party and/or the Arbitral Tribunal.

As provided by Guideline 20, a Party Representative may assist in the preparation of Witness Statements and Expert Reports, but should seek to ensure that a Witness Statement reflects the Witness's own account of relevant facts, events and circumstances (Guideline 21), and that any Expert Report reflects the Expert's own views, analysis and conclusions (Guideline 22).

A Party Representative should not invite or encourage a Witness to give false evidence (Guideline 23).

As part of the preparation of testimony for the arbitration, a Party Representative may meet with Witnesses and Experts (or potential Witnesses and Experts) to discuss their prospective testimony. A Party Representative may also help a Witness in preparing his or her own Witness Statement or Expert Report. Further, a Party Representative may assist a Witness in preparing for their testimony in direct and cross-examination, including through practise questions and answers (Guideline 24). This preparation may include a review of the procedures through which testimony will be elicited and preparation of both direct testimony and cross-examination. Such contacts should however not alter the genuineness of the Witness or Expert evidence, which should always reflect the Witness's own account of relevant facts, events or circumstances, or the Expert's own analysis or opinion.

Finally, Party Representatives may pay, offer to pay or acquiesce in the payment of reasonable compensation to a Witness for his or her time and a reasonable fee for the professional services of an Expert (Guideline 25).

Remedies for Misconduct

26. If the Arbitral Tribunal, after giving the Parties notice and a reasonable opportunity to be heard, finds that a Party Representative has committed Misconduct, the Arbitral Tribunal, as appropriate, may:

(a)   admonish the Party Representative;

(b)   draw appropriate inferences in assessing the evidence relied upon, or the legal arguments advanced by, the Party Representative;

(c)   consider the Party Representative's Misconduct in apportioning the costs of the arbitration, indicating, if appropriate, how and in what amount the Party Representative's Misconduct leads the Tribunal to a different apportionment of costs;

(d)   take any other appropriate measure in order to preserve the fairness and integrity of the proceedings.

27.   In addressing issues of Misconduct, the Arbitral Tribunal should take into account:

(a)   the need to preserve the integrity and fairness of the arbitral proceedings and the enforceability of the award;

(b)   the potential impact of a ruling regarding Misconduct on the rights of the Parties;

(c)   the nature and gravity of the Misconduct, including the extent to which the misconduct affects the conduct of the proceedings;

(d)   the good faith of the Party Representative;

(e)   relevant considerations of privilege and confidentiality; and

(f)   the extent to which the Party represented by the Party Representative knew of, condoned, directed, or participated in, the Misconduct.

Comments to Guidelines 26–27

Guidelines 26–27 articulate potential remedies to address Misconduct by a Party Representative.

Their purpose is to preserve or restore the fairness and integrity of the arbitration.

The Arbitral Tribunal should seek to apply the most proportionate remedy or combination of remedies in light of the nature and gravity of the Misconduct, the good faith of the Party Representative and the Party whom he or she represents, the impact of the remedy on the Parties' rights, and the need to preserve the integrity, effectiveness and fairness of the arbitration and the enforceability of the award.

Guideline 27 sets forth a list of factors that is neither exhaustive nor binding, but instead reflects an overarching balancing exercise to be conducted in addressing matters of Misconduct by a Party Representative in order to ensure that the arbitration proceed in a fair and appropriate manner.

Before imposing any remedy in respect of alleged Misconduct, it is important that the Arbitral Tribunal gives the Parties and the impugned Representative the right to be heard in relation to the allegations made.

* * *

E. EUROPEAN CODE OF CONDUCT FOR MEDIATORS (2004)*

This code of conduct sets out a number of principles to which individual mediators can voluntarily decide to commit, under their own responsibility. It is intended to be applicable to all kinds of mediation in civil and commercial matters.

Organisations providing mediation services can also make such a commitment, by asking mediators acting under the auspices of their organisation to respect the code. Organisations have the opportunity to make available information on the measures they are taking to support the respect of the code by individual mediators through, for example, training, evaluation and monitoring.

For the purposes of the code mediation is defined as any process where two or more parties agree to the appointment of a third-party—hereinafter "the mediator"—to help the parties to solve a dispute by reaching an agreement without adjudication and regardless of how that process may be called or commonly referred to in each Member State.

Adherence to the code is without prejudice to national legislation or rules regulating individual professions.

Organisations providing mediation services may wish to develop more detailed codes adapted to their specific context or the types of mediation services they offer, as well as with regard to specific areas such as family mediation or consumer mediation.

1. COMPETENCE AND APPOINTMENT OF MEDIATORS

1.1 Competence

Mediators shall be competent and knowledgeable in the process of mediation. Relevant factors shall include proper training and continuous

---

*   The European Code of Conduct for Mediators (2004) can be found at http://ec.europa.eu/civiljustice/adr/adr_ec_code_conduct_en.htm.

updating of their education and practice in mediation skills, having regard to any relevant standards or accreditation schemes.

1.2 Appointment

The mediator will confer with the parties regarding suitable dates on which the mediation may take place. The mediator shall satisfy him/herself as to his/her background and competence to conduct the mediation before accepting the appointment and, upon request, disclose information concerning his/her background and experience to the parties.

1.3 Advertising/promotion of the mediator services

Mediators may promote their practice, in a professional, truthful and dignified way.

2.   INDEPENDENCE AND IMPARTIALITY

2.1 Independence and neutrality

The mediator must not act, or, having started to do so, continue to act, before having disclosed any circumstances that may, or may be seen to, affect his or her independence or conflict of interests. The duty to disclose is a continuing obligation throughout the process.

Such circumstances shall include

— any personal or business relationship with one of the parties,

— any financial or other interest, direct or indirect, in the outcome of the mediation, or

— the mediator, or a member of his or her firm, having acted in any capacity other than mediator for one of the parties.

In such cases the mediator may only accept or continue the mediation provided that he/she is certain of being able to carry out the mediation with full independence and neutrality in order to guarantee full impartiality and that the parties explicitly consent.

2.2 Impartiality

The mediator shall at all times act, and endeavour to be seen to act, with impartiality towards the parties and be committed to serve all parties equally with respect to the process of mediation.

3.   THE MEDIATION AGREEMENT, PROCESS, SETTLEMENT AND FEES

3.1 Procedure

The mediator shall satisfy himself/herself that the parties to the mediation understand the characteristics of the mediation process and the role of the mediator and the parties in it.

The mediator shall in particular ensure that prior to commencement of the mediation the parties have understood and expressly agreed the terms and conditions of the mediation agreement including in particular any applicable provisions relating to obligations of confidentiality on the mediator and on the parties.

The mediation agreement shall, upon request of the parties, be drawn up in writing.

The mediator shall conduct the proceedings in an appropriate manner, taking into account the circumstances of the case, including possible power imbalances and the rule of law, any wishes the parties may express and the need for a prompt settlement of the dispute. The parties shall be free to agree with the mediator, by reference to a set of rules or otherwise, on the manner in which the mediation is to be conducted.

The mediator, if he/she deems it useful, may hear the parties separately.

3.2 Fairness of the process

The mediator shall ensure that all parties have adequate opportunities to be involved in the process.

The mediator if appropriate shall inform the parties, and may terminate the mediation, if:

— a settlement is being reached that for the mediator appears unenforceable or illegal, having regard to the circumstances of the case and the competence of the mediator for making such an assessment, or

— the mediator considers that continuing the mediation is unlikely to result in a settlement.

3.3 The end of the process

The mediator shall take all appropriate measures to ensure that any understanding is reached by all parties through knowing and informed consent, and that all parties understand the terms of the agreement.

The parties may withdraw from the mediation at any time without giving any justification.

The mediator may, upon request of the parties and within the limits of his or her competence, inform the parties as to how they may formalise the agreement and as to the possibilities for making the agreement enforceable.

3.4 Fees

Where not already provided, the mediator must always supply the parties with complete information on the mode of remuneration which he intends to apply. He/she shall not accept a mediation before the principles of his/her remuneration have been accepted by all parties concerned.

4.   CONFIDENTIALITY

The mediator shall keep confidential all information, arising out of or in connection with the mediation, including the fact that the mediation is to take place or has taken place, unless compelled by law or public policy grounds. Any information disclosed in confidence to mediators by one of the parties shall not be disclosed to the other parties without permission or unless compelled by law.